Country Roads

Printed in the United Kingdom by MPG Books, Bodmin

Published by: Sanctuary Publishing Limited, Sanctuary House,
45-53 Sinclair Road, London W14 0NS, United Kingdom

Web site: www.sanctuarypublishing.com

Copyright: Brian Hinton, 2000

Photographs: © Pictorial Press and Redferns
Cover: front © Philip Gould/Corbis; back © Rex Features and Redferns

ISBN: 1-86074-293-9

Country Roads

How Country Came To Nashville

Brian Hinton

For Dave Eyre, who told me about The Alabama 3,
and for Neil and Emma,
who helped with the soundtrack

Acknowledgements

The primary acknowledgment is to Jeff Hudson, my editor at Sanctuary, who put to me his idea that someone should write a book on the Celtic roots of country music. I have merely filled in the gaps. Also to Alan, Dan, Eddie and Michelle, and most of all Penny, who offered sanctuary to an apprentice rock critic.

We all pick up the enthusiasms of our friends, and much of what follows is the result of recommendations, suggestions and arguments with (among others) Julian Bell, Dave Caddy, Martin Carthy, Alan Clayson, Mike Cole, Mark Cooper, Neil Gammie, Amanda Hemingway, Jim Hanlon, David Harris, Stephen Hayward, Chris Heasman, Tom Jeffery, Bruce Laker, Ellie McCarthy, David McKee, Eileen McManus, Neil Philip, Neil Sowerby, and the priceless Geoff Wall, whose archive I have plundered but given it all back, honest. Special thanks also go to Nicky Dabbs, who read the entire manuscript and made extremely helpful and constructive comments throughout. Any follies are of my own making.

Particular thanks go to three musician friends, who have all been crucially involved in the English side of country and its roots: Ashley Hutchings, Martin Stone and Dick Taylor.

Any music promoter deserves a medal, so fond regards to the Isle Of Wight Three – Vic King, Pete Turner and Mike Plumbley – and those anonymous souls responsible for fine gigs I've taken in at the Brook, the Joiners and the Gantry in Southampton, the Tower in Winchester, the New Forest Arts Centre, the Town And Country Club, the Mean Fiddler, the Rainbow, the Hope And Anchor, the Marquee, the Angel Islington, the Irish Centre in Leeds and many other homes for country wayfarers.

I owe a particular debt (literally!) to Jeff Lewis, whose musical emporium in the Victorian Arcade, Union Street, Ryde, has provided all kinds of vinyl rarities, and is well worth a visit from any collector. Roger Careless from Glastonbury is my premier source for alt country CDs in England, and his expertise has been a great help, as have similar contributions from John Delaney.

One-man record shops like Snu-Peas in Bournemouth, Roger in Bristol, Spillers in Cardiff, Ferrets in Southampton and corporate enterprises like Tower Records, Record And Tape Exchange and Reckless in London have all helped me in tracking down some extremely rare items. There's nothing to beat a knowledgeable bloke (as they usually tend to be) behind the counter.

In exchange, I have blown my advance, and more, on country music – but that's the point, isn't it? Some of the most exciting discoveries, however, have come from riffling through the LP racks in charity shops and second-hand emporia. Country music – especially on vinyl – forms a kind of cultural slick which slops around the roots of our culture. It needs an archaeologist like me with time on his hands and determination in his heart to dig down and sift through these rich deposits.

In terms of print, *Backnumbers* has provided its usual excellent service in digging back into a barnful of old music mags. *Helter Skelter*, just off London's Charing Cross Road, has kept me up to date with *No Depression* and much else, so thanks to Sean Body for all of his help. I have plundered – with due acknowledgements – my own copious archive of back issues of the peerless *Zigzag*, as well as such other pathfinders as *Comstock Lode*, *Dark Star*, *Liquorice*, *Strange Things Are Happening*, and *Unhinged*. Most of those are long gone, but the totally unique *Ptolemaic Terrascope* continues as a benchmark of excellence.

Folk Roots has been a wonderful source of material, right back to its earlier incarnation as *Southern Rag*, although that estimable magazine also has the regular power to infuriate. Respect also is due to *Folk On Tap* (for whom I reviewed some of the CDs discussed here), *No Depression* and the ever-impressive *Bucketfull Of Brains*.

Cecil Sharp House is an invaluable source of material on the British folk traditions, the Bodleian has been a place of last resort, and nearer to home the Isle Of Wight Library Service – in particular the special music collection at Ventnor – has proved extremely helpful, both for books and CDs.

Thanks for technical help go to Dave Griffin and Kenneth Matthews of Solent PCW Services of Waterlooville, who provided invaluable technical assistance and serviced my trusty old Amstrad.

Last of all, apologies to my neighbours, as various strange sounds have drifted out over the cliff-top at all times of the day and night, most with a country twang. If those sounds continue due west, they will eventually hit America (there's nothing between me and the Appalachians but cool, cool water). At least it has replaced the more usual sounds of psychedelic rock and electric folk, or even worse my own free-form meanderings on the electric piano.

Contents

	Introduction	9
ONE	Will The Circle Be Unbroken?	11
TWO	Country Roots	45
THREE	Country *And* Western	89
FOUR	Country Fringes	135
FIVE	Country Outlaws	181
SIX	Country Rock	241
SEVEN	New Country	343
EIGHT	Full Circle	413
	Further Reading	455
	Index	463

"Even while you wept there by your fallen harp by the grave,
What you wept for was translated, pass'd from the grave,
The winds favor'd and the sea sail'd it,
And now with rosy and new blood,
Moves to-day in a new country."

Walt Whitman, 'Old Ireland', *Leaves Of Grass*.

"Violence was all: our day-glo badges winked a constellation
  as we goggled at Kimo Sabbi, Davy Crockett, the Caped Pretender.
They went down blazing, but lit a mighty conflagration
  in our souls – playground wars were flints struck on dry tinder:
I wore a coon-skin cap, shot the world with my Winchester Repeater
  – such times are gone."

Brian Hinton, 'Flints', *The Heart's Clockwork*, Enitharmon, 1989.

"Country is the last authentic goddamed shit left for us to rip off."

Bob Neuwirth.

Introduction

This book is a rock fan's voyage of discovery into the worlds of country and traditional folk. To further skew the balance, I have taken a British viewpoint on what is usually perceived as a purely American form of music in order to show how closely intertwined the two actually are. The journey ahead will take us through many strange byways and musical backwaters before the full pattern emerges. Nothing is quite as it seems.

Country music is at the root of a staggering variety of new voices breaking into the mass media, many of them female, many frighteningly young: it is for more than just nostalgia that The Dixie Chicks utilise banjos and fiddles. On the other side of a musical divide which this book hopes to bridge, there is a whole slew of wonderful singers and bands operating under the label of alt country or Americana. Many are much too good for the cult obscurity such packaging ensures.

It goes further. On the wilder shores of dance music and new wave frenzy, there has been a recent interest in adopting Appalachian murder ballads to electronics. The strange fusion which results is both timeless and timely. In the wake of the movie *Urban Cowboy*, even Nashville has turned back from the light pop it embraced to adopt a more rootsy sound. In many ways, country is now the music of choice of white America, with mass marketers like Garth Brooks selling 75 million albums so far, and rising.

When I was growing up in the Sixties, country was knowingly cringeworthy singalongs on *Children's Hour*, or Jim Reeves on my parents' radiogram, all cosy choirs and sexless monogamy – the very epitome of boring middle age. When that same radiogram pounded to the delights of *Blonde On Blonde* or Jimi Hendrix or 'Strawberry Fields', it was music from a different universe. Little did I then notice that Dylan's surreal tales were recorded in Nashville.

Now the tables have turned with a vengeance. Contemporary country is literate, witty and sharp. It both mocks and celebrates its own traditions. It has a vast audience of teenage fans, and its chosen audience is growing younger, while rock is largely moribund, and dance music a wave which has already peaked. After all those electronic bleeps, country is as refreshing as a mountain stream – it has emotion, it has human voices, and it has words. Big hats are the future!

As we shall see, the very image of country was a triumph of post-war marketing, where an anarchic musical form was tidied up, its originators sidelined and its wild men silenced. Jim Reeves was ideal because he was singing from beyond the grave, in a tuxedo. Even Hank Williams could be posthumously neatened and the feisty Patsy Cline sanitised. But, like all images, it began to crack: self-destruction was too juicy a fruit, for both performers and audience. Tales circulated about George Jones and Johnny Cash, and the audience loved them for it. It brought them down to earth.

The rock music which seemed fit to destroy country – and was partly its bastard child – instead re-energised it. All kinds of outlaws and misfits began to crawl out of the woodwork, and even if Nashville again tried the same trick there were too many loose ends to quite fit into a neat package. The music rediscovered its roots. At the start of a new millennium, country has learnt again how to speak to us intimately and act as a source of consolation, in a way in which rock can no longer manage and dance avoids by battering the senses into oblivion. In both the USA and Britain, the last decade has seen an enormous increase in personal stress, uncertainty, downsizing and overwork.

Country Roads has, then, an extraordinary history to relate, tracing the tangled origins of the music which emerged from the Appalachians in the early years of the 20th century and where it has gone since. Pure as a mountain stream, the underlying strength and humanity of country music has continued, sometimes quietly underground, sometimes like a river in full flood. It has also run into brackish shallows, and been muddied to the point of insult.

For now, though, let's get really sacrilegious – after all, the Bible continues to be the book of choice of country songwriters, old and new. Bill Malone's magisterial *Country Music USA* is the Old Testament of country music history, stately and canonical, laying down the ground rules. Nicholas Dawidoff's awesome *In The Country Of Country* is its Gospels, bringing the word direct from all of country's finest voices whom its dumbstruck author could track down, many of them on the edge of mortality. By that token, Nick Tosches' scabrous *Country* is the Apocrypha, collecting all the legends and dodgy tales which aren't quite accepted gospel but play round the edges of the accepted texts. *Country Roads* is country music's Acts Of The Apostles, an account of how the good news was broadcast to the heathen nations. Beware, though: often the zeal of the new converts can startle those back where the damned thing started, and twist it into something new. Some of the music we are going to consider would make an excellent soundtrack for the Apocalypse.

The heresy herein is to open up to anyone with ears to listen and a heart to understand a music which has too often been the tightly guarded secret of its own initiates. Happy trails to you all…

Chapter One

Will The Circle Be Unbroken?

The response of the British media to the 1999 Country Music Awards was all too predictable: total respect and whispered titbits of gossip in the straight country magazines, the occasional snide aside in the posh monthlies, and total silence in the kids' weeklies.

Jools Holland went to Nashville with a TV crew, but his initial concern was with what to wear on the big night. Various stars suggested ever more extravagant monstrosities. Reba McEntire greeted him regally at her mansion, Starstruck, and directed him to Manuel, where Kim Richey gave him a lovey's hug, and The Mavericks urged him to adopt red glitter lipstick. Hopes that Julian would appear at a spare piano during the awards themselves, and give it some boogie – as happens on a weekly basis on BBC's *Later...* – were sadly disappointed. This seemed short change for a man on whose own show, in recent memory, a solo Willie Nelson was good enough to freeze the blood, Lucinda Williams – as mean and dangerous as a rattlesnake – sang like knives being thrown, and Shelby Lynne proved dirty, vulnerable and sassy all at once.

Unlike the quality control of *Later...*, the Nashville show had the sickly charm of all awards ceremonies, with an audience cool in formal dress and live acts ranging from the witless to the mesmerising – step forward Dolly Parton. The "spontaneous" chat between prize-givings was so false that it froze in the throat. Everyone played to their image, with Vince Gill so affable it was suspicious, and Shania Twain shedding real tears. The Dixie Chicks acted young and foxy, a cross between The Spice Girls (if they could sing in tune) and The Corrs with an electric banjo. To neutral eyes, everyone looked under strain.

The Dixie Chicks open the show, as befits the newest brand. Their dance routine literally defies belief, even after much use of the Repeat button. A painted cityscape parts to reveal ruined masonry and a starry night sky, and three small girls appear, holding hands and dancing in a circle to flute-driven Irish folk music, vaguely. The children then plunge beneath the skirts of three giant, ten-feet-high flamenco dancers (don't ask!), from which, after a certain amount of bustle, the three fully-grown and short-skirted Dixie Chicks emerge. Singing. Meanwhile, an all-female troupe of dancers prance behind, like extras from an amateur production of *Riverdance*, some literally flying through the air on hooks, dancing a mutant jig in Scottish tartan. Having acted out the theme for this book, they all disappear, and the original three small girls re-emerge, only to suddenly lie down on the floor, either dead with the plague or asleep, and dreaming this whole farrago (presumably after some extremely potent potcheen). At one point, the only Dixie Chick not encumbered with an instrument goes into a wild punk dance, like Siouxie Sioux after too much amyl nitrate.

On comes the compere, likely lad Vince Gill, neat in his tux and boyishly round-faced, but careful to stress that he's a good ole boy. Almost his first words are "y'all", and for all of his genuine affability you can imagine him ordering you out of town, the smile suddenly absent. He has a banjo around his neck, his reasoning apparently being that if the Chicks can sell seven million records with one… He then reckons that he knows what killed the instrument, and launches into the first few chords of the theme music from *Deliverance*. Gill, a man who could have once joined Dire Straits, is certainly a dire straight as a comic. He later makes light of his ignorance of the Internet, reckoning that he had previously thought that "Y2K was a jelly you used for sexual aids". The last word is particularly unfortunate.

As we are still trying to work out what Y2K has to do with the Internet, Trisha Yearwood appears, statuesque in a glittery dress, with a string section, to croon a new song straight out of the 1950s. Dwight Yoakam appears in trademark stetson and blue jeans, singing a Queen song, with his similarly-clad dancers breakdancing on video, in slow motion. By now, the sound of Hank Williams revolving in his grave is like a jet engine. Other highlights include Alan Jackson singing 'Pop A Top' in white stetson and DJ but over a rich musical bed of fiddles and steel guitar, and a short-haired Martina McBryde bouncing around the stage like an American Julie Andrews but with better lyrics.

The music on show is typically Nashville: slick on top but somehow not quite attaining the New England sophistication to which it aspires. Deep down there isn't that baronial sense of cool: a shit-eating grin keeps breaking through. Hey mother, look at me in this posh suit. That *is* charming, while the lyrics have a sharp edge largely blunted by the plush surroundings. Dolly Parton and a grizzled Merle Haggard (with haunted eyes a thousand years old) aside, though, it's all much of a muchness. Dolly is introduced with old video clips and a voice-over, in which she declares proudly that she has remained true to herself: "There's always something going on in my head, and I've got to write it down." Even so, one piece of advice for mass acceptance is: "She's got to get rid of those wigs." Dolly's reaction to her award is: "I feel like I died and went to Hillbilly Heaven." To prove that this is more than just words, she proceeds to sing bluegrass with an acoustic band and Alison Krauss on backing vocals. She also gives thanks to her maker.

With Dolly or Merle on stage – or with Willie or Waylon, for that matter – there is always the sense that something could go wrong, or they could sing something you could remember for the rest of your mortal days. Otherwise, the whole thing has the risk element of a major golf tournament, with every performer colour-coded, a millionaire and in expensive leisure wear, doing extraordinary things with their hands. A wedge shot from the bunker, a slalom-fast bluegrass riff – it's all much the same thing, really, effortlessly professional. Ciely Wright is young and slim and kittenish, and sings 'Single White Female' like a siren. Alabama merge for the night with Nashville boy band N-Sync, and could be their fathers. Its all pre-planned and pre-digested. The old Nashville naffness – Tammy Wynette in tired crimplene or George Jones' chipmunk face – is much too jarring, too strange to fit in here. Ditto their talent and their vulnerable, wounded humanity.

Country has moved on. Those tuning into the relevant time slots on Radio Two will still hear the very occasional Jim Reeves or Patsy Cline track, but only in the context of some new tribute album. More historic sounds – smatterings of Bob Wills, Hank Williams, or even Jimmie Rodgers – are played back to back with the latest from Garth Brooks, Ricky Skaggs or Reba McIntyre. Former folk club organiser Nick Barraclough sticks close to current mainstream Nashville, while former *Old Grey Whistle Test*er Bob Harris is more aroused by the softer side of country rock (alternative country remains off the agenda). Both exude a trainspotters' enthusiasm and a redeeming, English wit. In Nashville, chatting backstage at the awards, they managed to upset Brooks and Dunn by suggesting that they'd won once too often, but all else was companionable, keeping things within the family.

Equally predictably over on Radio One, at the witching hour to which his world music show is now exiled, Andy Kershaw spluttered with Northern rage. The whole thing had been a disgrace, an insult to real country, with only Dolly deserving the title. It was just corporate muscle, sliced white bread when Andy wanted honest stoneground.

As for me, watching in a kind of dazed horror – and let's not even remind ourselves of the pseudo ballet at the start, like the Two Ronnies on LSD – it all reminded me of New Labour. Talk softly, look neat, wear smart suits, smile, and ultimately say nothing. Control everything and banish the wild men. Nothing must threaten the family demographic, so no Steve Earle, no David Allan Coe and no "no-show" Jones, let alone that jackass Beck. No conflict. No danger. In short, no bloody fun.

And so, in order to pursue our enquiry as to from whence this music sprang, and where it is possibly going, let us start as far away as possible from the tuxedo-clad suburbs of modern Nashville, and hopefully stay away. True country springs up when it's least expected, or even much wanted. It's like a virus: quick to infect, difficult to kill.

I time-travel in my mind back to the summer of 1999, and the heart of England. It's a sodden evening on the banks of the River Stour, where we're standing on a grassy field between Tesco's and the flowing river. The rich Dorset soil has been churned into mud by a midsummer storm the night before. Here at Blandford, now celebrating music week, a fairly typical cross-section of the counter-culture have had their ears bent by typical late-Nineties festival fare – anything to escape the drab confines of Englishness, and not a stetson or tuxedo (or steel guitar) in sight.

Gaz Mayall is stripped to the waist and brandishing an assegai, with some kind of animal skeleton over his private parts and war paint emphasising his chalk-white skin and lack of muscle. Vince Gill he is not, although his sense of musical heritage is just as proud as the Carter family or the Judds. Dynastic, in fact. Everyone here knows that Gaz is the son of John, the very-much-alive father of the long-deceased British blues boom. Gaz Mayall is genuine and boyish enough for everyone to tolerate his impersonating an African "ju-ju man" – it's all part of the game. Already this weekend we've had kletzmer set to a punky beat, dub reggae from the inner city, folky violins, folky accordions, even cocktail jazz from the former sax man of Hawkwind. Or was that last year? These things all begin to blur together. Everyone is trying to be unusual, or threatening, or charming. No one quite succeeds.

The alcohol and chemical level of the crowd has been rising steadily as darkness falls. As I drank coffee and tried to read *The Guardian* I was pelted with bits of burnt toast by adolescent urchins from Spiral Tribe, and violence almost ensued. I've had Raki in the healing field; I've watched a movie powered by solar power and been literally unenlightened. Something pulls me back to the tented stage, though, among the off-duty soldiers, standing up-tight and looking for a fight, and the ponytailed, rainbow-clad middle class who are here at play. All have been drawn to a stage still empty except for scurrying roadies, while techno music pounds from the PA. We crowd together, knowing that something is up, as the Saturday-night headliners prepare themselves backstage, donning their cowboy hats and dark glasses.

All that I know in advance about The Alabama 3 is their most recent single, and a buzz: a friend has shouted down the phone from the badlands of South London, far more their natural environment, ordering me to see them at all costs. There's a flurry of movement at the back and two very large and threatening men lumber to the front of the stage. They glare at us – I hardly dare look back – like a pair of twin headlights on full beam, silent and nasty, two dodgy bouncers who have accidentally strayed into a Sam Peckinpah movie. They're dressed straight from the Wild West, and they spend the whole night glaring at the audience in what seems to be half wind-up and half genuine menace. One thing is sure already: this is not Hank Wangford.

British attempts at "country and western" (as it is still nostalgically called by some) have always been a little weedy at best, or at worst an outright parody. This, though, has the itchy malevolence of the real thing, when it's not being tamed by the CMA. The men on stage tonight might well be refugees from a post-hippie dance trance, but they're more than just white men in stetsons: this is more than yet another witless parody.

There's a touch of evil in the air, a match for the sneer in Waylon's throat, or the aggression of the young Johnny Cash, or Hank's sarcasm. There's something about a festival at night, a hint of danger, the sweet smell of grass and sweat and the night air. It's the nearest we're going to get in England to the wild frontier, however far we travel, with firelight and insects flying and strange shadows. The wilderness is all used up: the only place we've left to discover is our own back yard. Cue, then, The Alabama 3 as a strange posse indeed stalks into view.

However shabby, brief and unknowable the American Wild West might now be, Hollywood caught its dying embers and worked them up into myth. At the edges of the new frontier, its inhabitants became gods or devils, violence was a purifying force, and male bonding a non-sexual form of love. It was a new world, up for grabs and with no apparent history, and such things could become as archetypal as Monument Valley. Rock music has always been quick to pick up visual cues from pulp fiction or cheap television, and the idea of the rock band as a gang of outlaws, defying society, is something that will resonate throughout this book. What country music invents, or borrows wholesale, rock culture merely steals the surface of, chews on briefly, and then spits out.

For the new rebels of British trip-hop, a large part of their self-image was that of being a posse, multi-racial mates from the badlands who ganged up together, for friendship and self protection, excluding everyone else. This was hardly new; The Beatles exuded just such cool under all their wisecracks: "We're The Beatles, and you're not." In an era of unlicensed premises, with virtually everyone on illegal drugs and playing music which was at that point not tolerated by society (and yet fawned over by advertisers and programme makers ever since), such an attitude was commendable. Later, Bristol's self-styled "Wild Bunch" gave the world the slow menace of Massive Attack, Portishead's sweet ache and Tricky, as cool and nasty a musical gunslinger as could be imagined.

With the Wild Bunch, the cowboy image was not accidental. Here were a trans-racial bunch of ne'er-do-wells, rough and rowdy, steering their drugged listeners through the wildest parts of their minds before safely bringing them down to the pasture of chill-out. As to their music, it was merely an over-amplified, technology-rich version of home music making, an odd combination of things – not so different from Jimmie Rodgers, really.

As for The Alabama 3, not for nothing would this wild bunch later provide the theme tune to television's *The Sopranos*, that affectionate but violent picture of the mafia at work, at play and under stress. The rabble that gather on stage at Blandford exude swamp fever and nasty habits; there are no men in white hats up on stage tonight (though there are plenty of stetsons and dark glasses). Most obvious is the former bass player from punk band The Ruts, in dark hat and long black coat, swinging his guitar high like a machine gun while the rest of the band skulk. Lead singer Larry Love is everywhere but stage front, but from whichever dark corner his voice is coming it's hypnotic, slippery and too sincere, sounding like Robert Mitchum in *Night Of The Hunter*: the killer priest, replete with fake US accent; a TV evangelist. And yet, and yet...

The music dips between the two ruling musical genres of the rural South: gospel soul and deep country. There is a mixture of both black and white sounds which takes us back to the roots of Americana, while 'The Old Purple Tin' conversely has a touch of Celtic in the mix: on the album Brit-country veteran BJ Cole adds a little sweetening on steel guitar, while on stage it is mainly led by the harmonica, wailing over a deep electronic beat, congas and flurries of synthesisers. Sometimes it sounds like an amped-up Mungo Jerry, while at other times the music is almost strong enough to levitate the stage, and I glance around to see everyone in the tent dancing themselves into semi-unconsciousness, myself included. Yet the lyrics are not the platitudes usually associated with Nashville but are instead a mixture of flagrant bad language, delivered straight deadpan – indeed, almost dead – along with intellectual self-analysis ("your own narcolepsy") and namechecks to Charles Mingus.

What comes through most obviously is a scrabbling despair, half acted and half genuine. When I finally track down their CD, The Alabama 3 are even more conceptually weird than they first seem. Their very name is a strange conjoining, juxtaposing the name of one of Nashville's smoothest country bands – typified by a preponderance of harmonies and pale regret – with this seven-man band, while rebranding a metal sign bearing that name with the number three, indicating a gang of convicted criminals seeking justice. Some of the band photos have the wild, chemical thinness of Hank Williams, who is mentioned on one song; elsewhere, reference is made elsewhere to his "cold, cold heart".

The central image is that of a boy breakdancing – or perhaps plunging to his death – on a metal railing in central Brixton, with the railway bridge pictured behind. There are no race wars here, though, with both black and white faces commingling alongside painted skulls, body piercings, a boy with a massive bruise on his face, a man seemingly without eyes reading Lenin, a feral tramp, a tattooed man (one of the bouncers at Blandford, no less) and images of Jesus.

The opening track, 'Converted', picks up the Biblical motif: sin and salvation. There are odd slices of sound, and then the deep voice of the Reverend Wayne Love slithers through the speakers, with an adopted accent straight from primitive America, speaking of degradation in the jungle. The song itself opens with Christ's temptation in the wilderness, translated into drug paranoia, and picks up assurance with the chorus of "Let's go back to church". A gospel choir sings, and the effect is oddly mesmeric. There's "a train a-coming", and it's coming for your soul.

John Prine's 'Speed On The Sound Of Loneliness' is more junky lament, tuneful self-pity set to steel guitar and a country swing. It ends with a rap from the Deep South (of London), hymning "sweet goddam pretty motherfucking country acid-house music all night long. Hank Williams on the jukebox, Jack Daniels in your hand, you ain't never goin' home." Whiskey flows like crystal streams in heaven.

It's dawn in Coldharbour Lane, after three days of drinking. 'Woke Up This Morning' samples Howling Wolf, Mississippi Fred McDowell and Muddy Waters in the style of a hungover swamp blues, country music's emotional and geographical neighbour. In the next song, a girl gets on "the last train to Nashville" to a country strut, but 'U Don't Dans 2 Tekno', and it turns out that she is actually "strung out in suburbia", waiting for a fix. Somehow, miraculously, the subject matter – the way in which the singer misses his girl's "ultraviolet smile" on the dance floor – is perfectly encompassed by the stately sadness of country music.

It's not all this serious. 'Hypo Full Of Love' is a seduction disguised as a church service, and 'Ain't Goin' To Goa' rejects the "consciousness expansion" of smoking dope on a Third World beach for God: "I go to my local tabernacle, and I sing." But underneath, these home-grown Steve Earles are fixated on what they jokingly reject.

Before the final song, there is birdsong, church bells, a steel guitar and the Reverend Love reciting his desperate vision like a man possessed: "Whatever your particular anaesthetic is, that you hold onto so desperately…that keeps you from screaming out at this very moment in absolute and sheer horror, whatever you fuck your brain with…it's a lie. It's a lie." 'Peace in the Valley' is full of country consolation (although the singer's boasting that "I have ecstasy" can be taken two ways) and the promise of a new dawn, waiting for "the light to shine on a brand new day". The last time this line is uttered it is by a child, hopeful and innocent – pure Nashville corn.

The Alabama 3 were interviewed by *Wax* after everything had fallen apart, when 'Ain't Goin' To Goa' had been remixed seven times on the same CD single (none as good as the original take), and the record company was prepared to "chuck money at handbag, shite mixes in an effort to get into the club charts". For Larry Love, alias South London DJ Rob Spragg, a trip to Italy with fellow noise terrorists "taught us how to operate as a collective. This ethos helped us to run parties back home – you get into a building, you squat, you run your sound system, and you leave on Monday morning before the police arrive." These are modern outlaws, in other words. "When we wore cowboy hats, spoke in American accents, it was the climate of Blur and Oasis. We were an antidote to humourless rock bands and DJs. There's nothing more boring than two skinheads with Maglites on their heads pressing machines. For us, playing live is about showing some love and respect for the audience." Through using country and blues samples, the band can tell "urban English tales of everyday underdogs", from Stephen Lawrence to a dealer of crack cocaine.

Half parody and half menace, The Alabama 3's set at Blandford screamed unanswered questions. What exactly fuels this music, with its deep sarcasm unable to completely cover over a huge sense of absence at the heart of things? Is dressing in cowboy hats childish or brave, a way of avoiding reality or neatly sidestepping it? Where did this monumental wildness first come from, musically, and where is it off to now? It was to explore such mysteries that I needed to write this book, and there, in that cold field, a bunch of druggy misfits opened up a whole new world for me. And I don't mean acid-house.

First, though, a government health warning. The trouble with country music is that you might to sneer at first, but it's like an octopus: once you're in its slithery grip, you might think you can escape, but it only needs the sigh of a steel guitar, or a lonesome fiddle, or sweet female harmonies drifting on the night air, and you're hooked again. This book is going to cause you to add a whole new limb to your CD collection, some of it from near the start of the last century, but much recorded in the last few months, or available live on stage right now. The Alabama 3 are quite right: this is a more heinous addiction than anything you can buy in a Coldharbour Lane back alley.

In Nik Cohn's words, country music presents an "elaborate sentimentality" which is still largely derided by the mass media. Its audience is often stereotyped as provincial and dim, badly dressed and easily taken for a ride. Both country fans and singers have long played up to this supposed dumbness, hence the coining of the phrase "Grand Ole Opry" in the first place, when it followed on from a programme of grand opera highlights on the same radio station.

The best case for the defence is put forward by Tex Sample (a name that would fit a country star, but instead possessed by a professor of theology, no less), in his book *White Soul*, subtitled "Country Music, The Church And Working Americans", although it is in fact a book of sociology, not music criticism. Sample was himself born in Mississippi, and his book was published in Nashville, so he is close to his subject. According to Sample, playing dumb is "a way of showing up a sophisticate": when he hears someone claim that they aren't too smart, "my first thought is to go home and 'lock up my goat', because I figure my protagonist is out to get it".

A recent guide to the Internet urges us to "forget the stereotype of a country music fan as a redneck married to his cousin and driving a pickup truck", but in fact such a stereotype is proving a contemporary role model. On 10 July 1999, *The Times* covered a report headlined "Hicks Are Hip As US Plunges Into Redneck Revival". The annual Redneck Games, in Dublin, Georgia, sees grown (and extremely large) men competing at mudpit belly flopping, hub-cap hurling and bobbing for pigs' feet in a bowl of vinegar. Trophies are made not from silver and gold but crushed beer cans. A local radio station host commented: "The games are tongue in cheek, and people seem to like that." The article went on to report that rednecks are "people who work extremely hard to make their living. We are everyday people and we like to have a good time."

It's a culture in its own right, spawning comedians like Jeff Foxworthy (a name straight out of Jacobean comedy, signed up by Steven Spielberg's Dreamworks film company) and even a "redneck rapper" in the form of Kid Rock. For Foxworthy, a redneck is someone "with a glorious lack of sophistication" – he's also climbing the social ladder. Georgia Brown's, President Clinton's favourite Washington restaurant, now serves up grits and fried greens to the ruling élite.

For Dan Fesperman of *The Baltimore Sun*, "all the things that, years ago, a North Carolina boy intuitively knew he'd have to leave behind if he was ever to be accepted in a wider world have become mainstream. Everyone drives glorified pick-up trucks and four-wheel drives." As if to prove his point, *The Observer* recently carried an advert for just such a beast, with the caption: "Country Boy With City Manners". Fesperman even sees Bill Clinton as emblematic of the breed, "a paunchy skirt-chaser from the foot of the Ozarks". Perhaps this is all a reaction to political correctness, in which to be white and male is already to have two strikes against you. There is even a rumour that a new initiative fiercely prohibits employment discrimination not only against non-whites, the disabled and native Americans, but also people "of Appalachian origin", thus proving its existence.

For Tex Sample, such "redneck nationalism" is of no account. Being a country music fan is itself a "form of resistance" to the national consensus. It's because of this, he reasons, that the audience support their stars most ardently when they're at their lowest: when George Jones was wasting away, his weight down to 105 pounds, his record sales enjoyed an all-time high. Those who see only self-pity in country music are writing from positions of privilege; the music "shouts suffering, it laments, it opens up a space, it breaks numbness and often insinuates hope".

Tex identifies country lyrics as part of an oral culture, an attempt to make things "memorable". It's also defiantly working class, with a chip on its shoulder. Songs can be an act of revenge, thus Garth Brooks' 'Friends In Low Places', which describes a former girlfriend humiliating him because he came to a party in the wrong clothes. It was only after the song had already been released that Garth went back and added a final verse, suggesting that the lady in question "kiss my ass".

Among the antidotes to a dead-end job are drinking, illicit sex and a good fight, all of which are staples of country music. When money is short, you want value for money – "more flash for the cash". Tex cites 'Blue Suede Shoes' as an example, and the kind of ostentation beloved of successful country stars. (However, he fails to recognise a similar tendency in black culture). Here, again, there's a large measure of irony and self-awareness. As Dolly Parton says about her own stage gear, "It costs a lot of money to look this tacky."

The archetypal ghosted biography takes the young singer – whether Dolly Parton, Johnny Cash or Loretta Lynn – literally from rags to riches. Country music expresses a love of outlaws and mavericks (even the names resonate), but is deeply conformist at heart: no pretensions, no bullshit, good honest folk with names like Waylon and Garth and Kathy, stars who never forget their roots and are always willing to sign an autograph. No arrogant rock star behaviour here. It could just as well be us.

In her book *Sing Your Heart Out, Country Boy*, Dorothy Horstman explains why country music has largely avoided party politics, despite some media reports to the contrary. Its fans tend to be individualistic, "suspicious of governments and 'movements'", and keen to keep their privacy. A deeply-rooted Calvinism, stressing our innate sinfulness, leads people to blame themselves rather than the system for their misfortunes.

Country music comes into its own as a friend in misfortune. Tex Sample writes movingly of examples of violence from his own life. After an uncle shot himself through the head, his sister became obsessed with Kris Kristofferson's song 'Help Me Make It Through The Night', and how his family failed to heed its message. As Sample points out, it's a song which can be read as a request for either sex or consolation, or both, and yet it doesn't suggest that anything will improve. Sample regards such songs as more intrinsically spiritual than yet another rendition of 'Peace In The Valley'. They help us survive.

At certain crisis points in my own life, country lyrics relevant to being dumped, being visited by the police or feeling vengeful have started to play in my head without being invited. They just won't budge. At times the form is tacky beyond parody, but it also deals with the nuts and bolts of life in a way at which classical music would turn up its nose and current rock 'n' roll would be either too cool or too callow to attempt to tackle. This high seriousness about the darker side of life feeds through into the best of the new country as well, fuelling my argument that such alternative bands are more the true heirs of Hank or Woody than some of the glittering clowns at the CMA awards.

As we have seen, The Alabama 3 address contemporary drug culture with an awareness of both its pitfalls and its highs far beyond The Shamen's punning tribute to ecstasy. As it just happens to be playing as I write, 'Weightless Again' by The Handsome Family opens with the singer stopping off briefly in the woods, calling forth all kinds of images of freedom. The singer makes us realise that "this is why people OD on pills, and jump from the Golden Gate Bridge". It's sung brilliantly, with a laugh at the back of the throat, or maybe a tear.

Country music is based on a series of such oppositions. Hard work is set against hard drinking; family commitment clashes with a self-destructive quest for freedom, the right to drink and screw and mess up wherever and whenever one chooses; and salvation is a everyday reality, but so is sin's sweet temptation.

There is a cynicism and worldliness to country songs, a feeling that the singer has seen it all before, that, after being hurt so many times, there is a danger that they could be again. There are very few songs of first love. The country world view shares a fatalism deep in Celtic culture that, even when things are going well, tragedy might just be around the corner. It's a music which was bred in poverty and violence, and is the polar opposite of the Broadway philosophy that everything will come out all right at the end. Baseless optimism is not on the agenda.

The poet Gerald Locklin, who once taught Phil Alvin, described the basic "plot" of a country song to me as: "My baby done left me, and I feel like home-made shit." It's all there: self-pity, a broken heart, down-to-earth language and farmyard imagery. Nothing fancy.

The balance between a life going good or bad can be paper thin. The hours after work can see a man sit quietly at home with the wife or drinking himself to distraction in some seedy downtown singles bar with a honky-tonk angel. In country songs, the Bible is not just an unread book which you only find in hotel rooms but a handy roadmap for the soul, with instructions and warnings. The speaking-in-tongues of Pentecostal sects feeds directly into the music. (It's no coincidence that Jerry Lee Lewis' cousin was the disgraced TV evangelist the Reverend Jimmy Swaggart.) When Lewis sings about the hellfire which awaits him, it isn't just some kind of smart metaphor.

The result is a nightmare to our current pieties. There isn't much room in country culture for liberal self-doubt, or excessive education; although Gram Parsons made it to Harvard (for a few months, at least), and most recent stars of alternative country have graduated (Nanci Griffith in Education, Garth Brooks in Marketing and Kris Kristofferson as a prize scholar at Oxford), they don't exactly wear their academic gowns onstage.

We're back with Tex Sample's "ritual of defiance", and it becomes clear that even Johnny Paycheck's 'Take This Job And Shove It' (actually written by David Allan Coe), which on the face of it seems to be very uncomplicated, is not so much an actuality as a daydream – these are words which never materialise outside his own head.

It goes deeper. Country songs can break into the emotional reticence which lies at the heart of working-class culture. As Conway Twitty points out: "I like a song that says things a man says, and doesn't know how to say it." This goes for women, too, as a new generation of female singers take off from the tough, no-nonsense attitude of Loretta Lynn, with songs like 'Don't Come Home A-Drinkin' (With Lovin' On Your Mind)'. This isn't to say, however, that male sexism doesn't play its part in the country world view (although it can hardly match the brutality of some of the early blues singers); Sample quotes another line sung by Johnny Paycheck: "God made men for himself, and he made you for me."

Certainly, there's still little celebration of single-sex relationships in country, alternative or otherwise, which is why kd lang remains so subversive – one can barely imagine, for example, a country version of Boy George. In song and on stage, the sexes still divide into hunky but modest men and pretty, self-assertive women. Just look back at the audience at the Country Music Awards: tuxedos for the men, little black numbers for the women, and not too many stetsons, except for those shortlisted for prizes.

A survey has indicated that country fans tend to make love more frequently than rock or MOR fans, but with fewer partners and in less deviant positions. Behind closed doors they like it straight, simple and often.

This same sense of personal loyalty feeds through into a desire for family values. Although the medium celebrates the strong-minded loner, in no other musical form is the duet such an enduring favourite, especially between husband and wife or mother and daughter. This itself expresses an in-built desire for continuity and friendship. It's no accident that 'When The Circle Is Unbroken' has proved so enduringly popular a song.

Yet this espousal of family values goes hand in hand with materialism, even veniality. Nashville came early to the realisation that it could successfully market albums short enough to be a criminal act, with lots of filler, and sell much the same record over and over and over again. Consequently, country stars tend to be prolific.

Let's take the case of one of my own favourite singers, Lacy J Dalton. The latest edition of the *All Music Guide To Country* lists a Greatest Hits, a Best Of and one new CD: 1991's *Crazy Love*. My own personal collection boasts none of these, just eight albums on crackly vinyl. Unlike encyclopedias, very few of us have complete runs of any artist's work, just a patchwork gathered by happenstance, and all different.

Dalton began her career as a protest singer and then fronted a psychedelic band, until a voice like "honey laced with whiskey" found its natural home in the country market. This change in career is not at all unusual, as we shall see. The *All Music Guide* reckons that Lacy's wide-ranging musical influences have denied her the stardom she deserves, which is judicial. After a debut LP under another name, Lacy has recorded at least twelve other collections. I have eight of them, spanning between 1979-1987, and I'm not bored of her yet.

The first, *Lacy J Dalton*, presents a tough-voiced strutter with a Southern accent, performing songs about the lack of real cowboys, and her love affairs with young "mavericks" rather than "the touch of a man who'd brand me to keep me around". On the inner sleeve, Lacy is presented as a woman in control, as befits someone who has her "shimmy shaking" and who, on a song which commemorates "the fallin'-down-drunk time", gets out "my guitar and a bottle of Lone Star". It all rings true, and while the backing has country sweetening it still packs a rhythmic punch. The track selection is varied in emotion and pacing, and Lacy's sassy vocals are high in the mix. This is life-enhancing stuff.

The latest, *Blue-Eyed Blues*, is, as one would expect, less fresh and up-front, more measured, sadder and wiser in tone, emotionally richer, and there are jazz overtones to the title track. Overall, the sound is tamer, more choir besmirched and string laden. It's just what one would expect of Nashville and producer Billy Sherrill, although on the Dylan cover 'Gotta Serve Somebody' Lacy sounds like Janis Joplin's younger sister. The low point is Lacy's song about meeting little green men from Mars (which is only saved by the lascivious way in which she adds, at the end, "some have two of 'em"), while the highlight is her self-defining 'Hillbilly Girl With The Blues', sung with such feeling that it breathes new life into old clichés: "If you think my song's too rough, please recall the road's been tough." She sings about how city lights can blind a country girl, and she has "never tried to hide how I really feel inside". Dalton's position in Nashville's pecking order is indicated by high-power duets with Bobby Bare, George Jones, David Allan Coe and Earl Scruggs. Each actually sounds as if they are in the same room – a rare thing for Nashville.

Each album sleeve has colour photographs of Lacy, front and back, and if her hair has grown less naturally frizzy over the years she still looks much the same, her own woman. Six of the eight were produced by Sherrill, while all feature the usual suspects among Nashville session men. After the largely self-written debut, the rest rely mainly on outside songwriters, and although the quality of these vary, it is certainly higher than any matching pop LP. Each album follows the same formula: five songs on each side, like a meal which leaves you still hungry.

Lacy's voice remains striking throughout, and the backing is professional, without drawing attention to itself. 1986's *Highway Diner* is the only one with an obvious theme; with its motto "I Believe In Harley Davidson And The American Working Man", it seems to be moving into Bruce Springsteen territory, songs about getting your hands dirty. Lacy gives special thanks to two men (presumably her managers) "for choosing the direction of this record". Even with such an original and self-willed singer, there is a sense of her being part of a production line ruthless enough to match Tamla Motown, with each new release being only a slight variation on what went before, and with plenty of filler. Why change a winning formula?

With CDs replacing vinyl, the best way to buy a country album if it emanates from Nashville remains in the form of a greatest hits collection. Of course, every now and then an artist like Willie Nelson forces through a concept album, just as Marvin Gaye did with Motown, but such exceptions do nothing more than prove the rule. It was once accurately said that the true sound of country music is that of cash jangling in a pocket.

Country entertainment was associated with patent medicine shows right from the beginning, just as early radio shows were sponsored by laxative manufacturers (*The Health And Happiness Show*, indeed!), and the hard sell continues.

In a review of the best-selling double CD *Country: Modern To Timeless Country Classics*, a cunning matching of new and old mainstream examples, Paul Du Noyer commented in *Q* that: "The only difference between old country and new country is that old country used to make money by accident, whereas new country makes it on purpose." He even predicts that, any day now, the genre will shed the country title: "Many have suggested that 'crap' would do the job quite nicely." Another English critic, Peter Doggett, wrote in the early 1990s: "Country is perched precariously between transforming America in its own image and sacrificing its soul to Hollywood." The jury is still out.

Perhaps, as Du Noyer suggests, the clue to all this lies in the name. The music was originally marketed as "hillbilly music", and then "country and western", both of which contain important clues. The music first came from the mountains, but it then expanded to include elements of life on a frontier stretching ever further west.

Many elements of "new country" – the stetsons, the boots, the love of wide open spaces – are derived not so much from folk music as it endured in the Appalachians as from the songs and imagery of the prairies. Perhaps the magic of the form comes from this strange combination, forged in the public imagination. In much the same way, black music was to take took the African influences which permeated slave plantations and set them in a new, urban context. Eventually, the two forms imploded, becoming rock 'n' roll. America was the catalyst of all this, a new land which stretched from ocean to ocean, where people could re-invent themselves.

Although it's easy to sneer at them now, the supposed home visits between The Carter Family and Jimmie Rodgers speak volumes. Here Virginia meets Texas. The first is at Maces Spring. As the broadcast opens, The Carters are singing tonelessly about living far away on a hill, as they do. Their patriarch suddenly warns them "Hey girls, stop that noise, here comes a strange car up our road," and Maybelle comes to the obvious conclusion: "Lord, it may be the revenue officer." These are outlaws, too, in their own way. Sara, though, points out that the strange car has Texas licence plates, and out steps Jimmie Rodgers. He sounds as cheerful as they are lugubrious, and yodels full in their faces with a friendly "Howdy, folks."

Like the family from hell, The Carters return the visit, although one is surprised that AP can travel during daylight hours. The visit opens with Jimmie yodelling a lonesome cowboy song, with a particularly throat-stretching whoop at the end. There must have been many such passages of boredom before the modern media conspired to over-fill our lives: "It's lonesome up here in these hills. I wish we had some company, that somebody would come to see us, that something would happen." Unfortunately, it's The Carters who come a-calling.

Rodgers did not, in fact, live in an old shack (although he was born in the tiny village of Pine Springs), but instead lived near the railway tracks in Meridian, Mississippi. Although it was temporarily obliterated from the map by General Sherman in 1864, Meridian was and is the crossing point of the two major railway lines in the US, north to south and east to west. In his book *In The Country Of Country*, Nicholas Dawidoff writes beautifully of how Aaron Rodgers had his son carry water to the black gangs of "gandy dancers", the labourers who kept the rails in order and sang in unison as they worked. Nick Tosches, who is more imaginative and less trustworthy, has Jimmie scattering marijuana seeds from the caboose of the trains on which he served as a brakeman.

Whichever is true, Rodgers was part of an industry which opened up America like no other, while The Carters lived largely static lives in their mountain homes. It's a contrast – and perhaps even a conflict – which is still at the heart of country music: a love of wide open spaces, but with the accompanying desire to settle down. Total self-reliance, as against being able to trust one's life in the love of family and friends.

Going back to *Lacy J Dalton*, just such a dichotomy runs through all of the songs on offer. It's unfair to analyse songs meant for mere entertainment, except that country cuts deeper than that. Lacy's voice suggests utter conviction for as long as she sings each song, first asking herself "Why do I fall for those crazy blue eyes?", choosing freedom over true love, while in another song confesses "I'm high like an angel, but the devil's got my soul." She celebrates restlessness in the 'Honky Tonk Man', a man who is ever on the road, or a Louisiana lover whom she plans to engage in "Texas rock in a Tulsa roadhouse." Flip the album over, and Lacy is asking why there's no stability in her life: 'Late Night Kind Of Lonesome' is a search – as yet unsuccessful – for "long-time lovin'". The final song, 'Turn My Head Around', is by someone wasted and lonely: "I need someone to help me get back home." She escapes safety only to want it back. It seems that Carter family values are just as seductive as those of the gadabout Jimmie Rodgers, with a girl in every town.

Railways – along with the freeways which to some extent replaced them – are a central image in country music, and indeed of the Hollywood western. Their coming usually marks the point when civilisation comes to town, and just like the road movie they link to one of the deepest mythic archetypes: the journey of the soul. Hank Snow's *Railroad Man*, an early concept album, has mean-faced Hank oiling giant wheels on the front and a purple piece of prose on the back: "Hank Snow rode the silver tracks to a place in the hearts of millions. The train is real and the songs about it are real. No matter how fast man travels, nothing will ever replace the peaceful reassurance of a lonesome whistle crooning through the night."

It's all oddly reminiscent of Dylan's notes on *Highway 61 Revisited* ("On the slow train, time does not interfere"), and his classic song title 'It Takes A Lot To Laugh, It Takes A Train To Cry'. Snow covers country classics like Hank Williams' 'Lonesome Whistle', Rodgers' own 'Waiting For A Train', or Roy Acuff's 'The Streamline Cannonball'. The spookier side of rail history is already rich with its own folklore, represented here by song titles like 'The Crazy Engineer', 'Ghost Trains' and 'The Wreck Of the Number Nine'.

To take a train ride is to visit another place, somewhere different, and going somewhere else is right at the heart of the American dream. Kentucky and Tennessee – the twin cradles of country music – were incorporated into the Union in 1792 and 1796 respectively. In many ways they served as the jumping-off point from which settlers moved north, south and – most crucially – west in the early 19th century. Again, one thinks of the Carter family, rooted and hidebound, rather than Jimmie Rodgers, mobile and free spirited. That shouldn't be seen as a criticism of those who settled in place once they had reached the

Appalachians, however; if you think you've found paradise, there's no point in moving on from it.

Country music has long derived its strength from this combination, with one part of its mindset celebrating a static world of eternal family values, and another energised by motion, danger and sexual freedom. It would be turgid if only the first were adopted, and trivial if only the second. The greatest performers in the genre – Johnny Cash, Bob Dylan, George Jones – have spent a lifetime oscillating between the two.

In just such a way, a growing interest in the potential of the new lands to the west proved one of the points of friction which sparked the American Civil War in the early 1860s, a war in which the "slave states" of Kentucky and West Virginia stayed with the Union. Not that there were too many slaves, or plantations, in the mountains; in Appalachia, small-scale farmers tended to slave for themselves.

"As cotton crops quickly exhausted the soil, the Southern farmers planned to expand into the newly-discovered Western Territories, taking slavery and cotton with them...most Northerners were totally adverse to slavery extending to the New Territories...Southerners felt that, unless they acted, they would become the 'poor relations' of the North." I take that passage not from a ponderous historical tome but from another concept LP, *White Mansions*, which was put together in 1978 by exiled Englishman Paul Kennerley. Exemplified by the Canadian Robbie Robertson, some of the deepest slices of Americana have been cut by those born elsewhere.

The white mansions of the title are both graceful Southern residences, hymned on celluloid as Tara in *Gone With The Wind*, and the whitened skulls which littered the battlefields. Photographs of the time resemble waking nightmares from Bosnia or Cambodia. For all of that, however, it's a sumptuous package, in which the likes of Waylon Jennings and Jessi Colter are seen dressed in period costume in faked up "old" photos , as well as heard singing the South's defeat, while Bernie Leadon leads the pit orchestra. More to the point, its hero – played by John Dillon – loses his gentlemanly status along with his money, and becomes a desperado in the new west.

What was at this point little more than wilderness has since become the location of the greatest mythology of the 20th century, a dream world of heroism, excitement and sudden death. The vision has darkened with time (it is largely an invention, anyway), but it has seeped into the subconscious – a little bit of us all is forever Davy Crockett or Calamity Jane.

At first, the territory to the west of the Appalachians was seen, in the words of one poet, as "a waste and howling inhabited/where none inhabited". Benjamin Franklin was among the first to see the potential of such land to a country whose small population was already set to explode. When Lewis and Clark battled their way to the Pacific coast in 1804, they merely lit the fuse.

This was a new Eden, free from social divisions, just as predicted by St John de Crevecoeur, when he settled west of the Hudson in the late 18th century: "The meanest of our log-houses is a dry and comfortable habitation. We have no princes, for whom we toil, starve and bleed; we are the most perfect society now existing in the world."

It would be a mistake, though, not to realise that mountains were not part of this new frontier. In 1784, John Filson wrote in *The Discovery, Settlement And Present State Of Kentucke* of a "land of promise, flowing with milk and honey, a land of brooks of water, a land of wheat and barley, and all kinds of fruits". Once the native American inhabitants – presumably not included in this catalogue of natural delights – had been bloodily pacified, an anonymous poet could write of "our soil so rich, our clime so pure/sweet asylum for rich and poor". In much the same terms, he also wrote about "an asylum for the distressed of mankind".

It's not too great a leap of imagination from this to John Denver's song 'Take Me Home, Country Roads', written two centuries later but with much the same message: "almost heaven, West Virginia". Denver also catalogues the delights of his Rocky Mountain home: "all my memories gather there". What Denver adds is a modern note of regret and exile. Like Wordsworth's daffodils, the "misty taste of moonshine" is recollected in the city, brought back to his mind by a song on the radio.

Three staples of the country music diet are offered here: firstly, there is the sense of the mountains holding an ancient wisdom, unavailable elsewhere – "Life is old there, older than the trees"; secondly, the landscape and a the body of his loved one become as one, so that the phrase "I hear her voice in the morning hour" could refer either to the breeze through the trees or a woman waiting, and "mountain mama" could be either; thirdly is the sense of a journey, so that it is literally country roads which he will take home.

Denver's own version of this song is bouncy and optimistic, with a hint of banjo in a backing that is otherwise quality pop. It's a performance *about* country music rather than really *of* it. The Carter Family's 1970s recording of the same song is much more delicate, more of a lament, with four female voices in harmony, so that they do not so much yearn for the feminine spirit of the mountains as exemplify it.

Despite his upsetting resemblance to the Milky Bar Kid, Denver should not be underestimated. In the retrospective *Rocky Mountain Collection*, he complains that most of his critics "are people living in big cities. I come in singing about the mountains, the wilderness, about love and family," hence the use of his song for the title this book. Those very themes fuel most of the musicians about whom I enthuse, although he isn't among them. Colin Escott writes that "his music offered us a vision of America before the fall". May paradise not be so bland, though.

Denver's grandfather was a German immigrant to Oklahoma, and after an unsettled childhood John studied architecture in Lubbock, Texas, before joining the

LA folk scene. There was even talk about him joining the embryonic Byrds, but he ended up with the less intellectually challenging Chad Mitchell Trio and writing 'Leaving On A Jet Plane' for Peter, Paul And Mary. Escott praises the fact that, when he set off as a solo artist, Denver "didn't try to sound like a 70-year-old Appalachian hog farmer" (which, in my own prejudiced view, would have made him much more interesting). This book celebrates those who did!

Denver was marketed as a safe alternative to such things, and in his own words appealed to those who "still liked a song with a lilting melody and an affirming, unconfrontational message". He and his wife moved, not to a shack in West Virginia, but to Aspen. In fact, his underlying message was extremely confrontational to those obsessed with market forces. The line about how his heart "still knows some fear" was about the plan to bring the Winter Olympics to Denver (the town), and the "resculpting" of the mountains required. Denver (the person) put his money where his mouth was, buying land in Colorado as a nature reserve, though he was also a ruthless businessman. Money came first.

Denver was never really accepted by the country music community, though he recorded an album in Nashville and made many appearances in the country charts. On 'Wild Montana Skies', a song about an orphan, he duets with Emmylou Harris, although her voice has an ache which his lacks. Now, after being killed when a light aircraft which he was piloting crashed (making his song 'Flying For Me' sadly ironic), it's possible to see Denver as a whole. His singing style might have been bland to the point of anonymity, but he was deadly serious as a pioneer of ecological awareness. He used his music as a soft covering for hard messages.

Denver's image, with over-sized glasses and wide smile, is close to that of a country bumpkin. His ever-present grin makes him look slightly vacant. As he was, in fact, extremely sharp, this brings us back to Tex Sample's theory about country folk acting dumb in order to confuse sophisticates. It certainly beats knowing irony, hands down.

Country remains an easy genre to parody, although its too-obvious wigs and garish clothing were once gross enough to do the job directly. Billy Connolly is a proud Celt who spends most of his time in America. He started off singing with Scottish folk duo The Humblebums, whose 'The C&W Super Song' neatly gathers all of the cliches together in one place. It's all here: a granny who is "a cripple in Nashville, friends" (the last word in a dreadfully sincere American twang), and whose wheelchair falls over a cliff, as do in turn little blind orphan Joe, the support services and the congregation at the funeral service. Connolly makes the sound of a lonesome coyote, he yodels, and the audience join in on the chorus. There are no dogs, but he makes up for that in his version of 'D.I.V.O.R.C.E.', where his pet is going into Q.U.A.R.A.N.T.I.N.E., after having caused a family split. (Connolly also adds some deliberate misspellings.) Even better is his spoken rap in 'Tell Laura I Love Her'. He's also respectful to the listening "ladies and gentlemen" of the audi-

WILL THE CIRCLE BE UNBROKEN?

ence, in the best country boy tradition, while descending into realms of bad taste perhaps best left to the imagination.

Like many great comedians, Connolly's humour dwells on simpletons trying to act smart. This is just as true of Hollywood's depiction of cowboys in the big city, and city slickers in the country. *Urban Cowboy* deals with the first, with much the same plot and title of *Midnight Cowboy*; but where the Jon Voight figure there ends in degradation as a male prostitute, just another pretty boy in a cowboy hat who ends up escaping with his dying friend to Florida, it's impossible to think that any character played by John Travolta would be allowed to fail so sordidly. Rather than psychedelic New York, the action here is in downtown Houston, its oil refineries, trailer parks and "Gilley's".

This must be the mother of all honky tonks, wonderfully dim and cavernous with punchball and bucking bronco machines, along with – less convincingly – women of startling beauty waiting for a dance and live entertainment, which includes Bonnie Raitt and Charlie Daniels. If *Midnight Cowboy* threw its vulnerable young hero into a world of aliens, "Bud" Davis seems to be always in control here, his main problem being how to get back together with his young wife. It's basically a story of trailer trash, with a rich man's daughter present merely as temptation, and a villain who is merely there to show how sensitive and non-violent to women the taciturn Travolta character is in comparison.

Gilley's Club really exists, in Pasadena, with a capacity for 4,500 patrons, and has spawned its own *Official Guide To Country Dance Steps*, from "that old slave tune" 'Cotton-Eyed Joe' to music "for true shit kickers", which is just as well, as the participants of these dances don't face each other except when whirling around at the end to the Bunny Hop and the Texas Two-Step. Here, too, is a use-ful guide to the "kicker fashion and cowboy duds" worn by US athletes as their casual wardrobe during the 1980 Winter Olympics: checks, denim and the linked ring symbol, courtesy of Levi Strauss. Ideal for Celtic cowboys everywhere is the Highland stetson, complete with a pheasant feather and branding pin. Other delights include Gilley's belt buckles, cowhide pants, lizard boots, leather lariats, ostrich jackets and deerskin pullovers.

This is not just a matter of attire, though. "The basic behaviour dictated by the cowboy code" appeals to people tired of the modern world, discussing the prob-lems of "relationships", "self-fulfilment", anxiety attacks, along with "today's lack of morals, and an ever-increasing crime rate". The first is questionable – Travolta beds four of his dance-floor conquests, including a twosome – and the latter provides the plot of the film, but the basic point is unarguable.

It takes us back to my original argument, that a large part of the attraction of country music and its trappings lies in its simplicity, as a kind of prozac for the ears. It's conservative, too: "Here no one has any trouble telling the men from the girls [and they do mean girls]; one needs little more than a lot of energy to dance adequately; everyone drinks as much as he wants; and anyone can go home with anyone he or she pleases."

The whole line-dancing phenomenon can be traced back to urban dance halls like Gilley's, although the *Guide*'s author, Tony Leisner, takes dance in America right back to the contra dances of New England: "democratic in form – with everyone pretty much equal on the dance floor". This is exactly the pleasure of line-dancing, that it is democratic and non-sexual. Early dances, on the other hand, were political, "styled around American Revolutionary themes and paeans to early American heroes". These rounds united all those on the dance floor to a single cause, while providing onlookers with "a symbol of America's fight for independence".

This idea of dance as a spectacle and metaphor is crucial to any subculture: think of the "fuck you" of bikers as they lock horns, hippies waving their arms around like palm fronds, embracing the air and life itself, or punks pogo dancing in a solitary, speed-fuelled, aggressive display of freedom. By that token, country dancing is about togetherness.

Leisner shows how dance in the American West took on other influences. Immigrant Scots and Irish brought their jigs and reels, while those already resident in Virginia brought the cotillion, with dance steps called out aloud by a solitary fiddler, as the mood took him, and which gradually evolved into the square dance. Just like country music, it's a process which is both spontaneous and planned. These traditional dances of the old west were consciously reworked in the 1940s by such revivalists as Lloyd and Dorothy Shaw, with their Cheyenne Mountain Dancers. The Gilley's crowd consciously recreate cowboy steps but add their own modern gloss. Fundamentally, it's all about seduction. As Leisner delicately puts it: "Young fans are looking for a good time that may not end with the last call from the bar."

Urban Cowboy capitalised on this sub-culture, as Hollywood always has. Its success was to integrate country values and pursuits as a trendy part of big city life, and its soundtrack was so good (particularly Charlie Daniels' song about the devil) that it made the music briefly fashionable. As a part-time rodeo rider, Travolta just happens to turn out to be a world-class dancer, and magnetic to women. The most interesting comments are by the rich bitch, when she first lures Bud back to her uptown apartment. She likes cowboys because "most men today are too complicated", and presumably cowboys aren't. Not for nothing is the central image of this film the bucking bronco, and Debra Winger brings out its sexuality – and hers – in a few climactic minutes.

More to my own taste is the less renowned film *Pure Country*. George Strait stars as a country singer bloated with success and fame. One night he walks out on it all, cuts off his "outlaw"-style pony tail and – *Urban Cowboy* to the letter – and meets a pretty young woman in a honky-tonk bar, after which he gets into a spot of fisticuffs. She takes him home to her family's ranch, and he breaks in some cattle. (Strait had grown up on a ranch in real life.) Lines become tangled, but it all comes out all right in Las Vegas when George reveals himself as a famous country singer, just like that good old ballad storyline of a king in disguise. He sings a heartfelt – and actually very good – song to his sweetheart, she melts, and everybody cries, including this hard-hearted writer every time he sees it. Sentiment aside, there are some sharp insights into the modern country industry, and exactly how cynically it is marketed. However, Strait shows that, beneath every country star, there's an honest farmhand who just happens to have a good voice and movie-star looks.

If both of these films deal with country values coming to the big, bad city, *City Slickers* sees the process reversed. Three jaded city folk, all with personal problems to resolve, go on a cattle drive, the latest kind of yuppie holiday. Things get tougher than expected, but they all emerge from the wilderness healed and rejuvenated, though saddle sore. As an antidote to the selfishness of the Reagan era, they discover the importance of friendship. That makes the film sound trite, but the quality of writing and acting take it deeper: the cattle drive, from New Mexico to Colorado, is straight out of Howard Hawks' *Big River*, and as the three friends bring the beef on the bone safely home (it turns out that the herd is on its way to be butchered) they hum the theme tune from *Bonanza*.

It's a genuinely heroic contrast to their first fumbling attempts at being cowboys, overseen by a taciturn Jack Palance. As Curly, a rugged exemplar of the old west, Palance's performance sums up the toughness and implacability of the breed, before literally dying in the saddle. As Mitch Robbins (Marty's city brother?), Billy Crystal is a man looking for the meaning of life, and finding it.

City Slickers is part of a Hollywood tradition, in which holy fools such as the Marx Brothers or Bob Hope enter the dangerous world of the Wild West, surviving through their own innocence. The musical highlight of this peculiar take on frontier life, exuding child-like wonder, is Laurel And Hardy's duet 'Trail Of The Lonesome Pine' from their 1937 movie *Way Out West*.

Much of the same fantastical spirit pervades the song 'I Wish I Was A Cowboy', performed by SE Rogie, a "palm wine guitarist" from Sierra Leone, and laid down in a tiny African studio sometime during the Sixties. Rogie tells his incredulous mother that his chosen career is "roaming with my guitar all day, with the prettiest women around me, singing my little cowboy songs". He then produces something close to a yodel. He also whistles, exactly where you'd expect. Both of his parents are horror struck, until a letter arrives offering him "thousands of dollars outright" to do just that. The whole family celebrates. Rogie sings with a sweet conviction, accentuating all of the "wrong" words. Both you and he know that the whole thing is a fantasy, but even so normal time stops for the couple of minutes that the song lasts.

Perhaps the best way to treat the Wild West is as a fairy story in which we can all pretend to believe. For Jorge Luis Borges, "the epic has been saved for us by the

Westerns, has been saved for the world by, of all places, Hollywood". The rules of such movies are simple and unchanging, but anything is possible within them. In his book *Westerns*, Philip French brilliantly shows how the form holds a mirror to the politics of the time in which each film was made. This was a genre equally loved by Richard Nixon – "good guys come out ahead and the bad guys lose" – and Joe Stalin, watching in his home cinema in the Kremlin.

The taming of the West began with Thomas Walker's discovery of a pathway through the Appalachians in 1750, a natural gap at 1,665 feet to the south and west of which the native Americans had already established trails into the wilderness, which he named after the Duke of Cumberland. (By a delicious musical parallel, Lonnie Donegan's crazed renditon of a song of the same name blazed a similar trail through the blandness of 1950s English pop.) It took Daniel Boone – the real equivalent of Fennimore Cooper's Leatherstocking – to first survey this wilderness, and the wooden hut to which he would retreat back in the Great Smoky Mountains – little more than a glorified dog kennel – still exists.

The paradise which Boone began to unlock for other pioneers soon degenerated into a bloody playground, where, as the governor of Arizona noted in 1881, a month before the shoot-out at the OK Corral, "the cow-boy element predominates, and the officers of the law are either unable or unwilling to control this class of out-laws, sometimes being governed by fear, at other times by a hope of reward. At Tombstone, the county seat of Cochise County, I conferred with the Sheriff upon the subject of breaking up these bands...so largely disturbing the sense of security, and so often committing highway robbery and smaller thefts. The opinion in Tombstone (shared by Deputy US Marshall Mr Wyatt Earp) is that the civil officials are in league with the leaders of this disturbing and dangerous element." One doesn't find here the outlaw nostalgia which was to invigorate the music of Willie Nelson and his friends – these things are doubtless more romantic after the event than they are when being faced with the nasty, slobbish reality.

That most potent symbol of the West, the gunslinger, only flourished for around 40 years, from 1850-1890. To the west of the Appalachians, English common law no longer applied. In 1876, the Supreme Court of Ohio passed a law that a "true man" was "not obligated to fly" from an attacker, but could kill him legitimately in self defence. However, this was merely giving legal status to what had long been a fact of life. As Oliver Wendell Holmes put it, "a man is not born to run away". Therein lies the essence of country values to this day.

"Wild Bill" Hickok gave some sage advice to fellow gunfighters in 1865: "When you get into a shooting row, be sure and not shoot too quick. I've known many a feller slip up for shootin' in a hurry." The names of famous gunslingers resonate through movies and song, and also the action-packed paintings of Charles B Russell: John Wesley Hardin (1853-1895), who shot his first man when he was just 15; "Billy The Kid" and his own killer, Patrick Garrett; and "Wild Bill" Hickok himself (1837-1876).

The James brothers, Frank and Jesse, are the subject of another Paul Kennerley piece of epic vinyl, *The Legend Of Jesse James*, featuring Levon Helm, Johnny Cash, Emmylou Harris, Charlie Daniels and a crack band led by fellow Englishman Albert Lee. Like *White Mansions*, it traces the sense of bitterness among defeated soldiers after the Civil War – "we might have lost the war, but we're going to end up with an awful lot of Yankee money before this thing's over" – but lacks the tragic sense of Kennerley's earlier sonic opera: outlaws tend to get shot in the end, but this is hardly a surprise, more like part of the job. The project feels like a movie for which the pictures have been lost. The essence of the Wild West as it lingers in our minds is visual, a Frederic Remington painting come to life, what John Ford described as "colour and movement".

Meanwhile, the West was slowly being colonised, with railway lines and telegraph poles and agriculture civilising the landscape. It was a gruelling life. As Hamlin Garland wrote in 1891, the settlers "rose early and toiled without intermission till the darkness fell on the plain, then tumbled into bed, every bone and muscle aching with fatigue, to rise with the sun next morning to the same round of the same ferocity of labour"; or, as Andrew Rissik put it more recently, "out there, bodies became harder, minds simpler", and this male ideal of "haltingly-articulate, unsophisticated decency" – exemplified by James Stewart – reflects the country music archetype. Say less than you feel, reveal less than you're thinking.

The most sympathetic musical celebration of the sheer hardness of the pioneer spirit comes not from Nashville but appears on *American Gothic*, a bitter take on contemporary America recorded in England by David Ackles, with the help of Bernie Taupin. The title refers to the famous painting of a pioneer couple, which Ackles and his wife recreate on the back cover, a pitchfork between them. The closing 'Montana Song' takes us back to that rural simplicity, after all manner of modern horrors and sadnesses (Ackles never looked on the bright side of life), and its epic grandeur still blows me away every time I hear it.

Ackles goes out to Montana "with a bible on my arm", searching for his roots. Robert Kirby's ever-changing orchestral score picks out each emotion, as does Ackles' rich, weather-beaten voice. At first he finds nothing, just a long-abandoned farm, a ghost town; but the family bible tells the story, of a pioneer couple "who made the land obey", then saw their children leave, which broke their hearts. He stands at last by their grave, "with young green tendrils in her hair, and seedlings in her hair". Truly, the singer has found "what I came looking for".

This is another example of the "perennial rebirth" identified by Frederick Jackson Turner as the West's unique heritage. In 1893, Turner delivered an address to the American Historical Society on "The Significance Of The Frontier In American

History", which set the seal on this process: within a few years, Hollywood was cranking into action on the farthest shore of the new frontier.

In the movies, of course, nothing is too ridiculous to throw into the stew, so we have tiny-town Westerns played by midgets, and a dinosaur starring as *The Beast Of Hollow Mountain* until the hero entraps him with some smart use of his lasso. Even that fits into the archetype: the gruesome death of the scaly villain, sinking slowly into quicksand, sees harmony restored and the hero reunited with his girl.

The cowboy, like the gunslinger, really came into his own after the Civil War, and took much of his role – and even his vocabulary – directly from the Spanish *rancheros* of New Mexico. (For example, the word lariat comes originally from *la reata*, and lasso from *lazo*.) Johnny Cash gives a useful glossary of 'Western Lingo' on his second album of *Ballads Of The True West* – thus "axle grease" is butter, to "bake" means to ride a horse too long, the "gunman's sidewalk" is the middle of the street, and a "high lonesome" is a big drunk.

To research cowboy songs, Cash followed western trails in his Jeep and by foot, sleeping under mesquite bushes and in gullies: "I heard the timber wolves, looked for golden nuggets in old creek beds, sat for hours in an ancient Indian burial ground, breathed the west wind, and heard the tales it tells only to those who listen." The result is Johnny talk-singing stuff like 'Stampede', 'Mean As Hell', 'Bury Me Not On The Lone Prairie' and 'The Blizzard'. There's a lot of sudden death, and Cash pulls off his usual vocal trick of sounding 150 years old.

His voice is as rough as a badger's backside, and the backing guitars prickle the ears like cactus spikes. Musak this is not, and it takes the spikiness of Cash's depth-charge tones – which no backing choir can sweeten – to properly evoke the world sought here. He even looks like a gunslinger on the front cover, unshaven and slumped against a tree, with mean eyes and a long-barrelled pistol – all in black, of course.

The original cowboys worked mainly on the plains, herding their cattle where buffalo had once roamed. It was a landscape which was dry and hot in the summer (the dust storms could literally choke a man to death) and windswept and freezing in the winter. It was a lonely job, and cowboys tended to be stoic and taciturn, displaying a rough camaraderie when they met and a rougher sense of humour. No wonder they have been so mythologised to fulfil every fantasy, from the all-singing, all-dancing Broadway he-men of *Oklahoma!* ("now the farmer and the cowman must be friends") to one of the gay icons of The Village People.

One of the loneliest men on celluloid is Ethan Edwards – played by John Wayne at his most brusque and haunted in John Ford's *The Searchers*. Ford's work is suffused with music: the movie opens with a choir singing "What makes a man to wander?...ride away" – a country theme if ever there was one – and later there is a wedding with a barn dance, corn liquor at the bar, and a swing band in embryo: string bass, fiddle, accordion and guitar. They switch from 'The Yellow Rose Of

Texas' to a sacred song without missing a beat. Ethan comes to break up the party and silence these instruments of joy, but at the end of the film it is he who has the door quite literally shut in his face.

Ford was born Sean O'Feeney, and if his Irishness is given fullest reign in *The Quiet Man* – with John Wayne the star as ever, here as an American prizefighter – it also peeps out of his Wild West epics through odd snatches of music, or with a comic Celt somewhere in the ranks.

At the heart of the black-and-white action painting *Rio Grande*, there is a massive and bemused Irish sergeant major. The movie also boats a particularly subtle soundtrack. In quick succession, three civilisations are "placed" by their music. Firstly, the native American Indians give vent to a wordless and blood-curdling chant, which presages a bloodthirsty attack (and an interpreter shot in the back with an arrow). Savage and untrustworthy, then, and alien to all that is human or decent.

Next, the young men under Wayne's care – boys, really – sing in their tent, a comical song about the Alamo and fried chicken, to the backing of a single guitar. Good fellows all, with a proper sense of American history, and a matching sense of humour.

Slower and more stately, and extremely manly, is the patriotic song with which the cavalry enliven their ride out into the wilderness. Like their good formation and neat uniforms, this is part of the civilisation which they are intent on bringing to the West, whether the locals like it or not. Here are fighting men, proud of themselves and their heritage, and their voices match the clip-clop of their horses' hooves.

Subliminally, the orchestral scoring on the soundtrack shifts from this martial progress to flutes, Celtic flourishes and an Irish jig. Maureen O'Hara washes her clothes in a convenient waterhole – the scene is all about maternal values, nurturing and domestic. It's the Indian "music" which will be silenced by the end of the film.

In another self-consciously epic Western, 1980's *Heaven's Gate*, this cultural diversity is presented not as a marriage but as civil war, literally. It takes as its subject the 1892 Johnson County wars between cattle-rangers and immigrant settlers, and the latter are defined through the native culture they bring to the prairies, with lots of polkas and celeidhs. It's a lifestyle which doesn't so much charm the locals as infuriate them, resulting in bloodshed on an epic scale. Such connections go back a long way: a cattle raid forms the basic plot of the ancient Irish poem 'The Tain'. In turn, the films of Sam Peckinpah are such myths brought bloodily to life. If one can look beneath the bloody surface, one sees an elegy for the dying West: hence the slow-motion gunfights and Dylan's ultimate death-song, 'Knockin' On Heaven's Door', mournfully intoned in *Pat Garrett And Billy The Kid*. The Magnificent Seven ride to glory, while The Wild Bunch merely roister on their way to being wiped out.

The finest country singers, both old and new wave – Johnny Cash and Will Oldham – have caught this elegiac note. In a post-modernist world obsessed with the lack of a future and only able to endlessly recycle the past, it is the current orthodoxy. Think again of the cowboy in *City Slickers*, like an Arthurian knight, dying quietly out on the range. As John Wayne got older, so the parts he played took on this same sense of a man raging against the dying of the light. Even spookier is *The Misfits*: here again cowboys are working themselves out of a job. They drive a pickup, and look for odd jobs. It's as if the atmosphere of the movie seeped into the bones of its stars: Clark Gable died before filming was even complete, Marilyn Monroe shortly afterwards, and Montgomery Clift before he reached middle age.

This sense of foreboding and transcendence is a counterpart of the "high, lonesome sound" which can be found in both the mountain music from which country derived and the British folk tradition from whence it sprang in the first place. It is a note which also resounds throughout the literature of the West.

It's something untranslateable. It's in the very timbre of the voices of Johnny Cash or Willie Nelson, but it's also in Clint Eastwood's performance in 1992's *Unforgiven*, a movie where pain really hurts, and the only way we can identify with the psychotic cold-as-snow hero, William Munny, is as representing the beast inside all of us. It's a film about scars, and that part of our nature that can never be domesticated. In country terms, it's Will "Palace" Oldham rather than Willy Nelson; terror rather than grace. The landscape is rough and unyielding, and the shanty town squalid and cheap. Where is forgiveness in a world without mercy?

There is a similarly unforgiving feel to the Westerns in which Eastwood made his reputation. Fresh from playing Rowdy Yates in the unremarkable (but fun) TV series *Rawhide*, he flew over to Europe to act in a low-budget film, made for peanuts by unknown Italian director Sergio Leone, with an operatic score by Ennio Morricone. Based on a samurai epic (itself with a plot stolen from Dashiell Hammett), *A Fistful Of Dollars* hit the world at much the same time as The Beatles, and with much the same impact. It immediately established a new genre, as visual and atmospheric as any country song. Indeed, soundtracks by Morricone or Ry Cooder are now the music of the West.

This is a world peopled by strange and frightening characters, with few clues given as to their inner workings. They inhabit huge and empty landscapes which seem subtly (and rightly) un-American, but over which they tower like giants. Spooky and highly dramatic orchestral music largely replaces the need for dialogue, so that gunfire speaks more eloquently than words. There is no morality. Almost everybody dies.

At their most ridiculous, such films resemble the recent craze for easy listening music with pretensions, such as The 50 Guitars Of Tommy Garrett's LP *Border Town Bandido*, with a mean, sombrero'd Tommy running through Western movie themes – one laughs at them, not with them. At their greatest, they resemble a waking dream – or, indeed, nightmare – which stirs the soul. Every rock star from U2 to Eno has appropriated them: Dylan's 'Man In A Long Black Coat' is surely more Leone than Hollywood. The boldest Spaghetti Western of all was Sergio's masterpiece *Once Upon A Time In The West*, in which the cast acts to a pre-recorded score and each character has his own musical trademark: harmonica for Charles Bronson, banjo for Jason Robardes, electric guitar for Henry Fonda. Of course, everybody dies – apart from Bronson.

These films in turn unleashed a nastier breed of Western back home, brooding and full of grotesqueries, embodying alternative country to the letter. The presence or not of such a sense of pessimism currently acts as a litmus test as to what is mainstream and what is "alternative". If it's hopeful, it's Nashville; if it's depressing, it's Americana.

The most unexpected and sickening violence of all, though, rounded off a movie produced by and starring Fonda's son, Peter, which was also made on a tiny budget. *Easy Rider* was released just as flower-power was wilting, and its counter-culture heroes (actually as expressionless and amoral as anyone in Leone's cosmos) smoked dope, took LSD and funded their ride across the South, from Mexico to New Orleans, on a cocaine deal. Replacing horses with two gleaming motorbikes merely brought the myth up to date a little. What took it back into the dark ages was the seemingly motiveless shooting of both longhairs, Fonda and Dennis Hopper, by a truck-load of crop-headed, redneck reactionaries.

Wyatt and Billy (perhaps The Kid, reborn), rode the highways to a soundtrack of The Byrds, Steppenwolf and weird folkies The Holy Modal Rounders. Perhaps their killers were listening to a country station, playing Merle Haggard as they took aim. With this movie, battle lines were being drawn and stereotypes established. One description of meeting Charles Manson in jail mentions his "crazy Appalachian face, all strange angles and points". The real shocker, though, was the movie *Deliverance*.

The Appalachians look remorselessly beautiful, while the banjo duet with the weird-eyed child suggests a heartening bond between the four city slickers and inbred mountain men. There is some jovial banter, and one old man engages in an odd little solo dance. Both the tune and the dance are oddly Celtic, a connection we will trace further throughout the pages to come. Meanwhile, although these fellow Americans do not seem to actually share a language, music is perhaps the medium through which they can communicate. Woodstock here we come.

But when the music's over the boy's eyes turn hostile, and in that strange scene where he looks down from a bridge – like an angel of death, or ET with a grudge – it's as if they have never met. What actually emerges downriver is a fight to the death, both with river and the locals, one of whom performs an act on Piggy demonstrating what he feels about strangers. The weekenders enter a private hell, where the kind of family values celebrated in *The Waltons* turn threatening – "All these people are related!" The atmosphere is closer to a horror film like *The Wicker Man*, in which the stranger from the mainland is set up as a sacrifice. As there, the beauty of the landscape only makes the events more horrible. What these city slickers discover deep in themselves is a shared gift for cunning brutality, and covering up the truth.

We're back to the debate in *Unforgiven* about what exactly in each human psyche makes a man able or unable to pull the trigger. Here the cold-eyed killer who emerges is not the proto-survivalist, all rippling muscles and testosterone played by Burt Reynolds – a western outlaw with a change of clothes – but quiet John Voight, and it brings him not triumph but nightmares. The music is crucial to the action, not a comic device as in *Bonnie And Clyde*. The weekender doomed never to return home picks out 'Moonshiner' on his guitar only a few minutes before the fateful encounter with the two bootleggers in the woods.

As to that banjo/guitar duet, at first it acts to dilute the tension of the first real meeting between city sophisticates and outback throwbacks, but then it really begins to grate on the nerves as the tune mutates on the soundtrack. It was quite something for an English-born director to turn a pleasant little bluegrass instrumental into something as fearsome as the theme tune to Jaws.

We were spared another horror, however, as at one time Burt Reynolds tried to launch a second career as a country singer, a failure he shares with Clint Eastwood, Twiggy and Tiny Tim. Here, fortunately, he confines himself to acting. With *Deliverance*, Appalachian folk became the new Indians. They were white, they were male, they were supposedly dim, nasty and mutant: easy prey when other minorities were starting to raise hell.

Another frontal assault – this time on the country music industry directly – came with Robert Altman's movie *Nashville*. The country music industry serves as a metaphor for modern America, venal and corrupt. The film links an open-air country festival with the presidential campaign of the Replacement Party, its leader based heavily on right-wing zealot George Wallace, who in real life obtained the endorsement of many country stars, including Hank Snow, Tammy Wynette and Marty Robbins. It's said that Snow is the model for the rotten-to-the-core veteran Henry Gibson, and Loretta Lynn (to her understandable fury) for Blakely, trying for a comeback but still on the edge. Both are gunned down during a charity show for the Replacement Party.

Replacement is indeed the underlying theme, with Blakely facing the surrender of her crown as Queen Of Country to the poisonous Karen Black (said by some to be based on Tammy Wynette or Lynn Anderson), and a lecherous folk singer played smarmily by Keith Carradine, bedding the wife of his singing partner. Tim Brown plays a black singer, obviously based on Charley Pride, and members of the Nashville Chamber Of Commerce play themselves as audience to a strip show performance, which sees the ritual humiliation of a would-be country singer. The whole thing is being supposedly reported back to English fans – distant and hopeless colonials – by an aggravating BBC reporter, played by Geraldine Chaplin.

This is a world of false smiles and backstage backstabbings, a hell of failed ambition, and it is poetic justice for a crazed fan to exact revenge on the objects of his fantasies. (The movie was released four years before John Lennon's assassination at the hands of just such an inadequate.) *Nashville* is an antidote to country music, not a spur. The on-stage music is the worst type of country-pop, the wigs and costumes are as tacky as can be imagined, and Altman traces a conspiracy between country music and right-wing politics which is patently untrue – the majority of country fans did not vote for George Wallace. For all of that, this is the image which contemporary Nashville has attempted to update, but maybe the new gloss witnessed at the CMA Awards is even worse.

Randy Newman's album *Good Old Boys* is an exploration of the Southern point of view, in which sarcasm meets understanding. 'Rednecks' establishes the tone: here is a song of the South, for those who drink too much and laugh too loud, men with no necks and no brains, whose one aim is to "keep the Niggers down". But Newman suggests that such racism is just as prevalent, albeit quieter, up North. Everyone knows where the ghettos are, even if marked on no map.

As usual, Newman performs a monologue of a person far from himself, whom he both skewers and pities. The whole album is a catalogue of the Southern dispossessed. 'A Wedding In Cherokee County' describes a back-porch bride, out in her "rocking chair" and surrounded by freaks, while her bridegroom prepares for a disastrous wedding night, as if it is ordained by fate. In 'Louisiana 1927', Newman squeezes the words out like toothpaste, and sympathises with the poor white trash, "crackers", down in the flood. (The Crackers was also the name taken by Dylan's musical compatriots on the 1966 tour, once The Hawks and later The Band.)

All of this is far from Newman's own life, as the resolutely middle-class, LA-based son of a Hollywood composer, but it rings true. Back on his debut album, 'Cowboy' was a richly-orchestrated elegy for the pioneer spirit: "City faces haunt the places I used to roam." Newman's peculiar slant is to suggest that the cowboy is too worn out and disillusioned, "too tired", to even resist.

By *12 Songs*, Randy's slurred vocals were backed by a country rock band comprising Clarence White, Gene Parsons, and Ry Cooder on slide. By this time he was writing from inside the skin of psychotic outsiders: a pyromaniac in 'Let's Burn Down The Cornfield', who "will love you while it's burning"; and the rapist who narrates 'Suzanne', waiting "in the shadows". Is Newman reinforcing stereotypes about country folk, or re-inventing them? 'Old Kentucky Home' is a bouncy tale, replete with steel guitars, about a family of alcoholics. Newman sings with relish about Sister Sue ("She didn't grow up, she grew out") and Brother Gene ("Big and mean and don't have much to say"), who kicks Mama down the stairs. Everyone is a retard, shooting at the birds on the telephone line. Or should that read Byrds, of whose underlying optimism this is so obviously a parody?

39

Newman's greatest monologue is 'Sail Away', a slaver's come-on to a "little wog", words missed out from most of the cover versions. Even with full knowledge of the dreadful reality, this version of paradise – all sweet watermelons and buckwheat cakes – can still enchant. Though the lines "In America every man is free/to take care of his home and his family" are deeply ironic, they also explain the lure of a land where it's possible to make up one's own identity. The young Randy appears in cowboy hat and two drawn pistols on the cover of the appropriately-named *Land Of Dreams* – it's as if he praises the delights of America despite himself.

In *Good Old Boys*, Newman focuses on the prejudices which continue to swirl around the genre. Supposedly, country is the music of choice enjoyed by poor white trash, male or male dominated, under-educated and illiberal. Merle Haggard's notorious song 'Okie From Muskogee' appears to revel in just such a mindset, sneering at the peace movement, long hair and marijuana, and bowing down to God and the flag. Here is a man who fits the stereotype: Haggard's parents were part of the diaspora from Oklahoma to California, seeking manual labour, living in a converted boxcar. When he wasn't serving time in the Preston School Of Industry, Merle's education was largely learned on the streets. (He later graduated to San Quentin Prison.) In fact, Merle went on to write and sing a multitude of songs which exude tolerance and love of his fellow (working) man, but let's not allow reality to intrude here.

It's a stereotype which both singers and audience at the CMA Awards were careful to avoid, but which in far-off Brixton helped to energise The Alabama 3, who were drawn to the innate puritanism of the form. The case against country music is threefold: that it is dumb, racist and sexist – and one also doubts that its attitude to wildlife would impress the Animal Liberation Front.

As we have seen already, dumbness is merely a kind of peasant's revolt, appearing stupid in order to fool the real dimwits, who are acting sharp. Sharyn McCrumb writes of her character the attorney Bill MacPherson that "most of the time people forgot what an intelligent fellow he was, because his unassuming nature allowed them to do so. In the South, 'simple country boys' are often the sharpest and most dangerous people – it is a pose particularly favoured by aspiring politicians.

As to racism, it is now held true in any serious study of country music's origins that black culture was crucial to its development. The most eloquent history comes in the chapter entitled "Cowboys And Niggers" in Nick Tosches' book *Country: Living Legends And Dying Metaphors In America's Biggest Music*. As he points out, the first musician to perform at the Grand Ole Opry was a black man, Deford Bailey, the "Harmonica Wizard". When on tour, he had to pretend to be Uncle Dave Macon's servant to gain sustenance, which merely shows that Macon was in on the conspiracy. Tosches takes us through minstrel troupes, fiddle-playing slaves, the common links between slide guitar and pedal steel in Hawaiian music, right up to the deep connections between R&B and blues.

My particular brief in this book is to redress the balance by exposing the continuing influence on country of the European folk tradtions, but even here Tosches finds evidence of black singers adopting ancient British ballads. In a version collected near Hearne, Texas, Barbara Allen has become a black boy called Roderick, while the ancient song 'Our Goodman' was remade by Coley Jones as 'Drunkard's Special' and by Blind Boy Fuller as 'Cat-Man Blues'. It's true that the only post-war black star in country is Charley Pride, and that, with his debut single 'Just Between You And Me', RCA were careful not to publicise his particular skin colour. When he did start to appear in public, it was with the protection of Willie Nelson, who introduced him onstage by kissing him squarely on the lips.

A less well-defined history is that of the input of native Americans in country music – far more the natural enemy of the original settlers than fellow immigrants, whose skin just happened to be another colour. Johnny Cash is surely not the only country star who has Indian ancestors somewhere in his family tree.

The bravest incursion remains Buffy Sainte-Marie's *I'm Gonna Be A Country Girl Again*, recorded in Nashville with the cream of local musicians and dedicated to Chet Atkins. On the back cover, Buffy poses under the Grand Ole Opry sign, recolonising her past. Almost all of the songs are self-composed, and the ironies of the title track defy description. It is a song about missing the rural delights of living "with an old brown dog and a big front porch and rabbits in the pen" in the heart of the city: all of the lights on Broadway "don't amount to an acre of green". This is a theme which one finds back as far as Shakespeare, and is a deliberate performance. Buffy bounces into the song like a young kitten, and her voice purrs like Eartha Kitt over a backing of steel guitars and back-porch fiddles; but to exactly what kind of country does she want to return? Here she might learn "happiness, peace of mind", but it all sounds too much like a fantasy ever to come true.

She puts some of her old songs into an electric setting, and the words of 'The Piny Wood Hills' – which already sounds part of the tradition – deal subtly with her own upbringing as the adopted daughter of parents of mixed race, far away from the landscape of her birth. Country music works its usual magic, and it all suddenly feels like going home, even Buffy's mouth-bow plucking away in conversation with a sawing fiddle on the one cover version here, 'They Gotta Quit Kickin' My Dog Around', which follows directly – and ironically – after her passionate and angry lament for Indian culture, 'Now That The Buffalo's Gone'.

Yet Buffy's clear, high tones soar above the backing like those of Nashville's finest, and, as the sleeve notes testify, once music making began, "all the walls came tumbling down...Nashville has found a new citizen". Sainte-Marie was also involved in the creation of FAIR, the Federation For American-Indian Rights, along with fellow Greenwich village folkies Peter La Farge and Patrick Sky. Her later album

41

Moonshot was again recorded in Nashville, with a full horn and string section, featuring the driving 'He's An Indian Cowboy In The Rodeo'.

A similar act of rediscovery is Candace Savage's book *Cowgirls*, studded with rare photos of girls working on the range or in rodeos. Here is Bella Star, the Bandit Queen – billed as "a female Jesse James" – and Calamity Jane, looking more like David Crosby in drag than Doris Day, . There is a whole section on Patsy Montana, the "yodelling cowgirl from San Antone" who prepared the way for such post-war singers as Patsy Cline and kd lang. Her songs are full of girls who refuse to settle down, whether a "man-hatin' lassie" or the subject of her 1939 number 'Rip-Snortin' Two-Gun Gal', who makes the most of being "as tough as I can be".

Of course, casualties litter the process like corpses on a battlefield. Randall Riese gives a brilliant pen portrait of Norma, who came to Nashville in 1939 at the age of 23, deserted by her husband and with two young children in tow. For years she underwent the usual round of auditions and singing in bars. At last, in the slipstream caused by Kitty Wells, she was signed by a small, independent label which went bust before they could release her debut single. Now, 50 years on, she sings along with the jukebox in the coffee shop where she works, full of industry insiders, still hopeful. "'Listen honey...y'come back here, anytime." And then she goes back to entertaining some of her other customers with the story of her days in the music business, or her sudden discovery, and of the dress that she never got to wear on the Opry.

Around and around, like a record spinning in hell.

It takes an outsider to see all of this clearly, as if on a laboratory slide. Stephen Walsh's book *Heartache Spoken Here* was published during the fall-out from *Fever Pitch*, Nick Hornby's love-letter to Arsenal Football Club. That literary bombshell was itself part of the debate about what men were for, exactly, in a post-feminist world. Walsh gets over his wife leaving him and his disillusion with the rock music of his youth by plunging into country culture, and the humour comes with the context.

After a brief visit to Nashville, and a rather snobbish (if understandable) horror at the crassness of Twitty City, Walsh's wife walks out on him, so he plunges into a love affair with country as a substitute. All of the fans he meets are similarly hobbled by illness, loneliness or being inadequate. Country and western in a purely British setting sounds like a fish out of water, absurdly shrunk, its wide open spaces cramped into out-of-season holiday camps and a semi-deserted "cowboy city" and mock gunfights in pub car parks. It's like Lilliput, and he quotes – apparently without irony – a fan's argument that East Anglia is the English counterpart of Tennessee: "there's so much country music around". Not too many mountains, though. Walsh fails to make the final connection, that his own Scottish childhood is just a source for this new obsession, which is just as potent as anything he found in America. Falling in love with country music was really simply a form of homecoming.

The best dramatic representation of all of this was Jimmy Nail's self-written BBC TV drama *Crocodile Shoes*. Nail stars and sings like a bird with a broken nose. Over two series, we trace Jed's progress from working in a Tyneside factory to stardom in Nashville, encountering many pitfalls on the way, like a modern Tom Jones (the subject of the book, not the singer, England's other country superstar as was). He is betrayed by his manager, screwed in every sense by manipulative women, but ultimately comes into his rightful inheritance: fame. The grittiness of Jed's working life in a dying industry gives him just the experience he needs to write real country, not just a local imitation. In Nashville, he meets a range of convincing oddballs, from alcoholic star Carmel to Scots songwriter Andy, who talks in rhyme and is driven to excrete violently whenever he writes a new number: "I can usually judge the quality of the song/by the pungency of the pong." The Celtic connection can take the weirdest of twists.

Andy Bull's *Coast To Coast* is a rock fan's tour of the USA, and although Nashville is not to his taste, neither is country music. Here is the home of Country Music Television, "the hillbilly's MTV", typical of a town which is "America at its shallowest, most schmaltzy, money-grubbing and exploitative…it would have made me puke if I wasn't already puking".

Bull is good on detail: in Bob Martin's Country Store, even the condiment bottles wear cowboy hats, and the Rose Loan Company specialises in pawning guns and guitars as if they were interchangeable. At Conway Twitty's shop you can buy a 3D Last Supper placemat, while in Hank Williams' place you can buy a hat with "shithead" printed on it and a fake turd on the brim, and The Elvis Presley shop resembles a thrift store. *The Country Music Hall Of Fame* does little to explain where the music came from. The one ray of illumination appears when Andy meets record producer Jim Rooney, who explains that the then-new wave of Garth Brooks and his like are "all guys in their 20s" who grew up on a mix of Southern rock and folk. (He himself started by producing Nanci Griffith.) "That sound, a country and folk combination, just started to blossom." Bull takes a pile of tapes but finds them disappointing, although "most of the time I could forget this was country music, which made it bearable". Even Garth Brooks, the great white hope, is "just too comfortable, too down-home, too corny". Bull's book is a minor example of a recent growth area in British publishing: the turning of what would otherwise have been a private diary of one's annual holiday into book form.

Another author who was already well known for his studies of British eccentricity was Roy Kerridge, who took the same mindset to the USA for *In The Deep South*. Later, Kerridge is driven through the Kentucky Mountains to see the Cumberland Gap by a local family who openly despise country music, viewing it as being something beyond the social pale. Their guest fits in well. As he passes the open sores caused by open cast mining, he ponders that, in England, "it is a safe rule to assume that trades unions are always in the wrong, but in America the bosses apparently stoop to union-like tricks themselves". To no one's surprise, the name Woody Guthrie fails to trouble the printers of this book. Kerridge sees the settlers pouring through the Gap to the West as representing "Peasant Power, unhampered by the civilising restraints of feudalism and aristocracy". (Fortunately, he doesn't express this opinion in any of the local taverns.) Such thoughts, though, drive him to an even more disturbing question, one which he fails to answer: "Is America a mistake?"

Down in Arkansas, Kerridge attends the Southern Swing Jamboree, and its sheer happiness suggests that such a question is a misguided one, that America is a melting pot in which cultures swirl together to form interesting new patterns.

To classical buff Roy's amazement and social outrage, "the musicians wore their everyday clothes". We're back to the Celtic connection. "Everybody looked Irish, if you can imagine Irishmen content to sip Coca-Cola." The fiddler leads the band into a chicken reel, then sets of waltzes and country ballads, along with a Gene Vincent medley. Rock 'n' roll, once "too black" for the country establishment, is now "as archaic as Elizabethan ballads". It has been absorbed into the mainstream.

Kerridge notes: "I had seldom seen people with such a delight in dancing", as the band throw themselves into 'The Arkansas Traveller' ("the fastest fiddle I had heard in my life") and couples spin around the floor to "falsetto howls, whoops and yips".

So how does one define country music? For Hank Williams, it needed to remain true to its rural roots, however messy that might be: "You gotta smell a lot of mule manure before you can sing like a hillbilly." Perhaps the problem with a lot of neo-country stars is that they simply look too clean.

Chapter Two

Country Roots

The poet Gerald Locklin sees the current craze for Americana, which has grown out of country, as "white people searching for their roots". In *Roots*, of course, Alex Haley followed his black ancestors back to Africa, like a film run backwards. The chains which shackled those white settlers – who, by their own decision, sailed over from Europe at much the same time – were less cumbersome but just as real, even if they did choose their own fate. They weren't driven by bullwhips or for profit, rather by a cocktail of fear, religious intolerance, poverty and starvation, mixed with a hope for something better.

This was the crucial difference, that these immigrants were (to misquote Jefferson Airplane) "volunteers" to a new land. It offered a dream of freedom instead of the living nightmare into which the slave population were suddenly thrust, the shock of which still echoes through black American music. Everything turns around, and one of the positive outcomes of political correctness is that the sufferings of those first-generation African-Americans have now been properly examined, although the sin of causing them can never be expiated.

The story of white incomers is less culturally sexy, and has been left largely for musicians to tell. It's a story largely untold in fiction or movies: in *Titanic*, Leonardo diCaprio could be seen as a late migrant, and there's a lot of rough Celtic culture on the lower decks, more smoothly expressed on the soundtrack – but the iceberg puts an end to that. It's true that the *Godfather* trilogy brilliantly examines how Sicilian culture endures in a new world, but that story is spiced with extreme violence.

The eve of the millennium saw various media exercises in looking back. Tom Russell's 1999 CD *The Man From God Knows Where* is far more than that, less exercise than expiation: "So rise up all you ancestors, and dance upon your graves." In the lyric booklet, photographs from his family album appear behind the printed words, like ghosts. Russell's manly vocals are delivered in a kind of hush.

Uilleann pipes, tin whistle, Hardanger fiddle and Swedish harp bring flavour to a new country soundtrack of guitar, dobro and banjo. The new-world tones of Iris Dement, Dave van Ronk (as a circus barker) and Tom himself, along with plus a crackly Walt Whitman, are offset by Irish traditional singer Dolores Keane and the Norwegians Sondre Bratland and Kari Bremnes, representing the twin sources of Russell's parentage. The album was actually recorded in Norway, and released by a label in Oakland. The Atlantic shrinks to a small pond in the process.

It's subtler than it sounds at first: in 'Patrick Russell', which recreates an account that his great grandfather wrote on his death bed, the guitar takes on a Celtic twistiness. Russell sings of a happy Irish boyhood, then starvation and "six cruel weeks" on the ocean, with each man bringing with him a sack of new potatoes and a spade. In the new world, a frying pan can serve as a washing utensil, and an oatmeal pan as an illicit still. In his new farm out on the prairie, with wolves howling in the distance, he meets the Malloys. Cue some unaccompanied singing from Dolores, an Irish jig, and we're into Mary Malloy's tale of coming to judgement at Ellis Island, then being shipped west as breeding material.

And so the album continues, linked by the repeated chorus of "I'm an American primitive man". It's all carefully done: on the opening song, "Old Tom" passes "Bill Cody's circus ships, European bound," on the high seas. A later song deals with "Sitting Bull in Venice" – complete with appropriate photo – with one of Custer's troupe in his "gondola canoe". Russell also adds Norwegian and Irish ballads, along with the American hymn 'The Old Rugged Cross', so that the whole thing becomes a kind of folk opera, and has indeed been performed as such by Tom and his musical partner, Andrew Hardin. As Russell told *Rock 'n' Reel*, "the project points out the mongrel history of America. The fact that we came from so many different places, and how we assimilated and brought together this brand new culture."

The way in which he weaves in the different immigrant families is masterful, and to untangle it here would damage the listener's own pleasure in working everything out. As a writer, Russell is too sharp-eyed to be sentimental, and can bury himself in other people, so that, for example, 'When Irish Girls Grow Up' is written supposedly by an older settler in sniffy disapproval, and country girls are corrupted by city ways and "sneak their whiskey in a cup". The whole thing has the organisation of an epic poem, but with good tunes on top. It also neatly alludes to the theme of this book, with cultures crossing so that children – lost, wide-eyed and in the middle – see "Jesse James a-comin through the rye". John Henry meets Barbara Allen. The last photo in the booklet sees Tom as a boy with his family, now full Americans, in stetsons and checked shirts. Even the horse is called Texann.

Tim O'Brien's *The Crossing*, also released in 1999, is another ghostly history of those who fled starvation in Ireland to risk the Atlantic crossing and brought their music with them – no Scandinavians here. It's another milestone in the links between country and folk, to which Tim was first alerted when he heard Kevin

Burke play fiddle on an Arlo Guthrie album. He was already aware of how Irish music and bluegrass influenced each other during the 1960s folk revival, and here he goes further back in time. The Hot Rize mainman is joined by country music's finest, among them Earl Scruggs, Jerry Douglas, Del McCoury on flying acoustic strings, and Kathy Mattea on vocals. To this mix Irish master musicians from Altan, De Danaan and Planxty are added, along with singers of the calibre of Maura O'Connell and the uncategorisable slide guitarist Kelly Joe Phelps, some electric bass and occasional light percussion.

This is a less formally ambitious project than Russell's, but then so is *Tommy* or anything by Andrew Lloyd-Weber. It lacks a narrative, but instead catches odd parallels between Celtic music and the bluegrass and "old time" US tradition, to which O'Brien himself belongs. (His very surname is a clue to his own Irish roots – his great grandfather emigrated in 1851.) It's a more spontaneous affair than *The Man From God Knows Where*, with little that has been pre-planned, except for a basic track listing. A crossing can be one way only or two paths merging, as here: "Once the players met in the studio, success was a simple matter of letting the magic happen." And it certainly does happen.

The most interesting moments happen when the Irish component re-colonise the material, thus Frankie Gavin's fiddle on a Danny O'Keefe song encapsulates all of the rich sadness of a land left behind, and Paul Brady's reclaiming of 'Down In The Willow Garden' – an American variant on a Celtic original – sees his voice soar in harmony with O'Brien and balance itself against a Hawaiian guitar. It is a cliché to say that the instruments almost speak, but here they do.

Tim's erudite sleeve notes are further evidence of the family connection between British folk song and country. The opening track, 'Ireland's Green Shore', is placed in pole position to exemplify the "freezing" of Celtic music in the Appalachians. "A certain culture" developed after Scots-Irish immigrants moved there in the late 18th century and stayed put. "Isolated and proudly sufficient, they held on to the old ways long after their disappearance in the lowlands." Forestry, hunting and fishing continue to provide their basic needs, and little else besides.

For O'Brien, the melody "suggests an intersection of old and new worlds", a division neatly seen in two versions of the same song already given commercial release, Maggie Hammons' unaccompanied rendition in the ancient Irish style of *sean nos* and Ralph Stanley's "driving fast waltz" mountain style. His own wistful vocals sound Irish here, backed by the "high, lonesome sound" of American bluegrass. The tune alone is later reprised as a gentle duet for clawhammer banjo and mandolin, definitely settling on the US side of the pond and as intricate as a spider's web: "Sometimes simpler is better."

The overlaps continue. From the Harry Smith *Anthology*, that primer of the 1960s "folk scare", Kathy Mattea duets 'Wagoner's Lad' over Irish fiddles and accordion. The title track was written by Tim during a British tour, after "a rough overnight ferry ride across a stormy Irish sea". 'John Riley' is not the traditional tune but instead a true story put into song by O'Brien and Guy Clark, concerning an Irish emigrant who deserts during the war with Mexico and founds "The San Patricos", who fight under a banner which combines a Celtic harp and the cross of St Patrick. He is captured by US troops and scarred on the cheek with a branding iron.

'Rod McNeil' is O'Brien's lament for another Irish-American, one who "developed a large audience for bluegrass in the Pittsburg area". Tim admits that the strict discipline of bluegrass means that he cannot play traditional Irish music quite right, until he realises that 'Yew Piney Mountain', a "crooked" old-time tune from Virginia with uneven bar lines, sounds Irish. He pairs it with 'Dusty Miller' as a tribute to Bill Monroe, the father of bluegrass. Monroe was proud of his own Scottish heritage, and featured Scots-Irish dance tunes throughout his career.

The real sting in the tail, though, comes with O'Brien's spoken blues (cue Woody Guthrie) describing his own return to the ancestral home: "digging up roots, you could call 'em tubers". He drinks in Mollie O'Brien's Bar, and meets an Anglo-Irish bigot and a cousin ten times removed who is just as unfriendly: "A cabin man...a lot of people wouldn't admit to that." He ends his quest by finding a rusty shack, no longer in human habitation. Tim realises that "saying you're from Cavan is as socially questionable as saying you're from West Virginia. (I'm both.)"

No wonder, then, that the final song is a tribute to the Irish travelling people, "displaced famine-victims", with its unstated parallels to the life of the professional musician. This is a much more personal album than Tom Russell's, though at the same time less autobiographical, with Tim revealing a great deal of his own psyche. However bitter some of the lyrics, the music flows like a mountain stream, whether in Kerry or Kentucky.

O'Brien points out that the first Irish settlers in the Appalachians were mostly Scots-Irish Presbyterians, who, "like the later post-famine wave of Roman Catholic immigrants, were also fleeing changing politics and the religious persecution which went with it".

To simplify hugely, these were the three great waves of Celtic immigrants. In as early as the mid 17th century, the invading British shipped off Irish refugees to work as slaves on Southern plantations. Many died in the alien climate. As Nuala O'Connor notes, with a deliberate lack of passion, "it was soon realised that black slave labour was more suited to the purpose".

The 18th century saw a large influx of Scots or Scotch Irish, "mostly small farmers, Presbyterians of Scottish stock, and recently arrived at that". Most of them had moved to Ireland in the 17th century as part of the Ulster Plantation, but they suffered discrimination for their faith under the ruling Anglo-Irish elite. This same elite also imposed intolerable rents on their poor tenants. A new land, which inscribed tolerance into its Bill Of Rights and where one could cheaply buy land of one's own, seemed a fitting destination. Those who remained back in Ulster now make up the majority of the population in Northern Ireland, and yet are still a race apart in their homeland.

Van Morrison is a product of one such family, and, while himself resident in America, developed the theory that "soul music originally came from Scotland and Ireland". Not so much soul music as music from the soul. As the composer Micheal O'Suilleabhain puts it, "The thing at the heart of the music making is something which is in the fingers or in the throat technique of the singer."

From 1700 to 1775, about a quarter of a million Protestants emigrated from Ireland to America, and spread themselves wide. Those who concern us most here were those who did not stray too far from the East Coast where they landed, settling in Virginia, North and South Carolina and the inland states of West Virginia, Kentucky and Tennessee, in particular in and around the Appalachian mountains.

The term *hillbilly* is said by some to refer to Protestant folk songs brought to these hills, which celebrated Prince William Of Orange after his defeat of a Catholic force led by James II at the Battle Of The Boyne in 1690. Certainly, the tune 'Battle Of The Boyne' was later renamed 'Buffalo Gal', just as the Celtic tune 'The Mountain Top' became 'Cotton-Eyed Joe' in its new home. During the Civil War, the Irish lament 'Johnny, I Hardly Knew You' was converted into the jaunty 'When Johnny Comes Marching Home', and the jig 'Garryowen' was adopted as a marching song by the Seventh Cavalry.

These last two songs came over with a third wave of Irish immigrants: Catholics, driven by hunger and poverty, who chiefly arrived in the mid 19th century. They poured into the ports of New Orleans and Boston, after which some moved on to the urban jungles of Philadelphia, Chicago and New York while others went west. As one Irish-American worksong put it: "In eighteen hundred and forty one/I put my corduroy breeches on." As well as farming, they found ready employment on the canals, in the mines, and on the railroads. Country music has become popular with many descendants of this third wave of Irish settlers, but is itself much more an outgrowth of the second.

Ulster had been a melting pot of Scots and Irish traditions, with the result that many songs evolved with words in English but tunes from the Gaelic. The Ulster singing style, too, was a hybrid: "the music would run to a more rhythmic line...you wouldn't have the same number of grace notes or decorations" as in Gaelic song. This plainer, more energetic style, was the one which came to the Appalachians.

It proved to be the still axis of a changing world. At the start of the American Civil War, the population of the USA was 30 million; within 30 years it had doubled, reaching 100 million during World War One. Life expectancy among the white population rose by ten years during the same period, while the rate of infant mortality was almost halved.

This population explosion was fuelled by mass immigration, of which the Irish was by far the largest group. Around 5 million Irish folk arrived during the 50 years before the Civil War: half from England, most of the rest from Ireland, and around ten per cent from mainland Europe. Another 10 million came in the 25 years after the Civil War, again most from Britain or north-west European, and a further 15 million arrived before the First World War, although these mostly from eastern and southern Europe, including many Russian Jews fleeing the Tsarist pogroms.

Resistance was growing to the numbers now pouring in. The Naturalisation Act of 1790 had always denied entry to the USA to non-whites, though it didn't deal with those non-whites who came involuntarily. In 1882, Congress refused entry to paupers, criminals or the insane, while those found in the closely-packed emigrant ships to be suffering from a contagious disease had already been weeded out and taken off in a quarantine boat for immediate despatch back east. From 1892, those who remained were processed at Ellis Island, "the isle of tears".

Would-be citizens were lined up like cattle, and doctors marked any obvious infirmities in chalk, directly on their skin (a circle with a cross in the middle meant that the victim was "feeble minded"). Those who remained unbranded were then lined up to face a verbal examination, often given a new name, and then handed over to the railroad companies in order to embark on their new life.

It wasn't an ordeal which had been faced by earlier settlers, though many of those had faced a yet more pitiless welcome. On one quiet morning, in July 1755, the Scots-Irish inhabitants of Draper's Meadows, Virginia, were massacred in their cabins by a war band of Shawnees.

Within little more than a century, the West had been truly won for the white man, and its prairies turned over to agriculture. Under an amended Homestead Act, new settlers could acquire land for free after having been resident for a preset number of years. By 1910, 50 million people were gaining a living from agriculture. In terms of Irish emigration, the figures speak for themselves. In 1820, 3,614 people came to America; eight years later, the figure had quadrupled. The real catalyst was the potato famine of the late 1840s. In 1847, 105,000 people fled across the Atlantic; four years later, the number had more than doubled. Two million Irish settlers alone arrived between 1840 and 1860.

But why America? In France, the abolition of the monarchy merely prepared the way for a self-appointed emperor, but in the United States the Revolution held. There, those blighted at home by absentee landlords from the Protestant ascendancy could become their own masters. The ideas of freedom fighters like Tom Paine had taken root in the Constitution, and such sturdy self-determination was a pointer to the modern world. In 1817, Madame de Stael told a Boston scholar that "you are the advance guard of the human race".

Ireland's troubles in the 1850s largely stemmed from the country to which so many of her population then fled. The success of US agriculture depressed prices, while the potato blight which was to claim a million Irish lives also came over from the US – just the kind of Atlantic Crossing that Ireland did not need. Disease was also exacerbated by the Whig's *laissez-faire* policies towards their closest colony, creating the kind of disaster which, in another century and on another continent, another Irishman – Bob Geldof – attempted to parry with Live Aid. There was no such relief here.

It was hardly surprising that the failure of Daniel O'Connell's campaign to establish home rule for Dublin led to a growth in Fenian activity and the botched uprising of 1848. Thomas Meagher had been one of the instigators, and was transported to Tasmania for his pains, but escaped to America, where he founded the Irish Brigade, who fought for the Union during the Civil War. By 1865, they had reached Virginia and were fighting fellow Irishmen on the Confederate side. Meager ended his days as the Governor of Montana, but his dream of taking his brigade back to liberate Ireland had evaporated. There was no way back, except through collective imagination in nostalgia and in song.

Over a century later, Joseph O'Connor traced the results in his book *Sweet Liberty: Travels In Irish America*, the title coming from an Irish folk song: "May heaven be her pilot and grant us strong breezes/'til we reach the greenfields of Amerikay." In a New York night club, O'Connor first encounters line-dancing, a "bucket of sick", which to his horror is soon taken up back home as the latest craze: "It is said that even Bono of U2 'regularly wears spurs' and has installed swing doors in his south Dublin home…Irish toddlers are being dressed up in frilly-fronted shirts and taught to kick their little legs in the air to the corrupt and demonical outpourings of Clint Black and Travis Tritt." Even worse, a friend's baby had come back from its crèche and uttered its first words: "Garth Brooks". His nephew, when asked to write down the name of his home town, Youghal in County Cork, spelled out "Y'all".

Back in New York, he encounters a female victim of this plague, with all of the usual symptoms: "the wide-eyed, vacuous stare, the stetson hat, the jeans so tight you could read the dates on the coins in her pockets". He threatens a slap on the head for anyone who thinks that this has anything to do with Irish set dancing, which is both more courtly and more physical, but even so this sets O'Connor thinking…

Irish dance music and American country are, indeed, closely related: "Jigs, reels, slides, hornipipes and polkas appear in both traditions, and not simultaneously in any other." Equally similar are the fingerings used by fiddlers and guitarists; indeed, the violin's use as a folk instrument "hardly existed in America before the first Irish immigrants arrived". They share with some English traditional tunes a modal scale, which is largely inimical to the classical tradition.

Where both part company from English native music – which also came over to the Appalachians, of course – is the frequent use of improvisation. Because this music was played for dancing, it might go on for hours and, "as much to avoid boredom as anything else, the musicians would change and rearrange tunes, turning them on their heads to keep themselves interested".

This same point is expanded in *Last Night's Fun: A Book About Irish Traditional Music* by the poet Ciaran Carson, a book which weaves beautifully through anecdote and history with no discernible logic. This is exactly the point: "Such is the character of Irish traditional music that many ostensibly distinct tunes, distinguished by separate, idiosyncratic names, might be cousins, nephews, nieces, variants or mutations of each other." Each tune is played at least twice, and its very names are marked by strange comminglings, "in their slips of the tongue, in their Chinese whispers, in their curious accretions of proper and improper names". Logic quite goes out of the window: "A good musician can produce a pulse against the ostensible rhythm of the tune." The result is a kind of *double entendre*.

O'Connor reminds us how there is a similar toing and froing between American country and Irish traditional folk, so that Emmylou Harris had a profound influence on Mary Black, who went on to record with Tammy Wynette, who put on record her admiration of Paul Brady, and so the circle turns.

He makes a fascinating study of one song in particular, which we have already encountered on the Tim O'Brien CD. 'Rosey Connolly', the tale of a man who murders his lover beneath a "salley" (a willow tree), was first noted down by a folksong collector in 1811 in County Derry. A variant surfaces later in Sligo as 'The Rambling Boys Of Pleasure', and it is now "by yon flowery garden" that the young lovers meet. Yeats reconstructs this as his poem 'An Old Song Resung', with its opening line "down by the salley gardens", although now it's a song about love rather than murder. His poem was soon put to music as a parlour piece, and was much sung in the USA. There it passed into the tradition as a true folk song, as these things are wont to do. Much the same was to happen with Padraic Colum's 'She Moves Through The Fair'.

Over in America, the collectors Flanders and Olley noted down a "New England ballad" called 'Sally's Garden', in which Sally has become a girl's name and she tells the singer to "take love easy" – no murderous intent here. However, on the TV series and the best-selling album *Bringing It All Back Home*, The Everly Brothers sing 'Rose Connolly', a country waltz they had learned from their father, and we're back with the "willow garden" and bloody murder.

It's exactly this kind of mysterious process with which Clinton Heylin gets to grips in his book *Dylan's Daemon Lover: The Tangled Tale Of A 450 Year Old Pop Ballad*. Clinton is always scholarly, but here he becomes obsessive, taking the entire book to trace Bob Dylan's 1961 performance of 'House Carpenter' back through innumerable printed collections and archive recordings on both sides of the ocean. His judgement is damning: "The surreal symbolism originally imprinted on these ballads has been gradually subsumed 'neath the homespun philosophising favoured by the white rural folk of the American plains." All of the wildness of the songs has been homogenised, just like Walt Disney's repackaging of old European folk tales into cartoons.

The real "co-efficient of change" was the strange mating of European folksong and African tribal music, the harmonics of one and the rhythm of the other. Heylin quotes Dylan himself on his links with traditional music, both black and white, "race" and "hillbilly", as 78s once characterised them: "My songs, what makes them different is that there is a foundation to them...those old songs are my lexicon and prayer book." As to his own successors, the likes of Bruce Springsteen, "they weren't around to see the end of the traditional people – I was".

The heritage of these "traditional people", as it crosses and re-crosses the Atlantic, is the subject of two recent multimedia events, with major television series backed up by CDs and a souvenir book. The music for *Long Journey Home*, the story of the Irish in America, was put together by the peerless Paddy Maloney. It is interesting to note that, whereas English folk maestros like Martin Carthy do not appear to have any cultural agenda other than inclusiveness, Maloney is driven by a pride in his native music which drives him endlessly to put it in other contexts, from the European classical tradition to Nashville, as if to prove that it can hold its head up high anywhere.

If the direction of *Long Journey Home* is mostly due west, with many an elegiac look backwards, then the earlier series *Bringing It All Back Home* deals much more with the music itself, and how "it inevitably wound its way back home again". The music for the series is full of such cultural transformations and minglings: Emmylou Harris sings two songs of emigration (one by the Englishman Cyril Tawney) in Nashville, alongside Dolores Keane and Mary Black: "She felt there was something in the spirit of their singing that she could relate to...the feeling that they were coming from the same place as herself."

Richard Thompson, a folk-rocker of Scottish parentage who is also deeply immersed in country and western, joins the same two Irish singers in Nashville to sing funereally – as only he can – on the haunting 'Dimming Of The Day', in a version even slower and more lovelorn than the original recording. The song, and indeed the performance, is redolent of the Appalachian "high, lonesome sound".

Ricky Skaggs believes that this sense of underlying sadness is due to the music remembering where it came from: "It was as if those first- or second-generation children that grew up playing those tunes started missing their homeland, and missing their folks. There was a sadness and a pining and a lonesomeness that just seemed to enter the music." As the extraordinary, hushed concerts of Dennis Hayes and Martin Cahill have recently reminded us, this sadness is in fact endemic to some strains of Irish music. Like a virus, it crossed with the musicians who carried it to take root in the Southern mountains and mutate into a new musical form. Skaggs is bang on the money, however, when he says that, "when your heart's broken, you're gonna play from your heart, you're gonna play much more lonesome feelings, and to me that's where the Appalachian Mountain, that High Lonesome Sound, came into being".

Skaggs is himself one of the finest products of that tradition, both as singer and instrumentalist, and is joined here by the Irish fiddler Paddy Glackin and the American fiddler Mark O'Connor on two tunes found in both countries. Perversely, both are joyous in the extreme, and have a vaguely Scottish lilt, serving to further shake up the musical kaleidoscope. Conversely, The Lee Valley String Band is an Irish group which plays plaintive music from the Appalachians, here recorded live in a Cork pub. Mick Daley joins them for a rendition of 'Carolina Star', a Celtic take on Nashville – both the place and the music it markets. The performance is effortlessly sad: this song which deals with a country singer feeling homesick not for Ireland, but for Carolina.

If this was all a mere technical exercise, as many such projects become, it would be of no real interest. However, the whole thing is shot through with a latent passion. To return to the Everly Brothers, Don remembers his father singing from "a great big song book with hundreds of songs in it. We never asked him where the songs came from, but I guess many of them must have come with the settlers." A song like 'Rose Connolly' "just always seemed to be there", and even if the Everlys haven't been able to trace their own ancestors in Ireland, they are clear about where this music came from: "You can really see the influence of Irish music in the harmonics…there's a lot of fifths and what I call 'spreads' in Irish fiddle playing, and you can hear that, and in the pipes too." As if to prove the point, the brothers are joined here by the uilleann piper Liam O'Flynn, and together they bring the song alive.

When O'Flynn's keening wail cuts through the slow strum of Nashville standard 'Don't Let Our Love Die', rather than the expected violin or mandolin, it's both a musical shock and yet somehow appropriate. The Everlys' country harmonies sound even more high and lonesome as a result. Like the man said, bring it all back home.

When Joseph O'Connor reaches Roanoke, West Virginia, he finds poverty and squalor, but once in the woods: "What a transformation. The forest was electric with life and colour. The smell of the pines was sweet and heavy, like some kind of drug." A spring gurgled at his feet, "turning the earth into rich, red mud. I stood very still, breathing the sweet straw-scented air deep into my lungs, and I have to tell you, I felt happy."

One of the earliest arrivals in Dublin, Virginia, was one Samuel Caddle, who crossed over from Downpatrick, Ulster, and wrote down some of the songs he and his friends had composed to pass the time. Here is a man in transition, halfway between the old world and the new:

> "The Lark is my morning alarmor,
> You jolly boys now who follow the plow,
> Drink long life and success to the farmer."

Caddle sits "like a king" in his new land. Let's drink, he writes, for "dull thinking will make a man crasey".

Nick Tosches' ground-breaking book *Country* (1977) is crazy too, so you can never tell what's true and what's pure invention. John Laydon arrives in Jamestown in 1607 with "grain and oil and axes and guns and knives". He also spells his surname Lydon, just like the future lead singer of the Sex Pistols. Laydon brings with him his father's violin, and fiddles "as a Man wilde by Fever" tunes from his homeland and "wondrous newe songs. Asked their Names, he reply'd the first Song is 'Devil's Bitche' and the other is 'Drunk Negar', and then laught."

Charles Frazier's novel *Cold Mountain* is set towards the end of the American Civil War, as Inman – a man injured while fighting for the Confederates – escapes from a military hospital, and begins the long trek back to his lover, Ada. This is literally a retelling of Homer's *Odyssey*, also set in the aftermath of a civil war. A happy ending can only be imagined by those of "glad temperaments", and cannot happen here because of the very nature of the landscape which Inman so painfully traverses.

A soldier dispatches lines of injured Federals with a hammer to the head, whistling 'Cora Ellen' as he works. Inman hums 'Hallelujah, I'll Live Again' as he goes through a dead man's pockets. Sara lullabies her child with 'Fair Margaret And Sweet William': "I dreamed that my bower was full of red swine/and my bride bed full of blood". (The same grim song, performed unaccompanied by Evelyn Ramsey in a cracked country accent, was taped by the English collector Mike Yates in Sodom Laurel, North Carolina, in 1980. It's a song first alluded to in a play first performed in London in 1611. Thus does history endure.)

Lee Smith's *Oral History* opens with the folk song 'Fair And Tender Ladies', and with the firmly communal nature of Appalachina culture is told by a procession of voices, as the family tree in a family bible begins to fill out. One of the voices is 'Little Luther', a crippled but natural singer, "in a high bluegrass falsetto". The instigator of this detective story in reverse is Jennifer, a college student who arrives with a tape recorder to catch the dying embers of folk tradition among her own extended family. What begins to reveal itself is much more disturbing than anything which could ever be captured on tape, although a final twist turns the whole thing into a tall tale, a shaggy dog story from the hills.

Perhaps people are turning back to country music because, as opposed to the supposition of dumbness which the media erects around it, it's the most intelligent pop music going. This goes all the way back to country's roots in folklore and ballad, no matter how removed from such things Nashville songwriters may now pretend to be. The very pulse of this history is buried somewhere in the music, and the finest contemporary country musicians are trying once again to find it, and dance to its beat.

In Joseph O'Connor's travelogue, when a Nashville bar band receives a request from the audience for the Hank Williams song 'Just A Closer Walk With Thee', they immediately launch into "Just a plate of butter peas/a toasted sandwich with Swiss cheese/just a nice big steak, oh please". The audience is delighted but he is shocked, thinking that, "for a traditional country buff, this would be every bit as blasphemous as Sid Vicious singing 'My Way' was to Frank Sinatra fans". But of course, that's the point; if O'Connor had got up and parodied Hank, he would have barely got out of there alive, but this is Hank's own people being affectionate. You're allowed to poke fun, but only if you're already one of the family.

Country music uses certain stock phrases, and every performer who adds to the tradition puts them together again in a new and unexpected way. It's just because country is generally perceived to be played by and for simpletons that Carson goes over the top in the opposite direction.

Sharyn McCrumb's introduction to *Foggy Mountain Breakdown* declares proudly that she comes from a race of storytellers: "My father's family settled in the Smoky Mountains of western North Carolina in 1790", travelling across from Scotland. "They seemed to want mountains, land and as few neighbours as possible." Like Appalachian singers, she recycles Celtic myth as American narrative. Her short story 'John Knox In Paradise' is the old Scots border tale of Thomas The Rhymer retold: True Thomas and the queen of Elfland become a modern Scot and a young American woman, but she still weaves her spell.

Sharyn traces her Celtic ancestors as they first migrate from Switzerland to the wilder shores of Europe. They unwittingly meet again in "the great American cultural stew" of the late 18th century: "A folktale here, a superstition there, or a snatch of an old fiddle tune there" – by such means they recognise one another. "Always flat-landers thought them strange and backward, because they'd rather live poor and free in the beauty of mountains than grow prosperous in the fertile lowlands…there's a word for 'hillbilly' in the language of every country with highlands."

McCrumb's novels are a country fan's delight, with all manner of sly references to musical heroes: *If Ever I Return, Pretty Peggy-O* even has a retired folk singer from the Sixties trying for a comeback at its centre, while *The Ballad Of Frankie Silver* describes parallels between the first woman to be hanged in North Carolina and a man lingering on death row – both choose to die rather than betray their families. The latter even comments, with the ghost of a smile, that, after his execution, "they can play 'The Green, Green Grass Of Home'. That's a real tearjerker."

The Folk Song Society was founded in London in 1898: "the members were mainly professional singers, musical journalists…most of them not distinguished for their knowledge of folk song", though they included the composers Edward Elgar, Antonin Dvorak and Edvard Grieg, all of whom were to incorporate traditional folk tunes into the classical canon. Early collectors were almost exclusively interested in the words, not the tunes which accompanied them.

Cecil Sharp, however, was a professional musician. In 1903, he had been staying with his friend the Reverend Charles Marson when he heard the vicarage gardener singing 'The Seeds Of Love'. (By the way of such things, the singer's name was John England.) By the dimming of the day, Sharp had arranged the words and music of the song for choir and piano, and had performed it to an audience, one of whom said approvingly that it was the first time that the song had been put "into evening dress". The song was copyrighted to Sharp, not to John England, as the piano arrangement was deemed to be an artistic creation in its own right. Thus opened a century of musical cattle raids on the public domain.

Cecil then cycled through the West Country like a butterfly collector, catching songs and country dances in his net. As his contemporaries explored darkest Africa and plundered it for booty, so he plunged into the "peasant" culture of his own land. Almost by chance he captured the dying embers of a culture which sounds closer to the American Wild West than Victorian England, "when the village had a more or less independent existence, built its own church, hanged its own rogues, made its own boots, shirts and wedding rings, and chanted its own tunes".

There were other folk song collectors, but none so single-minded. Only the Australian composer Percy Grainger thought things through fully. He sought to capture the performances as well, realising that these singers were not just there by chance, wild birds, unconscious of the tunes they piped, but artists in their own right.

Sharp also recorded some of his singers on a portable machine, but for him they provided rough diamonds for him to polish. In *English Folk-Song, Some Conclusions*, published at his own expense, he claimed that these "folk-ballads" were much the same throughout Europe: "Some have been traced to an Eastern origin, and they all appear to have been drawn from a common storehouse." After certain events in Germany, Sharp's supposition that this was the heritage of "the Arian race" has tended to fall from the cultural agenda. Ultimately, Cecil Sharp is to folk song what Darwin is to the theory of evolution, and he used the same patient method, immersing himself in his subject matter, from which he then evolved a theory to explain everything.

Sharp identified three principles determining the oral transmission of the music of the people down through the years: first there was continuity, as musicians attempted to reproduce what they had heard; then there was variation, as they brought their own personalities to bear on the material; and finally there was selection, when the next person to take up the song chose which of these new variants they liked most. For Sharp, folk songs change almost by accident, and the best singers act in an "unconscious" way as they alter the songs they pass on.

By the start of the Great War, Sharp had founded the English Folk Dance Society and taken over the Folk Song Society. His health was already failing, but his greatest musical adventure still lay ahead. He had just finished hosting a summer school in Maine, and was laid up with an attack of lumbago (caused, no doubt, by all that country dancing) when he was visited by Mrs Olive Campbell. During visits to the Southern Appalachians, she had been startled by the songs of the mountain people. Sharp was at first unenthusiastic, but once he had read some of the songs she had noted down, he turned back to her with an "almost lenient look", amazed by what she had found: "I am told he improved from that day." He first visited the area for himself in 1916, and over the next two years journeyed by horse and trap to 80 or so settlements along with his secretary, Maud Karpeles, who kept a record of this great adventure.

At White Rock, Sharp found that "the singers are just English peasants in appearance, speech and manner. It is most refreshing to be once again amongst one's own people." Two weeks later, he decided that, "although the people are so English, they have their American quality. They are freer than the English peasant. They own their own land, and have done so for three to four generations, so that there is none of the servility which unhappily is one of the characteristics of the English peasant." Such praise was unusual for a people usually referred to as "mountain whites" or "poor white trash" in those unenlightened times.

Karpeles is just as clear-eyed: "Like all primitive people, they mature at a young age and they marry young; often at the age of 13 or 14. The first marriage is often not a success, and the couple separate, usually without any ill feeling."

Very few of the mountain people could read or write, "but they were good talkers", using uncommon expressions, "many of which were old English". Their "charm of manner is a constant delight – they have an easy, unaffected bearing". Sharp and Karpeles were welcomed everywhere they went, and were treated with great hospitality. The locals had no notion using of music as an entertainment; it was part of everyday life, like breathing. "There now," said a woman struggling to remember a song for Cecil, "if only I were driving the cows home, I should remember it at once." Almost all of the tunes heard during their travels were "of surpassing beauty".

Some of the best songs were provided by children. One small boy amazed them by singing the whole of 'Young Hunting', in a way "which would have shamed many a professional singer". Sharp noted down the tunes in ordinary notation, while Maud took down the words in shorthand. Sharp put aside his earlier preconception that such music was universal among mountain folk. It was, ironically, a by-product of "bad economic conditions. When there is coal and good wages to be earned, the families soon drop their old-fashioned ways." In Clay County, frame houses had replaced log cabins and the inhabitants "received my remarks about the old songs with a superiority of air that was almost contemptuous". One ballad singer described such folk as people who "have got rich before they have any money".

Sharp's lust for country dance was satisfied in spades when he saw and noted down "the Running Set, an unsophisticated form of the now-popular American Square Dance". Sharp himself wrote of how "the moon streamed fitfully in lighting up the mountain peaks...casting its mysterious light, seeming to exaggerate the wildness and break-neck speed of the dancers, as they whirled through the mazes of the dance". This was a dance without music, just the stamping and clapping of the onlookers, but the very air seemed to vibrate in rhythm: "Over and above it all penetrated the even, falsetto tones of the Caller."

Dancing had such a bad reputation as a prelude to heavy drinking and shootouts and the like that it was called "playing" by participants as a form of disguise. Maud joined in on a "bean-stringing", performed in a "small, unventilated space about twelve feet square into which 30 or 40 people besides the dancers managed to squeeze themselves".

Practically all of the songs collected by Sharp and Karpeles can be traced to English or lowland Scots sources, but they are subtly different to variants of such songs he had collected in England a few years before. "Whether they have suffered a sea-change, or whether they represent English folk music of an earlier period, is open to argument. On the whole they are more austere, possibly less mellow, but no less beautiful, though their beauty may not be so obvious. Many of the tunes have a primordial intensity of expression, which strikes at the very root of our being." That high, lonesome sound.

Sharp was to collect the cream of his findings in the two-volume work *English Folk-Songs From The Southern Appalachians*, "comprising 273 Songs and Ballads with 968 Tunes", which also includes the tunes collected by Olive Campbell. As Sharp writes in his introduction, these are the produce of people "immune from that continuous, grinding mental pressure due to the attempt to make a living, from which nearly all of us in this modern world suffer". This, in 1932! Right at the start of this book, I argued that country music could provide a balm for the chafings of a post-Marxist world of downsized companies and "hot-desking", temporary contracts (like this book, in fact) and multitasking; and here is Sharp making exactly the same point when discussing the music from which country music – of which he seems blissfully unaware – was just starting to emerge, like a fossil found deep in ancient rock but a fossil fully alive nonetheless, rowdy and wearing a cowboy hat.

The songs themselves form a fascinating study in how a culture can move continents – almost, one might say, how it can move to another language – and be gently transformed in the process. This is Sharp's own theory of continuity, variation and selection, preserved in aspic.

In one of the 16 variants of 'Little Musgrave And Lady Barnard' collected during this trip, the one delivered by Mr Doc Pratt of Knott County, the tiny adulterer is invited to "strike the very first lick". Having chopped off his errant wife's head, Lord Darnel "stove it" against the ground. Most startling of all are the lines "It's just my uncle's negroes/herding my sheep to the barn," which certainly appear in none of the Scottish versions.

Other versions depart from the Celtic originals, like a bagpipe tune played bluegrass style: Mrs Sudie Sloan has "my little footy-page", and lovers who "fell to hugging and kissing", while Delie Knucklese watches how the foot page "dingled on the ring", Effie Mitchell has Lady Darnell as "my pretty little Miss", and for Jane Gentry she "raised up about half a doze asleep".

Here is a songbag which continues to be raided to this day, and doubtless will be continued to be plundered long after the book you currently hold in your hands has turned to dust and you likewise. The two volumes are full of echoes of the future. Thus does 'The Death Of Queen Jane' predict Bob Dylan's 'Queen Jane Approximately', and 'Gone To Cripple Creek' The Band's song of almost the same title, with the same sense of happy contentment: "gone…to have some fun".

Here is jovial racism: in 'The Old Grey Mare', half nonsense, half ancient ritual, when the singer puts her hide in a loft, "up came a nigger and stole it off". Here is the flora and fauna of a new land: "The raccoon's tail is ringed around/the opossum's tail is bare", and the squirrel eats up all the farmer's corn. Here, too, are mountain delights, so that, in 'Sugar Babe', "I got drunk and I reel against the wall/good corn liquor was the cause of it all." And here is just the kind of down-home surrealism which will resurface in the Harry Smith *Anthology* as country blues and in *The Basement Tapes* as drugged humour: "Sally in the garden was shifting sand, all upstairs with the hog-eyed man." Pure innuendo, if Cecil had but known it. As Dylan once put it: "Something is happening here, and you don't know what it is."

Maud Karpeles returned to the Appalachians 40 years on, but "the log cabins have nearly all disappeared. People no longer ride mule-back, but they go spinning along the roads in motor cars. The serpent, in the form of the radio, has crept in, bearing its insidious hill-billy and other pop songs." Had she but realised, it was into this so-called hill-billy that the music she loved so much had disappeared.

The English Folk Song Society felt it beholden upon itself to issue some printed *Hints To Collectors*, which say much about the nature of such cultural raids on the underclass. This refers to folk songs as if they were rare birds, fit to be stuffed: "Although folk music may be preserved in different strata of society, the classes from which the most interesting specimens are most readily to be obtained are gardeners, artisans, gamekeepers, shepherds, rustic labourers, gipsies, sailors, fishermen, workers at old fashioned trades, such as weaving, lace-making and the like, as well as domestic servants." Add cowboys and factory workers and you've got pure country.

Of course, sometimes the chosen victim cannot sing, so "may be asked to whistle the airs, or play them upon a violin". The kind of material to be collected has been decided in advance: "It will be found that the word 'song' often suggests something modern; it may be necessary to point out to them that nothing they learnt at school, or heard at a concert, is wanted." It is to Cecil Sharp's eternal glory that he ignored such demands, and wrote down a dollop of nonsense ditties and hymns and childrens' songs from the Appalachians which, if anything, are even more fascinating than the "big" ballads. They, too, endure.

One mystery remains: a large proportion of the tunes collected by Sharp in America are in the pentatonic scale, a scale without semitones. Many Gaelic tunes correspond to this scale, but this was true of few in England at that time. Sharp had two theories about this: firstly that this more "primitive" scale was in common use among the English peasantry at the time at which the ancestors of these mountain people left for America; or secondly that these songs had originally come into the

English-speaking world from the Scottish or Irish Gaels. Maybe both are true, or maybe neither. Whichever applies, it is incontrovertable that the musical backbone of country has Celtic roots.

Scholars have since found that such ballads were not unique to the southern Appalachians. Many have also since emerged in New England and the plains of Mississippi and Texas. The mountains acted as a barrier rather than a cradle, like a rockpool left exposed by an ebbing tide. Country music has evolved all over North America.

The first person to properly categorise these ancient ballads was an American, Francis James Child, although he restricted his examples to those collected in England and Scotland. His source material was mainly drawn from oral sources, and largely tended to ignore "broadsides" (roughly-printed street poetry which disseminated many of these songs in the first place). In his wonderful *Come Day, Go Day, God Send Sunday*, the life story of the Irish traditional singer John Maguire, he remembers his father buying a ballad from an itinerant singer: "They sung lots of songs and told you before what the song was. And there was a wee boy would go about with a great lot of them in his hand…they were priced from about twopence to threepence apiece, and I remember they used to get them all sold, every one of them. Nearly everyone bought a ballad." The Nashville marketing juggernaut starts here. It's interesting that the punters sampled the wares first, so to speak, so that these ballads weren't so much an equivalent of the modern paperback as a concert souvenir.

One of these professional ballad singers stood out: "He wore a fairly long beard and he had a young girl with him who played an ordinary fiddle. Sometimes he would dance a step to her playing, as well as singing the song." Dwight Yoakam, eat your heart out. By happy chance, the broadside which his father bought that day was 'Thousands Are Sailing To America'.

The itinerant singers seemed to disappear in the early 1920s, at just around the time when the American phonograph industry was setting itself up to release the work of "hillbilly" artists. Perhaps all of the ballad singers went off in search of recording contracts.

When he came to put them into printed form, Cecil Sharp divided the songs he found in America into ballads, songs, hymns, nursery songs, jigs and "play-party games". His collection starts with 'The Elfin Knight' and ends with 'Some Love Coffee', a jovial piece of nonsense verse: "Some loves coffee, some loves tea/some love's money, but they don't love me/singing in the lonesome comboy-ee/singing in the lonesome sea." All human life is here, in two blue-bound hardbacks with gold lettering courtesy of the Oxford University Press, but if the coffee song is the hobo of the world of traditional song then the Child ballad is the aristocrat; its grace and majesty secures it top billing in Sharp's collection, and everywhere else.

The classic ballad, honed by long immersion in the folk tradition, tends to plunge into the action and end just as abruptly. Broadsides, the writers of which were paid per word, take more time to set the scene, and usually end with a moral homily. They are often told by an identified narrator – "My name is Daniel Martin, I'm borned in Arkansas" – and relate a real-life event, usually a brutal murder or a hanging. This is popular journalism, rather than a feature film. By their very nature, ballads tend to be edited down by those who sing them, and they end up cut to the bone. Country songwriting has inherited this same self-discipline, which makes its products so memorable. Every word counts.

Over in America, however, the broadside also took on a whole new lease of life. There were lots of new murders and hangings to commemorate, such as the Taylor gang's slaughter of Gus Meeks and his family in 1894. The resulting ballad takes on a supernatural edge, as young Nellie emerges from the grave to denounce her killers: "She stood before the doorway with that awful gash in her head/While she sobbed and wept most bitterly, these were the words she said." This, as yet, lacks the conciseness which Child demands of his entries.

Closer to his demands are the blues, which use formulaic language and speaking almost as a form of shorthand, but unlike British folk music the blues were usually accompanied on banjo or guitar, with instrumental breaks to provide breathing space, elements which would soon cross the racial divide. To demonstrate quite how subtle these cultural shifts can be, David Atkinson compiled a "song trail" for 'The Unfortunate Rake' in *Root And Branch*, a new publication by the English Folk Dance And Song Society, which was founded to explore just such things.

The song was first published in 1808, as 'The Jewel, My Joy', a single-verse piece about a military funeral: "Sound the dead march as my corpse goes along." By the mid 19th century, the song had been printed as a broadside under the title 'The Buck's Elegy', set now in Covent Garden, London. It's clear that the "sad death" of the buck is due to a sexually transmitted disease: "Come all gallows whores who do mourn after me…" The song enters oral tradition, and is variously collected as being about the mourning of a trooper, a sailor and a young girl, all cut down in their prime. The nature of the fatal disease is explained boldly enough (though not directly), either by the stench of the corpse or a warning that "flash girls from the city was the ruin of me". The old songs are nothing if not plainly spoken.

And so over to America. By now the dying man has changed profession again, and the song is now known under titles like 'The Streets Of Laredo', or, more specifically still, 'The Dying Cowboy'. Cecil Sharp noted down an English version in 1909, from "Shepherd" Haden in East Meon. Nine years later, over in Peaks Of Otter in Bedford County, Virginia, he took down 'St James' Hospital' from two female singers, Almeda Riddle and Texas Gladden. Now, though, the cause of the cowboy's demise is a bar-room brawl, not syphilis.

"O once in my saddle I used to go dashing,

62

O once in my saddle, I used to be gay,
I first commenced drinking and then to gambling,
I'm shot through the breast and I know I must die."

The song moves across the genre divide to jazz and blues as 'St James' Infirmary', with "16 coal-black horses/all formed in a line". In this version, dating from around 1910, there are no suspicious circumstances, and the dying lover has changed sex.

Then on to the logging camps of Pennsylvania. 'The Wild Lumberjack' was published in 1923. Lines like "Once out in the forest I used to go slashing/once in the big timbers I used to be gay" are closer to Monty Python than to Cecil Sharp. Meanwhile, a variant from Montana sees our hero die of silicosis.

In 1957, the professional folk singer Rosalie Sorrels taped a song which her husband had learned from a colleague in the telegraph industry. 'The Lineman's Hymn' is a deliberate parody, and one of many in which the song is adapted to new professions.

"T'was once up the poles I used to go dashing,
T'was once up the poles I used to go gay:
First up the 60s and then up the 90s,
But I fell off an 18, and I'm dying today."

Such songs are strong – and commercial – enough to leap the great divide between traditional folk and Nashville's version of Tin Pan Alley. Nick Tosches explores two examples: 'The Bottle Preferr'd' was collected in Scotland in 1737, and is sung by a supposed monarch of the public bar, while Shel Silverstein's song 'Queen Of The Silver Dollar' was a country hit in 1973 for Doyle Holly, and has exactly the same central image: "Her sceptre is a wine glass/and a bar stool is her throne."

Just as strange is the tangled history of country favourite 'Deck Of Cards', a maudlin recitation in which a quick-witted young soldier explains that, when he is found with a pack of cards during a church service, he is not playing Sergeant Bilko but instead deriving spiritual satisfaction. (Believe that, and…!) A hit for Wink Martindale in 1959, the tall tale had already seen chart action for its author, T Texas Tyler, and for Tex Ritter. Like a hot bluegrass riff, it had already mutated into 'The Viet Nam Deck Of Cards', 'Hillbilly Deck Of Cards' and 'Cowboy's Deck Of Cards', but Tosches puts time in reverse, finding the same idea first in a 19th-century sermon and then as a British folk tale, 'The Gentleman Soldier's Prayer Book', which dates back to the Middle Ages.

Now Tosches pulls his most spectacular rabbit out of the hat. Warren Smith's 1956 B-side 'Black Jack David' remains one of the toughest rockers to come out of the Sun studios in Memphis. "I wrote it," claims Smith, and he also copyrighted the song, but Tosches traces it to Cliff Carlisle's 1939 song of much the same name, and further back to a British ballad 'The Gypsie Laddie' which was printed by Robert Burns in 1808, and right back to the pre-Christian myth of Orpheus. Warren Smith is confronted with all of this, and admits to having heard something vaguely similar in the cradle, "but I changed it around altogether". He was in the studio, searching for inspiration, and "I set down then and started writin' it then, and we cut it the same night. I was kinda halfway crazy about it, y'know?" And so the circle turns.

By just this kind of alchemy, the accents of British folk turned into an American twang, up there in the hills. It is the pivot on which the music turns. From here on in, it's country music all the way.

The Frenchman Jacques Vassal described the hillbilly style as if handling it with sugar tongs. The first thing to notice is "an extremely nasal tone in a constricted and high-pitched accent. The final syllables of each line are often stretched out and exaggerated to produce an effect which is partly comical, partly insistent. To add to the strangeness, there are various cries in the form of yodels, common to certain mountain peoples of Europe, as in the Tyrol, designed to exploit the echo effects produced by the mountains."

Be that as it may, the singer Jean Ritchie is a *bona fide* traditional singer, even if she now lives in New York. She was the youngest of 14 children, and wrote a beautiful account of growing up in Viper, Perry County, in her book *Singing Families Of The Cumberlands*: "My father's name was Ritchie and my mother's name was Hall…She was English and he was Scottish, and there were a lot of Irish, Welsh, and a few German families, and we all got intermarried so the music got sort of intermarried, too." Following the British tradition, these were still songs without anything added: "There weren't even any instruments, we didn't even have a dulcimer…In the old days they just sang, they didn't have any accompaniment to their voice." This was partly due to a religious prejudice against such wicked things as banjos and fiddles, popularly viewed to be "instruments of the devil".

Unlike back in England, in America there was some unison singing, and this spread into other forms of home entertainment: "When you danced and you didn't have a fiddle, you made the rhythm with your hands and you just sang the song, and the people who weren't dancing would stand on the side and help sing and help do the rhythm."

In 1952, Jean Ritchie was granted a Fulbright scholarship to visit Britain and research the origins of the culture in which she grew up, where she found that insight could strike at the strangest moments. On one evening she was sitting in Sara Makem's kitchen, in County Armagh, and as the bacon sizzled on the stove Sara fell into 'As I Roved Out', which transported Jean back to her childhood. "It was a play game that we played back home; it was called 'Old King Cole Was A Jolly Old Soul', and it used almost the same tune. So that's how the music got there! Sometimes the words were changed, but the tune remained the same. They had a way of keeping the Irish tunes, mostly because the Irish tunes were far superior, of course."

From this point on, one must be careful to keep in mind the difference between traditional singers like Maken and Ritchie – who both literally learnt the music at their mother's apron strings – and revivalists. Many whose work we will discuss later have come to the "old-time music" through a conscious decision rather than through the rediscovery of an heirloom. The meaning of the words "folk singer" has crossed over from one to the other, but when no less an archetype than Joan Baez was asked if she was such, she replied tartly (as is her wont) that, if she really was a "folk singer", she would live on an old farm in the Appalachians, wear dated clothes and sing with a nasal whine, which is hardly Joan's style. There is a profound difference between being moved or influenced by the sound of The Carter Family, for example, and actually being one of them. Many pretend, though.

The Edward Gibbon of country music studies is Bill C Malone, and with the publication of his book in 1984 he largely traces the music's decline and fall until that time, and cites Ricky Skaggs and Emmylou Harris as two hopes for the future. There isn't a stetson in sight. He ends by quoting country DJ Hugh Cherry: "Let us remember what happens when you kill the roots of a tree – it dies." In the time since, those roots have been well fertilised and the tree is branching into all kinds of strange configurations. It is merely a reflection of my own innate good taste that I have shamelessly used Malone's magisterial *Country Music, USA* as my guide through much of what is to come. That said, however, it's not exactly a snappy read.

Malone points out that "Indians of the back country; Spanish, French and mixed breed elements in the Mississippi Valley, the Mexicans of South Texas; and, of course, blacks everywhere" all added something to the melting pot from which country music emerged. White Southerners, to whom the very idea of socialising with Afro-Americans would be anathema, have nevertheless joyfully taken black music as their own: "a whole host of dance steps, vocal shadings, and instrumental techniques".

This practice pre-dated the gramophone. Whites met blacks at county fairs and on street corners, at work and at worship. Even in the mountains, "both the guitar and the blues form may have ventured…with black labourers who followed the highways and railroads as they gradually inched their way up the ridges". Way outside the scope of this book, but nonetheless worthy of mention, is how black culture has also impacted back on Irish and Scottish traditional music, with the trail-blazing work of Afro-Celtic Sound System and many black musicians now making regular tours of Ireland and Scotland. As always, such things work both ways; the mystical poet Aidan Dun told me about Celtic music from the Appalachians flowing down into the Delta, like a holy river of sound.

Malone reminds us that the mountains were not devoid of visitors: Methodist preachers, singing teachers with their shape-note hymnals, salesmen and pedlars visited them. Here were travelling shows, the "physick wagon" with its smooth talking "doctors" selling snake oil, or the "tent repertory" with its acrobats and Swiss yodellers and dancing bears. Malone's own father remembers a tent show visiting his home town in East Texas for a week, and the locals coming night after night, "bartering eggs, vegetables, or canned goods for the price of admission".

Thousands of country boys ventured into the big cities to work or play, and came back with what they had found. Here was black culture, from the street-corner blues singer to the abhorrent "blackface" minstrel shows, with their banjo extravaganzas. Here, too, were vaudeville troupes, with a whole repertoire of well crafted songs, Hawaiian string bands, and silent movies with pianola accompaniment. There were illicit musical pleasures in the red-light zones of Dallas or Memphis, and uplifting ones in the hymns of Isaac Watts and British methodism. Through the oral tradition, all of this was simplified into country: "Complex chords were eliminated, melodies were flattened, and words were often forgotten, or unconsciously changed." The "rural conservatism" of the South helped to preserve all of this music long after it had been "forgotten or scorned elsewhere".

The result was like a richly-stocked stewpot, brought slowly to the boil, and the essence was participation, not just passive listening. In open-air "camp meetings", those attending were encouraged to add their own call-and-response patterns to the hymns, while a "folk fatalism" coloured songs like 'The Old Rugged Cross' or 'Farther Along'. Central to the Southern gospel tradition was a deeply nostalgic sense of home and chapel, as a "bastion of security in a world of constant change". It is still so, and country music has taken this vision deep into its heart.

In the spiritual wake of the 'Great Awakening', the word of God was carried to the people by travelling evangelists, often at huge outdoor camp meetings, and the impetus spread to a whole nexus of chapels and sects. Joseph O'Connor steps into a local tabernacle to find a scene straight out of the most lurid imaginings of The Alabama 3. The congregation sing "morbid" hymns, then a Jerry Lee Lewis lookalike mounts the pulpit and rains down hellfire: "You've got yer young people all a-pokin' and a-snufflin' and a-dancin' and a-prancin' in the stinkin' manure heap of sin and filth." O'Connor leaves quietly, reckoning that some sin and filth would suit him just fine.

The final elements to go into the musical blender were parlour songs. These were sentimental ballads quite unlike those from traditional sources, songs which Malone characterises as dealing with "dying orphans, neglected mothers, blind children, maidens who died of broken hearts and eastbound trains that carried penniless children to see their poor blind convict fathers". These songs provided balm to a nation which had just undergone a bloody and pitiless civil war, but their sickly content has stained some country music to this day.

Fortunately, country music contributes an ironic edge, so that a song which sounds at first to be of this ilk turns around neatly on a pun, to reveal its true nature: 'I Keep On Missing You (But My Aim Is Getting Better)'.

The most important instrument was still the human voice. Early country stars like AP Carter had first learned how to sing in gospel quartets, though even this, the purest of heart of all musical genres, was driven by money. By 1930, the music publisher James Vaughan was paying at least 16 male quartets (comprising first tenor, second tenor, baritone and bass) to travel around the South, promoting his songs. Even today, scratch a country singer and you'll find a gospel fan underneath. All-day "singing conventions" would be held at local courthouses, with dinner served in the grounds, almost like a kind of Woodstock without any electricity, nudity or drugs. It has been convincingly argued that the elaborate metaphors so beloved of country songwriters stem in part from 19th-century hymns, and it's true that the kind of singing usually only heard on a Sunday embedded itself deep into the Southern soul.

It's almost part of the climate. Methodism was known popularly as "the singing church", and a collection of "shape-note" tunes, published in Georgia in 1844 and titled *The Sacred Harp*, went on to give its name to a whole tradition. These are songs which can still pierce the heart when one encounters their mournful affirmations.

With a new century, however, such music began to sound a little out of date. The evangelist Dwight Moody and singer Ira Sankey joined forces to create a new genre, the "revival hymn". This was more subjective, and stressed personal salvation rather than a communal ecstasy, a precursor of the "me-generation". When Sankey, died in 1908, she had sold around 50 million hymn books, and had earned royalties to match. The country music establishment is not unaware of such sales figures, and God has continued to do well for both man and mammon.

Settlers brought over the fiddle from Europe in the late 17th century. Even though traditional tunes were passed on without the benefit of musical notation, the tunes tended to stay much the same, while their names were democratised, so that 'Lord McDonald's Reel' became 'Leather Breeches' (supposedly about farting), while even an American sounding tune such as 'Flop-Eared Mule' was probably taken from a British tune. The new world inspired tunes of location, such as 'Cumberland Gap' or 'Sourwood Mountain'. There were, however, other sources – black fiddlers were common in the 19th century, while 'Over The Waves' was written by a Mexican, 'Fisher's Hornpipe' by a German, and 'Under The Double Eagle' was originally an Austrian march in praise of the Emperor.

Distinct fiddling styles evolved in different regions, and its players were in great demand for dances, which would often follow "work gatherings" or "moonlights", which were basically pie-and-ice-cream suppers. A description survives from 1793 of a local Tennessee adept called Gamble: "He had a sack of doeskin, in which he placed his 'fiddle and bow' when not in use. He could make his fiddle laugh and talk. There was such potency in its music that he often charmed away the pains of the body and silenced the groans of the sick." For dances, a fiddler would be paid according to how many sets he played, "ten cents on the corner". There were also other inducements: Uncle Jimmy Thompson claimed that "I just naturally need a little of the white lightning to grease my arm".

Some fiddlers would sing as they played, or called out the dance steps. A more usual accompaniment, however, was the five-string banjo, although when Thomas

Jefferson wrote in 1781 of a "banjar", Malone believed it to be something close to a "gourdlike device" brought over from Africa. Early Appalachian examples were made out of groundhog skins, and a fifth string was added by the minstrel entertainer Joel Sweeney the 1830s. This variant became closely identified with mountain music, to "lend pathos to a lonely lament, or give driving excitement to the wild hoedown".

Other instruments later found favour, once they became available through mail order firms like Sears Roebuck. Guitars were originally considered to be too upmarket for country music, but they started to appear in the hands of black construction gangs at around the time of the Great War. For this reason, the most complicated style is still called "nigger picking", or at least it was until people realised quite how offensive this was.

The dulcimer probably came over with German immigrants, and in Malone's words "beautifully complemented the singing of lonesome ballads", although it had a sound which was too delicate to be of much use to the wild. Italian immigrants, meanwhile, brought the mandolin, which rapidly became fashionable, and the autoharp was originally a simple instrument for children, until it escaped the parlour when "ingenious musicians" learned how to pick individual notes on its strings.

Other instruments which found a new role in country music ranged from the piano to the jew's harp. Virtually anything that could play a note, or somehow came to hand, was re-invented and put to the service of reproducing these home-grown rhythms. When we now look back on the scraps that survive it is a strange music indeed, somehow even more remote and savage than country blues, like a mad thing released. It's easy to read back into it the pulse behind early rock 'n' roll (punk, even, if you add electricity and drums), but it's more interesting to look backwards rather than forwards. There is a driving quality which isn't even to be found in Celtic music, equally wild though that can be. Something happened up in those hills. Maybe it was the whisky, or maybe the devil really did come a-calling one day, on his way to find Robert Johnson.

Southern musicians began to group themselves into *ad hoc* string bands, usually comprising fiddle, banjo and guitar, the players of which were often members of the same family. The unbridled savagery of such music, made by string bands with names like Walker's Corbin Ramblers, still crackles out on historic 78rpm singles. It's music that was just caught on the brink of recording history, but it was recorded nonetheless. With the advent of the phonograph, the country music industry was about to be born.

In the early 1920s, the phonograph boom was in temporary decline and facing competition from the wireless, which didn't have you bobbing up every few minutes to change the needle or turn over the record. On the radio someone else did that for you, or you could take in a live concert brought directly to your sitting room. You could even join in yourself; to quote Malone, "a wave of barn dance programmes began appearing on radio stations throughout the United States".

Almost in desperation, US record companies began to seek out the ethnic music of their own homeland. Ironically, the delights of "hillbilly" music were only discovered as a by-product of a sudden craze for the blues, after black vaudeville singer Mamie Smith had an unexpected hit with 'Crazy Blues'. Ralph Peer, one of the "recording scouts" who had discovered her, set off for the rural South in search of raw talent.

Meanwhile, Texan fiddler Eck Robertson had turned up at Victor Records in New York in June 1922 with his friend and rival Henry Gilliland from Oklahoma, dressed for the part in cowboy suit and Confederate uniform. Robertson's solo version of 'Sallie Gooden' is still startling, and certainly in contention for the first commercial recording of country music. When Eck performed this and another early recording, 'Arkansas Traveller', on the Southern radio station WBAP – the "square dance shows" of which could be picked up as far afield as Hawaii and Canada – he created another first, that of plugging his "product" on country radio. Many have since followed, like flies on roadkill.

The first country hit established another tradition, that of the carpetbagger moving in on the music for pure profit. Vernon Dalhert was one of the hundred or so stage names adopted by a classically-trained Texan singer called Marion Try Slaughter, and slaughter the music he sure did: Dalhert jumped on the hillbilly bandwagon with 'The Wreck Of The Old 97', backed with 'The Prisoner's Song'. It was the perfect commercial release: a train-wreck ballad and a hard-luck tale from behind bars, and it literally sold a million.

Dalhert had already ripped off black music with songs like 'Can't Yo' Hear Me Callin'', and 'The Wreck Of The Old 97' was taken note for note from a performance by the Virginian harmonica player Henry Whittier. However, Dalhert had found his niche; from then on he sang plaintive songs, also managing to sound as if he had a broom handle poking up his rear end. Dalhert established another country music tradition, that of squeezing your hits dry, and 'The Prisoner's Song' was re-recorded for at least a dozen different labels, alongside overwrought nonsense such as 'The Fatal Wedding' and 'The Dying Girl's Message', which, just to confuse things, went on to enter the tradition. Later folk song collectors recorded homespun versions of these songs, as if they were ancient masterpieces, but it was so much fool's gold. Like many who followed, Vernon made and sold millions but died in abject poverty: his music sounds impossibly dated now, while the real thing merely sounds timeless.

Meanwhile, Ralph Peer had reached Atlanta in his quest for new talent, and in June 1923 he recorded the first undistilled mountain singing ever committed to wax, when Fiddlin' John Carson walked into the temporary studio they had set up. Carson, already in his fifties, had been born and bred in Georgia, where he had won many "old-time" fiddling contests and was a local star on WSB radio, but Peer was still dismayed by the raw and anarchic sound of John's solo singing and scraping, which he reckoned was "pluperfect awful". Peer passed up the chance to issue the rustic delights of 'The Little Old Log Cabin In The Lane' and 'The Old Hen Cackled And The Rooster's Going To Crow' on his Okeh label, instead pressing up 500 semi-bootleg discs purely for local distribution. They had sold out within a month, however, and Peer reissued the disc on Okeh, immediately summoning Fiddlin' John to New York to sign on the dotted line and record more songs. He also released the Henry Whittier material which had, until then, languished in the vaults. A trend was set, and hillbilly was firmly on the national agenda.

In the way of such things, Carson's work is now available on a series of seven CDs, their sound lovingly remastered. The equally meticulous *F Roots* gave a rave review to "the sort of music which people really wanted to hear sung by one of themselves instead of the dreary crooners and dance band versions foisted on them by record companies", although it admits that Carson's fiddle was "visionary in the way it ignores conventional harmony" (like a cat on heat, perhaps), and that the recording quality is such as to make "much of the music quite painful to hear". For modern ears, Carson's later work with his band The Virginia Reelers and his daughter, Moonshine Kate, is far more palatable. That said, the Document re-release illustrates the full range of the hillbilly palette: blues, square dances, cowboy tunes, minstrel numbers, "comic" songs like 'It's A Shame To Whip Your Wife On Sunday', and old British ballads. Just to list some of Fiddlin' John's repertoire of tunes – including 'Cotton-Eyed Joe', 'Old Joe Clark', 'Fire In The Mountain', 'Turkey In The Straw', 'Charming Betsey' and 'Cripple Creek' – is to hear the sound of history.

Ira Spain had the onerous job of transcribing his music – so much part of the oral tradition – onto sheet music. It must have been like taming a wild mule; this music was not made for polite recitation: "Poor John couldn't make a record unless he was a little more than half drunk, and he always had to have a 'jaw-breaker' – a candy ball about half as big as a golf ball – in his mouth, and he would roll that around when singing. His words were so muddled up at times that we had to almost guess at what he was saying."

In the wake of John Carson, a whole slew of singles on 78rpm shellac were sold as a commercial proposition (in some cases, much to our 21st-century incredulity), and these show the wildness and grace of mountain music. The carefully-posed photographs of these musicians that survive provide an ironic contrast with their unhinged music. They sit uneasily, as stiff as boards, with shoes well polished and ties tight on the collar. Only the presence of fiddles, banjos, harmonicas, mandolins, cellos and mountain dulcimers – mostly held like weapons – indicate that these same white men (as they all are) are set for musical mayhem.

Before marketing neatly divided acts into "race records" and "old Southern tunes", when the catalogues of the time indicated which was which by the colour of the folk depicted on the sleeve, there were many Afro-American string bands. Some of the best were documented recently on the Folkways CD *Black Banjo Songsters*, with traditional songs like 'John Henry', 'John Hardy' and 'The Coo Coo Bird' on their set lists.

Volume one of Yazoo's *The Cornshucker's Frolic: Downhome Music And Entertainment From The American Countryside* mixes and matches both ebony and ivory. To be brutally honest, some of the music here could have graced a torture chamber: the shrill mix of scratchy violins and weird shoutings could be the soundtrack to bedlam. It's also amazingly exciting, with a wildness completely at odds with the CD sleeve, a 19th-century painting of a couple dancing in an open barn to music supplied by a solitary fiddler, with the look of a poet about him. The sleeve notes are po-faced, and are given their own colour bar: one critic for white, one for black. Matching them to the individual tracks would defeat Umberto Eco. Here, though, are the likes of The Red Headed Fiddlers, Walter Coon And His Joy Boys and The Binkley Brothers Dixie Clodhoppers. These are names that you really couldn't invent, and probably wouldn't want to.

There are all kinds of rough delights here. It's like dipping a bucket into a mountain stream and then looking closely at some of the weird a quatic life-forms with the microscope of time. To plunge in at random, Crockett's Kentucky Mountaineers – a father and his five sons – look like the Wild Bunch, in belts and braces. Their music mimics a rabbit hunt, and bounces along with a strange duet between fiddle and jew's harp.

Freeny's Barn Dance Band is also a family affair, with two cousins on duelling fiddles, but they both sound as if they're scraping directly onto the bone and there's an unsettling series of gruff shouts directing the dancers. It sounds as ancient as America itself. The rural blues can be just as unsettling, but the Western listener is more prepared for that in a way – this has a kind of weird jet propulsion, with a strummed banjo. Meanwhile, the black duo Andrew and Jim Baxter are mellifluous in comparison, with a song about corn whisky. Without photographs of the artists, you really couldn't tell the two musical traditions apart.

Stoneman's Blue Ridge Cornshuckers open with a bit of staged banter that sounds like Laurel and Hardy on acid. The first few sentences are so slurred, and so full of ancient slang, that they could be in a foreign language. Then things come into a vague sort of focus: "We've got a nice fence rail for you to ride, Jinx." This doesn't sound like a tea party, and the newly-married Jinx nervously lives up to his name: "Now look here, don't be too rough." But Ernest "Pop" Stoneman sounds like a man with mischief on his mind: "Ride around the house two or three times, boys, and if the old man don't ask us in, we're gonna cab the wash-tub over the chimney and tote off the wash pot…" Another voice chimes in: "If he let's us in, we'll dance 'til daylight and then go home in the morning…Hot dog!"

Like a train chugging along the tracks, in comes the fiddle of Uncle Eck Dunford and the banjo of George Stoneman, with Pop on mouth harp and guitar and what sounds like somebody kicking an old fence. Jinx lets them in, and Pop immediately rearranges the furniture: "All right, dad, move the beds and the tables, we need plenty of room to dance." The new Mrs Jinx shouts out from another room "Don't break that light", and they all swing into 'Love Somebody'. "Everybody get your partners..." They then wish the newlyweds the best of luck: "See you at the next log-rolling."

In comparison, Bascar Lunsford sounds as sane as a practising lawyer should, with a voice as deep as the ocean but just as full of joy, and set to a rippling banjo so that the love song 'Kidder Cole' is as happy as could be, and you suddenly think this is the greatest and truest music in the world. There really don't seem to be any barriers between the singer's inner emotion and the music he produces , something you usually get in rock music only when someone like Syd Barrett or Skip Spence is on the edge of a nervous breakdown, or so drugged as not to care.

This is music without self-consciousness, and Fiddlin' Cowan Powers And Family could be in your front parlour, each showing off their instrumental prowess and – in the case of Charlie, the banjo player – his cornball humour: "I'll play this piece in style with the way that girls wear their skirts: short enough to be interesting and long enough to cover the subject." Cowan is, however, self-conscious enough to realise that it's now time for the listener to turn the record over: "On the other side we will give you a real Virginia reel." When they do, it suddenly feels good to be alive.

To dip the bucket into the stream in for a second time, volume one of *The Music Of Kentucky* represents white culture only, and includes recordings made by Alan Lomax in 1937, alongside remastered 78s of a generally Christian hue. It reminds us that many of the original settlers had headed west as religious dissidents, and brought over a fierce belief in sin and salvation with their luggage, as well as the old songs from home. This in-built puritanism echoes throughout the music to come. Meanwhile, Alfred Karnes is bound for the Promised Land, "his soul with rapture filled", and he does indeed sound truly uplifted, almost drunk with godliness, as his voice whoops and lurches skywards. Karnes was a barber who later became a preacher, and one wouldn't like to meet him either with an open razor or an open bible. He isn't user-friendly.

Ernest Phipps was a minister to the Pentecostal Holiness Church, and here is joined by his Holiness Singers. On 'A Little Talk With Jesus' they sound like a slightly tipsy (mixed sex) Salvation Army choir vocally, and a dry run for The Bonzo Dog (Doo Dah) Band instrumentally. The tempo is taken just a fraction too fast for comfort. When they ask 'If The Light Has Gone Out In Your Soul', this is to handclaps and again at a fast strut, so that one can imagine marching behind them, banging a tambourine. The image of sunshine and darkness is one that struck home with the musicians, for whom this risible but joyful sound opened a musical trail to follow. One thinks of Hank Williams desperately testifying to having seen the light, or of

The Grateful Dead in 'Truckin'": "Sometimes the light's all shining on me/other times I can barely see."

'Shine On Me', Phipps testifies along with wailing women and rolls on the piano, opening his throat wide for the Lord . He can't keep up the gloom too long, though, and they up the tempo to their usual hurtle. In one of those weird strokes of history, The Kentucky Ramblers consisted of Elmer Bird and his father, Louis, plus (if the sleeve notes are correct) Connie Byrd – folk rock starts here. They tinkle cheerfully with 'The Unfortunate Brakeman', and on 'Glory To The Lamb' mandolins chuckle and a three-part vocal harmony breaks out into a smile. Every day is happy when you're with the Lord, even the "holy gloom" of Saturday.

Another strain of early country music which perserved into Nashville is maudlin corn, with the death of close relatives and furry pets a speciality. Here The Kentucky Ramblers take us through the lament (and lamentable) 'With My Mother Dead And Gone', with plenty of references to the grassy mound and suchlike and a cloying vocal delivery, although there is a certain instrumental bounciness in evidence and the song ends with a banjo strum. Maybe they're stoned on the produce of their much more up-beat 'Ginseng Blues', complete with yodel. They then sink back into misery with 'Do Not Wait Till I'm Laid Beneath The Clay', which is more a threat than an affirmation ("mourn early" is the message here), but again the sombre words are contradicted by jaunty mandolins.

WM Stepp is a fiddler "whose playing represents the earliest and most archaic style of American traditional music", and here he makes a British traditional tune, 'Bonaparte's Retreat', totally his own. Along with another Lomax discovery, Luther Strong, "their tune repertoires are comparable to the ancient ballads in tradition, modal in character with a good deal of use of the counter note". Certainly Stepp's 'Callahan' sounds Celtic in its trills and constant return to a bass note, sounding like the drone of a bagpipe.

BF Shelton has "the mountain tenor quality" often found in Kentucky, and his 'Pretty Polly' is sung to a gently plucked banjo, but it ends in a violent murder all the same, and one pre-meditated. It is the details which make it so terrifying, such as the reference to the spade lying by the newly-dug grave, or the "six hours" it took to dig it. Back in England, this ancient ballad was already a myth rather than a piece of journalism, and featured a talking bird, but through some kind of weird alchemy Shelton's matter-of-fact rendition lends it truth, as if he himself is Billy, whose soul goes straight to hell. It makes you think that he must be either simple-minded or a genius.

Since the folk revival, professional singers like Martin Carthy, Dick Gaughan and Jody Stecher have studied, polished and lived out these songs, in the manner of method actors searching out their inner motivation. Their renditions are emotionally moving, totally involving the listener, but still remain performances, and at the end we applaud their skill. BF Shelton has none of that, however: he's not looking for applause; he's simply telling it like it is, a young girl led off to her death.

The CD does a remarkable job of assembling a picture of what the hillbilly life must have been: early marriages, sudden deaths, large families, infant mortality, bootleg whisky, evangelical churches, front parlours, back-breaking work, hunting in the woods, mountain homesteads and family feuds. The archive photos, meanwhile, tell their own story. Bill Stepp is huge, in braces, collar and tie, and sits on a frail wooden chair in front of a china cabinet with his legs full open. Grim faced, he grasps his fiddle with his huge working hands, firmly but gently, while his wife – whom he subsequently abandoned – grins in another room, in front of hideous wallpaper. The cover shot is of four unidentified Kentucky musicians in the 1930s, the unknown hillbillies, again on a home-made bench, with a one-storey shack and flat-roofed shed behind them, and the wildness of Nature rising up behind them. One strums a mountain dulcimer across his knees, one holds a guitar side-saddle, and another in a denim boiler suit blows on a harmonica as if chewing on a chocolate bar.

I know these people. Not from the Appalachians, but as my own country cousins in deepest Gloucestershire, where I have spent many a summer. This, too, is like taking a step back in time, where they talk funny and live partly off the land, partly from running slaughterhouses and the like, and remember working along-side the mass murderer Fred West ("he were a funny bugger") and live in ancient houses with 14th-century wooden beams the length of the attic and garish wallpaper, with babies everywhere, and where everyone is related, with brothers who haven't spoken to each other for 30 years. It's a world of hard work and heavy drinking, and a good-heartedness which is seemingly lost elsewhere. As the token intellectual of such an extended family, someone they occasionally see on the TV, I have gradually come to realise that it is they who had the wisdom and myself the mere book learning, but also how cut-off and anti-intellectual a place it can be. You can't over-romanticise pig shit.

Bill Malone, that archivist of the undergrowth of country music, is a sure-footed guide through this first recorded generation of hillbilly sounds. The word "hillbilly" first appeared in print at the turn of the century, used as a term to describe inhabitants of the Southern backwoods. Al Hopkins' string band was recording for Ralph Peer in 1925, and when asked for a suitable name for the group Al answered: "Call the band anything you want. We're nothing but a bunch of hillbillies from North Carolina and Virginia, anyway." Their publicity shots play on this, showing them garbed in overalls, funny hats and neckerchiefs – another case of deliberately playing dumb, perhaps?

Country music had been called anything but that name, with "hill country tunes" coming closest, but now "songs from Dixie", "old familiar tunes" and "old-time music" gave way to this slang term, which was originally one of abuse. Even so, "hillbilly" was a word used by its own practitioners rather than the record companies, which were busy marketing this music for a wider audience. It's like black rap musicians reclaiming the word "nigger" or gays the word "queer", transmuting it from a bigot's insult to a self-description. To say that you're some kind of throwback from the hills is a sign of self-confidence, and it's fine if you use it yourself, while from an outsider it's still an insult that would need to be avenged in blood.

Scholarly adherents of Al Hopkins And The Hill Billies may still be battling it out with those who prefer the claim of George Daniell's Hill Billies, who broadcast on WSB a month after Al Hopkins met Ralph Peer. Hopkins was the better pioneer, performing in New York and playing for the president, starring in a 15-minute movie short, adding a Hawaiian steel guitar and a piano to the musical mayhem and basing his band in Washington DC, far from hillbilly country. In other words, they established a career.

But at what cost? The folklorist Archie Green discerns a continuing ambivalence in the very term "hillbilly", a pattern in which the urban dweller rejects this rural culture while at the same time sentimentalising it: "We see the eroded land with its rotting cabin; at the same time we cover it in rose vines of memory…unite under one rubric the songs and culture of the yeoman and the varmint, the pioneer and the poor white."

Malone argues that, just as the music was shaped into a commercial product at a time when the South's "reputation seemed at a particularly low ebb", decadent and culturally degenerate, these hillbilly sounds were filed in the popular imagination along with "Ku Kluxism, prohibition, sharecropping, racial violence and religious bigotry". It is a debate to which we will return when we reach the late 1960s, when two counter-cultures – redneck and hippie – clashed, even though they in fact had much in common.

Malone draws attention to the industrialist Henry Ford and his attempts to revive "old-time fiddling and the dances of his youth". This was partly an outgrowth of his hatred of ragtime and jazz, and a concern for "pure" white Christian America alongside the backwoods views espoused in his magazine *The Dearborn Independent*, indeed by the sheerest chance in its very name. When not churning out motor cars, Ford put the same energy into publishing a book of old-time dance steps, bringing traditional musicians to Dearborn to perform, and persuading his vehicle dealers to hold a series of fiddle contests, from which Uncle Bunt Stephens emerged the national winner, with 'The Old Hen Cackled'.

When it came to recording their material onto disc, a whole generation of singers seemed largely to turn their backs on traditional ballads, although as we shall see they remained firmly part of the repertoire of back-porch players. Perhaps such material already seemed too old-fashioned for popular tastes. However, the examples that did make it onto shellac are now like rare and precious jewels. From them, Harry Smith made what can only be described as a New World diadem.

Folk scholars Anne and Norm Cohen sampled almost 300 hillbilly recordings made between 1922 and 1924, and found that only one song in 50 was originally from Great Britain: over 30% came originally from Tin Pan Alley, and 60% was home-grown "folk" by anonymous songwriters. However, after AP Carter showed them the way, musicians learned to copyright their arrangements of these "old familiar tunes". There was literally gold in those hills.

The advent of recording saw the birth of the professional songwriter, though few were yet to see the wealth that some contemporary Nashville hacks take as their due. Carson Robison came out of vaudeville, where his on-stage description of "The Red-Headed Music Maker" suggests Celtic ancestry. He recorded for Victor in New York as a whistler, a tradition which has largely lapsed in pop music except by the likes of the Rogers Miller and Whittaker, and then only between verses rather than as an act in itself. More successful were the songs that Robison wrote for the likes of Vernon Dalhart, a category which Bill Malone describes as the "event song", and sees as a throwback to the British broadside tradition.

Robison supposedly wrote newspaper accounts of an event (just like Phil Ochs was to do 40 years later when looking for something to protest about), but then songs to an iron-clad formula which "began with a happy mood, then degenerated into tragedy". These included songs such such as 'Wreck Of The Number Nine' and 'Blue Ridge Mountain Blues' Again, 40 years on, one thinks of of Bob Dylan's 'Talking Bear Mountain Picnic Massacre', which starts as a joke and then ends bitterly, with the message that we put ourselves into the hands of con men masquerading as businessmen at our own peril: "There's a bran' new gimmick every day/just t' take somebody's money away."

But whereas the Sixties bards would extract the message that the powers that be are corrupt, Robison's moral homilies point out simply that fate is unkind, and that death can come to us all at any time. Whether or not he himself believed it, his message was deeply conservative, to suit his audience. Thus in a song about the John T Scopes trial, which attempted to rule whether mankind came from monkeys or God and sought to determine whether man should believe the word of Darwin or the word of Genesis, he decrees: "Mr Scopes will know, wherever he may go, that the old religion's better after all."

Malone reprints a wonderful photo of Robison, hands on hips and dressed like a prequel of Nudie the tailor: cowboy boots patterned with hearts and flowers, gauntlets with the lone star of Texas, an embroidered jacket, a kerchief and a giant cowboy hat. The effect is not so much John Wayne as high camp. He casts a giant shadow, and so did Carson in the country field – every train wreck or mine explosion or kidnapping song looks back to his influence. He turned the folk tradition into an art form.

Bill Malone also identifies some early singer/songwriters, though hardly with the fame or wealth of the likes of James Taylor. All four of those he identifies are blind, and the greatest was Dick Burnett, "a valuable link to country music's folk past", who preserved and rewrote traditional songs like 'Willie Moore' and distributed his ballads on paper about the size of a postcard. Burnett's 'Man Of Constant

Sorrow' re-entered the folk pool via the bards of Greenwich Village. Unlike Robison, Dick wrote from the heart.

If one form of music typifies the hillbilly approach at this time it's that played by the string bands, part of a line which stretches directly from "the folk entertainers who played for house parties, barn dances, church socials, tent shows and political gatherings" before 1920. In some cases they were literally the same musicians, now professionally packaged.

Malone contrasts two of the finest ensembles: Charlie Poole And His North Carolina Ramblers and The Skillet Lickers. Poole established a country archetype, from Hank Williams to Gram Parsons, of "the hard-living, hard-drinking young man who burns his life away". He was dead at the age of 39, although the music his band played was infectious and controlled, the kind of music which wiped its feet and called you "sir".

Their greatest hit was 'Don't Let Your Deal Go Down', a future live favourite for The Grateful Dead, and Malone's description of the Ramblers' sound – "a bluesy fiddle lead, backed by long, flowing, melodic guitar runs, and the finger-styled banjo playing of Poole" – could indeed be The Dead on autopilot, if you just change the instruments around a little and add a couple of thousand watts and two drummers.

The Skillet Lickers were musically just about the opposite, and more like a precursor of Bruce Springsteen, "a wild, raucous but highly infectious style…famous for their rough, hard, driving sound". Fiddle player Jim Tanner was a showman, a chicken farmer from Georgia who "whooped, sang in falsetto, and in general played the part of a rustic fool". Some observers reckoned that such antics tended to detract from the music, but it was all part of The Skillet Lickers' freewheeling anarchy, and this was just the kind of sound that was later smoothened out into bluegrass by Bill Monroe, never to be quite the same again. Louis Armstrong did much the same for jazz.

The Skillet Lickers also boasted among their number the fiddler Clayton McMichen, who, as his name suggests, was of Scots-Irish ancestry and learned tunes like 'Nancy Rollin' and 'Billy In The Lowground' from his father. He resented the "narrow hillbilly focus" to which he considered his band were confined, although he co-wrote some of the corny skits in which they indulged, thus reinforcing the stereotype. He updated his own musical style when he formed The Georgia Wildcats, playing the same hot dance style as Bob Wills, but, as Bill Malone points out, "it was always a point of some bitterness to him that later generations of listeners who discovered his music were more interested in what he called 'swamp opera' than in his attempted pop fusions".

The Skillet Lickers' guitarist was the blind Georgian Riley Puckett, many of whose songs came from traditional sources. On the 1924 recording 'Rock All Our Babies To Sleep', he was the first hillbilly singer to yodel, pre-dating Jimmie Rodgers by three years. The singer Bradley Kincaid had a smoother sound, and was attending college in Chicago, but his recitals of "old songs from back home" such as 'Barbara Allen' saw him become a regular on WLS's National Barn Dance, and when he later published a songbook of this hillbilly material it sold almost half a million copies nationwide. Louis Jones toured with Kincaid, and his own renditions of "old-time" material, while playing the part of an equally old man ("Grandpa" Jones), gave him a lifelong career as a supposedly ancient mountain man. It was a role into which he aged.

Meanwhile, Kincaid was paddling in deep waters, often speaking of "the pure 'Anglo-Saxon' blood of the mountains", which he seemed to equate with an equally pure morality. Malone traces this back to settlement teachers in the Appalachians, "who preferred the older British or British-derived material".

Buell Kazee was born in Kentucky, where he grew up with traditional songs as part of his birthright. After graduating in English, he brought great erudition to his treatment of such material, but then resented record companies' insistence that he perform such material in the voice of his youth. This is very much like the problems faced by contemporary West Indian poets, for example, whose publishers expect them still to write in patois while using quite another voice than the one with which they speak at their jobs as university lecturers. For Malone, he was "probably the finest ballad singer found on early commercial records", performing songs like 'The Lady Gay' (an American variant of 'The Wife Of Usher's Well'), 'The Waggoner Lad' and 'The Butcher Boy'.

Kincaid's producer at Brunswick forced him also to record hillbilly melodramas like 'A Mountain Boy Makes His First Record'. Malone compares him with Bascom Lamar Lunsford, a professional lawyer whom we've already encountered on the turbo-charged 'Kidder Cole'. Here was a man who had "only a fleeting relationship with commercial hillbilly", and recorded a mere handful of 78s, but was much more extensively captured on disc by the Library Of Congress and academically-minded folk song collectors. He also wrote the words of 'Good Old Mountain Dew', which entered the popular repertoire. When traditional songs were "rediscovered" in the 1960s, it was ironically those singers who best captured such ancient material who also captured a new audience.

John Cohen recorded singers who were either too young or too obscure to have been picked out by talent spotters during the hillbilly boom, notably the grim-faced Roscoe Holcomb, who epitomised the phrase "high, lonesome sound". Even Bob Dylan praised his strange, elongated phrasing as showing an "untamed sense of control, which makes him one of the best". Dock Boggs, the most untamed of them all, was later rediscovered, as was Clarence Ashley, a five-string banjo player who had recorded such song relics as 'Coo Coo Bird' and 'The House Carpenter'.

Such maverick talents have endured the longest, and their music fuels many of the alternative country bands. The showmen and hick hillbillies gained immediate commercial success, but took their music up a historical blind alley. That said, it was the highly commercial talent scout Ralph Peer, who, during four days in August 1927, discovered two brand new acts, after having set up his stall in Bristol, Tennessee, which between them helped to define country music: The Carter Family showing where it was coming from, and Jimmie Rodgers where it was set to go next.

As "new country" singer Gillian Welch explained in *Mojo* magazine, "imagine how powerful it must have been to hear The Carter Family on the radio and think, 'This is my music, this is speaking to me.' Then to go out and buy the record and play it again. That's part of why it exploded, that people heard it and thought, 'These people are singing about my life.'" The problem is that, while they were as revolutionary a force as The Beatles, with a smoothness of harmony and rhythmic thrust to Maybelle's guitar which put hillbilly music into focus, when examined retrospectively their music is about as much fun as having your teeth pulled.

On first hearing, there is a deadness to Sara's voice, a kind of sober propriety which irons out all the wrinkles – emotion, meaning, that kind of thing – and makes everything sound the same. She has the same distanced response one often finds in psychopaths. What seems to be missing is joy, the crackle of feeling which less-revered performers produce. For any new listener, the most stunning revelation is the nimbleness of Maybelle's guitar playing (and, indeed, the sweetness of her singing), which sounds as if a modern player has overdubbed ancient recordings. (This was an acknowledged influence on the playing of the likes of Chet Atkins and Merle Travis.) But you'll soon find that Sara's deep, almost male voice is like a drug, and you'll find yourself wanting more. A version of 'No Depression In Heaven', from an album of 1936 radio transcripts, has her sounding more unhinged than usual, hanging out the notes on the wind. It is followed with 'Jealous-Hearted Me', in which she sings about a man on his "midnight creep" with a glint in her eye. Morally pure this ain't.

AP Carter, too, has a striking voice when he bothers to sing lead vocals, but usually stuck down at the bass end of things. In publicity photographs he stands as stiff as a tree trunk. A precursor of the slacker generation, he plays nothing and would often wander off stage mid-concert, while Maybelle plays rhythm, lead and bass guitar all together, and Sara adds a rhythmic strum on guitar, banjo or autoharp.

What at first sounds like a lack of engagement is actually resilience, a refusal to bend to the overpowering emotions built into the songs that they sing. John Fahey once asked why Sara sang in such a mocking and satirical tone on 'John Hardy', but it's probably just that she's singing in a higher register than usual and consequently sounds more shrewish. By the time The Carter Family stamp has been applied, everything sounds much the same and is taken at a uniform and stately pace. It's a perfect soundtrack for the Depression, and the 1930s saw The Carter Family at their most popular. Essentially down-home itself, this was music which could console, if it rarely excited. As Nicholas Dawidoff puts it, "Sara Carter's voice brought a little sunshine to people in the shadows."

The most sombre CD in Rounder's magnificent repackaging of all The Carter Family's Victor recordings is *Worried Man Blues*, from 1930. As if seeking safety in numbers, the trio sing as a threesome more than usual, and there is a surprising preponderence of songs drawn from Afro-American sources, both blues and spirituals, while others are "made up" by The Carters. ('No More The Moon Shines On Lorena' was learned from a "song ballet", a broadside sold in the street.)

Alvin Pleasant Delaney Carter's importance lies not so much as his talents as a musician – in which role he was really only a frontman for his wife and sister-in-law – as in the wide repertoire which he gathered for his family to dip into. A British release is subtitled "folk, country, blues and sacred songs", and its sleeve notes refer quaintly to their playing "numbers that their mountain neighbours found most popular – old hymns and sacred gospel songs, regional legends, sentimental ditties, and the lusty ballads of railroading, hoboing and cowboys". I have yet to hear much lust on any Carter Family recording, even on later releases under the family name, which feature granddaughter Carlene. The family rarely performed anywhere other than schools or community centres, and AP's posters assured potential ticket buyers that "The Program Is Morally Good".

A more sinister interpretation is put on all this in *I'm A Man: Sex, Gods And Rock 'n' Roll* by Ruth Padel, the latest in a long line of books which sees everything from a modern feminist perspective and judges everyone accordingly – and pitilessly. (Yoko Ono is among those thanked for her help.) It also reminds me of Joan Baez's reported unease about being in the same room as a poor, white, Southern male. Padel takes a sinister bearing on the passage in Steinbeck's *The Grapes Of Wrath*, about a guitar picker: "'Heavy hard fingers'? Male ones. The tenderness of something rough, despairing, violent."

Padel looks at male pain in country music like an aristocrat handling something distasteful: with tongs. There is Hank Williams, the *"ame damnée"* who drank himself to death; there is the "flat and grim" voice of Johnny Cash; and there is George Jones, violent to women and with a voice like an "open razor". All of the feeling in early country music is "not just any feeling, it is male. Women are betrayers: love means male pain." And therefore, it is implied, secondary. The big theme of country is one of crying over someone, "a male-voice lament over a treacherous, hard-hearted female flirt". It might be beyond Padel and her like, but most listeners identify with emotion and meaning in a song independent of the race or sex of the singer. It's called stretching yourself; empathy, even. It's why I can listen to the music of "poor white trash" and let it speak to me, as it does to anyone prepared to listen.

So who does Padel blame most? Step forward AP Carter. Women in country were not allowed to be "loners" like Hank Williams: "Country music laments the status quo, but supports it to the hilt. Family values reign: female playing like female life is ruled by men."

And who exactly was this patriarch? AP was born in (and did not stray far from)

Maces Spring in Scott County, Virginia, situated at virtually the dead centre of the Southern Appalachians. He could trace his ancestry back to the 18th century, which suggests that he was of English or Scotch-Irish extraction. A restless man, he worked mainly as a fruit tree salesman, and used his job to go on exhaustive collecting trips to the mountains, sometimes accompanied by the black singer Leslie Riddle, who had also taught Maybelle how to play the slide guitar. Carter would take down songs from his informants, many of them traditional British ballads like 'Black Jack David' and 'Rambling Boy' or their American equivalents, songs like 'Cowboy Jack' and 'Rambling Hobo'. Often he or Maybelle massively rewrote the originals, or made a patchwork out of various traditional fragments. AP would then copyright them to himself, sharing the royalties 50/50 with Ralph Peer. Thus did he protect his repertoire.

In turn, songs like 'Will The Circle Be Unbroken?' entered the popular imagination. It's ironic that a group who proclaimed family values so fervently saw AP and Sara divorce, although they still toured and recorded for another ten years, bringing their daughters in on the act. In the late 1930s, they moved to Texas and recorded songs on transcription discs for broadcast on the Mexican station XET, which could be heard all over America. The family sound less stiff on these late recordings, literally more at home.

Their show was sponsored by the Chemical Corporation Of Chicago, and adverts for Kolorbak hair dye and Peruna tonic interrupted the pure mountain sound. In *When We Were Good*, his history of the folk revival, Robert Cantwell compares AP Carter's collecting of songs from "the grandparent generation" – the furthest we can usually reach back into a living past – with what Harry Smith did in his *Anthology*: "to reach into the past and retrieve it, assimilating the historical gap to the temporal gap that lies behind any musical performance and a recording of it". One thing about appearing live on the radio, whatever products one has to plug between songs, is that such a gap is non-existent, which is why broadcasts by The Carters or Bob Wills or Hank Williams all feel as if something has been trapped alive.

Cantwell is on surer ground when he writes about the way that women sing at the time gives insight into their social entrapment and its release in song. These "pinched, narrow voices", tutored in the "surges…of shape-note hymns", contain an "emotionality that seems only to belong to the intimate occasions in which communities revisit the spiritual bond that holds them in its embrace" – ie that they are most themselves when singing, and for no audience other than themselves. It explains the oddly repressed yet troubling vocal style of Sara Carter, which gives me so much trouble, "the voice of the young woman behind the desk at the public library who steadfastly refuses to believe that she is beautiful", surging with "sexual power" despite itself. This connects with early photos of Sara, a girl then in her late teens who wore "the short dress, anklets and cropped hair of a schoolchild" as awkwardly as a convict wears his stripes. But isn't that just the fashion of the time, Robert?"

Ruth Padel draws a similar Freudian connection with Maybelle's guitar, "held on the woman's lap, close to her body, domestic as a pet...the guitar as hearth, womb, a babe in arms, flanked by the family-group which is guarded, like a bison herd, by males".

Sara and Maybelle were reunited for an extremely emotional gig at the 1967 Newport Folk Festival – with not a bison in sight – and divided their repertoire between gospel and traditional songs. They had acted as a template for a new generation of singers, with the likes of Joan Baez re-recording many of their songs, while Woody Guthrie took their tunes and put new words to them so that 'Wildwood Flower' became 'Reuben Jones', and 'When The World's On Fire' transformed into 'This Land Is Your Land'. Woody was merely continuing a process which AP Carter had himself initiated, and which Billy Bragg trumped by later putting his own tunes to some of Woody's own lyrics.

Maybelle and her three daughters, Helen, June and Anita, formed an all-women Carter Family in the Seventies, with Carlene eventually replacing her grandmother. Anita died in 1999, and June commented that "my sister had the greatest voice of anyone in this town, absolutely the prettiest. She was perhaps the greatest stand-up bass player, until her arthritis made her stop playing." Her mother's instrumental dexterity had obviously been inherited. Mother Maybelle And The Carter Sisters toured with Elvis Presley in 1955, as part of the Hank Snow show, and it was said that Elvis fell for Anita. Now that would have been a match made in country heaven!

When June married Johnny Cash, a country dynasty was established, just as when English folk singer Martin Carthy married Norma Waterson. In both cases, it's the daughters (step-daughters, in the Cashs' case) who have taken up the musical baton. Cash has sung with The Carters, just as Carthy joined the Watersons. This is something more primeval than showbiz: music meshes with time, love and death. It's like English traditional singing group The Coppers, where long-time adherents like myself can watch generations of the same family pass through, still singing literally from the same songbook.

The Carters exemplified the pioneer spirit. *Guardian* journalist Martin Kettle flew to North Carolina to meet another such exemplar, Ray Hicks, who married his cousin 50 years ago and lives half an hour's rough drive from the nearest town, without a telephone, in "the same wood-frame house his father built, on the same land his grandfather tended, in the same country his ancestors settled in when they arrived from Northern England seven or eight generations ago". Hicks is huge, six feet seven inches tall, and he lives off the land and is a renowned storyteller. He and his wife "feed themselves from their own fields and on animals that they kill in the woods. They entertain themselves and visitors with the stories and songs that have made Ray into a minor celebrity." He has recently been besieged by writers and academics.

Here is the mountain man personified. Ray is now officially designated a national treasure, the very word suggesting that such men are now rare and in need of being closely guarded from predators. Here, though, is the whole Carter family lifestyle boiled down into one old man. "He has a musical, almost mesmerising, way of speaking. He even bursts into song, and sometimes he will suddenly start playing his harmonica. When he talks about the past, it is impossible to tell whether he is talking about something that is within his own memory or something picked up along what he calls the 'rough and rocky road'." As to modern life, "they're living so fast now they can't help one 'nother no more. I learned to feel as good as anybody and better than nobody, regardless of race and colour."

Such generosity of spirit informs the best of old-style country music. With nothing to market and nothing to sell, this kind of music is still made simply for the fun of swapping tunes and gossip, just for "the crack". John Maguire's memories go back to before the Great War, when "every house was a ceilidhing house at that time. They just danced in the kitchen, or maybe, if they had a big barn outside...if there came in many ceiliders to a house, they'd strike up a wee bit of a dance. If there wasn't a music man there, they sent for him."

Ciaron Carson's book describes the same process in Ulster, 50 years on. His parents drag him away from a low dive off the Falls Road, full of bohemian types reinvigorating this music, just as he is launching into 'East Virginia'.

He also loves and understands old-time music-making in the Appalachians, and how the two traditions connect: "It is not music to be consumed, but to be played and danced to...instrumental breaks are rare... If old-timey has frills, they are subliminal...its purpose is to close the gap between the dancer and the dance; yet its wildness summons up the mountain gaps and airy distances between the scattered settlements of Appalachia."

If the music we have discussed so far was all made for commercial release, we need to return to the one exceptional case: the recordings made by Alan Lomax in rural Virginia. Like Cecil Sharp before him, although this time armed with a tape recorder rather than a pad and pencil, other intrepid musical explorers have scoured the mountains for down-home music, the equivalent of Ray Hicks' fireside chat. What some have captured is as close as we are now ever likely to get to Appalachian domestic music-making, which, in comparison, makes The Carter Family look like pure Las Vegas.

In August 1958, the folklorists David Mangurian and Don Hill arrived in Delaney, Arkansas, commandeered the old school house and spent a day recording local musicians. The results were captured for posterity on a Folkways LP, released six years later. This is music which doesn't date; it's also a scratchy, unlistenable row, made not by the wizened old men one would expect but by local youths, who arrived with a mandolin, a brand new Gibson electric guitar and a large amplifier: "The guitar playing, foot stomping, and washboard-woodblock playing was so loud in the large, bare-walled room that vocals were almost inaudible and had to be recorded with the mic very close to the singer." One of the boys' uncles turns up later with his fiddle and a pick-up, which he plugs straight into the amp. Two youths duet on harmonica.

The repertoire is, as ever, a mixture of ancient and contemporary, "an odd product of the influences of the older members of the community and modern-day country and western recording artists heard on radio and juke boxes". The songs they play range from 'Wreck Of The 97' to the Johnny Cash song 'Red River', while the style is basically old-time music with modern amplification. The guitarist, John Mounce, is 21 and works on the family farm, raising broiler chicken – "I've played for square dances – parties – clubs and family gittogeathers."

The songs often end with a kind of musical breakdown. Young and old join in on all of the traditional favourites: 'Wildwood Flower', 'Casey Jones', 'Cripple Creek', 'Old Joe Clark', 'In The Pines', and even a snatch of 'Jingle Bells'. Most sound like a cat being skinned alive, and to derive any listening pleasure you'd have to be either criminally insane or a relative, but that really isn't the point. Here is home-made music, released by an ethnological record label to prove a point: that such music is timeless. It's a literal example of my earlier image of dipping a bucket into the live music of the region and studying the results. The players enjoyed making a racket with their friends. It's part of growing up – you could go into any British youth club and find boys in their mid to late teens playing the latest cult music. What's different here, though, is that their uncle joins in, without anyone minding, and that so much of what they play is ancient and folk based. It's in the blood.

The album cover looks like something from the Depression, with three youths posing – Marlon Brando style – in denim work clothes and dirty boots. These are not middle-class dropouts but full of testosterone and rough energy.

In the footnotes (it's that sort of album), John Cohen sets out Folkways' mission to represent "the seeds and sources for a dynamic aspect of American folk music...mountain music derived from the rural South". It's the kind of in-crowd sound now gaining approval among the hip know-alls in city lofts and college bars. (I'm paraphrasing a little here.) "It is part of an active and progressive tradition, yet it has always maintained a terrific sense of respect and preservation for its own past."

The Doc Watson Family, studio recordings released by Folkways the year before, justifies that last sentence, a near miraculous throwback to what family music gatherings must have sounded like at the turn of the century. The extended family of twelve perches on a rough wooden porch, and they look like the Beverly Hillbillies did before they struck oil, but the music they produce is as noble and chilling as anything you've ever heard.

These are not so much performances as something overheard, scoring over the Arkansas din through the intense artistry and passion here on show. Things don't get much more frightening than Annie Watson's crackly 'House Carpenter' set to spooky solo violin, a Child ballad she had learned in her childhood. The whole thing sounds feral. 'The Triplett Tragedy' is a savage tale of two brothers who kill one another, and

Sophronie Greer's *a capella*, matter-of-fact, pitch-perfect rendition, with the innocence of birdsong, is accentuated when you find out she actually the widow of one
of them. As you listen in horrified wonder, it's like history coming up and punching
you in the face, the sheer relentlessness of this tiny rustic voice which should be
laughable but gives you the shivers long after she's finally shut up.

Even the jovial, fatherly tones of Doc himself turn apocalyptic on the ancient
hymn 'The Lost Soul', as the womenfolk tonelessly repeat every threat: "Doom",
"I'm paying now" and "The unredeemed must ever pay". From this it's straight into
Gaither Carlton's jovial 'Keep To The Middle Of The Road' and the nonsense song
'Old Man Below' ("Had an old hat that he wore year round/had neither hat nor the
brim nor the crown"), and then Dolly Greer totters up and sings 'Pretty Saro'. Here
is the mysterious heart of what *Country Roads* is all about: she sings in a cracker-
barrel Appalachian accent, yet effortlessly works herself into the skin of an Irish
immigrant forced to leave his lover behind in the old world. It could have happened
yesterday. "I came in this country, eighteen and forty-nine, I thought myself lucky to
be alive". This isn't as much singing as possession by spirits.

Here is the whole gamut of the Appalachian musical tradition: shape-note
hymns, British ballads and string-band tunes, banjo struts and strums, old 78s by Al
Hopkins And The Hillbillies, songs learned in the cradle, songs picked up at folk festivals, and songs by Doc's son Merle. A family group singing and playing a bunch of
their songs – lots of showing off, but not an ego in sight.

It suddenly strikes me that the drug-soaked, cynical, hardened members of The
Alabama 3 captured just that kind of odd togetherness that night back in Blandford,
while the CMA Awards was trying so hard for it that it fell right on its face. At heart,
everyone there was competing, both for prizes and for attention. At heart, the greatest country music is about sharing, and passing the spotlight around.

Nothing is ever quite what it seems. When the folklorist Ralph Rinzler discovered him, "Doc" Watson was playing electric guitar in a rockabilly band. Persuaded
to plunge back into the music with which he grew up, and later becoming a fixture
at the folk festivals of the 1960s, Arthel "Doc" Watson stood out from everyone else
through his blindness, his good humour, the warmth of his voice and personality,
and the precision of his playing. When you listen to his actual material, though, it
can be as deep and as cold as the ocean.

Many people have compared Loudon Wainwright III's anguished yelp to a scalded cat, though not one being skinned alive (Joe Strummer, perhaps), so it's
appropriate that he takes part in the 1998 release *The McGarrigle Hour*, which is
opened by one of his old songs. This is a more polite event than the Watson family
get-together, and with more songs drawn from the Broadway tradition – Cole
Porter, Stephen Foster – than from the folk tradition. Nevertheless, there is a
Charlie Poole number, lots of banjo, the participation of the McGarrigle sisters,
Linda Ronstadt and Emmylou Harris, and the same family feeling pervades through-

out – literally, as Kate and Loudon's children Rufus and Martha Wainwright represent the younger generation.

Family history entwines itself around these songs. The traditional song 'Baltimore Fire' was busked by the McGarrigles and Chaim Tannenbaum in London's Portobello Road, "sharing a pitch at the tolerance of Scotch Bob. You only needed to know one or two songs, providing they were rousing, up-tempo numbers, and this was one of them." Other public-domain songs include a Bahamian rhyming spiritual learned from a Sam Charters book, and a New Orleans children's game first heard in a Greenwich Village coffee shop. The world is their oyster. You can almost picture the participants, grouped around an upright piano, singing sweet harmonies as the light fades outside and the door is safely locked. Perhaps this is the music of the future, as we all increasingly dread going out into crime-infested streets. It's certainly a more self-aware and sentimental affair than the Watson hootenanny.

Both albums, though, tap into a deep well of American music-making, of community songbooks kept in the piano stool and sing-songs around an open fire. The poet and guitarist Carl Sandburg compiled *The American Songbook* in 1927, which is still in print and is dedicated, as this book should also be, to "those unknown singers – who made songs – out of love, fun, grief – and to those many other singers – who kept those songs as living things of the heart and mind – out of fun, love, grief". Sandburg analyses what lies at the heart of American song, an otherness: "There are persons born and reared in this country who culturally have not yet come over from Europe…ballad singers of centuries ago and mule-skinners alive and singing today helped make this book".

It's a book made for active participation, accompanied by both words and music, and also for private study, providing a history of each song and including many old sketches and woodcuts. There's a promiscuous mix of black and white musical genres, with one section, 'The Ould Sod', sampling songs brought over from Ireland which remain unmarked by their journey. More interesting is the way in which songs from Britain mutate into those collected by Sandburg, in categories like "Pioneer Memories" and "Kentucky Blazing Star". 'Fair Annie Of Lochyran' becomes 'Who Will Shoe Your Pretty Little Foot?', set now on the plains of Indiana. 'The Dark-Eyed Sailor' turns into 'The Lousy Miner', with "lousy" here meaning that he's covered with lice, not hopeless at digging.

The Appalachian sound is heard full-on in "Southern Mountains", ranging from the sublime 'Gypsy Davey' to the ridiculous 'I Got A Gal At The Head Of The Holler': "Geese in the pond and ducks in the ocean/ho-dee-ink-tum-diddle-ah-dee-day/Devil's in the women when they take a notion." The first is a traditional song from England (the character re-emerges in Dylan's 'Tombstone Blues') and the latter a hybrid, with the kind of nonsense words which mean either nothing or everything. In "Tarnished Love Songs Or Colonial And Revolutionary Antiques" are songs transmitted orally, and caught in transition. The piece usually known as 'Love

Henry' betrays its racial origins here through its title 'Little Scotch-ee', although it entered the oral tradition in North Carolina.

Strangest of all is the 'The Dead Horse', which Sandburg has collects in Philadelphia, from the daughter of a sailing master: "At the end of the first sailing month, a canvas bag shaped like a horse was stuffed with straw, hoisted to the main yard arm, and given a sea burial." The English original is a remnant of an ancient ritual, maintained in the annual May Day prancing of the Padstow Hobby Horse, with a man inside snapping the horse's jaws at passersby. It goes back to who knows what strange gods, an incursion into American culture as odd as Haitian voodoo.

Garrison Keillor wrote a new preface for the Sandburg anthology, and is also largely responsible for *A Prairie Companion Folk Song Book*, which draws on the Department Of Folk Song, a short segment of the radio show which he invented in the mid 1970s after visiting the Opry in Nashville. As well as his own spoken monologues, the show actively searched for folk songs as they are still being performed.

There are plenty, although the communal nature of the enterprise means that most are either comic or deliberately nonsensical. Many are variants of themes to be found 50 years earlier in Sandburg's book. The editors here, the 1960s stringband troubadours Marcia and Jon Pankake, cook up a storm and create a series of new menus: 'Songs Of Misrule', or 'Greasy Grimy Gopher Guts'. (Maybe we'll drop the food pun right here!) These are songs in a continual state of transition; when mountain man Roscoe Holcomb played John Cohen a "new" song, Cohen commented that it was largely made up of phrases from traditional ballads. "Well," Holcomb countered, "that's how you write a song – you take verses from other songs and put them together to make a good story".

Keillor admits that the show – unlike the folk tradition – eventually ran out of steam, but it tapped into a mass unconscious: "Folk songs are beyond our approval, they occupy a realm of art that borders on religion, where applause and personal attention are not wanted." We're back to the Watson family. Garrison's own immersion in folk music came when he attended the University of Minnesota in 1960, much the same time as Bob Dylan, and began to take an interest in the (female) descendants of Scandinavian settlers in the area, hence the statue of the "Unknown Norwegian" in Lake Wobegon. It's a heritage cheerily alluded to in songs like 'I Been A Swede From North Dakota', and it takes us straight back to the Tom Russell album, with its celebration of a mixed Irish and Norwegian ancestry.

Stranger still are the "Celtic cowboys". As the magazine *Living Tradition* put it incredulously, "intoxicating Gaelic melodies drifted through the evening air at many a cowboy campfire...cowboys chose like the drovers of the old world, only the slowest and most haunting songs to bed down their scary herds at night".

This is yet another example of the complexity of links across the ocean. The Prairie Land And Cattle Company had its headquarters in Edinburgh, and would send out cattlemen to the States. The Chisholm Trail, meanwhile, is named after a trader who was half Scots and half Cherokee. The music of such pioneers has been revived by the Canadian David Wilkie, and he recently undertook his first tour of Scotland and Ireland, bringing the music back home.

The strangest connection of all is put forward by Joseph O'Connor, who takes it from a record assistant called Bert, who works in a Nashville record shop. Elvis Presley was influenced by Tennessee hillbilly – "which had a big Irish traditional strain in it" – and gospel music, even auditioning unsuccessfully for The Blackwood Boys.

Mainstream country gospel is now largely a spent force – just think of The Statler Brothers or The Oak Ridge Boys, and how they've declined into MOR over the years. The music now shines through mostly where it's least expected, like during Dylan's brief years of religious terrorism or on my own favourite, *George Hamilton IV's Bluegrass Gospel*, released by a Christian label and sung from the heart. It's hard to resist songs like 'I'm Using My Bible For A Roadmap' or 'Gathering Songs For The Master's Bouquet'.

Even this isn't exactly imbued with the vital force revealed by bootleg tapes of legendary Robert Ackers. Ackers was of Irish descent, a pathfinder who sang with an electric band but never recorded, and whose performances enthused both Presley and Jerry Lee Lewis. Ackers went in for hysterical tears and frantic screaming and wild flights into speaking in tongues. It wasn't really gospel singing in any normal sense. O'Connor is reminded more of traditional keening, a sung lament "which used to go on at funerals in rural Ireland".

Next, Bert plays a video of Mickey Gilley, also part Irish and a cousin of Jerry Lee, who too "liked to stir 'em up a little". Bert dashes back into the commodious back room from which all these goodies are appearing. Most American musics have "a little bit of Irish in them", he claims; even some of the blues has "an Irish heart". To prove his point, he reads out a section of Texan bluesman Mance Lipscombe's autobiography. Lipscombe suggests that "seance" – supernatural ability – was brought to America by the Irish, as well as by the blacks, while already possessed by the native inhabitants. "Irishman do thangs whole lot funny than other nation. Everybody nated to his nation. His instain, thats seance too, see. Got it inside." The problem with Lipscombe's statement is that, while insightful, it could be pushed into the suggestion that most white people – those without red hair, in particular – have no soul!

There is also the whole problem of how Celtic culture has recently been marketed as a product in its own right, in the post-*Riverdance* period in particular. One thinks back to that weird ballet at the CMA Awards. Cultural change is a far more subtle force than that, and, as we have seen (to generalise wildly), the first wave of traditional folk music to hit the Appalachians had Irish tunes and English words. There has also been a wonderful strain of English country music, which has fuelled yet another musical wave. Waves on the ocean, first one way and then the other. Country roots can also be transplanted.

Chapter Three

Country *And* Western

If early country music spoke with an Irish accent, it also had a black face – literally, in some cases, or with the aid of theatrical paint, in one of the many minstrel shows of the time. This was how Jimmie Rodgers, for one, started his professional career. Certainly Rodgers supports out the oft-said comment that country is the white man's blues.

It's not a case of endless twelve-bar patterns, more that this is a music which enabled poor whites to find a voice, and in the case of Hank Williams this was raised to the point of genius. A different kind of country performer, of whom Dock Boggs dived the deepest, plunged into the blues as such, and a blind test of his music would suggest an Afro-American with a nasal twang. The glory of Harry Smith's *Anthology Of American Folk Music*, released some 30 years later, was that he brought together forgotten gems from the dawn of the recording industry, and combined them so as to reveal a shared folklore and a stylistic unity. Many people thought that "Mississippi" John Hurt was a white man until they saw his photo, something which Harry Smith was careful not to provide.

Each music has borrowed from the other, so that the banjo is a direct descendant of the African griot's *bania,* and whites in blacked-up faces used banjo and fiddle music from the plantations as a form of affectionate (if condescending) parody of dem ole folks at home. In turn, black dancers re-invented Celtic reels and jigs to include an African sense of timing, and adopted Scots-Irish material like 'Ballad Of John Henry' – a contest between a railway worker and a steam drill – to a black context, featuring a black hero.

This chapter will later discuss what happened when R&B collided with country gospel in the Sun studios (though if you don't already know the answer then you're reading the wrong book). In between were pioneers like Ella Mae Morse, whose obituarist described the American popular music scene in the early 1940s as "notable for several strange collisions of blues, jazz and country music". At the age of 17, this white girl fronted the Freddie Slack Orchestra with her tale of "a swing half-breed...who sang a most peculiar cowboy song...come a-ti-i-i-ay...get along, get hip, little dogies".

The old piano piece 'Cow Cow Blues' was given a western context, and brought alive with a Forties jive-like "truck on down". A generation later The Grateful Dead were keeping on trucking and doing much the same, although the join was so seamless that few people noticed, and American music of black and white was shaded with "a touch of grey" as its performers aged into their material. Ella Mae went on to form the Nelson Riddle Orchestra, and plunged full-time into R&B.

Country music now belongs firmly to the "silent majority", and adopts contemporary black music only as a form of parody – look, if you must, at the name Run C&W, and one member's visual parody of a fat black rap star, clad in purple and adorned with neck jewellery. The actual music is black songs done bluegrass style, to the enhancement of neither. I can't recall seeing one black face at the CMA awards, and if the techno warriors of The Alabama 3 found country congenial it is largely because both forms of music are now white music *in extremis*: on the beat, with no syncopation. At least they put it back where it belongs, a double feature with Memphis soul.

The country mainstream has lost its swing. A friend of mine can remember people dancing to techno at the Glastonbury Festival breaking into a spontaneous bit of line dancing. As she says, "the whole world feels the country and western riff in its pelvic girdle. There's a kind of strut to male country dancing, like a cockerel patrolling the farmyard. Square on the beat, and square on the floor."

The Rounder CD *Deep River Of Song: Black Appalachia* draws on Alan Lomax's field recordings to gather such country blues delights as Brownie McGhee and Sonny Terry, Blind Pete and The Nashville Washboard Band. Although it is outside the range of this book, the ghost of this music passed over into country soul. There's always one exception to every rule, however, and Charley Pride's "easy" singing style took him from life as a cotton picker in Mississippi to being the best-selling singer on RCA since Elvis Presley. His skin colour, too, was obscured in early publicity photos, but by the time of his 1969 LP, *The Country Way*, a perceived disadvantage had been spun into a positive image.

The cover shows him playing the electric guitar in a tuxedo, with neat short hair and with the subtitle "The Warmth Of Charley Pride..." "You may think it's unusual for a negro to be singing real country songs in the true country way," the sleeve notes start, pitching a message towards the country fans (no great crossover potential here), but Charley's father was "a long-time fan of the Grand Ole Opry", so he's okay. Charley himself is full of country values ("some say he has never met a stranger"), and his "friendliness permeates the air wherever he goes".

It's a shame about the music, though, where the only difference from the standard Chet Atkins production and the usual sub-standard songs is Pride's careful enunciation, which at times has a touch of Nat King Cole's elegance and at others the soporific quality of Jim Reeves.

If The Carter Family were a throwback of a pre-electric age, Jimmie Rodgers still sounds modern: witty, full of beans and sly as a possum. For Bob Dylan, "his refined style, an amalgamation of sources unknown, is too cryptic to pin down. His is a thousand and one voices yet singularly his own." Rodgers was one of those rare popular artists, like Dylan himself – or, more recently, Beck – who was a musical sponge as a young man, soaking up all kinds of music from which he later constructed his own identity: "Jimmie is at the heart of it all with a seriousness and humour that is befuddling."

Rodgers was country music's first home-grown star, although he never performed at the Grand Ole Opry. He started in a travelling medicine show, as a speciality yodeller, and later played banjo in a "hillbilly ork", a string band called The Teneva Ramblers, whom he later renamed The Jimmie Rodgers Entertainers. When the call came to audition before Ralph Peer, his band decamped and tried for stardom without him, so it was as a solo singer, with just his voice and an acoustic guitar, that Jimmie turned up that day in August 1927.

His first single was a sentimental ballad, 'The Soldier's Sweetheart', backed with the lullabye 'Sleep Baby Sleep'. It sold well enough for him to travel to New Jersey to record at Victor headquarter, and here he laid down 'Blue Yodel', now better known as 'T For Texas', and featuring – in Dylan's words – "that infamous blue yodel that defies the rational and conjecturing mind".

When Ralph Peer signed up Jimmie in 1927, he tried to stop him performing so much "race" material, but it did little good. Young Jimmie had grown up with the blues in rural Mississippi, and there they are inscribed in his first major hit. While his singing voice is bloke-ish, down to earth and deliberately undramatic, Rodgers' yodel is quite indescribable. It's a musical instrument in its own right, on which he uses human breath directly – no brass, no tin, no wood – to perform solos of great variety and musicality, rather like Louis Armstrong without a horn. Perhaps even closer is Dylan's approach to the harmonica, where again it is singing by extension, without words, carrying on the song into a realm of pure emotion.

Many of Jimmie's performances make direct reference to his being a yodelling man, and the effect is much like George Formby boasting about his little ukelele. Imagining Rodgers without his yodel is like thinking of Eric Clapton without his guitar. Some people even reckoned that the tuberculosis which filled his chest with sputum also helped to make it sound so rich. For all of that, Rodgers civilises the blues; there is none of the savagery of Howling Wolf, say, although there is a lost quality to his voice on the slower songs which makes him a much truer exponent of the "high, lonesome sound" than Sara Carter. On a song like 'Sleep Baby Sleep', his yodel is like some lone beast at night, howling into the dark emptiness.

Among Rodgers' million-selling discs was 'Brakeman's Blues', and he even made a movie short, playing on his image as the singing brakeman, making up songs as he traversed America. In fact, his sister-in-law was brought in to write material, and he continued to plunder the public domain – cheerful filth preferred.

In 'Looking For A New Mama', the song's narrator is looking for "a woman who will cook and won't tell me dirty lies", and boasts a sound that's as lost as any you will ever hear. There's something innately cheerful to Rodgers, however, and by the end he has cheered up and is demonstrating a sexual explicitness which would blow The Carters back up Clinch Mountain: "I want a girl who will rock all day, she won't even stop to eat".

What Rodgers and AP Carter have in common is an ability to homogenise all kinds of music into their own peculiar style, the craftsmanship of which is understated but rigorous. Through both men, country music learned how to be literate, and this love of words is true of the best of the genre to this day. Country lyrics are adult, witty and truthful, even when the arrangements are dreck. Both men wrote (or, more accurately, rewrote) words which could connect directly with ordinary folk while satisfying the most rigorous professor of poetry. It was a trick which was passed down to Hank Williams: the art of not wasting a word.

He established a now well-worn pattern by pretending to be just an ordinary guy, whereas in reality he was anything but. The singing brakeman lacked his father's ability to stick at his job, however, and when Nicholas Dawidoff went to Meridian to gather reminiscences he was startled to hear of his dead hero as "a drunk on the street, a tramp". Spells on the railroad – as itemised on his song, 'Jimmie The Kid' – were only to make him enough money to survive his next assault on showbiz, touring the boondocks of east Texas. The brakeman's cap was part of the image.

It's certainly a mistake to see Rodgers as some kind of early John Mayall or Paul Butterfield, a white man giving his life to the blues, as he was also immersed in vaudeville, jazz and parlour music as well as hillbilly sounds; but in him there's an inner refusal to recognise musical boundaries, which at the time earned him such insults as "a white man gone black", and a "busboy in a roadside cafe singing nigger blues", which aren't so much insults as the highest praise.

The Rounder re-release programme of his life's work shows just how musically promiscuous and how self-conscious an artist Rodgers was. At first largely a solo performer, he later recorded with jazz bands, with John Westbrook on a tingly steel guitar, with a Hawaiian band, with a jug band, with blues guitarist Clifford Gibson, famously with the young Louis Armstrong on 'Blue Yodel No 9', and with The Carter Family. He is aware of both himself and his audience, so that the 'Blue Yodel' series extends itself through his recording career. (*Number 8* is now better known as 'Muleskinner Blues'.) Jimmie could be by turn either a jovial railroad man or a cheerful cowboy, a man with "grinding" on his mind or a lovelorn drifter. However, cheerfulness keeps breaking through; is there any song about betrayal as sweet as '15 Years Ago Today'? If I die and go to heaven, I hope to find Jimmie Rodgers there, singing like a bird.

Rodgers himself died young, soon after tuberculosis had been diagnosed, the disease which killed his mother and the subject of one of his deepest songs: "I've been fighting like a lion, looks like I'm going to lose/'cause there ain't nobody ever whipped the TB blues." Here is the John Keats of country, burning up inside and cramming in every morsel of joy before he goes into the dark. He made and spent a fortune on fancy clothes, Cadillacs and a custom-built house in Texas called Yodeler's Paradise.

This was conspicuous spending, now that the Depression was taking hold. Jimmie joined the humorist Will Rogers for a tour of the dustbowl on behalf of the Red Cross, and in a rare photo they stand together, both in white cowboy hats, Jimmie dapper in bow tie and white suit but as lean as a whippet. As a posthumous album title put it, *My Time Ain't Long*.

His final recording session, in New York in 1933, is almost too sad to discuss, as he was so weak that he had to sing seated, and rested in a cot between takes. He stood up defiantly for the aforementioned 'Years Ago', the final song of the day and, as it turned out, his career – the next day he lapsed into a coma, from which he never awoke. The song opens and closes with a yodel – the best way to go.

As a tribute, you can't get much more English than the reviewer for *Let It Rock*, who reckoned that Rodgers "took shitkicker music a little way uptown". His spirit lives on, not so much in the mainstream now as in fellow mavericks like Michael Hurley, chuckling in the face of the abyss. Jimmie's monument is not in the dusty museum in Meridian, with his peaked cap, his Martin guitar and railroad memorabilia, but in the musicians he inspired, an array of whom – including Dylan, Van Morrison, Steve Earle, Dwight Yoakam, Bono and Mary Chapin Carpenter – collaborated on a recent tribute album.

It wasn't only Ernest Tubb who started his singing career as a Jimmie Rodgers imitator. Hank Snow and Lefty Frizzel joined that company, and Slim Whitman was another in this mould, though one gone syrupy in a way which Jimmie never did himself – he was sweet, but that's different – and one of the funniest moments in the movie *Mars Attacks* is one in which Slim unleashes a terrifying yodel to scare off the monsters from outer space. Maybe that's where it came from in the first place.

The greatest musical tribute is Merle Haggard's double LP from 1969 *Same Train, A Different Time,* comprising songs by Jimmie and chat about him. He can't quite manage the yodel (and his voice whines where Jimmie whooped), but Merle catches the joy and the pain of these songs. He also throws some Dixieland jazz into the mix.

Michael Nesmith once joked that Jimmie was a "dreadful, dreadful man" who would travel around the country "and go into prisons and steal tunes. Everybody who knew the man personally wished they didn't". However, by some process of alchemy, Rodgers' spirit is still full-on in these musical borrowings.

On the cover, Haggard poses at the open door of a boxcar, with a double thumbs-up, customised guitar and denim hat, as in a painting of Rodgers which is propped up behind him. However, while Jimmie looks genial, Merle looks mean – the smile could also be a sneer. Jimmie's folksiness is now a thing of the past.

To those now spoilt rotten with choice reissues, it comes as a shock to read in the sleeve notes that, when Merle was growing up, Rodgers' "recordings of a generation were not easy to come by". It's hard to disagree with the assertion that "the unique manner in which Rodgers merged traditional white balladry with the black man's blues helped produce a new art form: an art form which has had an influence on the music of the world undreamed of in Rodgers' time".

If Jimmie Rodgers took the blues one way into the country mainstream, the far more obscure singer Dock Boggs took it straight down to hillbilly hell. In an essay printed in *Country Blues*, the Revenant reissue of Boggs' recordings from the late 1920s comprising a book and CD bound to look like an old photograph album (which, in part, it is), Greil Marcus reckons that Dock "sounded as if his bones were coming through his skin every time he opened his mouth". It sounds like wordplay until you look close into Boggs' cold, cold eyes on the front cover, or listen to the sounds coming out of those cracked country lips. "A deep well of violence within himself opened: he began a war with himself that, despite long interludes of peace, would last the rest of his life."

When you remember that Greil was a spectator at Altamont, as well as (less terrifyingly) at The Sex Pistols' final gig, this takes on an extra significance. Marcus is used to things dying. He reports dispassionately that Dock once beat his brother-in-law half to death over a debt of $52. An onlooker reported: "the blood was just squirtin' – I guess sometimes squirtin' three feet high. Looks like Dock had a little mercy on Dave. He's part human."

Greil gets a bit carried away by all this, making comparisons with the surrealists' manifesto. Jon Pankake, who actually knew Boggs, remembers a "gentle, thoughtful and articulate retired miner", even if he did sometimes get restless. Marcus superimposes the persona of the man singing onto the man himself, which is like thinking that Lawrence Olivier beat the French at Agincourt. Boggs was an artist who exorcised God knows what inner demons by putting them harmlessly into music. He was a popular entertainer among his own kind who once proudly told Mike Seeger how he had once busked for petrol money. He had his own band, The Cumberland Mountain Entertainers, complete with fiddles and guitar, and would buck-dance flamboyantly as they played.

However, on with the music. Dock opens with a driving 'Sugar Babe', sung by a voice as craggy and cold as a mountain top. He sings with the same mystical urgency as Robert Johnson, but an octave or so lower. There is a hypnotic quality about his voice which does strange things to the hairs on the back of the neck. The song is taken at a fast lick and with a blues-style plucked banjo (he learned his strange two-fingers-and-thumb technique from a black musician in Virginia) so that he picks out the melody as a counterpart to his voice. It's slightly slurred, as if drunk, and taunting. You looking at me?

Whereas the vaudeville-trained Jimmie Rodgers is always aware of his audience, Dock seems to be singing purely for himself – and, indeed, most of the time probably was. Stranger still, this song – which has so much of a blues feeling, if not a blues structure, with most lines repeated twice – shares at least one verse in common with a Child ballad: 'The Lass Of Roch Royal'. In Dock's voice, though, it sounds like an aristocrat slumming in the gutter. Mike Seeger analyses the modal tunings Dock used as "a style possessed by no other recorded player. It perfectly fits a lot of the older, previously unaccompanied songs in mountain tradition."

A song from another tradition, 'Down South Blues', was itself learned from a gramophone record, and the original 78rpm release is billed as "voice and banjo with guitar". There is something archetypal about the way in which the songs are presented – this is a voice we all have somewhere about our persons, which we reserve for the very worst times. In just the same way, the banjo – which sometimes sounds if he barely knows how to play it – is somehow just that, pure banjo, and every chord hurts the ears, hard as rock, no frills. The song is told from a woman's perspective, but the homesickness is unisexual: "I'm going a-back South, where the weather suits my clothes".

The album is an odd mixture of white man's blues and British ballads, the styles of which overlap to the degree that 'Pretty Polly' is reduced to a holler. Dock's voice manages to slide off the tune at all points, just enough to grate, and he captures a sort of dumb pitilessness: "He threw the dirt over her and turned away to go." The banjo, meanwhile, picks out a remnant of the Shaker chant 'Come Life, Shaker Life'.

The CD concludes with four tracks performed by an East Kentucky mountain duo, the brothers Bill and Hayes Shepherd, which were recorded separately. (The latter was given the pseudonym "The Appalachian Vagabond".) Both men were felt to be "too intense and too archaic for the record companies", though after Dock it is as if a violence has lifted. As the sleeve notes point out, Bill's vocals pre-date Bill Monroe's singing style by ten years, and you can just about hear them over the crackle of the only copy of his single record release. Bluegrass music also succeeded in removing the metaphorical crackle of this primitive music.

The most instructive contrast, though, is with Dock's near namesake, Doc Watson. Both learned much from the blues, and both re-interpret traditional ballads in their own peculiar style; but where Boggs is a brooding presence, literally in your face, Watson is a panacea, a musical cure-all with a friendly-sounding voice and dazzling instrumental prowess. I could listen to him forever purely for pleasure, while I have yet to play *Country Blues* all the way through in one go – it's just too unsettling. Doc, on the other hand, can happily play on as background music. If you tried that with Dock, you'd merely get a headache. This is music to which one must listen intently, if at all. Somehow, it's very hard to imagine this singer as a buck-dancer.

Just imagine what it would be like if he turned up for real, in your living room. It would be like the scene in *Rear Window*, when Raymond Burr steps out of the frame and comes into Jimmy Stewart's room, a beast rising out of the blackness, blundering in with murderous intent. Doc had his family and his son, Merle; Dock had a wife who glares at the camera with her lips pursed and an upside-down smile. Doc Watson I play for pleasure; Dock Boggs out of duty and to be scared witless.

A review of *Country Blues* which appeared in the genre-busting magazine *F Roots*, written by its guiding spirit the white blues singer Ian A Anderson, recalls that early exposure to Boggs made him "amazingly excited to find that we had role models from 40 years or more before". As a man who now champions such musical fusions as the magnificent Afro-Celtic Sound System, Anderson also places Dock on the cusp of two separate traditions: "His banjo playing was somewhere between blues guitar technique and the rolling rattle of Uncle Dave Macon, and his voice rasped out from somewhere else." Here are blues as "black" as they come, "in both mood and racial style", rubbing shoulders with Appalachian murder ballads, "where nobody comes to a happy end". Bob Dylan, meanwhile, reckoned that Boggs' music was just about "as deep as it gets".

Moran Lee Boggs was born the youngest of ten children in West Norton, Virginia. A photograph of him at the age of nine sees him standing up to attention, ramrod-straight and blank-faced, under such apparent strain that this could just as easily be a photo of a refugee in someone else's country. When his musical dreams faded, Boggs went back to work as a miner, refusing to become a company man and fighting hard for union recognition. He later gave up playing altogether, and pawned his instrument to a friend. (His religious-minded wife regarded his banjo as an instrument of the devil, and after listening to these early recordings it's possible that she might have been right.)

He re-emerged in the 1960s, after being rediscovered by Mike Seeger, and after that long silence rapidly recorded three albums for Folkways. One comprised interviews, drawing on for 40 hours or so about the old times before radio and records liberated this music from its mountain fastnessess, which have also been recently resurrected onto CD. With better recording apparatus and a more mellow singing style the sound is milder, though it's still not exactly Jim Reeves. It is, however, hugely exciting. He actually manages to smile in one photo.

Ian A Anderson grabbed this release for his review, too, and reckons Boggs "a treasurehouse of variants on old American folk themes", even if not quite as "haunted" and other-worldly as before. As a listening experience, it's just as startling as *Country Blues*, but easier to take, and most of those early singles are recycled here. The mixture of blues and traditional folk is as before, though like the five later tracks on that album are a little smoother and more professional. The song which stands out above all others is the traditional 'Oh Death', later covered by the LA band Kaleidoscope, which centres around an extremely unsettling dialogue with the Grim Reaper: "I'll fix your feet so you can't walk, I'll fix your mouth so you can't talk." Dock passed over in 1971, on his birthday.

One can understand the excitement displayed by folklorists like Mike Seeger and myth-makers like Greil Marcus at this music, which so radically overturns all kinds of cultural preconceptions.

Another singing miner to emerge blinking into the glare of public acceptance during the folk boom of the Sixties was Roscoe Holcomb, Eric Clapton's "favourite country musician". When Folkways reissued *That High Lonesome Sound* on CD, *Mojo* found a "job lot" of old mountain ballads – 'Little Birdy' and 'In The Pines' – and "wiry blues". Together they made up a short collection of Appalachian life, "before highways and hot dogs". The unaccompanied 'A Village Churchyard' is a performance "so absorbed that the words become almost unintelligible, and the listener is left with a thick residue of emotion expressed in pure, stark music".

Just like everything else, music progresses by a chance succession of forward, sideways and backward leaps. The kind of spooky music made by Dock Boggs and his 1920s counterparts had disappeared from the public agenda by the 1940s, when warehouses were being cleared of ancient 78s, and a few (very) odd collectors began sifting through them. The oddest of all was Harry Smith, and his release of the sumptuously packaged *Anthology Of American Folk Music* in 1952, comprising six LPs and a booklet, not only pre-dated the CD box set by some 40 years but also gave this music a public authority it had never enjoyed before.

Smith wasn't some dusty folklorist recording ethnic sounds which would only be of interest to the Smithsonian Institute; he was a cultural terrorist, tipping over the dustbin of popular taste before the Depression all over the back porch, picking out the strangest items. The whole point was that people had actually paid money for this stuff, and Smith erected his private horde of rare shellac as a monument to the forgotten. Here, wittily annotated and sequenced into a kind of rural soap opera with occult significance, was a whole secret tradition of American life. It was the enemy within, a counterweight to the bland, 1950s world of sliced white bread. Here was some gritty wholemeal.

By being classified on library shelves under the guise of anthropology, the *Anthology* was out there in the public domain for whoever wanted to recycle it. Through it, a whole generation of folk troubadours found a repertoire and a voice, while many later took the country road home.

With the *Anthology* now transmuted into a new medium – the blank purity of CD sound – and with as brilliant a carnival barker as Greil Marcus praising its wares, the music is once again publicly available and once again ripe for plundering. To be sure, artists such as Beck, Nick Cave, Freakwater and The Handsome Family have done just that.

Meanwhile, the country music mainstream failed to stagnate, as some doubtless would have hoped, but instead moved rapidly in new directions, consigning such as Dock Boggs, The Carter Family and even Jimmie Rodgers into dusty halls of fame. It began to cast off such faded trappings. The future was Nashville.

At this point, Nashville wasn't the centre of the country music industry, such as it was. It was pushed into a prominence which it otherwise might never have enjoyed by a matter of sheer chance. George D Hay was hardly Nashville born and bred; he came from Indiana and, after a career as a journalist, switched to working in the newest media in town. As the "Solemn Old Judge", George had already presented a barn-dance radio show while he was based in Chicago. His gimmick was to blow a steamboat whistle when things were getting tedious, but the show was based on his genuine love for this weird music, which so many others found laughable.

In 1925, Hay moved to the Nashville station WSM and, despite early reservations by the station's gentlemanly directors, put together a downhome variety show. What swung it was commercial endorsement from the National Life And Accident Insurance Company, who saw a huge potential customer base up in the hills. The show later gained its name from an off-the-cuff pun by Hay, at the end of NBC's Musical Appreciation Hour: "For the past hour we have been listening to music taken largely from grand opera, but from now on we will present the Grand Ole Opry."

The first attraction was a fiddle player called "Uncle" Jimmy Thompson, almost 80 years old, who was accompanied by his niece Eve on the piano. Whether this was before or after Hay had had his bright idea is not quite clear, but supposedly Thompson turned up at the new radio station on the off-chance and asked to be shown round, and Hay put him on the air there and then. This is the gospel according to *Newsweek*, although this story smells to me as just that: a folksy story to embroider what had been decided earlier as a matter of pure economics.

After an hour of country fiddling, Hay asked if the old man was tired. "Shucks, a man don't get warmed up in an hour. I just won a eight-day fiddling contest down in Texas." The audience loved it, and the gates to country heaven were suddenly wide open. The legend goes that Hay then asked Uncle Jimmy to come back and bring a few friends next time. Thus was the show born. Hmmm…

Uncle Jimmy's appearance was certainly real enough, and it acted as bait. Soon every string band, banjo player and country fiddler alive seemed to be coming down from the mountains, seeking admission. Hay was savvy enough to establish a team of regulars, like the black harmonica player DeFord Bailey and the comic banjo plucker "Uncle" Dave Macon with his son Dorris. All the more surprising was the fact that Macon was often billed as "the gayest old dude in town". He certainly dressed flamboyantly, in a waistcoat and winged collar – thus establishing a Nashville trademark – but was no feckless fop.

Uncle Dave's repertoire was a valuable repository of American folklore. Rather than retreads of British ballads, here were new songs about life at the sharp end of this brave New World. Here were descriptions of labour disputes in the Tennessee coal mines, life on the chain gang, life on Henry Ford's factory line, local political scandals and the Great Depression ('The All In Down And Out Blues'). Not for nothing was Macon known as the king of the hillbillies, although he also cast into the musical stewpot a vast repertoire of vaudeville songs. He also lived locally, and ran a successful mule and wagon company. Displaying another country characteristic, he was much shrewder than he looked.

Macon was also well schooled in Southern gospel music, and was a member of The Dixie Sacred Singers. (The flipside of country fooling and a thirst for liquor has always been a genuine thirst for God.) Hay showed the nous of Malcolm McLaren in telling his new stars to play down such spirituality and act dumb. He also rebranded them under titles like The Fruit Jar Drinkers. Thus did amateur music slowly begin to turn pro.

There is an excellent salute to the late Uncle Dave by Stringbean (aka David Akeman), added extra poignancy by the fact that Stringbean – who is photographed playing Macon's old banjo – was murdered shortly afterwards by a man burgling his home, a "beautiful 134-acre farm near Goodlettsville, Tennessee". As for Macon: "Underneath the mask of the clown was the character of a true Christian gentlemen (*sic*) who practised the Golden Rule." And for Stringbean: he was "born and raised in the hills of Kentucky".

Akeman learned "the old mountain folk songs from his daddy", and taught himself to play "the old mountain balladeer type of banjo the way it has been played for generations in the Appalachian Mountain area". He later joined Bill Monroe, and very much represents banjo playing before Earl Scruggs revolutionised it. It is still like a rusty wheel being dragged through the mud here, not a sleek limousine purring down a highway. Stringbean rattles and ratchets and strums like a true old timer, and also sings – which is perhaps putting things a little strongly – the old songs, from 'John Henry' to 'Hesitation Blues' (hardly Appalachian, but fun), and from 'Cripple Creek' to 'Ida Red'. He makes that banjo ring and strut and jangle. There's a good family tale about moonshining, too: "just one way you could get in", and no way to get out.

Stringbean's voice attempts the tune of 'Take My Hand, Precious Lord' like a tired cross-country runner desperately trying to keep up with the pack, and the effect is oddly moving: a man about to die caught on disc singing in tribute to one recently passed over. The album emerged on the Starday label, from Nashville, Tennessee, "The Musical Heart Of America: Country * Sacred * Bluegrass – INTERNATIONAL". No wonder the album was distributed by Gusto records.

Guest stars began to move to Nashville in order to be close to their main place of work. In their wake came all of the carpetbaggers: agents, promoters, A&R men, and of course the record companies. It was like Hollywood, which had started almost by chance among the orange groves a few years before but soon also found itself the hub of a new industry. Silicon Valley with a yodel.

Like any industry, it also established its ground rules early on, so that for many years drums were banned from the stage. If an act deviated from what it had agreed to play, as the Gram Parsons-led Byrds did in 1968 when he veered into 'Hickory Wind' rather than the Merle Haggard tune agreed, it would never be re-invited. (It's appropriate that the show should ban Gram Parsons and a drunken Hank Williams, as both took the early road to self-destruction.) The Opry moved from a tiny studio to an in-house auditorium with seats for 500, then to the Hillsboro Theatre, and then and on to various local churches and auditoria before settling at the Ryman in 1941, a former tabernacle and at this time "the mother church of country music". The audience even sat in the original pews. The Ryman had been built by a river-boat man following his conversion at the hands of the evangelist Sam Jones – this was not a place for addicts or drunkards. Like the Church, country music always maintained family values.

In principle, if not in reality. One of the most extraordinary chapters in Nick Tosches' book of "living legends and dying metaphors" is the one dealing with a kind of sexual innuendo more usually linked with black music. Here is Jimmie Davis, a contemporary of Jimmie Rodgers. In 'She's A Hum Dum Dinger From Dingersville', his lover is a "mowing machine", and an impatient bride "throwed me down" at the church. In 'Sewing Machine Blues', "It's the way you do/Just before the break of day." Davis went on to co-write 'You Are My Sunshine', to serve as Governor of Louisiana (on a segregationist ticket), and is now best known as a singer of gospel music.

Another early pedlar of smut was Roy Acuff: "I wish a diamond ring upon my Lulu's hand/Every time she'd take her bath, I'd be a lucky man." A year later, he had changed course radically and released 'The Great Speckled Bird', a curious but deeply spiritual song the tune of which is "ancient and British". The first commercial recording was by The Carter Family in 1929, as 'I'm Thinking Tonight Of My Blue Eyes', already a rewrite of the original ballad. Persons unknown put fresh words to the old tune, and in Oklahoma it was sung as a hymn by The Assembly Of God. Acuff had bought the new lyrics for 50 cents from The Black Shirts, a country gospel group.

Acuff first performed at the Grand Ole Opry in 1938, and he gradually changed its musical direction from a celebration of the old music, which was largely instrumental, to what Tosches describes as "the new vocalists and their new and synthetic country songs". It's a battle that hasn't stopped since. Acuff's chosen nickname also changed with the times, from "the king of the hillbillies" to "the king of country music". On such slight verbal variances does a whole civilisation shift.

Another form of cultural seepage was from blues to country and back again (Sam Chapman of The Mississippi Sheiks recalls his father playing 'Turkey In The Straw'), while some songs entered both the blues and country repertoire, so that 'Frankie And Johnny' was recorded both by Mississippi John Hurt and Jimmie Rodgers, and 'Casey Jones' by both Furry Lewis and Fiddlin' John Carson.

The "common ground between the testifying black gospel singer and the fid-dling hee-hawing hillbilly in overalls" was explored brilliantly by Barney Hoskyns in *Say It One Time For The Broken Hearted*, a book which takes as its subject "coun-try soul in the American South". It's a story of contradictions, in which "Charley Pride sounds white, and Eddie Hinton could easily be black". Hoskyns notes that country music is based largely on nostalgia for rural life, which could be "the very voice of malicious redneck bigotry... Fiddlin' John Carson played for the Ku Klux Klan, and the link between 'hillbilly' song and white trash racism has always hung over Nashville." It's a misconception which I hope my own contribution to this debate will help scotch.

Others have been here before. Tony Russell identifies a "'common stock' of bal-lads, train songs, hymns and fiddle/banjo tunes" shared by poor whites and poor blacks, a common musical gene pool, and Paul Oliver adds that, while many white singers have acknowledged their debt to the blues, "the reverse influence of whites on blacks is less frequently stated". Hoskyns puts it down to "that old white liberal guilt", and I am myself so culturally embarrassed that I would prefer to quote others here than make any personal assertions, as a guilty white liberal. Hoskyns is one such, too, but points out that Blind Willie McTell sang hillbilly songs, and in as late as the 1930s John Lomax "could still find a black Texan convict singing old English bal-lads like 'The Farmer's Curst Wife' and 'The Maid Freed From The Gallows'". It is a shared repertoire, which emerged in as late as the 1960s with another Texan singer: Mance Lipscomb.

Brownie McGhee was raised in the Appalachians, and recalled "'jookin', or country quilting parties, where songs were traded back and forth between blacks and whites". John Cohen refers to recordings of a negro string band from Tennessee "that use fiddle, banjo and guitar, and sound much like the Old Opry string bands...the local style of music is dominant over any differences that would be racially determined". 'Gray Eagle', recorded in Indiana in 1927 by The Taylor Kentucky Boys, has been described by Charles Wolfe as "the first racially integrated session in American music history".

The "borrowings" widen in scope. In *The Grapes Of Wrath*, John Steinbeck writes of a man picking guitar in his open tent while an audience gathers around him: "And then he sang 'Ten-Cent Cotton And Forty-Cent Meat'. And the circle sang softly with him. And he sang 'Why Did You Cut Your Hair, Girls?' And the circle sang. He wailed the song 'I'm Leaving Old Texas', that eerie song which was sung before the Spaniards came, only the words were Indian then." He continues with 'McAlester Blues', and the gospel song 'Jesus Calls Me To His Side', as his singing enters their dreams: "And each wished he could pick a guitar, because it is a gracious thing."

This is the passage which was so disgracefully misinterpreted by Ruth Padel, who left out the blessing. However much modern media types might sneer (peo-ple whose nearest encounter with hunger was waiting for the food to arrive at their table at the Groucho), country music was one of things that got people through the Depression. Record sales plunged alarmingly, but poverty has that effect. Acts like The Blue Sky Boys, The Monroe Brothers and Mainer's Mountaineers continued to perform traditional ballads, but in the wake of Jimmie Rodgers singers began to prioritise self-written material. Many made a good living just from the sale of their picture songbooks. Ralph Peer, the man who had discovered The Carter Family, was now principally a music publisher. It was the way of the times. The American company Decca took over his previous role of scouting for new talent.

As ever, Bill Malone helps us through the dense thicket of country music history. The catchment area shifted west, so that "new performers were more influenced by 'western' styles, cowboy songs *ersatz* and real, and by the eclectic 'hot dance' music that evolved in south-western dance halls". In such music the fiddle was still dominant, while the five-string banjo was mostly notable for its absence. Country music was becoming country and western.

The National Barn Dance, broadcast from Chicago, was building a huge audience in the South-west. The target audience can be surmised by the kind of advertising tie-ins which were directed at them, comprising ads for flour and farm clothing, alka-seltzer and laxatives. Of the latter, Crazy Water Crystals came from a well in Texas and gave its name to the likes of The Crazy Hickory Nuts, which tended to devalue the *gravitas* of the music they played. One can hardly imagine The Crazy Carter Family.

No one man or woman could fill the empty boxcar in which Jimmie Rodgers once rode the rails, but many tried and some duos came close. The Delmore Brothers performed the rowdy blues and ragtime styles which he made his own, alongside front-parlour weepies and traditional ballads. The Callahan Brothers were duet yodellers but came from Madison County, "one of the richest storehouses of traditional music", and as their name suggests were probably of Scotch-Irish blood. They learned 'Katie Dear' and 'Banks Of The Ohio' literally at their mother's knee, but combined such songs onstage with an early version of 'House Of The Rising Sun' and the hillbilly blues song 'Rattlesnake Daddy'.

Closest of all to the old music were Bill and Earl Bolick, who perhaps sensibly went out under the name The Blue Sky Boys. They originated from Hickory, North Carolina, "the land of the sky". Here was a continuation into the modern mass-media world of the kind of oral transcription which shapes a traditional music and moves it on. As Malone sagely notes: "Bill Bolick viewed his songmaking role as a folkloristic one of collecting and preserving the ballads and gospel songs of earlier years." He also reckons that their harmonies were "the closest and certainly the sweetest in country music history", with Bill's mandolin adding a third "voice". Their repertoire included the British broadside 'The Butcher Boy', along with other songs which had fled west.

Kentucky-born Lily May Ledford was a five-string banjo player who led the all-female Coon Creek Girls, who sang gospel and "hard-driving" mountain ballads like

'Pretty Polly'. Meanwhile, old-time string bands like Mainer's Mountaineers were pre-serving such traditional material – "breakdowns, reels, ballads, folksongs" – while preparing the way for bluegrass.

There were other routes back into a shared past. Bill Malone notes that the Great Depression helped to prompt "the rediscovery and consequent romanticism of 'the folk'". Poor Southerners, "ill clad, ill housed and ill nourished," emerged as a people "whose folkways deserved commemoration". The Farm Security Administration sent in photographers, while the father-and-son team of John and Alan Lomax began to make field-recordings of traditional musicians, under the auspices of the Archive Of American Folk-Song.

The newly unemployed haunted relief offices. Hobo cities started to appear outside every town, and some weren't that passive. Okie farmers trekked west to California through the dust storms, the Southern Tenant Farmer's Union was formed, and Appalachian miners and textile workers both engaged in industrial action, drawing down young radicals from the North to bolster support. Archie Green's sleeve notes to Sarah Gunning's Folkways LP *Girl Of Constant Sorrow* point out how important music was to this campaign: "From this setting came a group of topical songs using old melodies to set off intensely stark and militant texts...Piedmont mill villages and Cumberland mine camps became meeting grounds for the ideologies of Andrew Jackson and Karl Marx, Abraham Lincoln and Mikhail Bakunin."

Every cause had its bard, and one, Ella May Wiggins, was shot dead. When the young idealists returned home, "they took a body of songs, such as Florence Reese's great labour hymn 'Which Side Are You On?' and John Handcox's 'Roll the Union On', which have ever since served the cause of justice in the United States". Many Southern balladeers, like Aunt Molly, also moved north when the cause they so passionately believed was defeated. A young man called Woodrow Wilson Guthrie, "Woody" for short, was born in Oklahoma and learned a heritage of traditional folksongs from his parents, later forming a hillbilly band of his own in Texas. In 1937, he moved to California and sang on KFVD radio with a woman called "Lefty Lou".

He was still cast from the "old-time music" mould, basing his guitar style on Maybelle Carter and his songs on AP and Jimmie Rodgers. Even when he came to write his own songs, he tended to put them to traditional tunes, just as his disciple Bob Dylan was to do. Malone points out that "'Oklahoma Hills' follows the melody of 'The Girl I Loved In Sunny Tennessee', 'The Philadelphia Lawyer' is set to the melody of 'The Jealous Lover', 'This Land Is Your Land' is to the melody of 'Little Darling, Pal Of Mine'. Guthrie's hillbilly emphasis, however, was accompanied by a flowering of radicalism." When he returned to New York, "the radical community felt they had discovered a 'new Joe Hill'", and Guthrie was known forever after as a protest singer. These were seeds that would blossom into the "urban folk revival", and they had been planted and nurtured in the rural heartlands.

Meanwhile, there was little respite from the great slump. The Carter Family were close to the ground, and recorded 'No Depression In Heaven', offering a last line of refuge to beleaguered people: that if there is little hope in this world, there is always the next.

After the events laid out in Roy Acuff's song 'Cowards Over Pearl Harbor', American servicemen took country music with them as they fought across the globe, and even Bing Crosby began to record hillbilly songs like 'Pistol-Packing Mama'. *Billboard* began to list hillbilly records alongside blues and jazz artists in a section they called at first "Western And Race", and then, more appealingly, "American Folk Records".

Roy Acuff emerged further as the leading traditionalist, with songs like 'The Wabash Cannonball', taken straight from American folklore. It was a musical direction encouraged by his A&R man, Arthur Saverley, who was born in Britain and came west as a young man "filled with visions of cowboys and romantic isolated mountaineers". Acuff kept his Smoky Mountain Boys acoustic and dressed casually, without any of the cowboy affectations that were creeping in elsewhere. His harmonies and repertoire were straight out of mountain gospel, and struck a chord at a time which *Billboard* noted had "caused people to turn to simpler and more fundamental things".

Acuff was the son of a Baptist minister from Tennessee but grew up in Knoxville and learned much of his material from hillbilly records. He joined a medicine show peddling Moc-A-Tan, and – like Jimmie Rodgers before him – performed in black-face or playing Toby, the red-haired rube who was the butt of everyone's jokes. (A Celt, perhaps?) Ironically, Acuff's long-term influence – particularly through Acuff-Rose, the publishing house which he formed with the "non-rustic" Fred Rose – was to take country music away from such rural simplicities and into the mass marketplace. *Billboard* accurately predicted that country "will be the field to watch".

Indeed it was, but you needed to know just where to look. As the war ended, Rose turned his main energies towards promoting a new young singer called Hank Williams. Seemingly in another world, Bill Monroe's Blue Grass Boys had been quietly changing from the old string band style to something new. With the addition of the more bluesy fiddler Chubby Wise, guitarist Lester Flatt in early 1945 and banjoist Earl Scruggs a few months later, they found it.

Bluegrass is really the invention of one man, Bill Monroe, although he had many influences and many helpers on the way. It's now generally agreed that black fiddler Arnold Schultz, with whom the teenage Monroe played square dances, was a lasting influence, while another of Arnold's admirers was Ike Everly, father of Phil and Don.

When Elvis Costello caught a gig in a hotel ballroom by an elderly Monroe, the angry young punk (retired) was amazed by the sheer savagery of Bill's onstage performance, the way he attacked his mandolin like a man possessed. Bill Monroe's groundbreaking years were back in the 1940s, after he had split from his brother Charles and founded the Blue Grass Boys.

The highlights have been brilliantly captured on a recent budget CD issued by Living Era – every home should have one. The CD draws on five sessions, from 1940 to 1947, and you can hear the music evolve and solidify. The first couple of sessions have backing from guitar, fiddle and bass, with Bill on mandolin and a high tenor voice, sounding almost like a castrato. The sound is part blues and part traditional, and it drives along, with lots of unforced laughter. They open with Jimmie Rodgers' 'Mule Skinner Blues', with a strange mix of sadness and triumph in Bill's voice and jaunty fiddle sawing over the top.

By 1945, he had added an accordion (played by Sally Ann Forester, though she still counts as a Blue Grass Boy) and Dave "Stringbean" Akeman's banjo to the mix. There's a lovely sense of delicacy to the music, and Monroe's songs are a compendium of blues and folk phrases, shaken into a new pattern. The "high, lonesome sound" is full-on here, a melancholy which seeps through largely thanks to Bill's voice, which leaps around the register but never draws undue attention to itself. 'Footprints In The Snow' is a traditional song, and somehow archetypal, with love blooming in winter and Monroe following his beloved's tracks. It could also be a murder ballad but isn't, even though it ends with the girl in heaven.

These recordings sound as if they could have been made yesterday, timeless because nothing extraneous has been added to the mountain sound. How different to the Nashville sound soon to evolve, which has no place in this book. This is music which looks back to those original settlers traversing the ocean, and forward to music being made right now. I played this album back to back with Dolly Parton's bluegrass excursion, and they are cut from the same cloth.

On both sessions, recorded almost 50 years apart and with an ocean of "old-time music" made in between, the key word is restraint. The arrangements are subtle and carefully worked out in advance, with everyone featured but no one actually soloing. Stage clothes are Sunday-best, not flashy, and everything is subservient to the overall vibe. There's a deliberate quietness going on. This is ego-free music, not least Bill's singing, which wastes no emotion and yet is full of it. It's like John Wayne at his most matter-of-fact: "That'll be the day." You can imagine each lead performer, whether singer or instrumentalist, stepping up to the mike in turn, doing their thing and then retreating back into the ensemble.

This careful use of dynamics is central to bluegrass, and is achieved by the way in which the singer and players stand, controlling the pitch and sound of what they are creating by the way they approach a central microphone. It's a method seen recently on *Later...* with Steve Earle and The Del McCoury Band almost dancing around each other. Bob Dylan, a repository of ancient musical wisdoms, has tried to do much the same, from the 'Rolling Thunder' tour onwards, playing with the microphone like a champion football player toying with the ball. He understands the communal nature of what is going on here: this is music as a team game. Stubborn individualists like Dylan, Van Morrison and indeed Bill Monroe seem strangely to understand and need this, though all three have gone through many backing musicians during their long careers. Once they have a perfect sound, it seems almost impossible for them not to change things.

In Bill Monroe's case, two final elements needed to be added to the final mix for that perfection, and it certainly wasn't drums or electricity. Both were in place on the next session, a year later. Lester Flatt had played with Bill's brother Charlie in The Kentucky Pardners, but it was the revolutionary banjo playing of 22-year-old Earl Scruggs – as far away from Dock Boggs' style as could be imagined – which really ignited the flame.

By now all of the songs were being written by Monroe, except for one backward nod to Jimmie Rodgers' 'Blue Yodel Number Four', which is as profound a musical revolution as Jimi Hendrix covering 'Hey Joe' but quieter – the same words, the same yodel, but underneath it all a chugging, rapid sound, a banjo with no air brakes on. All of this from an old-time instrument already largely outlawed from post-war mainstream country music. 'Heavy Traffic Ahead' starts with each instrument introducing itself, then that same banjo chuckles in the background, moving forward to syncopate the tune, almost like Dixieland jazz. It then sinks back into the mix to provide a counterpoint to Bill's voice, and then has a cheerful conversation with Bill's mandolin. Under Scruggs' nimble fingers, the banjo has become remarkably fluid, his three-finger roll as rapid and jaw-dropping as the three-card trick.

Bill Monroe later revealed to *Acoustic Music* that "I wanted to have a music of my own to start with, where I could say I wasn't copying no man. So I went to putting different sounds, from the time I was a kid on. I put some blues on it, a little bit of jazz, Scotch bagpipe, Baptist-Methodist and the Holiness way of singing in it." (Note the bagpipes.) "I really put a solid beat in it, a driving beat, so it would be different, a driving music." Charlie Poole and Jimmie Rodgers were particular influences.

When the next generation came along, and Elvis recorded one of Monroe's songs on the flipside of his first single 'That's Alright Mama' (country meets blues, all over again), "they wanted him to get a style of his own, so he picked 'Blue Moon Of Kentucky' to start on his new style and it just worked out perfect". He later apologised to Monroe, who was gracious (and certainly didn't decline the royalties) and copied the copy. Monroe re-recorded the song, speeding it up on the last verse just as Presley had: "It done fine, it sells the number better. Yes sir."

On Monroe's death, *Acoustic Guitar* reckoned that his influence would live on, through those lucky enough to work with him and strong enough to take both the endless touring and his sometimes abrasive personality. For David Grier, "Bill always had an idea of what he wanted, and he wasn't shy about telling you". Nevertheless, "he did hand down its essence" to everyone who ever played with him, and they passed it on in turn, like a game of pass the parcel.

Peter Rowan was one of those who played with Monroe, and he later put together his own musical tribute, the album *Bluegrass Boy*, and confirms the spookiness of the form, mountain magic: "Bluegrass is a moment that happens, and sustaining that moment is a real challenge. The quality of bluegrass that raises the hairs on the back of your neck has always been in the music waiting to happen". On working with Monroe: "Bill was the ultimate Zen-bluegrass man. [You had to] let his fire infuse and enthuse you. Everybody who worked with Bill had to surrender." His pet hate was too much ornamentation. He once warned Rowan: "Pete, don't go out on that limb; there are enough flowers out there already."

To Monroe's fury, Flatt And Scruggs soon dropped off the limb altogether, forming their own bluegrass combo in direct competition. Nicholas Dawidoff's indispensible *The Country Of Country* encounters Monroe in later years, still busy on the road. Onstage at the Ryman, he transforms his frail body into a "defiant performance posture, with legs set firm, upper torso thrust forward, head tilted slightly upward, eyes hooded, lips apart and turned down at the corners". Here is mountain man personified, and he dedicates 'Uncle Pen' to his uncle Pendiver, a country fiddler and "the man I learned to play from". He even engages in an onstage display of the Kentucky backstep.

Dawidoff notes that "only with a very few string-powered instruments can a band play the sprinting breakdown arpeggios and lilting refrains that sound like bluegrass". The piano, drums or the electric guitar would disable it. The Blue Grass Boys were mainly "poor country boys" whom Bill knocked into shape on the road, and played faster than anyone else around. Monroe used unusual keys, and carefully arranged the instruments so that it was as if they were having a musical conversation: "When the banjo said something hot-tempered, the fiddle responded cheekily, and then the mandolin rolled its eyes and tweaked them both."

On live recordings, the audience can be heard through "surprised bursts of applause...nobody had ever heard country musicians play with such speed and precision, and such personality". The drive of the stand-up bass, and these "whimsical bursts of harmonic expression", lift this music far above the scrapings of the string bands discussed earlier. Monroe has somehow smoothed down their scratchiness, yet retained the excitement. As the Appalachian singer Jean Ritchie observed: "Bill used the old music, but he invented bluegrass with it. In that day it was punk, it was hip-hop. He took the old music and made it new".

Ritchie is more prescient than she realises. Later sections of this book will show how both punk rock and hip-hop – as well as British R&B, psychedelia, heavy rock, folk and grunge, along with certain country stars – have taken this same "old music" on board and made something new themselves. New lamps for old.

Meanwhile, there was Flatt And Scruggs with their Foggy Mountain Boys, a name inspired by The Carter Family song 'Foggy Mountain Top'. Born in Flint Hill, North Carolina, where things get mighty foggy in winter, Scruggs was steeped in such music from early childhood: "the old songs" – 'Sally Goodin', 'Cripple Creek' and the rest. The Carters were a particular influence, especially Maybelle's "simple" guitar style, one which he so spectacularly failed to follow. He also would hear his mother sing from old shape-note gospel books. His father, meanwhile, farmed cotton. At the age of eleven, Earl Scruggs was playing 'Reuben' on an adult-sized banjo when he suddenly found his fingers and the notes flowing. This was the basis of the style which had him later introduced onstage by Bill Monroe as "the boy who can make a banjo talk".

It was not the kind of miracle seen occasionally in Southern baptist churches. From his two elder brothers, Scruggs had already picked up a style pioneered by North Colorado string band players like Snuffy Jenkins, who began to use his middle digit as well as the thumb and index finger on his right hand to pluck the strings. Scruggs used his left hand to add a cascade of grace notes, like droplets from heaven. As a further party trick, he would sometimes "pinch on", simultaneously plucking two strings at once. He has had many imitators, but no one has yet improved on that chance discovery, or his skill.

As always, it was a case of something being personally passed on up in the mountains, and then a stray genius working out how to refine it. By adding drone notes, Earl learned how to put together a flowing melody rather than something that sounded like a donkey cart stumbling down a dirt road.

Lester Flatt had also started off on banjo, which he learned from his father, but after falling prey to no such miracle he soon switched to guitar. He also began to sing lead vocals with The Blue Grass boys, although it is interesting that the singing which cuts the deepest on those mid-Forties recordings is Monroe's. Flatt is more nasal, more "country", and has a nice trick of going upwards at the end of a line when you expect it to drop down, but it lacks the sense of reined-in emotion which we have already seen with Monroe's style. Lester is a more straightforward storyteller.

The band he formed with Scruggs dressed respectfully, with cowboy hats, but with no set uniform, and some stand jacketless onstage. Flatt And Scruggs themselves often dress like identical twins, and in a slightly different style to the rest of the band, so maybe it is a uniform after all, with subtle differentiations of rank. Even so, onstage the group look like a bunch of friends, clustered together but with the two stars slightly in the front. Of all things, it reminds me of Neil Young and Crazy Horse on the 'Weld' tour, dwarfed by giant speakers and sticking tight together like the last gang in town, but with Neil thrust forward a little: the main man.

They refused to be confined by the bluegrass tag, referring to themselves instead as "country musicians". On the road, they advertised Martha White biscuit flower. By this time, Scruggs was writing original tunes for the banjo. His speciality was "breakdowns", quicksilver instrumentals like 'Foggy Mountain Breakdown', which later became the theme music to *Bonnie And Clyde*. Alan Lomax called such music "folk music in overdrive". Not country, you will notice. There's a lot of jazz in the mixture, as well as old-time music. Young musicians like John Hartford learned to copy this style from records played at half speed: slowly and painfully, note for note, then next time a bit faster, and the next time faster still, and...

The Complete Mercury Sessions shows Flatt And Scruggs at full stretch, and with fire in their bellies: it is a freer, more flowing music than their work with Bill Monroe, less intense and less meticulously arranged, less sad, high and lonesome. Even so, it's sad, high and lonesome enough. The 28 tracks – without a dud among them – have resurfaced on two LPs released by Rounder and also a CD from Polygram – yet another essential selection, I'm afraid. Most of the songs are written by Flatt, sometimes with the help of Scruggs or their contemporaries, with a handful stretching back to the repertoires of JE Mainer's Mountaineers, or New Orleans jazz, or timeless settler music.

'Old Salty Dog Blues' was written early in the 1940s but was "based on an earlier folk song", while Preston Young's 'Roll In My Sweet Baby's Arms' is a composite of traditional phrases. Young admits that "I used to hear it around these old country dances, and, you know, you could add a verse and here and yonder and all." The Appalachian ballad tradition is just as strongly felt in this music as in that of Bill Monroe, but it's like a river which has gone underground: you cannot see or hear or bathe in it, but you know that it's there.

The band then switched allegiance to Columbia records, and the 1950s saw perhaps their finest hour, when Flatt And Scruggs and what was now retitled more sonorously The Foggy Mountain Quartet turned to country gospel. There is a strengthened vocal attack here, with help from Curley Lambert of The Jordanaires. Some of the songs were rearranged from the common stock – collections like that of James D Vaughan – and some written for the duo as a special commission. When Lester sings so hopefully of heaven, and asks plaintively if there will be room for him "when the Earth will meet the sky", you feel that this is more than simply the work of paid entertainers.

Like fog around the hills of Scruggs' childhood, melancholy swirls around these performances, the best of which were collected on *You Can Feel It In Your Soul*. Yes, you're right, I'm sorry, it's indespensible, and unfortunately these aren't the kinds of records that ever crop up in second-hand shops, unless someone is clearing out their entire vinyl collection or dies. Personally, I blame The Alabama 3 for leading me into financial penury through an addiction, for which the dealers exist openly on every high street and pay full business rates.

By the 1960s, Flatt And Scruggs had lightened up and were recording folkier material, like Woody Guthrie's 'This Land Is Your Land', or the campfire sing-song 'Down In The Valley'. They also released an album of such material, *Folk Songs Of Our Land*. Mike Seeger devised a precursor to the celebrity tribute album – still very much amongst us – with Folkways' *American Banjo Scruggs Style*, and students everywhere took up the music. One of the holy grails of this youth cult was the album of *Flatt And Scruggs At Carnegie Hall* from 1962, even answering a request for the 'Martha White Theme' and "tunes still alive with the old-world, jig-tune bounce in them". Here too is the "heart" song 'Footprints In The Snow', from that ground-breaking session with Bill Monroe. They look back in time – "it hadn't been too many years ago" – to when a group of musicians grooving together at home, with only fiddle and banjo, used to be called a band. What goes around comes around.

With Merle Travis as support, and Joan Baez as their cheerleader in the audience, the warmth of the response to their third major appearance in the Big Apple comes over still. By now, Buck Graves was on board playing dobro, "a steel guitar fretted in the Hawaiian manner", while "Cousin Jake" Tullock plays bass – and the fool. Even *Time* reckoned that "the best bluegrass (a polite synonym for hillbilly) is being done by Nashville's Lester Flatt, Earl Scruggs…cultural descendants of Tennessee's Carter Family… Scruggs is the world's most famous banjo player."

The album is packaged not like earlier Flatt And Scruggs releases – with the band neatly attired in front of the tour bus, well scrubbed, serious and old fashioned – but with Tom Alan's modernistic montage of photo strips and watercolour sketches. The "Pick" and "Sing" of 'Pickin' And Singin'' are marked out in stencil, while the stetsoned musicians mingle with young fans queueing for autographs, not a stetson among them.

There was a worm in the apple, though. Just as Earl Scruggs in particular was trying to update his repertoire, and even jammed with R&B saxophonist King Curtis, a new audience was out there, hoping to hear the old sounds and nothing but. Lester Flatt was also unsure of this new direction, including the addition of a drummer and recording songs by the likes of Bob Dylan, who by now had his own Band. The duo parted in 1969.

Flatt went back to playing more traditional fare with Nashville Grass, which included some former Foggy Mountain Boys in its ranks. Earl alienated many bluegrass fans by founding The Earl Scruggs Review with his two sons. Their debut electrifies the guitar and bass, adds a drum wallop, and covers songs by the likes of Michael Nesmith, Steve Young and Michael Murphey, the new young turks.

Unfortunately the whole thing now sounds a bit of a pig's breakfast, albeit an interesting one, with Scruggs senior largely drowned out, or simply providing musical colouring. The best track is a reprise of 'Salty Dog Blues', which swings rather than thumps. The veteran Uncle "Josh" Graves takes risks with his banjo, and while not on this album, Vassar Clements shone onstage, with a supersonic 'Orange Blossom Special'. Indeed, with this album one feels that this is a dry run for music which could really blossom on stage. Bluegrass, whether modern or progressive, remains essentially a live music, and the sparks need to fly from one musician in real time. These recordings now sound cluttered and out of date – much like the haircuts on the cover, where an open-necked, "casual" Earl looks far less at ease than on the more formal studio portraits with Lester. He sits in the middle of his band, cradling his banjo, with Josh Graves behind him with a perfect Fifties sneer and the younger members looking truculent. There isn't a smile in the place, and the music inside lacks both the joy and the melancholy of earlier recordings. This was a transitional stage: Earl went on to heavily influence the "newgrass" movement, playing a major part in gathering the veteran contingent for The Nitty Gritty Dirt Band's *Will The Circle Be Unbroken?* project and starring in his own television documentary, *Earl Scruggs: His Family And Friends*, with friends which included Dylan and The Byrds.

So what, then, is bluegrass? Bill Malone considers that, although it is now a "catch-all term" which includes any country music played acoustically and looking back before World War Two, "in fact it is not an old-time style at all: it did not begin to take shape as a distinct entity until the mid-Forties, and it was not named until a decade later". It's not a direct outgrowth of mountain music, and takes on other influences. It is instead "a dynamic and ever-evolving form", which appeals to those fans "with a traditional bent who have repaired to it for a refuge" and who love its "high, lonesome sound" and "down-to-earth songs". To me, this sounds as if it is a direct outgrowth of mountain music after all, just one which means that, in this world of global communication, all of us can live in the Blue Ridge mountains. In our heads.

Nothing changes, and nothing stays the same. Just as British folk music mutated in those hills to become something else, so "old-time music" (to use a less contentious term) also develops – and, after having had to listen to some of the more atonal recordings, thank goodness. Each revival brings something new to the template. Every musician is different. That's the fun of it.

Jazz-rock fusioneers The Don Ellis Orchestra recorded 'Scratt And Fluggs', a "sort of breakdown in 5/4 with the various sections taking up banjo and guitar lines. Various friends and wives were allowed to cheer the band on." It's messy but fun, and just as "authentic" as anything else which catches the spirit of the original form. (We'll look later at The Byrds, who took country music into outer space, and then back to the prairies.)

My own favourites among the many others dropped into the bluegrass box is the high-voiced Jimmy Martin, who joined Bill Monroe's Blue Grass Boys in the early 1950s and sounds as if he is straining for heaven, even on secular songs like 'The Little Girl And The Dreadful Snake'. His solo work sounds as if he is playing and singing with a hot poker up his backside. This is music which is rocket fuelled, and *respectful* is the last word you would ever use for it.

In quite a different firmament, though, is the spectral music left by two brothers from a mountain village in Virginia. Ralph and Carter Stanley couldn't have had more impeccable traditional roots. Their father was "a sawmill operator who sang old songs, like 'Man Of Constant Sorrow'", while their mother played banjo, clawhammer style. After the war, The Stanley Brothers recorded a few singles for Rich-R-Tone, which combined the influence of Bill Monroe with ancient material like 'Little Glass Of Wine', "a murder-and-suicide ballad that was very popular with their hill-country listeners".

Ralph's celestial tenor voice, "in the classic back-country pinched-throat style, with a variety of affecting vocal turns and note embellishments", soared over Carter's lead vocals. When they moved on to Columbia Records, Carter began to write songs which evoked loneliness and loss, of which his 'Lonesome River' is typical: "The lonesome wind blows and the water rolls high." The Stanley Brothers are not noted for their rib-rattling sense of humour, and Carter died at the early age of 41, almost as his own songs had predicted.

All is not quite as it seems. Ralph's 'I Worship You' is directed at an unfaithful wife, not God, while Carter's 'Calling from Heaven' – as he now is – ends with a question: "Are you lost in sin for ever more?". His 'Baby Girl', meanwhile, is also "sent from heaven". The duo recorded a surprisingly rocky – or rockabilly – 'Blue Moon Of Kentucky' shortly after Elvis, but there is no flash of teenage rebellion here, no snarl in the voices. If The Stanley Brothers found it hard to manage wit, sheer happiness is very much part of their world-view, offsetting the gloom. Here a banjo plucks and a violin dances, and the song slows where Elvis would speed it up.

Their unique sound is best described by a traditional song in their repertoire, 'Angel Band', which was a title also used for a CD reissue of their Mercury recordings, until they were dropped in a corporate manoeuvre. The brothers pose in matching fringed white jackets, pasty faced and looking dead already. However, the music inside is as full of life as anything you'll ever hear. Malone describes this sound as "sharp, bright...full of verve and energy", with The Clinch Mountain Boys pulsating in the background. Oddly, this is the same "high, wild, mercury sound" for which Dylan was searching a decade later and which helped to define psychedelic rock – crystalline. There are many different ways of getting high.

Three decades later, Dawidoff watches Ralph onstage, singing "the old songs...just like my mother taught me". He has sounded like an old man since he began, but by now he has aged into his voice. Another old man, Bill Monroe, listens in his dressing room, over the tannoy: "He's got a good voice. Sings like it should be sung. Keep it pure, you know. You see the music really touching them, being sung like they want it to be."

It takes us back to that crucial distinction between imitations and the real thing made by Ciaron Carson. If these undramatic performances which pierce the heart aren't mountain music, then I really don't know what is. Neither does Ralph Stanley, who emphasises that "what he sings is old-time mountain music – not bluegrass". Ricky Skaggs, a younger child of the mountains and one who has recently taken his muse back there, explained it succinctly: "When you hear Bill Monroe you hear the fire of the music. When you hear Ralph Stanley, you hear the high, lonesome sound of the mountains."

Cowboy music has very little to do with cowboys. It's also the kind of music which is lovely in small doses and yet aggravating at length. To become commercially successful, though, country music needed to escape itself. No-one was ever going to make a fortune out of the Stanley Brothers, or even Bill Monroe. As Malone sagely notes: "Given the pejorative connotations that clung to farming and the rural life, the adoption of cowboy clothing and western themes was a logical step."

And yet to play a Roy Rogers compilation straight after Angel Band is also to see the links: here, too, is a high-voiced man, a chunky backing played with a light touch (but no banjo), and songs about a dead mother, his "worried mind", and a final round-up "in the sky". What has evaporated down on the plains is the intensity of music, which cried out to be made. What is added is a sense of inner calm and a new landscape, with "dogies" and sleeping in the saddle, and "one more ride". It sounds like a Hollywood fantasy, and indeed it was.

John A Lomax had gathered a large body of western folklore in his book *Cowboy Songs And Other Frontier Ballads*, and it was from such printed sources or from professional songwriters that these "cowboys" took their songs, not the family tradition that one finds in the mountains passed down from father to son. True, there are a few exceptions, like Carl Sprague, who learned material from his Texan ranch-owning uncle, and Longhorn Luke, who had actually worked as a cowboy. Curley Fletcher was a rodeo rider who sold his poems as broadsides, while Goebel Reeves, the Texas Drifter, ran away from a middle-class background to become a hobo and write songs like 'The Cowboy's Prayer'.

The fascination lies in the way that cowboys, like mountain men, tended to be a race apart: such tightly-knit groups tend to develop their own folklore, or adapt that with which they arrived. On a recent Radio 2 series on *The Singing Cowboys*, Mike Harding mentions that "cowboys sang Mexican songs, Irish songs, English/Scots folk songs. They sang the blues, hobo songs, railroad songs, minstrel songs. You name it, they sang it." He then plays Lee Marvin wandering around the octaves, desperately seeking a tune in 'Wand'rin Star' as an example of what these singers on the range probably sounded like in real life. Harding himself is responsible for the song 'It's Hard To Be A Cowboy In Rochdale', a funny but true account of northern country and western fans in England who recreate the Wild West on Saddleworth Moor: "Spurs don't fit right upon my clothes."

In the sleeve notes to a 1959 album by The Sons Of The Pioneers – big screen smoothies with a full orchestra – Yellowstone Chip, a real pioneer, writes of how for 50 years he has watched cowboy songs enter "the folk music of our country", not showbusiness. "The cowboy sang then, as he does today, to calm

113

his restless herd of cattle, to soothe his horse, or simply keep himself company on the lonesome trail".

It's like the young Victorian bird-scarer who sang in the fields, "to keep myself from crying". Hence the soothing and up-beat nature of mainstream Nashville took off from these songs, not those of sin and retribution. It is literally hypnotic: "A sentimental song could bring close any animal, from an elk to a long-tailed lizard, and make him stand like a statue – and that changing to a quick-time piece would make him sway and wag his tail like a rattlesnake." This way to the line-dancing class.

The really important westward trail, however, was Jimmie Rodgers' journey to Texas for his final years. Here he immersed himself in cowboy myths, leading to the concept of the singing cowboy and western music as a genre all of its own.

Rodgers' imitators included Hank Snow, who even back in Canada wore cowboy clothes and called himself The Yodelling Ranger, and even farther afield the Australian Tex Morton, who went under the nickname The Boundary Ranger. Of this strange hybrid, Malone writes that he "sang cowboy songs with a bizarre, trilling yodel about both the Australian bush and the Texas Plains".

Back in the USA, Ernest Tubb wore cowboy boots and a stetson hat, and sang very few cowboy songs. Gene Autrey, however, did all three. Autrey's father was a horse dealer, and was descended from the earliest white settlers in Texas, contemporaries of Davy Crockett. His mother taught him hymns and folk songs from the cradle upwards, but he fled to find work as a railroad telegrapher. Supposedly discovered by Will Rodgers, singing as he swayed up on high, Autrey got a job on a Tulsa radio station as The Oklahoma Yodelling Cowboy. His early repertoire was largely in the mountain tradition, including self-composed songs such as 'A Hillbilly Wedding In June'. Hollywood gave Gene a new image, starting with *The Phantom Engineer*, a weird blend of cowboy tale and science fiction.

Songs about the mountains gave way to titles like 'Riding Down The Canyon': "There was a definite smoothing-out of presentation – a lower vocal pitch, well-rounded tones, honey-coated articulation." The same happened musically, with "soft guitars, muted violins, a melodious but unobtrusive steel guitar, an accordion, and occasionally even horns".

Born Leonard Sly in Duck Run, Ohio, Roy Rogers was subject to the same process. Brought up on a farm during the Depression, he first sang in public at farm socials, performing traditional cowboy songs. He also acted as a caller for square dances, and would send them home sweating in the time-honoured way, in his own words "having knocked splinters out of the floor". Sly worked for a US shoe company before moving to California, where he picked peaches and started singing on the radio with a band called The Rocky Mountaineers. His next band was called The Pioneers at first, until a radio producer renamed them Sons Of The Pioneers because they looked so young.

Young Len's first cowboy role was in the 1936 film *The Old Corral*, in which he appeared with Gene Autrey, whom he replaced at Republic Studios. *Under Western Stars* saw Roy Rogers appearing under his new name, perhaps in a half-conscious nod to Jimmie Rodgers. Here, in Mike Harding's phrase, he "shot the straightest, rode the fastest, and sung the sweetest". He appeared with his horse Trigger in all of his 180 pictures and TV shows, for which his second wife, Dale Evans, wrote him 'Happy Trails', a clip-clop theme song which remains archetypal. (Quicksilver Messenger Service used the same title for their own album tribute to the Western myth.) Rogers sung 'A Four Legged Friend' in tribute to Trigger, but at times managed to escape from his cowboy image, as in the World War Two movie *The Dark Command*, in which he appeared with a young John Wayne. The circle turns.

Rogers set a country precedent by signing an early – and extremely lucrative – deal which allowed him to retain full rights to his name, voice and image. This gave him full control over all merchandising opportunities, and he was second only to Walt Disney in the money stakes. His brand name began to appear everywhere, giving further impetus to the myth.

Again typically "country" was his open espousing of an uncomplicated Christian faith. With the tragic early death of his first wife, and two adopted children, he sure needed it. Each week he would read out a 'Cowboy Prayer' for The Roy Rogers' Riders Club: "Dear Lord, when trails are steep and passes high, help me to ride it straight the whole way through." After his retirement from acting, Rogers still kept up with country trends, recording songs by the likes of Merle Haggard and Kris Kristofferson.

There were some far stranger singing cowboys to be seen on the silver screen, all of which were variations on the myth. Few fed back into the country mainstream, but they are too much fun to miss. Marlene Dietrich smouldered with a teutonic accent as she serenaded 'The Boys In The Back Room': nobody believed that she was singing about poker. She wasn't the only woman to bring sex to the stetsons, either. Mae West vamped through 'My Little Chickadee' with WC Fields, and gave a new meaning to sung asides like "I could hardly contain myself" in 'Go West, Young Man'. Even more likely to stiffen any saddle was Marilyn Monroe singing 'The River Of No Return'.

Male comics also pounced. Groucho Marx sent up the whole genre when he sang 'Go West, Young Man', with plenty of rollicking yippees, while in *The Paleface* the cowardly Bob Hope crooned 'Buttons And Boys' between engaging in horseplay with Jane Russell. His fellow Roadster, Bing Crosby, gave a jazzy reading of a Johnny Mercer song about an urban cowboy "who never saw a cow" at a time when John Travolta wasn't even born. In *Way Out West*, Stan Laurel and Oliver Hardy sang lovely harmonies almost worthy of The Stanley Brothers, about a girl called June from the Blue Ridge Mountains in 'On The Trail Of The Lonesome Pine', then goofed it up.

Then as now, there were some crossovers. New York sophisticate Cole Porter, of all people, wrote 'Don't Fence Me In', a song which then entered the country repertoire through Roy Rogers. Through such devices, Hollywood fixed western music in the public mind. This same description also came to be used for mountain music, especially that by those ashamed to use the pejorative term "hillbilly". As Malone pointed out: "Most hillbilly singers became fascinated with the western image and eventually began to believe their own symbols." Bespoke tailors like "Nudies" in Los Angeles learnt to satisfy such yearnings.

Country singers were no longer men next door named Bill or Jimmy, but honest cowpokes: Tex, Slim and Hank. A singer and fiddler from Arkansas called Rubye Blevins changed her name to Patsy Montana, and had the first big hit by a woman country singer: what else but 'I Want To Be A Cowboy's Sweetheart'. Groups were no longer good old boys, but went out as The Riders Of The Purple Sage or The Sons Of The Pioneers. After Roy Rogers left, the latter continued to concentrate on cowboy themes, even though their principal composer, Bob Nolan, was a Canadian. But then so is Shania Twain, the CMA's last Artist Of The Year before the millennium. Nolan got well into character on songs like 'Cool Water', and such songs entered the folk tradition through countless amateur singalongs.

Radio stars The Beverly Hillbillies did the reverse. Long before the TV series of the same name, they were an LA band based around Zeke Manners, and pretended to be "a group of strange and primitive musicians...unearthed in the hills of Beverly". By a coincidence so odd it seems pre-ordained, the Bostonian songwriter Billy Hill (his real name) composed *ersatz* hillbilly songs like 'They Cut Down The Old Pine Tree', and then went on to tap the cowboy market with 'The Last Roundup'.

Maurice "Tex" Ritter was born in Texas, where he attended college for five years to study Law, not a subject with which the Wild West was very familiar. He moved to New York to work as an actor on Broadway, singing some folk-based material. Tex then came back west, but to Hollywood, not the Lone Star State. He won an Oscar for his appearance in *High Noon*, and his stirring recording of the title song, complete with strange female wails, reached number one. "I only know I must be brave/and I must face a man who hates me/or lie a coward in my grave".

Ritter was a rightly-acclaimed interpreter of cowboy songs, "with his thick Texas accent and storehouse of cowboy lore". Bleak cowboy tales were a speciality, on albums like *Blood On The Saddle*. The title track has a weird sound, which recalls in advance spaghetti western soundtracks or the pop psychedelia of Joe Meek, as the tape is artificially speeded up and slowed down. Tex comes in with what the sleeve notes describes as his "ten-gallon bass-baritone", and you're not quite sure whether he's serious or joking as he solemnly intones lines like "Oh, pity the cowboy, all bloody and red/for the bronco fell in on him and mashed in his head".

On the 1961 album *Hillbilly Heaven*, Ritter re-records his greatest hits with an "augmented rhythm section" – which sounds pretty much country to me – and a 14-voice chorus. Not an orchestra in sight. Tex is presented as somehow mythic, "more than a man and a voice – he's the sound of the great Southwest, the heart of the South and the hide of the West, the singing cowboy who rides the wide and open spaces of fact and fiction". Miles away from Texas, but close in its bloodthirsty theme, is the folksong 'Barbara Allen', which is set in London. It's not revealed on which side of the Atlantic Ritter found it.

Tex almost speaks this one. He made a speciality of what others called "recitations". The sleeve kindly tells us that "Tex calls them 'talkin' songs and that's a lot closer to what they are." From the way he sings, and sometimes what he sings, one wouldn't want to contradict Tex too firmly, so that is just fine by me.

'Deck Of Cards' was the first such recitation, which as we saw earlier was a tale of ancient lineage indeed. "The soldier boy said sir…" Later came 'Ol' Shorty', set to what sounds like a gypsy violin, but this is not the usual tale of a furry friend coming to the rescue. Quite the reverse: "Come to think of it, you can just have Ol' Shorty too." Tex has a slow-burning sense of humour.

'Hillbilly Heaven', though, is "a maudlin epic", with Ritter dreaming that he is greeted by "the old cowboy philosopher himself, Will Rogers". The Big Boss has asked Will to show Tex around, and he meets dead friends: "Boy was I glad to see…the Mississippi blue yodeller Jimmie Rodgers". Here is a Hall of Fame better than anything to be found in Nashville, with "all the gold guitars and fiddles hanging on the wall".

The more recently deceased are here, too, Hank Williams and Johnny Horton, "standing side by side, smiling at me". It's like the end of the film *Titanic*. Who else is expected in the next hundred years to have their names branded in pure gold in a "big tally book" covered with stardust? The list goes on: Gene Autrey, Roy Acuff, and Tex Ritter. A whoop of surprise from the chorus, and Tex wakes up. It has spawned innumerable parodies, but Tex himself can not have been totally serious. When Ritter had joined the immortals for real, his voice was described as like "a lonely wind blowing across a landscape populated only by tumbleweeds, rattlesnakes and human vermin".

"Western" quickly replaced "hillbilly" as a sales term; it had a better ring to it. It suggested that the music originated with the cowboys of the Texan plains, not from inbred backwoodsmen. This in turn fitted in with a typical American's self-image of living a life that was "open, free and expansive" – John Wayne rather than Jed Clampett.

It was also a better sales pitch. The original cowboy guitarists were probably Mexican *vaqueros*, crooning in Spanish as they rode the range. The "cowboy guitar" evolved as a commercial product in the 1920s, when the mail order company Sears Roebuck offered its "Bradley Kincaid Houn' Dog" model. It was a brilliant marketing exercise, as Sears also sold phonographs and records through the post and signed up stars to its own label. Sears also sold radio sets, and owned the Chicago radio station WLS (World's Largest Store), which gave saturation air time to its products. Then they bought the guitar manufacturer Harmony, and the trap was sprung.

117

Stencilled onto early models were scenes of cowboys on the range and the like. Brand names included the Red Foley Smooth Trailin', the Old Santa Fe – with Gene Autrey's signature under the tailpiece – and the Home On The Range. In the 1950s, cardboard and plastic models began to hit the marketplace, and what had originally been a working instrument became a child's toy. I had one myself, along with a Davy Crockett hat made of fake fur and a Winchester Repeater rifle with no bullets. I watched cowboy epics at my childrens' Saturday morning cinema club.

A world view was being peddled straight out of the Cold War. Indians were merely target practice. Women knew their place. Might was right if dealt out by a smiling man in a white stetson. He would strike up a cheerful ditty as he rode into the sunset. To a cowboy guitar.

Music percolates down, like water through rock, and by the 1950s had finally settled to my level on the radio programme *Childrens' Favourites*, with Uncle Mac – a nickname which could have come straight from the Appalachians. Here, like a residual sludge, were songs which echo within me still: Vernon Dalhert's 'The Runaway Train', Frankie Laine's 'Champion The Wonder Horse', 'The Deadwood Stage' by Doris Day, and 'Ragtime Cowboy Joe' by The Chipmunks, a singing group legitimately on speed. My own favourite was 'Ghost Riders In The Sky', an eerie tale indeed, with the glorious dead made visible. Mythical or what? Rock 'n' roll rumbled away in a different room.

Marty Robbins journeyed in the opposite direction, from the likes of his teenager-in-love hit 'A White Sports Coat (And A Pink Carnation)' – closer to loungecore than rockabilly – to three albums of tough and cinematic gunfighter ballads, steeped in the folklore of the Wild West. The young Marty would walk 15 miles to catch a Gene Autrey movie: "I'd sit so close to the screen I could've gotten sand in my eyes from the horses and powder burns from the guns." He was born out in the Arizona desert in the small farming town of Glendale, one of eight children. His father played the harmonica while his grandfather, "Texas" Bob Heckle, was a former travelling medicine man with a headful of tales: "A lot of the songs I've written were brought about because of the stories he told me. I wrote 'Big Iron' because he was a Texas Ranger. At least, he told me he was!"

Robbins started by playing country music, was signed by Acuff-Rose for his songwriting and became a regular on the Opry, where he returned in 1970 following a serious heart attack, receiving a 45-minute standing ovation. Then found himself relaunched as a teen pop sensation. He switched tracks again with 'El Paso', a four-minute single when such things were virtually unknown, which had Mexican-style guitar and was as economically written as a movie in brief or an ancient ballad – the same thing, really. Robbins' gravelly and authentic-sounding vocals are offset by a Nashville production which somehow takes off the top edge. I'd love to hear these songs remixed with a bit more strangeness thrown in. Robbins could hardly object, having died in 1982, but his voice has a resonance which sounds bigger now than the oohs and aahs of The Glaser Brothers, or the too-light rhythm section.

The single became the central tale of 1959's *Gunfighter Ballads And Trail Songs*, a beautifully-varied collection of closely-observed short stories set to music. The devil is in the detail: "I see the white puff of smoke from the rifle/I feel the bullet go deep in my chest." Robbins credits songs like 'Billy The Kid' and 'Utah Carol' as traditional, and they certainly sound that way. 'The Strawberry Roan' is, too, although I always mishear the line about the rogue horse being "the worst bucker I've seen on the range". The 1976 single 'El Paso City' brings the saga up to date, with Marty flying all over the place as he experiences *déjà vu* and a flash forward to death. It's 'Hillbilly Heaven' all over again.

The sleeve notes talk of how the Western tradition, "even when it is prettied up, is a strong and rousing one...reflected in their ballads", which are predominately melancholy, even when the tune itself is lively. Heroes or villains, in white hats or black, all have "an aura of romantic daring that clings to them still". Their tales build to a high-action climax, "as inevitable as those of Greek tragedies".

Does this sense of archetype explain why "Europeans have been even more enthusiastic about the American West than Americans"? Robbins certainly possesses it in spades, and one thinks of the Gallic worship of Hollywood B-movies, of English new wave directors like Lindsay Andersen coming to see John Ford as a myth-maker of genius, or of all those spaghetti horse-operas.

Maybe it's because all of this came from Europe in the first place, and comes into focus under the burning sun – the Western concept of the individual, as against the native American birthright of being part of one's tribe. In a global marketplace, as the nanny state withers away, we are all gunfighters now.

So who are the cowboy singers now? The answer is as unexpected as you would expect in the hall of distorting mirrors that is country music. Michael Martin Murphey emerged as a cosmic hippie, and 'Geronimo's Cadillac' was just one of many songs he wrote in sympathy for native Americans, hardly friends to the cowboy. And then one thinks a little deeper. Hollywood and a few early massacres (on both sides) excepted, both communities had much the same lifestyles: rootless, tangling with the landscape, living largely in the saddle. Both were outsiders to the real American dream, however much they fuelled it.

The young Murphey (surely from Irish roots, with that surname) had worked on family ranches, and he later retired as a Nashville "outlaw" to follow the lifestyle for real and buy his own ranch in New Mexico. He has made three numbered albums of folklore on the range: the first resurrects cowboy standards , the second is a Christmas special – one of the few you can listen to in July – and the third focuses on outlaws past and present. *Sagebrush Symphony*, taped live, binds together traditional songs and Murphey's own greatest hits.

Plenty of other singer/songwriters have dealt with the lifestyle, with scholarship and empathy, but with no blood on their own saddles. Mud, but no blood. We have already looked at Johnny Cash's two gritty concept albums on the subject, replete with a dictionary of cowboy talk. Willy Nelson's sparse *Red-Haired Stranger* set the outlaw agenda, fleeing not the law but Nashville. It is no coincidence that it is this aspect of those two otherwise deeply conventional country stars which endeared them to a new audience of disillusioned hippies, psychopaths and punks. Cowboy, then, is now partly a state of mind.

It is little surprising that the most scholarly look so far at the cowboy heritage is by Tom Russell, a man with the taste for a big intellectual range to ride. *Song Of The West* misses the star guests of his emigration epic, and is one of those albums which seems to fade into the wallpaper when you actually put it on – its the very best kind of musical wallpaper, though: an acoustic symphony. When you start actually listening, and reading the typically ornate booklet, the ambition of what Tom is doing again startles you awake.

Here are traditional songs like 'Rambler, Gambler' (itself a variant on 'The Wagoner's Lad'), cover versions, new songs inspired by a cowboy museum, working tales heard from his brother, a poem from the Lomax collection, and a cowboy prayer. If you can get over the sameness of Russell's matter-of-fact voice, or rather connect with the passion that throbs underneath, every song takes a different slant, so that the whole album ends up as a three-dimensional experience. It's better than the movies, although Russell avoids epic. It's the small details that tell the story.

The closest to a full-blown saga is a setting of Steven Vincent Benet's poem 'The Ballad Of William Sycamore', put to music by Steve Young, which has the inevitability of the great Celtic tales, though it lacks a supernatural edge. Russell sings this to a simple guitar, and the musical bareness makes it all the more stirring. His own ballad, 'Claude Dallas', has the same inner gravity; the shock is that this "last outlaw" is still on the run: "Come gather round me buckeroos…"

There's a nod to Marty Robbins in 'Gallo Del Cielo': "It's a *corrido*, a long 'running' story in the Mexican style." Most interesting of all is 'John Bull Tin', a kind of country, seedier version of the situation in Joni Mitchell's 'For Free', of all things. Tom gets drinking with a tramp on a London park bench, but finds his abandoned tobacco tin the next day: "I guess he rolled a final smoke/and went on to his reward." We're right back with The Alabama 3 and their old sacred tin. As to what this song is doing here, Russell asks the question himself in his sleeve notes: "Is this a cowboy song? You bet. That old coot was as cowboy as they come."

Some of the songs here are co-written with the Canadian Ian Tyson, once of Ian And Sylvia, who left the music business disillusioned and became a rancher in Southern Alberta. It's not that simple to escape, and Tyson has made a new career recording albums – such as *Cowboyography* – which are based on a close knowledge of working with the land. Essentially simple and unromantic, their bareness touches the heart. A whiff of the open prairie, a lonesome song as darkness falls, and the coffee pot brews. No-one brought up near a TV can escape it. We're all cowboys or cowgirls inside, even if we've never felt a saddle and hot horseflesh beneath us, with the ground a long way down.

I, for one, intend to keep it that way. The sheer dangers of the cowpoke lifestyle are best seen on a screen or imagined, but, as in *Urban Cowboy*, it is in such violent endeavours that the range-riders continue to take part. Leaving aside horse-racing and its updates on two and four wheels, the rodeo is probably the closest people can now get to cowboying, even if the real thing now usually roams the range in air-conditioned comfort.

Ian Tyson was trained as a rodeo rider as a boy. Red Steagall took the whole thing a bronco further and made *For All Our Cowboy Friends*, a concept album about the professional rodeo, and it can still make your jaw drop open. It's great, once. The music bursts out of the speakers like a bullock out of an open gate, and Red – "I refuse to say 'cowpersons'" – sounds like he gargles with spurs. He's like a tough old uncle, giving you a grin and a wholesome message: "Rodeo, you're a part of America/the outdoor dream that every youngster needs."

The rodeo riders study each other on the cover with an admiration close to the homo-erotic. Indeed, women seem redundant when all you need in life is "a good horse, fresh air, plenty to eat, and good friends". That, and having "a good horse between my knees". The humour is rough as sagebrush: a bar-room bully semi-poisoned with coffee grounds, in a place where you're not even allowed to spit out your spent tobacco. Just remember that, "buried deep within every man, whether he wears a business suit or a pair of faded jeans, there's a little bit of cowboy within us all". Then you look at the paleface clown on the cover, with one red sock, one blue and ludicrous braces, and the listing of local heroes, and the lovingly-recreated jargon, and the well-honed stories, and realise that this is folklore, alive and kicking.

It is already ritualised, though played for fun. Truckers are where the cowboys really went, still working the range for real rather than for a paying audience; alone in the cab, and then back telling tales in the truck stop. Male camaraderie and cheap beer. Dave Dudley's voice is as deep-down masculine as Red Steagall's, and he too is full of tales which go back to the ballads and probably to before anyone had learned how to write words onto paper. Lust, greed, cunning and stupidity: the kind of stuff that lasts.

Dave's 'Counterfeit Cowboy' has a dressed-up dude stepping into a local bar and conning the clientele with fake $50 bills. 'Rollin' Rig' is the story of a knight of the road: "Call my life a simple one, my world it ain't so big...I've seen it all, from the deck of a rolling rig." It neatly encapsulates country and western, "from the mountains of Virginia to the California coast" – these people don't just watch road movies; they live them.

Both songs are on *Special Delivery*, an album about "those on the move", and divided into "Uppers" and "Downers". It also includes a muscular version of 'Six

Days On The Road', the song which started the whole "modern truck song cycle". It's a matter of reality and not play-acting, taking little white pills on the highway and rushing back to his baby. Dudley's own career was put on hold for a while after he was hit by a car while packing away his guitar after a gig.

Dudley is officially endorsed by The Trucker's Union, and according to the sleeve notes has "captured the lonely life and hurried romance of the man in the cab", probably because, as a working musician, he shares the lifestyle, "the sweat and toil, the frustrations and despair, and that awesome, overwhelming feeling one gets when nearing home".

For Bill Malone, despite "the fabric of usable symbols which surrounded him, the cowboy contributed nothing to American music. The 'western' music which became fashionable in the mid-Thirties came from other sources." Out in the west, old-style string bands developed a unique style by soaking up local influences, in particular from Mexican-Americans – the original cowboys – and polkas and other dance tunes brought over by immigrants from central Europe, who formed tightly knit communities out on the plains.

As with the Scots-Irish, holding tight to one's native music was an antidote to homesickness. Home is a state of mind, and you can pack it up and bring it with you. It's a standard characteristic of the immigrant lifestyle anywhere.

What emerged from the stew was a sound that became known as "Western swing", dominated by fiddles and guitars. By adding a polka beat and lots of jazz, the music put on muscle: it was gutsier, sexier and with a stronger beat than early Appalachian string bands. More fun, too.

The Oklahoma Cowboys were formed by Otto Gray in 1924 as a "fiddlin', sin-gin' and dancin' unit for the purpose of bringing back to the present generation the music and songs of the early days of the West". Not for them the poorhouse look, real or assumed; these musical cowboys travelled from gig to gig in a posse of cus-tom-built cars, led by a three-ton sedan, like a railroad observation truck. No boxcars, no hobos, not a singing brakemen in sight. Country flash starts here.

Bob Wills was the man who made this new style famous. He was a fiddler who teamed up with the singer Milton Brown to form the nucleus of The Aladdin Laddies, renamed The Light Crust Doughboys when sponsored by Burris Mills Company. Wills had learned to play from his father and grandfather, both champi-on fiddlers, and then honed his trade in local dances, joining a medicine show in the time-honoured way. He even played blackface comedy. More crucially, he began to holler and joke with his musicians on stage, just like the black musicians did when he was a kid.

Wills founded The Texas Playboys and acted as bandleader, leaving lead vocals and lead fiddle to others. He whoops them along in a high-pitched manner that I thought at first was a lady on the edge of orgasm. Photos of the time see a relaxed combo, with Bob very much the focal point and a banjo still in the band. His music remains fascinating because of such recklessness, not so much crossing musical barriers as leaping over them, so that you have a breakneck version of 'Cotton-Eyed Joe', or a smooth take on 'Corrine, Corrina', next to rags and two-steps.

The band take this mixture of blues and traditional folk into the electric age, literally. Gibson had began to market their electric guitar in 1936, and Wills brought Eldon Shamblin into the band on that barnstorming instrument, which meant that it could compete with a brass section, steel guitar and drums. Shamblin wrote down musical arrangements for this augmented line-up just as carefully as Bill Monroe was about to for the more restrained timbres of bluegrass: "You can change the name of an old song, rearrange it and make it swing." The result was at first called "Okie jazz", or "Western jazz", with much the same sense of (mock) modesty as the Grand Ole Opry. How dare these country hicks act sophisticated! An early anthem – and million seller – was 'San Antonio Rose', also a hit for that most unlikely country star Bing Crosby (although he almost certainly had Irish roots, with ears like that!).

When Bob Wills came into town with his hundred-dollar boots and shiny band bus with logo painted on the side and steer horns on the front, the rustling sound in the background was that of country singers throwing away their old dungarees. It was the decisive step in the country makeover – which was ironic, as Nashville had previously shunned "the hollerin' yahoos of the Southwest".

One wonders quite what Wills – increasingly prone to alcohol abuse – was like as a band leader, as the changes in line-up would fill this book. When he added the fiddler Johnny Gimble, the brew was steaming, alternating jiving vocals with instrumental solos. Get any good compilation of his work (dozens are available, but only one is enough) and you will hear trademark songs like 'Time Changes Everything', with lots of whooping, a smooth overall sound which takes you immediately back to the war years but encompasses old-time fiddle pieces like 'Lone Star Rag', light blues, and traditional songs like 'Take Me Back To Tulsa'. It's upbeat, it makes you smile, it sets your foot tapping, and it leaves your brain alone. This is commercial music, with all of the appeal and shallowness which that term implies, and Wills got the blend right for a mass market. (He also marketed his own flour and rodeo, using the same principles.)

During the early war years, Bob moved his band to California, where they played to huge ballrooms, packed tight with munitions workers and people from the shipyards looking for a good time. After the war, he cut down on the brass, got back to fiddlin' and played smaller venues. This was his natural habitat, dance halls, with a thousand or so people jammed in, sweating and dancing to the dim lights and loud music, making that old wooden floor bounce.

Fortunately, we have nine CDs of the *Tiffany Transcriptions* recorded just after the war in California, which capture the interaction of a live band, hot to trot, and exuding a huge sense of well being. The band veer from corn-fed instrumentals like 'Sally Goodin' to Tommy Duncan's mellow crooning. He sounds unconvincing when he sings about driving cattle down from Nebraska, but chuckles his way cheerfully through 'Roly Poly', a joyous song about a boy who eats all day. This leads into a hotshot guitar break from Junior Barnard, a slice of steel guitar, then a tooting sax – all this to the feral howls of Bob Wills – and then the steel guitar player imitates The Glenn Miller Orchestra all by himself. The overall effect is close to Spike Jones or The Bonzo Dog Band. You suddenly realise that these people are sending up the whole thing.

Wills had a sad end for someone who made such happy music. He was about to reform The Playboys, conducting them from his wheelchair, when he died. His spirit is unquenchable, and Merle Haggard resurrected it on his 1970 album *A Tribute To The Best Damn Fiddle Player*. More recently, Ray Benson of Asleep At The Wheel – one of the many post-hippie bands to soak up his influence – has been engaged in a one-man resurrection mission, with many of those artists featured at the CMA Awards taking part. The Dixie Chicks steal the show, as there.

Darker shadows intrude on an album from Bloodshot Records of Chicago, *The Pine Valley Cosmonauts Salute The Majesty Of Bob Wills*, not so much through the bar-room renditions and studio backchat – which catch the essentially rough and ready nature of Wills in a way that perhaps Benson's over-respectful renditions do not – as in the cover art.

You really need to be as smug as me and buy the limited edition vinyl issue, but Jon Langford – art school terrorist, head honcho of The Mekons and The Three Johns and Bloodshot mainman (don't worry, we're coming back to him) – studs it with his obsessive oil paintings of Wills, a cross between holy icons and scrawled graffiti. "Traditionalist"/"Avant-Gardist" appears at the top, "Pioneer"/"Magician" at the bottom, and on the back cover Bob is painted in pure white, like a ghost, his fingers like bones. It exudes the same love affair with another culture as fellow Brit Duncan McLean's book *Lone Star Swing*, which, as we have already seen, traces memories of Wills through Texas – the light emitted from a dying star – and pastes a rare item of memorabilia at the start of each chapter. Like I said, icons.

Langford writes a gospel entry on the back cover which I can't improve on, so I'll simply copy it here word for word: "Bob Wills once rode 50 miles on horseback to hear Bessie Smith sing the blues. He was the first man to use drums on the Grand Ole Opry...when asked what he thought of rock 'n' roll, Bob said he'd been rockin' since 1928." The presence here of alt country stalwarts like Jimmie Dale Gilmore, Alejandro Escovedo and Robbie Fulks, plus the totally wonderful Sally Timms, shows that the rock goes on.

Western swing really died with Wills, though. 'Spade' Cooley built a big-band sound based on The Dorsey Orchestra and named himself King Of The Form, although the closest he got to the Appalachian ballad tradition was when he killed his wife, stomping her to death. His biggest hit was called 'Shame On You', which figures.

It can't have been too easy in the 1940s to have the Christian name Adolph, but the Texan Adolph Hofner is far more representative of the musical cross-currents of the time than a man nicknamed Spade. He is one of those figures whose influence has outlasted his music.

Hofner's grandparents came from Czechoslovakia to live near Praha, one of the oldest middle-European settlements in the States. Young Adolph couldn't speak English when he first went to school, and at home was subjected to a sole diet of Bohemian music, waltzes and polkas, played by his mother on her accordion. It sounds like a recipe for child abuse, but he learned to love it (well you'd have to to, wouldn't you, or go mad), and when he began to play in public, the Bohemian tune 'Dreamland Waltz' would sit next to 'Cotton-Eyed Joe'. Adolph's natural habitat was local beer joints, nicknamed "honky tonks" shortly after the repeal of Prohibition. Along with the likes of Ernest Tubb, Hofner prepared the way for the rough 'n' tough Bakersfield sound of Buck Owens and Merle Haggard.

For Glen Campbell, who has played more than a few in his time, honky tonks are "the fightin' and dancin' clubs". Malone describes them as "out-of-the-way dingy bars, but many contained dance floors. All were emblazoned with neon lights." They gave their name to a lifestyle, "Honky-Tonkin'", which was a weekend of social-ising, drinking and dancing. Music was indespensible, but more often than not supplied by one of those new-fangled jukeboxes (so called because of their popu-larity in Southern roadhouses called juke joints) rather than by an actual live band. The music had to change in such new surroundings, for, as Malone adds, lyrics about "poor old Mother" or church-going seemed a little redundant, giving way to songs which reflected "the problems and changing social status of the ex-rural dweller...family fragility, the insecurities of love, marriage dissolution, drinking and having a good time". Like us all.

Its not so easy to shake off the Appalachians. Malone adds that "Protestant cul-ture still gripped the lives of the honky tonk musicians, colouring the lyrics of even their drinking and cheating songs". Guilt is not an easy ghost to exorcise, but I would argue that the traditional roots of this culture also provide a deep-down resilience against adversity. Both things are ingrained in country music, like strata in ancient rocks, the impulse to self-pity and the matching impulse to turn one's back on self-doubt and ride away.

The 1950s certainly saw musical turmoil, with the emergence of rock 'n' roll on one side and the smoother sounds of the likes of "Hank" Thompson on the other, weeping in the honky tonk . His hit 'Wild Side Of Life' provoked an answer song by Kitty Wells, the pre-feminist 'It Wasn't God Who Made Honky Tonk Angels', which put the blame firmly back on the men. Strange things were stirring, and over in Hollywood the electric steel/electric guitar duo Speedy West and Jimmy Bryant were playing sessions in which western swing mutated into futuristic sounds. Left behind, like creatures in a rockpool, were bands like Hoyle Nix And His Cowboy

Band, who had played every Saturday night since 1946 at the Stampede Club, still serving up those swingin' sounds.

We need to fast forward, as time and blank pages start to narrow ahead. So much good music, so little time! In the case of post-war Nashville, this is no bad thing.

By one of those historical twists which make perfect sense when you look closer, singers with the deepest musical roots – and they don't come any deeper than Hiram "Hank" Williams – are those whose work has lasted the best. There is all kind of crap, the stuff that gave country music a bad name in the first place during my own youth: I don't intend to waste much time on it, whatever its huge sales figures its time of release. Go into any charity shop and it's full of records that were over-hyped a generation before, whether it be Richard Clayderman, Sir Harry Secombe or Jim Reeves. Few people want it now. It's the sort of stuff I had to clear out when my mother died, and she used music as a kind of librium, bless her.

An industry was being built. When *Billboard* changed the name of its chart from "Hilllbilly" to "Country And Western" in 1949 it was part of the sweetening process, drawing out the music's sting. Of course, what you shove out of the front door sometimes slips in through the back porch. Merle Travis is now best known for his thumb-style guitar, plucking the bass strings with that digit as his forefinger picks out a lead line. It was heavily influential on the likes of Chet Atkins, and was used to add weight to the sound of cutting-edge bands, particularly when playing live, to become an early form of country rock. Travis learnt the trick back home in Muhlenberg – the coal hole of western Kentucky – from Ike Everly, no less.

Merle himself had started by playing fiddle and five-string banjo. When it was suggested to Merle that he should record some "back home" folksongs, he decided instead to write his own. The results, as on the solo and acoustic 1947 album *Folk Songs From The Hills*, have entered the country canon through countless cover versions by those who have followed. Other songs of Merle's tend towards the whimsical, such as the anti-nicotine diatribe 'Smoke! Smoke! Smoke!', while the search for God on the adapted hymn 'I Am A Pilgrim', or lyrics sung from a miner's point of view (as was his father) on the 1962 album *Songs Of The Coal Mines*, are as serious as your life, despite Merle's own jovial singing style.

This was the same year that a supposedly traditional musician, Doc Watson, played New York for the first time, while acknowledging the huge influence that the supposedly commercial Travis had had on him. So who is the more authentic of the two? For gritty reality, Merle's own 'Dark As A Dungeon' or his "fun song" '16 Tons' are closer to Dock Boggs than Tex Williams, who, with his band The Western Caravan, was among the first customers of the tailor "Nudie" Cohen.

Country stars were learning to become snappier dressers, and other things were also changing. Just as the country blues had mutated in Chicago to something wilder and more dynamic, so country music on the West Coast of America was learning how to rock. Merle played a guitar built by Paul Bigsby and developed by

Leo Fender: "I got the idea from a steel guitar. I wanted the same sustainability of notes, and I came up with a solid-body electric guitar with the keys all on one side." Merle used it to make animal noises as a party piece, and by the early 1950s he was double-tracking in the studio, anticipating Les Paul and a whole progression of unreal sounds, from psychedelia to acid house.

Fender had by now perfected the Telecaster, with its piercing tone and staccato bursts like automatic gunfire, and had developed an electric bass to match. Rickenbacker had also developed a solid-bodied guitar. Here was the sound of the beat boom and folk rock, 20 years before its time.

Meanwhile, the Grand Ole Opry had also changed, for good. Bill Malone notes how the show's original down-home ambience was long gone: "George D Hay's dream of an uncommercialised 'folk' format had long been obliterated under an avalanche of commercial advertising, and 'stars' had proliferated." This, despite a carefully-planned air of "organised confusion". Another Kentucky boy, Red Malone, was now acting as host. His dying dog song 'Old Shep' reduced a young Elvis to tears, and my mates and I to tears of laughter when we found it years ago as a B-side on a student jukebox.

As I prefer to rely on discs, live tapes, interviews and memorabilia actually from the time (Malone aside), rather than on so-called histories written from this or that political agenda, I turn here to a mono LP, *The Red Foley Show*, supposedly recorded live on the road, and imported into Britain by the short lived Stetson label (whose parent company also brought jazz albums on the Impulse label across the ocean). What we have here is not city cool but country bunkum. There is an air of insistent bonhomie, as Red "won't you answer from your heart?" Foley provides the links between a cross section of the available country talent: Kitty Wells, The Wilburn Brothers, Ernest Tubb and a young Patsy Cline.

America's "finest country gentleman" sings his theme song and then dispenses some pre-written folksy charm: "I'd like to get acquainted with you in one big wad." Just as I'm about to sling the record, we have 'Sugarfoot Rag', an infectious and indefinably Celtic strumalong, which does indeed warm the heart.

More country shenanigans are next up, with the super-rustic Uncle Cyp Brasfield, who comes up with some extremely dubious jokes about a man with cold hands milking a cow. Off he goes, thank goodness, and now Red gets serious with 'Born To Lose', his foghorn voice offset by a heavenly choir, and a tinkling piano. Speedy Haworth plays some "fast guitar", Patsy Cline sings with a tremble in her throat, and then Red raids his "keepsake album" for a warning against communist dictators in 'The Message'. In America, "a kid that's born in the slums can climb a tree with a rich man's child, and fight for the juiciest plum," so push off, Russkie. Red's voice takes on a hardness here, and he warns his Marxist foe that "all you will gain in this land is a little plot just about six by three". And Mr Foley will dig it for you, personally.

There is not a whisper of audience reaction here, and after the intermission we have a "little ballad song" from The Wilburn Brothers, whom Red comically confuses: "In this business it's easy to use big words", but Red introduces Kitty Wells as its undisputed "Queen", and Ernest Tubb – whom Uncle Cyp tries to bamboozle – as giving us "a little tad" of his latest song. It turns out to be witless rubbish, smeared with a pedal steel guitar as sticky as vomit.

The show ends with an image of country togetherness, as Red gives us a bouncy, spiritless take on the spiritual 'He's Got The Whole World In His Hands'. First, though, a closing homily: "Friends, we'd like to leave you with a little thought that's been handed down to me through the years. Just remember that, when you lay down and take your last [a slight pause here] breath and go on into the great beyond, that everything you own, all your earthly possessions, will belong to someone else, but everything that you are and everything you have been will be yours forever." Has Appalachian wisdom come to this?

Countless songs, paintings, movies, poems, sermons and parents have said much the same (Lowell Folsom's threatening blues 'Mother Earth' is the scariest rendition that I know), but never before can it have been stated with such smarm. The only thing that's missing from Foley's similar role at the Opry is that show's commercial breaks, which he also recited. The best thing about this album, then, and the country mind-cast which produced it, is that you can't take it with you.

Pure corn from Nashville. It was true then, though is less so now, as when Nik Cohn wrote in the 1960s that "basically it's the centre of country music, but it handles a lot of pop as well, it carries more recording sessions than anywhere outside New York. It's a strange city – filled to overflowing with guitar pickers by the thousand, and scuffling. Once you've made it, you're in for life, and you're looked after." Red Foley helped to popularise Decca's Castle Studios, then Owen Bradley opened his "barnlike" premises in 1953 and in came the suits to handle A&R, concert bookings, and publishing rights. Acuff-Rose hit gold when Patti Page recorded 'The Tennessee Waltz', which was not, as its title might suggest, a traditional song but a composition by accordion player Pee Wee King.

It was another sign of the times. Professional songwriters were moving in, like the husband-and-wife team Felice and Boudleaux Bryant, although their own country roots showed through on songs like 'Rocky Top'. In general, Nashville kept things musically simple and lyrically close to everyday life. Bill Malone shrewdly notes that this new country was less pre-occupied with "mountain cabins, village churchyards and sunbonnet mothers', and closer to urban concerns, though seldom political. It was more personal, less communal.

This is crystallised in the frankly self-obsessed work of a young country singer/songwriter born Hiram Williams. Hank was largely self-taught: "I have never read a note or written one. I can't. I don't know one note from another." As a lyricist, he was about as functionally illiterate as Shakespeare.

Hank's career was masterminded by Fred Rose as carefully as Brian Epstein shepherded the Beatles, except that Fred also helped with his songwriting and Hank himself had the old mountain man's trick of being able to hear a good tune and then copy it. He joined the cast of a new radio show, *The Louisiana Hayride*, and shot to immediate stardom, but then decamped to the Opry. Johnny Cash, George Jones and Elvis Presley were to follow that same rising curve. It's some list, but even in that exalted company Hank Williams rules supreme. His music has a simple surface, but it's deep as the earth, and you can listen to it – and learn from it – forever.

Williams is the pivotal point of this book, and of much else besides. That gangling frame contained a heart that ached, a body that knew all of the pleasures of the flesh, and a brain that could take the wit, sadness and vision of the best country music and infinitely compress it to the core. When he sings 'I'll Never Get Out Of This World Alive', a fiddle scrapes and a steel guitar sobs and Hank sounds playful, jaunty almost, with a whoop to his voice and every syllable carefully enunciated. There's the same essential liveliness as with the young Bob Dylan, though the later singer's (assumed) rustic accent is much more accentuated than Hank's, who plays down the hillbilly corn. As an exercise in song interpretation, it is worthy of Sinatra.

It's the sound of a man taking pleasure in his own bad luck, or at least in his ability to put it all into tight rhymes (shades of the young Pete Townshend with The Who), but underlying it all is a dreadful sense of fatalism. The song is over so quickly that you hardly notice its passing, but you know in your gut that he has lived every word. Next up on the CD is 'You Win Again', again with the musicians starting at a lively trot, but here Hank seems to drag the pace backwards as his voice plunges deeper into melancholy and gets wilder at the edges, spiralling down to the word "sin", then rhyming it with "again". There is something yearning and hurt trapped in the vocals here, something almost too intimate. The same voice can express the purest lust too, in songs like 'Hey Good Looking'. A live version has him holding the long notes – especially the last syllable of "recipe" – like a wolf howling at the moon.

In my own mad scheme of things, Hank Williams is the only possible link between The Alabama 3, as they held court on that cold English field, and the glossy millionaires at the CMA Awards, busy congratulating each other. Dolly Parton excepted, I know towards which of the two lifestyles Hank would be more likely to gravitate.

His father was part Choctaw Indian, a small-time farmer who also worked for a lumber company, but brain damage suffered in the First World War made him a distant figure to his son. Hank grew up singing sacred music in the Baptist churches of Alabama, and that style of rural gospel singing is buried deep in his music, however secular – and sexual – it gets. So is the sense of damnation.

Hank Williams came out of rural Alabama like a hurricane. As a boy he had cleaned shoes and soaked up the blues – a street singer called Rufus "Tee-Tot" Payne taught him guitar for 15 cents a lesson. Barney Hoskyns hears in Hank's voice "all the rawness and pinched-animal pain" of Robert Johnson, and certainly Hank influenced black artists from Otis Redding to Al Green, but what I hear when I listen to him now is the whitest music imaginable.

Hank had his own hillbilly band from the age of 14, combining country gospel and honky tonk, and as a fervent Roy Acuff fan he understood the power and truth of the old music as well as anyone: "It can be explained in one word: sincerity. When a hillbilly sings a crazy song, he feels crazy. When he sings 'I Laid My Mother Away' he sees her a-laying right there in the coffin. He sings more sincere than most entertainers, because the hillbilly was raised rougher than most entertainers. You got to know a lot about hard work." Hank himself worked as a labourer and a welder, despite suffering intense pain from his spina bifida.

He had a lot to overcome. One biographer, Chet Flippo, describes Williams' folks as "tough Southern white trash, absolute bottom-of-the-rung peckerwoods". Another, the Canadian writer Colin Escott, understands the damage that such stereotyping did. He describes the advert for Hank's debut single on Sterling's "new Hillbilly series" as two rustics "from the shallow end of the gene pool, holes in their britches and a bottle of hooch between them". I can only add that at least they are playing violin and upright bass, and look lost in their music. The *Billboard* review played along with its description of "backwoods country gospel singing – way back in the woods". Both the singing and the song were "entirely funereal".

No wonder that Hank adopted another stereotype, named his backing band The Drifting Cowboys in a moment of pure poetry – one can imagine them drifting out there forever – and began to sport either western attire on stage or a smart suit. Always a snappy dresser, he usually wore a white cowboy hat (which hid his premature hair loss) and had the slightly reptilian good looks of a young Clint Eastwood. Not an ounce of fat, just like in his songs.

Hank was himself in the ballad-making tradition, and as good as stated it: "A song ain't nothin' in the world but a story just wrote with music to it". Like his anonymous precursors, he knows just how to set a scene and give it life in a few deft words. He even put his name to a book titled *How To Write Folk And Western Music To Sell*. For Emmylou Harris, "he brought that real high lonesome sound to country music".

What he also added to the genre was sexual magnetism. This is not something that we associate with, say, Dock Boggs. As Chet Flippo describes it, "he really stretched out the yodel on the word 'blues' and hit them with a little of that piston-like pelvic action and looked those women in the first rows right square in the eye and gave them a half-smile that was also a defiant half-sneer. Country music had just opened a door it hadn't known was there…" If that is reminiscent of Elvis a few years later then it is probably no coincidence that the jailbird who Presley plays in *Jailhouse Rock* has a photo of Hank stuck on the wall of his cell.

Hank was a mass of inner contradictions. He could be sour or generous by turns. He loved being on stage, but was also later banned from the Opry because of drunkenness. He was in nearly constant pain and developed a taste for morphine, but hosted the *Health And Happiness Hour*. As "Luke The Drifter", Hank gave sombre recitations in the style of Red Foley, but could also take himself less than seriously. Tony Bennett put strings to 'Cold, Cold Heart', had a massive hit with it, and Hank phoned him to ask "Tony, what's the idea of ruining my song?" He would play it on his local jukebox, though.

Roger Cook, an English songwriter now based in Nashville, reckons that his early death made him immortal: "He didn't wear the public out, like Elvis did." He passed out for good on the back seat of a chauffeur-driven car on New Year's Day 1953, at the age of 29. A film about his last hours, *Hank Williams, The Show He Never Gave*, stars the Canadian folk singer Sneezy Waters, much influenced by Woody Guthrie, and in the middle of a show, Hank – or Sneezy – breaks into the haunting folk ballad 'Alone And Forsaken'.

The writer Mikal Gilmore, whose brother Gary was executed for murder, reckons that, by the end of the film, "we have come as close to a reckoning with dissolution...as film – or pop music – has ever brought us". At Hank's funeral, Bill Monroe, Ernest Tubb, Roy Acuff, Red Foley and The Statesman Quartet all sang country gospel laments. His music was later overdubbed on a succession of duff LPs, but all was put right on a magnificent ten-CD box set. Paul du Noyer reckoned that it was an "archive" rather than listener-friendly, but "there's a palace of pleasures in here...it may cost you an awful lot of time and money, but nobody ever said that pilgrimages were meant to be easy".

The compiler Colin Escott reckons that "Hank could only sing in a go-for-broke way". People "looked beyond the hillbilly accent and saw that Hank had touched them. He wrote about himself, but he was really writing about everyone." A musical based on his life, *Lost Highway*, has been running in Los Angeles for over ten years. Those who have covered his songs range from The Grateful Dead to The Carpenters, Richard Thompson to The Bee Gees. It is a continuing influence, not least on the new stars of that which I regard as real country music.

Lucinda Williams, born in the same month that Hank died, remembers her own father's story of how he had met Hank after a show, and Hank telling him not to drink whisky, "'cause you got a beer-drinking soul": "I always related to this story in a way that would help me form my view of the world, and the way my music reflected that. Hank was one of us."

Jason Rindenberg, of The Scorchers, was working on his father's hog farm when he heard 'Cold, Cold Heart' "coming out of the barn and filtering out over the cornfields". Ever since, he has performed "hopped-up versions" with his band "to rock and roll and punk audiences all over the world, and they never fail to rock the house". For Mike Mills of REM, "simplicity, honesty and pain run like rusty trains through a very dark night; nobody said it like Hank Williams".

Plenty have tried, and some have even been driven to record whole albums of his songs. The latest at the time of writing is Irish singer Bap Kennedy's *Hillbilly Shakespeare*, with BJ Cole on pedal steel, but the three that really count are all by absolute masters of self-destruction, one of them Hank's own son.

The strangest and perhaps the truest is by Matt Johnson of The The, a man who himself came out of the London badlands like an electronic hillbilly, "an East End visionary successfully staring out adversity, himself and the void". Sounds just like The Alabama 3. The The's album *Infected* attacks the Thatcher/Reagan years with infinitely bitter and intimately sung lyrics about sexual misfits, bombings, impotence and a stained heartland: "I'm just another Western guy/with desires that I can't satisfy." One particular danger, ironically, is that of being screwed by American culture: "This is the 51st state of the USA".

Matt was never a country fan, and "didn't want to go to Nashville. I wanted to come at it from the viewpoint of a guy from London a couple of generations later." He praises the way that Colin Escott – who told Johnson that the versions of Hank Williams' songs on *Hanky Panky* were the most original he'd ever heard – had laid bare how the Nashville establishment re-wrote Hank's life story after his death, to make him commercially palatable. The The return him to the gutter: "I think he was a very dark guy, very intense, but sensitive and brooding." The oddest thing is that the graveyard guitar and lonesome harmonica take these songs back to the Appalachians, into a kind of primal soup of emotion. Where Hank's own versions skate dangerously on the surface, not drowning but waving, Matt plunges right in, with righteous gloom.

'Honky Tonkin' becomes a dirge. 'I'm A Long Gone Daddy' turns psychotic. 'I Saw The Light' is like a junkie refusing a fatal fix, screaming on the edge of reason. Guitars crunch, and Matt testifies so that you're forced to sing along, with a tear in your eye and joy in your heart. This album was meant to be the first of "an occasional series of albums celebrating great singer/songwriters", but nothing was heard from The The for seven years. It was as if Hank put his lovesick blues voodoo on him and Britain's own finest singer/songwriter of the 1980s disappeared, or was swallowed alive. Actually, he moved to New York. The last song he covers here is 'I Can't Escape From You'. Ever.

A promo that I particularly treasure interleaves Hank and Matt on each song. The vinyl release is deliberately antique, two ten-inch albums in heavy cardboard. A single version of 'I Saw The Light' has bonus tracks, and a cover photo of Matt in the shadows, his mouth set in its characteristic scowl. He wears a white hat.

Hank Williams Jnr's tribute to his father is a lighter beast. He principally remembers his father as a practical joker, not a melancholic. There are pop orchestral arrangements, and young Hank poses on the cover with a pout, a silver lamé jacket and brylcreemed hair, like a younger Jerry Lee Lewis. The sleeve notes are by Fred Rose's son Wesley. (Fred, too, died young, having cleaned up Hank Snr's smut content – on record, at least.) Hank Jnr's career has been "guided by his mother, and each and every decision has been 100% correct". Hank Snr found the same domineering presence in his life, and Audrey's behaviour inspired many of his most lovelorn songs before he divorced her.

However over-polite these familial versions, Hank Jnr went off to live the The The lifestyle until, in 1975, he fell down a 500-feet-high Montana mountain and needed to have half his face rebuilt. He had just released a hard rocking album with Charlie Daniels and other Southern boogie-merchants, much closer to his father's spirit than countrypolitan: "They were polarising times, and the music was the cutting edge of the times. If you listened to country music you were a redneck, and if you listened to rock 'n' roll you were a hippie freak. So what happened to The Allmann Brothers, in Macon, Georgia, was of no concern to the pickers in Nashville, Tennessee, just a couple of hundred miles up the road. But it was important to me because those Georgia boys were trying to tell me something."

He also began to follow in his dad's image, and just like him was at odds with, say, the clean-cut hat acts of the 1990s. In 1992, he spent a curtailed live appearance drunk onstage and cursing his audience. That's my boy.

George Jones sobbed when told of the death of Hank Williams, Snr. A Texan from the oilfields, but a hillbilly in his soul, Jones was born in Hardin County, named after some Tennessee outlaws who fled there to escape a murder charge. It figures, somehow. Jones' own career also seems to have been carried out on the run. He has been infused with the same demons as Hank, though unlike his mentor each fleck of pain and self-hatred, each moment of alcohol and substance addiction, has been etched onto that extraordinary voice.

Forgive the fact that the man looks like a nasty and narrow-eyed chipmunk, or that he seems to sing without any intervention from his brain. When George sings *My Favourites Of Hank Williams*, every one a downer, his voice does what one reviewer defines as seeming "to rise from the knots in his stomach, the words seeping through clenched teeth", and another as "an out-of-body voice". Just listen to 'You Win Again', the way he glides in and downwards, a swan landing on water. Jones breaks "then" and "sin" in two, just like Hank, but with greater craft (in both senses). Barney Hoskins sees his vocal as "more like the bowing of a fiddle player than the diction of a singer". That's the one problem, that you don't feel that he is properly weighing each word or living it afresh. This is a performance, not interpretation. He does a good train whistle imitation, though – more of a cluck than a cheep.

My own favourite George Jones album is one that does feel totally from the heart, 1974's *In A Gospel Way*. In the song 'A Man I Always Wanted To Meet', George proudly talks of how he met Babe Ruth, John Wayne and "the great Hank Williams one night backstage at the Opry house/He looked down and grinned when I said 'I'm your biggest fan.'" He – Jones, Braddock and Putnam, who wrote the song, or everyman – also shook the hand of JF Kennedy in Dallas on that fateful day. (Is this man jinxed?) Whoever is telling this song has been lucky in his celebrity conquests, even if they haven't, but he still waits to meet Christ face to face. And look what happened to him.

The awful 'Release Me' – as slimily oozed by the unspeakable Engelbert Humperdinck – is here reclaimed for Jesus, with new words that suggest a love beyond sex, or even flesh itself. Jones sounds truly transported, and his very lack of hammy over-acting makes it all the more true. As to a string-enriched 'Amazing Grace'...well, if Jones' measured voice here doesn't bring you close to tears, you are truly made of stone. Ruth Padel, who has stigmatised him as a violent Southern man, is mute on the kind of grace and tenderness you hear here. God knows what she would make of the next track, 'Mama's Hands', a male response to a female guiding presence which is almost divine.

Such things are not in the current script. I like to think that they will be, and that a rich debate will emerge as a result, across the gender divide. The kind of scholarship Padel represents is all too current, unencumbered by the facts. First establish your prejudice, then search out evidence to support it. I was taught to look at all the evidence first and then take a view. I'm sure that Hank would have "done it that way", too: he knew how uncomfortable the truth can be.

Just before the century ended, Steve Earle and friends turned up at the Lisner Auditorium, Washington, to perform a tribute concert to Hank. As *No Depression* commented, "when Steve turns up wearing a freshly-pressed shirt and looking downright respectable, you know something unusual is going on". Lucinda Williams and Kathy Mattea were there too, alt country and new country at their best, and Kim Richey stole the show: "all this up-temp stuff just pisses me off when I'm in a bad mood". She sang her own song, 'Home', a gospel song in the Hank tradition. It's just another sign that flowers continue to grow on the master's grave.

A "downright grumpy" Steve Earle introduced 'Mansion On The Hill' as "a hillbilly, bad-attitude version of Romeo and Juliet", and his rendition took on that "keening, high lonesome sound, a vocal remnant of his recent bluegrass collaboration with Del McCoury". As Hank himself signed off from the 'Health And Happiness' hour (selling alcohol-powered laxative): "Friends...if the good Lord's a-willing and the creeks don't rise, we'll see you 'fore long". Then The Drifting Cowboys light into a short burst of the traditional 'Sally Goodin'. It all comes together. Country and Western.

Chapter Four

Country Fringes

Wayne Hancock, the greatest honky tonk singer currently stomping the boards, did a live stint with his band on BBC Radio Two in February 2000. Steel guitar and slap bass and whacked drums, like a freight train down a rusty track; blues and rock 'n' roll and country swing; Wayne singing like a man with a sore throat – now that's my kind of country.

Hancock's rough Texan urgency jostled happily with Andy Kershaw's usual mix of spiky world music, but it was in the more mellifluous pastures grazed by Bob Harris that he really opened up. I love both shows, literally taking the rough with the smooth, but sometimes wonder why the BBC tries to soothe you to sleep at seven pm and then shake you rudely awake in the early hours. Wayne was like a shot of raw electricity, and told Bob that, despite a recent bout of pneumonia, he couldn't give up touring: "I don't care if I die. If I'm true to my music, then my music will live on after me." Hank Williams III once admitted that Hancock had more of his grandfather's spirit than he did, and he's no slouch.

The former marine and tug-boat operator now follows the Nick Lowe recording mantra, banging out his last album in two eight-hour days: "That's the only way to do it. If you're going to do this music and get the spiritual feel to it, it's got to be from the heart. If it's not in the studio live, it's not worth a dank, it don't sound any good, it sounds rehearsed and like Nashville."

This, it turns out, is not a place he would choose to dwell: "I hate Nashville. They think they can just buy anybody, that everybody has a price. What price are you willing to put on your soul and your integrity? You can't buy this kind of a feeling , you have to give it away. So I pretty much give it away. I myself went to Nashville in '89. Big mistake. But it was good for me, because for two years after that I did nothing but drink and work. It was such a turn-off." He counts off the beats to Jimmie Rodgers' 'California Blues', and yodels like a drunk at midnight.

By the time Hank Williams had turned his tour car into a hearse, the dark empire was already on the rise. By 1958 it had won, and erected a monument to itself called the Country Music Association, which Malone in turn calls "wholly com-

mercially orientated, and little concerned with the traditions and historic importance of the music". One of its own brochures openly boasted that the C in country
music "means cash". Carlene Carter thought that it was the initial of the body part
she herself brought to the music, but such thoughts are exactly those that the CMA
was created to stamp out. Judging from the 1999 awards ceremony, nothing has
changed in two generations. The CMA *did* inaugurate the Country Hall Of Fame,
and a museum to match, but this was exactly where it tried to consign the old
music: a museum.

The chief architects of the 'Nashville Sound' were Owen Bradley and Chet
Atkins. In 'Music City, USA', they created a smoother sound, played down the country twang, lost the banjo, and replaced scraping fiddles with mellifluous string
sections. The roughness of mountain vocals were sandpapered down, losing all of
their Celtic weirdness. Songs of rural life were now a no-go area. It was extremely
palatable to mass audiences, but was essentially background music and essentially
crap. Worst of all, perhaps, was the studio chorus – gospel music without God, as
bland as white bread. It ensured high sales, but, to quote *Rolling Stone*, Chet Atkins
in particular "has issued more dross than anyone in Nashville". This is supper club
music. And let's not even mention Eddy Arnold. It's interesting how camp it all now
sounds, something that kd lang – another outsider – picked up on by using Owen
Bradley to produce her deeply ambiguous pastiches.

Dawidoff calls his chapter on Chet Atkins "Taking Out The Twang". From the
very start, Chet "didn't want to be pigeonholed". Now, with almost painful symbolism, he sits in a rocking chair in his office, surrounded by his guitars. One must
separate the man from his influence. Atkins played with Hank Williams and on
Presley's 'Heartbreak Hotel', and appeared on Garrison Keillor's *Prairie Home
Companion* radio show, which was about as down-home as you could get in the
1980s. He grew up in rural Tennessee, a sickly child in an archetypal shack.

Sophistication is something at which he has had to work. Chet's father, James,
was a classically-trained Irish tenor with no love for country. Chet himself now has
doubts about what he did to the music. Nashville today is just a branch of the pop
industry. "Then a good country singer comes along, a Ricky Skaggs, a Randy Travis,
and gets us back to where we should be." Over, and over again.

Atkins worked best with Don Gibson, a professional melancholic who influenced Neil Young. Atkins used his studio as another musical instrument so that
everything was subservient to that lonely voice. This was great, once, but then
everybody else piled in. Gibson himself grew up in North Carolina, close to Earl
Scruggs, and played bluegrass until he entered the mainstream via a contract with
Acuff-Rose.

'Oh Lonesome Me' still sounds wonderful, not least because there is a roughness to the strummed guitar and Gibson's vocals, a real forward push to the music
which still connects to earlier country music. It's resilient. Gibson makes fun of his

sadness. All of the melancholy here is in the words, none in the music, as the guitar break chuckles and the male chorus chortles: it's a vibrant sound. Neil Young later gave the same song a heavy dose of mandrax and slowed down it to half speed. This was the high-water mark, though; other examples of Gibson's work sound studio bound, the kind of stuff that can only exist behind glass. Those who followed upped the chorale and downed the beat, to coffin that "high, lonesome sound", making it sound as if it had been locked up in a kennel.

In a stroke of bad luck, Eddy Arnold's 'I Wanna Play House With You' is currently seeping through my speakers. It starts off okay, with some sweet fiddle and steel guitar, but his voice is pure Fifties eunuch corn – all 'gal' and 'chickadee' and raised eyebrow – and there's something truly horrible in the basic *double entendre* here. Eddy is talking child-speak, but it's really all about wanting to have sex with the girl. Because she won't, it makes him all the hornier. He's like a kid up a tree, "but my baby days are through". A whole university department could waste a year just deconstructing the line "I'll pay the bills and you provide the thrills". Paedophilia, here we come.

Jim Reeves was raised in Galloway, Texas, one of nine children. He was devoted to the singing of Jimmie Rodgers, but was more interested in basket ball than music. However, he gave country a go after various blue-collar jobs, and early his recordings from the Opry sound almost tough. After all, he started singing in honky-tonks, which aren't known for their love of polite sounds. His real asset was the silky smooth talking voice with which he "sang", and he first marketed this as announcer and "hillbilly DJ" in east Texas. What happened next is too true to be good. "Gentleman" Jim stepped in for Hank Williams one day on *The Louisiana Hayride* after Hank failed to show. It was at RCA records that Reeves began to develop the countrypolitan duvet of sound which made him a superstar, lowering his voice to a baritone and dropping the fiddle and steel. He and Chet Atkins began to write new songs for this new voice to sing, "a touch of velvet". He was particularly popular in white South Africa, where anything rockier was banned as negro music. Jim then made the final perfect career move and died in a plane wreck – just outside Nashville, of course – in 1964. Why, as I write all this, do I feel strong male hands tightening around my neck?

On the posthumously-released, Chet Atkins' produced album *Distant Drums*, Reeves is presented as a seer from beyond the grave. At the time it was recorded, the title song seemed "too remote – almost unreal" to be released. In 1966, these words about a call-up are "mystically prophetic", and the studio drum taps like someone knocking on a coffin lid. Meanwhile, a mile from where I was born, in a quiet Southampton suburb, a lady has turned her whole house into a shrine for Reeves, and garners much local media attention as a result.

Another album to emerge from the tomb is *The Country Side Of Jim Reeves*, with the "earthy traditional Americana" of 'Railroad Bum' (which sounds more like childrens' hour to me) and an actually quite good take on Jimmie Rodgers' 'Waiting For A Train'. It is almost lively. Here, too, is 'Blue Side Of Lonesome' by blind Nashville songwriter Leon Payne, whose much stranger song 'Psycho' was covered by Elvis Costello. To say – as the sleeve notes do – that Jim chose "never to stop singing the songs of the hill and the range" is, on the evidence here, wide of the mark. More accurate is the injunction: "Quiet. Here is a pro at work."

If you're a pro, why allow death to stand in your way? *Jim Reeves And Patsy Cline: Greatest Hits* is a truly bizarre concoction, with the two deceased stars duetting thanks to studio trickery. Or maybe they were both still alive, locked in a Nashville basement with the tapes running. Maybe they were even forced to wear iron masks.

Bill Malone is no lover of Nashville smoothies, and points out that, before Owen Bradley began to mould her on disc with lots of echo, Patsy Cline dressed like a cowgirl on stage and loved a good yodel. She actively disliked her hit 'Crazy', written by the young Willie Nelson.

Live At The Cimarron Ballroom from 1961 presents a big-voiced shouter singing over some hot guitar picking, sexy saxophone and smooth violins from Leon McAuliff And His Cimarron Boys. Patsy is still recovering from a nasty car crash – "I said: 'Well don't cancel it, I'm gonna be there if I gotta crawl'" – but she sings with that trademark crack in her voice and hits a few wrong notes along the way. Steel guitarist McAuliff and his band have already played a couple hours of instrumentals: "This is strictly dance music." Needless to say, the ballroom is now a parking lot.

The CD is a precious time capsule, though, and here we have everything from an exuberant 'Won't You Come Back, Bill Bailey' to Bob Wills songs and a most unladylike 'Shake, Rattle And Roll'. Dawidoff writes particularly well about Cline, her rough background singing in the lowest bars, "skull orchards", and her raw sense of humour. She might have described herself as an "ol' hillbilly" from the Shenandoah Valley, but frankly there is none of that in her music, which Nicholas describes as "the first down-home torch singer. By living hard and singing smooth she fully inverted country's expectations of a woman." Even here, on stage, she goes into some detail about the extent of the plastic surgery she is going to need.

Nashville made Cline into a star, but her voice still has enough life in it to survive both that and the Tennessee plane crash that killed her outright, along with Opry stars Cowboy Copas and Hawkshaw Hawkins. I've searched long and hard for the worst-ever countrypolitan disc, for use as a torture implement, and must report that so far *Como In Nashville* tops the poll. This is definitely a bad case of tuxedo music, again beautifully put together by Atkins again, with Perry singing in his sleep.

At this point, we will leave the mainstream of country music history to pursue a mazy path indeed – trust me. As we dip alarmingly in and out of the picture, taking elements of the old-time music wherever we can find them (and this is sometimes in the strangest places), we will encounter a lifetime's worth of wonderful music, guaranteed to feed your soul. Somewhere in all of it, still, is that "high, lonesome sound" which first emerged in Britain's outer fringes and then got weirder still in the remote mountains of the American South.

One figure of whom I'm still on the trail is Kenneth "Thumbs" Carlile, who played guitar on his lap, like a dobro, and influenced the young Richard Thompson when he was throwing country and blues and rock into a psychedelic mix. Carlile laid down two albums produced by Les Paul, and three more under the tutelage of Roger Miller.

The really exciting music from down over the years, though, has come not from weird insiders, and certainly not from the Nashville production line, but rather from a procession of outsiders. Either they have come from another music and given country music a dose of their own personality – it's like a blank canvas on which those individual enough to dare can inscribe their visions – or they've tried to take country music itself back to its first principles. The Alabama 3 would correspond to the first, and Dolly Parton's bluegrass excursion at the CMA Awards to the second.

Ray Charles certainly invented his own music, a blend of R&B, big-band jazz and gospel which made him perhaps the first soul singer. He went a step too far for the toffee-nosed Nik Cohn, though, when "in 1962 he committed verbal hara-kiri, cutting a slop S&W ballad, 'I Can't Stop Loving You', complete with strings and chorus". Others take a more charitable view, throwing around words like "genius", or something close.

It still sounds extraordinary, and as the proud possessor of an original British pressing – in glorious mono and on the His Master's Voice label, with a very-much-alive dog staring down that gramophone horn – it has a depth and richness, a liveliness of being, which makes Jim Reeves sound like so much dog meat. It seems like a long way for that high, lonesome sound to reach us, and the only traditional song here (with new words written by Ray) is 'Careless Love', but when Charles sings "and when I was down/you just left me there" it's the essence of country music and the blues all rolled into one.

The liner notes reveal that Ray phoned Sid Feller, A&R man at ABC, and asked him for "top country and western hits from the past 20 years". Feller made a tape of 40 songs and Ray liked them all, so he simply chose the first twelve. Two are by Hank Williams – 'You Win Again' is sung sweet and slow, with the slightest of country burrs – and one by Don Gibson, the aforementioned 'I Can't Stop Loving You'. True, the choir come in a bit strong at the start, but they only make Ray sound all the more sly and bluesy when he answers them. One reviewer compared it to the sound of John Coltrane. Certainly, his voice slides up and down the octaves as smooth as a trombone, and the clicking sound is of jaws dropping in Tennessee.

There's certainly not a banjo in sight, but in place of Nashville politeness the arrangements here are at the top of the range, with sweeping strings and the punch of a big band. Even the choir sounds more soulful than the country norm. No Nashville music accountant would sanction as many as six songs per side, though, especially when not one of them is filler. That's the kind of dangerous, commie idea which can wreck an industry.

Rhino Records recently issued a four-CD box set centering on this album, its follow up – *Volume Two*, with big-band numbers on side one and strings and choir on side two – and *Country And Western Meets Rhythm And Blues*, one side of each, with a cover mock up of a Charles dressed as a cowboy shaking hands with a Charles dressed in a tuxedo.

He not only led the sessions from his piano stool but also oversaw the final mix. The results were so emotionally devastating that it's no surprise that two later country covers by Charles, 'Born To Lose' and 'No Letter Today', were banned from Washington jukeboxes in case they upset serving GIs. So what fuelled these country excursions?

Charles himself writes in *Brother Ray* that "you have to understand that the South was full of country and western sounds and I can't recall a single Saturday night in those days when I didn't listen to the Grand Ole Opry on the radio. I loved Grandpa Jones and those characters. I could hear what they were doing, and appreciate the feeling behind it. I wasn't fanatical about it, but I certainly dug it and paid it some mind".

A young Ray played some gigs on piano with The Florida Playboys, billed as "The Only Colored Singing Cowboy', even learning how to yodel. For Barney Hoskyns, Charles "takes the Nashville Sound to new heights of Hollywood superkitsch", and the singer himself admitted to being a "sentimentalist at heart". Certainly some people at the time felt that this musical cocktail was an "abomination": "Others even called me sacrilegious. I got a lot of reaction. But that was nothing new. I heard the same bellyaching when I did my first gospel/blues songs. In both instances…I just happened to hit some good timing."

Ironically, the fact that Ray Charles had chosen to explore this genre of music suddenly made country music fashionable to some ears. He was not the only black artist to cross a supposed racial divide here; Chuck Berry was "a black who could sound like a hillbilly", and spent his early days on the road attempting to appeal to both black and white. 'Maybelline', his first hit single, borrowed its tune from an old country song called 'Ida Red'.

Barney Hoskyns – good initials for a rock scribe – has a whole chapter on 'Nashville Blue', about the black music recorded in Music City, but of greater interest here is the career of Dan Penn and Spooner Oldham, whose recent CD *Moments From This Theatre* captures them in concert and still firing on all cylinders. Both were white Southern boys who had grown up on a mix of Hank Williams and bluegrass, but they got together at Muscle Shoals a couple of hours' drive north from Nashville. There they began to specialise in slow, bluesy ballads in 6/8 time, for the likes of Percy Sledge and Joe Simon. Gerri Hirshcy saw such songs as "part church, part hills", part of an unspoken heritage, all the weirder because, as fellow songwriter

Donnie Fritts put it: "I can't explain how the country feel crept into our songs 'cause, apart from a few guys like George Jones, we didn't like country music."

Rick Hall put the Southern soul sound together, and admitted that "my country background had an influence because I was quite melodic thinking, and Hank Williams records, for example, had a lot of melodic fill on them – the arrangements would answer the vocal". Sideman Barry Beckett reckoned that Hall "would think white lines on top of black tracks. Instead of usin' the steel guitar, we would use the organ. You can't bend an organ, but you've got the same transparency that steel provides in country." They used country piano stylings too, but the essential difference was that while Nashville musicians played "on the beat" – the Muscle Shoals style was to lay behind it a fraction.

One studio musician who took these things back to Nashville was Billy Sherrill, who adopted this same laying back style for Charlie Rich and, later, the likes of Lacy J Dalton (at whose work we glanced in chapter one) and Elvis Costello, too, but we'll come on to him later. In fact, many of the Muscle Shoals sessioners eventually gravitated back to Music City and its higher rates of pay, so that the likes of Norbert Putnam became Nashville stalwarts.

Country soul later evolved into the likes of The Allman Brothers, "balancing Gregg Allman's blues against Dicky Betts' bluegrass", whose early psychedelic recording of 'Spoonful' – Willie Dixon via Eric Clapton – was produced by the country songwriter John D Loudermilk, whose own song 'Tobacco Road' was given an R&B makeover by The Nashville Teens. It is a dialogue which echoes back and forth, so that Janis Joplin started off in Texas singing Carter Family songs with a bluegrass band and ended up as a white blues shouter, and Joe South played both on Aretha Franklin sessions and on the Nashville nights that produced Dylan's *Blonde On Blonde*.

Hoskyns considers the finest white R&B singer to be Alabama's Eddie Hinton, and I agree. "I believed a Caucasian singing negro music could make a lot of money" Hinton commented, but drink and drugs got to him and he died flat broke. Doubtless there's a blood connection somehow, and I'd love to know where and when his ancestors took the boat from England – Hinton is an old West Country surname.

When I bought Eddie's 1978 album *Very Extremely Dangerous*, out of a sense of family solidarity, I took it for granted that he was black, partly because he sounds it and partly because there is an Afro-American lurking at night in a squalid alley on the front cover with three white men across the road. It's not quite clear who is menacing whom, and it's certainly not an appealing image. One wonders why Hinton seems so careful to hide his real identity. On the back cover it's daytime, and the alleyway is empty, except for a giant hound dog.

Which, of course takes us to Elvis Presley. So how did hillbillies learn how to rock? Bill Malone trawls through history for those singers who adopted the "stepped-up" rhythms of black music in country. Two pairs of siblings led the way:

the kazoo-led Allen Brothers from Tennessee in the 1920s – they sounded so authentic that their discs were sometimes categorised under the "race" label – and Alton and Rabon Delmore from Alabama a decade later. The Delmore Brothers went on to record 'Hillbilly Boogie' in 1945, featuring Rabon on tenor guitar. Arthur Smith's 'Guitar Boogie' was a jukebox favourite after the war, and there was even a 'Gospel Boogie' released by The Homeland Harmony Quartet.

Both races met on the King label, often recording each other's songs. The rockiest of all was The Maddox Brothers And Rose's 'Hangover Blues', a precursor to rockabilly, with the same mesh of electric lead guitar, slap bass and high-energy vocals. Rockabilly added something even more untamed than drunk hillbillies: the sound of teens on heat. Meanwhile, there was poor old Bill Haley, who most books have as a failure for eight years as a country musician before finally having one bright idea: that of putting Western swing together with jump blues, calling it "cowboy jive" and thereby finding himself an angle.

After couple of hits, he was back in the shadows – end of story. Well, actually it's not, as a typically thorough (I almost said Germanic) Bear Family box set and a couple of biographies set the record straight. As for me, one of the first records I ever owned was Haley's ten-inch *Live It Up* LP, issued by London in 1955. The front cover depicts a cartoon cowboy, with checked shirt, jeans and kerchief, playing a guitar and grinning widely. Even though it sat oddly among my Beatles and Dylan albums, I loved this record to bits then, and I love it to bits now. Even today it struts out of the speakers with a clickety-clack, friendly style of singing from Bill and a real sense of fun. No menace, though.

The notes say that "this isn't quite rhythm and blues, not quite hill-billy, not quite Tin Pan Alley, not quite anything for which there is a standard definition. It's a kind of shaking, rattling and rolling music that shakes a lot of people, rattles others and rolls along all the time." Haley was raised in Delaware, and made his first guitar out of cardboard. Continuing the British connection, his mother came from Lancashire. Haley left home at 15, with a more serviceable instrument, and "worked at an open-air park show, sang and yodelled with any band that would have him, and worked with a travelling medicine show".

This is starting to sound familiar. Bill even won the prize for best yodeller in the state of Indiana. He joined The Down Homers, worked as music director for a radio station, then formed his own band, Bill Haley's Saddlemen, "indicating their leaning toward the tough Western style". In 1952, they looked up to the skies and renamed themselves the Comets. There's a touch of mountain music in the mix, too, if you listen hard enough.

Appropriately, he was the first rock 'n' roller to take the boat back east, and landed in Southampton, my own home town. It all connects. Photos from that tour show the whole band in vile tartan jackets, with saxophone, accordion and steel guitar on the bandstand. Peter Doggett wrote a typically well-informed article for *Record*

Collector, in which he draws attention to some early 1950s recordings on the Essex label, in which Haley and his band "create a blueprint for rock 'n' roll'", including a cover version of 'Rocket 88', 'Rock This Joint' and Haley's own 'Crazy Man Crazy', all released before Presley first set foot in Sun studios.

It hardly bears repeating, but Elvis Presley was born in Tupelo and once played as bottom of the bill to Haley, whom he modestly asked if he could sing with on stage. Haley was like a fond uncle that night. Elvis liked Red Foley, and admired the Louvin Brothers, but his greatest musical influence was country gospel, in particular such white acts as The Blackwood Brothers from Tennessee and The Stamps Quartet. He would often attend all-night singing conventions.

At the Sun recording studio, supposedly built over an old Indian trail and thus adding a third race to the mix, Sam Phillips put Elvis together with two "hillbilly musicians", Scotty Moore on electric guitar and Bill Black on string bass. No drums. The sound of huge doors, opening up wide. With sales at first largely confined to the South, he then moved to RCA and got famous, and fat, and died, and became even more famous still. As an adolescent, I could never stand the way he over-finessed a tune, like a man over-combing his hair. It was the kind of stupid, stodgy and slow music that The Beatles came into being to blow away. I didn't realise then that it had been a totally different Elvis – along with some Appalachian skiffle, some blues and some girl groups – that had got them excited in the first place. The young are crueller than anybody else, as they know deep down that they own the future. By the time that he entered my consciousness, Elvis sounded well and truly like yesterday's man. The very worst aspects of Nashville, too.

Back when he was a god, all five of Presley's Sun singles combined a blues tune on one side and a country song on the other. Elvis had already been over to see Scotty Moore – the guitar picker who Sam Phillips decided would best fit his voice – and had messed around at his house on some recent hits by Eddie Arnold and Hank Snow. Bassist Bill Black turned up, too, but wasn't very impressed by this "snotty-nosed kid". The next day they all met again at Sun studios, and the first thing they actually taped was the plaintive country ballad 'I Love You Because', now associated indelibly with Jim Reeves. Elvis came up with 'That's All Right (Mama)" during a refreshment break, and the first take was a spontaneous one, as the other two took up the beat. Phillips' quest for a "white singer who could sound and feel like a negro" was at an end.

So much for a master plan, cunningly thought out by Phillips. It just happened, as strokes of genius often will. All that was needed now was a flip side, and 'Blue Moon Of Kentucky' was the next number up for transformation – "Fine, fine, man, hell, that's different! That's a pop song now, little guy! That's good," Sam chortles from the control booth, while Elvis laughs proudly at what he has just done, and Moore gets racist, imitating a black falsetto and saying (in admiration) "Damn, nigger". Bingo: the millions of dollars are set to roll in – though not to Sam Phillips.

Meanwhile, Bill Monroe's bluegrass anthem has gone to Mars and back. Elvis hustles things along, smarmed with echo, his voice howling worse than a feral cat out on the tiles at night, then gliding like a swan. There's the click clack of the double bass, with Scotty adding a descant melody on his chunky electric guitar, and Elvis' sneering, exuberant voice breaking the lyrics up into gibberish as he mangles them, rocks them up, then throws them away.

It reminds me most of Barry Humphries' weird book *Bizarre*, which describes 50 different ways to destroy the 'Mona Lisa'. It's as if his voice and the lyrics are at war, like a vandal wrecking a bus shelter, and the staid safety, home pride and homesickness encoded in those stately words is all torn up. The young Presley sings over the beat, around it, even inside it, and by the time he has finished bluegrass is old fashioned. That, or course, remains its charm, and we will see others taking it in strange directions, although none ever as strange as this. The only thing you could do with such a dangerous young iconoclast would be to lock him away, kill him, or stuff millions of dollars down his throat.

When Elvis appeared at the Opry a few weeks after the single was released (it reached Number Three on the Memphis charts and sold around 20,000 copies), he was told by the head of the talent office that he should go back to driving trucks for a living. Presley cried that night, but laughed last and loudest.

The most extraordinary moment on the Sun tapes is when Elvis starts a conventional, heartfelt-sounding country blues renditon of 'Milkcow Blues Boogie', then breaks off with "that don't move me, let's get real, real gone for a change", and they rock it up. His second B-side, 'I Don't Care If The Sun Don't Shine', is a country ballad also "jumped up", in more sense than one, with bongos, and Elvis crooning lasciviously. He even throws in an "oh boy", and you could breed babies from his vocals here. There's lots of space in this music. Scotty plays pure rockabilly guitar, set loose to throw in fills, solos and (almost) power chords. The modern world starts here.

'You're A Heartbreaker', on the flipside of the third single – the aforementioned 'Milkcow Blues Boogie' (also recorded by Bob Wills) – is drenched with echo and the Sun speciality reverb, with drummer DJ Fontana now added to the mix. Elvis' voice curls like smoke as it hits the higher registers. One British repackaging of the Sun sessions is dedicated to Led Zeppelin, and one can see why, but country music is being left way behind.

Elvis spits out 'I Forget To Remember To Forget' – which backs his last single for Sun, 'Mystery Train', released in August 1955 – with a venom later rediscovered by Bob Dylan. Dylan rewrote Presley's first hit as 'It's All Right Mama, I'm Only Bleeding', while John Lennon threw in a direct quote from these sessions on *Rubber Soul*. These songs are now biblical texts, the rock 'n' roll Old Testament. Presley doesn't have the gift to write his own words, so invests those he is given with renewed emphasis.

Other Sun session tracks were bought in for his first RCA album release. Leon Payne's 'I Love You Because' has lovely flowing guitar, and Elvis sings it straight, in the quiet voice he would develop for the rest of his career. Greil Marcus paints on a wider canvas, hearing in the Sun recordings two conflicting emotions and ways of life. The country material captures "the affection and respect Elvis felt for the limits and conventions of his family life, of his community and ultimately of American life". The blues songs recognise "his refusal of those limits, of any limits". It's the same conflict that I myself discerned as being at the heart of country music, back in chapter one, and which is often symbolised as the difference between Saturday night and Sunday morning. Country music recognises the attractions, and limitations, of them both. It's not only Elvis Presley who, in Greil's words, gives voice to "a rhythm of acceptance and rebellion, lust and quietude, triviality and distinction".

Forget the blues, forget country songwriting, and forget smooth lounge-bar singers like Dean Martin, whom Elvis already idolised. Presley's abiding musical love was gospel. He said that his "was a religious family", which regularly attended open-air camp meetings and the First Assembly of God Church. The hillbilly cat later starred in just that roll in the film *Kissing Cousins*, where he doubled as a USAF pilot. Born in a shack, Elvis' mother had picked cotton to keep the family alive, and his father spent time in jail. When he was a grown man, Elvis had to be taught how to use a knife and fork to eat. His main nourishment was music, listening to the likes of The Carter Family. Later, he toured with "Mother" Maybelle and daughters, along with Jimmie Rodgers and The Louvin Brothers.

He was also out on the road with the Louvins, who at that time were still topping the bill, when Elvis sat down at the piano backstage and began to softly croon an old hymn. Dawidoff has the full story of what happens next. Ira Louvin comes up looking for a fight: "You fucking white nigger. If that's the kind of music you like, who don't you do that out there instead of that shit you do." Elvis replies, reasonably enough, "When I'm out there, I do what they want to hear. When I'm back here, I do what I want to do."

A fascinating CD exists of Elvis' first recorded live date in 1954, booked by C&W DJ Bill Collie at the 'Hoedown Club'. He was already "doing the 'hip thing'", taking on where Hank Williams left off, "and the girls went crazy. The people reacted vehemently." Introduced as the "bopping hillbilly", Elvis rocks his way through 'Blue Moon Of Kentucky' with lots of vocal hiccups, prolonged "oh wells" and verbal gymnastics. At one point he gets the words wrong and sings about the moon "shaking" rather than "shining". He does it much the same way on *The Louisiana Hayride*, to loud whistles of approval from the audience.

One day, Johnny Cash – who had just been signed to Sun – was present at a Carl Perkins session when Elvis sat in on piano, "and he was asking me if I knew any Bill Monroe songs. So a lot of those songs on there are old bluegrass things. Then we got into gospel, especially when Jerry Lee [Lewis] came in. Jerry Lee sat down at the pee-ana, and then it was all gospel after that." The result was the so-called Million Dollar Quartet, and the vocal jam session which resulted tells you all you need to know about the musical roots of these four young Sun firebrands.

Pure country. As Cash said elsewhere, "Elvis and Carl and I would sit in the dressing room before shows and sing those Blackwood Brothers gospel songs." History has since rewritten the script. The latest "Ultimate Collection" to appear under the title *Elvis Country* concentrates on slop like 'Green Green Grass of Home' and 'Gentle On My Mind'. Revolt had hardened into style, and the late Viv Stanshall – once a Teddy boy – could cruelly parody the lot, the way in which Elvis suddenly pauses for emphasis, the rubbish words, the hammy singing, and a moronic choir which bleats out each echo of its master's voice. If all popular music is drug fuelled, then the speed (natural or otherwise) of the Sun sessions has given way here to a stomach full of downers. It's worse than Jim Reeves. Music for a Russian state funeral. The sound of sleep.

It doesn't come much worse than 'Old Shep'. The tone is pure gospel, and maudlin memories of a boy and his dog catch at the emotions like a would-be religious experience: "If dogs have a heaven, there's one name I know, Old Shep has a wonderful home." Truly outrageous. When Elvis made his brief artistic renaissance in the late Sixties, country music was not part of what so briefly flickered and then went out for good.

Elvis' Sun sides were pure rockabilly, a potent blend of the rumble of rock and the emotions of hillbilly. It was certainly a long way from Dock Boggs. My own favourite is Billy Lee Riley's 'Flyin' Saucer Rock 'n' Roll', full of brittle shards of lead guitar, the odd scream, and Billy at the edge of his tether, seeing little green men. Shy-eyed genius Richard Thompson would later couple this on stage with a traditional English morris-dancing tune. It sounds like a perfect fit, so maybe rockabilly wasn't as far from its folk roots as sounds plausible in print.

Also on Sun were the likes of Jerry Lee Lewis, Carl Perkins and Johnny Cash, all of whom put country music at the heart of their later work, in very different ways, but all of which put Elvis to shame. The Sun original of 'Folsom Prison Blues' is as fascinating for what Cash has kept in (the rackety rhythm, the casual pace, the feel of it being light on its feet) as what he has lost (the high, sweet portion of his voice, for a start, a dead ringer for Dylan *circa* 1969). When he dives deep at the end of each verse, it's pure Cash. There's a sadism at work, not just the line about shooting a man to watch him die but also in the way he drives a story, forcing the listener to hang onto every word.

Jerry Lee's Sun recordings range in time from 1957's 'Whole Lotta Shaking Going On' to 1963's unlikely 'Carry Me Back To Old Virginia'. Jerry sounds unconvinced as he sings it; his real self is just like the cockerel on the Sun logo, proudly crowing at the dawn. There's something feminine about that voice as it glides and swoops, always holding something back, and something masculine about its macho chuckles and sly innuendo. In just the same way, his piano pounds in the left hand and tinkles in the right. When he sings about rockin' and rolling with Ruby all afternoon, there's not even the pretence that's its about dancing. As to country roots, they surfaced early on the *Old Tyme Country Music* LP, with remakes of songs he probably first heard in the cradle, like 'Crawdad Song' and 'Deep Elem Blues' (a cover of the Shelton Brothers hit), while 'Crazy Arms' was a direct cover of Ray Price's Number One country hit.

Jerry Lee told Joe Smith: "I was raised Pentecostal. You learn that God is a big God. You don't put him in one corner. He spreads himself out. I went to Bible college in Waxahatchie, Texas, and I preached for three years. A lot of people were saved under my ministry."

With Sun, he had a different pulpit and a more openly sexual bible from which he read. The whole lotta shaking could be religious conversion as well as two bodies at it like knives, and 'Great Balls Of Fire' is about more than having your testicles on fire. After the label was sold off in 1969, in the next year they released an album of Lewis singing gospel, *Sunday Down South*, and for a while in the 1960s he embraced country full time. It's like his closest black equivalent, Little Richard – the only other person in history to make playing the piano sexy – who gave it all up to become a preacher. And yet… Nick Tosches quotes a friend who knew the teenage Lewis in Memphis: "Jerry Lee was always a shitkicker. There were always horror stories. There was always an aura of extreme violence to Jerry Lee." Jerry Lee himself puts history straight about Jim Reeves: "A strange person. We had some pretty good times together. Yeah, he drank." He even threatened to tell RCA to "kiss my ass", and upstaged Jerry Lee. "There's a pro."

In his autobiography *Killer*, Jerry Lee proudly proclaims that "I ain't no hillbilly guitar from Nashville. I am an artist." Born in Louisiana, "my family were poor, we grew up in a shack, we didn't even have a bathroom. My mother used to pick cotton all day." His father was a bootlegger among many other part-time jobs, spent time in jail, and – more to the point – was "a fantastic singer as well as guitar player. We would have family sessions all the time when I was a little boy, gospel songs." It's the same old story; only the details change. Jerry Lee can still recall his parents singing in church, "and I have never heard people that sang that good in my life". His brother was killed by a speeding truck, almost in front of Jerry's eyes, and at the funeral his Dad turned up, under armed guard and "all chained up".

As for his ancestry, Jerry Lee proudly claims Dutch, Indian, English and Irish roots, while his sisters remind him to add Indian and Jewish to the mix. One of his best albums was recorded back in the old world, at the Hamburg Star Club, with British R&B combo The Nashville Teens. I once bought Jerry Lee Lewis' *Country Concert*, a cheap exploitation job without any details included about where it was recorded or even why, apart for a desire to squeeze a little more juice out of the withered fruit. Truly, The Sex Pistols had nothing on these boys for making cash from chaos. The results are truly awesome, a mix of bravado, drunken asides, swearing, self-pity and wonderful trills and hand-swipes on an electric piano. He gets words wrong, he slurs them, he stretches them out, he interrogates the audience and his band – he sounds like a man about to hang making his last confession. In the middle of it all is a version of 'Will The Circle Be Unbroken?', and as that hearse takes his mother off to the graveyard Jerry puts a chill through the soul as he sings about a better home "in your precious sky" with infinite sadness, as only he can. There's plenty of Hank Williams' covers, too. The whole thing is as mesmeric as a car crash, and best listened to after a few beers (as doubtless it was made), when it's truly heroic.

'Will The Circle Be Unbroken?' also turns up on Gene Vincent's terminally sad swan-song album for John Peel's Dandelion label, although here it is retitled 'Circle Never Broken' and features Red Rhodes on pedal steel. Long gone are the glories of Cliff Gallup's razor-slash guitar. Gene sounds washed up and fed up, and where Jerry Lee railed against the hearse Vincent sounds hopeful about that new world "in the sky".

Generally with these old rockers, nothing became them so much as their manner of leaving. The finest hours of Roy Orbison and Carl Perkins are both TV specials filmed late in their lives, surrounded by celebrity guests who suddenly look like fans and both surrounded by a country sadness.

Buddy Holly never had the chance to grow old, but he broke through all kinds of barriers, the first being Nashville itself. Born in Lubbock, Holly started as half of a hillbilly duo with Bob Montgomery and went on to record some rockabilly in Nashville with the likes of Grady Martin on lead guitar, and Boots Randulph on saxophone. Having failed there, he went to Norman Petty's studio in New Mexico with his new band, The Crickets – Waylon Jennings was one of many who passed through – and experimented with multitracking, an echo chamber and standing a mic right up against the body of a double bass in order to capture that deep twang.

Holly was frozen in time after his death in an air crash, and his music now sounds pure Fifties, for good and ill. One brief tour of England – during which Holly played his Fender lead guitar louder than anyone had previously ever imagined – ignited a spark which later broke out in a forest fire of British beat. The inevitable tribute album made fellow Lubbock boy Joe Ely realise what a pioneer Buddy actually was, despite his gawky image: "He really was one of the first singer/songwriters. He wrote and arranged 'em, and played guitar and sang. He kinda changed the course of music. Right after that came The Beatles and The Rolling Stones, the first superstars who played and sang their own songs…and Buddy Holly songs."

Holly's time in Lubbock was a "well-kept secret", but his memory fuelled a new generation of singer/songwriters there, too, with Ely prominent among them. "Jimmie Dale Gilmore and I were playing together, and LO Holly, Buddy's father, came to see us." At one point, Ely was mooted for the role in the Buddy Holly biopic, but Gary Busey got the role in the end, and did a near-perfect job. Joe Ely continues to find things to surprise him: "he just continues to surprise me, like the way all the guitar leads are almost like Northern Mexican leads. That's a real Texas thing." In 1955, he was rehearsing in Lubbock; two years later, he was opening for Elvis. "That was such a short time. It always leaves me wondering how much of that stuff he really invented."

Ricky Nelson was the son of a jazzman, and came to fame on a radio soap opera. This sounds as far from country as you can get, until you listen to his records, which all have that indefinable lonesome sound. Even if born elsewhere, Ricky grew into it, and died tragically in a plane crash to fully live the myth. He acted as a gunman in the film *Rio Bravo*, and his subsequent single, 'Lonesome Town', was about Hollywood, not Dodge City. There was even an EP of *Ricky Sings Spirituals*, and two albums of country music, *Bright Lights And Country Music* and *Country Fever*. It's still showbiz.

Meanwhile, back in deep country, gospel – or something quite like it – was blessed with the sharp voices and close harmonies of The Louvin Brothers. The keystone to their vision is the 1959 album *Satan Is Real*. Both the cover art and the opening track are pure Alabama 3 – surely they heard this album before inventing the Reverend Love? The two men stand in white suits and as if embracing invisible women, with a horned giant standing behind them, his pitchfork at the ready. The original sleeve note has it that "The fiery setting pictured on the cover of this album was conceived and built by The Louvin Brothers using chiefly rocks, scrap rubber, and lots of imagination. The scene became a little too realistic when Ira and Charlie were very nearly burned while actually directing the photography."

Charlie adds the information that Ira was the architect of this bizarre construct, and that the devil was twelve feet tall and made of plywood. "We went to this rock quarry and then took old tyres and soaked them in kerosene, got them to burn good. It had just started to sprinkle rain when we got that picture taken." As the rocks heated up, they started to explode. It looks like an exhibit from inside London's Millennium Dome, cheap and tacky and forcing a moral message down your throat. As to the title track, Ira gives a short but nasal sermon over dramatic organ chords. The little old man, "bent with age, his hair thin and white", who stands up during the sermon and testifies to the devil had actually done just this when the brothers were attending church in Alabama. "Once I had a happy home. I was loved and respected by my family, I was looked upon as a leader in my community, and then Satan came into my life. I grew selfish and un-neighbourly, my friends turned against me, and finally my home was broken apart. My children took their paths into a world of sin." As the listener shifts uneasily in his chair, he goes for the emotional jugular: "Sinner friend, hell is a real place, a place of everlasting punishment."

The album is all the more shocking when you hear later Louvin Brothers material, where electric guitars, secular lyrics and the modern world intrude. Just look at the LP sleeves, though: these were two sharp dudes from the start, always dressed as twins rather than just brothers, usually mirroring each other in shiny Italian suits or snakeskin boots, divided by the shapes of their bodies and the hard glint in Ira's eyes. When they appear in yellow, open-necked shirts in front of a field of slightly menacing plants in *Country Love Ballads* they look like they're in costume, and there is an electric charge – in both senses – to the songs of rural love enclosed there. The two voices are like a man and woman duetting. When Gram Parsons first introduced Emmylou Harris to their music, she asked who the girl was "singin' the high part". The music is more up-beat than you would imagine, however sad the words. No wonder that "many people who usually prefer other types of music have become enthusiastic fans of the Louvins". Me, I could listen to them forever.

The Louvins have the gift of giving whatever they are singing a kind of emotional bounce. Even the world of sin depicted on *Satan Is Real* is a good place to dwell, far from lonely street. They rescue The Carter Family's 'The Kneeling Drunkard's Plea' from its piety and somehow make it real, not moral massage. (Ira knew all about drinking.) Even traditional material like 'Dying From Home, And Lost' is reborn, in the joy of the mandolin solo and the speedy shuffle rhythm. Their 1956 album *Tragic Songs Of Life* concentrated on such mountain songs, including 'The Knoxville Girl'. This is music which burrows backwards in time, and no wonder that the brothers both vehemently rejected any connection with bluegrass (although they had once unsuccessfully tried to adapt to it). This is music which comes alive whenever you put it on the stereo, but the world view of which is about as close to most listeners now as a sermon from the *Taliban*. Bluegrass rarely consigns its listener to damnation or puts the devil on its record sleeves.

Ira and Charles Loudermilk were born in rural Alabama. Their father played the banjo, their was mother a shape-note singer, and the brothers sang wherever they could raise an audience. The early repertoire was drawn from centuries past, comprising songs like 'Hole In The Bottom Of The Sea'. The Louvins later added a bass and fiddle and formed The Foggy Mountain Boys. Charlie briefly played with Bill Monroe after the war, before signing up with Fred Rose. Years later, Charlie took Hank Wangford – who had asked where their harmonies had come from – to listen to some Sacred Harp singers, "about sixteen of them: he just walked around these people trying to figure out what each of them was singing. And it just blew his hat in the creek, those harmonies."

At first the brothers sang pure gospel before broadening out, but Charlie now says "I think my brother was tortured by religion". It is central to the Southern dilemma. Dawidoff brilliantly paints a verbal picture of the two sides of Ira, a grandfather by the age of 31 and subject to savage beatings as a child. On one side were "his gorgeous voice and songs of heart, hearth, Mother and Saviour", while on the other was "the stereotypical cracker – a fiery son of the dirt-poor lower Appalachian hill country who could not control himself around women or drink".

The same man who sings so trustingly that "there's a higher power" also tried to strangle one of his wives with a telephone cord. Nowadays, he would be undergoing psychiatric treatment (and would probably be mute); back then, singing provided the therapy.

Even the more appealing Charlie reckons that welfare payments are ruining the Republic, believes in "frying" criminals, and calls scrub pines "nigger pines": "I don't mean nothing by that", he protests in vain. As to hippies: "I don't care how good a man plays, I wouldn't hire him with long hair." Needless to say, his own son is now in his forties and wears a pony tail. Charlie, too, moves with the times; his 1996 album *The Longest Train* was produced by English singer Julian Dawson (as bald as a brush, so he's okay) and features Barry Tashian, once of The Remains, a long-haired band *par excellence*. The finest track is his cover version of Sandy Denny's finest song, 'Who Knows Where The Time Goes'. When I first saw Fairport play it, they were the shaggiest, most sloppily-dressed band ever, with both Sandy and Richard Thompson lost in a halo of curls. Musically, there was just the same kind of chill in the air as there was with the Louvins, despite the difference in haircuts.

Charlie Louvin remembers a "poor kid" with overalls but no shirt on his back, tanned as a "moon pie", who came to a show in Arkansas. It was the young Johnny Cash. The Louvins remembered their own musical heroes, Roy Acuff and The Delmore Brothers, in two concept albums. The latter in particular was a sparse and haunted affair, full of mountain harmonies and that high, lonesome sound, sung fast. Even a slow song like 'Blues Stay Away From Me' has a kind of inner propulsion, and then dies away almost to a halt. Two more were planned but never recorded, to The Monroe Brothers and The Blue Sky Boys.

Ira and Charlie were consciously passing on a musical baton, and it was grasped next by a warring couple of brothers from Kentucky, probably of Irish descent, with the surname Everly. As the sleeve notes to their 1959 album *Songs Our Daddy Taught Us* put it, "the boys are the sons of Ike and Margaret Everly, veteran folk and country singers…and their parents before them". Ike had left the coalfields for a life in music, "and there's hardly a town in Tennessee that hasn't eaten its breakfast" to his show. Ike started teaching the boys "as soon as they could hold a tune", bribing them with a quarter for each hour's practice. As to the "old, old songs" here, "Don and Phil Everly are just the newest crop of sons to get this treasured heritage". They appeared on their father's radio show singing close country harmonies, though by now the brothers were closet R&B fans. Add the fact that Phil had written a Top Ten song for Kitty Wells at the age of 14 and you have a career set for take-off.

The trick of it was to use their youth and good looks – like two ferrets on heat, one dark-haired and one light – to disguise their country roots, so that session men like Chet Atkins and writers Felice and Boudleaux Bryant suddenly found their work high up in the pop charts. A song like 'When Will I Be Loved' is a wonderfully resonant rehash of the high, lonesome sound, but presented as a teen disc. An early recording session with Columbia had included hillbilly fiddle and duo singing straight out of the Louvins, but did nothing chart-wise. Cadence dropped the fiddle but added a steel guitar, and bingo, 'Bye Bye Love' was at Number One for seven weeks in the country chart, then at Number Two on the pop charts, and was finally listed as R&B as well. Suddenly, the brothers were touring not with their elders and betters in the country ghetto but also alongside Chuck Berry, Jerry Lee Lewis and Buddy Holly – rebels, all.

The pop world specialises in brothers who are not: Walker, Righteous, Doobie, Bollock – Waco even. Here were the real thing, however, and the ensuing tensions led to Don attempting suicide in a London hotel and then, ten years later, drunk onstage at a nightclub, as Phil smashes his guitar in sheer aggravation. When they do reconvene in 1983, at the Royal Albert Hall, they enter from opposite sides of the stage, and keep it that way. It is a homecoming in more ways than one, with a British backing band including Pete Wingfield on keyboards, Mark Griffith of Matthews' Southern Comfort on bass, and the incomparable Albert Lee on lead guitar. They blow up a storm.

Perhaps as a way of retaining their sanity through the rock 'n'roll years, the Everly siblings dropped a musical bucket into a deep, deep well on *Songs Our Daddy Taught Us*, a quiet and largely acoustic affair, with the old mountain songs performed sweetly but straight. No drums. It is an extraordinarily bold move for a pop duo, especially as this is only their second album, and one issued on three EPs to boot. Their harmonies are like honey, oozing out of the speakers.

Here are 'Barbara Allen' – mentioned by Pepys in the 1660s – and 'Roving Gambler', as first sung in "the taverns and wayside inns of Henry the Eight's England". How different to their first album for the same label, where the brothers are passengers on the back of the latest motor scooters, speeding away, guitars strapped to their backs like rifles. Here, too, is 'Who's Gonna Shoe Your Pretty Little Feet?', "an ancient ballad…from the Highlands of Scotland", of God knows what antiquity, alongside music hall songs from the turn of the century and long-forgotten Nashville hits by the likes of Bradley Kincaid and Gene Autrey. All from the two hottest young kids on the block. If only Boyzone were so adventurous – although one of them, to give him his due, did present a surprisingly erudite history of traditional Irish folk on Radio Two.

This is a different kind of seriousness, bringing "these ageless songs of a family fireside to the jet-propelled age of today". Ten years later, The Byrds went in reverse, swapping the sound of a Lear jet taking off for banjos and Louvin brother songs. At the 1983 reunion concert, the brothers play 'Barbara Allen' and the like, the first time this acoustic material had ever been given a proper live airing, but only a few verses of the first. "That song goes on and on and on." One of the brothers comments sardonically that, on his death bed, the modern Barbara would reach for his cheque book. "Those songs when I first heard them, they made me cry." The voices match high and low in the Appalachian tradition, and both seem to float over the bed of two strummed guitars.

Tim Rice, no less, describes how "they made it on pure sound. The two voices in one were irresistible, unequalled for beauty or precision in pop music." As Phil later said: "I think that, if people are so happy remembering things from yesterday, maybe there's something wrong with today." As the sleeve notes say, these performances were forward looking, the antithesis of nostalgia, when first released: "There's the beat and rhythm of today in the wonderful way Don and Phil sing them." They still sound fine to me, and tied to no time zone.

What the brothers quietly achieved remains extraordinary, pure mountain music at heart which fed straight into the Beatles' singing in particular and harmony pop in general. This from two brothers who, before they hit the pop charts, were playing a tent show with Bill Monroe: "It cost fifty cents to get in and another quarter to sit in the segregated seats. And it cost another 25 cents to see the rock 'n' roll portion of the show".

Strangest of all is their 1968 album *Roots*, which includes archive sound footage from a 1952 family radio show, with 15-year-old Don and "baby Boy" Phil two years younger. Then electric instruments crash in, with a souped-up version of Merle Haggard's 'Mama Tried', which could be The Byrds or The Grateful Dead singing in tune. The brothers appear in archive photographs from their boyhood, in cowboy hats, throwing snowballs and holding a litter of puppies. The music, though, is bang up to date for its date of release, a curiously open-ended experiment which sold poorly at the time and has yet to receive its proper due.

Here are songs by the likes of Jimmie Rodgers and Glen Campbell, and the less-expected names of Randy Newman, and Ron Elliot of The Beau Brummels – America's first Beatles' copyists – who also helps out with the arrangements. An acoustic work out from 1952 will suddenly blossom forth in stereo, and with a post-psychedelic edge. "This work is an attempt to explore the roots, explain the aesthetic, chart the progression and capture the incomparable beauty of The Brothers Everly." The traditional song 'Shady Grove' is copyrighted to Venetia Everly, and after a psych-country version Ike sings it straight, as "an old fashioned toe-tapper", somewhere out on the time coast. The album ends with 'Kentucky': "I miss the hound dogs chasing [rac]coon". The way they welcome the advent of death – "I will be coming soon" – is a little too enthusiastic for comfort.

I'm reminded of Stuart Hall, the (black) doyen of cross-cultural studies. When talking about the Jamaican influx into Britain, he stated a wider truth. Traditions do not develop in isolation. That only brings stagnation, an ossification of the vitality which keeps a culture alive. Conversely, traditions evolve through outsiders who bring about change. Any living culture is in a "process of becoming".

Whether such incomers are welcome or unwelcome hardly seems to matter; it is a more a question of the shock they bring to the system. As on the *Windrush*, which brought West Indians to Britain to staff the hospitals and buses in the middle of the century, so on the boats to Appalachia.

Professor Hall takes us on from the point we reached before we started to look at myths of the Wild West and the Nashville music industry. He sees the movement of people *en masse*, whether refugees, work-seekers or adventurers, as the crucial element of cultural change. "Routes" is a synonym for "roots". Both processes lie at the heart of a civilisation.

It's just the same dichotomy that we keep finding at the heart of country music: "should I stay or should I go", in the words of The Clash. The impulse to settle down in comfortable domesticity, and the matching impulse to stray out on the wild side. One naturally follows the other. It's there in our myths – Odysseus' long journey home from the Trojan war. It underlies the key movies or TV soaps with which we now tend to underpin our lives. Choose your own example, but think of the way that each James Bond movie starts properly only when he is back in those drab offices, receiving instructions for his next foreign assignment. Or Dorothy, blown from Kansas over the rainbow and back, but finding the people from home – suitably transformed – in new guises but really just the same.

Think above all of *The Searchers*, half movie and half myth, in which Ethan Edwards pursues his quest for five years, brings the girl back home, and then has the door of domesticity slammed in his face. It's even deeply encoded in the stories we tell our children, so that Bilbo Baggins or Peter Rabbit or Mole and Ratty leave their comfy firesides and have thrilling adventures out in the wild wood, which they contemplate in old age, back in front of the fire. If they have survived, that is.

In chapter two, we traced some of the roots of mountain folklore back east to Britain. We need now to follow the second Irish diaspora, led largely by poor Catholics this time around, as in the post-Famine years they fled across the Atlantic to find work and a new life, taking their instruments and their music with them. Then we will bring it all back home to Greenwich Village, and a wave of youthful anger which deluged the world.

Farewell To Ireland is a magnificent four-CD set of ramshackle, life-enhancing dance music and songs first captured on rare 78rpm singles. It's like a resurrection to hear this jovial melange, crackling with the same spirit as *The Cornshuckers' Folly*, and much the same scrapy, slightly out-of-tune fiddles. This is music for public entertainment, not contemplation, and neither high nor lonesome. The mind behind this regathering belongs to the tireless Ron Kavana, who does for the sounds of the second Irish diaspora what Harry Smith did for mountain music and the rural US blues.

First up is Pat White, who sounds like a right old scamp, and whose 'I'm Leaving Tipperary' is buoyant and joyous and sly and hopeful, even if it does seem that he's left his teeth somewhere in the Atlantic. However, Pat was born in Chicago in the 1860s, of Irish parents, so that "the anchor's aweigh, the gang-plank's up" is only a memory learned from others – hence, perhaps, his lack of regret: "Now, folks, we'll just have time for one more shindig before I take the boat for America…so fire away." He calls one last dance, and a steam whistle blows. It's all like something out of *Toytown*.

Kavana's scrupulous notes trace White's career as a professional entertainer, through medicine shows and into variety theatres as a "comedian, singer, dancer and fiddler". The song here was taped in the 1930s, the same time zone as Harry Smith's trawl through more rustic sounds, with Pat already over 70 but as full of life as an old rooster. Of the rest of the four CDs, the songs come sometimes as a relief from a relentlessly cheerful programme of airs and dances, many based on traditional tunes but with all the melancholy rinsed away. Stage Irishness, per-haps, but also as tuneful and stirring as the day they were recorded.

The Flanagan Brothers update a folk song of huge antiquity in 'The Beggarman' (and Richard Thompson later updated it again, changing the sex of the jolly seeker after alms), while Packie Dolan sings a hymn to the delights of 'A Drink In The Morning' – something stronger than tea, that's for sure. 'The Night Pat Murphy Died', meanwhile, has some edgy dialogue, with one man trying to turn another's fall from a skyscraper into farce and the victim refusing. The song into which they launch together is a weird account of high-jinks at the wake.

It takes a certain leap of imagination to conceive how music as proudly Irish as this could evolve thousands of miles to the west, but it did and here is irrefutable evidence. This is a music in transition, proof of Stuart Hall's theory. What is ironic is that a puritanical campaign instigated by the clergy back in Ireland had helped to drive native dance music and song there virtually into extinction. Bishops outlawed the crossroads dance, and clergymen were docu-mented as "breaking into private houses, smashing musical instruments and even physically attacking musicians 'in the Lord's name'". Taking it in vain, more like.

The music still lived on in the Appalachians, and these new emigrants helped fund a fledgling recording industry, so that Ellen O'Byrne would order Columbia to press up batches of 500 discs of authentic traditional sounds at a time, which she then sold through her music shop in New York. Its nickname was the "Sinn Fein" music house, indicating something that Kavana glosses over: the political nature of this revival of interest in Celtic sounds. It was all part of fighting for a nation state.

Not that the music was kept as pure and free of foreign influences as it had been in the Appalachians – and even there it was slowly distilled into something stronger. Kavana writes of the "ragtime, stride, jazz and even boogie woogie influences heard in Dan Sullivan's piano playing". The piano is often the chief rhythm instrument here, thumping away like a big accordion. Other instruments to be incorporated include the tenor banjo, the cornet and the guitar, all alien to the Celtic tradition.

As compared to the first Irish wave of emigrants, this has the feeling of urban music played in variety theatres and dance halls – like New York's notorious Tub Of Blood – rather than something hanging on like mist in the mountains.

Don't expect Nigel Kennedy, though. Paddy Sweeney's fiddle wanders off key, like a cat being scraped alive, but there's an exuberance which gets him through. Michael Coleman follows, and suddenly you're in the hands of a master. Kavana pays warm tribute to Captain Francis J O'Neill, flute player, police chief of Chicago and the compiler of what remains the standard work, *The Music Of Ireland*, known in traditional circles now simply as "the book". He followed this up with *Dance Music Of Ireland*, subtitled "1,001 Gems". Each tune was given the barest of entries, a "skeletal outline of the tune" as Mick Maloney put it. Considering what was happening back home, it was all the more vital that O'Neill made a record of all these tunes before they evaporated.

The collections did not recognise regional differences, and thus set the basis for a truly national amalgam, one which was later imported back to Ireland. Many a "traditional" musician learned his repertoire from this book, then customised it. O'Neill had taken the opposite course to most collectors, who go out in the field to search out material. In O'Neill's case, the fields came to him, principally at the Chicago Irish Music Club. He also consulted printed sources, and professional pipers like Patsy Touhey when they passed through town.

After a rural childhood in County Cork, O'Neill took to the sea, perhaps when his local priest banned all crossroads and house dances. He was shipwrecked in the middle of the Pacific and reached America from the east, working as a cowboy, a teacher, a railwayman and a shepherd before joining the police in 1873 and helping to root out corruption in the Chicago force. He was also responsible for the first promotion of a black officer above the rank of patrolman in the USA.

His own personal life was far from happy, however, with three of his ten children dying from diptheria on the same day. Once O'Neill had worked his way up to being boss, he would employ virtually any Irishman who could hold a tune, and his force were called "the most musically-informed body of men anywhere".

As to Irish dancing in America, the formalities imposed by the Gaelic League formalised things in a way unknown in the set dancing back home (or, indeed, up in the Appalachians), while non-Irish dance measures, like the waltz, were gradually assimilated. Group dances were taught by professional dancing masters in the pay of the League, and thus the *ceili* was born. Perhaps the most important influence on the course of Irish music, though, was the advent of the gramophone, and the dance music now collected on *Farewell To Ireland* and other fine collections, like *Ballinasloe Fair* and Topic's *Irish Dance Music*, flooded back home on 78rpm singles. Here was another example of cultural change, and Frankie Gavin remembers how, when he was a young man, his father – also a fiddle player – would cycle to Galway every Saturday "with the price of a 78".

Gavin junior and senior agreed on Michael Coleman as being their favourite fiddler. One Irish exile in New York in the 1930s wept in sheer joy when he heard Coleman playing 'Lord McDonald'. "It cannot be, it cannot be," he cried out, "no earthly man could make music like that." Those of us fortunate enough to see Martin Hayes tuning his violin to that high, lonesome sound in concert recently feel much the same.

As to Coleman, Frankie Gavin still maintains that "the approach he had to any tune just can't be beaten...nobody can play like that today. I work towards trying to recreate it in my own playing." He has done just that in his work with De Danaan, the subtlest of all Irish traditional groups. The first is 1989's *The Star Spangled Molly*, and if anyone thinks I am straying too far from country music in all this I would merely point out that the lead singer here is Maura O'Connell, now based in Nashville and a star of new country. It all connects, I promise you.

The Star Spangled Molly is a fond and tongue-in-cheek look back at the 1920s, when – as the title suggests – Irish music was opening itself up in the USA to a new world of influences. The "frantic era of the Charleston" was also the heyday of John McCormick, and his "innocent and idealised vision of a lovely past, tinged with sweet regret". (It sounds like Jim Reeves.) They play 'Maggie' almost straight: O'Connell draws out each ounce of sweetness, bringing clichés back to life – next stop, Nashville. She does the same to 'Come Back To Me, Mavoureen', sung dead slow and as sentimental as hell, and from that "last bastion of genuine mid-Atlantic nostalgia", Leo Maguire's show on Radio Eireann. It would be ideal for the McGarrigle sisters, who had that same trick of laughing gently at the sentiments therein and making them ache all the same.

"Songs our fathers loved" was the show's catchphrase. It was balm for sore limbs and minds, that's for sure. 'My Irish Molly-O' was first recorded by the rumbunctious Flanagan Brothers, whom we encountered singing about Pat Murphy's comic wake. This is equally cynical, about the financial penalties of love, and "definitely from the taproom end of the music spectrum". Almost a foxtrot, the band throw in accordion, bouzouki and banjo – although Joseph O'Connor imagines that he is hearing trumpets, tuba and piano, which simply aren't there. Maura finds a harder edge to her voice, Johnny "Ringo" McDonagh plays bones, and the middle eight is almost worthy of the Bonzo Dog Band. As infectious as a rash, it rightly reached Number One in the Irish singles chart.

Being perverse, De Danaan next light into a version of The Beatles' 'Hey Jude', as if it had been written in the 1920s. It works just as brilliantly as Mike Seeger, John Hartford and David Grisman's recent backdating of 'When I'm 64' in the old-time style of playing topsy turvey with the timing – don't look forward!

There's a lot of solid research behind all this merriment. Jackie Daly, a famously inscrutable man rarely known to waste ten words when none would do, has built a melodeon from scratch to mimic that played by John Kimmel, who billed himself "in an age rampant with racism" as "The Irish Dutchman". His sound was described at the time as somewhere between a Scotch bagpiper and a jazz band.

What De Danaan brings to the originals is a greater professional smoothness, an ensemble playing far beyond the reach of those they emulate. Even the record sleeve is a pastiche of an earlier and more gracious age. 'I'm Leaving Tipperary', though, is "that rarity in an age of sentiment, a tear-free emigration song", and this version – taken from an original rendition by The Shamrock Band – is even quicker, funnier and more joyous than Pat White's: "Ha, ha, ha," goes the refrain. "Goodbye now," and the disc ends.

Two years later, De Danann took this experiment even further on *Half Set In Harlem*. The set and half set are "the earthy versions danced in Irish country kitchens" – and presumably the American homes of Irish immigrants, too – "of the courtly European dance the quadrille, a favourite of Napoleon". Lewis Carroll applied it to lobsters in the Alice books. The album matches the pun of the title – dance and intent combined – with a series of musical mismatches which draw on some of the stranger hybrids to emerge in North America. Irish music is matched in turn with Jewish *klezmer*, with jazz, with the Celtic tradition transplanted to Cape Breton and with Southern black gospel. The featured vocalist this time around is Eleanor Shanley, with a small gospel choir on a cry to God on 'Operator' and a different one on two contemporary folk songs, on which to my ears they sound a little misplaced. Gospel only works properly when put to divine purpose, whether or not the musicians or audience are true believers. Anything else sounds sacrilegious. De Danann themselves remain resolutely acoustic.

The growth of a commercial recording industry in 1930s America, along with rent parties (drinking sessions in private houses) and the usual rounds of weddings and wakes, meant that Irish musicians in America were starting to earn a living. They weren't the only ones. O'Connor quotes a Boston newspaper editorial in 1850 to the effect that "the raw Irishman in America is a nuisance, his son a curse. They never assimilate. They are a burden and misery to this country." In reality, it was Irish sweat and toil that helped to build it.

The Irish folk-rock band Horslips said as much in 'The Man Who Built America', the title song of an album all about emigration and its consequences. Loneliness is the basic mood, and the title of the first song, with Charles O'Connor's fiddle and Jim Lockhart's flute providing the high sounds. The band pose moodily, casting giant shadows, and their music is as far from De Danaan's gentle complexities as could be, a guitar-driven wall of electric sound for singer Barry Devlin to climb, but tuneful for all that. Live, Horslips were one of the loudest (and best) bands I ever saw, with powerhouse drumming. It matches the working fury of their hero, building a railroad track to the stars: "See him driving those golden nails/that hold together the silver bars." There also is a poem in Gaelic bidding farewell to the shores of home, "since fate had forced us to go". The front cover is a photo taken in the aftermath of the assassination of John F Kennedy, just one among millions who could trace his family back to the old country. The inner sleeve has an abstract design, based on the ships which took away the emigrants, and the final song goes back 'Long Time Ago' to lazier summers. There's no way back in the previous song, though: "It's just a letter from home, telling you things that are changing."

Bringing It All Back Home points out the heartbreak behind that title song: "dangerous and pestilential sea voyages had killed thousands", and from then on the only work going was "menial, hard and poorly paid". They lived in city slums and worked on house construction, in the docks, in machine shops, down the mines, and building canals and the railroad. As a song which pre-dates the Irish Famine has it: "In eighteen hundred and forty one/I put my corduroy britches on...Poor Paddy works on the railway."

Some construction teams were wholly Gaelic speaking. In the lumber camps, outlaw songs like 'Brennan On The Moor' were popular, and "the English-speaking Irish seem to have been the principal bards". Even more interesting as a sign of cultural change are the "macaronic" songs found in the lumber camps. This is a term which refers to a set of words somewhere between Irish and English, not a song about pasta, so that the Gaelic song 'Siuil, siuil, siuil, a Run' becomes in English 'I'll Sell My Hat, I'll Sell My Coat', and is collected as such in America. Another version taken down in the Catskills substitutes "a nonsense-word rigmarole to approximate the sound of the Irish words" and the song's meter, so that the Irish – literally translated as "walk, walk, walk, my love" becomes "Shule, shule, shule, I rue."

Pete Seeger took two separate songs from the oral tradition and put them together under the title 'No Irish Need Apply', in which a bigot is routed, to public applause. Stereotypes lingered, though, and "Pat" was portrayed in cartoons as an ape man, though this later softened into the image of "a lovable rogue with the gift of the gab" and the comically dim stage Irishman. A generation later, The Clancy Brothers and Tommy Maken turned up in New York in trademark Arran sweaters and a hearty repertoire split between rebel songs and traditional ballads, with some comic chat in between. With a banjo playing a predominant role, it could be straight from the Appalachians, apart from the tin whistle and aggressively Oirish accents in which they declaim the songs, each word a punch in England's face. "Without England on our backs, they would never have been made", Liam Clancy writes on *The Moonshiner* EP, with Pete Seeger joining in on banjo and Bruce Langhorne on lead guitar. (The latter would later perform the same function for Bob Dylan.)

Roots music with an Irish accent. This construct in turn influenced Dylan's early attempt at songwriting, and he borrowed many a tune: Dominic Behan's adaptation of 'The Patriot Game' becomes 'With God On Our Side', and 'Brennan On The Moor' turns into 'Rambling Gambling Willie'. It is also music purged of anything high or lonesome, and made over for a mass audience. All three Clancy brothers had moved full-time to the East Coast from Ireland, with Paddy recording Irish singers for Folkways and then setting up his own label, Tradition, releasing records by Odetta and Josh White, while Liam went on song-collecting trips to the Appalachians. When they flew home to "return to the source of their work", they recorded a live album at the Ulster Hall, Belfast, during which Tommy Makem danced a jig onstage during 'Beggar Man', a variant of the song performed by The Flanagan Brothers 30 years before. At the time of this visit, The Clancy Brothers were responsible for one in three of all albums sold in Ireland.

Back in America, they were part of the urban folk revival which made cult figures of even more unlikely figures – Dock Boggs and Doc Watson, for starters. The Clancy Brothers' ultimate importance lies not in their rousing but unsubtle singing – involving lots of whoops and good-hearted maleness – but in the care they took in researching their native material, which includes poetry as well as song. Collectors like Mike Seeger directed a similar intensity of purpose back onto the music of the Appalachians.

The left romanticises failure just as the right idolises brutality, and when Franklin D Roosevelt's National Recovery Administration – which closed banks, fixed prices and wages and suspended anti-trust laws – was itself closed down by the Supreme Court, he targeted government relief instead to such projects as the Works Progress Administration, which sent unemployed scholars and historians throughout America to study a shared past, and in musical terms to record it. As Malone points out, it was at this point that "social activists began using folk songs as a political weapon".

More immediately, Roosevelt paid Southern farmers to diversify, built enormous dams and encouraged workers to organise into unions. Here was a man of largely English descent, I should point out with my own inherent racial pride! It was the world according to Woody Guthrie, and a time of change reflected in the murals of Thomas Hart Benson in the New School in New York. It showed that *laissez faire* was not the only possibility.

If this proved to be much too close to socialism for the American establishment, its echoes rippled on, into the secret America celebrated by Harry Smith and into the folk revival, itself largely based in big cities and on college campuses. There were other sources, other legends. Joe Hill was one of the first of the American unionist singers, connected with the "Wobblies", the Industrial Workers Of The World. Hill was born Joel Hagglund in Sweden and emigrated to New York, where he played the piano in a New York café. Under his new pseudonym, he wrote and sang dozens of political calls to action, soon collected in a little red book snappily entitled *Songs To Fan The Flames Of Discontent*. The songs themselves had titles like 'Casey Jones The Union Scab' and 'The White Slave', which was about a young girl reduced to prostitution: "Who is to blame? You know the name/It's the boss that pays starvation wages."

Hill worked in the Utah copper mines but was falsely accused of murder and was killed by a firing squad in 1915. His memory lingered on, however, and became myth in the song 'I Dreamed I Saw Joe Hill Last Night', which Dylan himself transmuted into 'I Dreamed I Saw St Augustine'. Rebel, martyr, saint: the usual progression.

At about the same time that Bill Monroe was inventing the essentially conservative bluegrass, singers like Burl Ives and Josh White were becoming fixtures on the alternative circuit, as were Woody Guthrie's toneless paeans to a better nation, often in collaboration with Cisco Houston and bluesman Sonny Terry. (The fact that most of Guthrie's songs have no or the same tune dates his music now, while the nobility of his lyrics is timeless.) Pete Seeger and The Almanac Singers followed up Hill's activism with talk-songs like 'Talkin' Union' – "If you wait for the boss to pay, we'll all be waiting for Judgement Day" – and provided practical advice: "you can pass out a leaflet and call a meeting".

Seeger's deliberately plain-speaking vocals and harsh banjo picking have an Appalachian sound to them. He originally learned four-string banjo after he dropped out of Harvard, then virtually rediscovered the ancient five-string variant. Seeger's father, Charles, was both a musicologist and a political activist, and both Pete and Mike took different routes from this influence. It is doubtful that any Appalachian picker could even spell, let alone have "this machine surrounds hate and forces it to surrender" emblazoned on his instrument. On *The Bitter And The Sweet*, a period piece recorded at the Bitter End, Seeger sings not only the expected 'We Shall Overcome' but also 'Barbara Allen', "our best-known English-Scottish-American folk song", and 'Around And Around Old Joe Clark', "a well-known old square dance tune, brought alive again with Peter's fleet fingers". It was hardly a tune that had died, but it ties in with Seeger's claim that the turning point in his life came in 1935, when he attended a folk festival in North Carolina run by Bascom Lamar Lunsford.

Suitably inspired, Pete later joined The Weavers with Lee Hays, who had a massive hit with their version of Leadbelly's 'Goodnight Irene' and then attracted the sinister attention of the House Of Un-American Activities Committee. As such things go, he later turned into an edifice of musical conservatism, and reportedly took an axe to the power cables at the 1965 Newport Folk Festival when Dylan first went electric in public, and trashed the protest boom by outpacing it.

Back in the 1950s, under the politically committed Moses Asch, Folkways proved a willing label to release such material when it was still dangerous and "issue led". One recent compilation of Seeger's work divides his songs helpfully into themes of unions and labour, peace, civil rights and "hope". Listening to this stuff now, one admires the nobility of purpose but misses anything like poetry, excitement, or love songs. Especially love songs. What these singers – now based in the Lower East Side of New York – provided was an example of good practice: that one should use one's own privileged position to sing about – and for – the poor and dispossessed. It is a message which has echoed through the best folk and country music ever since.

Seeger's half-sister Peggy got together with Guy Carawan for the ambitious *We Sing America*, a jazz-blues-folk fusion recorded in England with the legendary Joe Meek on sound balance and with notes by AL Lloyd. It's a bold enough hybrid to be a forgotten antecedent for alt country, with everything from the big city sound of 'Big Rock Blues' to the voice and banjo of 'Cripple Creek'. Lloyd admits that some people find this "city-adopted folk song" distasteful, "but the fact is the folk have always been at work on the folk music". As another folk pioneer, John Tams, told me a few days ago, "it bends back".

In much the same vein, Burl Ives' *Ballads And Folk Songs* includes The Carters song 'I'm Thinking of My Blue Eyes' and a fine mix of ancient ('Foggy, Foggy Dew') and modern ('On The Grand Canyon Line'), with what sounds like Acker Bilk on clarinet, jazzing things up. "This latter-day minstrel of Falstaffian appearance has brought sudden and vivid life to the Anglo-American folk tradition." Ives was the son of tenant farmers in the bible belt, and his "tobacco-chewing grandmother" taught him British folk songs from the cradle. By the age of four he was singing them in public for money. He remains an enigma, an over-polite singer most famous for his comic movie roles, but also a serious scholar of folk music. Popularisers sell at the time, but date horribly. It depends what you want: lots of money or respect.

One of Guthrie's disciples whose work has certainly lasted is Rambling Jack Elliott, born as he himself jokes "on a 4,000-acre ranch in Brooklyn" and about as authentic as Bob Dylan, whom he joined on The Rolling Thunder Review. Elliott is a one-man template for the wandering folk singer, always hitching a ride somewhere else. His early repertoire extends from folk songs like 'Roving Gambler' to a version of 'Will The Circle Be Unbroken?', combining banjo and harmonica, and a live version of 'I Belong To Glasgow', of all things. He once serenaded some kids on an English railway platform, one of whom turned out to be a pre-teen Mick Jagger. The first American folk singer to tour Europe, he recorded his debut album for Topic on an eight-inch format – surely one of only a very few pressings ever made – called *Woody Guthrie's Blues*, a tribute to his master.

Back in the States, Dylan was listening hard and stealing what he could, as fooled as anyone else by Jack's claims to have been brought up as a cowboy. (The Byrds learned their version of 'Mr Tambourine Man' from a demo tape of Dylan and Elliot singing the song, hence the lack of the final verses.) He learned to fingerpick from an impeccable source – Elizabeth Cotten, the Seeger family's maid – and also developed the talking blues: "to speak like that you have to be around country people, do the things they do. Those cadences do not come from learning to speak from the Berlitz method."

Onstage, Jack still rambles between songs in much the same way, so that "a gonzo rap about Walden Pond somehow logically segues" into an account of how he once performed a gig down the phone. So what's country about him? I hear a disgruntled reader ask. Well, for a start, 1998's world-weary *Friends Of Mine* ranks at or about the top of the dreaded Nashville tradition of an album of duets with famous friends. The likes of Peter Rowan, John Prine and Jerry Jeff Walker howl along with his gravelly vocals, while Emmylou and Nanci Griffith sweeten them. At times, he sounds as laconic as WC Fields. Country enough? Rambling Jack also recorded an album of traditional songs, *The Long Ride*, with people like the ubiquitous Tom Russell, who is in many ways his natural successor.

Another offshoot of the Guthrie world-view was The Whiskyhill Singers, who accompanied The Kingston Trio onstage but whose only album was a learned affair, with scholarly readings of such songs as 'The Bonnie Ship *The Diamond*', another Rolling Thunder revival. The Singers also contributed to the movie score of *How The West Was Won* before disbanding.

Dylan said of Woody Guthrie that "he had a particular sound, more or less a Carter Family-type sound. And he had something that needed to be said...for me, he was a link in the chain." The Carter Family, parents of protest – it all makes sense. Dylan talks about Woody's "innocence", one that he himself never regained. Peter Guralnick makes the same point in his sleeve notes to *Folkways: A Vision Shared*, confusingly issued by CBS. Woody's songs "could not stand without a clear awareness of Jimmie Rodgers' or The Carter Family's music going before". It makes a mockery of the false division which has arisen between country and folk, a split which this book is at pains to reconnect. Guralnick writes movingly about how the discovery of such music was like coming out of a darkness (one into which Will Oldham is gleefully plunging back), "a cant-free, plain-speaking place, naked and unadorned, a world where...you could shout your beliefs from the nearest building or the highest mountain top". City meets country.

In 1958, the clean-cut Kingston Trio had a number one hit with 'Tom Dooley', an Appalachian murder ballad about a man called Tom Dula. Suddenly folk music was hip, hootenanny was the word in vogue for a folk-song session, and an all-star (and fake) album of that name defined it as being "for the young and for alert individuals who are rediscovering their American heritage – and enjoying it". Enjoyment was the key. After some of the over-worthy academic inquiries, this came with the force of punk rock, a blast of raw energy. Before the divisions came down, it was possible for CBS to bring together the part-singing of The New Christie Minstrels (complete with banjo) on a Woody Guthrie song, Flatt And Scruggs with Mother Maybelle Carter, The Clancy Brothers, Johnny Cash, Pete Seeger and Bob Dylan. Largely or totally acoustic, though, Leon Bibb combines a banjo and a full orchestra, and the even more operatic Orriel Smith (a friend of the Seeger family, though, so she's okay) murders 'Down By The Glenside' – "it has that certain elusive quality of much Anglo-Scots-Irish balladry".

Cash snarls 'Nine-Pound Hammer', "a white blues written by Merle Travis: the construction and content make it as valid a folk song as any which could have evolved through the oral tradition". Cash delivers it "with a native Arkansas twang and a natural ease", which is almost as good as having natural rhythm, like those poor folk do.

Another cash-in album of the time, busy cornering a market in this kind of sound, is equally eclectic. On an album released by Elektra, here are Jack Elliott and Judy Collins, Eric Wissberg's banjo strut 'Flop-Eared Mule' and Oscar Brand's hail fellow well met 'Squid-Jiggin' Ground'. As if aware of its own daring, the sleeve note quote Big Bill Broonzy's reply to whether the song he had just performed was a folk song: "Well, I never heard a cow singing it".

Peter, Paul And Mary certainly stretch the definition of that term about as far as it can go, only beaten by Australia's The Seekers, a miserable bunch who emigrated north to England and cover on the same side of the same album the British traditional song 'The Water Is Wide' and the same music via the Appalachians in 'Lady Mary': badly, and with an orchestra. As to Mary Travers and her two male stooges, they do mischief to traditional songs of the likes of 'Stewball', which Martin Carthy has spent a lifetime since rescuing and returning to good sense. The trio sing such stuff over-politely, as if it is already in a museum case and needs dusting. This is easy listening and hard politics.

They're still surprisingly listenable, though, with choral harmonies, but that's not really the point. Their main historical importance is as an early conduit for the early songs of Bob Dylan. He repays the debt with a back-sleeve poem to the album that broke him through, 1963's *In The Wind*. It's a nostalgic look back at Greenwich Village before fame hit home, when "I remember Luke playin his banjo and singing 'East Virginia'," though no rooster ever crowed on MacDougal Street; "there was no dew on the grass, an the sun never came shinin over the mountain". Note the dropped d and g – authentic or what? From this "subterranean world" (that's a good phrase, Bob, you should use it again sometime), the music is now coming up the steps into daylight. Or down the mountain.

The folk revival inspired first the search for sources and second the spotlight of public adulation sweeping back to illuminate some of the original pioneers – hence the rediscovery of Dock Boggs, Buell Kazee, Jimmie Tarlton and Clarence "Tom" Ashley. The last-named's 'Coo Coo Bird' opens volume three of the Harry Smith anthology, 'Songs', issued by Folkways in 1952, and his influence spread as slowly and insidiously as a stain.

When it was reissued yet again in 1997, once more to infuse – or infect – contemporary music, John L Walters wrote in *The Independent* that this might be a song that you can trace back to 18th-century Sussex, but "with its repetitive, mesmerising banjo accompaniment, its atmosphere is not far from 1960s Steve Reich or 1990s dance music. Lyrics such as 'Jack O'Diamonds, Jack O'Diamonds, I've known you from old' sound as alienating and weirdly familiar as anything by Underworld's Karl Hyde." John Fahey describes Ashley as probably the best mountain five-string banjo player ever, "also the scroungiest and most forceful".

It's certainly a thought: mountain musicians as the first sound terrorists, mixing traditional words together in a post-modernist way. But then, the more you immerse yourself in the weird world of the *Anthology Of American Folk Music*, the more anything becomes possible. You need only to look at the list of those who came together at the Royal Festival Hall recently in tribute: Jarvis Cocker, Bryan Ferry, Nick Cave, Van Dyke Parks, Eliza Carthy, Beth Orton, Mary Margaret O'Hara...more enigmas per square inch that night than anywhere else in the known world. The reissued *Anthology* comes with its own critical apparatus, and it's enough for me that musicians like Peter Stampfel (who first heard it under the influence of peyote), and John Fahey (who puts it above the Dead Sea Scrolls in cultural importance), testify to its occult power.

The six-CD set is certainly the very antithesis of a cash-in anthology, with every song in its rightful place, a huge if odd abundance of footnotes and sidelights, and from bang out of nowhere a folk canon put together in front of your eyes. This is magic, in every sense. Not many record compilations quote Robert Fludd, Aleister Crowley and Rudolph Steiner, and few are as meticulous concerning sources, or have song summaries that are so amusing. The Child ballad 'Our Goodman' becomes Coley Jones' 'Drunkard's Special', and is given the footnote: "Wife's logic fails to explain strange bedfellow to drunkard".

Scholarship and poetry, meanwhile, meet in the passages on Buell Kazee and his 'Brilliancy Medley': "One of the pioneer rural recording artists, with unaccompanied solos issued by Victor thirty years ago, his playing in the present recording is quite archaic in its studied and exaltant formality, but the medley of traditional tunes is more suited to the popular dance steps of the 1920s than to the square dance." The new edition adds further information, including Eck's dates of birth and death, his later collaboration with The New Lost City Ramblers, his appearance at the 1965 Newport Folk Festival, and what appears on his tombstone: 'World's Champion Fiddler'. It also informs us that Fairport Convention, The Dixie Chicks and Sam Bush have all covered the tune on record.

Fahey believes that Smith "was acutely aware of a fairly simple truth...certain musicultural traditions were sympathetic to each other while others were not". Hence *canun* but no *conjunto*, and no Jewish-American; the real meeting place here is black and white music "of the unschooled variety", despite the "persistent protestations of many White artists". Bill Monroe is named as someone who "would have us believe he invented bluegrass...nearly true, of course". I first learned of the *Anthology* from Greil Marcus' wonderful book on *Dylan's Basement Tapes*, having discovered the Situationists through the same writer's book on The Sex Pistols, so expected something rich and strange, and got it in spades. It's just a shame he didn't spend as much time discussing the *Basement* tapes, but you can't have everything.

The *Anthology* was reissued in the same year as *Invisible Republic*, and Greil's insights on "the old, weird America" are recycled in both. He places its release – at the height of McCarthyism – as a form of mute resistance. Its alchemical colour coding and raising of lost music and musicians from the dead "made the familiar strange, the never-known into the forgotten, and the forgotten into a collective memory". Here was the enemy within, encoded in this "repertory of the past".

Harry Smith was also a fanatical collector (including his own semen, frozen in jars), a long-term resident of the Chelsea Hotel (rent unpaid), an artist and the maker of avante-garde films which now look like precursors of Monty Python. His mother sang Irish folk songs. Ed Ward pointed out in a review exactly what and whom he dared to exclude here – Robert Johnson and Bill Monroe, for two. The "great roar of voices" whom he did choose included many that – almost beyond belief – were still alive, and got a second bite of the cherry thanks to the *Anthology*. John Pankake talks of meeting eleven of the participants here, and of how "folk song revivalists of the 1960s began to search for and locate the surviving artist". It also unleashed a whole generation to play their own versions of the old-time music here, and take it on again. As Paul Oliver observed in *Jazz Monthly*, back in 1963, "there's many a folknik who has added 'Willie Moore' and 'Old Dog Blue' to his repertoire by lifting the words from the collection". But that's simply the folk tradition, theft with attitude. For those not blessed with an Appalachian family home, this was the next best thing as a song source.

Jeff Place carefully lists all of the versions recorded since, and confirms what I myself felt when I first heard the thing: that my complete record collection – Dylan bootlegs in particular – was coming alive, and revealing a whole forest of roots. "The secret script of so many familiar musical dramas," to quote Elvis Costello. In no particular order, I already owned or knew versions of these songs by Joan Baez, Sam Hinton, Bert Jansch, Nick Cave, Jody Stecher, Ewan MacColl, Pentangle, Fairport, Michael Martin Murphey, John Fahey, Merle Travis, The Grateful Dead, Johnny Rivers, Bill Haley, Boiled In Lead, Del McCoury, Spike Jones, The Blood Oranges and Bob Dylan – and that's just the first of six discs. To hear The Bently Boys' 'Down On Penny's Farm' is a particular revelation, as it gave Dylan the germ of 'Maggie's Farm', and here also is one of his earliest songs, 'Hard Times In New York', previsited. He simply updates the references to his own life.

Marcus points out that Harry Smith ignored "all field recordings, Library Of Congress archives, anything validated only by scholarship", but plenty of others were doing just that, and the most important of all was Alan Lomax. Growing up in Texas in the 1930s, he slipped into blues joints under cover of darkness. His father, John, collected cowboy songs. They joined forces for the Library Of Congress, at first collecting "black secular music", but broadened their range to cover Britain, where it all started, the Far East, the Caribbean and, in 1959, the Appalachians. They were joined for part of their quest by the young English folk singer Shirley Collins, whose first album sounds like a Sussex-born singer imitating American dirt farmers as a result, imitating folk songs from…Sussex.

In a recent talk at Cecil Sharp House, Shirley talked memorably about what it was like following in Maud Karpeles' footsteps – another subservient woman in the wake of a great man. When she told one resident that she came from England, "England over the water?" was the question that came shooting back. The preacher EC Ball subjected her to threatening quotes from the book of Revelations, and she was told wild tales of murder and mayhem, about Ada Coombes shooting her husband's fancy woman in the foot on the sabbath and being given an extra sentence because she chose to do so on the seventh day. Lomax ordered her to covertly tape some call-and-response singing on her trusty Niagra recorder after the preacher, a hard-shell Baptist, had made them remove the more obvious Ampex. As he began to use words like "abomination", and referred disparagingly to Shirley's bobbed hair as "sinful", then started "sobbing and wailing, his voice breaking as he threatened eternal damnation", she was so nervous that she pressed play rather than record, and his voice came back in stereo, so to speak. "Serious mistake," reports Ken Hunt, Britain's foremost "old music" expert, from the front row.

In her forthcoming account of this trip, *America Over The Water* – a response to that mountaineer's question – Shirley admits that "the truth was that in Kentucky I started to feel afraid. The beauty of the place was undeniable, the mountains high and steep, heavily wooded, greeny-blue deepening to purple at dawn and sunset, when pink clouds nestled down in the hollows or haloed the peaks" (there speaks a great singer), but amidst it was hardship and deprivation. She was told of "feuds between families and neighbours", with one farmer shot dead because his cow strayed into another man's field, and at night she heard gunfire in the hills, "and I didn't know whether the prey was animal or human". You don't hear this sort of thing from Cecil Sharp.

The results, as recently compiled on a series of CDs under the joint title *Southern Journey*, are less stark than the Harry Smith archive from 78s made some 30 years earlier. Volume two alone has instrumentals like 'Old Joe Clark' and 'Sourwood Mountain', plenty of fiddles and banjos, and lots of British ballads, lullabyes and blues licks, often all at once. What impresses most, even today, is the self-confidence and zeal of the playing, and the rusty tunefulness of the singing, as serious as your life but also a normal part of life, as if it's an everyday occurrence to break out in a tale of murder or adultery from the Elizabethan age. In these hills, it is.

The winds of change and time passing also blow even through these remote mountains. It bears out Stuart Hall's point about how change can enrich a tradition and keep it alive. 'The Burglar Man' is a fairly recent song composed for a local vaudeville entertainment, part of the heritage left by the medicine shows, and Bob Carpenter describes it as "one I wouldn't want to get involved in, and I don't think you would either. This is a very sniptious sight here." Lomax notes that most British versions of 'The Girl I Left Behind Me' end happily and almost all American variants unhappily, with the man betrayed and no new true love to console him. One dreads to think what Ruth Padel would make of that – the incipient anti-woman bias of the American male, or what?

As often happens, it is the snippets of conversation which entrance – "Did you ever catch any foxes?" Shirley asks, and Wade Ward replies "Hardly ever" – and the unaccompanied female voice which cuts the deepest. Here Texas Gladden sings 'Three Little Babes', more usually known as 'The Wife Of Usher's Well'. It has you on the edge of your seat even now, 40 years on, and even though you somehow know from her tone that the children are already dead. Lomax's original sleeve notes are reproduced here, which explain how the Blue Ridge Mountains were a wilderness "braved" only by "Scotch-Irish from Pennsylvania and English from the lowlands of the Carolinas", looking for land and the freedom to worship as they chose. The rural folk singer has a great regard for old-time music: "He likes a song all the better if it reminds him of his grandparents, the hills of home and the free way of life of the mountains." It is just this respect for the past which has kept the music going.

Lomax was a singer in his own right, with albums like *Alan Sings Great American Ballads* to his credit. His daughter Anna is following the family trade, still collecting. As another preacher said to Shirley Collins, who had fled from the Baptist meeting to the safety of her car and was then called back to tape the rest of the service: "This young man and his little contraption might be the means of someone knowing that the songs of Zion are still being sung."

In 1953, another young man had been listening to, and had then recorded his own, brand-new versions of *Folksongs From The Southern Appalachian Mountains*, a ten-inch album on Elektra. Tom Paley was a postgraduate in Mathematics at Yale, and as such hardly fitted the stereotype of the ignorant moonshiner, especially as he had been born in New York. At Yale, "we had a department string band on the campus, and one of our professors liked to call square dances". It all sounds a little like the compulsory Tudor dancing in Kingsley Amis' sarcastic novel of university life, *Lucky Jim*, but Paley was made of sterner stuff. People talk of his arrival in the New York folk scene as if John The Baptist had blown into town – which would make Mike Seeger the Messiah!

Paley sang and played banjo and guitar, and another friend at Yale, John Cohen, would sometimes join in. Paley haunted New York record shops, searching out the old music, as he later told *Folk Roots*: "Interesting thing is how I got interested in old-time country string band music as opposed to what most of the people were doing in the so-called 'folk revival' (it wasn't called that, back then)". He found an obscure radio show which played the old sounds, *The Hometown Frollick*, and started to get familiar with the likes of The Carter Family and Uncle Dave Macon, like diamonds in the rough. "I'd listen through hours of stuff that I didn't really care for in order to hear a few of the older things".

A particular favourite was Charlie Poole And The Carolina Ramblers: "they had this interesting syncopated way of playing those runs…and The Ramblers' whole approach to a string band, the way the fiddle took the melody, the banjo plucking a brittle rhythm, and those runs going off the bass strings of the guitar". Paley also loved the work of Riley Puckett in The Skillet Lickers, the way he would back up the other musicians. These influences fed direct into The New Lost City Ramblers, a trio of young upper-class zealots hungry for old-time music, namely Paley, Cohen and Mike Seeger, Pete's half brother.

Tom Paley had been part of the folk revival right from the start, having joined American Youth For Democracy straight after the war. Here he attended concerts by the likes of Pete Seeger and watched, enthralled, as Pete started to hold "hootenannys", or the more informal "wingdings", in union halls. Tom began to play concerts with Woody Guthrie, but the most crucial meeting was with Mike Seeger, at a "hoot" in Yale. No wonder that Dylan got such a laugh when he announced that he got one song from Rick von Schmidt, whom he had met "one day in the green pastures of...Harvard University".

A photo of the young band sees three over-serious young men in collars and ties and with neat haircuts, with Tom holding his banjo like a weapon. Like The Charlatans or The Band a decade or so later, the look was the message. Robert Cantwell describes how, in addition to "newly esotericised discographic sources and a performance style as exotic as a Tibetan prayer", the band dressed "like railroad stationmasters or telegraph operators" and posed "with the blank faces and straight spines of a portrait studio of the last century". They were clowns, too, full of self-parody, swapping instruments onstage like bubble-gum cards.

The Ramblers made a great deal of albums but were never a full-time affair, and so Paley split off in the early Sixties, moved to London, and is currently obsessed with Swedish fiddling. Such are the whims of genius, for the echoes of what he and his two fellow zealots achieved still rumble around America.

That being said, those albums I have heard by The New Lost City Ramblers – and most are now very hard to find, which explains how they have largely fallen off the cultural map – now sound a little stiff and unconvincing. They are too respectful, lacking the wild exuberance of the mountain men they ape. Tracy Schwarz (a man) replaced Paley, and typical of the new trio is *Modern Times*, a concept album of industrial folk songs which, like the Harry Smith *Anthology*, almost all come from commercial recordings, "popular songs, sold in the popular marketplace". The vocals sound a little mannered, but the acoustic sounds of banjo, violin, guitar and harmonica run as clear as a mountain stream, and as fresh.

A description of the band's debut in 1958 at the Carnegie Recital Hall mentions "a peculiar nostalgia for 1932. They are not, in this year of 'Tom Dooley' at all like that other trio. Their clothes lack fashion, and they look a bit dishevelled, despite the vests and ties. Their music is kind of dishevelled too – not pretty like the greeting card pictures painted in song by other 'folk' singers. Rough around the edges, kind of gritty, kind of real. Kind of...old timey." That comes from the sleeve notes to their 20th anniversary concert from 1978, which includes appearances from two celebrity guests: Pete Seeger sings 'Barbara Allen', a song that "came out of Scotland about 300 years ago", while Elizabeth Cotten – who cam from North Carolina and was the Seeger family's cleaner – sings a cracked rendition of her own song 'Freight Train'. As sung by Nancy Whiskey, it later reached the UK Top Ten. Otherwise, it's the usual mix of mountain breakdowns, Carter Family songs and similar rural intimacies. 'The Soldier And The Lady' is "about as close to bluegrass as we get", though. The best description of Mike Seeger comes in Robert Cantwell's wordy but beautifully researched *When We Were Good*, itself particularly good on the left-wing activism – summer camps and youth guilds – which underlay the folk revival. Like most academics, Cantwell is obsessed with sex and class, and neatly pins down Seeger as an emigré from his own social group. More to the point, Cantwell stresses how original Seeger is, far more than the sum of his borrowings, and how "he creates a strange, swimming, otherworldly sound that might…suggest the image of a sun-blinded western wagoner of the 1850s at the edge of his endurance". Even if such a sound was never actually heard on the prairies, it could have been, perhaps. Seeger "can come most fully into possession of himself only in disguise".

He later formed The Strange Creek Singers, another part-time band, and has continued to put out solo albums of solo banjo playing and the like, always beautifully annotated. He refuses to allow that old-time music has ossified: "If you play it yourself and learn it by ear, it can't be static." Talking to *Folk Roots*, he echoes Stuart Hall's views on the beneficial aspects of change: "One doesn't need to go outside the field to have evolution or even revolutions. People like The Horseflies reach outside, and I find that entertaining." He prefers old-time music to bluegrass because "it seemed like, and is, much richer, because it draws on hundreds of years of musical tradition". All he has ever wanted to do is to share the music he loves so much.

There is a photograph of an intent Seeger and his young black assistant recording a mountain-banjo-playing old man, on his back porch in West Virginia, with the wonderfully appropriate name of William Bragg, but this is no relation of England's premier folk bard. Well, maybe a distant one… After his boyish recording of Libby Cotten, Mike went on the road with his tape recorder, and the cream of the result are found on the CD *Close To Home*, a portmanteau collection which includes the likes of Dock Boggs and Maybelle Carter, and on which that same photo appears on the front cover, and a close up on the picture disc inside.

This is a very personal project, and his notes reflect this. Seeger asks himself where his "love and preoccupation" for such sounds came from. At first it was pure rebellion: "I was the son of two modernist composer-musicologists who with great joy had just discovered the wonders of traditional Southern rural music." (Note the word "joy" there.) But it goes deeper: "I was singing 'Barbara Allen' by the time I started school. My mother was transcribing folk songs from field recordings for her publications." Not, you see, for the pleasure of herself or of her son. There was no radio in the house, for reasons of culture, not poverty, so he listened to field recordings and then graduated to making his own tapes at bluegrass and country music shows. He then tracked old-time music back to its source. This was all done while Mike and his young family were living a hand-to-mouth existence. Here is a man who has literally gone hungry to pursue his art.

As to his relation to the likes of Dock Boggs, for which the re-recording of whom alone Seeger would rightly deserve to be remembered, they also collect and perform songs to play at home: "I'm a collector-performer too, but with an urban perspective and a slightly different agenda".

Jacques Vassal saw the effect of this renewed interest in traditional music as three-fold, firstly as the "transfusion of fresh blood into the veins of a moribund culture". It is the same argument as Stuart Hall's, and in this context "pop" music extended itself enough to reflect social realism. Hence the protest style of Barry Maguire's 'Eve Of Destruction', at its most strident, but also a renewed strain in country music that reflected contemporary reality, songs like 'Harper Valley PTA' or even Roger Miller's portraits of hobos and failures, winsome but fun. We will come back to Sixties country at the end of this chapter.

It was secondly a two-way process, with some folk singers becoming rock stars, most notably Bob Dylan. The return to traditional sources unleashed a new breed of singer/songwriters, who invite "each of us to become not only an heir or a lis-tener, but also one of the members of an eternal process of collective re-creation". We all become members of the traditional music community, even those of us who have never been to Tennessee. By this argument, even as massive an event as Woodstock was in reality half a million crowding around a big back porch.

Vassal's third point is that "authentic folk music and its interpreters were stim-ulated in their convictions and revitalised for at least a generation", and the example he names is Arthel "Doc" Watson and his son Merle. As we have already seen, Doc was discovered in the Appalachian heartlands in 1960 by Ralph Rinzler of The Greenbriar Boys as part of the crowd of musicians surrounding Clarence "Tom" Ashley, a man revered by folklorists but who could not gather "20 flies" among his peers. Watson was playing an electric Gibson Les Paul, much to Rinzler's disap-pointment, but when the young man started picking at a banjo Watson climbed out of the truck, grabbed the instrument off him like taking candy from a baby and "ripped off some of the best mountain picking imaginable. Here was the context of the folk music I had heard in recorded and concert performances for 20 of my 26 years". Within a year, Doc Watson was guesting at the Newport Folk Festival.

Dawidoff fills in the gaps. The Watsons had fled from Scotland in the early 19th Century, "when the lairds began enclosing their farmland and renting it in cast tracts to English sheep farmers". They settled in deep Gap, North Carolina, in a landscape much like that of the Scottish highlands, a comparison of which Sharyn McCrumb – of similar stock – has made much in her detective novels, as demonstrated back in chapter one.

Watson was born blind but was persistent and, having learned music at his father's knee ("so country you could smell the frost on the sweet-potato vines"), he played in a swing band, The Country Gentlemen, with a repertoire which stretched to such non-mountain songs as 'Tutti-Frutti' and 'Tea For Two'. This was no "hick from Deep Gap", however much he became associated with childhood ditties about groundhogs and muskrats and chilling murder songs, all sung so sweetly as to inoculate them, at least until the words have slipped down, by which time it's too late. As I've said before, I can't be critical here; I could listen to the Doc forever, and what Dawidoff identifies as a "slightly plaintive tremor" in his voice infects everything he sings. If there's a better, more mellifluous example of the high, lonesome sound than his versions of 'Shady Grove' or 'Omie Wise' then I can't imagine it. Just don't patronise him, as if all this came with his mother's milk.

Watson's music is a cunning musical construct, about as spontaneous as Elgar, say, in which blues, Dixieland and new-style country lend a riff here, a lick there. As the fiddler Mark O'Connor points out, "Bill Monroe and Doc Watson are as progressive as anybody I've ever heard", and to listen to the two men duet on mandolin and guitar on 'Soldier's Joy' in 1964 is, according to Dawidoff, "to hear the very limits of the instrument expanding". Merle was a perfect rhythm guitarist and companion on the road, until death took him young. Their albums together are numerous, if sometimes shockingly short on playing time, wonderful collision points of blues, country and folk, and I've yet to hear a bad one.

Of particular historical interest are live recordings from various Newport Folk Festivals in the early Sixties, which have the crackle which only live performances can give, however rackety, and in which Doc plays with an ever-changing array of friends, performing everything from Jimmie Rodgers to Dock Boggs and Charlie Poole, from the lonesome 'Blueridge Mountain Blues' to the sprightly 'Handsome Molly'. Doc later recorded with Michelle Shocked on *Arkansas Traveller*, and immediately put her at ease: "I said, 'I'm just people, I'll make a lot more mistakes than you will when we put it down. Don't worry about it, just get in there and pick it and sing it like always.'" And she did.

Jimmie Dale Gilmore reckons that Watson "brought an open-mindedness to the folk world by being both the real thing and a genuine innovator…he was one of the first people to play real country music for the city crowd". It's an influence which endures. When Gilmore plays supper sessions at Threadgills, "at least four songs a night" are drawn from his repertoire. Doc himself is still progressing while seemingly standing still, and one of the tracks from his recent, sparkling session with Mac Wiseman and Del McCoury – with the likes of Alison Krauss in support – was nominated for a Grammy. *Folk Roots* opines that "they play like old friends", and you can't say much better than that. A new release of old home recordings by Doc and Merle was overdubbed later by such contemporary maestros as Sam Bush and Marty Stuart, but somehow it crosses an invisible line. Doc is best heard unadulterated, and live.

"Doc" Watson was the most palatable of the old-time musicians to emerge or re-emerge at this time. More in the Dock Boggs mould of rural grimness was the singer and mountain banjo player Roscoe Holcomb, whose 1965 Folkways album *The High Lonesome Sound* was championed by Bob Dylan, among others. Another band to borrow from such music were The Greenbriar Boys, who numbered Eric Weissberg (later of *Deliverance* fame) as well as Ralph Rinzler among their number, and veered closer to bluegrass than the early string-band style of The New Lost City Ramblers. TV was another new medium to give impetus to old music, with *The Wilburn Brothers Show* presenting the former child singers performing gospel and traditional songs, and Porter Wagoner on his rival show, and in his Nudie Cohen suit, presenting Mack Magaha's old-time fiddling and a young Dolly Parton. The show was sponsored by the Chattanooga Medicine Company, maker of Wine Of Cardui, for "women's complaints".

A weird hybrid of blues and old-style country surfaced in England under the term "skiffle", first as an offshoot of the Ken Colyer group. Sessions recorded between 1954 and 1957 feature Alexis Korner on some tracks, Ken's brother washboard player Bill Colyer on others, and songs which include folk material like 'Casey Jones' and 'Old Riley'. Resolutely English, it is nevertheless a dream-like recreation of an America that never was, at the same time heartfelt and implausible.

In as early as the late Forties, Colyer had presented skiffle music as part of his nightly history lesson in New Orleans-style jazz. The origins of the music were as a form of busking, or that made by a "bottler", who took the money for entrance to private parties: from the start, it was a communal music; everybody could join in. In 1953, Colyer took on a banjo player called Tony Donegan to perform this set within a set, and Lonnie, as he became, went on to do the same with Chris Barber's Jazz Band, though Colyer beat them to the studio by a couple of weeks. However, it was Donegan's nasal, urgent version of 'Rock Island Line', recorded during 20 minutes of dead studio time, that hit the charts, as he injected a new exuberance, even a sense of danger, which made Alan Clayson seriously compare his stage act to Jimi Hendrix, "generating a sweaty, exhilarating intensity never before experienced in British pop".

Donegan's repertoire reflects the kinds of discs brought back by merchant sailors like the young Tommy Steele, everything from Woody Guthrie and Leadbelly songs to slave hollers and British folksong bounced back from the Appalachians, from the 'Cumberland Gap' to the 'Wreck Of The Old 97'. Billy Bragg, no less, later describes the skiffle craze as a forerunner of punk, and part of a DIY ethic which still applies to dance-music pioneers who put together computer programmes in their bedrooms: "It seems to me that skiffle was the first genuine teenage cultural manifestations in this country." The Beatles met while playing skiffle, in The Quarrymen, as did The Rolling Stones and Led Zeppelin. "It's a totally derided form of music today, but was actually a reaction to trad jazz. People in Britain didn't meet Americans, there wasn't the cosmopolitan culture we have today." It was also a political music, tied in with the "ban the bomb" marches on Aldermaston.

For Bragg, watching kids of your own age "playing fast music on acoustic instruments was as revolutionary as me seeing The Clash at their peak. It was fucking revolutionary." Having myself seen The Clash in 1977, and noting the gap between their magnificent stage gestures and pitiful music, I'm sure it was more exciting than that. Mind you, Joe Strummer did emerge from a better band, the far rootsier 101ers. I have a 1959 78rpm single of Lonnie Donegan's version of 'The Battle Of New Orleans', "trad arr Jimmie Driftwood" and published by Acuff-Rose, more mainstream country than whom you cannot get. On the back sleeve, Parlophone trumpet discs from Eve Boswell to "Jimmy Shand's Party", but set among them is an EP by The Vipers Skiffle Group, one track of which is archetypal: 'Don't You Rock Me, Daddy-O'. Now, I'd love to hear Doc Watson sing that! Some of the early skifflers went into pop, some (like Wally Whyton of The Vipers) into country, and some (like The Spinners) into traditional folk, as did weightier figures like Martin Carthy, a man fully aware of the Appalachian dimension.

Carthy joined the likes of Ewan MacColl and AL Lloyd in a new rash of folk clubs opening up in Edinburgh – birthplace of The Incredible String Band – and London, often open through the night and often underground, both literally and figuratively. These clubs played host to visiting American performers like Tom Paley, Paul Simon and Bob Dylan, and in them traditional music met drug-fuelled contemporary folk, and the results exploded the known musical world, influencing everyone from The Beatles to Jimmy Page. There were firm transatlantic links between this scene and the parallel one in Greenwich Village, the coffee houses of which acted as playpens where the likes of The Fugs, The Holy Modal Rounders and similarly weird acid-fuelled acts took mountain music to Mars and back.

Technically speaking, Harry Smith was the producer of The Fugs' first album, *The Village Fugs – Ballads Of Contemporary Protest, Points Of View And General Dissatisfaction*, which is best described as wild drugged men with beards running amok in a studio, bashing a few instruments on the way. One listen is great; a second is redundant. Smith's contribution was simply to be there, the guardian spirit of this collage of weird sounds, plus also to smash a wine bottle against the wall on 'Nothing'. British beat poet Mike Horovitz later picked out Ed Sanders' "ecstatic hillbilly falsetto", although to be accurate the music only gets countrified – indeed only gets musical – on the band's later records for Rounder. Sanders' two volumes of short stories, *Tales Of Beatnik Glory*, are a wonderful picture of lowlife on the Lower East Side, The Fugs' natural habitat: disease and drugs and bad rock 'n' roll.

It was also the chosen haunt of Guthrie and Pete Seeger, who lived on East Tenth Street, and the natural habitat for the coffee-house scene, where old-time music was given artificial resuscitation, with not a mountain in sight.

Fugs 4 is a collaboration with the Holy Modal Rounders, a duo of Steve Weber and Peter Stampfel who suddenly came up with the idea in 1963 of "combining Harry Smith *Anthology*-era music and rock 'n' roll – the basis of much of the music I've been doing ever since". Stampfel started playing banjo in 1958, and learned fiddle by playing along with the *Anthology* (although some listeners reckon that he needs more lessons, but he certainly gives his all), and found that, while "post-bluegrass fiddlers tend to sound similar, these guys sound like they come from different planets". Like Dylan, he put new words to these old songs, and thus taught himself songwriting. Unlike Dylan, he stopped right there.

Stampfel's note to "Long John" says everything you need to know about the oral tradition: "It evolved in the usual way – hear song, forget song, try to remember song while adding your personal wrinkles, bingo! New version."

The Rounders, too, set a flame burning. When Ian Anderson reviewed *Too Much Fun*, their Nineties reunion CD, he describes the duo – whose name was misheard by a stoned friend after they had decided on the 'Total Modal Rounders' – as being the "ancestors of alt country, though they made most of the current crowd sound "like wet fart painty-waist wimps", and Stampfel's highly individual "yelping wall of a voice" was like the "bastard offspring" of Charlie Poole and the Larry The Lamb bleat of English folksinger Peter Bellamy. This is certainly not the kind of music which you can put on in the background and forget, although compared with the Fugs it's Beethoven.

No Depression, no less, reckoned that their early albums used the *Anthology* as "a roadmap to a shadowland, leaving our heroes free to explore long-forgotten, mouldy corridors and dirt paths, heedless of place and time". On The Rounders' 1964 debut album, Stampfel cites his influences as "Grandpa Jones, Charlie Poole, Little Richard, The New Lost City Ramblers, Robert Graves, Lenny Bruce, Donald Duck, various roots and herbs", and that mix of old country, humour and mind-expanding drugs neatly describes his music. It's also a masterpiece, with Harry Smith staples like 'The Cuckoo' rewritten to accentuate Stampfel's zen wisdom. In the sleeve notes, he writes: "This song is very old. It's about everything." The standard words gradually mutate into a personal observation about Peter and his woman moving to the mountains to die together, then the general observation that "some times I wonder what makes women love men/then I look back and I wonder what makes men love them". It's a bold move, to put your own personal mark on the tradition, and only a man as deeply-learned and chemically-altered as Stampfel can pull it off.

The trick is to get the music right first, and the combination of harshly-played banjo – it hurts your ears to hear it – and strangled, ominous vocals could be straight out of a mountain holler. 'Blues In The Bottle' was later reduced to sanity by The Lovin' Spoonful, but the original almost falls to bits as you listen, then unleashes words like "rooster chews tobacco/and then the hen uses snuff", which leaves you just sitting there, speechless. 'Same Old Man' relocates 'Leatherwing Bat' to contemporary New York, 'Hesitation Blues' mutates into a discussion of the "psychedelic blues", while 'Mr Space Man' rewrites 'Mr Bass Man', and pre-dates The Byrds: "How do we end?" "Like this?" *Clunk*. "Gee, Captain". All good, mad fun, but the smile drops when you hear Stampfel point out that, the day after they ended recording this life-enhancing stuff, Kennedy was shot dead and euphoria would never be quite the same again.

After a second album – which reprised Uncle Dave Macon's 'Old Plank Road' so that the vow "I'll never get drunk no more" is sung over a barely-suppressed chuckle, and which took on Bill Monroe's 'Hot Corn, Cold Corn' and wrestled it to a draw – the band temporarily split up, and were never quite as simple again. *The Moray Eels Eat The Holy Modal Rounders* was a college favourite of mine, in that at first I simply could not believe that any serious record company – let alone Elektra, at the height of their powers – could have actually released it, and then its dissonant madness was embedded deep inside me, like a hook. It's as if the first two acoustic albums are spiralling from eccentricity into downright madness. 'Bird Song' turned up on the soundtrack of *Easy Rider*, and was just right in that context. Stampfel sounds dangerously unhinged, and there's an edge of danger behind the exuberance. The song's middle section is not so much deliberately archaic as plain out of tune. Only in 1969 could an album contain tracks like 'My Mind Capsized'. Skip Spence's material will be covered later.

This kind of stuff – in particular their almost unlistenable concept album *Indian War Whoop* – sounded appallingly dated for a decade or so, but has now snapped into focus as a kind of musical test tube, which could only have happened in the 1960s, and which no one would dare now but which nonetheless has a period charm – just like the Harry Smith *Anthology*, in fact. As Stampfel puts it, the Rounders were "the first really bent traditional band. And the first traditionally-based band who were not trying to sound like an old record." Here lies The Holy Modal Rounders' greatest legacy: that they set other musicians free to use this old music as building blocks for something else.

The Youngbloods, a tough New York inner-city country band, recorded their own version of 'Euphoria', and then moved to California to follow the lifestyle hymned therein. The looser combo that resulted jammed wonderfully on 'Give A Fiddler A Dram', here "learned from the Folkways album *Mountain Music Of Kentucky*". The Rounders recorded the album *Good Taste Is Timeless In Nashville*, but the thrill had gone. Stampfel continues to sporadically record his strange vision, and he remains an antidote to those who try to reproduce mountain music too solemnly, as he himself once had: "I mean, a lot of this music was not serious, you know? Besides the murdered-girl songs and the tragic ballads, all the music was quite light-hearted. And I felt that I was being true to the tradition of music being fun."

The banjo player Luke Faust first emerged at the Washington Square in Greenwich Village, alongside two old-music pioneers already mentioned, Tom Paley and Eric Weissberg, along with Paul Clayton, whose 1956 LP *Bloody Ballads: Classic British And American Murder Ballads* was perhaps an unconscious influence on Nick Cave, and features a blood stain on the front cover which, like Mr Potato Head, has been converted into a cartoon face, on which the two "o"s in "bloody" have become its eyes. Luke Faust is also credited for "banjo accompaniments and all" on two traditional songs recorded by Dave Van Ronk. Faust was part of The Insect Trust, a strange New York electric band who have much of the full-hearted sound – and combination of woodwind and driving bass – of early Fairport. The late, lamented *Strange Things* magazine described them as "the missing link between the Shetland fiddlers and Appalachian hillbillies". Certainly 'Foggy River Bridge Fly', with its bowed violin and answering banjo phrases – though not overstaying its welcome on their debut album – combines those two. 'Mountain Song' adds an Eastern influence to banjo heroics and a plaintive song from the Appalachians.

The Insect Trust's guitarist, Bill Barth, also worked with John Fahey, with whom he was responsible for the rediscovery of blues legend Skip James. Fahey himself, who writes so brilliantly about the *Anthology*, holds a PhD in American music and folklore. His early phase as a "hillbilly" came to an abrupt halt when he heard Blind Willie Johnson playing and discovered the blues, so much so that early albums were released under the persona "Blind Joe Death", in much the same spirit as Harry Smith's concealing of the racial origins of his chosen singers.

On the sleeve notes to the reissue of the two versions of *Blind Joe Death* on CD (Fahey is an inveterate tinkerer with earlier albums), Glenn Jones writes of the "joy in sorrow" which characterises his work, not that far away from the high, lonesome sound. However authentic his sources, from the start Fahey was composing extended works for guitar which develop their own logic, as do their titles – let's hear it for 'Revelation On The Banks Of The Pawtuxent'. He has since pursued that same idea with full orchestras and sound collages, but many of us prefer his guitar playing undiluted. He, or course, disowns it.

Played solo, on a tune like 'The Yellow Princess', his steel strings can take a listener into realms of sheer narrative mystery which I can only compare with Martin Hayes at the current moment, and with him it is a matter of tone while for Fahey the tunes themselves are new but oddly familiar, a development of the tradition. The same old story.

The original notes to *Blind Joe Death* are a delight in themselves, with a biography and discography of the non-existent blues man, a prose account of a meeting with a devil woman, and notes to the effect that one song was written "in a fit of optimism which he later regretted" and another is "an attempt to reconstruct an old song from three lines imperfectly remembered by an old peasant woman in Sligo, who often sings them to herself". They comprise "Every hand is lunatic that travels on the moon." The three-minute tune drawn from this *does* have a kind of Celtic chording, and a particularly insistent lead line, but that's it. Otherwise, here among self-compositions like 'The Transcendental Waterfall' (a "ballet") is Fahey's usual slow, percussively-played mixture of blues tunes, non-conformist hymns from the Bible belt, Sacred Harp titles and versions of 'John Henry' and other traditional songs.

In a note on his sources, he writes of a debt to The Carter Family and the *Episcopal Hymnal*, plus of course the Harry Smith "miracle", which "justifies, by itself, the existence of Folkways". When I saw Fahey live, 30 or so years ago, he seemed to be moving and talking at half speed – while on the same bill was Nick Drake, who simply didn't seem to be there at all – but playing three guitars at once. Oh, those glorious Sixties. He started his adult life on field trips buying old "hillbilly" records from poor black folk, then played briefly with Canned Heat, and later founded his own record company, Takoma. More recently, his label Revenant has seen a steady trickle of re-releases of archive material, like that recorded by The Stanley Brothers, which "vividly recast the past, not as nostalgia but as American Primitive or Raw Music". Harry Smith lives.

Fahey recently revealed to *Wire* that a lot of his pyschological problems stemmed from sexual abuse by his father. This explains the turtle motif which echoes through-out his work. It's not some ecological message, as people like me formerly thought, but part of a personal mythology which built on his memory of a box turtle he saw at the age of five, and "I saw what I thought was a penis walking across the lawn". Heavy stuff – no wonder he finds the old hymns so comforting. "I play the best when my unconscious is altered", he reckons, and has now abandoned the acoustic guitar for the electric version. Ditto all his earlier music.

Whatever he might think of it now, Fahey's conceptual masterpiece remains *America*, augmented on CD to its original double LP length, but still with a dying tur-tle and poisoned fish on the cover. His native land is polluted, so he goes back in time to the country blues, to sacred songs like 'Amazing Grace' and Fahey's own 'Jesus Is A Dying Bedmaker', via Charlie Patton, plus the 14-minute instrumental 'Mark 1.15': "The time is fulfilled, and the kingdom of God is at hand." He was right all along: in his mixture of religious dread and the transcendental, Fahey is the near-est thing contemporary music has to a hillbilly, albeit one with a PhD.

Another guitarist with pretensions – although in his case they often stayed just that – was Sandy Bull, who made three solo, multidubbed albums for Vanguard in the 1960s which are virtually a blueprint for world music. On them he plays guitar, oud, bass and banjo, the last from seeing Mike Seeger play. "I liked the sound and idea of a long-neck banjo", and he ended up taking lessons from Eric Darling, of The Weavers. "Then I discovered the oud and didn't play the banjo again for about

20 years." If this sounds a strange decision, it is largely due to Pete Seeger, who acted as a catalyst towards musicians discovering other cultures, and the links between them. "I was playing banjo and guitar almost exclusively in my early years, so I played the mountain and modal stuff, and I saw the similarities between that and Indian and Afghani music."

Bull played Greenwich Village with a young Joan Baez, and recorded his debut album in 1963, *Fantasias For Guitar And Banjo*, which still sparkles: the 22-minute track 'Blend' carries out the Arab-bluegrass fusion he talked about, but it and its two equally listenable successors, *Inventions* and *E Pluribus Unum*, are still largely Bull playing with himself, in every sense. Somehow these records lack the inner discipline of Fahey, the ability to make something new from such fusions. It's the difference between an historical curiosity, which these three albums are – going for high prices, collected by sad people like me – and music which remains on the cultural agenda in its own right and clutters the re-release racks, like Fahey's.

It's almost a matter of personal arrogance, this practice of taking sources and then casting them away when you've extracted the nourishment you need and you've remade the music in your own images. We'll deal with The Mekons later. Meanwhile, Sandy's growing drug problems darken 1972's *Demolition Derby*, my own personal favourite, with its haunting cross-currents of Latin sounds and straight country – Floyd Cramer and 'Tennessee Waltz'. Bull joined the 'Rolling Thunder' tour and gradually came back into the world, continuing to plunder it musically. The soul covers of 1996's *Steel Tears* won him a nomination in Nashville for Best Folk CD. It's all a long way from those early banjo lessons.

That said, it was country blues rather than country music which became the ethnic music of choice amongst Greenwich Village folkniks, with pioneer acoustic acts like Koerner, Ray and Glover, whose work now sounds impossibly dated . The best recorded history of this brief fashion is the Elektra box set *Crossroads: White Blues In The 1960s*, which points out that "Spider" John Koerner was also schooled in "Anglo-American balladry", and this comes more to the fore in *Running Jumping Standing Still*, his messy (but fun) album with an electric band featuring John Wilce on banjo and mandolin, laid down in Elektra's lodge-cum-recording-studio on California's Feather River.

The same company promised a matching box set to *Crossroads, O Love Is Teasin': Anglo American Mountain Balladry*, but if it came out at all I've never seen it. Brian Hogg is a great rock archivist, so it should come as no surprise that he put together the definitive compilation of early-Sixties acoustic troubadours in *Blues In The Bottle*, which crosses over into Appalachian territory and smashes through musical categories with the Scots' usual élan. Traditional folk meets the blues on equal terms here, as it did in "folknic Bohemia", so that Tom Rush is represented by 'Barbry Allen' – as melancholic as it is mellifluous – and 'Baby Please Don't Go', and Dave Van Ronk by a passionate 'The House Carpenter' and 'Death Letter Blues'.

John Sebastian was actually brought up in Greenwich Village, and his father, a classical harmonica player, introduced him to the blues: he also played with Doc Watson before joining The Even Dozen jug band (folk music you could dance to) and then forming The Lovin' Spoonful. His manager, Erik Jacobsen – himself a five-string banjo-playing folkie in the bluegrass style – reckoned that John was the "folk musician who got to the electric guitar first". Jacobsen went on to extract country flavours from his other charges, The Sopwith Camel, Tim Hardin and Norman Greenbaum. Peter Stampfel wrote the liner notes to The Spoonful's first album as deliberately nonsense: "stiffness is dissolving". Their sound was a lovely mixture of blues and folk with a country tinge and English affectations, with electric autoharp wisps (rocking up The Carters) over a solid beat.

There's something wistful about Sebastian's persona, a man who sings with a smile in his voice and then turns on the sudden desperation of 'Darling, Be Home Soon'. You can even forgive him singing about "those yellow Sun records" from Nashville, in that definitive song about session men in Tennessee, 'Nashville Cats'. Country pickers "play clean as country water/play wild as mountain dew", but there is a certain sarcasm here, not least in Sebastian's deliberate hick accent and tangled grammar: "play twice as better than I will". Is that final line about being "glad to say a word about the music and the mothers from Nashville" a carefully-veiled and extremely rude insult?

The band tick like a grandfather clock or a Johnny Cash jogtrot, and the wonderfully eccentric Zal Yakonovsky – who reconnoitred with Sebastian to great effect at the 1970 Isle Of Wight Festival – shows off at the end. Sebastian turned down an invitation to join Crosby, Stills And Young (as their drummer), proved to be the saviour of Woodstock, drifted for years, and recently returned to his jug-band roots with The J-Band, still messing blues and folk together. "Okay, there may be a few guys who are record collectors and live in their mom's house and stay in the basement and play their records, and go 'You know, that was more of a North Carolina thing that you did, instead of a Memphis piece of music', and you go, 'Hey, I don't really care.'"

Chapter Five

Country Outlaws

Rusty Evans is one of the folk troubadours who has fallen by the wayside, but his 1962 album *Songs Of Our Land*, full of such Americana as 'Sloop John B' and 'Ox Driver's Song', states, tongue in cheek, that he is "a native of that community richest of all in folklore – Brooklyn".

It was a process of remaking. Happy Traum admits that "it was like a clique in Greenwich Village...we all left our neighbourhoods and gravitated towards Manhattan, and formed the nucleus of a folk revival in America". His own grandparents were German Jews on one side, English and Dutch on the other, but "most of the immigrants, let's say in the early 1900s, really tried very hard to lose the European background and become Americanised". He had no inclination to play the music of his ancestors, rather "we looked into blues and mountain music and cowboy songs and found in that a way of expressing ourselves". This, really, is this book's theme.

Of course, there were some genuine performers around, none more so than Jean Ritchie, as illustrated back in chapter two. Jean's family had been visited by Cecil Sharp in 1917, and her father taught her to play the dulcimer. Representing the public face of mountain music, she took a degree in social work and then moved to New York, where she was recorded by Alan Lomax. A Fullbright scholarship to Europe enabled her to trace the British origins of much of her repertoire. She even sang at Cecil Sharp House, in a neat case of cultural reversal. Her 1962 album *Jean Ritchie Singing Traditional Songs Of Her Kentucky Mountain Family* was the first folk album to be released by Elektra, and she has recorded and published multiple volumes of Child ballads and dulcimer tunes.

My own favourite of her many albums is 1977's *None But One*, which sees her paired with a rock band (really stretching out the title track) led by mountain dulcimer. The cover is a wraparound which blends an old photo of the annual Hall family reunion in 1928 with one of Jean in the studio with some longhairs. "Looking at the circle we all make, the stream of humanity, I take comfort in the thought that my ancestors are still present in myself...and that I shall be present in my own descendants when my body has worn out and moved on."

She comes over like the musical equivalent of Sharyn McCrumb, a wise old woman of the hills whose clear, youthful voice can span the maudlin sentiment of 'The Orphan's Lament', the ancient riddles of 'Nottamun Town' and her own, deeply savage 'Black Waters', about the mining of her homeland. She sings it almost tenderly, but the words cut deep: "Then they threw down my mountain and covered my corn/and the grave on the hillside's a mile deeper down." 'Wondrous Love' has some equally wondrous choral singing.

When another young folk singer first appeared in New York, blowing in seemingly from nowhere with the wind, some recognised Bob Dylan as an amalgam of Dock Boggs, Woody Guthrie, Rabbit Brown, Hank Williams and just about every American roots singer, mixing blues and folk and country into one ragged voice and songbag. Onstage, he had the charm and pathos of another small man, Charlie Chaplin. However, there was no great sense that he was any good as a songwriter, except as yet another Guthrie copyist.

Peter Stampfel told the *Rough Guide* that Dylan started his career as a songwriter just as Woody had, putting new words to old songs, and "he made up a whole bunch of songs to tunes on Harry Smith's *Anthology* just as a way of teaching himself to write songs". Others, watching the way he just seemed to pluck these songs out of the air, suddenly began to follow suit: before Dylan, only Tom Paxton and Pete Seeger were writing their own material. Another spur to creation was, as Stampfel earlier told *Zigzag*, "the time of the crystal. Hallucinogens had just cracked on the scene." Smith himself had released an album of peyote rituals, and suddenly peyote and LSD were openly advertised, and still legal.

Dylan arrived at much the same time, the summer of 1961, as did Ramblin' Jack Elliott. Fred Neil and Dino Valente were already on the scene, as was Luke Faust, later of The Insect Trust, "the first person from the city who sounded as if he was from the country". Stampfel first saw Dylan in a coffee house "that changed its name from The Commons to The Fat Black Pussycat to The Feenjon…he had this punk motorcycle hat" and looked much as he did on his first album cover, baby-faced, quizzical, and with pixie ears.

At Gerdes Folk City, Dylan started his set with "a fiddly banjo-type tune called 'Sally Ann', which just about took the top of my head off". His repertoire was still entirely traditional, "but his singing style and phrasing were stone rhythm and blues". This 20-year-old acoustic guitar playing singer of country blues and Appalachian ballads had already put folk and rock music together, five years before being booed off stages around the world for his pains. "The main thing about Dylan was that he was the first person who really knew traditional stuff, whose phrasing was rock 'n' roll". After him, the deluge.

Up to that point, rock music and folk music were "two separate, never-the-twain-shall-meet forms. And Dylan put them together where they obviously belonged. It was an epiphany." The rest of this chapter will trace what kind of musical explosion this spark set off. Meanwhile, back at The Gaslight, Dylan, Jim Kweskin and Stampfel all played residencies for a pittance, and other regulars there included Sandy Bull, Luke Faust, Jack Elliott and Ian And Sylvia. The summer of '62 saw John Sebastian and Phil Ochs at the Nite Owl, and lots of ladies of the night: "it was pretty hip to know a lot of hookers".

Happy Traum jammed on banjo with Dylan on guitar and vocals at Gil Turner's house, now widely bootlegged as the "banjo tape", which gives a valuable insight into the musical climate of the time: open, unsuspicious, and with lots of spontaneity. "It was just like throwing song titles around. It was very loose the way it is when people swap songs, drinking wine or whatever." Nobody knew then that, 40 years on, these things would still be of interest: "When I think of all the money I could have made if I'd taped conversations and followed him around, picked up his turds or whatever..."

Back in Minneapolis, a couple of years earlier, Dylan's repertoire was a mixture of blues, Woody Guthrie songs and traditional ballads straight from the Appalachians. A boy with the voice of an impossibly sick and weary old man gives us 'Wild Mountain Thyme' – "this is a Texas song I learned from Woody Guthrie". He laughs half-way through, then gives a performance which is half heartfelt, as if in a dream, and half self-parody, with rolled country "r"s. He also takes on 'Pretty Polly', which he personalises: "I used to be a rambler, I rambled all around." The trademark laugh and words cut short suggest a mountain retard.

It is brilliant, totally assured in a way that only the young and extremely talented can be, driven along by an urgently-strummed guitar and a tension in Dylan's voice, whereas 'A Long Time Growing' is hushed, reverential, and the song's narrator is reincarnated by Dylan, who acts out her anguish and anger along with her father's soothing retorts. If this music is still technically illegal then it's a disgrace. The official bootleg series, important as it was, barely scratches the surface.

'I Was Young When I Left Home' is also carefully annotated as traditional, but it is from a different musical universe than the three ballads just discussed: "It must be good for somebody, this song. If not for me, it must be good for somebody." What we get is a song about being on the road – which Dylan indeed is soon to do, abandoning his family, his creature comforts, even his name – which aches and throbs and moans, with Dylan's assumed Okie accent a mask through which the callow Jewish middle-class youth can transform himself into anything he wants to be, a bereaved English lady or a tramp on the street. Dylan's voice is rapt, hypnotised almost, and you feel that, to stop him singing, you'd have to break his fingers and gag his throat, but even that might not be quite enough. It's also beautifully recorded, by whomever was sensible to get this down, with lots of presence and the guitar much more full-bodied than the over-polite first album.

Bob strays outside his Guthrie fixation – which spans sixteen songs over three CDs – and the blues masters to attempt a slurred take on the first verse or so of The

Carter Family's 'Will The Circle Be Unbroken?', and give us a percussive but yearning 'Dink's Song', which was written by Alan Lomax and his father: "I heard that from a lady called Dink. I don't know who wrote it." The same Alan Lomax who later tried to pull the plugs at Newport in 1965, that's who, Bob.

Dylan – a name which some say comes from Matt Dillon, the TV cowboy – is like a young contender trying the whole musical fabric of the American people on for size. No one since – until Beck, perhaps – has dared as much, or moved on so quickly. But Beck is always tongue in cheek and self-regarding, whereas the singer here seems unafraid to give himself up to his material, like Orpheus to the pursuing horde of women bent on pulling him apart. The only artist I can think of who I've seen invest this level of passion and commitment was Jeff Buckley, and look what happened to him. Most artists know where to stop; the great ones just keep going, and that way lies madness, early death or, at the very least, riding your motorbike off into the dust.

Dylan has been compared at this time to a sponge, soaking up songs and accents, performing other men's styles and repertoires, and then squeezing them out in his own image. Bob certainly knew the Harry Smith *Anthology*, and performed songs from it, like 'Ommie Wise', 'The House Carpenter' and 'See That My Grave Is Kept Clean', which concludes his debut album. More importantly, he used it as a picture-book of images, so that songs like 'Down On Penny's Farm' could detonate his imagination.

They have often been quoted, but Dylan's views on the folk tradition are so germane to this book that they deserve repetition. He gave them in 1966, at the height of his own surrealistic weirdness, and they pre-date the stranger disjunctions that characterise *The Basement Tapes*.

> "Folk music is the only music where it isn't simple. It's weird...I've never written anything hard to understand, not in my head anyway, and nothing as far out as some of the old songs. Traditional music is based on hexagrams. It comes about from legends, Bibles, plagues, and it revolves around vegetables and death. There's nobody that's going to kill traditional music. All those songs about roses growing out of peoples' brains and lovers who are really geese and swans that turn into angels – they're not going to die. It's all those paranoid people who think that someone's going to come and take away their toilet paper – they're going to die. Traditional music is too unreal to die. It doesn't need to be protected. Nobody's going to hurt it. In that, music is the only true, valid death you can feel today off a record player".

He could have been talking about Dock Boggs. He could have been talking about himself. The same truth is put more wittily – and nastily – in the famous confrontation with his Scottish copyist, Donovan, who puts his own head in an open noose when he put new lyrics to a tune extremely close to 'Mr Tambourine Man', which Dylan immediately recognises.

"You know," says Dylan, "I haven't always been accused of writing my own songs. But that's one I did write."

"I didn't know, man. Thought maybe it was an old folk-song."

"No, it's not an old folk song yet".

Dylan put the process in reverse when he took the structure of 'Lord Randall' and changed the question-and-answer pattern from the murder of a son to the potential murder of the whole human race by nuclear warfare in 'A Hard Rain's A-Gonna Fall'.

Matthew Zuckerman pulled together the "folk roots of Bob Dylan" in a still-continuing series for the fanzine *Isis*, which is essential reading for its bootleg reviews alone. Zuckerman talked to Martin Carthy, who still smarts at the way Paul Simon copyrighted 'Scarborough Fair' to himself after having learned it bar by bar from him, but has no problems with Dylan's appropriations. Dylan had met Carthy while filming a play for BBC TV, and also learned 'Scarborough Fair' at Martin's feet, but in the fire of his imagination Dylan retooled it as 'Girl From The North Country'. For Carthy, "that was completely different, completely legitimate. Bob never hid anything. And he made his own song from it. That's what folk music is all about." The heartbreaking line "she once was a true love of mine" comes from another traditional song, 'The Elfin Knight', though it's impossible to ascertain on what side of the Atlantic Dylan first encountered the song.

The roll call continues: 'Ramblin' Gamblin' Willie' comes from 'Brennan On The Moor', about two lovable rogues, one a highwayman and the other a gambler; 'Nottamun Town' mutates into 'Masters Of War', despite legal action from Jean Ritchie (but then, who can copyright a folk song, and what is presumably Nottingham Town is certainly not in Kentucky); 'Lord Franklin' – a Carthy show-stopper – became 'Bob Dylan's Dream'; and 'Percy's Song' incorporates and refers to the traditional tune 'Wind And The Rain', learned from Paul Clayton.

Clayton himself took the song from the autoharp player Kilby Snow, whose versions appeared on a Folkways album. Dylan simply joined the chain. By a kind of back projection, as a teenage hippie I was turned on to Carthy's early albums with Dave Swarbrick – which are full of long and sometimes unaccompanied traditional ballads – precisely because I recognised so many of the tunes and, unlike Jean Ritchie, say, I found myself in tune with Carthy's urgent, austere vocals. I didn't know then that the king of the English folk revival was also a rock 'n' roller at heart, and that his all-time favourite LP was *The Brown Album* by The Band. By 1971, Carthy was playing electric guitar with Steeleye Span.

Zuckerman quotes William Blake on the nature of artistic influence ("The bad artist seems to copy a great deal. The good one really does copy a great deal"), and then Dylan from 1997. When he was young, he wanted to achieve something that nobody had before, and better. It led him to folk music, "at a time when it was totally off the radar screen". There were probably only a dozen or so people of his own age who had even heard of Woody Guthrie, Roscoe Holcomb or The Carter Family: "They were free spirits who took chances, and I never wished to annul any of that spirit." Bob duetted with Ralph Stanley, another such artist, on 'The Lonesome River', which Dylan claimed was the high point of his career that far. 'Ballad Of Hollis Brown' takes its tune from 'Pretty Polly', as performed by Dylan back in Minnesota, and probably learnt from The Stanley Brothers, who in turn learnt it from their father. As to Lunsford, his rendition of 'I Wish I Was A Mole In The Ground' appeared on the Harry Smith *Anthology*. The line about a railroad man who "can drink up your blood like wine" was recycled by Dylan in 'Stuck Inside Of Mobile' on *Blonde On Blonde*.

We are getting ahead of the story, though. I am now entering the tangled thickets of Dylanology, fiercely guarded by self-appointed guardians of the flame, spitting vitriol worthy of The Master in his 'Positively Fourth Street' phase. Taking the meticulous Clinton Heylin's *Dylan, Behind Closed Doors* as my guide, I shall venture there regardless. The Minnesota tapes were almost certainly laid down in Bonnie Beecher's apartment during two private concerts in 1961. They are preceded by a set taped in the previous year in St Paul, which remains about as inaccessible as the holy grail, with chance sightings – or, in this case, hearings – rare enough to keep people hopeful. Heylin reckons that what has emerged sounds "sweet and pretty", and is sung in a voice which would not reappear in public until *Nashville Skyline*. It must have felt like going home.

Traditional songs present in 1960 include 'The Two Sisters', 'Mule Skinner Blues' and 'Who's Gonna Shoe Your Pretty Feet?', all taken from the Lomax anthology and part of an imaginary immersion in the pioneer spirit, alongside Dylan's highly-exaggerated stories about running away from home to join a travelling fairground and playing piano with Bobby Vee. This from a youth who had started off doing Little Richard imitations with his school rock band, and then steeped himself in hillbilly 78s from the collection of Echo Helstrom's mother ("old cowboy songs"), with a special liking for Hank Snow. Anthony Scaduto reports that Dylan and his friend John Buckland would even take "a lot of straight songs and do them hillbilly style, like 'Somewhere Over The Rainbow'. These two guys would just start pick-picking on their guitars and off they'd go like a couple of mountain boys." By 1960, though, he was the "purest of the pure" in his search for traditional sources.

By February 1961, on a tape laid down at the home of the Gleasons, 'Remember Me (When The Candle Lights Are Gleaming)' is pure country corn, sung again in a voice close to that on *Nashville Skyline*, recorded eight years later, after he had changed popular music forever.

In November of that year, the boy still widely nicknamed "John Hammond's

Folly" entered the Columbia recording studios to lay down his first album. Stacey Williams' erudite sleeve notes present him as a performer steeped in folk and the blues, as well as with a massive fixation with dying young. 'Man of Constant Sorrow' is "a traditional Southern mountain folk song...probably never sung quite in this fashion before". Dylan gets deep inside the song and its noble self-pity, elongating notes both with his voice and on his harmonica to suggest the length of time in this wicked world he has left to suffer.

"A traditional Scottish song is the bare bones on which Dylan hangs 'Pretty Peggy-O,'" but in its move westward "the song has lost its burr and acquired a Texas accent, and a few new words and fillips by the singer". This doesn't catch the exuberance which Dylan brings to this hoary song, or his dismissive introduction: "I've been around this whole country, but I've never yet found Fennario." He whips up a party on his guitar and harmonica, laughing and whooping in sheer joy (it's almost a yodel) and reducing the original to matchwood, so that the lieutenant is now "riding down to Texas in the rodeo".

The country influences continue, with 'Highway 51' "of a type sung by the Everly Brothers" (though Dylan sings it like a black singer) and 'Freight Train Blues' "adapted from an old disc by Roy Acuff". Dylan's frantic rendition is close to skiffle, and he scrubs his guitar like a washboard while stretching the word "blues" out to infinity, like a train whistle heard out on the prairie. The sound in the distance is Jimmie Rodgers applauding.

Among the outtakes, with a matter-of-fact "Here's a story about a ghost come out of the sea", Dylan dives into a brisk 'House Carpenter', a song as old as time, and as scary:

"What are those hills as dark as night?
"Those are the hills of hellfire, my love,
"Where you and I will unite."

This is the song which led Heylin on a two-year search through its back pages, finding source material on both sides of the Atlantic but never quite where Dylan put together this version. In his own mind, perhaps.

In March 1962, Dylan appeared on Cynthia Gooding's radio show and lied through his teeth: "I used to travel with the carnival" – for six years, apparently, on and off. "I was the clean-up boy." But Cynthia probes him as to quite how he fitted this in with school, and he replies evasively "I didn't go to school a bunch of years. I came out even." This must be news to his mother. He is on safer ground with a slow burn through the traditional song 'Long John', though: "I learned this from Ralph Rinzler", he says, but then admits to adding "one or two verses...the rest just fell together". He also admits to an early repertoire of Johnny Cash and Hank Williams songs, including 'Lonesome Whistle Blues', with a mournful but somehow exuberant version of which he opens. This is the secret of the young Dylan, singing songs of melancholy and death, but with a massive life force coursing through. As to his current repertoire, taped to his guitar, "I copied the best songs I could find."

Youthful talent will out, and the ruling deities of the folk scene vied to promote, play alongside or bed the newest kid on the block. Joan Baez did all three, bringing her "little vagabond" Bob Dylan with her to concerts and then feeling – and singing and writing and talking about – a huge sense of betrayal when he moved on, as young men must.

For Robert Cantwell, folk song revivalists before Baez divided along lines of gender, "one that thrust the work songs, chants and blues of the levee, prison and juke joint, or the complex techniques of bluegrass, in the masculine sphere, with the 'remorseless authority' of such concern to patriarchy". Ballads and the spiritual realm were left for women. Joan's early repertoire of Appalachian ballads – "utterly pure, nearly sacrosanct folk songs", as the 1959 Newport Folk Festival programme put it – had her new fans see her as some kind of untouchable madonna (a "two-wheel gypsy queen", perhaps): "I looked like purity itself in long tresses, no make-up and Bible sandals."

Baez actually began her musical career playing the ukelele and singing country songs like 'Your Cheating Heart'. Her mother was Scottish, the daughter of an Episcopalian priest, but she was brought up in California rather than Virginia, and her father was Mexican. Joan learned her folk music at Boston University and in the adjacent coffee houses. Her early albums explore her own mixed heritage of British and Spanish traditional ballads, though Vassal points out that she doesn't customise these songs in the true mountain manner but instead prefers "a certain plastic perfection to genuineness". The care with which Baez sings can get right on any listener's nerves, that's for sure, but these performances are not as winsome as Baez later became. They're still too sweet, though.

Each song comes with copious notes by Nat Hentoff – "unlike many city-billies, as Charles Seeger first named the urban singers of folk songs, Miss Baez is not an eclectic." On volume two alone, 'Wagoner's Lad', 'Once I Knew A Pretty Girl' and 'Railroad Boy' are from versions first noted down in the Southern Appalachians. 'Old Blue' is pure Americana, a dog song as later recorded by The Byrds. Baez reaches a note at one point that surely only dogs can hear. 'Pal of Mine' is a song of mixed race, taken from a negro spiritual but "vocally in the Carter Family tradition, instrumentally in the modern 'bluegrass' style". Joan could be Emmylou Harris. The Greenbriar Boys, meanwhile, add authenticity and life, with rippling banjo and a hearty chorus. They do the same on 'Banks Of The Ohio', "a favourite with 'country' singers of several decades ago, and this performance is stylistically a re-creation of their approach". Baez seems to perk up a little as a result.

Baez next recorded two volumes of songs in concert, which see her moving towards performing material from contemporary songwriters, and this material also has much the same effect on me of a dentist revving up his drill, as do the compliant audience. Here too are three songs later rocked up by her contemporaries. 'Babe, I'm Going To Leave You' is an interesting racial hybrid, like Joan herself, "a white blues, a form which was created early in our century by the meeting of the Southern lyric lament (with its ties to the old ballads) and the negro blues" which was later covered by Led Zeppelin on their explosive debut album. Jimmy Page was an old hand at borrowing traditional folk tunes from the likes of Bert Jansch. 'Matty Groves', meanwhile, later became Fairport Convention's theme song, and 'Copper Kettle' was one of the few tracks to rescue Dylan's second-worst album *Self Portrait*. (The worst was its out-takes). It is described here as a "contemporary moonshining song" from Texas. The revenue officers have been having a hard time recently: "With the introduction of the party-line telephone into the hills, the word gets around pretty fast these days."

Whatever purists like me think, it is undeniable that Baez brought Anglo-American folklore to the heartlands of contemporary America. The album *5* is at least eclectic, with The Greenbriar Boys copyrighting 'Stewball' ("an American version of a British broadside ballad of the 19th century") but sadly not present to tone down Baez, by now in full vibrato. She also murders the Johnny Cash song 'I Still Miss Someone', dragging it along slightly too slow and adding unnecessary pathos. When Sandy Denny sang it a few years later, she was brisker and less emotionally self-indulgent, much like Johnny himself. The essence of country music is a tear held manfully (or womanfully) back, not splashing all over the listener.

Farewell Angelina had the immediate benefit of one of Dylan's best early songs, and one which, more to the point, seems to be a kiss-off to Joan herself. It also saw Ralph Rinzler back on mandolin and electric guitar embellishments from Bruce Langhorne, who, if not a Nashville cat, should be; he did exactly the same trick for Dylan. The downside was Baez's own icky sleeve notes: "I have two goats – Daisy and Cassandra...my life is a crystal tear-drop... You, Dear Reader – you are Amazing Grace. You are a Precious Jewel" etc. Even Nashville has never got quite this sickly. On the upside, we have a trio of Dylan songs to start with and Woody Guthrie's 'Rangers' Command', which is based on an Anglo-American ballad. To maintain the balance, 'The River In The Pines', a "traditional American ballad", is matched against the Scottish song 'Will You Go, Laddie, Go'. This is otherwise known as the long-time Dylan favourite 'Wild Mountain Thyme', as performed by him at his comeback gig, the 1969 Isle Of Wight Festival, where he sounds like a (just) slighter deeper-voiced Joan. It's creepy, like trying on an old lover's discarded clothes.

Baez went on to record *Any Day Now*, a whole double album of Dylan covers, with Nashville's finest, having previously made a whole Christmas special with a full orchestra. It's beautifully done, but somehow redundant even before it was laid down on tape. The country tag stuck, and *David's Album* has been described as showing "the most questionable characteristics of country and western", with platitudes rather than songs, and with the inclusion of 'The Green, Green, Grass of Home' – always a touchstone of inauthenticity. The logical extension of all of this was 1973's *Where Are You Now, My Son?*, on side one of which had some extremely palatable C&W versions of songs by Joan herself and Hoyt Axton.

Side two consists of a "ballad" of sound effects, literally without rhyme or reason, laid down by Joan on a portable tape recorder in a bomb-strewn Hanoi, with overdubbed piano and vocal warblings. It is bad beyond belief, and one even wishes that the Vietcong had aimed better. No wonder that the opening song on side one starts with the line "I have lost my way". Actually, Baez sounds very much at home with the country violins, which tone down her solo excesses, and sings deeper from her body and with more personality.

As will become clear, almost every important folk outlaw from the Sixties' folk boom later found temporary or permanent relief in country music, as a kind of numbing device. Looking more closely, of course, mountain music was already embedded deep in their work. It is a source of future consolation, an antiseptic already present in the bloodstream.

Meanwhile, Joan exorcised the demon of Bob Dylan in her song 'Diamonds And Rust', abandoning Nashville for the rock mafia of LA, and even parodying Dylan's voice on the same album. It is fit revenge: Dylan cruelly ignored her in his home movie *Don't Look Back*, then revisited their affair through a hall of mirrors in the completely impenetrable *Renaldo And Clara*, but rejoined her onstage in the accompanying acoustic footage from The Rolling Thunder Review.

Baez recently duetted onstage to the vibrant folk-rock of Eliza Carthy, Martin's daughter. At the Lyric Theatre in Hammersmith, Eliza's rough fiddle playing and spot-on, ice-cold harmonies transformed 'The Night They Drove Old Dixie Down' from the recorded travesty to a genuine lament. It was like a fast-forward trawl through Baez's back pages, from a solo 'House Carpenter' to 'I Dreamed I Saw Joe Hill' and then on to the sweet sadness of 'The Sky In Tennessee'.

They also featured work by some contemporary female country writers whose songs Joan has championed in recent years. Baez jokes about the professionalism of the Nashville scribes, like bespoke tailors, who ask her "what you gonna want, a rhumba, a waltz, a two-step?", so she just takes her poetry in and they make it into a song – "I use the term 'we' very loosely". Next up is one such song, about an old school friend who yodelled, and whose brothers Joan fancied. She has certainly loosened up over the years – the professional virgin has long gone.

For those lucky enough to see it, it was a practical manifestation of the folk tradition being handed down, before of our very eyes. Baez has aged into grace: as *The Guardian* commented, it is difficult to imagine Dylan "inviting Billy Bragg up to share half his set", though he certainly should. Wilco, too.

Judy Collins has followed the same path as Baez, from the purity of traditional folk to country to a sophisticated form of MOR. Trained as a classical pianist and the daughter of a radio executive, the closest she came to the mountain life was spending a summer vacation from college in the Rocky Mountain National Park, "and the sort of homesteading life in which folk music flourishes", with no electricity and baking her own bread – Marie Antoinette tending her sheep. Collins' voice is so rich that many feel the same way about her work, that it's a kind of artistocrat slumming, which isn't helped by a spectacular beauty which had boyfriend Steve Stills write 'Suite – Judy Blue Eyes' for her. When she released her third album in 1963, with Jim McGuinn playing guitar (and including 'Turn, Turn, Turn', with which he hit gold with The Byrds), she was leading the whole pack.

All of this was achieved on Elektra, virtually a one-man label under Jac Holzman, who had started by recording folk singers in his front room and for whom "poetry and music will change the world". His label was poor and flexible enough to take risks which no major company would have taken at the time, and he achieved his aim, first through singer/songwriters Tom Paxton, Phil Ochs and Fred Neil, and then with psychedelia performed by the likes of Love, The Doors and the definitely un-folky Stooges. Like Island in Britain, which was originally a reggae label, Elektra grew out of the genre that originally defined it and stood out in a crowded marketplace through its sleeve designs, its production values, even its logo (although it soon abandoned that of an acoustic-playing folk singer). It exuded the kind of "crystalline clarity", for which Judy's voice is praised on her debut, *A Maid Of Constant Sorrow*.

In this garden of delights, Collins grew from the clear-voiced, undramatic reteller of Appalachian ballads of her first album – a perfect primer for The Byrds and Fairport, who later put drums and bass and electric guitars to, in turn, 'John Riley' and 'Sailor's Life' – to someone who herself incorporated orchestras, country bands and whale songs, and acted as a talent scout for a generation of songwriters. There is a political edge already to Ewan MacColl's modern murder ballad 'Tim Evans' and the IRA sympathies of 'Bold Fenian Men', while Erik Darling's banjo ripples through as one of two "assisting musicians". Even the title song is a feminisation of the old folk song. The sleeve points out how Judy's "sense of the dramatic is always kept within the bounds of impeccable taste". It was to disable her music in the end.

Like Tom Rush, who followed a similar career from trad folk to cover versions and country, Judy was essentially an interpreter, and the work of such usually fades. On her second album, Collins shed the banjo but covered the full range of the folk tradition: a WB Yeats poem, whaling stories, nonsense verse for kids, Irish hymns, gospel spirituals, a Child ballad, one collected by Cecil Sharp, a song from the Polish, and American folklore in 'Fannerio'.

At her best, Judy seems to dream her way through a song, and nowhere better than on *Who Knows Where The Time Goes?*, recorded with a full electric band. 'Pretty Polly' starts as folk ballad and ends as a throbbing blues led by Steve Stills, while Sandy Denny's title song is even slower and more pensive than the original and Judy's own 'My Father' – written as he lay dying – sets infinitely sad lyrics to a filigree of keyboards and deep drums. Country meets Celtic on Robin Williamson's 'First Boy I Loved', and Ian Tyson's 'Someday Soon' opens with pedal steel, after which the band strike up a jog-trot rhythm, and Judy's voice has never sounded lovelier, or more in love. It floats in the breeze.

Shel Silverstein provides the sleeve notes to another Elektra album, Judy Henske's *High Flying Bird*. As a singer, Henske is obviously out of the Patsy Cline mould, big and brassy. Shel writes tongue in cheek (or some other aperture) as a native of Wisconsin, telling her that she will have to stop singing her current repertoire "and start singing nice, sweet, feminine, petite songs like 'Barbie Allen' or 'Greensleeves' or 'Who Is Going To Shoe Your Pretty Little Feet?'". She should change her plunging necklines for "blue jeans and a checkered blouse", and must stop singing about "women dropping their boyfriends into wells...to appeal to the hard hip hearts of today's hard hip hearted folk audiences". Silverstein works himself up into a lather of mock indignation, uncomfortably close to the way a country audience reacts when they feel they have been betrayed – this could be about Shania Twain! "You have made a mockery of marriage and motherhood. I wish you luck and happiness and hope in years to come you find that your 'career' was worth it."

As for the record itself, apart from topping and tailing Sandy Denny's musical life (who began her solo recording career five years later with 'Last Train to Yuma', here under the title 'Lonely Train', and closed it with 'Til The Real Thing Comes Along'), it is an odd mixture of torch songs and traditional folk songs rewritten by Henske. The sound is that of purists revolving at speed. 'Columbus Stockade' – "wish I was back in Tennessee" – features lots of banjo and a confrontational vocal style similar to that Dolly Parton adopted on her recent bluegrass album. 'Good Old Wagon' is a kiss-off to her horse-drawn conveyance – or, more likely, to a boyfriend – set to the sound of an out-of-control trombone. It is the obverse of Elektra's trademark sound of harpsichords, deadly strange lyrics and a drugged subtlety.

Carolyn Hester is also essentially inauthentic. Her debut album boasts that she is one of a new breed of folk singers, one that "doesn't live in the hills and never did. We earn our living singing folk songs, and we've been influenced by time." Her smoky voice weaves itself around Irish and Scottish folk material, songs in Spanish, Southern blues and a "freewheeling country-song", 'Swing And Turn Jubilee', featuring a very young Bob Dylan on harmonica and Bruce Langhorne on guitar. Hester's immersion in her material and her reasons for choosing her songs are as impeccably authentic as any old-time singer: "If I can't really love a song and it can't haunt me, then I know it can't haunt anyone else."

Talking of authenticity, the results of Buffy Sainte-Marie's Nashville sojourn still sound realistic enough, with her Eartha Kitt-style throaty growl fitting in well with steel guitar and sentimentality. An adopted child, Buffy grew up in New England and then moved to New York, where Dylan's stamp of approval helped her get bookings on the coffee-house circuit. Her early albums for Vanguard presented

Anglo-American folk material, such as her bare and spectral take on 'Reynardine – A Vampire Legend'.

Her debut album contained two magnificent examples, 'Cod'ine', a song about inadvertent drug addiction covered with relish by The Charlatans and Quicksilver Messenger Service, and 'The Universal Soldier', recorded by everyone from Donovan to Glen Campbell and which provoked Jan And Dean to provide a track in response: 'The Universal Coward'. She told *Record Collector*'s Mark Paytress that the assassination of John Kennedy was a death blow to the folk revival, too: "There was such hope before – even the President seemed to want social change. Everyone was tremendously high, there didn't seem to be any obstacles." The coffee houses were a symbol of this freedom: "They were terrific places where people went to think clearly, exchange ideas and talk about politics until the early hours. Everybody had a guitar." Suddenly, folk and protest music were just a marketing tool. Buffy then recorded the experimental album *Illuminations*, a strident and weird affair where "all the electronic sounds on this album have been synthesised from Buff's voice and guitar". By now, she had discarded her mouth bow.

It was at this point that she received a request from Chet Atkins to record in Nashville. "Although I saw a lot of male chauvinism down there, I didn't think that Nashville was any more redneck than anywhere else…it was an open-hearted adventure." She went on to work with Jack Nitzche on the soundtrack of *Performance*.

After *I'm Gonna Be A Country Girl Again*, Buffy returned to Nashville for 1972's messier, less focused *Moonshot*, with a full choir and orchestra and songs by Mickey Newbury and Towns (*sic*) Van Zandt, and her own exuberant 'He's An Indian Cowboy In The Rodeo'. This was one of the songs resuscitated for the recent *Up Where We Belong*, put together on computer in Hawaii and then bounced off a satellite to her record company in Britain, which features lots of sound effects, including croaking frogs, native chants and chirping cicadas: "It is the logical conclusion of a line in the title song, "I know a boy so primitive he can call me up without a telephone'."

Other female singers got lost in the rush, but time has been kind to the music they produced. Karen Dalton was from Oklahoma, played twelve-string guitar and banjo and made her name in Greenwich Village. She shares the wild beauty and 21st-century mystique of the English traditional singer Anne Briggs. Karen's second album, *In My Own Time*, is a dark affair indeed, as her other-worldly blues croak wavers over a country-rock band, like an unquiet ghost. Alt country starts here, and one can trace a direct line to Lucinda Williams.

Dalton died in the early Eighties of an AIDS related disease, and this album sounds sickly and drugged as hell, with traditional songs like 'Katie Cruel' and 'Same Old Man' side by side with a strange mix of country and soul – Holland Dozier and Holland rub shoulders with George Jones on the writing credits. Fred Neil pays credit to Dalton as a huge influence on his own singing style, and there is also – much as one would expect – a Holy Modal Rounders connection. When Bobby Notkoff makes his violin cry at the end of the Dino Valente song 'Something On Your Mind', it almost splits your head in two.

Rosalie Sorrells was described in the programme notes to the 1970 Isle Of Wight Festival as "a dark-eyed mountain girl from Idaho, with a face like an elf and a voice that reminds some of Billie Holiday". With age, it has developed into a quizzical, rustic rasp. Born in a log cabin in Idaho and left to bring up five children alone, Rosalie took a course in American folklore, which led to her collecting traditional song and following a career in which she is as much storyteller as singer, with songs for and about children a speciality. ('The Baby Tree' was covered by Jefferson Starship, on *Blows Against The Empire*.) Her recent albums are relaxed affairs, drenched in traditional songs and embarrassing in their intimacy.

On the concept album *Then Came The Children*, Sorrells recalls her father as a man of the land: "He was lithe and strong 'til the day he died. He could name every bird, flower, stone and tree on the skin of our western lands...and he could have waltzed with bears." She appeared at the Isle of Wight with David Bromberg on second guitar. At the same festival, Joni Mitchell played Appalachian mountain dulcimer on some newly-written songs which later appeared on *Blue*, although as her career nose-dived jazz proved to be her bolt-hole of choice.

It's certainly not a matter of skin colour. Odetta was the queen mother of the folk revival, and Dylan admits to having learned all of the songs from her debut album. Born in Alabama, she studied as a classical singer, sang in shows, and then discovered a passion for folk music in her late teens, forging a new career for herself. Her repertoire covered everything from black working songs to white Appalachian ballads, blues to jazz, and spirituals to children's songs. For Odetta, it was all part of a larger picture. The New World has evolved a "unique music form, because it is derived from a combination of different peoples. It could never have begun in just Africa or England or Scotland, because everyone came here from somewhere else with his own music. American folk music became a unique blend of all people's music". A blend, in turn, which she has passed down to musicians as different as Nick Cave and Nanci Griffith.

It is almost as if country finds its own victims. Eric Andersen started as a Guthrie-influenced folk troubadour, with songs like 'Plains Of Nebrasky-o', before moving into the influence zone of Dylan, even going as far as to re-record his acoustic album *'Bout Changes And Things* with a folk rock band, like his master. Apart from his theme song, the pretty 'Violets Of Dawn', his early songs are largely undistinguished developments of the folk canon. Most archetypal is 'Looking Glass', a domestication of the Child ballads, in which an impossibly pure lover conveniently dies and is mourned almost with gratitude – deeply adolescent. (That song alone would keep Ruth Padel occupied for days, if she ever heard it.) But then Eric grew up and suffered real heartbreak, and the face on *Blue River* stares out with eyes deep in chemical excess and suffering – an Appalachian stare. On the back, he stands, pencil thin, in a flooded timber yard, like just another piece of human detritus.

It is no surprise that the record is dedicated to those friends who "helped me get through it all when times were bad", and judging from this photo things were as bad as they can get. The music inside sobs and throbs and occasionally comes up with a bitter laugh, recorded with the cream of Nashville, and has rarely been bettered. It is an album which I put on first if I ever feel suicidal. This happens pretty rarely, it's true, but it's like a fire extinguisher: vital when needed. Until a few weeks ago I had the comforting feeling that I was the only person in the world who rated it, but with an impending CD release scheduled it turns out that many others feel the same, which is oddly annoying. This is personal.

No Depression described the CD issue of *Blue River* as "subtle and incandescent". On his arrival in Nashville, the musicians were completely excited. "here's a guy who doesn't want us to play Floyd Cramer licks!" They were hot for something new.

Cue The Alabama 3. Here is another example of country music finding its ideal interpreter, like a virus finding a carrier. A combination of harmonica, accordion and Nashville sweetness bring out something in Andersen's voice – a sadness, a self-pitying despair – which was always there but previously passed unnoticed. It has deepened noticeably from the folk days, and has become creepy. As he sings about "sitting here, like a book upon a shelf", it could be Norman Bates regretting his lonely life. Here are pleas to the Lord ("Jesus I'm falling"), a retreat to basics ("I spent the day with my old dog Moe/down an old dirt road") and deliberately bad grammar ("How many times do you gotta try?"). Here, too, is self-interrogation ("How many times do you have to die now?") and self-discovery ("That prisoner was me"). The way that Eric sings such lines leaves you in no doubt that there's more than entertainment going on here. Like so many others have said, this is white soul.

I'm reminded of Van Morrison's *Veedon Fleece* – another mysterious album – by the ways the musicians follow the singer's every mood swing, so that a riff is picked up in turn by bass, piano and accordion in 'Wind And Sand'. They seem stitched to Andersen's voice. His bad luck didn't change there; the masterful follow-up, *Stages* – which includes a love song to Patti Smith, one of the friends thanked on Blue River, and some newer material recorded with two members of The Band – was delayed for almost 20 years. 'Rag Mama Rag' was quoted in passing on 'Pearl's Goodtime Blues', presumably a tribute to Janis Joplin. The 1989 album *Ghosts Upon The Road* was a return to form, with songs like 'Irish Lace' and the ten-minute autobiographical title track, but Eric Andersen's albums do not exactly spill out of record store bins.

Another sub-Dylan artist to beat an artistically rewarding path to Nashville was David Blue, whose very (adopted) name suggests pain and misery. Eric Andersen gave him the name because his persona at the time was "gruff, nasty, unsmiling [and] suspicious", qualities which come across with full force on his self-named debut, following a few tracks on 1965's *Singer-Songwriter* project with Richard Farina and Patrick Sky. It has to be among the worst albums I possess, along with *Jasper, The Red Crayola* and other over-rated slices of psychedelia. Nashville never allowed anyone to play so out of tune. I keep it because it's on Elektra, so the cover design and session musicians are immaculate, and because it is so outrageously bad, a total rip off of the *Highway 61* sound, but with gibberish words rather than Dylan's mix of beat poetry, Rimbaud and surrealism.

Blue mirrored his hero's every move about a year too late, and so he went country in 1970, with another self-named disc, *Me, S David Blue*: "I did it in three days, which is very typical of Nashville records. You go in there and whip it out, which I liked." You don't fool with country, though, or it will find you out.

Blue joined other country rockers at David Geffen's new label, appropriately named Asylum, and here he made his bleakest albums, none more mournful than *Stories*, but no one really noticed. *Com'n Back For More* was subtitled "A Story", but he had abandoned country for LA smoothness, and the links are all missing. When he died, while out jogging, Blue's best memorials were his laconic appearances in the Dylan home movie *Renaldo And Clara* and in Neil Young's *Human Highway*. This is a perfect example of someone in the right place at the right time, and the legacy is as lacklustre as such people's usually are. Boston's Broadside saw through the emperor's new clothes early, saying of the first album: "Blues' melodies are non-existent, and he refuses to sing – I say refuses, because I believe that he can carry a tune, but he chooses not to in the mistaken idea that his untutored *sprechstimme* is somehow appropriate to our incoherent age."

Some of the old-time music vocalists couldn't sing either, but the joy comes in that they were at least trying very, very hard. The line-up of talent at The Turk's Head coffee house in Boston is mouth-watering: Eric Andersen, The Charles River Valley Boys, Buffy Sainte-Marie, The Blues Project, Jimmy Reed, Tom Rush, Jesse Colin Young, even Don McLean – all for a token charge, with a reading from Tolkein's *Lord Of The Rings* every Thursday. Blue says of Greenwich Village itself: "It's the original site of New York, where the Dutch were, and it looks like England or Amsterdam, very old, very charming." The same applies to Boston and other coffee-house coteries. We're back to those early European settlers again. Their old haunts seem to act as a magnet for new music. A magnet, or a trap.

Blue was born Stuart David Cohen, and Leonard Cohen is perhaps the most surprising Nashville nut among the singer/songwriter fraternity, although he emerged not through the coffee houses but as a published poet and novelist who drifted into a new career (and even his biggest fans – myself included – would never claim that he could sing in any technical meaning of that word). Unlike David Blue, the sound that did emerge, and the words it croaked out, mesmerised even more people than it alienated.

His voice has deepened to a world-weary croak, and after more love affairs than most he has now retreated to a mountain – not in the Appalachians but in California – where he lives a celibate life as a zen monk and put out occasional records like *The Future*, which sees it as murder. Tomorrow, the Wild West in your own home town. It's all a far cry from his student career as a third of The Buckskin Boys, a C&W combo.

Leonard had long listened to country stations, joining a long line of Canadians who yearned for the prairie life, from Hank Snow to Shania Twain. The future doom-monger played at square dances and church basements, with 'Laughing Len' proving something of a guitar wizard. His country roots occasionally peep through, as when his 1970s backing band, The Army, featured Ron Cornelius on guitar, Charlie Daniels on bass and fiddle and Dylan's record producer, Bob Johnston, guesting on harmonica. One of his most popular songs of around this time was 'Diamonds In The Mine', a country ramble. He also wrote Hank Williams' into 'Tower Of Song' in which he asks the country singer just how lonely things can get, and "Hank Williams hasn't answered yet/but I hear him coughing all night long."

Arlo Guthrie puts a cheerful, country-rock beat to his father's 'Oklahoma Hills', and turns Pete Seeger's tune 'Living In The Country' into a country strut. To say (as some did at the time) that Arlo was "re-inventing" C&W now seems a gross exaggeration – making it palatable for a rock audience is more likely. It all sounds a little lightweight, although the Woodstock hit 'Coming In To Los Angeles' (from London – where else? – the pilgrimage west as ever) remakes the outlaw in the image of a dope dealer. Having Chris Etheridge on bass is a kind of *grand cru* mark on country rock of this era, and here indeed he is. There is great lead guitar, too, but any album which boasts both James Burton and Clarence White has a head start on most. 'Running Down The Road' is the title song of the album on which all of these songs appear, and Jacques Vassal writes of its "impressionistic and quasi-spatial instrumentation". It sounds to me as if the band are in a different room from Arlo, like that spoof of the 'Banana Boat Song' that used to be a mainstay of childrens' radio. At the end, it sounds as if they are each in a different room from the other, and wearing earmuffs.

Arlo came back into focus on *Last Of The Brooklyn Cowboys*, which opened with an Irish reel and took in country, gospel, jazz and Mexican while remaining of the moment. *Amigo* did much the same, though by now nobody much was listening.

Tim Hardin was another of those shooting stars who burned out young, and seeing him play a support slot at Birmingham Town Hall – to Rare Bird, of all things – was depressing indeed, as dribbles of talent oozed out of his hunched frame. Born in Eugene, Oregon, and supposedly a descendant of true outlaw John Wesley Hardin, he learned early on to assimilate the music of the South, with Hank Williams a particular influence. Hardin's voice was full of that high, lonesome sound, and combined with his slight but word-perfect songs – about a real world of carpenters and black-sheep boys – it can still break your heart. His most challenging album is *Suite For Susan Moore And Damian – We're – One, One, All*, recorded in a "log house" and a folky version of the country theme of family values.

Susan, the lady from Baltimore, left him soon afterwards, and he moved to a house on Bear Cat Mountain, totally alone. The overall concept of this strange album, as with so much else, seems impenetrably locked into Hardin's own mind. Much was too personal to really connect with anyone else, but 'First Love Song' has a sad and quiet beauty which many singers strive their entire lives to find. His guitar seems to be out of kilter with Hardin's anguished voice; at times he seems to be fighting for control with it, as the words dig the depths of his very soul. Tim had tried to record some of this material in Nashville, though hardened pickers were bemused by his attempts to dragoon them into a new sense of rhythm. It's like a musical tug of war, with consummately professional sidemen and an out-of-control genius straining in opposite corners of the studio. It's fascinating, but the results didn't surface for almost 30 years. "This guy is really on the edge, maybe over the edge," reckoned David Briggs, who was just about to put together Area Code 615.

Hardin's final studio album, *Tim Hardin 9*, contained 'Shiloh Town', a magnificent song about the Civil War and birds leaving for the winter (it would make a perfect soundtrack for the novel *Under Cold Mountain*), and some hailed it as a return to form, but it turned out to date back to the abandoned *Nashvhille Sessions*, five of which finally appeared on the anthology *Simple Songs Of Freedom*.

'Thanks To Gideon' was supposedly inspired by Tim's reading of Proverbs 13 in his hotel room Gideon bible. There is some desultory studio messing about, then he counts "one", and they're off into a slow musical burn, with Tim free-forming a vocal over the top. He's stoned, one presumes, but there's nowhere like Tennessee to get you musing about sin. It has the same free-form verbal madness of Van Morrison's *Bang* sessions, and the cream of Nashville keep going where lesser men would throw up their hands in despair: "Well, with Timmy, it was always an adventure…"

Saddest and most majestic of all is his final *Homecoming Concert*. The string quartets have gone, and all we have here is that voice and some disjointed introductions between the old songs. It's the perfect antidote for anyone wishing to romanticise heroin and the human spirit. As Andy Darlington puts it, you can hear the "cracks and bruises" here, "the first time he'd played the town of his birth and the last time he'd perform anywhere". You can't get more country than that. Johnny Cash, The Everly Brothers and Waylon Jennings are among those to have covered his songs.

Country turns out to have been the music that dare not speak its name during the folk era, and now will hardly shut up. The saturnine Bob Neuwirth was Dylan's sidekick for much of the Sixties, and can be seen smirking alongside him on *Don't Look Back*. To him is attributed the advice to his master that "country is the last authentic goddamed shit left for us to rip off". Times change, though, and Neuwirth, who co-wrote 'Mercedes Benz' with Janis Joplin, re-emerged in the Nineties as a singer/songwriter in his own right, recording *Look Up*, a magnificent collection of country duets which *Bucketfull Of Brains* reckon that "anyone whose heart was touched by Son Volt would be at home with it".

1989's *Back To The Front* was recorded in the sitting room of fellow member of The Rolling Thunder Review Steve Soles, and it starts with the sound of a solo banjo. It is full of songs in which country meets folk, although this remains music delivered by a man in an emotional mask. Eric Andersen, of all people, came up to him and said that he wished he had the nerve to be honest about relationships in songs. "Hey, man," Bob replied, "I'm a writer. They're not necessarily my romances, my failures I'm singing about." No wonder he collaborated with that other enigma, John Cale – cold on the outside, burning with passion within.

Neuwirth was brought up on old-time country in Ohio, "more bluegrass than western swing, more mountain music than Bob Wills". (You've said enough to get a page in this book, Bob.) He remembers hearing Hank Williams on the radio, and a recent song deals with the Grand Ole Opry. He recently played a short European tour of improvised shows with Howe Gelb: "I saw Giant Sand once when Victoria Williams was part of the band." If ever a man still looked an outlaw, it is the craggy Neuwirth. The subject of Dylan is still out of bounds.

Dylan played harmonica with Fred Neil at the Cafe Wha?, and Eric Andersen told *Mojo* that Fred was "a cross between a rumour and a legend. I heard a story that his grandfather was Jimmie Rodgers, the Singing Brakeman." He had been a child star on the Grand Ole Opry, and perhaps as a reaction exemplified the stance that even to sell a few records was to become "culturally tainted" (although Paul Kantner of Jefferson Airplane remained a fan, and kept his songs alive). This was a pity, as Fred had a warm, friendly voice – supposedly at odds from his own personality – and wrote sweet, sad songs, like 'Dolphins' and 'Everybody's Talking', which became the theme song for *Midnight Cowboy*. Even there, however, it was sung by someone else. Fred Neil's self-imposed retreat to a Southern farm is symbolic of the way in which the political commitment of this generation came ultimately to nought. A man who once wrote 'Tear Down The Walls' ended by retreating behind them. Others found their own walls behind which to hide, and country music was as good a refuge as any.

Phil Ochs' sound was as different from Fred Neil's as could be, with a voice like a hiccup and a strange mixture of luxuriance and bitterness – as indeed were his songs. His written-by-numbers protest songs were really only apprentice work, and it was only after he had left Elektra that he began to capture that label's trademark sound, a decadent beauty. 1967's *Pleasures Of The Harbor* and the albums that follow have only been properly evaluated since two career retrospectives: a three-CD box on Elektra and a two-CD package on A&M, which amazingly hardly duplicate each other. Ochs can now be seen as a prophet of Americana, a singer bold enough to take on a rotting civilisation and expose its foibles and its soiled magnificence. Here is David Accles with a dose of vitriol.

Ochs was forced by his parents to attend a military academy, and then majored in journalism. Both served him well. His father was a doctor who finally settled in

Ohio, but Phil was schooled in Virginia. He returned home to take his degree, but abandoned this to pursue the risky life of an itinerant folk-singer. The young Ochs was a dreamer, with a sense of frontier morality largely drawn from the cowboy movies in which he immersed himself. Years later, Ochs would go with his (then-) close friend Bob Dylan, Dave Van Ronk and David Blue to catch a late night Western double feature at The Lyric. Here they would "OD on popcorn, and shoot back at the screen with finger pistols – their feet up on the chair in front, their dialogue better than the lines of the film", unless it starred John Wayne, in which case they would "sit in awe".

One night, they had a private audience with Marlon Brando and his native American girlfriend at The Dakota. Afterwards, a stoned Dylan could hardly contain himself: "He thinks he's an Indian. We passed the peace pipe around." Country music runs like a strong current under Ochs' his work: at college he immersed himself in the music of Johnny Cash and Hank Williams and, as it developed, his own singing style – like his speaking voice – had "an ever-so-slight Scottish lilt, which undoubtedly influenced his melodies".

At college, Phil joined banjoist Jim Glover in a duo, The Sundowners. Jim later formed 'Jim And Jean' with Jean Ray, an unjustly forgotten act who influenced the likes of Fairport, across the ocean, and covered some of Phil's early attempts at songwriting. The radical folksinger Bob Gibson was an early mentor on Ochs, and Phil showed himself a true son of the direct-action side of another hero, Woody Guthrie, when he went to Kentucky to support the striking miners. Marc Eliot's biography of Ochs – which is much more than a conventional biography, and is more an attempt to resurrect him – recounts that Ochs, Dylan, Judy Collins and Eric Andersen all went down there together and spent five days "singing, picketing, eating, sleeping. Phil talked with the miners. He visited their families. Whenever he had time, he'd be on the streets of Hazard selling copies of *Broadside*, taking whatever he could get."

On the way back, Ochs "was flooded with the romanticism of their adventure, their flirtation with danger, the luxury of safety. To quote his album note, "'Hills of West Virginia' was written on my trips to Hazard, Kentucky, with Eric Andersen. I found myself renewing an old habit of pretending I was taking pictures with my mind." The images which resulted "don't have any special message", presaging Ochs' sudden immersion in full-scale orchestrations and massive songs, like 'The Crucifixion' – a meditation after much thought about Kennedy's assassination – or 'Tape From California'.

Ochs' greatest work lies in the trilogy of albums he recorded over a mere two years with Larry Marks. *Pleasures Of The Harbor* was seen by some purists as a betrayal, and in hindsight is like a poisonous flower, a view of the death of Sixties idealism. Gone was the bareness of the early albums; here Ochs recorded painstakingly, one line at a time, with a full orchestra and tape loops. The title track was inspired by the John Ford movie *The Long Voyage Home*: "They've lived the tales to carry to the shore."

He went further still on *Tape From California*, in his own words "a comment on the spiritual decline of America". It's Gore Vidal set to music. The sailor is back from sea again, but this time "he must have lost his mind". As a result, it contains his bare and emotional song 'Joe Hill', taking the tune of Guthrie's 'Tom Joad' and with Rambling Jack Elliott helping out. One key line could describe Ochs' own career: "It's the death of a rebel that I died." *Rehearsals For Retirement* descends into the abyss, a "two-act musical" which saw democracy becoming dictatorship and Ochs himself 'King Of The Cowboys': "He wants to get me, he wants to hurt me."

Ochs seemed to go mad with pain at this point (a process which culminated with his suicide), appearing drunk and in a gold suit at Carnegie Hall, like a young Presley, baiting the audience. They were particularly annoyed when he attempted the old Conway Twitty hit 'Mona Lisa'. At the second show, he went into a long monologue: "And now, as we get towards a fascist America, which is coming in the Seventies in a big way" – hello, Ronald Reagan – "we start to see a change in the right wing." Their chosen conduit was "an artist who is a genuine songwriter, who's as good as anybody around. His name is Merle Haggard, and he has the possibility of being today's Hank Williams."

Phil goes on to sing a song by this new musical antichrist, and what else could it be than 'Okie From Muskogee'. The audience enjoy it, despite its "fascist" attributes, but when Ochs announces a Buddy Holly medley they boo for a good five minutes. He finishes with an Elvis Presley tribute, to match his suit: "If there's any hope for a revolution in America it lies in getting Presley to become Che Guevara. He is the ultimate American artist. He was the root of American music. I've lost my voice now, but I'm going to try to sing him anyway." The audience cheer and dance in the aisles. It is three in the morning. The management pull the plug. A career ends.

"Phil Ochs is dead!", someone shouts from the audience, and five years later, having been refused a place on the 'Rolling Thunder' tour, Ochs killed himself. He directed that his ashes be scattered from Edinburgh castle as a piper played the ancient Scottish lament 'Flowers Of The Forest'. Ochs' final album, the ironically titled *Phil Ochs' Greatest Hits*, was split between country rock backings – with Clarence White and James Burton – and songs orchestrated by Van Dyke Parks. "Fifty Phil Ochs Fans Can't Be Wrong" was the bitter sub-title. There are more than that now.

Dorris Henderson brought her autoharp and versions of Appalachian ballads from LA to London in the mid 1960s. A black girl, she had got hold of the Alan Lomax songbooks, "and they were my bible. I taught myself all the songs in there that I could maintain in my brain: 'Single Girl', 'Darling Cory' – they said something to me." She started singing professionally in The Ash Grove and The Troubadour, as well as in New York, "rushing from one bar to another, all over the village". Now she brought this material back home, to Greenwich from Greenwich Village.

She recorded two albums with her boyfriend, folk-blues guitarist John Renbourne, himself busy recycling songs by the likes of Dock Boggs, both solo and with Pentangle. (His version of 'Sugar Babe' is particularly fine.) As she told *Folk Roots*, "The stuff I heard in England was different from what I was hearing in the States." Davey Graham was introducing Indian raga to folk music, and collaborating with Shirley Collins – whom we last saw song collecting in the Appalachians – putting jazz stylings to traditional songs, sung in Shirley's soft Sussex burr.

Shirley's earlier 1959 album, *Sweet England*, features her playing an Appalachian banjo on the cover: "The Southern mountain people have developed an extraordinary range of techniques for accompanying their heritage of British songs. The most suitable and successful of these mountain folk arts is that of the five-string banjo, and it is this instrument that Shirley Collins, very properly, adapts to the mood of Southern English folk song." Her wistful, dreamlike tones are revered by some, hated by others. Me, I like them. Sometimes. Here she ranges over songs as geographically various as the "British-American jingle" 'Charlie', with a tune from Jean Ritchie; an English nursery song with pig *oink*s; the American mountain murder song 'Omie Wise'; a Gaelic song translated into English and learned by Shirley's uncle in the Eighth Army; and 'The Bonnie Irish Boy', "showing the recent influence of the Irish on Southern England". You can't get more cross-cultural than that.

Four of the songs here resurfaced on the collaboration with Davey Graham. For the riper-voiced Henderson, such experiments were "a great grounding in how music can cross borders", and came as a great relief to Dorris, who had found resistance in America because she was singing material "that I wasn't 'supposed' to sing". Dorris later joined the folk-rock band Eclection.

As for Graham, his modal experiments themselves fed back into the tradition, as well as into bands as diverse as Led Zeppelin and Buffalo Springfield. Just listen to 'White Summer', or Stephen Stills' guitar break on 'Bluebird'. Davey was one of the first folk troubadours – alongside fellow Scot Alex Campbell – who happily included Ozark folk songs like 'Willie More' in his largely Celtic repertoire, and he also played five-string banjo. In a fascinating concert recorded in the early Sixties at The Herts County Folk Music Jubilee, he jams with a mountain dulcimer player and Johnny Orange on autoharp.

Early folk-rockers in England had long schooled themselves in mountain music: Ashley Hutchings told me that, even before Fairport Convention were Fairport Convention, they had mastered the complete works of the likes of Doc Watson and Clarence Ashley – both of whom he saw playing London folk clubs – and then transformed them into something else.

Hutchings can remember seeing three contrasting Appalachian musicians in the London folk clubs of his youth. Clarence Ashley was straight off the farm, clad in braces and workshirt and with no attempt at stagecraft – he just got up when called and sang. Jean Ritchie was a huge woman, delivering genuinely comic anecdotes between each song, deeply knowledgeable with a very authentic singing style yet oddly polished. At times she could seem "almost showbiz". Best of all was Doc Watson, who was as natural as they came, but also a skilled entertainer. All three made an enormous impact on the British folk scene of the early Sixties.

Over in Ireland, Sweeney's Men's Terry Woods' style was half Celtic, half American mountain music. Their first album had 'Tom Dooley' and 'Willie Of Winsbury' (the beautiful tune of which Richard Thompson later borrowed for 'Farewell Farewell') as adjacent tracks.

Early Fairport also covered songs by Jackson C Frank, an American in London whose life was as self-destructive as any Nashville burn-out, and who died as a tramp out on the streets, but whose debut album was produced by fellow ex-pat Paul Simon, with Art Garfunkel as tea boy. I would still give Simon And Garfunkel's whole repertoire in exchange for one mysterious song like 'Blues Run The Game': "Catch a boat to England, baby, maybe to Spain." In Soho, scarred both mentally and physically by a classroom fire when he was still a boy, Jackson found a bunch of fellow spirits: "Eccentricity was something that was socially acceptable. It wasn't a matter of you being crazy". The musical form of this eccentricity was to set folk music from both sides of the Atlantic on a collision course. The echoes are still reverberating.

They recorded 'Idumea' on their folk-classical fusion album *Galleries*, and when their frontman, Peter Bellamy, moved to Keighley he became an occasional member of Sharon And The Students, "whose repertoire included Sacred Harp, shape-note and Balkan songs". Bellamy was also an adherent of the country blues, sung in his usual window-shattering voice with which delights he woke me up one morning. He also ordered me to go out and augment my already vast record collection with The Carter Family: "There's 20 titles available. You need to go out and buy the lot."

Bellamy is remembered fondly now for many musical extravagances, not least his version of the cowboy song 'Sante Fe Trail', first collected by Alan Lomax and sung in a piercing Norfolk accent. "Almost certainly written by an Irishman," Bellamy reckoned, "because it sounds like it. This shows cowboys had a real streak of poetry in 'em". *Wake The Vaulted Echoes*, Free Reed's magnificent three-CD tribute to Bellamy, ranges through lots of versions of poems by Kipling to another great poet, Bob Dylan, and his affirmative 'Death Is Not The End', which in this context is particularly appropriate.

By the mid-Sixties, Dylan was well into his stride as a songwriter and busy remaking everything in his path. Ancient tunes developed new and politically-charged words, Hitchcock's movie *Psycho* is relived as if it is a folk narrative, and songs like 'Desolation Row' seemed to stretch into infinity, bolting surrealism onto the ballad tradition. What, after all, could be more ballad-like than the opening line, "They're selling postcards of the hanging"? After all, many of Dylan's earliest songs were printed in *Broadside* magazine, and the whole underground folk scene existed – as such scenes usually do – through *samizdat* literature and word of mouth. When he first visited England for a proper tour, in 1965, *Melody Maker* welcomed him as if he was some kind of alien, and from the amount of conventional sense any journalist got out of him he effectively was. News conferences of the time sound as if Dylan is communicating in code.

Not many people outside the folk scene had heard of LSD, but you just knew that something odd was happening, as groups like The Beatles (successfully) and the Stones (disastrously) tried to follow suit, and tangerine trees flowered 2,000 light years from home. They were fine on places, transfused by acid – Strawberry Fields and Itchycoo Park and Penny Lane – but the pictures that others painted were usually static. Only Dylan could create situations, a bar-room scene in Juarez or sexual games in the back of a car in 'From A Buick 6'.

What could descend to mere word play in the hands of others kept true to its own strange logic in Dylan's world of carnival mayhem and endless distortion. 'Desolation Row' was a place every listener knew, even if it had a different postcode for each person. The discipline learnt from traditional song persevered; on *Highway 61 Revisited*, there are two blues and one ballad in the title alone. The musical structures remain simple, although they bear a verbal weight beneath which they start to buckle.

First there were three recording sessions in Columbia Studios in New York (the second of which is confusingly known in bootlegging circles as the "LA Sessions"), which were laid down with his road band, an untried and nameless group who had until recently been backing Ronnie Hawkins as The Hawks, with Al Kooper drafted back in January 1966 for 'One Of Us Must Know (Sooner or Later)'. This was the only track to survive on *Blonde On Blonde*, and featured Rick Danko on bass and drummer Sandy Konikoff replacing Levon Helm, who grew tired of being booed every night. There are two rejected takes of 'Visions Of Johanna', both subtly different enough from the later Nashville take to be essential, and all three of which assert that the country music station plays soft, "but there's nothing, really nothing to turn off".

In February, Dylan moved his operations across to Columbia Music Row Studios in Nashville. Thus it was that, in the very epicentre of what was generally perceived as the most hidebound and backward musical force in America, largely with redneck musicians, Dylan created the first psychedelic album, a double, so hot was the singer's muse at the time.

The album opens with a studio party, and the call for everyone to "get stoned" on 'Rainy Day Women #12 & 35'. For this track, the musicians entered into the spirit of things by swapping instruments: "Al Kooper played tambourine, bass player Henry Strzelecki played the organ pedals with his hands, Kenny Buttrey rearranged his drum kit, putting the bass and drum sideways across a couple of chairs and lashing cymbals to music stands." In general, his metronomic beat defined the whole album and kept this runaway train on the rails: "Everyone would fall in with the drums." The sessions also seemed to take no account of time (or studio fees), and at 4.30 in the morning, on the same song, Wayne Butler was called in to play the trombone.

On 'Most Likely You Go Your Way (And I'll Go Mine)', Charlie McCoy plays electric bass with one hand and trumpet with the other, both at the same time. Joe South and Wayne Moss provided the guitar licks, and the blind Hargus "Pig" Robbins the piano. There were three outsiders, besides Dylan: producer Bob Johnston, Al Kooper on trademark organ and (Robert) Jamie Robertson on stinging lead guitar. As Kooper later wrote: "Imagine how it felt to be playing on a session when you knew that whatever you played would last forever." To the backing musicians, 'Sad-Eyed Lady Of The Lowland' seemed to do exactly that.

The song closes affairs with Dylan squeezing out each word like toothpaste, recreating the nobility of a Scots ballad, as Nashville's finest keep things going with precise drum taps and a gospel organ. This is truly devotional music, though not to God. With her "cowboy mouth", what man could resist this cloistered image of womanhood? Not me, for sure. Whatever actually happened in the studio, the power of Dylan's voice and words makes it feel as if time has stopped. It sounds like both singer and players could go on forever, and that in a finer world they would. Everywhere is that "thin, wild mercury sound" that Dylan had still not yet quite achieved in concert.

Charlie McCoy and Kenny Buttrey returned on *John Wesley Harding*. They brought with them Pete Drake on steel guitar, an unimaginable instrument for *Blonde On Blonde*, where the Nashville input is mainly limited to that of laying down a rich background sound and no more. It is not country music by any reasonable definition, while the three succeeding albums undeniably were country, both in sound and intent. In between came *The Basement Tapes*, the pivot on which Dylan's whole career turns. Here is music of friendship and sharing, offering ancient wisdom and crude humour, ego-free and musically rich. The very last thing with which you would have thought the noise terrorists of those apocalyptic '66 concerts would have busied themselves. Then you listen more closely, and you realise that the Apocalypse is at the centre of what they're singing about.

Greil Marcus, the poet of rock criticism, ends the first chapter of his book on *The Basement Tapes* in Cardiff in 1966, with Dylan and Johnny Cash ("at 33 he looks like cancer") jamming on Cash's "lovely, seemingly traditional ballad" 'I Still Miss Someone'. Dylan suddenly begins a new song, "I bought me a ticket, for a one-way train", and "the song he's now singing sounds older than the grandparents of anyone in the room and more familiar than anyone's own face". It is a ticket that will take him away from the madness and danger of that tour, and whatever dangerous chemicals are coursing through his skeletal body. "Strap yourself to a tree with roots" will become his watchword. The music literally of his grandparents' generation – via Harry Smith – will guide him. Dylan is set to emigrate back west, into the past and a new homeland, "an America that exists only in the basement of a big pink house, a country that no one has exactly inhabited before".

Clinton Heylin, rock music's greatest sleuth, is never better than when making tangled things clear, and his chapter on *The Basement Tapes* is perhaps the most exciting of all. His chronological survey needs to be cross-referenced with Marcus' alphabetical track-by-track "discography", which teases out the historical roots of so many of these songs. So many of those musicians this book has dealt with are credited that one aspect of *The Basement Tapes* seems to be that of putting together a huge bran tub of Americana. Dip in at random and you will find Flatt And Scruggs' 'Come All Ye Fair And Tender Ladies', Hank Williams as 'Luke the Drifter', Sun era Johnny Cash, Marty Robbins, Roscoe Holcomb's 'Hills Of Mexico', Ian And Sylvia, The Skillet Lickers, Hank Snow, The Carter Family's 'Wildwood Flower', sea shanties and Appalachian ballads. Dylan chooses a different voice each time.

Dylan's own new songs partake of the same arcane knowledge of other musics, but slyly and nowhere more obviously than in 'Clothesline Saga', an answer to Bobbie Gentry's 'Ode To Billy Joe'. Marcus can inject as much interest in a chance aside as many others do in a whole book, and here he mentions in passing *Best Of Tragedy*, "a collection that links Appalachian murder ballads to the teen death songs so much in vogue in the early 1960s" (I'm still searching), then links this in turn to a 1990s performance by The Rock Bottom Remainders in which the horror novelist Stephen King takes lead vocal, with fellow rock critic Dave Marsh, "in bloodied prom dress, as the dead girlfriend". One hopes he isn't being literal here, but somehow knows that he is.

The best day-by-day recreation, however, is by Heylin, who posits some early sessions at Dylan's own house in Woodstock, in the Red Room, while a Levon Helmless combo fumble and glide through other men's songs. It is different again to the order of the five-CD bootleg. Symbolically, the first song fragment to be recorded is 'Lock Your Door', which sounds like it is recorded through a door, as the musicians within retreat from the world outside, and most emphatically from the "summer of love". For Dylan, that had already come and gone. In the same month they moved to 'Big Pink', and Dylan gradually begins to insert his own songs into the mix. The final session is in November, when Helm returns. The Band begin their own journey into songwriting, and Dylan concludes with some more traditional country and blues classics, almost as if saying farewell to this period of woodshedding. 'All You Have To Do Is Dream' is the final track, and is played twice, first as a "languid run-through with hints of Bing Crosby" and then "the pace quickens even if the tempo doesn't, and the floorboards lift off into the sky". It's as playful as a kitten.

The official releases of this material have been senselessly put into mono and robbed of much of the richness of sound which the five-CD set possesses. It really sounds like the best home jamming session you've ever heard, the kind of rough spontaneity The Beatles attempted and failed to get on the *Get Back* sessions.

There is a sense of the five participants – six, when Levon returns, and until that time only one of them a native citizen of the USA – as emigrants in a strange land (as Woodstock was them all), holed up in the hills, slightly stoned, remembering the good old days. They play beautifully together, an ego-less and comforting music, homely and controlled after the sharp ecstasies of the ear-splitting '66 concerts. Being booed and threatened night after night around the world had produced a camaraderie under fire. US soldiers were feeling much the same in the jungles of Vietnam, an escalating conflict whose dark shadows touched some of these songs, and all of *John Wesley Harding*.

Whatever had happened to Dylan on the road to Bearsville on 29 July 1966, where Striebel Road dips down sharply to the river, when he plunged over his handlebars after hitting an oil patch on the road, it was a new man who was photographed at the time, with a scraggly beard, rustic clothes and an interesting range of cowboy hats. When *Little White Wonder* hit the record racks a couple of years later, when Dylan's muse had gone walkabout, it was music that was already largely known from a fast trickle of officially-sanctioned cover versions by bands from Fairport to Manfred Mann and even The Tremeloes. The music held together, unfathomably mysterious and extremely male. Alongside music with much the same spirit recorded a few years later by The Grateful Dead and their like, it inspired a generation to get back to the land – to the mountains, even. It provided a key to the locked box of Sixties excess. This was music with mud on its boots.

The original fourteen-track edition cuts out all of the extraneous material we can now hear, and was drawn from demos sent around for other musicians to cover. There is a sense of unity here completely destroyed in the eventual official double album, salted ("polluted" is the adjective used by the fierce Heylin) with later tracks by The Band from that same basement, choosing secondary takes of 'Tears Of Rage' and 'Too Much Of Nothing' and some extraneous overdubs performed after the event. Much more serious was the complete omission of 'I Shall Be Released' – the cornerstone of the whole enterprise – and 'The Mighty Quinn'. One of my favourite versions is a 13-track UK pressing on Rover records, complete with Robert Crumb-type cartoons, one for each song. (It's much better than the official photo shoot, with Dylan and The Band posing in a boiler room with some circus freaks playing characters from Dylan's mind.) 'This Wheel's On Fire' has Dylan's head exploding, and 'The Mighty Quinn' depicts the old Dylan in a flashy suit and back in the city. The Band are renamed "The Bent", and are drawn as sinister mountain men.

Other tracks started to surface on bootlegs like *GWW 'VD Waltz*, and then on official compilations like *Biograph* and, much later, *The Bootleg Series*. Dylan allowed the Robertson remasters to appear shortly after *Blood On The Tracks*, just as the Manchester '66 concert came out shortly after *Time Out Of Mind*. It's as if he is aware of the suffocating quality of his past, and will only sanction its re-release when he has an album out in the marketplace which is equal to it. This would be easier if he did not butcher near-perfect albums like *Infidels* at the last moment, forcing his most rabid fans back to the same state exhibited by that man in the corner, which is probably the point of the exercise anyway. Where does all this stuff come from in the first place? *The Basement Tapes* started, as their name suggests, as a home taping project, although some suspected even that. Why should it be too easy to hear them as originally intended, Tiny Tim and all? "Too much of nothing can make a man feel like a king..."

Heylin – who is, of course, still searching – reckons that very little has gone missing which Dylan wanted to keep. He documents "the passage from drought to flood" and back again, with Dylan inspired by his return to his musical roots to start writing again. And what songs! If you want a distilled version of the odd mixture of traditional British folk and mountain music that this book is all about, listen to this. A good place to start is the uncompleted electric take of 'She's Your Lover Now' from January 1966.

With its "postcards of Billy the Kid", a friend "in a cowboy hat" and a girl standing on a bar with "her fish head an' a harpoon/an' a fake beard plastered on her brow", it's his wildest acid-fuelled freak show, and Dylan muffs it at the end, either because he gets the words twisted around – "your mouth cries wolf" – or just because he cracks up. Lyrically, the *Basement* songs are tighter in structure, more gnomic, with rapid thumb sketches of Turtle, Skinny Moo and Mouse, legendary creatures all. These are songs full of aphorisms: "lost time is not found again", and "too much of nothing/can turn a man into a liar". The usual strange people carry out the usual impossible actions, but now the surrealism has gone native, and this skewed reality takes place in a rural setting: "I bought my girl/a herd of moose."

Dylan writes as a bemused outsider, not as judgmental as before, just recording what he sees – although apparently fuelled with copious amounts of industrial-strength coffee and marijuana, in the absence of moonshine – and he is learning the art of concise understatement. When he sees a wheel of fire rolling down the road, the last judgement or maybe just part of his crashed bike seen as he lay there on the ground, he quietly notes "best notify my next of kin". He has certainly been getting out his C&W albums from cold storage: 'I Shall Be Released' is worthy of Hank Williams, each word like a hammer, awaiting redemption, while 'Please, Mrs Henry' has the sly wit of Jimmie Rodgers. It's that odd mixture throughout, a light surface and an apocalyptic undertow, so that 'Down In The Flood' is a natural disaster, the Biblical tale which saw Noah go sailing, and a leave-taking to a girlfriend. It's funny, cheerful and vengeful, with not a grey-flannelled dwarf in sight. This is people's music, so that "I" – or the "we" in 'Tears Of Rage' – is everyone.

The music is built to match the words it carries, bouncy and friendly, with Garth Hudson's organ like a warm wash of sound tying everything together. The stumbling rhythm section swap instruments and clip-clop along with the high spirits and occasional duff notes of an old-style string band. Dylan does his best to sound like a yokel, and there are plenty of choruses. Robbie Robertson has shed the screaming breaks of the '66 tour, sublimating the anger and vengeance behind those "premature ejaculations" into the songs he was beginning to write, at first much in the style of his master here. He comes to the fore on the slower songs, winding country licks around Dylan's lead vocal like a conversation, as on 'Goin' To Acapulco'.

The albums to emerge after both parties surfaced from the basement were both more sombre affairs, with the good humour here becoming chinks of light in the darkness.

John Wesley Harding, named after an outlaw, was supposedly written back in Dylan's study with a large family Bible open on a lectern and Hank Williams albums scattered around. Even if not true, it certainly makes sense, symbolically. After *The Basement Tapes*' carnival colours, the new album was black and white and grey, right down to the cover.

As to Woodstock, the word spread and it became just another tourist trap. They even held a rock festival just up the road, but Dylan had already fled to put on a white suit and sing soothing country harmonies with a still-seismic Band on the Isle Of Wight, and you don't get much more rural and out of way than that. I should know – I still live there. Dylan himself went back to live in the city.

The semi-acoustic mysteries of *John Wesley Harding* were recorded in four days in Nashville, only a few days after the death of Woody Guthrie. 'I Dreamed I Saw St Augustine' is based on 'The Ballad Of Joe Hill', but the Old Testament is the dominant influence here, with all kinds of half quotations. Matthew Zuckerman traces three to Leviticus alone: "Ye shall eat, and not be satisfied" is one, which comes fairly directly in 'I Pity The Poor Immigrant' as "who eats but is not satisfied", and it could be the response to any listener searching for clues here. Heylin quotes Dylan to the effect that he was trying for the same sound as the Canadian folksinger Gordon Lightfoot had achieved with Buttrey And McCoy: they were "astonished by Dylan's calm professionalism" in the studio this time around. He half smiles on the cover, but the short story on the back is deliberately opaque, as are those inside. People were reduced to turning the album upside down and seeing The Beatles as shadows in the trees. "Nothing is revealed", except perhaps in the simplicity of 'I'll Be Your Baby Tonight', a simple love song which closes the album, and points the way directly to *Nashville Skyline*, which is pretty much a musical non-event.

That album is almost a parody of Nashville product. It is confined to songs of lost love and fulfilled romance. It is short on playing time, with plenty of filler. To further pad things out, there is an instrumental and a duet with Johnny Cash on 'Girl From The North Country' (which is distinctly funereal – and Roy Harper does a far better parody of early Dylan singing this song than Dylan has since about 1964). Dylan smiles vacuously, tipping his hat, while the same sky appears over Nashville on the back and Cash's free-form "poem" babbles inanities. What, exactly is, "by math of trend"? And has he actually seen Dylan' "scar of mend", presumably from the bike crash?

Even the apparently self-revelatory 'I Threw It All Away' is damaged by its folksiness: "take a tip from one who's tried". The word-play in 'Peggy Day' is vacuous. Only 'Lay Lady Lay' stands out, with its blue-collar sympathies: "his clothes are dirty but his hands are clean". Dylan's echoing "new" voice, which reminded many old friends of what he sounded like before he became an honorary Okie, is like a rusty gate squeaking, with an awful *basso profundo* which rises to a whine. Even Elvis in Las Vegas was never as bad as this. Musically, it is the same old Nashville crew, plus Charlie Daniels, Bob Wilson and Norman Blake, but it is river mud after the crystal sound of *John Wesley Harding*.

It really proves my point that country music can save the soul but that the Nashville machine – which is not the same thing at all – can embalm those who enter its rhinestone-embroidered halls. Back to the mountains, Bob. The full tape of the sessions with Johnny Cash are even more depressing, two men singing out of tune and mangling such classics as 'Good Old Mountain Dew' and 'T For Texas', wrestling the life out of them. 'One Too Many Mornings', once a gentle protest song before becoming an apocalyptic howl in '66, is now like two old men singing in the bath.

Kris Kristofferson – hardly a better singer himself – was working as a janitor in Columbia studios at the time, and must have thought that surely he could do better as a songwriter than the fare then going down. And he did. Dylan's final Nashville excursion, *Self Portrait*, boasts a huge cast of musicians, some American folk ballads (to which it adds nothing), and a few live tracks from the Isle Of Wight Festival. It could happily be reduced to a single – a one-sided single, at that. The live version of 'Like A Rolling Stone' is a particular travesty, with Dylan draining out all of the vitriol and adding the word "girl" wherever he can fit it in. As someone who affected a dislike of country music at the time, this album failed to redress any of my prejudices.

Ever after, Dylan would touch one of the twin poles of country music and Western myth in passing, though rarely the two together. What were the Traveling Wilburys but a kind of outlaw gang, getting old together in the saddle? On one side is his soundtrack to *Pat Garrett And Billy The Kid* – haunting, death-droppingly slow – or his unreleased take of the talked-sung 'New Danville Girl', with its tribute to Gregory Peck's film *The Gunfighter*, which was co-written with Sam Shepard, or the floating imagery of *Blood On The Tracks*. The same album was due to feature Eric Weissburg's *Deliverance*, though they were largely left in the hospitality room, twiddling their banjos. Dylan did revisit some of his *Basement* songs with Eric for *Greatest Hits: Volume Two*. He literally resurrected Greenwich Village for The Rolling Thunder Review. He reinvigorated gospel in his "born again" shows in late 1979, with that indefinable crackle of a man up on stage confronting his audience, so that the songs come to life, whereas in the studio they lay around like heavy puddings. Maybe he always was a hellfire preacher.

Under The Red Sky was a return to the rustic surrealism of *The Basement Tapes* and the Harry Smith magic show behind it. "Wiggle wiggle wiggle like a bowl of soup" is about as direct a song about love-making as you can get. The whole album at first sounded like Dylan had finally lost his mind, until you realised that it was a collection of nursery rhymes, like the final refuge of an exhausted spirit. The Edward Lear of the acid generation.

Two albums of acoustic folk, blues and country dutifully arrived, all written by others or simply anonymous, dividing his fans as ever. The irrepressible Andy Kershaw suggested of *Good As I Been To You* that he would play one track each week, not from the album but of the original version of each song "which Dylan has murdered on his new record". The age and sadness of Dylan was plain for all to see on the cover photo, his eyes screwed up as if in inner pain, though Biba Kopf in *Wire* reckoned that, "scarred with a lifetime's loneliness", his "weatherworn tones give the older songs, which he shuffles through his constantly changing concert repertoires, the patina of experience he couldn't have had when he wrote them".

Just as Dylan got away with singing which would have had a busker arrested for being a public nuisance, the vocals here could clear a public square, or even a mountain porch. There's something dead about his voice, and he slurs the words so you have to fight to decipher them. Even the fanzine *Homer, The Slut* admitted that "it lacks range", which is much like saying that Danny de Vito lacks height. His vocal on 'Blackjack Davey' is genuinely terrifying, like the backwards-speaking dwarf in *Twin Peaks*, or a sly and deranged mountain man. These songs draw you in like a seedy carnival huckster – "come this way, I've got something truly horrific to show you, something you will never, ever forget".

There is also some X-rated stuff here. The guitar playing sparkles throughout, which makes the whole album even more horrible, and I defy anyone to listen to it all at one sitting. Dylan sings as if each word is costing him his life blood. Mat Snow's comments in *Q*, that the album is "a rocking chair...his new *Nashville Skyline*", seem to describe a different record to that which I can hear.

The album didn't start out like this. It was originally planned as an all-electric affair, with sessions booked at Chicago's Acme Studios and dobro maestro David Bromberg slated to take the producer's chair. 26 traditional songs were laid down, some with "a sort of bluegrass sound – mainly acoustic, with some fiddle and mandolin", while others had horns and a rocking rhythm section. These have yet to surface, even on the bootleg circuit. Instead, Dylan retreated to the home studio he had in his garage and recorded a new batch of songs, both solo and acoustic. Just as he had once openly used Martin Carthy's repertoire as a grab bag, here he took arrangements from Nic Jones – second only to Carthy as an interpreter of English folk song, with his soothing voice inducing a near hypnotic state in his listener – and the Irish singer Paul Brady. Both are masters at transforming the tradition. Dylan, however, seems more interested in transcribing it. The voices of the dead seep through.

World Gone Wrong might have seemed a (further) step too far, but it's actually a more listenable and varied record. What is most extraordinary is the youthfulness of

Dylan's tone, even if it also sounds as ancient as hell. To put it back to back with his first album is to hear the whole span of a human life, from exuberance to world-weariness. At times he sounds oddly sexless, much like some of the old mountain women taped by Mike Seeger or Alan Lomax. Just listen to the sense of waste in his voice as he sings the line "All the friends I ever had are gone". He has seen the very worst, and nothing left in life is any kind of threat. By looking backwards, one can go forward.

The album was recorded in "a couple of afternoons". Dylan writes his own arcane footnotes this time around, and 'Broke Down Engine' puts a Blind Willie McTell song in the voice of Dock Boggs: "It's about revival, getting a new lease on life." Of the Anglo-American songs here, Dylan attributes the "perverse tale" of 'Love Henry' and 'Jack-A-Roe' to Tom Paley (as was 'Little Maggie' on the previous album, all three taken from Tom's 1953 Elektra ten inch *Folk Songs From The Appalachian Mountains*), and also namechecks The Lost City Ramblers. Jerry Garcia introduced him to 'Two Soldiers', while 'Lone Pilgrim' was learned from a Doc Watson album. Greenwich Village, revisited.

Talking to *Mojo* in 1998, Dylan recalled that he heard the Harry Smith *Anthology* "early on, when it was very difficult to find those kind of songs". It wasn't a set which got into many record stores; "I imagine I heard it over at somebody's house, some older kind of person…it's all poetry, every single one of those songs, and the language is different than current popular language and that's what attracted me to it in the first place." If you can learn songs like those, from the inside, "then there's nowhere you can't go". Dylan also put out a Jimmie Rodgers tribute album on his own label, Egyptian, on which he performs a jaunty 'My Blue-Eyed Jane'. He next plans to record a Carter Family tribute.

As to his own new album, *Time Out Of Mind*, Elvis Costello traced much of it back to the kind of songs Harry Smith had resurrected: "It's living tradition and he's doing it in such a smart way, taking the rural poetry in these songs and adding his own bit of poetry – that's the way these songs probably existed in the first place." These are songs which have "travelled across boundaries". In America, "every kind of culture mixed up – I mean, what's Bob Dylan doing living in Duluth? His family had to get there from somewhere." Russia, probably. "There's folk music explained right there."

The album in question will last forever. When I first heard it, I knew that this was the vision of a man back from the other side of death, as actually turned out to be the case. It's not just lyrics like "I've seen too much", or "the lonely graveyard of my mind", or best and worst of all "I was born and I'll die here, against my will", but the way he sings them, almost cheerfully now that he has totally given up hope. The traditional songs from the two previous albums have entered under his skin. This is an album that begins "I'm walking through streets that are dead", to the same guitar chord repeatedly struck like a heartbeat, or clods of fresh earth on a coffin.

Isis disinterred its traditional sources, finding many pre-echoes in Alan Lomax's *Folk Songs Of North America*: "riding in the buggy, Miss Mary Jane" and "I went to

212

Sugah town…I shook that sugah down" are taken almost directly. The final, longest and most bizarre song of all, 'My Heart's In The Highlands', is modelled on a Robert Burns poem, itself based on a Scottish folk song, while the final strange encounter with a waitress is an echo of a much more recent composition by Texas oddball Terry Allen. This really is a case of bringing it all back home.

As if looking for absolution, Dylan donned a C&W tie, spangled suit and cowboy hat when he and his country-flavoured tour band appeared in front of the Pope. A few days later, he appeared in front of me, and a few thousand others, at a concrete leisure centre in Bournemouth. That tiny figure on the stage, the back of his natty suit drenched with sweat, moved like a rock 'n' roller and inserted some of these same new songs, alongside past classics, including – of all things – 'This Wheel's On Fire'. The stage seemed to levitate. It was one of the most life-enhancing concerts I've ever seen. The ghost smiling at the back of the hall was Harry Smith, seeing his investment returned a thousandfold.

Four of the musicians who appeared on *Blonde On Blonde* subsequently formed Area Code 615. They cut two albums of cool instrumentals in the run-down and rustic Cinderella Sound Studios, Tennessee, covering 'Crazy Arms' and 'Get Back' in half a minute for both, and running all kinds of country changes over 'Hey Jude', 'Lady Madonna' and Otis Redding's 'I've Been Loving You Too Long'. It seems somehow inappropriate for the good ole boys photographed on the cover, with short, brylcreemed hair, paunches and leisurewear, playing baseball in the shadows. It's nice at last to see what these musical shift-workers look like, previously so studiously anonymous, but they all look as if they've spent too much time in the studio and need a good dose of sunshine. You wouldn't want to meet the sunken-eyed Bobby Thompson on a bright day, let alone a dark night.

Today, the music stands up surprisingly well, powered by Buttrey's drums and Norbert Putnam's electric bass, with banjo, steel guitar, mouth harp and fiddle all jockeying for pole position on top. The second album, *Trip In The Country*, opens with the Celtic chording of Bill Monroe's bluegrass tune 'Scotland'. 'Katy Hill', which starts off side two, is a traditional song with a defiantly Scottish lilt, with shouted, almost desperate lyrics and a psychedelic lead guitar part from Wayne Moss. Its a *tour de force* in an arrangement, as careful as De Danaan or The Chieftains, so no wonder that the following track is 'Sligo', a strange melange in which the blues meet bluegrass, along with a touch of Irish.

The material is almost all self-written this time, more relaxed, less like showing off. 'Stone Fox Chase' became the theme tune to 'The Old Grey Whistle Test', forever identified with Bob Harris with his beardy grin 'n' pullover, back when this music was perceived as too dangerous for mass consumption. It still is; the only place you'll find alt country with any regularity is with the same Bob Harris, on his Saturday night show on Radio Two.

There are clues that the trip of the title is more than the kind you can get on a Greyhound bus. Mac Gayden sings 'Gray Suit Men', in which the usual dope-smokers sneer at the rest of the world, and 'Devil Weed And Me (Buffalo Herd)' is even more explicit. It opens with what sounds like a sitar, which is then replaced by a banjo, rising above a slow jazzy drone. A saloon-bar piano enters the mix, then a soulful fiddle, a piercing mouth harp and a playful lead guitar. The whole thing finally calms down and fades away with a grown-up kid's duet on recorder and kalimba.

Talking to Max Bell, Moss said: "I noticed that recording with Dylan was more relaxing and more enjoyable than the usual country things we did". (Moss had begun his Nashville career engineering a 1959 collection of country hoe-downs for Leon "Psycho" Payne, then played sessions for The Everly Brothers.) Dylan "looked very strange to us. We were still what you'd call rednecks and he changed a lot of heads. He also altered a lot of the studio techniques we were familiar with; the new projects that began to spring up in Nashville couldn't have happened before." Between takes, "we'd sit around and jam, playing stuff like 'Lady Madonna', adding dirty lyrics". Unfortunately – or perhaps not – Area Code 615 dropped the words. Moss began to work with the likes of Linda Ronstadt and Joan Baez, as well as learning something else from Dylan: "When he came to town, we were green as far as the dope culture went." Not for long, though.

Steve Burgess was the first English writer to properly link the second wave of psychedelia to the first, and he died (allegedly) in a morass of witchcraft and drugs. He wrote in *Dark Star* that "somebody must've been fooling with the water supply in Tennessee, because deep redneck country somehow caught the hippie ethic bug and suddenly people like Billy Swan, with his twisted rockabilly, and Dennis Linde...came lurching out of the backwoods clearly under the influence of whatever's growing out there in the briar patch." Neatly enough, Swan pens a sleeve note for Linde's self-titled album on Elektra, on which Dennis builds a spaceship and Wayne Moss supplies the other-worldly sound effects. Area Code 615 were a victim of record company politics: "At the end of that, we had 'ding dong the code is dead' 'cause Polydor were disenchanted with our lack of success and we said goodbye."

When they appeared at The Fillmore West, on a bill with Country Joe And The Fish, Bill Graham acted as the band's cheerleader. The problem was that the individual musicians could always earn more on sessions than out on the road, so they never really melded into a band. The same has continued to be the case with Nashville session men, and it also applied when Area Code 615 mutated into Barefoot Jerry, with Moss as their frontman, together with Ken Buttrey, Mac Gayden and keyboard-playing Doctor John Harris. Barefoot Jerry was named after an ancient Appalachian fiddle-playing grocer, who chose to sit outside his store awaiting customers with nothing on his feet and a fiddle in his hands.

On *Groceries*, which compiles their first two albums, Jerry is photographed with his fiddle, a straw boater and, confusingly, his shoes and socks firmly in place.

On the sumptuous inner sleeve, his shop fronts a single-lane highway, and then a rock-strewn mountain torrent which could have come straight out of *Deliverance*. Harvey Magee's sleeve notes say it all: "There has always been a mysterious haze that hangs over the Smoky Mountains that gives them a haunting quality...an eerie blue-green aura that can hold you spellbound and captivate your soul." Barefoot Jerry is "caretaker to these hills", a man whose "existence is a simple one. He'll offer up a tune from a beat-up old fiddle using a hickory stick for a bow, or he'll tell a tale about some 'haints' that live down in the 'holler'. The old man is in tune with his environment and his whole world lies in the simplicity of mountain life."

Moss and his chums came over from Nashville to take up residence in an old log cabin behind the store, and there put together the band which now bears his name. They came "to feed off the mountain magic, and feel the juices of their creativity stir" against a landscape of mountain streams, wild flowers and "the majestic presence of some higher guiding force". The six albums which resulted have yet to be given their proper due. Here is the very finest country rock ever made.

Barefoot Jerry was subtitled "Southern Delight", and side one is described by Burgess as "an almost single-minded PR job for homegrown weed", though the album is also much more. Guitars soar from a solid rhythmic base, with that extra touch of mystery and relaxation that the mountain atmosphere supplies, with consummate pros stretching out, taking the odd musical risk but letting their knowledge of ensemble work feed in too. Built up from loose jams taped in the cabin, this is probably the most "professional" music ever to evolve from the hills. There is also a hard-headed questioning going on here about what it means exactly to be a Southern man as the Seventies dawn.

First up, though, is a song offering hospitality in the mountain tradition: "We don't care what state you come from, we don't care what state your mind is in." Mellowness is the keyword, "calloused hands and open minds", so take a toke on the hash pipe and you can crash overnight if you want to. *Deliverance*, this ain't.

Mac Gayden's 'I'm Proud To Be A Redneck' is the key song, and its call to peace and love now sounds naive but optimistic: "We've got to renew this place...you don't have to be ashamed." Wayne Moss' 'Smokies' is sung in his laconic voice over a trademark Barefoot Jerry shuffle, and here is someone who took Dylan's injunction to go get stoned literally: "'Smokin' is their claim to fame/and that's how the Smokies got their name." The next song urges caution about such self-inflicted oblivion: "Quit while you're a Head/don't get yourself too high, and blow your mind." It's set to the kind of good-time, richly-chorded music which in England only Reg King And The Action (and, later, Mighty Baby) could quite match – good-hearted music. With 'Blood Is Not The Answer', we're into what Burgess describes as "Mac Gayden preaching truth devoutly" over a church-like chorus, and with a double-time instrumental break "that reaches several climaxes that would amaze and delight your lover". Gayden comes back, and the song seems to float its way to heaven.

The second, self-titled album was on a new label, but was much the same as before: lush, with instrumentals played with impossible precision, interspersed with Moss' realistic lyrics set to *Pink Panther*-style staccato rhythms. 'In God We Trust' has a middle section straight out of a church service, restating the Ten Commandments. Like a toked-up Carter Family, the band hymn the delights of a family night in. This is music without a message, "just for the body and the soul", like Little Feat at their loosest. It's as strange a brew as ever came out of Nashville via the mountains, incorporating dope idealism, questions as to where the South was heading, a bluegrass tune in the form of 'Little Maggie', the sound of a joint being lit, and a spot of smut. 'Fish 'n' Tits' was self-explanatory, but many English listeners were puzzled by 'Snuff Queen'. (A Nashville groupie, if you must know.)

Watchin' TV, on a third record label, ratchets up the funk and the vocal blend, leading all the way up to 'Mother Nature's Way Of Saying High', which Max Bell describes, without hyperbole, as involving "a melodic and spatial grace unparalleled in the rock idiom". Strummed acoustic guitar chords are followed by a meditative vocal about the morning sun, and then the band crash in. The lyrics lurch in and out of bad weather and praise the farmer, and then the ensemble start flying high, fuelled by thunderous drums – a redneck Grateful Dead – and faded out on full power.

It is this sense of space which defines Barefoot Jerry, the "blue haze" of mountain air translated into crochets and quavers. The next couple of albums marked time, but had that same mixture of delicacy and spunk. On *You Can't Get Off With Your Shoes On*, a song to Frodo is outweighed by Moss' 'Slowin' Down': "The mass transit of highways is eliminating the fields, with folks taking the speed limit to the level where you couldn't enjoy the scenery if your life depended on it." Take that, Dave Dudley. *Keys To The Country* has been described as having an "arrogant classiness", as it covers Jimmy Driftwood's piece of American folklore 'The Battle Of New Orleans' and Mac Gayden's joyous though simple-minded 'Appalachian Fever', a love song to a landscape. Wayne Moss comes on like country's answer to Kevin Ayers, with that same deep-voiced philosophising, on the deeply romantic 'You Can't Say It All'.

Barefootin' is both the band's swansong, and its ace in the hole. On the cover, six country boys – by now hirsute and a little broad in the beam – pose in white dress suits, with canes and boaters but still no shoes. McCoy is back, and here is acid country's finest hour. The good-time feeling here is redolent of life in Tennessee, which Bell himself finds "so slow that the average American would die of boredom after the briefest sojourn". Conversely, it's a lifestyle on which Moss and his musical colleagues thrive, though they are aware of the presence of snakes in Eden, too. 'Hiroshima Hole' is about Hartsville, the world's largest nuclear power plant, and Wayne sings as seriously as your life while the band swells behind him, urgent yet luxuriant: "The solar cell is a wishing well/on which no tax is due." The song ends with a gong being struck. Or is that an explosion? "They cool reactors using my drinking water", Moss complains to Max Bell; "if it leaks we all get cancer, and if terrorists seized it they could level one third of Tennessee. I took a lot of care with that song, 40 parts for acoustic guitar and six electrics. That's why we can't do it live." Only Barefoot Jerry could follow this with a gentle love song, and then with the urgent 'Tokin' Ticket', about the varying penalties for possessing marijuana throughout America.

The two final tracks see the band heading for the hills: "Your ulcer and your migraines won't get you anywhere/your doctor and your analyst won't help you keep your hair." Up at Jerry's grocery store, you can throw away your "tranquilising pills". Then back to the roots on 'Highland Grass', with its quick-fire Celtic banjo riff, and an abrupt end. It was 1977, and punk music was pushing aside such music forever.

Like dinosaurs sniffing their last breath of air, Dennis Linde was also continuing his caucasian soulful search for 'Everlasting Love' – the song of his which, bizarrely, the Scottish boy band Love Affair took to the top of the British charts. Better than any of his own songs, which now sound as if they were recorded through a bell jar, was a truly spooky cover of 'Ghost Riders In The Sky'. *Dark Star* described it as "cactus desert eerie, flickered with cold blueflame lightning guitar, echoed with phantom voices…a cosmick western with unearthly cowboys and demon cattle. Stay clear of that jimson weed, *hombre*." This was the kind of desert-bred weirdness that would resurface after punk with the likes of Giant Sand and some of the alt country bands.

Meanwhile, Mac Gayden had gone off the rails with a band called Skyboat, who projected ions at the audience and albums like *Hymn To The Seeker*, on the sleeve of which he mindlessly intones that "the east and the west wing whisper seek the summer where the nest is woven of immortal thoughts". The music is made to match, with lots of flute and some disorientating jump cuts. Come in, Johnny Rotten. Please.

The late seventies saw the sad decline of another band, The Band, which existed before Dylan but needed his creative spark to jog them off in a new direction. For so studiously mysterious a combo, Levon Helm's memoirs, *This Wheel's On Fire*, opened up a lot of windows onto dusty rooms. When you filter out the inter-band feuding, it emphasises how indebted The Band were to country music. It's like the whole of this book, on fast forward and retold by a great musician.

Helm was as country as you can get, born on his father's cotton farm near Turkey Scratch, Arkansas. Among his earliest memories is that of singing with his father – "a fountain of music" – and hearing 'Blue Moon Of Kentucky' on the family radio. The first live show he saw, in a tent, was Bill Monroe And His Blue Grass Boys: "They took that old hillbilly music, sped it up, and basically invented bluegrass music; the bass in its place, the mandolin above it, the guitar tying the two together, and the violin on top, playing the long notes to make it sing." The banjoist, who just happened to be Earl Scruggs, "backed the whole thing up, answering everybody". The rest of Helm's career was set there and then. It really "tattooed my brain".

Helm started earning money from music when he paired up with his sister, who played a broomstick bass, with himself on harmonica and Jews harp. As Levon And Linda, they played a mixture of current hits and "the old songs we'd learned at home". And then he saw Elvis Presley. Twice.

Helm differentiates between the two shows, as part of the movement from country to rock 'n' roll. In as early as the 1930s, his own father was one of those pioneers who began to sing the blues "with a twang, and it became something else, with a different bump to it. That was the seed." Then white people started requesting Muddy Waters and Sonny Boy Williamson. Sam Phillips began his billion-dollar quest, and the Sun sound "was country music, all right, but it had that good black backbeat in there as well". The first time he saw Elvis, it was just with Scotty Moore and Bill Black on doghouse bass. There were "no drums", as by law you could not have a drummer in a place in which alcohol was served.

The second Presley sighting was about six months later, at a high-school auditorium, and by now Black was playing electric bass, releasing Scotty to make his guitar strings "cry". DJ Fontana "played like a big-band drummer – full throttle. DJ set Elvis free." The effect was "devastating".

Local heroes Conway Twitty and Ronnie Hawkins made the same progression, and Levon joined The Hawks, watching new members arrive when Ronnie relocated to Canada. Rick Danko learned country music from his mandolin- and banjo-playing father, while Garth Hudson "sort of grew up with country music because my father would find all the hoe-down stations on the radio". When they started heading out on their own, Helm named his group The Crackers, a kind of fuck-you to anyone who reckoned them a bunch of simple country boys. Record company politics renamed them, but Levon's stories led Robbie Robertson to shape a whole mythology drawn from American history and folklore.

The Band never played country music, as such. What they did was to sound as if they were a hundred years old. Producer John Simon reckoned that they played an "Appalachian scale", while Robertson called it "mountain music", "because Woodstock is in the mountains", and Al Aronowitz dubbed it "country rock with the taste of Red River cereal and the consistency of King Biscuit Flower". The Band even dressed like mountain men, in "dark western cut clothes, string ties and black boots", with hats from Robbie's collection. On *Music From Big Pink*, one photo was deliberately aged while the other, 'Next Of Kin', included their families, young and old.

This is music that still sounds richly odd, almost static. Group members swap instruments and vocals seemingly with no attention to ego. That came later. The whole thing is mixed to show up ensemble playing rather than individual solos – there is lots of sustain – and the voices drip age and passion, with old-time harmonies and enigmatic lyrics as deep as a starless night. It is music which consoles and yearns. Manuel's 'In A Station' is about Overlook Mountain, and is a fine example of the "visionary" quality of the album, embodying country comforts after years on the road: "Once I climbed up the face of a mountain, and ate the wild fruit there." Richard's singing on 'I Shall Be Released' is just as other-worldly, a plea for tolerance, but as lost and lonely as a ghost. Here is true communal music – and The Band looked that way, too, on their rare stage appearances, tossing the melody line to each other like a superbly-drilled sports team. Everyone knows and plays their parts intuitively. The musical complicity here could only come from a bunch of musicians so long together that they are virtually telepathic.

It must be remembered that this music was created, like *The Basement Tapes*, during "a civil war, a time of conflict and turmoil in the United States. There was tension in the air, sometimes so thick you could barely wade through it."

When The Band moved to LA to record their second album, with the working title *Harvest*, some neighbours reckoned that the "grouchy, bearded mountaineers who had taken over Sammy Davis' house" were some kind of weird cult. Maybe they were. The resulting album inhabits its own universe, the ultimate example of Americana (created from their own guts by a band of whom only Helm was born south of the Canadian border), perfectly balanced, from its earth-coloured sleeve to its supernatural playing. The voices are more differentiated, with Levon a raconteur, Richard still questing for release and Rick the cowpoke, honest but embittered. Robbie is now silent, talking through his reined-in guitar (but when he occasionally gives it its head, it's "wall-of-death" time) and lyrics which can compress a century into a tightly-rhymed chorus. The music runs the full gamut, from the primal rock 'n' roll with which they all grew up to 'Rocking Chair', which sounds like it was taped on a back porch high in the hills. The album is a collection of short stories, based in rural life but never simply nostalgic. They are impersonal while presenting a whole cast of believable characters.

Like *John Wesley Harding*, these songs are also parables for life in the city, endlessly meaningful. Thus 'King Harvest' is about farmers banding together to form unions, and poverty ("don't judge me by these shoes"), but there's also a harvest moon and a carnival at the edge of town, and Levon reckons that "some of the lyrics came out of a discussion we had one night about the times we'd seen". The song is set in the past, but set precisely now: "It was that magical feeling that pulled us through." This was a conscious attempt to create a living mythology, and time shows Robertson as the editor of a collective effort, not a songwriter with five puppets playing and singing his creations.

In 'Rag Mama Rag', "we were trying to bring to mind the feel of those old acoustic songs like 'In The Pines'." Robbie and Levon went to the public library in Woodstock to research 'The Night They Drove Old Dixie Down', a "workshop song" planned and written over months, not minutes. It was a luxury which could only be obtained over long country nights, and no wonder that over in England bands like Traffic were doing much the same. When the shockwaves of The Band's music hit British shores, it made a lot of bands swap psychedelic mayhem for a similar search for roots. Fairport Convention were a case in point, simplifying their musical structures and plunging back into English folklore. When this proved to be not purist enough for Ashley Hutchings, he dressed his new band, Steeleye Span (an Irish-English hybrid), in old-style clothes and bin black. Undertakers to the 1960s.

Ironically, it was the pressures of fame and the use of heroin – that most unfaithful servant of them all – which wrecked it all. The songwriting and subtlety leached away from subsequent albums, Robertson jumped ship to produce the Tennessean draft-dodger Jesse Winchester up in Canada, and remnants of The Band continued to recycle the same old songs, to smaller audiences, until one night Richard Manuel hanged himself. A bootleg CD exists of his last New York gig, in summer 1986, *The Last Moving Shadows*, and that voice sounds even more lonesome and haunted than ever. If The Band were about togetherness, this performance is friendless and naked. Never has 'Long Black Veil' sounded so realistic, especially the way in which the mic suddenly catches his voice as he sings about the scaffold being near.

A rowdy audience at the Lone Star Cafe hear him and unspecified friends go through the same old songs yet again. It could indeed be Danko and Hudson up on stage with him, or their stand-ins: there's certainly lots of accordion. The drummer certainly ain't no Levon Helm, or even a second Richard Manuel. Whoever they are, nothing can touch Richard's slowed-down melancholy on a countryish 'You Don't Know Me', or his percussive electric piano on a gruffly-sung 'Stage Fright', although that song too is now closer to the bone than entertainment should be. 'Mystery Train' is a rockabilly ghost ride indeed, going straight to hell, while on 'Cripple Creek' he imitates Helm's country vowels. On 'I Shall Be Released' he is back to his own falsetto, as strained and vulnerable as a child in the cradle. Things end with a joyful 'Willie And The Hand Jive'.

Manuel also supplied a Randy Newman soundalike vocal – so deep and worn out on 'Country Boy' – on some of The Band's better-than-expected comeback album *Jericho*. Needless to say, this Jericho is in Kentucky, just as the Nazareth in 'The Weight' is where Martin guitars come from, not Jesus. They also cover Dylan's 'Blind Willie McTell' almost better than the original. It was a law of diminishing returns, however. By this time King Harvest has also claimed Rick Danko, but The Band's early music lives on as strong and potent as ever. 30 years has merely tested its mettle and found it sold as a rock. For the film of *The Last Waltz* – how typical for The Band to play their last gig all together as a party and Thanksgiving meal, with lots of old friends dropping in! – The Band added a separately-filmed sequence with Emmylou Harris singing 'Evangeline', their song about Minnie Pearl, that mainstay of the Grand Ole Opry: "She represented our homage to country music." Levon went on to star as Loretta Lynn's coal-miner father. It was a perfect match.

Helm went up to Kentucky to research the role, and found it like another homecoming. He had been with such people all his life, and "I knew that families like ours make up in love for one another what they might have lacked in material things". Robertson acted in *Carney*, then traced his own roots back to the native American forebears, tracing history backwards, as usual. Fine as the resulting albums have been, they feel like personal projects, while the joy of The Band was that they created a history for us all, a place to dwell as the Sixties imploded and all certainties and idealism had fled. Elliott Landy was the court photographer, and his book *Woodstock Vision* looked back 25 years or so later, to tell its own story. It progresses from scenes of high-society debauchery – with Lauren Bacall looking even older than The Band, but wrecked as well – through the hippie princelings lost in a world of drugs and psychedelic lights, and onto The Band, like a five-headed beast, out in Nature, and at home in their kitchen or playing up in the studio.

Here, too, is a fresh-faced Dylan with his young family, and even Van Morrison, uncomfortable in a blue mini-cloak, raises a slight smile as he stands out in the woods with a woman and child (not his own, but who's counting?). The book culminates with the so-called Woodstock festival, with the likes of The Band onstage, but it now looks less like flowering than it does compost, the city crowds fouling up all that good clean country air. I'm sure it didn't look that way from their point of view, but after all that sense of space here is the crowd who would later flood into Woodstock itself, driving the musicians further into the woods. Eden never lasts, here on Earth. Landy looks back now to a time of "innocence, belief, faith? I felt I was part of something that was changing the world." It's still there, in The Band's first two LPs.

Here was a "tree with roots" strong enough to which you could strap yourself, wherever you came from. The Band, slightly older than their listeners, acted as surrogate parents, none more patriarchal than Garth Hudson, with his preacher's beard. They played music rooted firmly in a rich and ancient soil, using instruments to match, and many former hippies went on to trace those same roots back to the country music in which they were first nurtured. Helm got together with Dr John and a mixed-race musical crew to make his Levon Helm And The RCO All Stars in 1977, the year that Barefoot Jerry gave up and punk thought it was blowing away all of this music and everything it represented – beards, Bob Harris, musical complexity, slowness, country delights. "I'm so bored with the USA," The Clash declared, seeing off what they thought of as cultural imperialism and playing the music of The Stooges, MC5 and Richard Hell instead. The cover is of snowy woodlands, in which is inset a log-built house, lights blazing, and alongside songs by Chuck Berry and Booker T is a heartfelt treatment of the public-domain song 'That's My Home'.

In the Sixties, despite the apparent dominance of Nashville 'n' strings, real country music was reinvigorating itself from the roots up. The Opry spurned television but others didn't, and another old friend, Red Foley, turned up as compere of the *Ozark Jubilee*, with the usual cast of rustic clowns, like Uncle Cyp, and sweet singers, Brenda Lee amongst them. Shows hosted by The Wilburn Brothers and Porter Wagoner were particularly rich receptacles for traditional country.

In 1969, three shows moved into the mainstream. *Hee Haw* was "hillbilly to the point of grotesque parody", perpetuating the image of the mountain man as buffoon, but it also slipped in a gospel quartet – including Buck Owens – each week, singing the old religious songs to a single acoustic guitar.

The Johnny Cash Show brought the likes of Bob Dylan and cajun fiddler Doug Kershaw to a family audience, as well as featuring Mother Maybelle Carter and a history section, 'Stop This Train', "a combination of history and song" which included archive film and photos. As in his music, Johnny Cash too was trying to give America back to its people.

Glen Campbell's Goodtime Hour was more 'countrypolitan', though he was still rootsy enough to feature his parents and give lots of prime time to his high-pitched country giggle. It was a signpost to the future.

Meanwhile, country music spanned the world, with Grandpa Jones playing with German musicians The Munich Mountaineers and Red Hayes gigging in the Japanese version of the "Gland Ole Opry". Foreign imitators soon followed, and however bizarre the country styles of the Belgian Kitty Prins or the Austrian Connie Tex Hat, it was really only them bringing the music back home. English songwriter Roger Cook, of the appalling Blue Mink and other light-pop harmony groups (he was the Flowerpot Men), moved to Nashville and became a millionaire in the process.

England took Slim Whitman to its heart, and a strong fan club still exists. Slim was a riverboat gambler lookalike, digitally challenged having lost some fingers in an accident, an old country smoothie, and the man whose yodelled 'Indian Love Call' repelled the aliens in *Mars Attacks!* I listened to a whole double album as "research", and it was like eating three boxes of sickly chocolates in one go. England also took as genuine that outrageous ham Boxcar Willie, a rambling man in hobo dress with a boxcar-load of railroad songs. He had been a civilian flight engineer in the real world, but regressed to overalls and a floppy hat and, more to the point, a repertoire taken from Hank Williams, Jimmie Rodgers and Roy Acuff. All this from a first visit in 1977 –again, that symbolic year.

Meanwhile, back in the late 1950s, there was a renewed interest in such Americana, alongside the urban folk revival. Bobby Bare could be, by turns, "mournful or raucous", but his rustic delivery did not prevent him from reviving the traditional mountain song '500 Miles', and he has gone on to interpret stories in song by his contemporaries. This is not an arcane or academic exercise, not with titles like 'Greasy Grit Gravy' and 'I've Never Gone To Bed With An Ugly Woman'. 1974's *Lullabies, Legends And Lies* presents folklore as comically re-invented in the songs of Shel Silverstein – "gather round fellows, I'll tell you some tales about murder and blueberry pies" – to the old-style backing of dobro, fiddle and steel guitar. Here is giant Paul, magic Marie (a "sure-hit songwriter pen"), Rosalie's 'Good Eats' cafe where time stops, plus a vomit-inducing duet with Bobby Bare Jr, who asks the questions. Bobby Thompson chugs along on banjo, and there's a live audience. Bare's delivery is sharp enough to cut open their ears. This is not relaxing.

Shel Silverstein acts as creative director for Bare's *Hard Time Hungrys*, which was released the next year, a concept album about life on the streets with spoken dialogue between songs, remembering one Depression and foreseeing another one. Bare looks careworn on the front cover, and a tramp goes through a dustbin on the back. Bobby's voice gains majesty is this context, and on these songs he sounds like a prophet of doom. The talk between songs is like a catalogue of (mainly) poor white-male sourness and despair, on which the songs in turn comment. A kid's chorus proceed to sing 'Daddy's Been Around The House Too Long". Bare himself sounds like Johnny Cash with a sore throat. This is the kind of music which refuses to melt into the background. "Talk about something else" – this from a farmer gradually going bust. "What do you want to talk about?" "Nothing."

The same year saw as different an album as is possible to imagine by the same artist, Bare's *Cowboys And Daddies*. "Today, being a cowboy is more an attitude than an occupation. Most of them ride up pick-up trucks or anything that'll hold still long enough for them to get on." Left-field songwriters like Terry Allen and Ray Wylie Hubbard have songs covered here, including Hubbard's deeply questionable 'Up Against The Wall, Redneck Mother'. It is the mother's son who is the real subject, "he's kicking hippies' asses and raising hell," and to Bare he's a hero. The next song is about a man who loves a cow, and that's alright, too. *Me And McDill*, meanwhile, leaves Nashville for Muscle Shoals, past "not so young good old boys in jeans and summer cowboy hats". This is Bare's constituency, both as subjects and as listeners. Bare has a new sheaf of songs by Bob McDill, writing for "that sad magic voice", and the concept here is the struggle to become, and stay, a country music star.

I find in Bare's work what everyone else says Merle Haggard gives you: a hard-eyed look at the world from a blue collar poet. Bare might not write his own songs, but he seems less sentimental than Haggard, more pitiless. These are two wonderful surnames, though, just right for the territory they set out to cover.

In 'Hillbilly Hell', Bobby returned some years ago as an unknown singer, scuffling for work with "a song and a guitar and a message to tell", and he does so with the utmost economy, over a rolling piano riff. The young hopeful watches limousines go by as he pumps gas, and sleeps in his car while living out in his head the usual Nashville dream, in (with a neat sideways look at Hank Williams) the "cold, cold heart of Tennessee". The trouble is, we only hear from those who have won through. As Malone points out, Bare went from petrol pump to microphone because he "reinvigorated the storytelling tradition in country music, and moved the music a bit closer to its roots".

This wasn't necessarily either a comfortable or a forgiving process. The title of another song here, 'Don't Think You're Too Good For Country Music (Just Because You Can Rock 'n' Roll)' carries an implicit threat, though whether ironic or not is hard to tell: "Your licks are neat, but you won't eat/until you learn one little lesson…they don't boogie much in Nashville." Don't waste our time here with your BB King or ZZ Top blues riffs, boy…

The 1950s saw a resurgence of "saga songs", mainly released on Columbia Records' 41300 series, as if someone had planned it. Johnny Horton's 'Springtime In Alaska' was in the Robert Service tradition of rough tales from the Yukon, and was followed by a series of cowboy songs from Johnny Cash, such as 'Don't Take Your Guns To Town', and then Horton again with his hit version of Jimmy Driftwood's song 'The Battle Of New Orleans'.

The song starts with banjo and electric guitar in unison, then military drums, Horton's nasal rendition of this military engagement with the English, and a manly chorus. It's half childrens' nursery rhyme and half comic monologue, and totally unique. Lonnie Donegan recorded a faster version, which somehow loses the charm of the thing (maybe because he was on the losing side). Jimmy Driftwood was a singer from the Ozarks who recorded a much longer version on an album with the tongue-in-cheek title *Newly Discovered Early American Folk Songs*, which he had supposedly used to teach his students key points in American history. It was based on the old traditional fiddle tune 'The Eighth Of January'.

Johnny Horton was first marketed as "The Singing Fisherman" and as another Presley, raised in a poor Southern family and fully in charge of things, whether he sang rockabilly or smoochier ballads. He caught the history bug from Driftwood and went on to write his own concept album of Americana, *Johnny Horton Makes History*, which was more fuel for the skiffle craze across the Atlantic. Horton was killed in a car crash in 1960, while Driftwood went on to establish a centre of Ozark folklore at Mountain View. Which leaves us with…

I've been putting off a proper discussion of Johnny Cash's nearly 50-year-long career for as long as I could. Anyone not reacting with respect and fear to his best work can't have been listening properly, while much of his output is patriotic dross. As an artist, he achieved everything that his fellow Sun pioneer, Elvis, muffed: his own distinct voice with a world-view to match, however pitiless and uncomfortable that might be. His role as a survivor now gives him the status of an Old Testament prophet, spreading threats and wisdom, someone you can't turn your back on. The original man in the long black coat.

Just ask U2. Cash is probably best approached as a raconteur, a man who carries the weight of the world with him but also looks and sounds as mean as a rattlesnake. Put next to him, the boastful, prancing Mick Jagger resembles a powder puff; at Altamont, Cash would have probably waded into the crowd rather than make a dash for the helicopter. The recent remastered and augmented *At Folsom Prison*, from 1968, is as good as any place to start, with its cover photo of that pitiless face looking down with half a smile and half a sneer, with a Fifties haircut and sweat rolling down his cheek. He does look like someone who would shoot a man in Reno "just to watch him die".

If anyone thinks I am simply peddling the authorised version, I would ask if they would care to hold a stage in front of an audience of convicted murderers, thieves, rapists and the like for an hour, let alone seem to taunt them with songs about hangings, dungeons and prison blues, not to mention two put into the mouths of executed felons, set to his band's jog-trot rhythm, and throw in some sexual innuendo. Now proudly uncensored is some of Cash's language, a long acoustic folk holler about John Henry, along with 'Busted' and 'Joe Bean'. Cash poses in front of the Victorian gothic frontis of the prison – alongside his wife, June Carter Cash – in a black three-piece suit, with shoes and patent leather hair to match, enters the gates like a dark prince, and then sings within touching distance of the felons and their armed guards.

Under the harsh strip lights he looks as hard as anybody present, and his voice is like granite: unmelodic but remorseless. The band comprise Carl Perkins, Luther Perkins (no relation) and Marshall Grant on bass, the latter two being the original Tennessee Two from the start of his career. Carl Perkins' drummer, WS Holland joined them in 1958, and he's here, too. Here The Tennessee Three, plus friends, stand ramrod straight, dancing to the beat. Luther was dead within the year. Johnnie's father – presumably not an inmate – is then introduced (to cheers), and then the assistant governor (to boos). Between songs, announcements boom out over the tannoy, then at the end: "Please hold your seats until released by the officer, then go out by the side door." It's like being back at school, but with gun law to keep control.

Johnny's handwritten note explains what it's like to be stuck behind bars, told from the inside: "All you have with you in the cell is your bare animal instinct." Hence his decision to play such gigs, for his "brothers". Suddenly all becomes clear, the joshing, the rough humour, the sudden bout of sentimentality and the shouts of recognition. These inmates, who know when they're being patronised, recognise one of their own up there on the stage. It's the mountain people's belief in family as the ultimate human organisation – hence the feuds – here taken to its logical conclusion. Steve Earle certainly recognises a father figure when he adds that, "in 1991, I dropped off the edge of the Earth, resurfacing in '95 by way of the Davidson Criminal Justice Centre". Later that year, he met Cash, who offered him a piece of steak, "as if nothing had happened..." and then, the sting in the tail, "...to either one of us".

Cash repeated the trick in 1969 at San Quentin, with Shel Silverstein's 'A Boy Called Sue' and Dylan's bespoke song 'Wanted Man', plus a John Sebastian composition, of all things, and the traditional 'Wreck Of The Old 97'. If anyone is entitled to sing about American history and myth, it is Cash. He was born in Arkansas in 1932, and has since traced his family tree to 17th-century Scotland. His early claim to be part Cherokee is now admitted to be a self-deluding fabrication, just like Shania Twain. Both artists are temperamentally nomads, though, so maybe this inheritance is based on soul, not bloodlines.

Dylan told Dawidoff that Cash remains "the kind of person you'd turn around and he'd be gone". Johnny himself puts this down to the influence of his father, who was always off on the next job. Cash also tours endlessly, but more psychologically interesting is his comment about how he broke fruit jars as a child "just for meanness". His older brother, Jack, walked into a saw blade, and Johnnie watched him die over the next week. When the ambulance found him, according to a serviceable biography by Christopher Wren, "he was holding his stomach in, and he said to the driver: 'I picked up as much of my intestines as I could, but there was about six feet that was all chopped off". They breed them tough down South. He then added, pathetically, "tell me something, because I'm going to die".

Dawidoff makes this the key to Cash's running away from his own talent – more specifically from putting these things down in lyrics – and a hollowness he perceives at his centre. One could equally erect all kinds of theories about Presley losing his twin brother at birth. Meanness, though, remains the key to Cash's whole career. Bill Malone sees Cash as a kind of precursor of David Bowie, a method actor who chose to dress in black and recycle folk-based material. His biographer stresses this folk element, with Cash meeting Dylan back in the early Sixties in Greenwich Village: "He came down to the Gaslight. I was struck by how tall he was. He was dressed in black, with a white shirt. I saw him again at Newport. He gave me his guitar." Cash wrote fan letters to Dylan, too, and was in the Village to learn songs from the Indian writer Peter LaFarge, of whose work he was an early champion.

Even Wren, when not writing on country music, "has travelled extensively through England and Scotland, singing American folk songs". When you listen to Cash's Sun recordings, it is neither the wild and sexual rockabilly, on which Presley failed to improved, nor anything that could be described as country music. However, it has the leanness – in its simple accompaniment, in Cash's stripped-down voice firing words like bullets, and in the verbal restraint of his songs – of the folk tradition. There are lots of Hank Williams covers, though, and Johnny grew up on the masters. When he married June Carter, Johnny told her: "I was a fan of The Carter Family back when I was a little kid." When he first met Maybelle, June told her "I think he's scared of you." In awe of her talent and historical importance, more like.

Cash is deeply country, in his family tragedy and the poverty in which he was raised in Dyess, a whites-only community created by the New Deal to resettle farmers on productive land. It was like being original settlers all over again, and Cash learned early how to get his hands dirty. True stories of rural hardship fed fairly directly into songs like 'Pickin' Time' and 'Five Feet High And Rising', about the flooding of the Mississippi River. Cash would make up impromptu songs where he stood. As his own autobiography bears out, he was also deeply country in his addiction to pills, and the fleshy over-keen delight he seems to take in his own weakness, matched with a fitful religious intensity.

Cash's concept albums for Columbia in the 1960s have been written out of country history, mocked as camp or ignored because they contain few of his hits. They can certainly be toe-curlingly embarrassing, especially when he starts narrating with that same patriotic sob in his voice as John Wayne, usually with a choir somewhere in the middle distance and the US flag flapping on his lawn. They're usually better on the drawing board than in execution, mainly because, like Walt Disney, they cut out all of the natural poetry and replace it with sentimental doggerel. At its worst it's more grown-up than most opera libretti, but it can still descend to the level of "Over fields of new-turned sod, and then communion with my God, I walked alone." As one would, if one went around reciting stuff like that.

They also reveal an ambition which puts other country artists in the shade, and a love of his native land which surely makes him the lost godfather of Americana. Aside from the two cowboy albums already discussed, my own favourite is *From Sea To Shining Sea*, a tour of forgotten places. The lines quoted above are unrepresentative, and are followed by genuine excitement in Johnny's voice as he describes finding primitive flint arrowheads. Far better is his prologue to 'You And Tennessee', which rings as true as his voice. It is presumably dedicated to June Carter, and after a lonely banjo starts up he speaks as if to himself: "Like a sweet rippling mountain stream goes the sound of the banjo on Cripple Creek. Never beginning, never ending, just rippling on and on. So does the land just ripple on and on. As the heart gets soft on a woman, so the heart can get soft on the land. And to fall in love with a woman as well as the land is to surely be in love."

Cash tackled the folk songs of his native South on two early albums: *Songs Of Our Soil*, with typical Nashville over-production; and *Now There Was A Song: Memories From The Past*, on the cover of which he wears a straw hat and rustic shirt, leaning on a fence – Huck Finn or what? Other subjects which he tackles – almost as if each is a wild animal to be shot and skinned in turn – is the development of transport in *Ride This Train* (forget the folk tales), unalloyed worksongs in *Blood, Sweat And Tears*, and the history lesson that is America. It's almost as if Cash is taking himself back to school, making up for what he has missed.

The odd thing is that Cash's own great gift as a songwriter is concision, so that in 'I Still Miss Someone' even the title suggests an evasion – who, exactly? – and each word counts like a silver dollar. "I never got over those blue eyes, I see them everywhere" says everything that a love song needs to, and has there ever been a bleaker opening than "at my door the leaves are falling, a cold, wild wind will come"?

Just by being there and surviving it all, Cash has become an icon for his grandchildren's generation. As he told Barney Hoskyns, out on the road, "college town audiences are my favourite – that's when it feels like the Fifties again. Then we go wild." One particular triumph was at Glastonbury in 1994, when he out-moodied the likes of Rage Against The Machine and Paul Weller. No contest! No wonder that he attracts tribute albums from the likes of The Pine Valley Cosmonauts on *Misery Loves Company*, or the likes of Faith And Disease and Kill Switch on *Americana*, advertised in *No Depression* above an album called *Mood Music For Snake Handlers: 13 More Songs About Murder, Drinkin' And Jesus*. Cash sings much the same in his two albums of contemporary songs, both produced by Rick Rubin, after he had been dropped by Columbia in a typical example of corporate crassness. The effect is startling, both parodying his own image and as serious as your life – which from the way he sings, he would be more than capable of taking away from you.

American Recordings is Cash unplugged, a small selection from 70 or so songs recorded with no musical accompaniment but that from an acoustic guitar, and recorded simply in Rick Rubin's living room in Southern California, the singer's cabin in Tennessee and the super-cool Viper Room, hang-out of Johnny Depp and the like. They cheer Loudon Wainwright's line about being "bullied and buggered" for the sheer joy of the way in which Johnny spits it out. He's been there. It was as if Cash closed his eyes and played whatever came to mind, so that his whole musical heritage spilled out, folk and blues and country and lots of gospel (his first musical love): "This is the way all country singers do it at first. We sit around and pick. It's very personal, up-front, one on one. It's very unforgiving too. You can hear every mistake I make." True, but they're like knotholes in wood, a sign of authenticity. An alternative set on bootleg, *Unsurpassed American Masters*, is just as spine-tingling as the official release, and contains traditional material like the murder ballad 'Banks Of The Ohio' and 'East Virginia Blues'.

The official set is cunningly divided into categories of new songs by Cash and material by new wave singer/songwriters like Nick Lowe (his one-time son in law), Loudon Wainwright III, Kris Kristofferson, Tom Waits and Leonard Cohen – the cream of the crop. There is even a spoken introduction to 'A Cowboy Prayer', here credited to John and Alan Lomax. There is also another fascinating handwritten message from Cash, with lots of deletions to prove that it's authentic. Like the album, it looks both forward and backwards at once. His first memory is of his mother singing him to sleep with gospel songs (they have much the same effect on some of us, still), and of joining in by the time he was four. He began to imitate songs he had heard on the radio by Jimmie Rodgers, Gene Autrey and "the Delta blues singers". He learnt to finger pick his guitar, and still knows only three or four chords, but soon organised an acoustic band, The Barbarians, with two other guitars and a mandolin, which he would force on local honky tonks, "until the place closed or we were too drunk to continue". His career ever after.

The cover is as much a genius piece of rebranding as the album. Like a preacher gone bad, Cash stands somewhere out in the badlands, in a long black coat which sweeps the ground, with two dangerous-looking dogs and the eyes of a psychotic killer. All you need to complete the shot is a sign saying: "This man is dangerous." Inside is a photo of the back of his hand, worn with age and playing. The Bible is much invoked by this surrogate preacher, even the number of the devil, 666, in Cash's own allegorical tale 'Redemption'. (Now just who was it who was saying that

JR couldn't write good songs any more?) Glen Danzig's 'Thirteen' is about an out-cast – Cain or everyman – and has been described as "a real Old Testament death blues". There's rough humour, too, as in the opening track 'Delia's Gone', a mur-der song as usual, but at least he is considerate enough to shoot her twice to put her out of her misery. Jimmy Driftwood's 'Tennessee Stud' is a love song to a horse. In all, there is lots of killing and child- (and foal-) bearing.

Lowe's 'The Beast In Me' is archetypal, surely more applicable to the older man, a real man wrestling with a real demon. Suddenly Cash is a second Robert Mitchum, with love tattooed on one hand and hate on the other. Here is all that inner rest-lessness, "caged by frail and fragile bars", and he sings in a world-weary *basso profundo*, like a man making his last confession. It's like Jeckyll fighting Hyde, almost schizophrenic, and the effect is totally unsettling. *Unchained* adds an elec-tric band – basically Tom Petty And The Heartbreakers – and songs by new wavers Beck and now-defunct Soundgarden, plus Dean Martin and Jimmie Rodgers, but it's a picnic after the soul-scrapings of the previous album.

Cash leans against a wooden fence, white haired and almost benign. On the back of the booklet is what I presume is Cash's Tennessee hideout, and it fits the rural rhythms here. Johnny's own song 'Country Boy', written back in 1957, is taken at a fast lick, rockabilly revisited, and looks back happily to good days, despite the poverty. Cash has rarely sounded more joyful.

Barney Hoskyns watches him try out some of the newer material on a frankly bemused audience out in the Midwest, then Johnny opens himself up in perhaps the most revealing interview he's ever done, about going back to his roots. Elsewhere he described the young Dylan as "one of the best hillbilly singers I'd ever heard", while here he reckons that Beck is much the same: "He had that Appalachian music like he really felt it and loved it." As to Nashville, he hasn't turned his back on it but "I don't know if they turned their back on me". The last album he made there had been pressed in an edition of 500. "I think there's a glut of songs that sound over-produced", though some stations are starting to play "the veterans again". His own new career as an alternative rocker has been comprehensively ignored.

As to the tradition: "I've always loved folk music. It's the backbone of country, or it used to be. It's where country came from and I think if country ever looks again at its roots and draws on that tradition it'll be in good shape." Prophetic words. Is he an American icon? "Shit, no. No. No. I see the pimples on my nose and the fat jaw from the pain where it's swollen…thinning hair, whatever. Icon? No. Not in my mir-ror." He wants to die on the road, with his boots on. Elsewhere, Cash proclaimed that "Hank Williams and Jimmie Rodgers were not as tough as I am. Both of them knew that they were going to die, and I always knew I wasn't". Some people acted as if they were proud when he "straightened up", but had been waiting for years for him to fall off the wagon "so they'd have a legend to sing about and put me in hill-billy heaven". At the time of writing, he's still down here on Earth, and still singing.

Cash is a prime jewel in the crown of "hard country", as more traditional sounds began to be called, a storyteller who looks back to his heritage. Lloyd "Cowboy" Copas kept the old music alive in 1960 when he had a country Number One with 'Alabam', an old ragtime tune. George Jones was at the centre of the honky tonk revival, as was his fellow Texan Ray Price, at first as a carbon copy of Hank Williams – a close friend – but soon establishing his own "shuffle beat" sound with his hit single, 'Crazy Arms', and his band, The Cherokee Cowboys.

Malone describes the Ray Price style perfectly, with pedal steel and fiddle defiantly taking the "lead passages, while a shuffling drum beat and an electric walking bass laid down a rhythm that no dancer could resist". It was dancehall music, and Price employed a whole generation of new songwriters to keep him supplied, including Roger Miller, Willie Nelson and Kris Kristofferson among them. (The first two also played with his band.) Price eventually defected to the quieter pastures of country pop. I have album his version of the Irish song 'Danny Boy' on a compilation somewhere, sung to a tinkling piano and lush orchestration. He could be Sammy Davis Jnr, except there's a country 'n' Celtic lilt in there somewhere.

Over in Bakersfield, the California sound took over, a rocking noise, though not as wild as rock 'n' roll, "distinguished by the clarity and high-decibel sound of its electric and pedal steel guitarists". Forget the fiddles, though; the natural ancestors of this sound were honky tonk acts like The Maddox Brothers And Rose, as tough as leather. There was a natural antagonism with Nashville, whose studios were seen as diluting the music. A blue-collar town if ever there was one, Bakersfield was at the heart of the California oilfields, and back in the 1930s had been a natural migration point for the Okies, who put their rural folk songs into the mix. This was definitely city music, though, growing to maturity in dark and sweaty bars. The tenor voice of Alvis "Buck" Owens and his band, The Buckeroos, will be forever associated with the place, and as a light illuminating the musical blankness of countrypolitan, even though today their records sound a little bland. I shall mention the name Lynn Anderson just the once, and then run away and hide.

Owens and his "All-American Show" were captured onstage in Reno, Nevada, on the album *Live At The Nugget*, and it sounds like a circus. No wonder that Buck appears on the front cover clutched in an elephant's trunk. It also sounds far from Dawidoff's description of Buck's sound ("like a broken beer bottle"), but this is the early Seventies and he has calmed down. This is music as escapism, not as social realism. They start off with a rocked-up 'Good Ole Mountain Dew', and a comic song about gambling to fit their surroundings. Next up is Lester Flatt's 'Rolling In My Sweet Baby's Arms', frantic rather than high and lonesome, but from "an album we have out that we think is the real honest-to-goodness American music".

Meanwhile, Buck tells a shaggy dog story about his banjo player: "I know that he don't look like much, he sure ain't no Raquel Welch." "It's a banjer," Ronnie Jackson informs him with a country twang. Another band member suggests that he "weld it", and yet another that if he put it where he, personally, wanted him to, "you'd be pretty uncomfortable". For all of that, however, he's all over the Cousin Emmy song 'Ruby'. Owens' vocal sounds like a train whistle, and the band kick up a storm, even in these polite surroundings.

Buck now introduces teenage sensation Kenni Huskey, who smoulders on a Kris Kristofferson song, and his own son Buddy, who struts through a song by John Fogerty. The focal point of the evening, though, is The Bakersfield Brass: "They play it country. They play it pop. They play rock. They play Bach. They play Buck." They also play bluegrass, on 'Flint Hill Special', with banjo flourishes. It's so bizarre – like a marching band in Tennessee – that it works. Once.

Buck And The Buckeroos recorded a whole album in the style, 1971's *Ruby And Other Bluegrass Specials*. They cheer up the music, described on the sleeve as "a special kind of note-holding, high-pitched harmony speckled with short fiddle and banjo solos. You'll also find fast, hard driving rhythm." And you do, but the high, lonesome sound has evaporated on its way down to Bakersfield. Buck's greatest legacy is his influence on those who came after, John Fogerty and Creedence Clearwater, Gram Parsons, The Grateful Dead and surrogate Bakersfield boy Dwight Yoakam. Don Rich on lead Telecaster was one of the progenitors of country rock – maybe even more than that, as The Beatles covered his song 'Act Naturally' when they briefly took their own country swerve. Owens himself made a brief comeback in 1988, with the album *Hot Dog*.

The hottest dog in Bakersfield, though, was Merle Haggard, one of the towns native sons. His father was a fiddle-playing rancher who had a particular love of Jimmie Rodgers but was forced to curtail his playing after marrying his devout wife. He died young, perhaps as a result. Before Merle arrived, his parents had left Oklahoma in an old car packed high with everything they owned, but Haggard rejects Steinbeck's view of such economic migrants as derelicts, with his usual pride: "Most of them weren't tramps. They were just people locating, proud people being transplanted because of a drought." Norman Tebbitt would have been proud of them. Where Steinbeck got things wrong, according to Merle, was "the ingredient called pride. My mother said when they got to the edge of Bear Mountain and looked over into the 'Garden of Eden', she said, why, at that moment she knew she'd made it – this was what they were looking for." Exactly the same phrase that David Ackles used in 'Montana Song'.

Perhaps Haggard has sublimated this implied reproof on his parents, suffering "some sort of a forced migration, like the Cherokees out of Tennessee", and it fuels his distaste for supposed freeloaders, or those who do not properly value the flag.

This love of America's native land – even if not always accompanied by his damp-eyed patriotism – has been a key influence on the new wave of country. Even more so than Johnny Cash, he hits a vein of working-class pride and gives it a dignity that is self-fulfilling. On his latest album, he chooses to cover 'The Roots Of My Raisin'

Run Deep', and sings it with blazing emotion, leaving irony to the hippies and draft dodgers. It is a stance admired by all who are liberal at heart, a strength of purpose which their own creed runs from as if scalded. We all have prejudices, it's just that the right wing are more honest in owning up to them.

There were two separate tribute albums to Merle's songwriting, issued almost simultaneously. *Mama's Hungry Eyes*, issued on Arista, is mainstream Nashville with Vince Gill (with a heartfelt version of 'The Farmer's Daughter'), Clint Black, Alabama and Alan Jackson, but also free radicals Emmylou Harris and Willie Nelson. *Tulare Dust*, on Oakland's tiny Hightone label, has roots singers like the slinky Lucinda Williams and the wistful Iris Dement, the urgent Joe Ely and the angry Peter Case. They seem to dig deeper into these songs, so that a man often traduced as a reactionary redneck looks more like Woody Guthrie's true heir. It's all here: down-home stories, humour, anger at the lot of the poor, the wish to escape. Like Dylan and so few others, each song is in a different voice.

Producers Tom Russell and Dave Alvin reckon that Haggard is "the last of a breed of great country songwriters...his kind ain't coming around again". Reviewing both CDs, another country rock pioneer, Sid Griffin, recalls seeing Merle reduce a small town crowd to tears. Here is a man with a perfect CV: a widowed Okie mother and an impoverished family background, a spell in San Quentin following a youth spent engaging in petty crime and as a small town rebel, and an unrequited love for Dolly Parton. His best songs are about failures, but failures with a determination to kick themselves right back out of the gutter.

Dawidoff reckons that Haggard's albums generally cut deeper than most, though I have yet to find one from his classic years that is good all the way through, except the partly live compilation *Songs I'll Always Sing*, performed with his road band The Strangers. A friend saw them almost by accident when Joe Ely was the support act, and was stunned by the determination of Haggard's singing – a little man, dressed from head to toe in black – and the sheer sense of energy generated by him and his band onstage. It is a contained wildness learned in the oilfields and honky-tonk joints of Bakersfield: "Tonight we'll kick the footlights out again." "The Hag" remains a specialist taste, though.

The reason is probably his song 'Okie From Musgokee', which he insists is partly a self-parody but was taken as a call to arms, with President Nixon a particular admirer. Along with the defiantly anti-peacenik 'The Fighting Side Of Me', the number certainly gets ecstatic whoops of assent on *Songs*, and would still go down well on the Republican campaign trail. Miscogie sounds an awfully boring world, and brings out a bullying element in Haggard's voice. The latter song is unambiguously thuggish – isn't free speech what the troops were supposedly fighting to protect in Vietnam? If he felt so strongly, he could always have volunteered himself.

Such titles seemed to bear out Phil Ochs' allegation that here was the Antichrist come to Earth, though both men exude an un-snobbish respect for working people. Like Hank Williams, Haggard remains largely unconscious of his own creative urges, a natural songwriter who would often dictate words he seemed to take straight out of the air to his wife Bonnie and then promptly forget them: "It's like God put them through me." He wrote for her one of his finest songs, 'Today I Started Loving You Again', scrawled on a paper bag.

Tribute albums to Jimmie Rodgers and his one-time employer Bob Wills tie Haggard in to a tradition which he is proud to continue. There's just something about his voice that renders me immune, a whine in all the wrong places. His one notable vocal trick is to wobble all around the note with a kind of deep sigh, which is meant to suggest emotion and instead sounds like a man preparing to vomit. For me – and I'm taking to the hills tomorrow, with no forwarding address – Merle as a vocalist sounds like the sum of all his influences. His genius (and that is not too high a word) is in the stories he tells, not the way in which he chooses to tell them. I'd give his complete works for *Tulare Dust*.

Oddly, then, my own favourite among Haggard's own releases is his nostalgic elegy for steam engines, *My Love Affair With Trains*, complete with spoken passages and lots of sound effects. It's sentimental and patriotic and totally compelling: "The train is called America, your ticket is a dream." As there the songs are mainly by others, but they all cohere and there's lots of Bing Crosby in Merle's voice. I presume that the use of toy trains on the cover, though, is the record company being clever rather than cheapskate.

The Haggard albums generally reckoned to be the best are those released by Capitol in the Sixties, although 1981's *Big City* has recently been repackaged as an 'American Milestone'. It came out in the same year as his unusually revealing autobiography *My House Of Memories*, and the songs also seem to be looking back, which is the posture at which he is always best. Here is the pain of a dull job, although the reference to "so-called social security" is, again, ambiguous. Would Haggard prefer the workless to starve? There's lots of escapist talk about becoming a hobo, but it doesn't sound real.

That regressive note sounds again in 'Are The Good Times Really Over? (I Wish A Buck Was Still Silver)', which is almost Nazi in its sentiments. Haggard sounds like his name, and to a funereal beat, as he rolls time backward to "when the country was strong", to a simpler world, before Elvis and Vietnam and The Beatles: they are all related in his mind. It was a time before hand-outs, "when a man could still work and still would". We're back with the angry, purist Okie: "I wish coke was still cola, and a joint was a bad place to be." We're also back with the male supremacist, "when a girl could still cook and still would". Merle, there's nostalgia for the past, which is nice, and retrogression, which isn't. Get your apron on, like the rest of us new men.

Coming up next, and far more palatable, is 'Texas Fiddle Song', sung staccato to a fiddle which plays out his praise of mountain tunes like 'Old Joe Clark' and 'Cotton-Eyed Joe'. It's his only real concession to old-time music, though, and that lack in his work explains a lot. If Johnny Cash remains the ultimate country outlaw then Merle certainly remains the archetypal redneck, and maybe he should apply some mountain balm to it. A bluegrass potion, perhaps.

What he did instead was to re-record 43 of his best songs on the double CD *For The Record*, in chronological order, with guests like Alabama and Jewel coming in to duet. It's perfect Sunday-morning music. Age and time have smoothed down the rough edges and enriched his singing: it now has the patina of a fine antique, slightly cracking at the edges, deeply sad and thrillingly emotional. It could be Willie Nelson at times, that way of lingering on a note, and they duet on 'Pancho And Lefty'. To listen through the two CDs is to hear a whole life relived – there's a wonderful Bob Wills imitation for a start – and no wonder, then, that Merle writes in the liner notes that "these recordings have drained my emotions. Maybe someone will understand the mental pain involved, and appreciate…the emptiness it causes, and the time it stole from my family." Deeply country, he now thanks the Creator, and Lou Bradley, the co-creator of this album.

Freed at last of filler, this gives a stunning overview of the sheer quality of Haggard's writing, and his reputation as the natural poet of the working class is vindicated: "It takes a special breed to be a truck drivin' man/and a steady hand to pull that load behind." These are plain tales from the hills, spoken by an army of inarticulate Merles to whom he gives voice, the kind of people proud to state, as in 'Workin' Man Blues', that they've "never been on welfare". Mothers loom large, as does poverty and family togetherness, the three combined in highly personal memories of the Depression. These are prejudices or values – depending on how you look at them – held in common with the music of the early settlers. Maybe Haggard is more traditional than he realises. On the cover, he looks like an older and more frightening version of Elvis Costello crossed with a mountain preacher, adorned with dark shades, hat and frown. He has the haunted eyes of a one-time jailbird. His beard is either white or red, according to the light. (Merle McHaggard, perhaps?) Needless to say, he looks both hard right and right hard. Here is pure country music, with all of its contradictions intact.

Much as he avoided Nashville – and as a loner and a natural rebel he wouldn't have been welcome anyway – Merle Haggard's prejudices are pure Music City, even when it's dressed in a DJ at an awards ceremony. In the 1960s, many new stars began to shine in that firmament. Again, I'm going to be wilfully selective and choose to deal with my own favourites, but that's one of the privileges of getting to write a book, anyway. It's certainly not for the money!

Well, I like Glen Campbell, and I don't care who knows it. There's something about the combination of his voice with a good Jimmy Webb song – and Webb is a great singer in his own right too, though in a painful, desperate kind of way – which hits the guts and soul of many more people than everyday housewives. Peter Doggett described his singing as "smooth but never bland". Where Haggard grates,

Glen slips down like silk, the godfather of easy listening, with sweeping strings to match. Neither are cloying. Aside from an acting role in *True Grit*, and a spell in The Beach Boys (Brian Wilson wrote and produced his 1965 single 'Guess I'm Dumb' as a dry-run for *Pet Sounds*), Campbell started as a session guitarist. His tribute album to Hank Williams raids the family photo album to show an archetypal rural child-hood, toting a banjo, violin or guitar, and skates over the emotional quicksand. Glen is a lovely singer, but as sentimental as hell: the everyday housewife turns out to be his mother. It's Jim Webb who shovels in the melancholy, though.

When not leaving wedding cakes out in the rain and providing grandiose musical confections for the likes of Richard Harris, Webb is a songwriter and singer who knows how to locate the high, lonesome sound which this book is really all about. It's there in the sound of the wind in the telephone wires, and in his most haunting song, 'The Highwayman'. Campbell's great skill, for such a naturally warm singer, is to find a chill in his voice to match.

On Glen's *Greatest Hits* he duets with Mississippi's finest, Bobbie Gentry, on a mellifluous take on The Everly Brothers hit 'All You Have To Do Is Dream'. Gentry is one of those singers who has got lost along the way, though not in my record collection. Here is the music of the people, the landscape and even the bugs of the Mississippi Delta. Add sophisticated arrangements by Jimmie Haskell (LA smooth rather than Nashville smoochy) and on her debut album, *Ode To Billy Joe*, the most famous track comes last, and has all kinds of pre-echoes. It remains a song which inhabits its own mysterious world, despite having provoked a novel. (Is it a baby they throw from that bridge?) After the fractured guitar intro and spooky strings, making you know something is up, as does the unnatural calm in Bobbie's voice, this is pure Appalachian horror tale in its family detail and inevitability, despite the Deep South setting. A Greek tragedy told in a matter-of-fact way.

Before she took early retirement from the industry, Gentry recorded two more albums which extend the concept. *The Delta Sweete* is more snapshots of down-home life, with songs by Mose Allison, John D Loudermilk and Doug Kershaw, with Bobbie doing strange things with her voice. 'Refractions' is country psychedelia, which then leads straight into the cajun family diary of Kershaw's 'Louisiana Man' and the folk-rock dream of 'Courtyard'. Being Bobby, the lover goes away and the dream dies, now seen as "illusions of all I'm living for", and the record ends with a sinister, unresolved chord. Or a cord. As a melancholy device, it's worthy of Tennyson. "Here is the dust, the fragrance, the molasses, grits and grit, the love, sorrow and humour of the Delta country," as the sleeve notes say. "What you do in the dark will be brought to light," as Bobby writes. These are not exactly comfortable songs – she's too sharp-eyed a writer – but if you're looking for a true heir of the mountain ballads then look no further.

Patchwork took her into the 1970s with a turn to the mainstream, but a Hollywood session man here plays banjo. Gentry is revealed as the blood sister of

Laura Nyro, another largely-forgotten maverick. Few seemed to notice the table of delights spread before them, despite the hopeful advert on the back of the album for the International Bobbie Gentry Fan Club. A CD box set, please.

In much the same territory of small-town revelations was Tom T Hall, with whose song of dirty secrets being washed in public, 'Harper Valley PTA', Jeannie C Riley had a massive hit. For Malone, Hall was one of a new generation of songwriters who combined "a sophistication acquired in college or military experience with an understanding of the plain people...restoring the old tradition of storytelling".

A JR Ewing lookalike, Hall was born in Kentucky, and while still a teenager he played bluegrass to accompany his uncle Curt's travelling cinema, later becoming a local DJ. Using such local knowledge, Hall brought stories from the hills up to date, but retained their conversational style. He wrote 'Harper Valley PTA' in the style of Gentry's hit, but using a childhood memory: "I wrote about a lady who had criticised a teacher for spanking her child to get at her." Hall has the archetypal country voice, deep and come-hither, laid back, conversational, and with strong consonants. His songs mix tragedy and comedy. Typical subjects include the tale of a city driver jailed in a hick town for speeding, a gravedigger burying a man who still owes him money, life in a Kentucky coal town, and a tribute to Clayton Delaney, "the best guitar picker in our town/I thought he was a hero and I used to follow Clayton around." So why didn't he make it, down in Tennessee? Alcohol, basically, and Hall is determined to avenge his memory. After all, "it could be that the good Lord likes a little picking too".

On *In Concert*, recorded at the Opry with The Nashville String Section, Hall revisits his bluegrass roots and follows this same song with 'Foggy Mountain Breakdown'. He is now a published author, with "punctuation and everything", but he reads them as well as writes them, and has recently been studying Roy Clark's *Big Note Banjo Book*. Before a supercharged rendition of the tune by his friend Earl Scruggs, he jokes, "if you all like this, I'll send Roy the money for his book". They certainly did, and Hall went on to record *The Magnificent Music Machine*, a bluegrass album which features the likes of 'The Fastest Rabbit Dog In Carter County Today' – about a chase – and 'Bluegrass Festival In The Sky'. It switches repeatedly from a Carter Family-style lament to a sprightly listing of all the greats in hillbilly heaven, some of them not even dead yet.

Lovely songs all, bringing the tradition up to date. Even Bill Monroe, one of the sacred list, comes along for the ride. One wonders what he would make of the cartoon cover – with Tom pulling the levers on a Heath Robinson contraption which plays fiddle, banjo and guitar all at once – or the back cover quote from Plato: "Music is moral law. It gives a soul to the universe." Listening to some of the fiddle playing here, one can only agree.

In his boldest album, *In Search Of A Song*, Hall took a guitar, notepad and tape recorder on the road, and went out to find America. The back cover has a

Jimmie Rodgers – 'The Singing Brakeman' – country music's first ever solo star

The first female country star, Patsy Cline died in a plane crash

Hank Williams, the hillbilly Shakespeare

King of Western Swing Bob Wills with his Texas Playboys

Johnny Cash, who successfully made the transition from Sun Records rocker to country music icon

Bob Dylan went to Nashville in the late Sixties and the world followed

Merle Haggard: blue-collar poet who showed his fighting side, too

Kenny Rogers and Dolly Parton, the king and queen of 1970s Nashville

The Eagles: where Gram Parsons led, they followed

The Byrds took a country detour as Sweethearts Of The Rodeo

Nanci Griffith, where country meets folk

Bright young things of country, The Dixie Chicks

Techno meets country with The Alabama 3 – the starting point of my search

Hellfire singer and organiser of the
Harry Smith Tribute, Nick Cave

The Nitty Gritty Dirt Band bridged the Nashville generation gap

Steve Earle, from Copperhead Road to a bluegrass resurrection

'New Country' superstar Garth Brooks, who has recently lost his way

Leading alt rockers Wilco, who helped bring Woody Guthrie's songs back to life

Shania Twain: she brought rock marketing to Nashville and country to the pop masses

Country soul that will rip your heart out from Shelby Lynne

Hip young gunslinger Beck meets the original Outlaw, Willie Nelson

road map – with Nashville at the centre – and polaroid snaps from the journey. The songs are its aural equivalent. 'Who's Gonna Feed Them Hogs?' has a farmer fretting in hospital and staging a miraculous recovery. It is sung as if written in a truck stop: "Waitress, before you leave, would you bring me a coffee and a hot ham sandwich, please?" One photo has Hall gripping the Hyden town sign, with a church above advertising: "Jesus is soon coming." "He'd sure be disappointed if he did". 'Trip to Hyden' starts with a nervous Tom driving up past hound dogs, temporary-looking houses with their "lean and bashful kids", stopping for beans and corn bread, and revisiting the site of a mining disaster – "just another country hillside". Hall buys a jacket – it is sunny "but somehow the town was cold". A survivor brings the accident to life: "it was just like being inside of a shotgun". This is magnificent writing, in any medium, and one can only guess its influence on everyone from Kris Kristofferson to Tom Russell. Modern country music starts here.

Hall has become a touchstone for new country. *No Depression* reckons that he reshaped the music, "deepened details, complicated narrative and followed colloquial voices further than they'd ever gone". *Real, The Tom T Hall Project* sees these songs strong enough to be radically rearranged, almost as if they are already part of the tradition. Joe Henry puts a nuclear charge under 'Homecoming', sampling a classic intro from Charley Pride and adding "staccato guitar, drum loops and scratchy moans, like border radio echoes breaking through a Dust Brothers mix". The results are menacing, over which Henry "deadpans every line with knowing resignation". Best of all are Victoria Williams and Mark Olsen, who best grasp Hall's "hard-to-pinpoint tone, that place between abjection and gaiety".

Hoyt Axton is another such songwriter, picking up the little details which count. He was also a deep-voiced country crooner who found an alternative career playing good ole boys on film and TV, from *Gremlins* to *The Bionic Woman*. His songs were covered by folk and rock acts as various as The Kingston Trio – who took the "damn" out of 'Greenback Dollar' – and Steppenwolf, with 'The Pusher'. Even Ringo Starr had a hit with his 'No No Song'. His own albums are a little lightweight for my taste, although *Snowblind Friend* has a nice visual mismatch, with a heavyweight Hoyt in a snowy scene and a Saint Bernard on the cover. The title track is an anti-cocaine song, its slumped victim having found nirvana "in some ungodly bathroom in some ungodly hall". Axton has the same gift as Hall in writing a line like a killer punch: "he said he wanted heaven, but praying was too slow". Mimi Farina and Tanya Tucker are among those who provide vocal support. As that combination shows, in Axton's world folk and country are back together, and good friends.

Much weirder are the late-Sixties albums of country exotica by one-time Nancy Sinatra collaborator the gruff-voiced Lee Hazlewood, which virtually unobtainable at the time and some of which are now being recycled on Smells Like, the label run by Sonic Youth's drummer. *Cowboy In Sweden* is just that, a deranged C&W album recorded during his self-imposed exile in Scandinavia, with titles like 'Cold Hard Times' and swathes of violins "sweetening Hazlewood's creepy, weatherbeaten baritone", as *Mojo* put it. It's as if Johnny Cash took the place of Glen Campbell. This is not a comforting body of work.

His latest CD, *Farmisht, Flatulence, Origami, Arf!!! And Me*, is influenced by Western swing, while 1963's *Trouble Is A Lonesome Town* centres around the inhabitants of a mythical Wild West town called Trouble, and each track is prefaced with a spoken word introduction describing them. On the front cover, Lee squats on a railway track with his guitar case, seemingly oblivious to any oncoming trains. An ominous message appears opposite, superimposed on a map of Colorado: "You won't find it on any map, but take a step in any direction and you're in trouble." Hazlewood kick-started country rock when he released the debut album by The International Submarine Band on his own label, LHI, and persuaded his one-time collaborator Duane Eddy to write an enthusiastic sleeve note. Lee was typically obscure when *Record Collector* asked him how he discovered them: "Suzi Jane Hokem found them. They weren't lost, but she found them."

Hazlewood made his debut as an actor in 1970's *The Moonshine War*, set in Kentucky during prohibition. More recently, he issued a single of 'Dolly Parton's Guitar', and appeared at the Festival Hall in "cowboy boots, jeans and sweatshirt" in front of such rock alumni as Jarvis Cocker and Primal Scream frontman Bobby Gillespie. In his strange, self-obsessed musical world, Hazlewood invented cowboy existentialism. Or maybe he's just a charlatan who finally got lucky.

Van Dyke Parks is a weightier and more enigmatic figure, who collaborated with Brian Wilson on the (luckily) still-unreleased *Smile*, and other Beach Boys projects. *Smile* goes back to the farmyard for such bizarrities as 'Do You Like Worms?' and the kazoo and quacks of 'Mrs O'Leary's Cow'. One of the few songs that emerges from the stoned morass intact is called 'Vegetables'. Country music is one element Van Dyke threw into the blender, so that, as he recently explained, "over and over the crow flies, uncover the cornfield" could refer either to the final, bleak paintings by Vincent van Gogh or his impression of "some great American prairie". He was certainly one of the pioneers of Americana. Who else but Parks could write a concept album around the Br'er Rabbit stories (on *Jump*), or set off to discover America through calypsos, or set a "paniolo cowboy in a field of sugar cane" in Hawaii with a native choir and a lush orchestra in support? He can't still sing, of course.

Meanwhile, back in Austin, The Derailers have recently revived the Bakersfield sound on *Full Western Dress*. Hard country is making something of a comeback, and it doesn't come any harder than Jim Ford's 1969 single 'Harlan County', rediscovered with huge enthusiasm by ace DJ Andy Kershaw and reprised on his compilation *Great Moments In Vinyl History*: "Just one listen leaves little doubt that Jim Ford has lived the hardship of Kentucky's coal country." Country meets soul, with bass like a piledriver, a full brass section, a father shot for cheating over 15 cents "to buy a loaf of bread", and a granite-voiced Jim "digging hard coal at twelve years old". The family pray together to escape a place where "the cold winds blow and the crops don't grow", and children dream of a pair of shoes.

It shares the same emotional universe as John D Loudermilk's clip-clopping 'Tobacco Road' (a man also responsible for the album *John D Loudermilk Sings A Bizarre Collection Of The Most Unusual Songs*, including 'The Little Grave' and 'Mary's Little Boy Child'). The Kershaw compilation follows with two African pieces (the second virtually unlistenable, but that's also par for the course), and then Dwight Yoakam sings an acoustic 'Mystery Train': "an old blues thing that was updated by the hillbilly kid that was Elvis Presley". Dwight's voice bucks and cracks like a rodeo rider. Add dub reggae and some of the more deranged singer/songwriters and you have the Kershaw show in microcosm.

It is not as bizarre a mixture as it might at first seem, however. The note to the SE Rogie track here points out that his greatest influence as he grew up in west Africa was Jimmie Rodgers, and the cover is another cartoon by the Wild West-obsessed Glen Baxter, depicting two cowboys drawing up their horses and staring at a distant plume of smoke. The laconic caption reads: "'Looks like the Sioux have got to another boxed set of James Last albums,' drawled the Kershaw Kid."

Before we move on to country rock, let's look at a quick overview. Bill Malone provides an overview of Nashville product at this time, its songwriting in particular, which has long been one of its strongest elements. The writers are mainly Southern men from rural backgrounds but who are well aware of the media mainstream. Nevertheless, "they have retained a sense of place that is refreshing in an age of ceaseless change and dislocation". They can "tease the universal out of the particular", seeing life as it is, not as they would like it to be, and writing topical songs about contemporary events.

As a legacy of its folk roots, such music is at heart nostalgic. As Loretta Lynn puts it: "we were poor, but we had love". It's also essentially apolitical, though generally in favour of the status quo. Compassionate but not liberal, with little time for gay rights or free love. In this they also share the morality of the old ballads. "In country music, individuals are usually left alone to confront life", hence the image of the cowboy out on the range. It's not a music afraid of wallowing in one's own personal pain, which has led to the parodies discussed earlier and charges levelled at it accusing it of being little better than soap opera. The late 1950s saw the rise of full-time Nashville songwriters like Harlan Howard, with titles like 'Pick Me Up On Your Way Down' or 'Don't You Ever Get Tired Of Hurting Me?', and Willie Nelson, servicing sob-singers like "Whispering Bill" Anderson.

The image of a music dominated by "adult male white Protestants" has been dented by the growing empowerment of women singers, the breakthrough coming with Jeannie C Riley, and her miniskirts and go-go boots, and the "country

Lolita" Tanya Tucker. There was also a wider ethnic mix with the likes of Kinky Friedman and Texas Jewboys, the "Cajun hippie" Doug Kershaw, and the Chicanos Freddie Fender breaking through.

Such changes were largely on the surface, however. As with Merle Haggard, the 1960s saw country becoming identified with the silent majority, as America divided itself down the middle into hawks and doves. In such a contest, Nashville had a pronounced beak, strong claws and two beady eyes. Hence the disillusionment of hippies like Gram Parsons and The Byrds, who loved the music and could not understand why the industry it had spawned did not love them right back. We're back with *Easy Rider*.

George Wallace came to a political arrangement with the likes of Hank Snow and The Wilburn Brothers, which is at the poisoned heart of Altman's movie *Nashville*. Even future Jimmie Carter supporters Kris Kristofferson and trucking Dave Dudley wrote songs supporting "our boys" out in Vietnam, while lifetime democrat Ernest Tubb attacked hippies in his song 'Love It Or Leave It'. The country view of those forced to depend on social security can be best seen in Guy Drake's 'Welfare Cadillac', a car which he patently hopes will drive over a cliff.

Ironically, then, the economic effects of Reaganism and Thatcherism, whose espousal of market forces is pure country, were most movingly put into words – and resisted – by these same C&W reactionaries. Merle Haggard's 'If We Make It Through December' is told by a man praying not to be laid off before Christmas. David Allan Coe's wonderful song to a tyrannical boss 'Take This Job And Shove It' – as I myself did – is hardly supportive of management's right to manage. Trucking songs generally support the man in the cab, not the men in suits who plan his schedules. What is 'Convoy' if not a song advocating direct action?

For Malone, a man alive to every ripple and cross-current in the genre he so evidently loves, it was an historical moment when "commercially, the music stood at the highest peak in its history", but stylistically it was at a crossroads. In one direction, pop music opened its bag of promises, providing financial well-being but a music so diluted that it eventually became unrecognisable. The other path – steeper, narrower and pointing back into the hills – was a fusion of traditional sounds and musical innovation. "One of these roads led towards bluegrass." It is that rocky mountain path which we will now follow.

Chapter Six

Country Rock

Bluegrass might sound like a music preserved in aspic, but it continued to develop and mutate, like a living force. The basic repertoire remains much the same, however, with endless fires on mountains, blue moons, Knoxville girls, older Joe Clarks and shady groves. Ralph Rinzler, of The Greenbriar Boys, was briefly Bill Monroe's manager, and began booking him into folk clubs and colleges. Mike Seeger continued to draw critical attention to Monroe, and there was a weird synergy between Bill and young musicians from the North, who were busy falling in love with this weird, purist sound. At heart, theirs was a romantic gesture, much like those musicians of a similar age in Britain rediscovering their folk roots, and there is no fanaticism like that of the young. Among those to work their apprenticeship as Blue Grass Boys were Roland White, Bill Keith, Richard Greene and Peter Rowan, both to make a 180 degree shift in the late Sixties and join psychedelic rock bands. The true musical revolutionary, though, was Bill Keith.

A Bostonian, Keith played with Monroe for only nine months, but during that time developed a chromatic style to enable the super-fast playing of fiddle tunes on his banjo. As Bill Malone explains it, this new style stresses the "exact and complete melody of a tune", as compared to the Scruggs technique of showering the music with notes almost at random. What startled audiences was the sheer speed and precision of his playing, with 'Devil's Dream' his theme tune much as 'Stepping Out' was that of Eric Clapton, who was much the same kind of innovator in a completely different music. Both musicians fuelled a musical avalanche – progressive rock for Clapton and progressive bluegrass for Keith.

Bluegrass began to spread far from the mountains where its roots lay, and where, as Stephen Price writes in his history *Old As The Hills*, "the men were taught to pick and sing by friends and neighbours". (Guitars, not their noses.) Bud and Ola Belle Reed established the New River Ranch in Pennsylvania, a country music park where old-style musicians could meet new-style fans, while Boston's Hillbilly Ranch was set in a notoriously rough area of town known locally as the "combat zone". Everett and Mitchell "Bea" Lilly moved there from West Virginia, and played seven nights a week as The Confederate Mountaineers. Malone notes how strange it was that "the clear, high Appalachian sound should thrive so long in the frigid, working-class atmosphere of a New England honky tonk"; but, given that many of the audience would be of Irish descent, it's not really surprising at all. Bluegrass is a music born in poverty and tooled by Monroe into a form of escapism, along with instrumental flash.

Like a particularly virulent form of mountain weed, bluegrass proved most stubbornly at home in Washington DC, and not just among the likes of old-time fiddler (no political comment implied) Senator Robert Byrd of West Virginia. The core of its fans had come down from the hills to work for the government or the military as part of a diaspora which had begun in the 1930s. Ernest "Pop" Stoneman was to be found in a naval ordnance factory during the day and playing autoharp and singing old-time music with his kids in The Stoneman Family in local bars and clubs at night.

The singer and guitarist Charlie Waller was born in Texas, was raised in the cotton country of Louisiana and came to Washington with Busby's Bayou Boys. Here he joined the locally-born John Duffy on mandolin, at first for a one-night stand at a local nightclub, appropriately enough on the 4th of July, 1957. They decided to form a band together, and became known as The Country Gentlemen. When sometime Blue Grass Boy Eddie Adcock – from Scotsville, Virginia – joined in 1959, the band really started flying. Duffy played two or three strings simultaneously to get a jazzy sound, while Adock attacked his banjo like Merle Travis picked his guitar, in a syncopated style, and Waller sang in a "throaty" style. Tom Gray came in on bass, but a fiddle player was notable in his absence, at least until a decade later when Ricky Skaggs joined. Bill Malone rightly calls The Country Gentlemen "the founding fathers of the progressive bluegrass style".

They were also the punks of bluegrass, speeding things up and relying on visceral energy. Malone reproves them for lacking pathos, but admits that they "restored vitality" to the form, and acted as a magnet to young players. The Gentlemen – their name itself a throwback to a British past – took risks with material ranging from the old ballad 'Greensleeves', through Dylan's 'Girl From The North Country', to the theme from the movie *Exodus* (oddly appropriate and relevant to Appalachian history), and displayed a satirical sense of humour between numbers which appealed to a college audience. The band is still going, with Charlie Waller still in charge, and recently played at London's Barbican Theatre.

The Country Gentlemen had a long-term residency at the Shamrock Club in Georgetown, which catered for a steady Irish clientele. There was certainly a strong Celtic element evident in bluegrass as it evolved, not least in the mixture of sentimental songs and quick-fire instrumentals. They continued to play at the Shamrock regularly, even when becoming used to selling out Carnegie Hall. Their early albums appeared on the Folkways label, and they then moved to the independent label Rebel. John Duffy went on to join The Seldom Scene.

Bluegrass blossomed during the folk revival and its quest for rural authenticity, real or apparent. While some purists dived back into The Carter Family or The Skillet Lickers, others chose what Malone described as "this dynamic sound, which seemed to represent a vital updating and reinvigoration of traditional mountain string-band and vocal styles". To quote myself, some of the albums of this stuff is so speedy you wonder if they used studio trickery. They didn't. In 1957, Folkways issued a book on American banjo styles, edited by Ralph Rinzler, and two years later Alan Lomax put on a concert at the Carnegie Hall featuring the likes of The Stoney Mountain Boys, playing what he deemed "the freshest sound" in America. Robert Shelton, the journalist who later helped break Dylan to a wider world, began to review the music in the rarefied pastures of *The New York Times*, and called Earl Scruggs the "Paganini of the five-string banjo".

The linking figure here is Bill Clifton of The Dixie Mountain Boys, a natural-born aristocrat from Maryland who first heard country music while visiting the shacks of tenant farmers, as the son of the man who owned them. After a private education, he learned to play while at the University of Virginia, and with his college friend Paul Clayton became a crucial link with the folk revival. Bill himself later served as advisor to the Newport Folk Festival, as such people do, and thus helped to obtain exposure for many a country singer there.

One shouldn't sneer too much at the Marie Antoinette aspect of all this, with lords dressing up as rustic locals, fun though it is, because Bill's love of the music was genuine enough, and one thinks of fellow figures in the blues revival – Alexis Korner in particular – who used the contacts brought to them by a privileged background to advance the music. And Cecil Sharp was hardly a simple farm worker.

How far, after all, would The Beatles have got without the guiding hand of Brian Epstein? Or The Who without Kit Lambert? Posh opens doors that the rest of us don't even know are there. Clifton brought a fine vintage of traditional songs to the bluegrass repertoire by The Coon Creek Girls *et al*, the cream of which he published in a book of *150 Old-Time Folk And Gospel Songs*, which came out in 1955 and has proved vital for just about every bluegrass picker. It was, of course, privately printed.

As the Sixties dawned, bluegrass acts started to appear at prestigious festivals and on the concert stage, as well as at honky tonks. It was the same for revivalist folk musicians in Britain, dragged from the druggy shadows of the Soho clubs to the brightly-lit stage of the Festival Hall. In both cases, they were generally a more reliable bet than the last straggling remnants of the old-time music, to whom an audience of strangers was a new and frightening experience.

When the likes of Harry Cox, Dock Boggs, Walter Pardon or Clarence Ashley could be persuaded into the public arena, it was a life-changing experience for many lucky enough to see them and feel the force of the tradition full in the face. However, most of the audience frankly couldn't tell the difference, and to cater for such arcane tastes the polished likes of The Stanley Brothers began to resurrect "antiques" and "evergreens" (as Carter called them), songs they had not played since childhood, while Ralph rediscovered the clawhammer style he had learned from his mother.

Flatt And Scruggs plunged cheerfully into old-time material, but Lester Flatt was less happy than Earl Scruggs, under with pressure from A&R men to record more contemporary material. Acceptance by a new audience, though, was matched by a cold shoulder from the dark empire of Nashville. Bluegrass – let alone the less palatable old-time music – virtually disappeared from country radio shows or jukeboxes, and thus from the charts. The only way to keep it commercially alive in this area was to smuggle it in, so Mac Wiseman's musical in-joke 'Charley's Pride And Johnny's Cash' incorporated the bluegrass style into a sound more to Nashville's taste.

The McReynolds Brothers, Jim and Jesse, make an interesting case study, and also made some excellent music. No wonder that a fan's biography of the siblings is subtitled *Appalachia To The Grand Ole Opry*. Born in a coal mining enclave in Virginia, and tapping into a music learnt at their mother's knee (indeed, other members of the clan had already recorded commercially back in the 1920s), they drew inspiration from older brother acts like the Louvins and the Delmores. Their early work is closer to mountain style old-time string band than the more contemporary sounds of bluegrass. Jesse learned his fiddle technique from old-timer Marion Summer, and their early repertoire was chiefly gospel and traditional, but this was unlikely to earn them a living outside the mountains, or even in them. The Brothers moved around the Midwest, and at one point sounded like a slightly more nasal Sons Of The Pioneers.

Jesse copied the syncopated style of Earl Scruggs on his mandolin, a style he debuted in 1951 on an album of gospel songs issued on a small label in Kentucky under the name of The Virginia Trio. At this point, things are still more Appalachia than Opry. They briefly jumped ship to Capitol, home of Merle Haggard, before burying themselves in the Nashville studio system and becoming Opry regulars from 1964. Mission accomplished. They were by now performing as Jim And Jesse And The Virginia Boys, boasting Vassar Clements on fiddle and banjoist Allen Shelton and his famous "bounce", although it was his predecessor, Bobby Thompson, who pioneered the chromatic style evident on their landmark 'Border Ride'.

Jesse's mandolin playing remained the focal point, "crosspicking" a tune, backing triplets and a background drone all at once. Equally innovative was the "mellow, soft tone" they brought to their vocals. Jim and Jesse were not ashamed to adopt such shibboleths as drums, pedal steel and amplification for purist bluegrass fans, alongside a hit single with a trucking song and a whole album of Chuck Berry songs, punningly titled *Berry Pickin' In The Country*. Only a band with such impeccable ancestry could risk so much. As ever, converts to the form were much fiercer in their conservatism than those who grew up in the fold.

Just as innovative, though sharper in tone, were market leaders The Osborne Brothers, from Hyden in Kentucky, the bleak town which Tom T Hall so memorably visited. Their father was as traditional as they come, a yodeller adept on fiddle and banjo, but like all true sons of the soil Bobby and Sonny extended their musical empire. One thinks more recently of Eliza Carthy, heiress to both The Waterson Family and Martin Carthy, embracing dub reggae and techno and conversely bringing a new and contemporary audience to traditional British song. Such music has strong roots: it bends back if you twist it out of shape, tougher than ever.

As The Lonesome Pine Fiddlers, the Osborne brothers crossed that invisible line from old-time to bluegrass. They covered songs by such Nashville-based songwriter as Felice and Boudleux Bryant, and pioneered a new kind of vocal harmony, as a trio with fellow Kentuckian Red Allen. Put simply, the harmonies radiate downwards from Bobby's high and piercing tenor, rather than upwards from a lower-pitched singer. When they went "modern" in 1967 and attached amplification to the banjo and mandolin, and then added electric guitar, piano and a set of drums, one irate fan cut the cord to the banjo's amplifier. Shades of Dylan at Newport in 1965. Like him, they later repented, and *Fastest Grass Alive* takes them back to a more traditional sound.

The Lewis Family "took up mountain instruments to spread God's word through music". In a photograph in Price's book, courtesy of Canaan Records' "Pops" Lewis, two of his three sons and three daughters pose in front of a fountain. The sisters look like a parody of backwoods fashion, with matching beehive hair as big as a Scots guard's bearskin and each in an enormous chequered skirt. The Martians have landed! At one bluegrass festival, Bill Monroe invited the banjoist, Little Roy, to jam with his band, but had to ask his parents' permission first. Pop finally agreed, "just as long as y'all don't play any profane songs". 'Cripple Creek' proved OK – after all, our Lord made the lame walk.

In a taboo that stretches back to The Carter Family, the only way for these ideologues to allow their womenfolk to sing is in a family group, and with material which praises the Lord: "This music is morally pure." Bluegrass remains a heavily male affair, as well as one performed solely by whites. As Price points out, like actors, "musicians have been associated with loose living, so playing in a band was considered too damaging to a woman's reputation". One of the first bluegrass musicians to smash through this prejudice was Hazel Dickens. Among her most recent admirers have been rockers like… "I just can't keep their names in my head, 'cause they're so strange. It's called Sonsomething – Son Dance? Son Volt, that's it".

Much like her Victorian namesake at the blacking factory, Hazel left to work in a factory – and live in a "hillbilly ghetto" – in Baltimore. Here, though, she met the omnipresent Mike Seeger, who was then a conscientious objector to the draft and working in a TB sanatorium, trying to save lives rather than take them, and keeping old-time music alive at night. (Is this the kind of man who brings out your "fighting side", Merle?) The contrast in lifestyle and attitude between liberal Mike and hillbilly Hazel is the stuff of either high comedy or low tragedy.

To his amazement, Seeger found a small folk song community tucked away on the streets of Baltimore, "a meeting of working-class bluegrass people, like Hazel and her brothers, and urban folk-music people who were often liberal politically". It was a rare meeting point: the two kinds of people rarely overlapped, the first usually feeling patronised and the second over-full of middle-class guilt. "It happened with The Almanac Singers, but this was bluegrass, and this was the Fifties, the middle of the McCarthy era." Hazel seemed a little on guard, but also with an inner determination: "I was still a country girl. Back home I had to have an escort when I went out, somebody in the family. I couldn't just say 'I'm going out on a date.' My father would have slapped me over, he'd-a took the belt to me… I would go to these sings and there would be people sitting around. I'd never seen people sit on the floor cross-legged. I had no frame of reference. Everyone I knew generally sat on a chair."

To have a woman playing bluegrass at that time was in itself both a novelty and, to some, a threat. Her new friends tried to rescue her from the "sweatboxes" in which she worked, and were genuinely in awe of her resilience: "You had a remarkable person, coming out of a family that was just destroyed by industrialisation." She started playing in bars on her own, covering Kitty Wells songs, and then started singing with the college-educated "sweetheart" of another of The Pike County Boys. Alice Gerrard looks like a Pre-Raphaelite painting in the photograph by John Cohen (another name with which we're already familiar) which now graces the Smithsonian Folkways CD *Pioneer Women Of Bluegrass*. For Alice, to whom the Harry Smith *Anthology* had been "big with all of us", Hazel acted as a mentor as well as a friend. She could be talking about someone of a different race, of which to all intents and purposes Hazel was.

The duo played private jam sessions before making their public debut at the Galax Fiddler's Convention, playing old Carter Family songs, and they cut their first demo tape in the basement of the magazine *Bluegrass Unlimited* with the help of two young folk revivalists, David Grisman and Peter Siegel. As Hazel told *No Depression*: "We didn't know how to polish anything. We didn't know what the word meant." Folkways were impressed enough to release *Who's That Knocking* in 1965, with Hazel and Alice singing tenor and lead, just like the men. It was as big a gender leap as The Coon Creek Girls way back when. To their surprise, Bill Monroe was extremely supportive. On a later album on Rounder, Hazel and Alice expanded their repertoire into country, folk and old-time music, and the duo teamed up with Anne Romaine's Southern Grassroots Revival Project, touring the country and awakening a political anger in Hazel, which began to feed into her own songwriting.

Her songs appear on the Oscar-winning documentary *Harlan Country, USA*, and the same director, John Sayles, gives Hazel a telling cameo part in *Matewan*, singing unaccompanied beside a miner's grave. She also became involved with the fledgling women's movement with songs like 'Don't Put Her Down, You Helped Put

Her There'. Conversely, her solo albums for Rounder saw a return to honky-tonk styles, and even the influence of George Jones. Jones is many things but bluegrass is not one of them.

Let's quickly jump to the cheery banjo sound of Don Reno, just to cheer ourselves up. On albums like *Fastest Five Strings Alive*, playing as I write, Don makes his instrument chuckle – and he grins on the cover, with apple cheeks. Snuffy Jenkins told Don, then a nine-year-old boy hopeful, to "put another pick on that third finger and use it if it kills you". He replaced Scruggs in the Blue Grass Boys, though reckoned that The Morris Brothers – with whom he had played earlier – were bluegrass' true originators. Here he slows down and makes 'My Old Kentucky Home' almost plaintive. Then it's back to maximum speed.

Bluegrass instrumentals entered the media mainstream through Flatt And Scruggs' soundtrack for *The Beverly Hillbillies* and the movie *Bonnie And Clyde*. Every moviegoer could soon identify at least one bluegrass tune, 'Duelling Banjos' (a variant of Dan Reno's 'Mocking Banjos'), after its starring role in *Deliverance*. The undertow of this was the music also became a shorthand device to indicate deep country – bumpkins at best, psychotic murderers at worst.

Bluegrass became a music for outsiders and mavericks, one which you needed to be eccentric or pernickity to follow, which is why ex-hippies were about to dive into it. As a result, major labels refused to touch it with a fencepole, so that small independents like Starday – and later Rebel, Rounder and Sugar Hill – became the main music carriers as a result, largely through mail order. When Dolly Parton was dropped by Nashville as being supposedly over the hill, she went instead to Sugarhill, plunged into bluegrass, and revived her career – hence her starring appearance at the Nashville awards, rather than the sad corral of a stage full of "veterans", seemingly carved in wax, which formed a brief interlude from the main event.

The music remains resolutely uncommercial. Bluegrass fanatics are keen home tapers, acting this way either as hardcore collectors recording each set as a historical document, as guardians of an electric variant of the oral tradition, or simply from stinginess. It's the kind of attitude which transferred itself over to The Deadheads. The Grateful Dead had close links with bluegrass, and themselves played a psychedelic, blissed-out variant, slowed down and stretched out almost to infinity.

Long before Woodstock, fans of the music chose to overdose on their favourite music at bluegrass festivals, held out in the countryside. There was a sublimated desire to imitate the original settlers, getting back to Nature for at least a weekend, in tents or camper vans, with sanilav and lots of fresh air. Bill Clifton put on the first bluegrass festival in Virginia in 1961, and it was a financial flop. Carlton Haney, a promoter from North Springs, Carolina, took over the idea but included a theme for each festival, bringing a sense of "drama and history to bluegrass", with tributes to individual musicians and long-defunct bands reforming for the night, plus an obligatory open-air church service on Sunday morning.

The idea spread like wildfire, with the Bean Blossom Festival – held on Bill Monroe's land among the hills of Indiana – being a particular favourite. These were and are family affairs, often teetotal, and as free of drugs, profanity and illicit sex as the promoters can manage. Malone compares these gatherings to the religious camp meetings back in the 19th century, where folk met blues with much the same fundamentalism (for music, this time around), but with one crucial difference: the "absence of black people". That aside, fans can meet their heroes face to face, and even join in with them in earnest, camp-fire jams.

It is much the same at British folk festivals, like Cropredy or Cambridge, which are much more likely to feature such music than big country festivals like Wembley but are without quite the same moral restrictions. The overall vibe in both cases is that of an extended family, with the musicians as friends or relations, not as distant superstars. Half of the audience bring their instruments with them, and after the main set the night air is full of plucked strings.

Price traces these "parking-lot pickers" back to corn-husking and barn-raising parties, "where music make the work go faster and the respite more enjoyable". Much later came Washington Square in the 1950s, "the Grand Ole Opry of New York's folk music set", with pickers clustered around the pool, on adjacent benches and under the marble arch which acts as a gateway to Greenwich Village. Roger Sprung learned bluegrass banjo here from Billy Faier, "who taught me to slow down records in order to hear all the notes". Friends in Philadelphia took him to New River Ranch, where Flatt And Scruggs were headlining: "The car was still going when I hopped out – I almost broke my neck in my eagerness." He travelled south to meet the likes of Bascom Lamar Lunsford, and then accompanied Jean Ritchie, joined Mike Cohen in The Shanty Boys, had Doc Watson guest on his first album, traded old-time instruments, and formed The Progressive Bluegrassers. He's learning still.

In the fierce crucible of such public arenas, bluegrass continued to change and grow, with elder statesman Ralph Stanley adding an element of unaccompanied singing to his concerts, looking back to the vocal phrasing of the Primitive Baptist Church and of mountain quartets. He also looked forward, bringing in young musicians such as the Ohio-born guitarist Larry Sparks (who sang with a "lonesome rural sound"), and the Kentuckians Keith Whiteley (who died young) and Ricky Skaggs, both raised on Stanley Brothers' discs with their mothers' milk.

Ralph's standing among a younger generation was shown when Dylan, Gillian Welch, Dwight Yoakam, Hal Ketchum and many others came into the studio to jam live on *Clinch Mountain Country*, a recording which Dylan reckoned the peak musical experience of his life. President Clinton commended his "heartfelt vocals and tradmark banjo", and Gillian Welch later reckoned: "It was one of the scariest things I've ever done – to sing with your biggest influence. My God! We sang a Carter Family song…when I finished I told everybody that I had gotten my ass kicked because he's so good."

Ralph was always on the lookout for new talent, and he hit gold with Ricky Skaggs, from Eastern Kentucky. Needless to say, his mother used to take him to Baptist services where, by the age of three, young Ricky could sing along in harmony. "My daddy bought me a mandolin when I was five." By the age of seven, he was guesting on Flatt And Scruggs' TV show, and his dad was refusing to allow Ricky to play baseball in order to protect his fingers. With his friend Keith Whiteley, they auditioned for Ralph. "Keith and I grew up the same way the Stanleys did, in fundamentalist Baptist churches and in rough country." On the way back from gigs, and to keep themselves awake, "we'd sing those old Baptist hymns. They came out as natural as can be for us." Stanley dropped his head with sheer emotion as he listened, invited them onstage, and "told us that our singing really brought back a lot of memories, just to hear people sing old songs." From the mouths of babes....

Older performers retreated to the music of their youth, with Jimmy Martin, Jim And Jesse and The Osborne Brothers all bringing in younger members of their family but easing up on the amplification. Skaggs himself married one of Ralph Stanley's cousins. Younger bands, like The Country Gentlemen (whom Ricky subsequently joined when he decided to become a full time musician: "they pay weekly salaries – they're a corporation") and the Seldom Scene, have remained strictly acoustic. When Duffey and Adcock both left The Country Gentlemen at the end of the Sixties, young and urgent musicians like Doyle Lawson and the aforementioned Ricky Skaggs took over the baton.

Meanwhile, back in the early to mid Sixties, bluegrass saw a whole blast of fresh energy emerging from the West Coast. This music pre-dated both psychedelia and country rock, but if you look closer beneath the beards and flowing hair of those later pioneers, and you'll see many of the same musicians, with neatly trimmed hair, forced grins and colourful stage uniforms. It was a revolution in waiting. Hip teenagers were embracing bluegrass as a mysterious and ancient source. Even if they had never been as far east as the Appalachians, they were already bringing contemporary folk material – and then, within a few years, new songs by The Beatles and other pop groups – into the accepted repertoire.

The Dillards – brothers Doug and Rodney, together with childhood friends Mitch Jayne and Dean Webb – left Salem, Missouri, in 1963 to head for California, fortune and fame. They travelled in a '55 Cadillac (the engine of which eventually "ate itself") with a one-wheel trailer, working their passage across the country. Back home, they had honed their craft at "pie suppers, hog-calling contests [and] turkey-calling contests". Talking to *Omaha Rainbow*, Doug first recounts playing for the Miss Nude contest, when he felt obliged to shed everything but his banjo, and then reveals that he started playing the instrument after seeing Uncle Dave Macon at the Opry. He got to know Earl Scruggs well enough for the older man to drill holes in his banjo and put in tuners. One senses a baton being passed on here.

Having won a residency at the Ash Grove folk club in LA, The Dillards gained a booking at the Newport Folk Festival. As they later told Dave Henderson, "That was like letting a dog loose in the chickens! Four guys from the rural mountains unleashed into the intellectual New York scene." Here they jammed backstage with Bill Clifton, landed a TV role as the Darling family on the *Andy Griffiths Show*, and prepared their debut album, the serious *Back Porch Bluegrass*, released on Elektra.

Here, however, was a group who proved too irreverent for the serious folk fans and yet too rough and ready for the mainstream. The solution came with a live album recorded in 1964 at the Mecca in Los Angeles, with a sleeve note by John Stewart, who is of the belief that bluegrass is like an antique car: "it can either be many hours of pure fun or it can sit in a museum and be a crashing bore". Doug "never plays the same part twice", while Mitch can reduce an audience to hysteria with his comic intros. This was not by chance: Doug reckons that this was a way to convey bluegrass "to people who were a sophisticated audience", who would not usually listen to the genre. "Comedy brought the bluegrass to them."

The album cover has the band in buckskin uniforms, with instruments held aloft and one of their member lying down as if dead. The effect is macabre but striking. The music inside is a combination of sparkling playing and laconic backchat and is the very opposite of polished, although instrumentally they are as precise as a medal-winning relay team. Introducing 'Old Blue', Mitch pokes fun at Joan Baez (practically a capital offence at the time), as being too upper class to have to visit the outdoor toilet on a winter's night and fighting the hound dog for possession. Hillbillies don't fluff up their dog like poodles, or give them rhinestone collars: "They're a status symbol down home." To sing this song properly you need to know about privvies in the Ozarks – "about a hundred yards too far from the house in winter, and a hundred yards too near in the summer" – and how they attract stray foxhounds.

Having taken on Baez, The Dillards also cover a Dylan song, 'Walking Down The Line', very early. He might sound "like a dog with his leg caught in barbed wire", but he writes real well. They sing it like four birds sitting on a branch, for sheer joy, and the acoustic instruments circle round each other as only bluegrass can. No wonder that Tom Paley's fellow mathematicians loved its fractal patterns so much.

Their update of a far older song, 'Pretty Polly' – "murder without punishment", in this version – is sung straight by Rodney, but with a comic intro by Mitch: "There's a need for murder in every culture, and back home we had that a lot. People needed it, and if they needed it badly enough they did it." Having got her in the family way, Polly's boyfriend reckons it cheaper to knock her on the head and bury her: "He was a very careful boy, apart from that." When they get to a dark hollow, he hits her in the head and kicks her, and she sees the open grave with the spade by it, and says "Willie, you're peeved at me, aren't you?" He then guts her – the audience are laughing extremely nervously at this point – and no good guys come round to take vengeance. It all makes the film *Shallow Grave* seem a little bloodless.

Mitch's macabre intro is the same trick which the folk singer Vin Garbutt learned ten years or so later. Vin comes from Teeside, the arse end of England, and makes no attempt to moderate his accent, but instead reduces the audience to tears of laughter with his irrelevant introduction to a local ballad, and then – and this is the real trick – brings them to tears with the full-on (and extremely loud) way in which he sings it, as if for real. Back at the Mecca, there is a running gag about Rodney's harmonica and where Mitch would like to stick it.

This is an album imbued with the old music, however comically introduced. 'Buckin' Mule' is a mountain song, "so old it has wrinkles, and our version is very likely to finish it off". Bluegrass is a communal music; it needs "the fun of a live audience to communicate itself" – and, yes, "we're all hillbillies", not the Budapest String Quartet. 'Sinkin' Creek' plays turn and turn around, with a banjo playing a fiddle tune and a mandolin the banjo part: "Those that like the lonesome, primitive sound of the old fiddle tunes will recognise the framework as one of these, with a lot of improvisation."

'The Whole World Round' goes even deeper, focusing on those settlers who "just couldn't abide their neighbour's axe", and moves on until the trees began to thin out. All over the Ozarks, "in woods and in churchyards, lie the graves of the people this song is about, the pioneers". It is performed with a kind of dignified sadness, and The Dillards' trademark vocal unison harmonies – like a blast of fresh, cold air – are already well in place. The traditional tune 'Liberty' is something which Mitch loves to play to "anyone who thinks hillbilly is degrading and simple, for I never heard a piece of music that had so much to say". It has no words, of course.

Mitch is only half-joking when he recounts that "nobody at home thought we could make a living playing this kind of music". Like The Beatles' music of the time, and for much the same reason (it captures youthful exuberance and a fresh, clean musical combo, with no loose ends), it hasn't dated a second since it was laid down. Even Mitch's quips are still funny, which is far from the case with all kinds of mainstream country fooling. When he says that Doug looks as happy on stage as a possum eating bumble bees, it strikes true – country wisdom, again.

Ironically, the later, more experimental albums by The Dillards now sound much more of their time, and tame compared to the live sparkle here. After *Pickin' And Fiddlin'*, a collaboration with fiddle player Byron Berline, Doug went off to play electric banjo with The Byrds, and then joined Gene Clark for a while in The Fantastic Expedition, still on that pioneer trail. The Dillards hired Herb Pederson on "Nashville rhythm guitar" and banjo, and went on to make two ground-breaking albums, 1968's *Wheatstraw Suite* and the later *Copperfields*, on which the vocal attack is upped a notch or two and the repertoire takes new songs by Eric Andersen, Lennon and McCartney and Tim Hardin, but chiefly includes those by themselves. 'Cottonfields' is a song of rural nostalgia by Herb Pedersen, complete with orchestra, and between some of the tracks of the previous *Suite* are snatches of Southern talk. The best of all is their version of 'She Sang Hymns Out of Tune', prefaced by a spoof report on snake prices – "all rattlers off one cent" – over a reprise of the opening song.

The Kentucky Colonels were an even wilder bluegrass group, and again were founded on family membership, with Roland and his brother Clarence – whose father worked for the Lockheed Aircraft Company – almost telepathic on mandolin and guitar respectively. A third brother, Eric, had been replaced by Roger Bush on banjo, Leroy Mack played dobro, and when Bobby Slone joined on fiddle and bass the line-up was complete. In 1965, they recorded the legendary album *Appalachian Swing*, which had no vocals because they were too expensive to record. However, this allows Clarence to take off on guitar. Born in Maine and raised in California, he is far from being a product of the Appalachians himself and, as one record guide puts it, "the White brothers played and sang with grace, total conviction and no irony whatsoever". The obvious highlight is 'I Am A Pilgrim', whose arrangement was taken wholesale by The Byrds for *Sweetheart Of The Rodeo*. The lack of a human voice here makes it all the more poignant, and White's guitar seems to fill in the gap.

When Roger Bush joined them, "I think we were called The Smoggy Mountain Boys, or something. Yeah. The One Night Only Boys." They played folk venues like the Ash Grove: "the big folk boom was on, and bluegrass fell right into it". Clarence had been playing guitar since the age of six: "My mother had tons of 78s – country music from the Twenties on up to the Fifties." His father played the fiddle, and knew lots of French-Canadian songs. (The family name was Le Blanc, so this is no great surprise.) The Kentucky Colonels played "with an intensity that bordered on chaos". Clarence was heavily influenced by the unchaotic style of Doc Watson, and a young Jerry Garcia accompanied The Colonels on a tour of the East Coast, captured on film on *Long Journey Home*.

Acoustic Guitar magazine described White's style as the next step on from Watson or Don Reno: "He deconstructed these phrases, punching holes in them, twisting and stretching them, and making them perform acrobatic feats of unequalled grace and daring." It can be heard in full flow on *Livin' In The Past*, a rag bag of live recordings from the early Sixties which somehow adds up to a complete show (but much longer than anyone human could physically play such music). The show is introduced by a soft-voiced Garcia in 1964 – before The Dead were even conceived – and then it's straight into an hysterically fast 'Fire On The Mountain', complete with whoops from the audience. This music makes punk sound geriatric. There's lots of homespun and slightly dubious wisdom – "applause is like making love to a widow woman: you can't overdo it" – and off they go, careering down both their repertoire and the years.

Being live, this is bluegrass un-embellished, warts and all, and although the vocals lack the chill of the very greatest (they're all too young to fully feel the tragedy in these songs) they succeed in displaying the weird family togetherness which the music demands. As to the instrumental interplay, it is simply jaw-dropping, extra-terrestial – you name it. It feels like the strings are on fire, and, like Hendrix, Clarence is so extraordinary a player that you somehow feel that he is not long for this world. The band reckon that their 1964 gospel concert at UCLA was their best gig ever, but 'Get On Your Knees And Pray', taped a year later, is even more spooky, with the vocal lines a cat's cradle and Billy Ray's high tenor like a shiver in the night. Being bluegrass, it's followed by a most un-sacred (and desperately unfunny) comic routine about a deaf mother, and then Scotty Stoneman – whom Garcia reckons to be the "bluegrass Charlie Parker" – showing off. There is also a photo collage: scenes from a lost world.

The Colonels, who look more like proud young lieutenants, went electric much at the same time as Dylan ("to get work"), with Bart Henry on drums and Clarence playing a Fender Telecaster. As Bush recalls: "we were doing in '66 what The Burrito Brothers are doing now. We just played country music" – just! – "but we rocked it up a little bit." They drew their new repertoire from early Nashville and Hank Williams in particular, with rock 'n' roll drums. "Clarence was being influenced by session musicians like James Burton and a really wild guitarist from the Paul Butterfield Blues Band, Michael Bloomfield", although his actual licks still came from the likes of Don Reno or Doc Watson.

According to Bush: "So we had really a different kind of a band, but who cared? This was a little town of Azusa, California, and we played in the bowling alley there in the lounge. It finally just got unbearable. I went to work in a machine shop there during the day and playing at night, and we finally broke it up about May or so of 1966."

Clarence White went on to work with Gene Parsons as a humble session man on the Bakersfield International label, where he invented the Stringbender, a device which enabled him to imitate a pedal steel by pulling down on the guitar neck. He and Roland later put other line-ups of The Kentucky Colonels together. The CD *Livin' In The Past* has a photo of their last reunion on the back cover from January 1971, although it's actually a compilation of live Sixties highlights. It also mentions some 1973 gigs by The New Kentucky Colonels, including a tour of Europe. Then, at the height of his powers, Clarence was wiped out by a drunk driver as he was loading his instruments after a gig in Palmdale, California, in July of that same year.

Country rock was never quite the same afterwards. Before he reinvigorated The Byrds, Clarence had formed Nashville West with Gene Parsons and Gib Guilbeau, and an album subsequently emerged, recorded on "Gene's living-room Sony" at the club of that name in El Monte. Nick Ralph reckoned it to be an essential archive release – "its raw sound can be both appealing and annoying" – despite songs like 'Green Green Grass of Home' and 'By The Time I Get To Phoenix', which is certainly a culture shock after the old-time material played by The Colonels. The recording is skewed so that the electric guitar drowns out most of the rest, but as a bar band they were years ahead of their time.

History could have been so different. White was offered a demo recording of

Dylan goofing about on 'Mr Tambourine Man' with Jack Elliott, "like a drunk man singing", but the others turned it down "because it was a stupid song and because they said electric folk was just unacceptable". So it went to The Byrds...

LA's Country Boys, or The Kentucky Colonels as they became, had a couple of local rivals. The Haphazards didn't amount to much but featured pre-teens Larry and Tony Rice, with Jerry Garcia on banjo. The Golden State Boys featured (again) the almost obligatory pair of brothers, Vern and Rex Gosdin, with Don Parmley on bass and mandolin-twanger Chris Hillman. They subsequently renamed themselves The Hillmen "after their 17-year-old genius," as Jim Dickson told the ultimate Byrds chronicler, Johnny Rogan. "I thought it would focus attention on Chris because he didn't sing much." During the years 1963-64, under this moniker they made some live recordings in LA, straight onto three-track and combining traditional bluegrass classics with newer material by Woody Guthrie, Pete Seeger and Bob Dylan. Hillman sings 'When The Ship Comes In', but he's so shy he's barely there and is carried by the soft harmonies of the Gosdins. The results – not issued until 1969 – make easier listening than The Colonels, less supercharged (isn't everyone!) but with more appealing vocals. It's also as mournful as hell, which is exactly what's required. Even earlier, Hillman had been a member of The Scotsville Squirrel Barkers (aka The Kentucky Mountain Boys), who recorded a budget LP of traditional bluegrass, which was sold in supermarkets and truck stops for $10 each, and was nothing special. Hillman, however, was.

He grew up in the country, near San Diego, and came to the music through folk, first Pete Seeger, then Leadbelly, then The New Lost City Ramblers. "I loved Mike Seeger's mandolin playing", he later told *Folk Roots*, and began to frequent LA's Ash Grove and take in sets by Flatt And Scruggs and The Stanley Brothers – a priceless apprenticeship. Hanging out with local surfers, none of whom condescended to listen to surf music, he also picked up what these "cool guys" were taking in: Jimmy Reed and flamenco. "I got to hear real rootsy, traditional kinds of music."

The Gosdin brothers were "real guys from the South", and served as Hillman's "window of authenticity". It was their record producer, Jim Dickson, who insisted they try some contemporary material, just as he was to force a new band whom he started to manage, The Jet Set (aka The Beefeaters, and then The Byrds), to record 'Mr Tambourine Man': "otherwise we could have veered off into a more Beatlesque path". Dickson brought Hillman in on electric bass. The new band was unusual in being drawn from a bunch of hardened professionals, mostly from an acoustic background in either the thickets of folk or country.

At this point, I hope, the patient groundwork the reader has invested so far is about to prove the launching pad for all kind of weirdness, so please stay with me. This music is about to go thermonuclear, and I just hope my prose can keep up with it. Just grab hold of your mental seat-belts.

While still at school, the Byrd who stayed in the aviary longest, Jim McGuinn, painstakingly learned five-string banjo and twelve-string guitar – an instrument he would make the heartbeat of folk rock – at Chicago's Old Town School Of Folk Music. The course also included the rudiments of country music: "They taught you everything – Earl Scruggs and the Sam Hinton basic beat...they had it really academicised." He also became an (underage) fixture at the Gate Of Horn folk club, then run by Dylan's future manager, Albert Grossman, and featuring the likes of Odetta.

On *Peace On You*, McGuinn looks back in the title track: "lisen to Mr Gibson play his fine old guitar". A twelve-string model, of course. There's even an Irish singalong thrown in. It was here that Jim acquired a taste for British traditional song – sea stories a speciality – which recently resurfaced on his internet-only release *McGuinn's Folk Den Volume One*.

Sid Griffin was surprised to find "only quiet renditions of the now-traditional Celtic ballads and rounds which inspired him in his youth" on this latest form of oral transmission, via a computer. He began by posting a folk standard every month on his web site, complete with lyrics and chord chart, like an electronic back porch. Thus was 'Space Odyssey' revealed to be an update of 'The Handsome Cabin Boy'.

As soon as he had left school, the young prodigy took up paid gigs with The Limelighters and The Chad Mitchell Trio, playing anodyne acoustic folk, before joining Bobby Darin to spice up the acoustic segment of his cabaret set. He also served an apprenticeship at the Brill Building as a songwriter, working 9-5. In a mohair suit, he played twelve-string guitar and banjo on various bluegrass cash-ins ('Banjo Bach' is an early example of his prowess at mixing and matching musical forms), as well as sessions for the likes of Hoyt Axton, The Irish Ramblers (from "the banks of the River Blackwater, separating the counties of Armagh and Tyrone") and Judy Collins, from whose repertoire The Byrds later borrowed 'Turn, Turn, Turn' and 'Deportees'.

Jim – as his name remained until he joined the Subud faith and renamed himself Roger – was already a folk club legend, and flying. His voice was a one-off, dreamy and almost bored, a vocal drone that was as unmistakeably Celtic as his surname. It was also the perfect sound for the drug generation. The Mamas And Papas' 'Creeque Alley' reckoned that 'McGuinn and McGuire couldn't get no higher', although this was supposedly out of jealousy of his hitting the pop charts and not a reference to personal indulgences. Meanwhile, McGuinn had lived in the same New York hotel as John and Michelle Phillips for a while. Commuting across America, he became a resident at LA's Troubadour, but a new-found love for The Beatles was seen at first as some kind of mental aberration.

Then one night, Jim was playing with his new musical friend Gene Clark, and a teenage tearaway whom McGuinn had known back in Greenwich Village, David Crosby, turned up. As Clark told Rogan: "we went into the lobby and started picking on the stairway where the echo was good, and David came walking up and just started singing away with us doing the harmony part...we hadn't even approached him." It was evidently sheer musical magnetism, even if three such egos would neither be able to stay together or stay apart afterwards. It's nice to know that so much wonderful music came about from such a chance meeting, even taking into account their common musical background. It was a spark waiting to ignite.

Gene Clark was born in Missouri and raised on country music and bluegrass, influences which would return to haunt him. He too became a folk fanatic, briefly joining The New Christie Minstrels (these last two facts are *non sequiturs*) before joining McGuinn to form an acoustic duo, *à la* Peter and Gordon. Sneer not: Jane Asher's brother later became a premier country-rock producer, and his later albums with Gordon touched on some very weird territory indeed, none less expected than the 1966 release *Hits Of Nashville*. Gene and Jim's future colleague, David, had been a spoiled brat in Hollywood (some reckon that he still is), saved only by having the singing voice of an angel, which is also still miraculously intact despite a lifestyle which even the more decadent Roman emperors would find excessive.

Back in the early Sixties, Crosby gave up an early acting career to sing in the local clubs: "I was a folkie, and I played because I loved it." In Venice, California, he shared digs with first Dino Valente and then Paul Kantner and David Frieberg – the San Francisco sound in waiting – before donning a red band jacket to join commercial folkies The Les Baxter Balladeers. We're not talking authenticity here. Jim Dickson became his manager and took Crosby into the studio to record a strange repertoire in his choirboy voice, which ranged from Ray Charles to Hoyt Axton and the Civil War song 'Jack O'Diamonds'. When he brought his two new colleagues to Dickson, he steered them into a midway point between British beat and American folk.

McGuinn is open about how The Searchers – themselves named after the John Ford film – were a big influence on his guitar style, telling John Tobler that he also liked "The Seekers and Dusty Springfield…it was hip to be English, but to be fair they were using folk music licks that I was already using anyway. So it's not a rip-off; they'd put a beat to it, but I was using those same suspensions in folk music. The Searchers were using two six-strings in octave harmony" rather than one twelve string. McGuinn eventually got disenchanted with folk, but "now the pure stuff is young again, and for me it's new again, and I'm just having a revitalised interest in it". (Why do all of these pioneers keep on stating the theme of this book, in far better chosen words than I can manage?)

McGuinn didn't lose his interest in folk music during those electric years; he simply transformed it into another medium, that of folk rock. It peeps through regardless, however. The brave new world of the Seegers and their like had grown stale and in need of renovation. As McGuinn told *Zigzag*: "I feel that most of the people in that movement weren't really interested in the music, they didn't want to get inside it, but did it rather to be there and be seen." It needed The Beatles to "clear the air of that strange outlook which evolved through the *Hootenanny Show* and things like that". A revolutionary music had turned into part of the status quo:

"it was getting very commercial and plastic packaged in cellophane". When The Beatles hit his consciousness, it was because "in their chord changes I could see degrees of complexity that folk music had gotten to by that time". Just add Dylan's lyrics and you have the template for a life's work.

The Byrds-in-waiting began to grow their hair accordingly, and Dickson brought into the fold Hillman and Michael Clarke (who had run away from home to play congas in coffee houses) on drums – or, rather, cardboard boxes, which was all they could afford at the time. *Preflyte* sees folk becoming rock becoming something else.

With 'Mr Tambourine Man', they mated a twelve string and a backbeat to a piece of Dylan's stoned poetry, although McGuinn was the only Byrd permitted to play in the studio at this time, while session men like Leon Russell filled in Monkees fashion. McGuinn's stoned, sneery voice floats over it all, as impossibly cool as he was himself in those days, his eyes hidden behind specially-tinted granny glasses, as far removed from an acoustic folkie as could possibly be imagined. The flipside was Gene Clark's haunted 'I Knew I'd Want You', evoking a primal melancholy. Country boy Gene was the first Byrd to emerge as a songwriter, and he found something of that high, lonesome sound in this minor-key moan.

As time went on, their blend of country and traditional roots began to peep through. Between the Indian ragas, guitar breaks in the style of John Coltrane, snatches of electronics and rocked-up Dylan lyrics, the first two albums saw a brace of jangly Pete Seeger adaptations: 'The Bells Of Rhymney', from a Welsh poem about a mine disaster (incorporating "temple music", a particular crowd favourite during their residency at Ciro's) and 'Turn Turn Turn'. For McGuinn, who sings it in best preacher mode, "it was a standard folk song by that time, but I played it and it came out rock 'n' roll, because that's what I was programmed to do, like a computer". The same album saw The Byrds cut the Porter Wagoner hit 'Satisfied Mind', at Hillman's insistence. The wonderful optimism of those celestial vocal harmonies – bluegrass on liquid oxygen – rather blunts the misery of the words, like young men singing the blues. Just give them time, though.

'Fifth Dimension', meanwhile, went about as far out as was possible in 1966, and here was the safe haven of traditional song, like a touchstone amidst the madness of jet flight engines, benign Mr Spacemen and extra-drugged dimensions – life in free fall, "to never hit bottom". 'Wild Mountain Thyme' came from the McPeake family via the coffee-house scene, where McGuinn "took it from Pete Seeger". He sings it with incredible tenderness, and a string orchestra shadows his vocal. They waver between cowboy theme tune and Indian raga – country and eastern.

On the cover of *Younger Than Yesterday*, Crosby wears a cowboy hat twice. Inside, Hillman's old friend Clarence White plays on 'Time Between', a country shuffle, the first song Hillman ever wrote and particularly Beatles-like. Hillman "sort of grew up with Clarence. Then, around the end of '66, I found him again living way out of LA and playing in country groups in bars and things, playing electric guitar

257

now". He's also on 'The Girl With No Name', providing grace notes and what is almost a solo on this tale of subdued bitterness.

Dickson particularly liked these songs "because of their country flavour. McGuinn has no sensitivity towards country music." *The Notorious Byrd Brothers* sees a viciously slimmed-down group posing in a tin-roofed stable, with Crosby supposedly transformed into the horse which gazes out here – wonderfully funny, if true! Don't worry, Roger, there's an even bigger egomaniac about to join your band and hijack it all the way to Nashville.

Pedal steel closes 'Going Back' like a distant memory, and Red Rhodes' electrically-treated instrument matches Hillman's chorus on 'Natural Harmony', as strange a vision of Eden as anything since Bosch. Clarence White picks bluegrass-style on Goffin-King's 'Wasn't Born to Follow', as pure as a mountain stream. A door closes at the end. White also plays on 'Change Is Now', working around Crosby's rhythm and McGuinn's explosive solo, blossoming forth in the middle of the song, like a needle plunged straight into an open vein.

True to an album all about change and growing up and looking back, the following track, 'Old John Robertson', is based on Chris' childhood. "I grew up in a small town of about 1,000 people. There was an old man, John Robertson, who retired there. He had been a movie director in the Twenties. He wore a Stetson hat and had a long white handlebar moustache. Quite an old cowboy character, but he was really nice to us kids." The thanks he gets is people laughing behind his back, but Hillman sings this song of second childhood with real affection. Originally conceived as a straight country tune with tickly guitar, "all of a sudden this harpsichord and baroque section walked in". This is pretty much par for the course on an album which starts with a drug song and then phases everything to hell, and on which the young men of earlier albums suddenly sound older than the hills.

McGuinn then made the biggest mistake of his life. He was already planning The Byrds next album, a double, and slated to be nothing less than the complete history of music. Once again, it follows the pattern of this book, from the British diaspora to The Alabama 3. "I wanted to use elements of early music, progressing to Celtic music, showing how that was distilled in North America to produce various forms of folk music, then to show the origins of country music and bluegrass, R&B and rock music, and finally going into the future and exploring the synthesiser and computer music."

To carry out this huge plan he needed more than the two Byrds left in the nest, so "when I hired Gram Parsons it was as a jazz pianist. I had no idea he was a Hank Williams character, too. He pretended to be a jazz player, too."

Gram Parsons was a true Southern aristocrat, heir to a citrus fruit empire in Florida and from a family of gothic dimensions. (His father, "Coon Dog" Connor, was an alcoholic who killed himself one Christmas day.) Gram started playing in teen bands like The Legends, whose 'Rip It Up' is pure rock 'n' roll with a wild guitar break, then played unplugged with The Village Vanguards and then The Shilohs, whose work survives on *Gram Parsons: The Early Years 1963-65*. They pose on the back cover, young preppies in neat matching suits and haircuts, with two acoustic guitars, string bass and banjo; but the crappy music inside is a teenage glee club plus water. The album, dedicated to the memory of Gram's mother, includes two early songs sung solo, in which he plays down his Southern accent (he sounds like a young James Stewart when he instructs the rest of the band during 'Surfinanny'), or perhaps before he played it up later. They also perform a gospel song and a glutinous 'Bells Of Rhymney'. There is little here to prompt his boast that "I'm sure my music is going to be as big as Dylan's". This is the sort of insincere rubbish which drove McGuinn out of folk music.

Parsons briefly attended Harvard, then put together The International Submarine Band to fulfil his vision of "cosmic American music": "We were always trying to do hard rock or rhythm and blues or country music at the same time, and nobody understood it, and we were nuts anyway." However, on the evidence of an early single 'Sum Up Broke' – a slow burner with some of the Who's malevolence – and its B-side 'One Day Week', a Zombies' soundalike with lots of electric piano and a great fuzz guitar solo, they were far from nuts. There's not a pedal steel in sight. Gram moved to LA, supposedly "to get out of the cold and be next door to some good country music stations".

Here he mimed in Peter Fonda's drug movie *The Trip*, and in Rogan's words "fulfilled his Hank Williams fantasies by appearing in various honky tonks and country bars while celebrating the Bakersfield music scene of Buck Owens and Merle Haggard". Another circle closes. Every Thursday he would drive out to the Palomino Club in his new rhinestone suit and sing Merle Haggard songs, although Barney Hoskyns reckons that most of the hardcore country audience looked at the foppish youth "and thought he was a honky tonk imposter". Indeed, he was one among many, and local bluegrass picker Chris Darrow, later of Kaleidoscope, reckoned him "an interloper on a Dwight Yoakam level". Everyone from Rick Nelson to the young Bernie Leadon was trying to fuse country and rock. "There was a different vibe about Gram, particularly because he wrote his own songs, but I don't think any of us thought of him as the Duke Ellington of our deal."

Meanwhile The International Submarine Band split, with some members renaming themselves The Flying Burrito Brothers, playing a mixture of rockabilly and western swing. Gram kept the old name to record *Safe At Home* in 1967, which was released a year later – undoubtedly the first country-rock fusion to make it onto album, though. Ignored at the time, it remains eminently listenable, recorded live and mixing and matching new Parsons songs like 'Luxury Liner' and rocked-up versions of country classics by Merle Haggard and Johnny Cash. The black element comes through 'That's All Right, Mama', from Arthur Crudup via Elvis. Earl Ball adds jingle-jangle piano and Jay Dee Manness contributes pedal steel, while Parsons has his Southern accent fully back in place and the others supply mournful harmonies. The album came garlanded with praise from Don Everly ("white soul") and Glen Campbell ("someone should have done this a long time ago"). Label owner Lee Hazlewood believed it "unique in concept".

Now that Gram was in The Byrds, like a cuckoo in the nest, he could try again. Byrds' roadie Jimmie Sieter flew down to prepare the Nashville studio: "we had two eight-tracks plugged together in sync, and no one had ever seen that before. All the players, like Ernest Tubbs' band, came from miles just to look at our machines." On 15 March, and with smart new haircuts, The Byrds appeared at the Grand Ole Opry, having been booked to sing two Merle Haggard songs.

A redneck audience sat suspiciously through 'Sing Me Back Home', with some even calling out "tweet tweet". "Nobody who was part of that scene wanted us to be there," McGuinn said later, "and you could feel the resentment. They didn't think we were real, and they were pretty protective of their little society." Just as it seemed that some of the audience might unbend, Parsons announced a change of plan – Tompall Glawer had announced 'Life In Prison' – and launched into 'Hickory Wind', which he dedicated to his grandmother. The result was an immediate ban from the Opry for singing the greatest song to emerge from the South for decades. The saying "pearls before swine" comes to mind.

Sweetheart Of The Rodeo was no sooner recorded than legal pressure from Lee Hazlewood forced McGuinn to re-record Gram's lead vocals himself, in a fake Southern accent, leaving only 'Hickory Wind' as it was first intended. Now that most of the originals have now resurfaced, however, I have to say I prefer the doctored version, as McGuinn's voice maintains a link with what has gone before. Otherwise, it would be Gram Parsons plus backing musicians. What we have is a country excursion, which – like Fairport's similar right-hand turn into traditional folk – became a one-way trip.

I can still remember buying this record – in mono – and being disconcerted by the look of the thing, with its lack of band photos and a lot of new names. When I smuggled it onto the family music centre, I felt an initial wave of incredulity and disappointment (the last thing about which I wanted to hear my counter-cultural heroes sing was the Christian life), and was then gradually won over by the grace and mystery of the sound, a good year before the release of *Nashville Skyline*.

I can't have been the only teenager to have felt that way. This was the first attempt by a major rock band to take the plunge into pure country, from the cowboy fashion parade on its front cover to the mournful, largely acoustic sounds inside to the wolf silhouette on the back, howling at the moon. To my mind, it has never been bettered. To top and tail it with two songs from *The Basement Tapes* was a masterstroke, both giving a country twist to a Byrds trademark and also tying things in with the other pioneer busy going back into the past, up in Woodstock. What could better describe the delights of country life – in every sense – as the chorus, "We're going to fly, down in the easy chair"? Drugs on the back porch. Never before had "going nowhere" seemed so good an option, ditto "take care of your health, and get plenty of rest". You need it after a bike crash, or after inventing acid rock.

A brisk note on the acoustic fiddle and we're into a bluegrass gospel song, written by the two surviving original Byrds and sung by Hillman like he's a lost soul, with McGuinn on Rickenbacker banjo. Five of Parsons' original takes have surfaced on the Byrds box set and the CD reissue of the album. (On CD-R, you can now put the original album together, if you must.) I still prefer McGuinn, in this context; he brings a kind of raised eyebrow to his renditions which helps rock 'n' roll refugees like me ease themselves into this alien listening experience.

On the released version, McGuinn sings instead with a pronounced twang, like a comic hillbilly, and his ironic joy on the line "others take pleasure in things I despise" is worth the price of admission alone. This comes from a man who later used to hand out cocaine like a candy bar. The country soul of 'You Don't Miss Your Water' is back to his sweet Byrds voice, crying into its beer in some run-down honky tonk, with marvellous clunking piano from Earl Ball. Here is another song of regret and looking back – this album has deep emotional links with *Notorious Byrd Brothers*, however different its surface. Gram *does* sing on 'You're Still On My Mind'. As Nick Barraclough was saying only the other night, country gets really serious when even heavy drinking doesn't blot out the memories. With steel guitar and piano predominant, The Byrds are hardly here at all.

Fortunately, Parsons' vocal was kept on 'Hickory Wind', as even McGuinn couldn't sing this tenderly or with such nostalgic passion. Country rock starts here, and frankly it doesn't get any better than this, with the climbing piano and sighing violins and whispering steel, let alone the plain man's poetry of "it's a hard way to find out/that trouble is real/in a faraway city" or the weary way Gram almost prays for the wind to follow him home. The grave is implied already. Even Emmylou couldn't improve on these harmony vocals, and McGuinn's genius as an arranger is in full flight. Sadness seeps through, high and lonesome as your life.

'One Hundred Years From Now' has Parsons looking forward, but he's hardly more cheerful. "Nobody knows what kind of trouble we're in." The Byrds have always been generally optimistic about the future, with McGuinn hardly able to wait to put on a spacesuit. A rehearsal take is more relaxed, almost to the point of tedium, and Gram sounds bruised, whereas the harmony Byrds who replace him are soothing, despite the lyrics. They can't help themselves delivering perfect lullabies for grown-ups. Hillman sings again on 'Blue Canadian Rockies', and the man whose vocals once had to be recorded without him knowing is now a confident and joyful singer. (The George Harrison of the group?) Merle Haggard's 'Life In Prison' is faster than the rehearsal tape but less emotionally penetrating, although it has a nice tricksy intro. If this is McGuinn imitating Gram, he's a bloody good impressionist.

'Nothing Was Delivered' could be taken as an ironic comment on the album itself, and if so is immediately contradicted by McGuinn's potent vocal, the sheer punch of The Byrds and their session chums, with Kevin Kelley crashing in at the end like a coda for his own career. All kinds of interesting material has since surfaced from these sessions, including Parsons singing lead vocal on Tim Hardin's 'You Got A Reputation' and his own song 'Lazy Days', but most interesting of all is the traditional ballad 'Pretty Polly', sung by Roger and presumably a track from his proposed concept album of "old-time music, not bluegrass but pre-bluegrass, dulcimers...nasal Appalachian stuff". He's certainly nasal enough, and gives the song just the pitiless treatment it needs.

(I've just been taking a break and reading today's newspaper, and there is an item about a middle-aged psychopath who gave his girlfriend poison, watched her choke to death and then forged her will. These stories are not just examples of antique folklore. They address something permanent in the human condition, and like driving past a car crash there's always a double reaction: both to look away and to stare in guilty fascination.)

The country Byrds then went on the road, and their gig in May 1968 at Rome's Piper Club opens with McGuinn introducing the new recruit. "His name is Gram Parsons. He's going to sing you a song, play the guitar." Then straight into a slow, intense 'You Don't Miss Your Water', with musical embroidery on the electric banjo by Doug Dillard, who is guesting tonight and indeed on the whole tour, in the absence of a steel guitar. Here is alt country 30 years early. It's like hearing a collision between a psychedelic band and an old-time folk combo, and it's wonderful.

Fairport were playing in town that night, and Ashley Hutchings still remembers how musically shocked he felt by this concert, and by the fact that, when the band disappeared, only Gram remained, chatting with fans (Hutchings included). He was shocked not only by his politeness – they typical Southern gentleman – but also by how young he was and how enthusiastic about the music. Later sightings seemed to be of a different person.

The same band, minus Dillard, appeared at London's Middle Earth Club on 6 July. Martin Stone remembers being turned upside-down by the music on offer, and seeing the cream of London's rock aristocracy – in particular a wide-eyed Richard Thompson – among the crush. The musical shockwaves of this gig radiated for years afterwards. It has been captured on the bootleg CD *Under Your Spell Again*, and is much heavier on the country material, including a sprightly reading of the Buck Owens song of the same name. There's more psychedelic guitar, a-slipping and a-sliding; 'Hickory Wind' is even more melancholy than in Rome; and 'Sing Me Back Home' is a dying man's wish, with a bass-heavy lead break while and someone makes a pedal steel sound (still missing in action) on their electric guitar.

The country material is now a section in itself, and The Byrds then lead into a trio of old favourites: 'Eight Miles High', 'Space Odyssey' and 'Tribal Gathering', the first with driving bass and McGuinn attacking his twelve strings with venom. Here is a fairground of sound, and fun for all the family: thunderous drums at the end churn up all that country air. The second is a gavotte in outer space, in parallel with the movie released in this same year, and with some electronic weirdness at the end. The third is pure psychedelia, chiming sounds with piercing guitar.

The next day, Gram played his final gig with the band at Sounds '68 at the Albert Hall. After this, the rest went off on a disastrous South African tour and Gram went back to the States to take over control of The Flying Burrito Brothers.

Gram Parsons flew away from The Byrds, having gorged on their fame and musical contacts and stealing Hillman for his new band. McGuinn, a man with no real feel for country music, was left with a bunch of country musicians who kept his band flying in a kind of creative half-life. More by luck than judgement, he obtained the services of Clarence White, now fully electrified – and still electrifying – and the band changed polarities. Before, they had made supersonic albums and played ramshackle concerts. Now they were as sleek and professional a live band as could be imagined, and each album had a couple of worthwhile songs at most. But what songs!

Dr Byrds And Mr Hyde suggested the schizophrenic nature of the new band, and this theme is reflected on the botched album cover, on which each member has a cowboy alter ego emerging from their own third eye. They open with another song from *The Basement Tapes*, 'This Wheel's On Fire', with McGuinn investing the song with all of the bitterness he must have felt when half his band jumped ship. It has that same slow carefulness of someone being tortured, with sinister electronics to follow.

Clarence White sketches out a nervous breakdown on fuzzed electric guitar, but was uneasy: "I felt I was faking it. In bluegrass music there is a lot of gospel and blues influences and flavouring." Too many white bands were now playing a stale variant on the blues: "I didn't ever feel that I could catch up with them, so I just wanted to play honest music in an honest style that I believed in." The last four years of The Byrds saw them, in effect, playing bluegrass rock, with McGuinn's jangle surrounded by sweet country picking. It might be heresy to say so, but this was a more revolutionary musical mix than Gram Parsons every attempted, and far more influential.

The new album saw the amped-up square dance of 'Nashville West', looking back to White's failed country bar band, which Rogan describes as "a drunken free-for-all". Handclaps lead off the traditional song 'Old Blue', as once performed by The Dillards: "We laid him down with a golden chain." You can't get more country than mourning a dog, though where Presley would have piled on the tears McGuinn sounds cynical, as if it's all a wind-up. Maybe it's just his voice. The new drummer was Gene Parsons (no relation), another former member of Nashville West, and as irony would have it Gram and Chris Hillman had recorded some tracks with Gene and Clarence as a prototype Flying Burrito Brothers. At the Carnegie Hall on one memorable night, The Byrds and The Burritos each played a set, then came together for the encore, with Bernie Leadon joining in on banjo for 'Pretty Boy Floyd'.

Gram also bequeathed to his old band a song he co-wrote with McGuinn in London. 'Drug Store Truck-Driving Man' is dedicated to the extremely right-wing radio WSM DJ Ralph Emery, a professional redneck: "He don't like the young folks, you know." It was more than personal, a "father to me" who spurns his son. The Vietnam war had exposed a fault-line running through the nation, with the peacenik Byrds on one side and the country music audience, by and large, on the other. Another fault line opened when Gram Parsons publically attacked McGuinn as being a musical carpetbagger, with no real interest in the music he was now espousing: "He doesn't live that life, and he brings you down. McGuinn wouldn't know Clarence White from Mighty Sam if it wasn't for Chris [Hillman]."

He mistook Roger's cautious and academic approach as betraying a lack of passion. The next album, *Ballad Of Easy Rider*, plunged deeper into America's folk roots. The title track expanded a few words scrawled by Dylan on the back of an envelope into a song seemingly as old as the hills. Next up is another dog song, then the traditional 'Oil In My Lamp' (of which the outtake is better), the sweet and sour 'Tulsa Country' (as previously recorded by June Carter) and McGuinn's sad retelling of the ancient British ballad 'Jack Tarr The Sailor', with a banjo in the background, and during which – to complicate the matter further – Roger adapts an Irish accent here. This is followed by the stirring country gospel of 'Jesus Is Just Alright', an elegiac version of Dylan's 'It's All Over Now, Baby Blue', and then a slow take on The Gosdin Brothers' song 'There Must Be Someone (I Can Turn To)'. Vern wrote it when he came home one night to find his house stripped of all its furniture and his wife and kids gone. It must have echoed around those bare walls – a truly country moment.

Add to this the poignant Woody Guthrie song 'Deportees', and this is the closest McGuinn ever got to his Americana double album. Two album out-takes of traditional songs enrich the mix: the jazzy version of 'Way Beyond The Sun', borrowed from British folk band Pentangle; and 'Fiddler A Dram (Moog Experiment)', which is fused with banjo and the kind of synthesiser pictured on the inner gatefold sleeve of *[Untitled]*. McGuinn leaves his voice untreated, and this was an experiment which the likes of Snakefarm have recently reinvigorated.

As new bassist Skip Battin recalls, "there was a real charge of energy that none of us expected". The studio album collects together (out of context) many of the songs which McGuinn and Jacques Levy wrote for a proposed rock musical, *Gene Tryp*. It is one of those fascinating concepts which got lost in the making, much like Spirit's *Potatoland*, and a much more coherent project than anything which Pete Townshend ever came up with. With Tim Buckley shortlisted at one point to play the lead role, Broadway doesn't know what almost hit it. McGuinn could have become as rich as Andrew Lloyd-Weber. The story transposes Ibsen's epic and restless drama *Peer Gynt* to 19th-century America, like those traditional songs which took on new colouring in the new world, and all of the ambivalence of Ibsen's folk hero comes through into his anagram. In the play, he finally comes to a kind of self-realisation through his picaresque travels.

In more recent solo concerts, McGuinn has taken the audience through the plot, and much the same happens to Tryp, a kind of proto-hippie – maybe even Roger himself – saved by country music. The hypnotic 'Chestnut Mare' corresponds to Peer Gynt's attempt to catch "a reindeer, or some animal like that". Here, it is a tall tale from the New West. In 'Lover Of The Bayou', "the scene was set during the Civil War, and Gene Tryp was smuggling guns to the confederates".

The studio set also includes Leadbelly's 'Take A Whiff (On Me)', sung by Clarence and with a guest appearance by fiddler Byron Berline, another former member of Nashville West. Good as the live album is, it pales besides the recently-discovered *Live At The Fillmore* from early 1969, complete with all kinds of country rock delights such as 'Buckaroo' and 'Sing Me Back Home'. 'Drug Store Truck-Driving Man' is introduced as being "about a DJ down in Nashville who told us he didn't like hippies".

The Byrds gradually coasted to a halt, with such old-time delights as the tune 'Green Apple Quick Step' and a final album which took its title from the traditional bluegrass lament 'Farther Along', as later sung over Clarence White's coffin by Gram Parsons and Bernie Leadon. There were various attempts to reform the original line-up, but lightning refused to strike twice, although McGuinn, Crosby and Hillman got together in a Nashville studio in 1990 to record some songs for the retrospective box set. The real magic, however, came one night at Hammersmith Odeon in 1977, during the heyday of punk, when a shiny-eyed McGuinn, a laid-back Hillman and a stumbling, heavily-bearded Gene Clark each played a set with their own band before joining together at the end for a short but explosive set, culminating in 'Eight Miles High'. It sounded like a valediction, on that night in 1977, as it does now, a glory departing this Earth.

Meanwhile, Gram Parsons hung out in England with Keith Richards. When he first met The Rolling Stones they took him off by Rolls Royce to Stonehenge, and he would later oblige them by taking Richards to Joshua Tree. Ever the musical pick-pockets, The Stones learned the wherewithal from Gram to compose 'Wild Horses', 'Dead Flowers' and 'Sweet Virginia', on which Parsons is said to sing harmony vocals. As Bud Scoppa wrote: "The Stones were willing participants in the same mythopoeic, imagined, country America." They in turn passed this down the line to Primal Scream, in the unfairly maligned emotional desperation and strength of *Give Out But Don't Give Up*, which is post-ecstasy, in every sense. Country music is an ideal soundtrack to those coming down from chemical highs, even if it has rarely fuelled them.

Parsons then talked with Richie Furay, from Buffalo Springfield, about forming a country rock band, to be called Pogo. Furay's ideas for what actually became soft rockers Poco were too bland for Gram, who instead reformed The Flying Burrito Brothers, "basically a Southern soul group playing country and gospel-orientated music with a steel guitar". Clarence White and Gene Parsons turned him down, so what we actually got was something close to what Gram had tried to force on The Byrds: himself, Chris Hillman and Sneeky Pete on pedal steel. Hillman felt that "the Byrds had really fallen flat for me. Even after hiring Clarence White, I felt it wasn't going to go anywhere," and so he jumped ship. There was no drummer as yet, but Chris Etheridge from the original Burrito brothers rejoined on bass, freeing up Hillman to play guitar.

Just like Eric Clapton, Parsons was transfixed by Delaney And Bonnie, a kind of country-blues conglomerate who jammed around small clubs in LA and signposted a freer, less egotistical music than progressive rock had become. It was a friendly, undemanding sound, and made Gram realise that "the Hazlewood thing had been a shuck": he needed to add "funk and stuff". "That's where the idea for big-time country music started hitting me. I realised that I could do it, too, and that people were not so hung up on sick music as I thought. There was a little bit of room for funk." Unfortunately, many of Parsons' own later live performances – both with The Burritos and The Fallen Angels – were relaxed and unrehearsed to the point of chaos. Gram was a trust-fund millionaire with no real need to work, except when his inner demons dictated, and it was almost as if it was only on the edge of personal disaster that he could finally find the inner energy to produce music of – to use a grossly overworked word – genius. A sound that was new to the world.

The rest was a druggy mess, and Gram's immersion in the emotional pain of his particular hero, George Jones, ultimately didn't do him any good. What he added to Jones' tearful tales of self-inflicted failure was the ability to write some of the greatest songs country ever produced, the voice of a bruised angel – totally without the edge of aggression of the older singer – and an intellectual agenda. In some ways, Parsons is the enemy of all of that for which this book stands. In his dysfunctional childhood in Waycross, Georgia, with rich parents, themselves descended from Swiss Mennonites and English gentleman Colonel George Reed, country music was regarded – to quote Ben Fong-Torres – as "laughable, the corn-poke outpourings of hillbillies and hayseeds". During their annual summer vacation at Beaver Dams Springs, Tennessee, they would listen to fiddlers at the local square dance, and that was that. Gram started as an Elvis Presley fan and worked his way back.

What we therefore get is his attempt to divest country music of its folk elements and substitute black music. As we have seen, everyone from Jimmie Rodgers to Dock Boggs had fused the two, but Gram added hippie idealism and an outright agenda: "We are playing roots music. It's a form of love music, a binding type of music between people. We're playing with white soul, and soul is universal. And the universality of roots music has stood the test of time."

Parsons came to praise the Nashville sounds he loved, and ended up making them sound outdated. The problem was that the music Gram loved – George Jones included – is rooted so deeply in that "high, lonesome sound" that Parsons came to epitomise it, as he sank deeper into the trough. As with Jim Morrison, you can't avoid reading the short and wilful life back into the lyrics and the way in which he sings them. The first step to hell, then, was The Burritos' debut, *The Gilded Palace Of Sin*.

On the cover, the Burritos pose self-consciously (Gram excepted) in their Nudie suits, illustrated with a pterodactyl, peacocks and marijuana plants, and with two come-hither girls hired for the occasion, all in front of what looks more like an outdoor toilet than a gilded palace. One half expects to see Old Blue sleeping inside. Gram leans against one of the women, his hand in his pants and a druggy, lecherous look on his face. No one smiles. These men do not look exactly welcoming, more like a cross between gunslingers and murders.

Although you can't see it, Gram had a huge shining cross "emblazoned on the back of his jacket". The others might have been in costume – like The Band, a thousand miles or so to the north – but Parsons was for real. Another shot from this session had them posed in front of a yucca or Joshua tree. The location here was the Mojave desert, which would fatally attract Gram back for his last shot of morphine, and indeed become his funeral pyre. The songs, too, are ominously prophetic, and for much longer than Parsons' own brief existence. Here, in one, poorly-selling album, he moved the country music agenda forward by about 50 years and mixed in sweet soul music. We're back with Barney Hoskyns' vision of Muscle Shoals and Nashville as Siamese twins, joined at the hip.

The cover might be a parody of Nashville – "ludicrously excessive", as one review had it – but the music inside is a kind of post-modern retake on that music, just as Serge Leone's movies take Hollywood Westerns and then mess them up. Here, Sneaky Pete's pedal steel is put through all kinds of special effects to make it virtually unrecognisable from the plaintive sounds of yore. The songs also take an oblique view of country obsessions: the "proud to fight" song turns into a young man escaping the draft in 'My Uncle', the woman as temptress becomes a "devil in disguise", and comic vengeance turns to hellfire at the door. 'Hippie Boy' is a parody of Hank Williams (aka "Luke The Drifter") reciting 'The Funeral'. Parsons cross-dresses on 'Do Right, Woman', singing as if female, and then, on his own 'Hot Burrito #1', opens up a vein of tenderness which others had previously been too manly to dare. "I'm your toy, I'm your old boy" has a playfulness new to the genre, and yet the way Gram sings these words makes George Jones sound like the Laughing Policeman.

At other times, the record reminds me of Procol Harum, all lush keyboards and an obsession with God's absence. 'Hippie Boy' – about the Chicago riots instigated by Mayor Daley (an archetypal C&W fan if ever I saw one) – brings together every "hippie, bum and hillbilly out on the street" over a church-like organ. Parsons sounds uncannily like the Reverend Wayne Love of The Alabama 3, and the album concludes with a communal singalong on the old gospel song 'Peace In The Valley', just like *Exile In Coldharbour Lane* 30 years on.

The band then hit the road, and their live sound – a ragged mix of "Dixie rave-ups and emoted, ragged, raw country soul" (to quote *No Depression* magazine 30 years on) – fell between every imaginable musical stool. As Hillman said, "it was too country for FM rock radio, and Nashville hated us. It wasn't slick, polished stuff." It changed the lives of many of the few who saw them, however. *No Depression* quotes James Austin, now a Rhino executive responsible for such worthy projects as collections by Roy Rogers and Buck Owens, who recalls more people onstage than in the audience at one gig: "Gram didn't seem to care that nobody was there: he just played his heart out."

Others were taking all of this in, with a view to the main chance. With former Byrd Michael Clarke now on drums, the band played small clubs around LA, and as Hillman told Barney Hoskyns: "I remember playing the Troubadour and Glenn Frey and JD Souther would be watching Gram. Glenn would watch him like he was studying him for a thesis. I think he was looking at The Burritos as this very raw, soulful but loose aggregation of guys and thinking 'we could do this but better'. Which The Eagles did, as a very successful, slick version of the Burritos."

Parsons was now wearing "outlandish scarves" onstage, "and doing this mild cross-dressing, playing these redneck country bars where people just wanted to kill us". He was hanging out not with Tammy Wynette but with the likes of Miss Mercy, of groupie group The Girls Together Outrageously, who loved his look of "true glitter-glamour rock". When The Rolling Stones came to town, Gram in effect left The Burritos.

Eve Babitz, who executed the weird arthouse sleeve of the Byrds' *[Untitled]* – half concrete observatory, half Monument Valley in the snow – says half jokingly that Parsons "went over to the Chateau Marmont and degenerated into the quagmire of Sunset Strip". Sin City had proved to be more alluring than keeping his own band rehearsed and on the road. (Or was it Celtic music HQ?)

In a 1970 interview quoted by Ben Fong-Torres – and this is so good I couldn't make it up – a spectacularly stoned Gram muses on how singing with Mick 'n' Keef brings country and ancient music together, like visiting Stonehenge in a cowboy hat: "It's all the same. That's what Keith said. When the three of us sing together, it sounds like Gaelic music. Like The Incredible String Band." They reversed the polarities, just like Jagger did at much the same time in *Performance*, changing shape with East End gangster James Fox so that you're not quite sure who's in the back of that limousine as it drives him away. "We were doing Hank Williams songs…Mick's Southern accent and my English accent. What does it all tell you? It's the same."

The Eve Babitz quote comes from her essay 'Eve's Hollywood', about a mythical country rocker called James Burns (as Gram indeed did), but the disguise is wafer thin. He makes her think of "yellow moons and magnolias", getting his cocaine "in sealed vials from Germany" and a man for whom "death could be tomorrow morning".

Here was a person whose sainthood came only after his demise; many musicians of the time simply couldn't stand him. Meanwhile, The Stones persuaded Parsons and his band to play at Altamont, where hellfire really did seem to be raining down to Earth. They even appear briefly in the film of that event, *Gimmie Shelter*, playing some sweet country tunes which fail to pacify the avenging Angels. The song in question is the trucking song 'Six Days On The Road', which is a little ironic, given the band's leisurely tour schedule. By now, they had a new guitarist, Bernie Leadon, another future Eagle. Another teenage bluegrass aficionado, playing with Chris Hillman in the Scotsville Squirrel Barkers and by now a veteran of LA country rock, Bernie had first seen the band live at the Troubadour, and reckoned "yeah, they got the look...the attitude...the record deal, everything. But they forgot something fundamental here: they just can't play or sing."

A surviving tape from the Avalon, which emerged as the bootleg CD *Sin City* after years circulating among fans, puts the lie to that, or more realistically captures a good night from this erratic combo. The music is a little sloppy, true, and this is nothing like the free-jamming Byrds with Clarence White. Parsons' voice dominates everything, with Sneaky Pete all over the instrumental sections, and the music is fully alive and passionate. "We'd like to do some country songs", Gram slurs in an almost comically exaggerated Southern accent after 'Close Up The Honky Tonks' and 'Dark End Of The Street', which are nothing but. "It's really great the way everybody sits around and listens," he opines from a narcotic inner world. "This is what it all comes from, nostalgia and sweet country music." He later comments: "We are so simple." There is a wonderful free flow to the sound, a lively simplicity. Shut your eyes and you could swear it was Wilco.

Shortly after the release of *Burrito DeLuxe*, a tuinol-soaked Gram was asked to leave his own band, having sabotaged a gig in the San Fernando valley. The cover is another Nashville parody, a humble burrito encased in rhinestones, and thus inedible. It would literally choke you.

The Burritos stand in the same costumes which Gram wore for his role in an unreleased and unreleasable movie about flying saucers filmed in and around Joshua Tree. Frankly, just like *Saturation 70*, the album is a bit of a mess. Etheridge is gone, Bernie Leadon appears on guitar and dobro, and Hillman is back on bass. He later reckoned that "Gram and I just couldn't seem to hook up again". The album was written and played "without any of the intensity of the first album, [and] it seemed we were walking on different roads".

It sounds that way, too. Side one opens with Gram's 'Lazy Days', first mooted for use in *The Trip* and now a confession of artistic lassitude, and ends with the traditional song 'Farther Along', as later covered by The Byrds but spiritless here, sounding like a rehearsal tape. The undoubted highlight is Parsons' reading of the Jagger/Richards song 'Wild Horses'. Keith had sent a demo to Parsons to see if Sneaky Pete would play on their version, but Parsons immediately grabbed it for his own band. With Leon Russell on "gospel-tinged piano", Gram sings it with sweet sadness, as if lost. Gram himself reckoned it was a song "you never get tired of". Tired of Gram's antics, Hillman opined that "he had the talent, he had the spark. He had no discipline." To redress the balance, A&M executives had the band straight back in the studio, recording a semi-live set of country standards, to which Gram insisted on adding songs by Larry Williams and John Fogerty.

Rick Roberts replaced Parsons once he had been ordered out of the band after missing one too many gigs. *Close Up The Honky Tonks* is a double album which couples one album of prime cuts by "the bad boys of country rock" and another of previously-unreleased songs, some from a still later line-up in which Al Perkins had replaced Sneaky Pete.

The Burritos then entered a slow and inevitable decline, one mercifully denied its founder. 1972's *Last Of The Red-Hot Burritos* is lively enough, recorded with Byron Berline and Roger Bush from Country Gazette, into whom The Burritos merged to become The Hot Burrito Review. Things then return to bluegrass, with the likes of 'Orange Blossom Special'. Also merging into this conglomerate were the reformed Kentucky Colonels.

Things then became very confusing, even testing Pete Frame to the limits. 1975's *Flying Again* has a front cover which makes a cowgirl out of butterflies and a band constructed in much the same way around Chris Etheridge and Sneaky Pete. The most recent album I've seen under this trademark is a double recorded in Sheffield, Alabama, as *Back To The Sweethearts Of The Rodeo By The Burrito Bros...1986-7*. Fiddler Gib Guilbeau is the lead man here, with guitarist John Beland on electric guitar. The front cover is an old photo of a cowboy and his horse out in the snow – half smothered by it, in fact, and so a good approximation of the music within. The effect is like modern Fairport Convention, keeping an old fire burning when it's long been lacking wood. There's still enough sparks and embers to keep us listening in the spirit of nostalgia, but a glory has long departed.

To further confuse things, back in 1976 A&M released *Sleepless Nights*, a Parsons retrospective based on the country standards recorded by The Burritos shortly before he left. For once, the sleeve notes get it right, bearing out Bud Scoppa's description of a "pure, honest country album". They sound exactly what they are: out-takes. The really penetrating music here comes from a later stage of Parsons' brief career, when he was duetting with Emmylou Harris, and it can break the heart in two just to hear them.

A live radio broadcast of Parsons and The Fallen Angels live in 1973, rescued from the archives by Rhino and put onto CD via direct optical digital transfer (whatever that is), is a revelation. Everything is relaxed, even 'Drug Store Truck Drivin' Man', and the duet with Emmylou on 'The New Soft Shoe' reaches a luxuriant sweetness which no one else in country has ever touched. "A great breath of fresh air," the DJ reckons. Kyle Tullis, "the pride of Tennessee", plays bass, and Gram carefully places each of the Angels in their geographical context: Emmylou from Birmingham, Alabama. There's also some sexy badinage about goings-on in the tour bus. He's still mixing up the medicine, though, so that 'Cry One More Time' is by The J Geils Band, as R&B as white men can get. It's the duets that really hit home, what Harris called "osmosis": "Just by singing with him, I learned that you plough it under and let the melody and the words carry you. Rather than this emoting thing, it will happen on its own. You have to have restraint in how you approach a song." And restraint is the watchword here: gliding on half power.

It's what they described to one hostile DJ as "regressive country music". Emmylou was still convinced that music should "very dramatic and that I must go up very high. Gram said, let's just voice it down. Basically, less is more." This, as it happens, is the secret of all great country music, from Jimmie Rodgers to The Handsome Family.

To arrive at such holy music, and to put a band of semi-unknowns in total control of what they intended – the 2/4 country shuffle which Gram discusses on the 1973 tape – he went through a couple of lost years when the light seemed to have left his muse forever. Restraint was definitely not the watchword hereabouts. Had Parsons died shortly after he had left The Burritos – as he almost did in a motorbike crash – he would be a musical footnote by now rather than the focus for biographies, tribute albums and endless namechecks.

Gram then met up with Byrds producer Terry Melcher, another self-destructive child of wealth, who said that "at that point in time the country world was seen as a reactionary group of people, and you've got this guy dressed in Nudie suits and sounding like Hank Williams, with the attitude of the psychedelic people". Here was "the white country Jimi Hendrix". The two men worked together, as Gram had once done with Chris Hillman, and recorded ten songs by the whole gamut of country writers, from Gram himself to Merle Haggard, performing titles made famous by Patsy Cline, George Jones and The Everly Brothers, with Ry Cooder and Clarence White on guitars. At one point, Gram threw up all over the piano. He later signed out the master tapes, and presumably destroyed them.

He moved to England for a while, first to a house in Kensington and then to chill out in Cornwall with Ian Dunlop, his former colleague in The International Submarine Band, who is now an organic farmer. Here Parsons found people more receptive to his music, perhaps because they recognised its roots. By the same token, such music has always had a fervent fan base in Holland. Gram's girlfriend paints an idyllic picture of finding old Roman statues in riverbeds and of being chased by cows. It's as bizarre a picture of a troubled and ultimately doomed American in deep English country as the poet Sylvia Plath, a decade before, living in a Devon farmhouse with Ted Hughes.

Gram felt weirdly at home. "They seemed to be ready for country music." He told Chuck Casell that "I always had this dream about starting a country band in

England. England is so unjaded that way. They're so open-minded, they're ignorant: they don't know." I'm not so sure about that. As we will see, many of the
pathfinders of psychedelic music – Iain Matthews, Andy Roberts, Martin Stone,
even Nick Lowe – fuelled the early Seventies British country-rock scene.

A more tangible form of healing came from the inimitable Dr Sam Hutt, veteran
of many free festivals – in the medical tent rather than on stage – and a one-time
member of archetypal hippie band Boeing Duveen And The Beautiful Soup, who
psyched up Lewis Carroll poems. At this time Hutt shared a flat with Roger Chapman
of Family. Gram was visiting him on a medical matter when Sam, as a fervent Byrds
fan, expressed his distaste for *Sweetheart Of The Rodeo*, at which point Gram picked
up a spare guitar and sang him 'You're Still On My Mind'. Result: instant conversion.
The two men jammed together whenever they could, and Parsons forced on him his
own particular medicine of George Jones' records. Once injected with this potent
drug, Hutt developed the loving parody, his alter ego Hank Wangford, and touched
his own flame to real country, one which still burns bright to this day.

Parsons also spent time with Keith Richards, trying to come off heroin together
and arguing over the right chords for 'I Fall To Pieces' as they put the pieces back
together. Of this strange time, Gram later said: "I was learning how to be invisible."
It was Family's Rick Grech who helped Gram regain his profile. They first met on the
plane back from the rock festival in Rome, where The Byrds are captured live at the
Piper Club. Grech, also doomed to die young, was of Ukrainian ancestry and, as his
wife, Jenny, told *Record Collector*: "it surfaced when he played the violin, and he was
naturally drawn to country music, because of the links between the American and
East European traditions". They met again when Gram flew back to London to help
out on a country album Rick was putting together with Sam Hutt. The project fell
through when Parsons – who even such an authority as Keith Richards reckoned
could get better cocaine than the Mafia – turned up with some prime grade heroin
and, as Hutt laments, "I could feel the dark shadow of smack blighting the air.
Unsmiling. Blots out laughter." So much for cold turkey.

Grech later took into safe custody two notebooks of lyrics and jottings which
Parsons rescued from his house in Laurel Canyon when it burned to the ground.
(Hellfire at the door, perhaps?) Here the words for '$1,000 Wedding' are decorated
with a cartoon of a man lying in his coffin, from whose mouth emerges the caption
"Collectors unite! The truth is at hand." Just as chilling is a note to himself: "Start
from the cover just like the old daze. Born just to die." No wonder Gram has been
called the James Dean of his generation.

Slowly and painfully, Grech got Parsons back into shape, first jamming with him
on lost Parsons songs like 'Ain't No Beatle, Ain't No Rolling Stone' and on material
which eventually surfaced on *GP*, co-produced by Rick. The two men moved to Bel
Air, where they jammed old-time style with Byron Berline and banjo player Alan
Munde. Jenny says: "That was what I called the pickin' and pukin' party, the combi-

nation of Gram and all the substances he was using and those lovely but incredibly straight country musicians." On a tape of this time, Gram "bitches about Merle Haggard's fiddle playing" as Grech and Berline weave around his vocals on the likes of 'Back To Alabama'.

He had already tried to record an album with Haggard in the producer's chair, but Fong-Torres tells the whole sad story. At first Gram could not recognise the author of 'Okie From Muskogee' in this "nice, sweet cat" who "doesn't hate long-haired people". The project fell through, though, partly because of Merle's own problems and partly because of just this cultural divide. As the veteran of prison and privation later told BAM: "He was a pussy. I thought he was a good writer. He was not wild, though. All these guys running around in long hair talk about being wild and Rolling Stones. I don't think someone abusing themselves on drugs necessarily determines how wild they are. It might determine how ignorant they are." Here is the Okie himself speaking, and in retrospect he's right.

Parsons was sharp-eared enough to reject the kind of bland sounds for which he had opened a door, though: "I keep my love for variations, even tho' I've some sort of rep for starting what has turned out t'be pretty much of a country rock (ugh) plastic dry-fuck." As to The Eagles, they were "bubblegum", and their music had "too much sugar in it. Life is tougher than they make it out to be."

Emmylou Harris had grown up around military bases in Virginia before moving to Greenwich Village as a folk singer, then on to Nashville, where she failed to break through as a country star, and then back to live with her parents. She played bars in Georgia, with a repertoire which stretched from Joni Mitchell to bluegrass, and barely made a living. Rick Roberts came in one night, was bowled over, and for a time Emmylou was seriously considered as being the first Flying Burrito Sister. Chris Hillman urged Gram to go see her, and in front of an audience of three people he joined her for a duet on 'I Saw The Light', which seems only appropriate.

Gram was now blown up like a balloon, off heroin and straight onto alcohol, a far more country addiction. As to their harmonies, which lift *GP* up to the heavens, Emmylou at first found him a little ragged, but "Gram and I just seemed to sing together. I wasn't aware that I was following him; at the same time I was. It was real natural." He tested her on the George Jones/Gene Pitney duet 'That's All It Took', and it quite literally was. After this introduction to the oral tradition, "Gram introduced me to a vein of music I call the 'high lonesome' – the beautiful heartbreak harmony duets you hear in songs by the young Everly Brothers, Charlie and Ira Louvin, Felice and Boudleaux Bryant." It's that sound which seeps through their work together, like blood through a bandage.

Gram's short tour with The Fallen Angels certainly polarised opinion, with Richie Furay recalling "one of the most pitiful things I ever saw", whereas Steve Earle hitch-hiked from San Antonio to Houston to see it and, as he told *Mojo*, "it was loose but it was tough. Gram's hair was frosted and his fingernails were painted red. He sang through his nose with eyes closed while the band played catch-up for most of the night. I saw and heard Emmylou for the first time that night. I left a little bit in love and absolutely certain what I was going to be when I grew up".

It's a bit like the first Velvet Underground LP. Not many people bought it at the time, but most of those went out and formed their own bands as a result. This late period of Gram's life was equally influential, even if the man only received one royalty cheque – via Joan Baez, of all people – in his whole life. He was certainly on a one-way track. John Lomax III, of another famous dynasty, told Barney Hoskyns: "He was blasted out of his gourd. He was putting everything into his system you could get without regard to anything." Gram wouldn't even reach Hank Williams' brief span.

"Death is a warm cloak," he told Crawdaddy in a now famous last interview, "an old friend." He could be Dock Boggs. With a serious heart condition now diagnosed, he worked on a final album, *Grievous Angel*, which came out posthumously and sounds like a goodbye note. It opens with the sheer joy of 'Return Of The Grievous Angel', an immersion in the C&W myth in which truckers and cowboy angels meet in porch or parlour, from "Cheyenne to Tennessee". The song is written on a night train, and Dylan himself appears as a king with "an amphetamine crown", set to unbuckle the bible belt. A glorious out-take, which surfaces on *Sleepless Nights*, is The Louvin Brothers' 'The Angels Rejoiced Last Night', which snaps the buckle back tight.

Emmylou floats over Gram's voice on examples of primal melancholy such as 'Hearts on Fire' like a swimmer. This has all the emotion of Nashville without the cloying sentiment, an arrow straight to the heart. 'Love Hurts' is even greater; the old Boudleaux Bryant song sounds here too intimate to be allowed out in public. Emmylou uses her folk background to be both spot-on and slightly out of sync – it's all very modal – and a country fiddle adds a third voice to the equation. If you know a sadder performance, I don't want to hear about it. The middle verse of the album's closing song, the singalong 'In My Hour Of Darkness', is supposedly about Clarence White, but Parsons too was "just a country boy" at heart. Even here, the chorus "Oh Lord, grant me vision, Oh Lord, grant me speed" can be taken either as a prayer or a plea for further chemical stimulation. Light trapped in a bottle.

When Parsons died in room eight of the Joshua Tree Inn, Emmylou felt like "I'd been amputated, like my life had just been whacked off". Phil Kaufman honoured a pledge he had made to the singer and, having kidnapped his coffin at LA International Airport while dressed in a cowboy hat and a Sin City jacket, built a funeral pyre out at Cap Rock, where he had watched for UFOs with Keith Richards. It's as far as can be imagined from the Appalachians, yet with its own "strange abstract geography…You wouldn't want to be sick in these mountains." Gram was like some Viking chieftain, placed on his byre of flames. He burnt like "an unbelievable fireball", and was mistaken for some hours for a burning log. As a later song pledged, Emmylou did indeed become "the keeper of the flame, 'til every soul hears what your heart was saying". It was obviously easier for someone like Elvis Costello, who had never known Parsons, to say "his exit was perfect". This for a man whom *Rolling Stone* once described as "America's greatest living singer of sad songs". Now the "Lord's burning rain" had visited him, once and for all.

The pyrotechnicians were later fined for stealing a corpse, and to gather funds, they organised a 'Gram Parsons' Funeral Party', starring old friend Jonathan Richman and The Modern Lovers, and with Bobby "Boris" Pickett playing 'The Monster Mash'. Guests were served bottles of Gram Pilsner. Next step, the *Grievous Angel* theme park. Sean O'Hagan visited the spot 25 years after, and found "that there is something revelatory, almost apocalyptic, about the deserts of the American West: an elemental spirituality that lends itself to thoughts of transcendence. Or damnation." No wonder that Captain Beefheart chooses still to live there. It is an appropriate place to burn and turn into smoke. Gram's charred remains were buried in New Orleans.

Phil Kaufman is now road manager for Emmylou, who organised the 1999 tribute album *Return Of The Grievous Angel*. A year before, The Coal Porters did much the same at the Garage, Islington, with an Irish compere and "the pride of East London", Rob Childs, on pedal steel. "The Bootleg Burritos", as Sid Griffin christened his band for the night, play respectful covers but add nothing other than respect. Once played, soon forgotten.

The CD is dressed with details from Gram's famous Nudie suit. The best music is when artists forget undue respect and do their own thing, as when The Cowboy Junkies carefully leach out any sign of life from 'Ooh Las Vegas'. Beck sings 'Sin City' relatively straight, and The Mavericks glide through 'Hot Burrito #1'. Almost inevitably, Elvis Costello is here, and I can only agree with *Folk Roots* that his version of 'Sleepless Nights' is so schmaltzy as to deserve capital punishment. Far better are alt country stars like Wilco on a saloon-bar 'One Hundred Years From Now', and Whiskeytown's slow Stones-like strut through 'A Song For You'. Whiskeytown got the slot because Emmylou – who knew nothing else about them – heard that, while looking for a deal, they would cross-examine A&R men to determine how much they knew about Parsons. "I said OK, that sounds like something Gram would do, only he would ask about George Jones or Webb Pierce."

Most interesting is the way that strong-voiced women have now come to take the lead role, not just the harmony vocal. Here the highlights are Gillian Welch's stern and haunted old-timey 'Hickory Wind', Chrissie Hynde's tough rendition of 'She' and Lucinda Williams slurring through the title track (during which David Crosby, of all people, soars above her soprano on harmony vocals). Sheryl Crow and Emmylou Harris duet on a sweet-voiced 'Juanita' like sisters. The instrumental sound is tough alt country throughout. *No Depression* reckons that the difference between Nashville and the alternative is that the latter "are much more likely to be influenced by Gram Parsons".

Something of the wildness of the great original has been lost here, symbolised by the way in which Victoria Williams and Mark Olson chose to record their contribution at Buddy Miller's studio – Dogtown, in Nashville – rather than at their own home in Joshua Tree. Chris Hillman reckons that, "of all the people out there, I sort of look at Dwight Yoakam as being the Gram Parsons that worked – the operating model. He planned his career out and did quite well, and never sacrificed any integrity doing so." Yes, but where's the shiver at the heart of the music? Elvis Costello, more reliable as a critic than as a singer in this context, hears Gram's sound in rock bands like Son Volt. Hillman, who should know, reckons that Wilco have really captured the early Burritos' sound: "Nobody was doing it then, it was so out of left field. It was loose but it was full of energy and life."

Talking to Nigel Williamson, Emmylou concurs, not hearing much of Gram's influence in Nashville, "but I hear it outside in the more diverse pop and alternative musical worlds. I went for people who are innovators in their field and listen to their own drum rather than following the pack." She left it up to each artist to record whichever song they chose to cover. Keith Richards agreed to join in, but was eventually too busy. The Eagles are notable by their absence. Beck, meanwhile, "does it even more traditionally than Gram. He sang it from more of a country place." Talking to England's Peter Doggett, she adds that Nashville never embraced Gram, and that the album is less a tribute than an introduction, "because few people in the United States have any clue who Gram was, though I know it's different over here. They've seen his name, though usually it's misspelled." Another interviewer asked her whether she was worried about stirring up ghosts with this project, one in particular. "I lived with the ghosts for a long time," she replies, "and I think they've moved on. I think they've got other things to do."

Harris now looks back to her collaboration with Parsons as "regressive country. You have to draw on the past and you have to come up with something new. Gram's music...tipped its hat to the heart and soul of traditional country." She herself came to the music late: "It was like I discovered this treasure that was under everybody's noses, and it overwhelmed me." As she tells Dawidoff, Parsons taught her the essential "restraint" of the music. However, she has never wanted "to restrict myself to what people called country".

When Emmylou started her own solo career with The Angel Band, "I was definitely gathering up everything that Gram had touched, almost like musical relics. I had just started to find my musical identity and my voice through Gram, and I was happy to be a student, alongside him." Her own career has been a long grace note to his brief incandescence.

In the best Nashville tradition, Emmylou writes few songs herself and so has to go to outsiders for material. *Profile*, a superior "best of" compilation, has songs by AP Carter, The Louvin Brothers, Don Gibson, Dolly Parton and Billy Sherrill – all "country" – but also R&B offerings from Chuck Berry and Delbert McClinton. Her voice is a hybrid, too, with country vowels but a folky glissando. It dodges around the notes like a bee gathering honey. Unlike Judy Collins, whose vocal purity she most resembles, there is never the sense that Emmylou is skating over the meaning of the lyrics. She lives every word.

A tape of a show at London's New Victoria Theatre from 1975, the year of her debut album *Pieces Of The Sky*, reveals a sound not that far removed from the Nashville mainstream, with prominent pedal steel and piano and songs which alternate between the weepy and the up-tempo. Emmylou is still most used to performing "in places with people sitting at tables and beer in front of them", and she brought honky-tonk intimacy to the concert halls of the world. There is a real twang to her voice, lots of songs from Gram Parsons and, best of all, her own lament for the dead singer: 'Boulder to Birmingham'.

She describes The Hot Band, put together to back her, as "the greatest country band in the world, if not the whole universe", with heavyweights like James Burton, pianist Glen D Hardin and Rodney Crowell, "a real good old boy from Austin, Texas". Here they glide beneath her voice like a Rolls Royce, with no apparent effort and no cock-ups. It is the very antithesis of rough mountain music. The Hot Band powered a succession of regal albums which straddle soft rock and country, which are lovely but rather outside the scope of this book. Mick Brown once complained that this was country music without enough dirt beneath its fingernails.

Emmylou got rooting, and with the help of the aforementioned bluegrass star Ricky Skaggs on fiddle she began a sharp left turn towards traditional sounds on 1979's *Blue Kentucky Girl*. James Burton is still performing arabesques on the electric guitar, but this is music which has been booted up the backside, even though the amps are turned right down. Western swing is in the air. Emmylou appears in front of a painted stage set of an old Wild West saloon wearing antique clothes and with rose-engraved boots and matching guitar. She sings with even more of a rural tremor, and 'Hickory Wind' – here slowed and toned right down – sounds like a fond farewell to more than her favourite singer. It is, of course, heartbreaking. Flip the disc and you have Jean Ritchie's 'Sorrow In The Wind', with The White Girls singing harmony and a mountain sound, alongside material mainly written in the Sixties. Even Rodney Crowell's contribution here, the sprightly 'Even Cowgirls Get The Blues', is deliberately old fashioned, as well as a nod to Tom Robbins' weird novel of the same name.

The following year brought *Roses In The Snow*, which really broke the mould, mixing bluegrass with Appalachian material. Emmylou looks underdressed on the front cover – she could get a cold on her chest, poor thing – but on the back she's wrapped up warm and sensible in front of a rough cabin, and singing mainly traditional music. Violins weep, acoustic guitars pick out simple riffs, and the whole thing is driven by God. Even Paul Simon's 'The Boxer' is incorporated into the tradition, although Emmylou's voice is perhaps a little too pure, too carefully tuneful, to really dig out the painful joy at the rough heart of these songs.

Again she is doing what she's always done best, interpreting an off-centre music for a mass audience, but with respect. Her voice flows smooth, but never bland. Emmylou won a CMA award for this album as female vocalist of the year but, as she told John Tobler, "they don't have a category for bluegrass. They just ignore it. It's getting to where they're finally starting to recognise Bill Monroe." The later *Angel Band* is a collection of acoustic country gospel in the steps of The Stanley Brothers.

Emmylou swapped husbands and producers (which amounted to the same thing), leaving Brian Ahern and an album of farewell scraps in *Evangeline*. On the back cover she looks like a trapped animal in the city, standing literally in the middle of the road. If this was some kind of act of vengeance, it failed; on the inner sleeve she is caught up in the air, dancing. She then married Paul Kennerley, the English composer of concept albums of Americana as who was touched on back in chapter one, which seems like an aeon ago. Together they wrote *The Ballad of Sally Rose* (which I always think of as "the pink album"), a final expunging of Gram Parsons' memory, whose story it tells, even if 'The Singer' is never named. Typically subtle is her long-awaited declaration of love, set to the AP Carter tune 'You Are My Flower'. Emmylou is 'The Sweetheart Of The Rodeo' out on "the longest road".

As this album is fiction rather than autobiography, some facts are changed, with Sally Rose the daughter of a Sioux Indian. Later, "she gives up everything and settles down" alone in a broadcasting tower, in retreat from the world like Tennyson's Lady of Shalott, sending out "the sound of the Singer" for the rest of her days, indeed forever. "I swung my hammer out in Joshua Tree." It's like an old Appalachian tale of doomed love, and like a ghost "she's just waiting for you to tune in…"

Rather than wallow in the past like her heroine, Emmylou went back further and dropped a rapidly-cooling Hot Band for The Nash Ramblers, an incandescent bluegrass band with Sam Bush on mandolin. They recorded a live and slightly over-polite album at the Opry in another vindication of Gram's memory. 1991's *At The Ryman* looks forward as well, opening with a Steve Earle song, although poor reviews led to her being dropped by her record label. She had stepped too far outside the expectations of her core audience. To be more exact, she had outpaced them.

Harris' music is too careful to impose false concepts on, as WB did with 'Songs Of The West'. Each album has its own inner logic, and Emmylou went on to record some of the greatest of her career. Producer Daniel Lanois sculpted *Wrecking Ball* with U2's drummer and his own guitar textures, using lots of antique instruments to achieve a haunted and mysterious sound, with the arrangements built up in his home studio out of live jams. Just as he filtered out every extraneous noise from Bob Dylan's voice on *Oh Mercy*, and helped take Robbie Robertson back to his Indian roots, so he helps Emmylou to look deep into herself, and the result is the highest, most lonesome sounds she has ever uttered. The title track alone chimes, aches, soothes, and chills the blood.

Here, too, is a repertoire of songs by heavy friends like Lucinda Williams, Gillian Welch, Rodney Crowell, The McGarrigle Sisters, Neil Young, Lanois himself, Bob Dylan and the rest. Here is rock, folk and new country: not a Nashville hack in sight. As the CD sleeve suggests, this is music in motion, with all kinds of hidden depths and echoes. Emmylou seems to be singing in a hall of mirrors.

A radio broadcast of her 1995 appearance with the Lanois band at the Shepherds Bush Empire prove that this sound is not the product of studio trickery. Performed live it's even more extreme, with Daniel's effects-laden guitar-work pushing Harris seemingly to sing with a new voice, like a woman possessed. 'Poncho And Lefty' and The Burritos' song 'Wheels' join songs from the record, which she told Brian Mansfield are based around one theme: "Yearning. That's probably always been a driving force in what I look for. If yearning had a sound it would be Daniel's production."

Mansfield points out the spiritual undertow of the CD with an opening song about walking "to the other side of desire". 'Sweet Old World' is a "love letter to a friend who has committed suicide", while 'All My Tears' is "an elegy written in the voice of the deceased". The final track picks up the "life in death theme" of the opening song. No wonder the disc sounds so haunted, so close to Appalachian ballads in spirit if not in sound, but Emmylou reckons that, if anything from it gets played on country radio, "it'll be nothing short of a miracle".

However, she intends to continue to make records regardless. "I still love country music, but the mainstream is just so squeaky-clean right now. I think people need to get a little dirty and colour outside the lines a bit." She reminisces for *Acoustic Guitar* magazine, and remembers how she first heard the likes of Hazel Dickens and Alice Gerrard on *The Dick Cerri Show* as a teenager, alongside The Carter Family and Mike Seeger. From this she was pulled into the folk revival, and Gram led her back home, "taking an un-traditional-sounding country voice that was perhaps overtly pretty and overtly sweet and putting it into the restraints of country music style". Rather than limiting her voice, "it opened it up".

As I write, Emmylou's latest venture is a live collaboration with the alt rock band Spyboy, featuring Buddy Miller on lead guitar and Brian Blade on drums. *Mojo* reckoned that it was "the sound of a band reconstructing country rock with a passion the young pretenders might well envy". Emmylou also continues as a harmony singer of genius, as recent acoustic collaborations with Linda Ronstadt and Dolly Parton have shown. The two Trio albums so far centre on mountain ballads, like 'Rosewood Casket', and love songs respectively. Co-producer of the second is John Starling of progressive bluegrass combo The Seldom Scene, and it could be a back-porch singalong in paradise with everyone's ego left at the front door. Nanci Griffith reckons Emmylou's secret as a harmony singer is that "she has a great capacity to listen", along with "the amount of heart she puts into it" and her own natural amiability. As her entry in *Rough Guide To Rock* points out, "she is as likely to be discovered singing harmonies with her friend Dolores Keane in a Galway pub as she is to be seen among the rhinestones at a Country Music Association awards ceremony". More likely, in fact.

At a 1994 concert in the Royal Concert Hall in Glasgow, her band played a couple of Bill Monroe tunes. "I've been waiting a long time to do this particular song here," she announces, and they launch into a lively version of 'Scotland' as the audience clap and whoop in time. Tours by The Hot Band brought to prominence a whole generation of young country musicians – generally lumped together as the "new traditionalists" – many of which have become stars in their own right, including Ricky Skaggs. Rodney Crowell also liked *Grievous Angel*, with all of its "kinfolk" singing, and was also aware that there was "a wound that was in the process of healing" deep within her.

So did some of her more fervent fans. One threatened to assassinate this pretender to Gram's throne, while another thought that he was Parsons' ghost. Crowell is briefly glimpsed at the 1999 CMA Awards, whereas Emmylou was clearly not, and who is the compere but another former Hot Bander, Vince Gill, now legit in Nashville eyes. Meanwhile, Emmylou's house in that same city has proved a refuge for the likes of Nanci Griffith, Steve Earle and Lucinda Williams, for whom she remains a surrogate mother – a "connoisseur of songs" in Earle's phrase.

Emmylou continues to "drink water from the deepest well", and her greatest influence on the music has been this sense of inclusiveness. The old folk would understand. As she told Dawidoff, nothing in current Nashville strikes her as "mysterious or creative". To her, a rock star like Bruce Springsteen is much closer to the country tradition "because of the way he phrases, the simplicity and passion of what he does – it's country even if he doesn't have a pedal steel guitar. Merle Haggard doesn't always have pedal steel, you know."

Meanwhile, The Byrds were flying separately and country music was the destination of choice. Not for McGuinn, though, who revisited his folk roots on the 'Rolling Thunder' tour "like a Fellini version of Greenwich Village". The show was also like a travelling hootenanny, or a tent show on LSD, or a recreation of the Pilgrim Fathers (and Mothers). With conscious symbolism, the first concert was to be held at Plymouth, Massachusetts, where they came ashore. They even pose on a mock-up of *The Mayflower*. The sprawling four-hour show traversed the nation, visiting places which rock or folk music had rarely penetrated before. It was carefully choreographed by Jacques Levy, Roger's partner in *Gene Tryp*, on Dylan's instructions: "The idea was that it should not look staged. The thing was to make it appear like a spontaneous evening…like a travelling vaudeville show or a travelling circus. There was almost a hootenanny feel. There was no tuning up between songs, there were no pauses. Big chunks of the show were the same every night."

Just add a sales pitch and you have the travelling medicine shows in which so many early country singers got their first commercial breaks. The guests here were old hands, though, just the kind of acoustic has-beens whom Dylan had supposedly disposed of in 'Positively Fourth Street'. Allen Ginsberg came along as "official bard", and was the nearest thing to God that they could find. Howard Alk filmed the proceedings, both on- and off-stage, and playwright Sam Shepard – who had co-written *Cowboy Mouth* with Patti Smith – helped to write the "script" for what emerged as the incomprehensible *Renaldo And Clara*, with David Blue as a kind of stoned Greek chorus playing pinball. Even though Phil Ochs was judged too far gone to be invited (and hanged himself partly as a result), the interest of all of this to the present book is a final gathering together of so many of the coffee-house traditionalists, like a parade of ghosts.

Dylan himself wears a cowboy hat and white paint on his face (the effect is not so much clown-like as of something dug up from the grave), and his eyes blaze like burning coals during 'Isis' and other new folk tales. Each singer – Ramblin' Jack Elliott, Joni Mitchell, Bob Neuwirth, Kinky Friedman – had their own guest spot before the main attraction: McGuinn sings 'Chestnut Mare', while Joan Baez duets with her former lover as well as singing 'The Night They Drove Old Dixie Down'. The tour is nothing less than an attempt to rediscover a lost, mythical America, from the Pilgrim Fathers to a Shaker village and on to Jack Kerouac's grave. Each night starts with David Mansfield on pedal steel leading the tour band through 'Flint Hill Special', electric bluegrass to "yee-haws" from the players. The final song is a mass rendition of Woody Guthrie's 'This Land Is Your Land'. The promise remains unfulfilled.

Mansfield's country-steel wailings and mandolin trills – along with Scarlet Rivera's electric violin and the deliberately ramshackle rhythm section – ties this music firmly to the string bands of the Thirties, rocked up and coked out. Such was the air of excess that many of the musicians herein converted to evangelical Christianity shortly afterwards, Dylan included. Jesus had the last laugh.

McGuinn recorded *Cardiff Rose* immediately after: "The whole spirit of the Review was that we had this wonderful energy. It was such a high place that we wanted to take as much of it into the studio as we could." Jacques Levy had a swing in his apartment, and as Roger was playing around with it "I said, let's write a pirate song, so we researched into pirates, got into the jargon and the whole rant and roar of it". The result was 'Jolly Roger', pun intended. Meanwhile, a real traditional song, 'Pretty Polly', finally saw an official release: "I recorded it like the madness of in-breeding, that crazed, glassy-eyed feel! The humour of the murder came across". Weird guy.

Roger told John Tobler that, after being "erased from the map" during the 1970s, The Byrds came back into fashion thanks to "the advent of REM and Tom Petty". 1991's *Back From Rio* saw McGuinn in total command of his material, and I'll leave him singing about the "high, lonesome sound" on 'King Of The Hill', a song about extinction.

Chris Hillman joined Stephen Stills in Manassas, a free-flowing blend of rock, blues and country sounds. With Al Perkins and Byron Berline, the band "could cover anything from a very hardcore Latin, salsa-type thing to very traditional blue-grass", but the huge promise of early live performances was never followed through. Drugs might have liberated rock musicians in the Sixties, but by now they were angels of destruction. Chris returned to his bluegrass roots in 1982 with the primarily acoustic *Morning Sky*, released by a newly-formed label which has since become the market leader for this kind of music: "I hooked up with Sugar Hill Records. Barry Poss is a wonderful guy to work with."

Desert Rose was more of the same with added electricity, but after initial success "our shelf life expired in Nashville. People's attention span has been reduced to that of a mosquito." Even so, with a band of that name "we ended up appealing to really hardcore country people, who had no idea who The Byrds were". He was still drawn to the music of his teenage years. 1985's *Ever Call Ready* collected country gospel songs, and chronicles the "born again" fervour which swept the bluegrass community in the mid Eighties. It was a new kind of addiction.

Dylan, as usual, had been there first, in his hellfire and damnation songs: 'Solid Rock' in the studio is a pale shadow of the fervour with which Dylan sings it to an audience of true believers. Like him, Hillman's ardour has now cooled, and he told *Record Collector* that "I got very frustrated with that particular evangelical look at Christianity. I didn't feel comfortable there." Nor, presumably, would he have been in the Appalachians, where such faith is almost part of the scenery.

The 1990's saw Hillman record two more retrospective albums with Herb Pederson, whom he had first met in 1963 when he was the banjo player in The Pine Valley Boys and Hillman was still in The Scottsboro Squirrel Barkers. The bluegrass album *Out Of The Woodwork*, recorded with Tony and Larry Rice, recreated these long-gone days. "I actually replaced their father as the mandolin player in a band, The Golden State Boys." Even so, Hillman now does not consider himself a blue-grass player: "I'm so out of practice. I can play the music but I can't keep up if they play a fast song." The previous year's *Bakersfield Bound* was a tribute not only to Buck Owens but to all kinds of singers from the 1950s. "We picked songs that we liked, a lot of songs that were done by brother duos like The Louvin Brothers." Here were the roots of *Sweetheart Of The Rodeo*, newly exposed.

Hillman is now in semi-retirement. As he told *Mojo*: "as soon as all the line danc-ing, Garth Brooks, Billy Ray Cyrus stuff came along, they knocked a lot of us off the radio. I don't call it country any more. It's too smarmy for me." The legendary LA radio show *Folk Scene* tempted him in to sing live in the studio, and Hillman's own version of 'Mr Tambourine Man', backed with an acoustic band, is cheerful, fast paced and the song of a survivor. He sure makes those guitar strings dance.

Gene Clark was the first of all to embrace country rock, on his 1967 album *Gene Clark With The Gosdin Brothers*, which is full of good playing, sad songs and sweet country harmonies. He later reworked the album as *Early LA Sessions*, where Clark's shaded face appears surrounded by antique postcards of California, like glimpses of a lost paradise. It appears in greatly augmented form as the CD *Echoes*: "we were all just a little bit ahead of our time". The Byrds and Rex and Vern Gosdin shared a management team: "Clarence White was playing guitar with them, and their act was just country enough for what I wanted to do." Chris Hillman helped on the arrangements, but now it's Gene's voice which cuts through the years. I first heard 'Tried So Hard' on Fairport's *Heyday* tape, but here it's even better – the curt way the lyrics start, White's twangy guitar carrying on a dialogue with Gene, who sounds both confidential and lost, and then those sweet country harmonies. High and deep and lonesome. The whole album is like a chance collision between The Beatles and Hank Williams.

Next, Clark teamed up with Doug Dillard, after the two men had been "picking together in friends' smoke-filled living rooms". Their first trip to Nashville together was symbolic in that both men were thrown into the local jail after a bar-room fracas. They were arrested by three armed policemen in front of the Grand Ole Opry building. You just can't make these things up. As Doug tells it: "We tried to plead not guilty – I hadn't done a thing – but the guy says 'well, you were with Gene Clark, weren't you?' I said yes. He says 'Throw 'em in jail.'" Dillard recognised the bailiff as having once played with Bill Monroe. "I finally ended up getting his autograph."

Gene told *Zigzag*: "bluegrass actually goes back all the way to the Elizabethan period in England. It's more European than anything else." As the composer of the wonderful phrase "tabernacle hillsides" (as good a description of the Appalachians as ever made), Gene makes a clear distinction between these early settlers, passing their music "by mouth and instrument, not on sheets of music paper like city country music". Nashville, in other words. As to their shift back to electric instruments, Clark reckons that "Country and western will go on because it is definitely an established heritage of this land...and we are trying to keep it pure. We can still play electric guitar and keep it that way."

The LP sleeve has the two in a motorcycle and sidecar (Clark is the driver), both wearing bikers' peaked caps, both laughing, and this is one of the happiest records I know. All the same, Clark's primal melancholy seeps through via his questing voice and mysterious songs like 'She Darked The Sun', offset by Doug's cheerful picking: "I lost ten points just for being in the right place at exactly the wrong time" – the story of Gene's whole life. There's a road song, a radio song, and a lot of bluegrass in the instrumental sound, not least in 'Git It On Brother', with Dillards-style harmonies on top, although both electric harpsichord and harmonica also make their presence felt. 'Don't Come Rollin'' has the swing of mountain music but an excess of words – a Clark speciality. It's like he's trying to force a quart into a pint pot.

When they played through the album at the Troubadour in late 1968, The Fantastic Expedition also included Bernie Leadon on lead guitar, Doug on a custom-made Rickenbacker electric banjo, Michael Clarke on drums and David Jackson on electric bass. "They were all drunk…and it wasn't pretty," one Byrd present commented. A reviewer wrote: "they play country music with a rock beat. I hope it isn't immediately classified as country rock." Some hope. After an extremely odd B-side, with Clark pastiching Presley on a breathless 'Don't Be Cruel', The Expedition went back to playing acoustic sets, with Donna Washburn on backing vocals and Byron Berline on fiddle.

Dillard and Clark's second album brought in Sneaky Pete on pedal steel as well, although this lacked the distinction of its predecessor. The title track, 'Through The Morning, Through The Night', is a slow burn with weeping fiddle. There are many more covers, including the fiery bluegrass of 'Roll In My Sweet Baby's Arms' (next step: Country Gazette) and the choral gospel song 'I Bowed My Head And Cried Holy'. The album is simply too eclectic, with Washborn recounting the moonshining tale of 'Rocky Top', then Clark's archetypal 'So Sad' in his role of folk singer/songwriter rather than country boy, and then straight into God-knows-who singing the mock-vaudeville 'Corner Street Bar'. (The Charlatans seem to have sneaked in, somehow – just wait, boys, you're in the next section.) 'Polly' is a slow lament, not the murder ballad, and 'Kansas City Southern' makes you want to ride those rails. It's so infectious it could go on forever.

Clark seems hardly to be there at times, as if he's already on that train. One reason could be that, between recording the two albums, the two men were foolish enough to revisit Nashville, and "they hit Gene over the head with a baseball bat! His eyes just kind of rolled around a little bit, but it didn't knock him out." When Clark left The Expedition, Dillard kept it going for a year or so, bringing in Bush and Byron Berline, whose Country Gazette was The Expedition's natural child.

Gene recorded a couple of songs with The Flying Burrito Brothers and then abandoned country for folky mysticism with his 1971 *White Light* set. Tracks from an abandoned album with a country rock band (including White, Etheridge, Sneaky Pete – all the usual suspects) for A&M emerged in Holland as *Roadmaster*. A Byrds reunion proved disastrous, and Clark went on to release his masterpiece, *No Other*, in 1974, an album I myself put on a pedestal alongside *Astral Weeks*, *Pour Down Like Silver*, Mighty Baby's *A Jug Of Love* and *Ijaman*, as being music genuinely of the spirit.

Gene has filtered out country music for a kind of multidubbed drone, and the lyrics are rich in mountain wisdom. Gene told Steve Burgess that it was originally a 13-track album, "but we weren't able to do a double record, so the rest of the songs were left unfinished". This is like being told that Hamlet is only half the original play. This, too, deals with madness, death and pretence. The glam rock back-cover photo is a "hoax", and deliberately bears no relation to the questing songs within: "I am always high, I am always low, there is always change…beyond the cosmic plain."

This is a long way from bluegrass, but its emotional power and transcendant singing is oddly close to some of the old-time music, albeit without a Christian God.

If anything, it is music – the "strength of strings" – which has replaced him. Like Johnny Rogan, whose *Timeless Flight* contains a brilliant description of this album (and which certainly helped me), I would put this record above anything even Gram Parsons was given enough time on Earth to achieve. Cosmic American music. The real thing. It's certainly the wildest shore that this present study will visit, but there is enough mountain wisdom here to force me into bending my brain around it. It's like catching quicksilver in your hands.

The front cover is a collage of people lost in thought, one of whom is half immured in the Sphinx. God alone knows the drunk or drugged states from which Clark drew these insights, though the fool on the back cover, in his tent-like flares, is impassive. Thomas Jefferson Kaye was intent on matching them with studio trickery, his own "Brian Wilson extravaganza", and he even had Clark's double-tracked voice sent down a telephone on the title track to get what Rogan calls that "eerie, cavernous sound". This is the realm of 'Tomorrow Never Knows', not Owen Bradley. Clark starts fully confident – jaunty, almost – on 'Life's Greatest Fool' after some Chet Atkins' style guitar, but Chet himself can have rarely played on songs about people looking into "the darkness of the day". Country self-pity turns suicidal, and Gene smiles. "Homely" is Rogan's analysis, a "rock Confucius" issuing home-spun aphorisms as a gospel choir sigh in the background, with Clydie King among them, who performed the same role for Dylan's gospel years.

A stretch of rich acoustic guitar, and we're into 'Silver Raven', with Gene's voice infinitely sad, bucking and cracking with the sheer majesty of his vision as it shakes him to pieces. Bell-like bottleneck guitar from Jesse Ed Davis recreates the flight of "wings that barely gleam", then almost weeps. No wonder Clark later sings about "the strength of strings". Notes fall as if raindrops from heaven, while rivers "wait their turn to die". The title track has Cuban cross-rhythms, and Gene fuses love for the divine with that for a woman, in the best Appalachian tradition. Only Clark's evident belief in lyrics such as "then the pilot of the mind/must find the true direction" – singing them as if his life depended on them – prevents this from descending into the realms of "progressive" boobies like Yes. Instead, it ends on a kind of scream.

John Rogan, student of Old English, sees 'Strength Of Strings' as a "rock equivalent of the music of the spheres", with its "ghostly chorale", over which Gene searches out the mysterious place that music can take you. 'From A Silver Phial' starts with what Rogan terms a "cocaine burn-out". If so, it certainly sums up what happened to country rock, and indeed to most post-psychedelic music, which that sweetest of drugs helped to put to sleep.

After more transcendent guitar, the words are full of imagery from the Tarot pack. When preparing for this album, Clark played Stevie Wonder and The Stones' *Goat's Head Soup* over and over again, alternating like an electric current between the light and the dark, God and the devil. It's just the kind of yin and yang around which we saw Jerry Lee Lewis construct a whole career. The "master's room" here reminds me most directly of an early song by that other C&W-trained folk poet Leonard Cohen, demonstrating power and control in the guise of spiritual exploration. This way for Charlie Manson and his female acolytes.

The whole of 'Some Misunderstanding' "was written in a dream". There aren't many songs which modestly mention that "maybe someone can explain time" and then talk of selling your soul (as he seems to have done here, never to record such powerful stuff again in a life which just petered out), and still find time for a guitar solo, like a bird in flight, while Richard Greene plays fiddle. Clark told Steve Burgess that the line "we all need a fix" was a reference to Gram Parsons' self-inflicted demise, was but also a metaphor drawn from navigating by the stars. The whole interview – between two men who are now dead – is perhaps the deepest that rock journalism has ever gone by this time. "Doesn't it feel good/to stay alive?"

Gene sings about these mysteries with his country-boy twang, which makes them all the more believable. Just when you think you might be completely leaving the known world, along comes the cooling country breeze of 'The True One': "I used to treat my friends as if I was more than a millionaire…but what's been flying high must always touch the ground." The word "treat" here can be taken two ways: in terms of giving out largesse, or in terms of bad behaviour. Surely it is pedal steel that powers the song along, but none is credited. Lyrically, this could have been Merle Haggard after 20 years in a Buddhist monastery and while on an unnatural high.

The final song, 'Lady Of The North', has a fiddle, a driving beat and words which take this former Byrd flying again, right into the mountains, and for Rogan this is "a transcendental flight into the heavens". Country roads sure take you a long way. It's also about making love in an open field, with the "silver" lady being real as well as imaginary. For all of that, Clark's lyrics are slices of zen wisdom (he pays tribute to David Carradine as another adept), and his soaring voice – its rural vowels seemingly emphasised to make up the words as it goes – searches for truth like a grizzled prospector after silver, over a wah wah guitar.

The search for precious metal is a metaphor for surfing the cosmic internet, and Clark even named his tour band The Silverados. (Silver is the colour of needles, too.) The album ends with the age-old image of a breeze which "whispers through the trees" – the same presentiment of death which Gram Parsons heard in a hickory wind, and which echoes through folk and country. It is the wind that shakes the barley, or Johnny Cash's 'Any Old Wind That Blows'. True to such Celtic mysteries, the last sound here is that of electronic bagpipes. Or maybe the Earth dying.

Gene is honing in on a mystical power he finds in the American landscape: "When I first went to Mendocino I found there is something in that place – like there is in the Rocky Mountains, or Big Sur: I even got it in Ireland just the other day."

Even so, the album's own mysterious inner landscape alienated many country rock fans. The thanks that Gene received for plumbing the depths of his soul was to be dropped by David Geffen for going over budget. The Eighties start here. In concert at Ebbet's Field in 1975, with a two-piece band, Clark gives us a passionate 'No Other' – all the more urgent for its bareness – and a 'Silver Raven' on which his voice has never sounded so countryish or so intimate. As the performance settles into a rhythm, he gives a kind of verbal wobble and then suddenly lets his voice go in a feral whoop, like Michael Hurley's werewolf, out of hiding and suddenly put in front of a microphone. This is Dock Boggs territory, and it's not a CD to play in the dark. Sweet harmonies appear at the end, but the damage has already been done.

Gene sings the same song for Mountain Stage in West Virginia in 1988, three years before his death, and, as the compere says, he's "just fine all by himself with his guitar". On the plane there it occurred to him to repeat a song "I wrote in northern California about 13 years ago", and the version here is effortlessly sad, almost whispered at times, while at others like a desperate, shouted warning of "when the sea begins to cry". He goes straight into 'Tried So Hard', and that accent is definitely hillbilly, with a Tom Rapp lisp. It's a voice which can still cut like a knife.

The two strands of Gene Clark's music – country boogie and folk prophecy – existed uneasily side-by-side on *Two Sides To Every Story*, again produced by Thomas Jefferson Kaye, and "kind of like an archive". On the sleeve, a heavily bearded Clark leans next to a child's spinning top as darkness starts to surround him. He grins on the back, like a man who knows the secret of life or, as some journalists wrote at the time, a fat old hippie who has smoked and drunk too much. The intensity has gone; here is some chuckling country rock, what one reviewer described as "a sweet blend of folk roots and muted orchestration".

'Home Run King' has Doug Dillard on banjo (the mind boggles when trying to imagine how he would have sounded on *No Other*) and is about self-definition: "You are either a newspaper boy or Babe Ruth." After the mental storm of the zen album, he is left here "coming down" to the crying sound of a pedal steel, alone on a 'Lonely Saturday', like Dylan in Nashville after the 1966 holocaust.

Clark visits the traditional song 'In The Pines', and revisits 'Kansas City Southern'. Unfortunately, he also took solace in heroin at about this time, as well as "running wild in Hollywood" on alcohol. Newly-emerging cowpunks like The Long Ryders took Gene as an icon, and, having guested with them on disc, he returned with *Firebyrd*, but "Gene wasn't there mentally", living in one room and hitting the bottle.

A 1985 concert with The Fyrebyrds, "featuring Michael Clarke", contains a ragged 'Silver Raven', reduced to a plod here with a disconcerting *oompah* beat. Another gig the same year saw Gene Clark onstage with Rick Danko and Richard Manuel of The Band and Michael Clarke again, four men waiting in God's exit lounge.

Rogan writes of Terri Messina taking a clearly ailing Gene up to the Californian ski resort of Mammoth shortly before the end. "He'd achieved a mescaline high and trudged up the snowy slopes to "have a word with the Big Man" (by whom we do not mean David Crosby): "He returned with one of the most extraordinary compositions of his career, a work which combined metaphysical speculations on the

nature of angels with alien visitations, reflections on the prophets…and other apocalyptic musings." Things sure get weird in the mountains. 'Communications' is a
twelve-minute song which has yet to see commercial release or trickle its way down
by one means or other to humble fans like myself.

It seems extraordinary that some kind of legal quagmire is preventing the
release of all kinds of unreleased gems, which Rogan lists meticulously in his book.
When you look through them, you could almost murder Rogan out of sheer jealousy because he's heard them. Then you remember that Morrissey of The Smiths
reacted to Rogan's fine biography of his band with a publicly-stated desire that
Johnny should die in a motorway smash. Meanwhile, Gene – a much greater artist
– rests in semi-obscurity. To misquote Can, we want more.

Gene Clark died in 1991, on his parents' 50th wedding anniversary, after starting
to resurrect his career with the young singer Carla Olson, of new wave band The
Textones. *So Rebellious A Lover* contains a gorgeous version of the traditional song
'Fair And Tender Ladies', sung to a gentle strum (hear Gene whistle – he'll be yodelling next), and Clark's own 'Gypsy Rider', sung like a ghost, with a country mandolin
break. The live CD *Silhouetted In Light*, taped at McCabes and issued posthumously, ends with a version of 'Will The Circle Be Unbroken?' with special guest Steve
Young, and this is a ramshackle encore with no thought of posterity. Steve forgets
the words at first, then some country picking leads us into those timeless words of
reconciliation. It's a nice way to leave Gene: onstage and singing but not alone.

John York remembered "a sweet guy who had to die to get the world to start
taking him seriously. His Missouri meets Elizabethan sensibilities, his courtliness
versus his drunkenness – it adds up to a real Hillbilly Shakespeare."

A later Byrd, Gene Parsons moved to a cabin home in California and "began
growing a lot of vegetables and tried to live as close to nature as possible – as a result
I became very healthy and very happy. It was a great state of mind." His solo albums
reflect this self-sufficient life, although the inner gatefold sleeve of *Kindling* is
ambiguous. Here is a landscape of tree trunks, with a mobile TV propped on one sad
stump with the picture of a growing forest on its screen. On the outside, Gene sits
with an axe and a wall of logs, with the same expression of pride on his face as in that
famous painting of a settler family which David Ackles parodies on *American Gothic*.
To his right is a wood-burning stove, and so the message here seems to be that of
planned management of Nature. When one thinks of the devastation which logging
and mining have wrought on the Appalachians, the message is even more powerful.

The music is made to match, opening with the lines "I've got a pig in a pen, and
I've got corn to feed her", with a chorus to the effect that Gene is trying to build a
"monument" to a productive life. This is true country music, and the acoustic
delights here are, if not bluegrass, at least something close. It's back-porch music,
with Clarence White on guitar, Gib Guilbeau on fiddle, and Nick de Caro's warm-
toned accordion to match Gene's own vocal timbre. Or timber! One song here is

actually called 'I Must Be A Tree'. Parsons can sure knock on wood, and he draws proud attention to his own prowess on banjo on track one. He truly combines the best that the names Gene and Parsons convey: a bridge between the two doomed troubadours and a man who, at the time of writing, was still happily alive.

All is not well, though. 'Sonic Bummer' sounds like a barn dance, but the words are bitter, about a sonic boom killing his chicken. If many of the Woodstock generation literally went to ground (one thinks of Ken Kesey parking his magic bus on his farm in Ohio, where it still rusts), then this is the perfect primer, a Whole Earth guide set to sweet country music, and not a million miles away from Barefoot Jerry.

In an interview at the time, Gene talked about his plans to move to a bigger acreage and to build a house in the middle, which isn't that different from the original settlers' dream, really. His greatest hope is to save the giant redwoods, although "I doubt if there will be any left by the time my daughter grows up".

As the Seventies kick in, there's an unspoken parallel with his views on the record industry. He went to a Columbia convention and heard an executive talking about albums as units to be shifted, "and for anyone knew he could have been talking about Firestone tyres, panty-hose or a packet of cookies". As companies grew and merged, a decade later this was exactly what happened. The same skills were applied to any commodity, with knowledge of or love for one's subject a decided disadvantage. As the century turns, though, it is those small independent record companies who know their product – whether Sugar Hill, Bloodshot or Cooking Vinyl – which have flourished, while the majors shed staff and acts. Any mountain farmer could have told you the same.

Philosophy aside, Parsons formed The Docker Hill Boys with Joel Scott Hill and Chris Etheridge, joined the reformed Burritos, and then returned to solo work with 1979's *Melodies*.

His hair is shorter here, and Albert Lee is following Clarence White's example on "electric string-bender guitar" (of which Gene holds equal shares in the patent, doubtless to the benefit of his acreage), but all is much the same. Gene perches on some giant tree trunks this time, which seem to be part of a house for giants – perhaps his wish was granted. On the back he gazes soulfully through a spiderweb of metal spokes. Technology is represented inside by the subtle use of moog, and as well as the obligatory cover of 'Hot Burrito No #1' Gene's own songs are given a good airing. The traditional content has been played down this time, to the album's detriment. A freshness has gone, and not just on this record. The Sixties are ancient history by now; the shutters are down. Gene's voice is just as deep and relaxed as before – melodic, in fact. On his tribute to White, 'Melodies From A Byrd In Flyght', it touches majesty, and his lead guitar break is almost worthy of the master.

Skip Battin re-appeared as a member of The New Riders Of The Purple Sage and then joined the reformed Burritos, along with Gene Parsons. His songs, co-written with jaded scene-maker Kim Fowley, continued to plumb the depths of banality. By the time of *In Don't Go Crazy* he had exhausted the English language and was writing partly in Italian.

Weirdest of all, though, is the debut and self-titled album by the Byrds' one-time producer Terry Melcher. Doris Day is his mother, and actually appears as a backing vocalist here. The name of the cowgirl she played so memorably – Calamity Jane – is eerily appropriate, but there's no deadwood stage in sight, just death in the air.

As if trying to exorcise demons, Terry dresses all in white, John McLaughlin style. He looks guarded, guarding his genitals with folded hands, which, as he was menaced by Charles Manson, is hardly surprising. With all the usual Byrds mafia in support, this is a spooky record indeed, with rich string arrangements, a choir, and fear at its heart.

The traditional song 'Roll In My Sweet Baby's Arms' has never been performed like this, with a big-band arrangement and Terry barking out unease at a funeral pace. He mines all of the implicit treachery in the song, which others usually gloss over. With sonorous chords on the violins, Jackson Browne's 'These Days' takes on a sinister tinge once you realise that Sharon Tate and her friends were butchered in a house in which he had once lived himself, supposedly as a warning from Manson. Terry had half promised to help his career as a folk singer. (Roll over, Dock Boggs). The line "I don't do too much talking these days" certainly takes on extra meaning, as does "I've not forgotten them". By now it is a lament.

Scared yet? 'Dr Horovitz' sounds cheerful, like The Plastic Ono Band, but it's about Terry getting very little help from his analyst. Hardly surprising. On the surface, 'Beverly Hills' sounds like a tourist guide to LA – "just plain folks living there" – but Joni Mitchell this is not: "You'll see the big mistake you've made" as you cruise down Sunset Strip. The whole album is like a secret code, which anyone who has read Ed Sanders' book *The Family* can break. Side one closes with 'These Bars Have Made A Prison Out Of Me', by Oldham and Penn from Muscle Shoals. It can rarely have been so badly sung or laden with such implicit meaning. The spoken middle section always brings me out in goosebumps, with the phrase "someone has to help me" howled out by a man whose memories and undeserved guilt will haunt him to the grave.

'Arkansas' is a beautiful ode to the Depression, with banjo, steel guitar and harmonica. "The brambles took the cabin I was born in", and for any other child of such privilege "the troubles I was born to" would sound a spoiled brat's moan. Here, though, it rings all too true. The string arrangement soothes the soul, and the whole thing rises to a beautiful climax, with Terry a child again, whittling a stick.

Not so 'Stagger Lee', that traditional song of murder, which takes us back into nightmare. Terry's untutored voice somehow makes the words he sings sound all the more true. A beautiful country rock backing – as crunchy as peanut butter, and with Ry Cooder on stratospheric lead guitar – makes it all the worse. Dylan's 'Fourth Time Around' – another vengeance song – is barked out, and Melcher takes it back home to Nashville (where the original was laid down in the first place) with mandolin and pedal steel. The line "Everybody must give something back for something they get" is positively sinister in the circumstances, and the choir emphasise it over and over again as the song fades away. Stand aside, Nico.

Roger McGuinn's 'Just A Season' is a typical vision of Eden as seen in childhood from that generally cheerful writer. Terry sings it staccato, if singing is the right word here. There's lots of cello, and the jingle-jangle optimism of The Byrds at their best, with a circus barker getting in the way: "I never got one star", he sings hopefully.

Melcher's own song 'Halls Of Justice" shares the measured language and sense of doom of *The Basement Tapes*: "I keep looking for some old place to hide." Here it joins hands with two of Dylan's best finger-pointing songs, 'Positively Fourth Street' and 'Like A Rolling Stone' (both slightly rewritten for the purpose) in a medley, albeit one that lasts less than three minutes. Terry builds a triptych here to false friends and the sense of being totally alone.

'The Old Hand Jive' rewrites a famous rock 'n' roll song – sad and slow here – to picture young Terry watching Johnny Otis on the TV and wishing he was anything like as good. It's two minutes long and perfect, pitched at just the same point of melancholy a microsecond before it turns to self-pity, as Eric Andersen's *Blue River*, but with a greater excuse than rock star excess. It fades out, but you sense that Terry will still be living this record long after you've put it back in its sleeve and returned it to the shelf.

Clarence White reformed The Kentucky Colonels after The Byrds hit the ground, but his great monument is the one and only album by Muleskinner, released (briefly) a year after his death, although it has since been reissued.

First, though, the TV broadcast. There is something about a great acoustic band which strikes a perfect, almost miraculous balance between its members. Some of their life-force gets captured on the recording tape. This is denied even to the greatest amplified music, where there is so much more room to hide. Early albums by British folk groups like Planxty, Boys Of The Lough or The Bothy Band pull it off – it's kind of *weightless* – and Muleskinner do the same here. To be heretical, the acoustic musings of Led Zeppelin touch much the same spot, and with the same Celtic tinge. It only seems to work when the players have a shared heritage in traditional music. Back to the old back porch!

Muleskinner were formed as a one-off for a TV show set to star Bill Monroe, and as a youthful warm-up band who would return at the end for a brief jam session. Bill's bus broke down, though, and after three hours' rehearsal this new bluegrass mafia set to work. Fiddler Richard Greene, banjo player Bill Keith (whose playing we discussed right back at the start of this chapter) and singer Peter Rowan had all been Blue Grass Boys, while Clarence turned down a job with Bill Monroe in 1967, with his brother, Roland, taking his place. Rowan and mandolin player David Grisman had played together in various teenage bluegrass combos before taking a drastic career loop to form Earth Opera, an archetypal hippie band, on Elektra records.

We'll take a brief detour to this musical freakshow – it's worth the view. With words like "every day is the same/going gently insane", and jazzy keyboard-led improvisations, it all seems as far from bluegrass as you could imagine. A masterpiece of the strange, Vietnam rumbles on in the background. Rowan's voice is like a concerned Martian, as he sings lyrics like "you wake up in the dark to know you're blind". One can only imagine the riot if this lot had been booked by the Opry, and it would have been purely intentional. Rowan later admitted: "Earth Opera was rather reactionary to what I considered the Nashville stranglehold, the commercial approach to music."

At one point, Peter's voice wavers like that of an Indian yogi (Indian as in Asian). Get to the end of the album, though – which now sounds like some kind of historical aberration – and there lurks 'Death By Fire', Rowan's first songwriting masterpiece, which demonstrates his uncanny ability to get beneath the skin of another culture. The song inhabits the same universe as The Strawbs' 'The Battle': nameless brutality in a warped Middle Ages.

Here is corrupt America as seen by the angry young, with treachery all around, religious faith a bad joke and the heroine crucified. It's a nightmare worthy of Mervyn Peake, with a room "full of white teeth" and a talking skull. Flip to the end, and the girl sleeps in "new-fallen snow", and suddenly you think of how many times the young Rowan must have played 'Footprints In The Snow'. Everything snaps into place. You can't escape the folk tradition just by filling your head with hallucinogenics and attacking the establishment. Those things are just on the surface.

It's too painful to contemplate quite what the patriotic Monroe would have made of this, or of his former wonder boy's 'Home Of The Brave', a sarcastic anti-war rant. Listen to the end of 'Dreamless', though, and suddenly there's a lovely mandolin break almost worthy of Bill himself. Bill Keith (that man again) plays pedal steel on *The Great American Eagle Tragedy*, of which the title track is an extended elegy for the state of a nation. Like many of his contemporaries, Rowan came to bluegrass out of psychedelia, and with radical, left-wing politics quite at odds with the conservative tenor of the music as Monroe invented it. The other stand-out track is 'Mad Lydia's Waltz', in which his vocal sends shivers up your spine. It's very European, like a settlers' lament.

Peter already knows how to spin a tale, throwing in telling details like "her laughter is ringing on the beach at low tide" while John Cale saws away on viola. On the collage cover, a tough US sergeant's face is replaced with a kitten's. At this point, one-time bluegrass purists Rowan and Grisman were blasting out avante-garde jazz on twin saxophones. Teenage rebellion, eh?

Greene and Rowan later joined Seatrain, an hysterical combo whose most interesting aspect is what Rowan describes as a "spiritual quest…a journey going out to the medicine man. It was going to the mountain instead of coming down from the mountains. Wandering and searching." For all of that, they murder Lowell George's 'Willin'' on their second album, steamrollering the song's slyness and turning it into a simple-minded country hoe-down. The rest is an attempt at fusing bluegrass with classical music. It now sounds a dated as the band look.

Not so Muleskinner. On their one and only TV appearance, Rowan contributes his own 'Land Of The Navajo' and Maria Muldaur guests on one song. It's all as sparkling – and rough around the edges – as you would expect, but when the same bunch reconvened in the studio to record Muleskinner something else happened. The music shoots out of the speakers with a fierceness that takes your breath away.

Part of this must be due to Rowan's energetic voice, which has a kind of feral yelp when he gets excited; but these players have brought the energy (and indeed the noise) of rock music to the subtleties of bluegrass. The band are now amped up, with Clarence's Telecaster "cracking like a bullwhip" and a heavy rhythm section. What you lose in purity you gain in visceral excitement – it's the polar opposite of those kids making mere noise in an Appalachian village hall by whom whom we skirted earlier. These are the best you can get, Monroe's musical children, with all of the cultural changes you would expect. They all play so fast on the title track that there seem to be notes missing. It's bluegrass on drugs, but what they're really mainlining is that high, lonesome sound. On every track.

Beg, borrow or steal this album. As Rowan writes in the sleeve notes to the Ridge Runner reissue: "We played as we felt it, coming out of a bluegrass rock tradition in those early days of the 1970s. Clarence's gentle soul was our unifying force, holding the music together. We had all the time in the world, and no idea how quickly things would change." All kinds of history collide on this record. The lonesome 'Rain And Snow' is a traditional song which Rowan learned from Obray Ramsey, "the great Appalachian singer", and made famous with The Monroe Band, from whom The Grateful Dead learned it, putting it on their first album. It's the kind of song that The Holy Modal Rounders would pervert in their own way, but here it has a grace and favour which brings a tear to the eye.

Another twist to the kaleidoscope: Grisman and Rowan both played with Jerry Garcia in Old And The Way, while Rowan's dope song 'Panama Red' was taken up by The New Riders Of The Purple Sage, another Dead offshoot. What The Grateful Dead burlesqued, though, is here played straight. After an apprenticeship in New York playing with the likes of Del McCoury and Jody Stecher, Grisman contributed mandolin to *American Beauty*, and with guitarist Tony Rice learned to add jazz and improvisation to bluegrass. He called the result "dawg music".

While growing up, he believed that "one day I'd be listening to *Foggy Mountain Banjo* and the next to 'Night In Tunisia'. Rice brought "robustness", a strict tempo learned from his time with JD Crowe, "who had picked it up from Jimmy Martin. It was really good for us – boot camp." Tony was later replaced with the more free-flowing style of Mark O'Connor and the "unrelenting pulse" of bassist Rob Wasserman. They added world music to avante-garde jazz, so that *Quintet '80* contains an (as always) acoustic rendition of John Coltrane's 'Naima' and Grisman's own 'Thailand'.

Although old-style music suffuses such progressions, the closest Grisman comes to treating his source material directly is on 1988's template of authenticity *Home Is Where The Heart Is*, with Doc Watson. In the more recent *Tone Poems*, made with Rice, antique instruments are the stars, vintage pre-war Martins and a Snow Queen mandolin from the 1930s. Grisman's best work is when – in Peter Rowan's words – there is "that sense of teetering on the edge of frenzy. Where you've got that band churning away, it's great. You can just ride on out there vocally."

As for Rowan himself, he went off on a strange odyssey (albeit patchy, with some albums red hot and others mildly tepid), which as yet shows no sign of coming to any firm conclusion. Grisman rejoins him on *Texican Badman*, with Jerry Garcia meeting Flaco Jimenez among the backing musicians. The album contains four early Terry Allen songs and a set list which ranges across the Texas-Mexico border.

It's oddly representative of his work as a whole, an interesting jumble. The whole record is best characterised as a weird update of western swing, with lyrics undreamed of by Bob Wills, such as "come see the dragon chase the autumn moon". The final track is a roll call of dead heroes, that old country standby, but here Eric Dolphy, John Coltrane, Otis Redding and Charlie Christian join Patsy Cline: "Lazybones" all, coming over the "blue horizon".

This sense of another world haunts all of Rowan's best work. As he told *Swing Fifty One* – itself named after a tune on the first album by the David Grisman Quintet – "That's why I said my albums are produced by Earth Opera because I think that my albums now represent that spirit of adventure and mysticism and mystery." So Earth Opera are more than a band, more like a way of life.

Rowan identifies with Robin Williamson's search for "ancient Celtic and pre-Celtic music: Old-World musics that have this sense of pathos and ecstasy. An undogmatic kind of music that has ancient feeling to it. It treats major poetical themes: love and death and what have you." Rowan's own work centres around the "what have you". Peter and his wife drove across the continent looking for "a spirit of American history and myth". They finally found it in Monument Valley, the land-scape endlessly revisited by film-maker John Ford. Here they found dinosaur bones and primitive wall paintings: "You look at your feet and there are fossils of seashells, and you realize that you're standing on the bottom of an ocean that is now the top of a mountain."

Much the same feeling comes across in a *No Depression* interview with Jimmie Dale Gilmore, who walks out of his back door to a ravine which meets up with Lick Creek, "the oldest known inhabited spot in North America". No wonder that Peter Rowan's album *Walls Of Time* is one of his finest, tracing a Celtic connection. He was born near Boston to a wealthy family: "We're descended from Sir William Wallace, the Scottish rebel who invaded England and was hanged, drawn and quartered at Tyburn. So ended the Scottish revolt." When Peter became involved in the music business, he was horrified by the way "they thought their audiences were a bunch of real hillbilly bumpkins". Also, "a lot of people who really loved bluegrass at that time really hated black people, and I really spent some sleepless hours trying to figure that one out".

Maybe this explains the variety of his work since. It has a strangely unfinished quality, ranging from the weird tales of *Medicine Trail* – a lyrical equivalent of his wild leap on the back cover – to the full-on rock of The Wild Stallions, and the intense acoustic ballads of *Dust Bowl Children*. On *Revelry*, he is joined by Greg Douglass on electric guitar and Tex Logan on fiddle. There is a Celtic lilt to 'The Holy Wells Of Ireland', the last stop on the trio's travels in Europe: "Smell the heather and the pine." Another Rowan piece, 'Rising O' The Bones', is surprisingly cheerful, interspersing the "dirty" protests at Long Kesh with the National Guard shooting students dead at Ohio, and then adding a jig. It's unsettling, but it ushers in the full-scale fusion of *Walls Of Time*. "When I was in Ireland the pieces just fell together in my mind." Meanwhile, back in Nashville, the "weight" of the players "pulled it in a bluegrass direction rather than going '*nouveau*-Celtic'".

Rowan's vocals are less grating than before, softened with sweet mountain harmonies and lots of banjo. Nothing is forced. "The thing about Irish music is that the ancient themes still exist in the music." He adopts a dreadful Irish accent on 'Plains Of Waterloo', a song about a dying soldier killed fighting Napoleon. It starts sedately and then speeds up into a mid-Atlantic strut, ending with slow sweeps across the strings, like a weary army marching home. It's almost a movie for the ears, all done acoustically. Astonishing stuff.

Rowan was careful not to over-rehearse his musicians – among whom are maestros like Sam Bush and Ricky Skaggs – so that they capture the "spontaneous feel" of true bluegrass. Peter was as careful in his song choice as Harry Smith a generation before. All of the religious songs here are different, but each is about "being alone and having a vision".

Where the young Bob Dylan moaned 'Moonshiner' like a dying geriatric, and stretched out each note almost to infinity, Rowan is more upbeat, keener to sell his wares: "A gallon for a two-dollar bill" seems like mighty good value. He describes this version of the old song as a "bacchanale". You almost believe him when he tells you that his product will leave you "with breath sweet as the dew on the vine". This is life-enhancing music.

Again, just like the Harry Smith *Anthology* the whole record has an underlying narrative, kept secret from those who skim over the surface of things. It is a parable, no less. Here the story is that of a man who emerges from jail, then goes up to the mountains on a search for spiritual redemption: "I ain't coming down in chains." He meets a mysterious woman, and here his troubles really begin. Even the hoariest traditional song becomes symbolic in this context. As Rowan explains it, "Maybe 'Walls Of Time' is him finding the grave of his sweetheart or 'The Plains Of Waterloo'…and maybe she didn't really die. Maybe it was love that was dead." Of course, this being Rowan, the CD issue brings in three tracks from an unrelated album in the middle, which break the flow completely. Certainly the title song (credited jointly to Rowan and Bill Monroe) is about love beyond the grave, in the best mountain tradition.

As Rowan told *Folk Roots*: "there were certain things that Bill Monroe passed on to me. It has a lot to do with feel; it's what Bill used to call the 'Ancient Tones.'" His 1996 CD *Bluegrass Boy* is a fine tribute, entirely self-composed, with a noticeably ageing Peter shown silhouetted against a darkening sky. He prints out the sage advice from Monroe which he has so spectacularly failed to follow in the years since: "Pete, don't go too far out on that limb, there are enough flowers out there already." But that's the whole point of it: the danger.

Meanwhile, psychedelia was erupting in California and spreading like a fever. It seemed at first to have nothing to do with mountain music, which dealt with limitations; this new sound was about the very lack of limits. Apart from a few pathfinders like Barefoot Jerry, it was a lifestyle which would take some years to hit Nashville, but when it did so the comedown in particular wold re-energise the music. Free love, brain-scrambling music and mind-bending chemicals – a wonderful cocktail from which to wake jaded and in need of confession and some soothing pedal steel. Remorse doesn't come much sweeter. The widespread use of hallucinogens unleashed a re-mythologising of American history in the psyche of those foolhardy enough to mess with them (and some who were just pretending). The drugged mind truly was the new frontier, and the newest gunslinger in town was the lead guitarist, combining blues structures with the freedom of avante-garde jazz.

Even a cursory glance at hip posters of time shows a matching obsession with the lifestyle of native American Indians. Forget the scalpings: it was their nomadic way of life, their long hair, their semi-nakedness and their use of natural herbs to get religiously high which struck a chord. Life in Haight Ashbury was tribal, with communal living the new fashion. Dances and happenings bore titles borrowed from Indian lore: the Be-In, for example, and the Gathering Of The Tribes. Country music needed no prompting here. As well as the obviously genuine Buffy Sainte-Marie, Presley, Johnny Cash and Shania Twain all claimed Indian blood (although Shania's turned out to be adopted).

English folk-singer Roy Harper later took this to its ultimate self-hatred with his song 'I Hate The White Man' and, by extension, the Christian God, "who turned you all loose". It was a call taken up by various ethnic extremists, and underlies political correctness right up to the present day. Harper was white himself (at least in skin colour), although he was alienated by spells in prison and mental hospital, and "liberated" by dope. Out in the desert, Charlie Manson took things a little further by carrying out his own Indian raids on rich settlers in the Hollywood Hills.

Scratch below the surface a little, though, scrape away the long hair of the new psychedelic bands, and the faces that emerge are long-term inmates of the Sixties folk scene. Listen carefully to the repertoire of bands at the Fillmore and you will hear songs or ideas or atmospheres from the Harry Smith *Anthology* given a new twist. It was as if Smith's vision of that old, weird America was coming true, with adventurous light shows and through a haze of dope smoke. His one-man resistance to the 1950s had borne fruit.

Nashville could have been in a different galaxy to all of this, although the likes of Willie Nelson were later to mutate from a suit and short haircut to would-be *brujo*. As the walls between different musical styles came tumbling down, and eclecticism was the name of the game, the country music establishment kept up their straight-backed stance of cultural apartheid.

For Chet Atkins it was a matter of them and us, and never the twain shall meet: "We were aware of what was going on, but their music came from rock, whereas the kind of changes we were making were firmly rooted in country music." But was it real country? Emmylou Harris remembered how Gram Parsons – a hippie boy if ever there was one, enslaved to love and drugs and family handouts – "had a vision and a real love for those old mountain harmonies. The idea was to keep the country pure but give it a rock kick." Other bands were doing this before *Sweetheart Of The Rodeo* was even a gleam in Gram's eyes.

It was not for nothing that The Electric Flag replaced The International Submarine Band on the soundtrack of the movie *The Trip*: they were much more of the moment, with their jazz-rock and driving guitar. Psychedelia was like a bunch of mad children in the attic, turning everything upside-down and inside-out. You could invent your own reality. You could forget the boring restrictions of tempo or key changes or tuning. If you wanted to put a banjo through a Leslie speaker, and then record it backwards, great. Nothing mattered as much as self expression. No wonder that much of the music that resulted is now unlistenable. Some is still amazing in its sheer grace and recklessness, breaking through philosophical and musical barriers which no one before had even realised were there.

My own exposure to this kaleidoscope world came via John Peel's wonderful show on Radio London, which presented bands with extraordinary names doing extraordinary things with huge conceptual seriousness. It was music literally from the other side of the world, and, as with C&W, the English variant had a charm of its own, although little connection with the real thing. LSD took people back to their childhoods and made everything fresh as new paint. You only needed to hear 'Penny Lane' backed with 'Strawberry Fields Forever' – Paul's chirpiness and John's pain, as if illuminated by lightning – to realise that something extremely strange was going on.

The electric Dylan had smashed open a door through which The Beatles emerged with a whole new magic box, and now all kinds of weirdness were seeping in. When Skip Spence came to Nashville, perhaps the weirdest of the lot washed up right in Music City.

Most people now trace the San Francisco sound back to the historic Red Dog Saloon in the ghost town of Virginia City, Nevada, on the Comstock Lode, in summer 1965. The poster for the opening night might announce "The Limit Of The Marvellous", but the accent is on the last word. The clientele already existed in a kind of impenetrable bubble, sky-high on their own youth, luck and talent. They dressed self-consciously in Wild West clothes and listened to a weird jingle-jangle bunch called The Charlatans, whose self-mocking glee was part of the joke. Their image had been put together with more care than their music. Photographer Herb Greene was amazed by the length of their hair, the coolness of their attitude and what they released in that run-down saloon. It was the new Wild West: "We were all post-adolescents playing at cowboys and Indians."

When George Hunter first met Mike Wilheim, "I used to hang out at his house, listening to Johnny Cash." What evidence survives of the original line-up shows a barely adequate, country-ish combo, but one producing music with strange undercurrents. Listen to Buffy Sainte-Marie's 'Codeine Blues', with its weird echo and clunking backing, over which Wilheim sings deadpan and slightly off-key about his helpless drug addiction. There is a guitar solo in the near distance, with an unsettling edge. If one word describes the mix of blues, folk and country which The Charlatans purveyed it is "Americana", which – given the place in which they played – is only too appropriate. Dancing was obligatory.

'I Saw Her' was also recorded for Kama Sutra in early 1966, a folk song set to auto-harp, but The Carter Family this ain't. It's much closer to The Stones' 'Lady Jane', awash with sarcasm. 'Jack of Diamonds' ("take four") is a rolling, thumping version of the traditional song, with vocals like a foghorn. And then there's 'East Virginia', done virtually straight, with tinkling piano. The Charlatans learned this song from The New Lost City Ramblers, and brought in bluegrass fiddler Hank Bradley on this version, with Wilheim imitating a dobro on his electric guitar. This is a music which looks backwards. The band planned their initial record release as a "little souvenir thing, a ten-inch record because it would look like a 78…real thick with a picture on one side and the grooves on the other". Like everything else, this is self-consciously a performance, in tune with Wilheim's image as "a rock 'n' roll Wyatt Earp".

A reformed line-up recorded an album for Philips long after the magic had evaporated. Songs by Johnny Cash and AP Carter indicate their country roots, and the band gradually mutated into the jovial western swing of Dan Hicks And His Hot Licks, with the singing drummer now in sole charge of proceedings. Meanwhile, other off-centre bands were emerging like buds on a tree.

A scruffy group of ex-bluegrass and jug band players went electric and called themselves The Warlocks. John Cippolina, his services turned down by The Charlatans, fell in love with their Wild West image and set about forming The Quicksilver Messenger Service. They moved deep into the rural wilds, proud to announce themselves as the only San Franciscan band with real mud on their boots, and propelled their twin lead guitar sound into something new and strange. Another guitarist who could make your back shiver, Barry Melton, met Woody

Guthrie fan "Country" Joe McDonald at the Berkeley Folk Festival, and they got talking. Meanwhile, bluegrass fiddler Rodney Albin met singer Pete Kraemer, and The Sopwith Camel began to taxi down the runway.

Flight was a metaphor for all kinds of other things, although when Jefferson Airplane began their residency at former pizza parlour the Matrix it was with a stand-up bassist and a repertoire largely of trad folk and blues songs. The lead guitarist, Jorma Kaukonen, told *Acoustic Guitar* that "the first music I played was old-timey and bluegrass". The Carter Family, too. "I was interested mostly in ethnic music or American traditional music." Seeing Merle Travis' cameo appearance in *From Here To Eternity* "kind of got me going". He always preferred acoustic music at heart, and with Hot Tuna was free once again to explore it, as he has done since in a series of unplugged (and to my ears increasingly boring) albums. This, though, was the essence of the SF sound: folk music, rocked up and with all kinds of odd borrowings from the blues, soul and what was not yet called world music. Particularly important were the sound and fury of the old honky tonks (this was essentially live music), and the same delight in jazz improvisation which had earlier invigorated western swing. Ralph J Gleason attended one early gig and saw Jefferson Airplane not so much as a rock 'n' roll band, more a "contemporary-popular-music-folk-rock unit".

Just after The Charlatans' residency had been cancelled following the inevitable drugs bust, a strange bus rolled in from Ohio painted in Day-glo colours and with the legend "Further" on the front – the new frontiersmen were rolling in. In December 1965 they held the first Acid Test, with a soundtrack by The Warlocks, who were now renamed The Grateful Dead and were at this point a heavy R&B band. As they began to play hippie hangouts like the Fillmore and the Avalon, The Dead began to loosen up and incorporate some of the music with which they grew up. Hell, even Jerry Garcia's girlfriend was nicknamed Mountain Girl.

It was all still a game, though, and on one night The Dead dressed up as Indians – war paint, feathers, the lot – and raided Quicksilver's remote ranch, setting off firecrackers and joining in with a large pipe of peace. Joel Selvin's book *Summer Of Love* describes how the return raid turned sour. One night at the Fillmore, "dressed as cowboys, they figured to tie The Dead to their amps, dance around and sing 'Kawliga', the Hank Williams song the band set about learning specially for the event". Unfortunately, when the police discovered a bunch of white youths carrying rifles in a black ghetto they threw them in jail, and David Freiburg was beaten up for his pains.

The early innocence of the scene was ebbing away, especially as the media wagon trains rolled into town. Former folkie Scott MacKenzie sang a musical travelogue about coming to San Francisco with a flower in your hair, to find Eden and the "gentle people". Eric Burdon hymned Monterey, where Hendrix and The Who flew over from England to join the party, with "Prince" Brian Jones parading around in his cape. Nashville turned its back, although I'm going to plunge straight in.

The Grateful Dead – like The Warlocks – is a name taken straight from the twi-light zone where folklore and the occult meet. A succession of chemically-altered graphic artists evoked just such a place visually with the skull and roses motif, which the band took as its own, representing growth from decay. Had The Dead been an obscure Twenties hillbilly band, Harry Smith would have had them straight onto his *Anthology* for their strange atmosphere and the wayward playing of their early songs, a code to which the listener doesn't quite have the key. Robert Hunter was one of the first volunteers to undergo trials under LSD, and it opened up the whole of Americana to him as a kind of cosmic playpen.

On their first album, Garcia's weedy but addictive voice ploughs through an unemotional update of 'Cold Rain And Snow', credited to the band rather than the public domain in which they found it. A lecherous-sounding Pigpen takes most of the lead vocals and goes through the gutbucket blues repertoire, largely to tedious effect.

By 1968, however, Hunter's baroque lyrics had blossomed into the rich incom-prehensibility of 'Dark Star' and the like. Phrases like "the transitive nightfall of diamonds" were perfect for stoned minds and for filtering out those who wanted words merely to make literal sense. Garcia's picking here is country clean, sticking on a riff then suddenly flowing up to the stratosphere, interacting carefully with the rest of the band, so that the music has the ebb and flow of the sea. As he himself said: "I would describe my own guitar playing as descended from barroom rock 'n' roll, country guitar." Don't try this at the Opry, though.

Even the album cover perverts the stars and stripes – old glory itself – into the word "dead", while a bare-breasted queen emerges from an open coffin. Inside, the band is literally playing in the street to people as far as the eye can see. This is gen-uine people's music, with 'St Stephen' a song remodelled from the folk tradition, with phrases like "in and out of the garden he goes" and "wrap the babe in scarlet colours" retaining some of that elemental balance, as does the key line "one man gathers what another man spills". If that isn't country wisdom, I don't know what is. It also applies to all of those who have spent the years since the Sixties cleaning things up.

Constant gigging in front of an audience as wild and unhinged as the band itself pushed them beyond their own talents into making music which is both absurdly cheerful – "our thought jewels polished and gleaming" – and yet aware of the psy-chic abyss yawning just a step away. Some of the guitar halfway through 'Dark Star' is like the soundtrack for a torture chamber, with textures like broken glass. It's even said that the weird *thwack* at the end of 'Dark Star', just before it picks up speed again as 'Saint Stephen', is that of an electrically-treated banjo note. All of this from a little white pill. It's literally schizophrenic, as spoofed in the marvellous audi-tion piece of the would-be hippie Hitler in Mel Brooks' movie *The Producers*, first hymning his flower and then stamping on it. It could be Jim Morrison on a bad day.

The continuing fascination of the musical flash of the late Sixties lies in this unresolved tension at its heart. Country music is the direct opposite, bringing consolation and constraint. And yet, on lead guitar, Garcia's bluegrass heritage was starting to pay dividends, as his maimed fingers conjured endless runs of electric magic. As fast flowing as a stream and as light as thistledown, his notes dance an endless duet with Phil Lesh's energetic bass over Pigpen's rich organ chords and the two drummers. Weir, ever the boy, pins things down on rhythm guitar.

Eric Pooley is chief political correspondent of *Time* magazine, and has also written the clearest description of the band's folk roots in *So Many Roads (1965-1995)*, the recently released five-CD box set of outtakes and live delights. He talks us through a 1993 rehearsal tape of 'Whiskey In The Jar', "a centuries-old Irish ballad that came to New England with the colonists", the penultimate track of the whole set sung here as if by an unrepentant highwayman.

Garcia used to sing it in his string band days back in the early Sixties. Here he sings it in a clear but wavering voice, carefully enunciating each word as the band feel their way into it, like blind men learning how to see. Weir comments "I haven't heard that one in 30 years," and Garcia retorts "I haven't, either. I just remembered it." From somewhere deep inside. "A folk song," Lesh comments. "A cool one," Jerry replies. Aren't they all?

Pooley comes in with the analysis. Back before LSD, such songs were "a ticket out of the mainstream, a link to what Kenneth Rexroth calls the 'old free America' – a country of limitless possibilities, a place that seemed tougher and stranger, more compelling and more fun than suburban Palo Alto." Mountain ballads, bluegrass, cowboy polkas and C&W all became part of the huge musical palette with which these "musical omnivores" began to paint: "The bizarre tales of the Southern string-band tradition (a girl drowns and her heartbone is turned into a fiddle) let them know there was room in this country for the weird and the inexplicable." As well as taking, they give back as well. Garcia points out: "Hunter and I always had this thing where we liked to muddy the folk tradition by adding our own songs. It's the thing of taking a well-founded tradition and putting in something that's totally looped."

Jerry had been "an absolute ferocious five-string banjo player" in his youth, and described The Dead as a "mutated bluegrass band...as in bluegrass, the instruments talk to each other". They added the kind of inner dialogue they found in the work of John Coltrane, and Jerry began soloing "in paragraphs rather than riffs and licks", but his more immediate influence in stretching out so productively was Scotty Stoneman from The Kentucky Colonels: "This is a guy who took an ABBA fiddle tune and extended it out for 15 minutes, with 17-bar phrases and unbelievable expressive shit. I couldn't believe what I was hearing. I never heard anything like it outside of jazz."

For Pooley, there is a "continuing lesson in both the old songs and the best Dead songs, a message of grace and spirit...of melodies sung in the face of grinning Death". Mikal Gilmore takes it further, believing that, like Merle Haggard, The Clash or Notorious BIG, The Dead "sang to embolden audiences that had been branded and treated as outcasts by a world outside".

As The Dead began to evolve their space-age music in the late Sixties, they used the energy of their supporters to push themselves to the outer limits. The band seem to have swallowed their folk roots whole, although they occasionally peep out. There is an out-take of 'St Stephen' on the peerless *Live Dead* – with bagpipes, of all things – in which one song turns into another, before it all comes back to earth with the traditional hymn 'We Bid You Goodnight'. It was not always thus.

A 1964 gig from the Tangent folk coffee house in Palo Alto survives, warts and all. Well, just warts, really. Mother McCree's Uptown Jug Champions are announced on the poster as purveying "fine old-time anthroposophical jug band music". Never was anthropology so beautifully fused with philosophy. The announcer introduces the band as "just a panic to watch. They fumble around on the stage, and they bicker, and eventually they come up with some pretty weird music." The first thing you hear is a banjo, followed by some fairly unlistenable cover versions, like slowed-down skiffle. Pigpen sings – sort of – and plays harmonica. There is washtub bass, washboard and Bob Weir blows the jug. Badly.

This falls on the blues side of the great acoustic divide, but Garcia was also well schooled in the Celtic tradition. He lived in a wrecked car for a while, playing "dippy folk songs. It was before I got into a purist trip." He also took a song-collecting expedition to the South, and then played bluegrass with The Hart Valley Drifters, alongside Robert Hunter on string bass, Dave Nelson (who would re-emerge in The New Riders Of The Purple Sage) and Peter Albin, a founding member of Big Brother And The Holding Company. Other names for this floating combo were The Wildwood Boys, The Black Mountain Boys and The Thunder Mountain Tub Thumpers, none of which rang quite true. These were city hipsters, not rustic innocents. They even won a prize as the best amateur bluegrass band at the 1963 Monterey Folk Festival before promptly splitting up. It's like the Portsmouth Symphonia throwing out any member as soon as they can play in tune.

Garcia had become "kind of froze up in bluegrass". He had also played in a folk duo with his wife of the time, Sarah, and Weir first encountered him playing banjo in a music store. Once The Dead had moved from Haight-Ashbury into the wilds of Marin County, Garcia and Hunter began to discover how to write tight and sharply-focused songs about getting back to the country.

At much the same time, the likes of Merle Haggard's prison song 'Sing Me Back Home' were entering The Grateful Dead's live shows, as they mutated from freak-outs to selections from a cosmic American jukebox. It's wonderfully ironic that just the kind of musicians whom the mythical Okie from Musgokee would most distrust, fear and spurn – wild men on drugs playing atonal hour-long jams – were now taking Merle seriously as a national bard. Under the tie-dyed attire and long hair, they were kith and kin.

Meanwhile, country influences emerged in the strangest places. The Quicksilver Messenger Service began as a vehicle of folk singer Dino Valente (aka

Chet Powers, a twelve-string merchant straight from Greenwich Village who wrote 'Let's Get Together' and ended up in jail after a dope bust) and emerged out of the ashes of Beatles' copyists The Brogues. Skip Spence passed through on his way to Jefferson Airplane, but the band's greatest moments came when John Cippolina unleashed his shivery lead guitar, like a pedal steel on drugs, with Gary Duncan as a trusty foil. You still really need to hear Cippolina on vinyl in order to capture every ounce of the bite, attack and glide he made uniquely his own, but there was definitely a country twang somewhere at the heart of his sound. On the majestic track 'The Fool', appearing on their first album, there is even what sounds like a lariat lashing rawhide used as percussion.

In another part of the wood, Glen Campbell of The Misunderstood was torturing a real pedal steel to make all kinds of unearthly noises, as his band drove straight at the sun. As their champion, John Peel, wrote: "At the tender age of two, he had been given a plastic guitar, and had begun to scrape cutlery and other steel object up and down its strings." This is what the Sixties were all about, grown-ups reverting to childhood. Years later, The Long Ryders picked up the baton.

Quicksilver moved to an 88-acre ranch at Point Reyes Station and took their collection of guns with them. Pete Frame chronicled what happened next. One of their roadies walked the range each morning playing the saxophone, accompanied by a pet wolf. Cippolina re-erected a hundred-year-old fence in his bedroom, "all covered with moss...I had to water my room, man". If these men were deranged, they were not the blissed-out hippies of stereotype.

When a neighbour came over to shoot the wolf, Quicksilver "all ran inside, went to the armoury and loaded up with guns and ammo. Then, in the best Western movie tradition, we smashed the windows with our gun barrels and began blasting. The farmer just freaked. Lit out of there like a rocket...but we followed him, all the time firing at the sky and the ground, followed him like he was a pheasant. We kept firing near him and he'd fall on his face in all the mud and horse shit, scared to death. Then he'd get up and run like a crazy man until he made it home." So who was the real John Wayne here? They followed him back to his farmhouse, "firing at his roof, picking off lumps of it, just like eating corn." After that it was time to leave Point Reyes.

The result was *Happy Trails*, a conceptual album put together in the studio from live tapes (just like *Live Dead*) and with a stunning sleeve designed by George Hunter – once of The Charlatans and now of Globe Propaganda – in which a cowboy waves farewell to his sweetheart in glorious technicolour. It is 1930s Hollywood as recreated in oil paint, and the album itself is described as a "movie", with two song suites based around two of the more unsettling compositions of Bo Diddley rather than Roy Rogers. Gary Duncan points his twelve-bore right at the viewer, and all four musicians are literally drawn from photographs, like long-dead heroes. Each one of them breaks through the frame that tries to contain them.

The music itself is just like that, unsettling and masterful, with the Fillmore crowd brought in as part of the soundscape on 'Who Do You Love?'. When Glen Campbell (of The Misunderstood, not the 'Wichita Lineman') turned his rocking pedal steel to this same splenetic song of human skulls and rattlesnake hide with 'Juicy Lucy', he got himself a Top 20 UK hit. He could make his instrument squeal with pain onstage. Quicksilver's greatness as a band was to visit both heaven and hell, often in the same song, and here the instrumental 'Calvary' sounds like the theme for a particularly bloodthirsty spaghetti western, complete with a tolling bell, a manic chorus and a symphony of feedback, before ending with a howling wind. 'Happy Trails' comes as a welcome respite, with rhythmic clip-clops, a honky-tonk piano and vocals dipped in syrup. After the unearthly noises of the previous 40 minutes or so it's like a blessing, no matter how tongue in cheek it sounds, and fades into silence as a man whistles on and around the tune.

Later Quicksilver albums were more notable for their cover art than the music held therein, especially after John Cippolina jumped ship to join Copperhead. A later album that he made with Terry And The Pirates is graced with a fine CM Russell painting of 'The Doubtful Handshake' between a settler and an Indian, who grins with menace. Cippolina played for a while with Free Light, a jazz band whose lead signer was Mel Tillis: "The guy's got 100 gold albums...I never heard of him, either...he stutters. You'd know every song that he wrote, but you'd never know the guy."

Cippolina also joined The Dinosaurs, a band of hippie veterans, as well as guesting with Welsh band Man and inspiring the subtle guitar tones of Richard Treece of Help Yourself, the UK's finest ever country rock combo. Like so many of those who gained fame in hippie rock bands, Cippolina died too young, but to the very end, "like a gunfighter who has left the limelight, he kept partying, playing music as often as possible, saying 'The easiest place for me to play is live and loud, to really feel the chord ringing through my body – I crave for that.'"

Joe McDonald grew up with country music on the radio and live at Involvement Park, where he saw the likes of The Maddox Brothers And Rose. His friend Roger Bush – the same one who later joined The Kentucky Colonels – taught him how to play guitar, "and he introduced me to 'Dark As A Dungeon'". When he formed a band of his own, McDonald told *Folk Roots* that at first he toyed with the name Country Mao And The Fish before changing it to Joe, after Stalin: "I thought that sounded more like a jug band." Country Joe's greatest gift is as a storyteller in song, whether about the sinister Martha Lorraine or quiet days in Clichy. He also drew the best out of his like, whether the poet Robert Service or Woody Guthrie, with whose music Joe grew up: "I made the Woody album during the time I was trying to split with the Fish. I wanted to make a simple record; a return-to-the-roots album."

He chose to do so in the Bradley Barn studios, just outside Nashville, and looked back in the company of John Tobler. "Those players didn't know a damned thing about Guthrie. Most of the players come from working-class Southern roots anyway, and they knew all the melodies, they just never heard those lyrics to them... The vehicles that he chose were country vehicles and those players just kicked butt." This was almost literally, in the case of session leader Grady Martin: "He was a total redneck. He tried to suck me in. He said 'so tell me Country Joe', right through the intercom – all the place could hear – 'You know where I can get any good marijuana?' And I said, 'I'm sorry, Mr Martin, I'm a stranger here myself, but maybe some of your friends know.' In his heart he hated me, because I was one of these new hippies and they were all traditionalists, but they played great."

After years of hippie jams, Joe was amazed by how "they swapped the leads in a way that rock players and folk singers don't do, which is to divide the verse up in little chunks", eight beats of guitar, then eight of piano and eight of banjo. "They were used to cramming all this into two and a half minutes. It was very impressive." It wasn't quite as impressive, though, when a black man came into the studio and hardly dared to speak.

Over in LA, The Doors were never folksy, although Jim Morrison comes close to country sentimentality on 'Orange County Suite'. His vision of America was essentially a mythic one, stuffed with the ghosts of dead Indians and poems urging the listener to re-invent the gods. His 'Riders On The Storm' have legs rather than fetlocks, and Morrison underpins his vocal with a whisper, to ghostly effect. Another dissident bunch from the city of angels was Love, whose 'Singing Cowboy' is a warning, not a promise: "Got a lassoo in your hand, will you ever understand/it's a do or die, boy?" Arthur Lee fired his own gun in public once too often and received something close to a life sentence. Youthful pranks look less jovial in middle age.

Back in San Francisco, Moby Grape had three lead guitarists, five harmony singers and Peter Lewis' C&W influence, which came through more clearly on later efforts like 1969's *Truly Fine Citizen*, recorded in Nashville. Central to the band was "demonic" Skip, the "maniacal core of the group" – in photos of the time he just looks cute and a little disorganised. He was responsible for the 1930s number 'Just Like Gene Autrey; A Foxtrot', which played at 78rpm. Quite what the singing cowboy had done to get a namecheck remains unclear – yet another example of the Americana imagery floating in the wind at this time, thanks to the collision between stoned minds and childhood memories.

There is a C&W clip-clop rhythm to Jerry Miller's short song which begins "Would you let me walk down your street naked if I want to?", although one can hardly imagine Johnny Cash singing such words – he would just do it. Skip Spence finally went over the top when he threatened Don Stevenson with a fire axe, and was committed to Bellevue mental hospital for six months. As his intended victim put it: "He was a visionary, and what happened was he broke through. And part of him didn't want to compromise, come back and rejoin the rest of us." So off he went to Nashville in late 1968, once discharged, and recorded *Oar*.

As to Moby Grape, the sleeve notes to the indispensible double CD *Vintage* – which sorts out the wheat from the chaff of this frustratingly uneven band – describe

Moby Grape '69 as a return to basics, "gussied up with nothing more than church bell guitar twang and fresh mountain-air harmonies". As always, country music comes galloping to the rescue of a band in trouble, like the US cavalry. One track, which was unreleased at the time but which hints at the ambience of these sessions, was 'Big', with the lyrics "They called me a weener, I called them a nerd/I called her a whore, and she called me a turd", along with a "yippee" in the chorus and hillbilly accents. The CD booklet calls it "a prairie camp-fire chorus".

Then powerhouse singer Bob Moseley ran away to join the marines and fight in Vietman (Merle would have been proud), while the remaining trio laid down the aforementioned *Truly Fine Citizen*, a great album in embryo but destined to remain forever unfinished. The band split up a few weeks later, and have sporadically reformed ever since. Moby Grape are one of those bands which you can never quite pin down, thank goodness. The cop on the front cover of *Truly Fine Citizen* – fat and threatening, just like the one whom James Dickey plays in the film of his novel *Deliverance* – was actually a security guard at a CBS studio in Nashville, the same one in which Dylan invented this kind of music in the first place. Far from being some kind of redneck fascist, he guarded them when they wished to smoke dope for inspirational purposes, "which we thought was a truly fine thing to do". So what at first looks deeply ironic is in fact deeply meant. Just like the Grape's finest music, as it happens.

Skip Spence was paddling his canoe down a far rockier river. I remember seeing Greil Marcus' rave review of *Oar* in *Rolling Stone* and then spending over 20 years trying to track down a copy. Until the 1988 Edsel reissue, it was an extremely rare artefact, even on the psychedelic collector's market, having sold a pitiful amount at the time. Marcus would make a good share tipster, having pointed out in his review that "someday it'll be as rare as 'Memories Of El Monte'," which Frank Zappa wrote for The Penguins. The problem is that doo-wop obscurity was but a career opener for that ultimate cynic, whereas this marked the creative end-point of the gentler, more spiritually inclined Spence. Marcus is right on the button, though, when he describes *Oar* as being "like the sort of haphazard folk music that might have been made around campfires after the California gold rush burned itself out – sad, clumsy tunes that seem to laugh at themselves".

Just listen to 'Cripple Creek', in which an ancient song is updated, through "streams of fire", and is now both "daydream" and modern legend. Through Skip's weird inner alchemy the song now possesses the stamp of reality, just as the dying man leaves "his wheelchair spinning deeper in the mud". For Greil, Spence's songs for Moby Grape sounded like musical versions of street fights, but here things are "quiet and insinuating…music that has much the same tone to it as Dylan's basement tape…Real music, not someone's half-baked idea of where it's at." Marcus deserves huge bonus points for having taken the trouble to listen to this groundbreaking album so carefully, when most people either ignored it or actively stepped away from it, like drivers swerving around a dead dog in the middle of the road.

As things go, you can now hardly move for CD reissues and musical tributes, while the album has more influence – and sounds fresher – than many multi-million selling acts of the time. America's own Syd Barrett captures just the same kind of fractured logic and ambient musical landscapes without the benefit of any musician other than himself, and thus captures the essence of old-time music better than a whole aviary of Eagles.

Skip sings with everything from a deep croak – like Lee Marvin on largactyl – to a comical pride on 'Lawrence Of Euphoria', always slightly out of tune. Officially diagnosed as a paranoid schizophrenic (the US war casualties of the late Sixties were not all in Vietnam), Columbia were generous enough to give him six days of recording time in that same Nashville studio – one can't imagine any such corporation nowadays giving such a person such a chance. The latest *Oar* reissue contains ten tracks recorded on that final day, though nothing compares to the spectral drone of 'Grey/Afro', which is about the furthest from country music that anything recorded in Nashville has ever gone. At one point, it sounds like he's playing the digeridoo. The last words on the final two-track reel are Skip's "We're out of tape? Did I just run out? Okay…"

Just like with the later musings of Syd, one wonders how much the cult which has arisen around this album is essentially voyeuristic, watching a man's last glimmers of sanity drown in the encircling darkness. Skip himself doesn't seem aware that anyone is listening. However, there is something everlasting in the record he laid down so quickly, just as the Sixties dream began to sour. In his time of madness, Skip provides a kind of ghostly commentary to *John Wesley Harding*, recorded in the same place a year before. As Peter Doggett points out, both "were baleful admirers of Johnny Cash, whose baleful presence seems to inhabit several songs cut during the presence", deconstructing his one-two rhythm while the out-take 'Furry Heroine (Halo Of Gold)' "dips in and out of 'I Walk The Line'". 'Weighted Down' is pure Cash, a man's slow lament of being encumbered by his gun and sinfulness. It's the kind of music which, once heard, one can never forget, much as one might wish to.

Shortly after Spence's death in 1999, a tribute album, *More Oar*, was released, with the likes of Beck and Alejandro Esccoveda providing sympathetic covers. The cover shot, of the original sleeve photo in negative, was peculiarly effective. With Skip now literally a ghost, it looks like him having the last chuckle. The madcap laughs. Even singers like Robert Plant or Robyn Hitchcock – less readily associated with this kind of music – are able to perform the act of self-abnegation necessary to recreate such odd songs sympathetically. It is – let's admit it – a much better listening experience than the original album, but less emotionally devastating. For example, Jay Farrer interprets the folk blues 'Weighted Down' much more professionally but loses its funereal sadness and Skip's stoned, dying croak. Buy both.

Another maverick on the edge, but one comfortably closer to genius than madness, was Captain Beefheart, from California's Mojave Desert. He called *Trout Mask*

Replica, his greatest creation, "bush music". To achieve it, he dismembered the "fascist" rhythm of rock music, as well as afterthoughts like harmony, and then put them back together again, in much the same style as the avante-garde painter that he is now. Music being a largely democratic art, to achieve this he had to half starve his Magic Band and virtually hold them hostage. The result is the wildest Appalachian music crossed with dirt blues and free jazz. Unrepeatable, thank goodness.

After a privately-produced EP, which contains Lawrence Hammond's song 'Orange Fire' (about napalm) and is now one of the most precious artefacts of the whole psychedelic era, Mad River went on to make the edgiest album of even those strange times. Matters weren't helped when the initial pressing was accidentally speeded up. Appropriately enough, 'Amphetamine Gazelle' starts with a speed freak's babbling before Hammond's keening wail of a voice cuts like a scalpel, and by the time we reach the horror story of 'War Goes On', it's been like a crash-course in Sixties culture, with titles such as 'High All The Time' and 'Eastern Light', a song about making love during the daytime which starts with the unanswerable question "Where does the sun come from, and where does it go?" Bognor, maybe. The twin lead guitars boil to a climax, as does Hammond when he proposes marriage.

Lawrence sounds in pain throughout, and on his Vietnam epic he conjures up a grisly picture indeed. Odd scrapings follow (this is the kind of record where the drummer is also credited with playing "fence and worms"), then atonal guitars snap into a brisk beat, and Hammond tells the story of a 15-year-old girl tethered in a truck, "her hair tied to her knees". After one of the wildest West Coast guitar solos ever unleashed, Lawrence returns to find birds picking the veins from her hands "like they were worms". He props her upright in a cornfield "to scare away the crows, I guess". Try listening to that on LSD! The album ends with a brief lullabye, which is just as well.

You may well have guessed by now that such things could only come to one brought up on bluegrass and folk music and who later sought mental consolation in sweet country sounds. Hammond grew up in Nebraska, and as a teenager was a keen fan of bluegrass combo The Blue Southern Ramblers, whom he saw "in a ragged honky tonk". As he told John Platt, he would place his face right up against their instruments and mutter: "I wonder, how d'you do that?" Later he became a folk singer in Greenwich Village, first opening for Jesse Colin Young and later duetting with the likes of Mike Seeger, who is becoming the secret hero of this book. Hammond even went on to study at Antioch College, where The Lost City Ramblers were then based.

He says, without any understatement, that the first Mad River album became "a juggernaut that was out of control" – and we're not talking about sales figures here. One day, as he leafed through a pile of Merle Haggard albums, he realised how much he preferred those kinds of songs to those which he was writing for his own band. On their second album, produced by his old friend Jerry Corbitt, "the most noticeable thing is the shift away from the long acidy tracks of the first album to a much more relaxed country-ish feeling", and *Paradise Bar And Grill* even features poet Richard Brautigan relaying downhome truths. Hammond later went solo, backed by The Whiplash Band, and then returned to bluegrass. There aren't many veins like worms here, but however oddly mutated and twisted, his quavery singing and startling words have that high, lonesome feeling in spades. He does advocate marriage, after all. His solo album *Coyote's Dream* is such that each song "tells a story on its own". This is no human carrion, though.

The Beau Brummels had started as shameless Beatles' copyists before going on to record some near-perfect West Coast harmony pop, and with *Bradley's Barn* took a desperate last throw of the dice by going to record in Nashville. The famous studios are converted to a real hay store on the cartoon front cover but are rural enough in real life, 28 miles out of town. The wildly over-optimistic sleeve notes refer to this album as marking the place where "what future generations may refer to as The Bradley's Barn Sound happened to pop music". Dream on.

True, some of the future Area Code 615 are on board for this largely acoustic delight, but to claim it as an important coming-together of "second generation young men" from Tennessee and California is a little rich, while "new music to help us all touch and hear and see" is definitely over the top. More realistic is the description of Sal Valentino as "looking Cherokee in a country where it's safer to look paleface", or stories of Ron Elliott learning guitar from country records but copying both lead and rhythm at once, as if both had been produced by the same player. No wonder Wayne Moss and friends were amazed to watch him at work.

The Youngbloods formed on the East Coast, although they never needed to go to Nashville because country music flowed deep in their veins, and what they did with it was quite unique. First, Jesse Colin Young – in his own words a "middle-of-the-road ethnic folk singer" living on the Lower East Side – teamed up with Jerry Corbitt, who was a bluegrass guitarist who had moved to Cambridge, Massachusetts, from his native Georgia. Then they met Lowell Levinger, a long-haired loon who renamed himself Banana, and who also had a bluegrass background but now played electric piano (and played it better than anyone else in rock, in my own biased opinion). With jazz drummer Joe Bauer, they started off playing good-time music, with a residency at the Cafe Au Go Go. RCA signed them up, but the company was then unsure in which direction to push them. As Jesse later told John Tobler: "I mean, we weren't Eddie Arnold or Elvis Presley, so they were a bit stumped." Tired of the slums of New York and seduced by the California ballrooms they shed Corbitt, moved west and recorded *Elephant Mountain*, 13 songs of freedom, as magnificent an album as rock music has ever produced.

Mysterious and welcoming, with lots of studio chatter, the disc combines jazz, country, bluegrass and white soul into one seamless whole, with Young's seductive, relaxed vocals poured like hot fudge over the top. The way he sings 'Quicksand' can break your heart. Songs break down, literally, and then pick themselves up off the floor. The downhome sloppiness only points up the razor-sharp interaction of the band, like men released from prison. Later studio outings became a trifle too relaxed, but this is an album in which the city and the country are held in perfect balance.

In exactly the same way, the cover painting depicts the three-piece band playing in an open field, with a bird their only audience and the aforementioned mountain behind them, and with bread and honey spread over an adjacent wall. The photo collage on the back shows the other side of this idyll, strewn with rural clutter and with Jesse buried alive in some kind of sump hole.

The band reach their free-flowing zenith and rode the wind on two live albums, one recorded on either side of the USA. By this time they were relaxed enough to revisit their roots: 'Sugar Babe' is a distant relative of Dock Boggs' version, still tough enough to have the words "your body's going to shrivel, Mama, when you come to die".

Traditionally-based lyrics like this and 'Fiddler A Dram' – first recorded by Cecil Sharp – rub shoulders with much newer songs by Tim Hardin, Fred Neil, Chet Powers and members of the band. It all seems to fit together, extremely modest "white" music, with Young's voice apparently knowing no limit to its sense of vulnerability or desire. Sadly, individual releases on their own label, Raccoon, began to split the band back into its constituent parts (the bluegrass of Banana And The Bunch, along with a couple of free adverts for Jimmy Martin and the jazzy noodlings of *Crab Tunes And Noggins*), as did their live set, which was now dividing itself into separate portions of rock, country and jazz, where before all three had been jumbled up together.

Two studio albums followed, largely comprised of cover versions, and then it was goodnight. Their swan song, *High On A Ridge Top*, has one of the finest record jackets ever – mountain beauty again – but not much going on inside. *Good And Dusty*, meanwhile, is a different kind of creature, a deliberate return to the old music which first inspired them, and with a more down-at-heel photo of the band set in a splintery wooden cabin. Everyone is smiling, and here are recorded the likes of 'Stagger Lee' and a delicate 'Will The Circle Be Unbroken?', alongside R&B classics. There's a lovely old-time feel to the music here, whether in the odd noodlings of the title track or in the casual precision of 'Let The Good Times Roll', which they really do.

One prominent track is Banana's answer in song to Merle Haggard's 'Hippie From Olema #5'. There's lots of good sense about the hippie lifestyle at its best, and an underlying good humour in lines like: "We still wear our hair long like folks used to, and we bathe often, therefore we don't smell." Here are people who don't hate blacks, who take in strangers if they're ragged – or "haggard" in the final chorus – and can't think of anyone to hate. So who is the truer American citizen, Banana or Merle? (I wonder what Mr Levinger is doing these days – he's too good to lose.) Another highlight is Young singing his heart out on 'Circus Face', while new member Michael

Kane plays mournful French horn and Banana picks at a banjo, bringing things full circle. Here is the same kind of innate majesty as The Band, who were also about to hit artistic free-fall. Jesse breaks out into a laugh at the end, despite everything.

Merle Haggard, Mel Tillis, Jimmie Rodgers, Hank Williams and the public domain all turn up on the composers' lists of an extremely odd album by The Blue Ridge Rangers, five men in silhouette. They all look even closer than siblings, which is true enough – they are all John Fogerty, no less, Mr Creedence Clearwater Revival himself. Despite his huge sales, he was never a comfortable part of the San Francisco scene, too blue collar and too genuine a poet among a crowd of imposters. His music always kicked like a mule, but it had previously been closer to swamp-rock than country music, ancient or modern. Here playing every instrument like Michael Oldfield in a stetson, he embraces the art form as a whole, stripping it back to its primal growl and thump.

Banjo and yee-haws open proceedings, and John has swapped his swamp slur for a hillbilly twang. Hailing from California, Fogerty's teen band, The Golliwogs, had played every two-bit bar and honky tonk in the state, and so claiming affinity with the Blue Ridge Mountains is a little rich, but Fogerty doesn't so much cover the song as inhabit it. He's even better on the gospel songs, testifying as if desperate. One critic compared it to Leon Russell's C&W album *Hank William's Back*, illustrated by just that body part: "It has sometimes been left to children of rock 'n' roll to rediscover the power of the best C&W."

Fogerty does a good George Jones impression, to a jog trot and seemingly disconnected from the words, howling like a wolf with its paw in a trap. His Merle Haggard is even better, and 'Today I Started Loving You Again' is a slowed-down exercise in self-pity which sheds blood.

As was increasingly becoming the case, musicians started using country like a chef uses seasonings, adding to taste. Serpent Power were an outgrowth of the San Francisco poetry scene, a band playing baroque folk rock, and their debut album ends with the 13-minute-long 'Endless Tunnel', a ghost-train ride with oriental sounds on the organ and JP Pickens on electrified five-string banjo. It gradually picks up speed like, well, a runaway train: "Mr Conductor, where are we going?" "I don't know, I'm just following the tracks." David Meltzer, who wrote those deathless words, joined his sweet-voiced wife – Tina, their lead singer – on *Poet Song*, which includes the one-minute poem 'Lamentation For Hank Williams', all the best lines of which come directly from the master: "There's no dreams but bad ones." Meltzer obviously thinks he's doing Hank a favour merely by writing about him, which is his first mistake. One minute? Surely the man deserves a couple of hours, at the very least!

There are all kinds of sidelights on C&W. The Steve Miller Band review past metaphors for their male allure – gangsters of love, and the like – and then settle on being space cowboys to keep on top of things: "Bet you weren't ready for that." On an album ironically entitled *Brave New World*, they realise that life is getting tougher as the Sixties come to an end. Sly Stone's *There's A Riot Going On* is also about the increasingly violent backcloth to the play of love. Here is a man who worked as sound engineer on Autumn records, when they were recording early psych, now singing the likes of 'Luv N'Haight' and 'Spaced Cowboy'. With the latter, we're back in the funky soundscape of The Alabama 3, but this time with a manic yodel thrown in on top and some harmonica straight out of Area Code 615. The next track is a vacuous parody of Burt Bacharach, with the album as a whole a picture of a culture in free fall. Even the title track is a wind-up: it doesn't exist.

Meanwhile, the next generation was coming through. Johnny Ciambotti had started his career playing bass with bluegrass act The Valley Boys, who had a residency at the Ash Grove playing alongside The Kentucky Colonels. He jumped ship for San Francisco, met John McFee and founded Clover, a perky bunch who sang songs about lizards playing rock 'n' roll and the track 'Chicken Butt', which became their theme song. After recording two albums for Fantasy, they spent five years in the wilderness before re-emerging in England just as punk was starting to rear its ugly head. They did for country music what The Flamin' Groovies did for rock 'n'roll, kicking it up the backside and refusing to take it too seriously while staking their very lives on playing it.

Texas also proved to be a seed bed for the next musical wave. *Take Me To The Mountains* by Shiva's Headband features electric violin and heartfelt lyrics about trading cement for trees, while on the back cover a man literally drowns in concrete. It's an album all about homesickness: "I Don't Hate California, but it's not my style." On the front cover, a crack in the sky reveals armadillos as far as the eye can see. Ten years later you could replace them with deep-voiced, country-style singer/songwriters in the Texan mould. There are just too many to count. The armadillo was by now a mascot of Austin and all who lived there: resilient and armour-plated but sensitive inside.

It was a town which had earlier sired Roky Erickson and his band The Thirteenth Floor Elevators: "It was sort of like being in Jesse James' gang. We had the cops after us wherever we went." Their meagre output appeared on the International Artists label, run by Lelan Rogers. Only in Austin could IA acid rock bands like Bubble Puppy appear on the same bill as Willie Nelson, who had moved there from Nashville. Lelan also produced his brother Kenny Roger's first hit, the quasi-psychedelic 'Just Dropped In (To See What Condition My Condition Was In)'. The Elevators, on the other hand, were so psychedelic that they set off as young men on a "quest for pure sanity" and got lost somewhere along the way. On *Bull Of The Woods*, Erikson performed his own mournful take on 'May The Circle Be Unbroken', sounding like a ghost singing. He repeats the title phrase over and over again, sad but hopeful, as he waves goodbye to his mind. On later albums, after extensive ECT, Roky inhabits a twilight world of Appalachian myth, but now folk tales have been replaced by cheap horror movies from the 1950s. It's fun at first, but...

Doug Sahm, born to German-American parents and a singing prodigy, was an altogether more cheerful creature, actually appearing onstage with Hank Williams at Austin's Skyline club in 1952. As he told Ed Ward, Hank "was wasted. He was so skinny he had to perform sitting down, so they made me get up on his lap...his legs were so bony they were hurting my ass." After a spell of pretending to be English with The Sir Douglas Quintet, featuring Augie Meyers on Vox organ, he went solo and became a regular at legendary venues like the Armadillo World Headquarters, as well as helping to launch Roky Erickson back to an expectant world.

Doug was the spirit of western swing personified – always good for a polka – and as a teenager he received encouragement from no less a figure than Adolph Hofner. He later reformed The Sir Douglas Quintet with two of his sons, one of whom went on to join The Meat Puppets. The circle is, indeed, unbroken.

Sahm put out a huge range of material, good-natured in the extreme, and if nothing is quite essential then nothing is fully dispensible either. His refusal to leave Texas for very long, after that first initial foray to Sixties San Francisco, led to sporadic gigs and one-off albums, which is hardly the route for riches and fame. My personal favourites include 'Texas Rock For Country Rollers', with songs like the lustful 'Cowboy Peyton Place' (in which the steel guitar is an aphrodisiac), and the sleazy blues of 'You Just Can't Hide A Redneck (Under That Hippie Hair)'. As if to further confuse his audience, he appeared under all kinds of nicknames; *The Return Of Doug Saldaa* is so titled because it was a name "the Mexicans gave me. They said I had so much Mexican in me that I needed a Mexican name."

Groover's Paradise sees him team up with the Creedence Clearwater rhythm section on a Tex-Mex trip. This is music which sounds just like lying in bed, and there's a great cartoon cover with lots of armadillos and even more in-jokes – "Austintatious", like the sleeve says. Doug is ready to board the tour bus, The Furry Freak Brothers are at the wheel, and there's a steel guitar and brass section on the soundtrack – paradise indeed. High, but never lonesome. In the early 1980s, Sahm and Meyers reunited and moved briefly to Scandinavia. Shortly before his death in 1999, Sahm formed The Last Real Texas Blues Band, although the blues were only part of his musical palette. You won't see his like again.

Much of what came to be known as that strange hybrid country rock can be traced back to Buffalo Springfield and the nightly guitar duels between Stephen Stills and Neil Young. It's a rivalry which has lasted, to great mutual benefit. Again, the band has folk roots, and openly celebrate their country influences on the back cover of their second album, paying tribute to Doc Watson, Hank Williams and The Dillards. Richie Furay began his working life in Greenwich Village, briefly joining Stephen Stills in The Au Go Go Singers – we're not talking strict authenticity here: "It was built to a formula: two girl singers, a deep bass voice, plunky banjos, tuneful folk standards and a little choreography." Stills then joined The Bay Singers, a touring version of much the same, and during a Canadian tour he met Neil Young, who ran a mile from such a musical straitjacket, and has been running ever since.

Among Neil's settler ancestors were a revivalist preacher and a fiddle-playing farmer. He formed a teenage band, The Squires, and then re-invented himself as a Dylanesque acoustic singer. Stills called Ritchie over to LA to help him put together a band with rock flash and folk subtlety. Independently, Neil Young and bassist Bruce Palmer drove Neil's trademark hearse down to LA, where there was a mythical meeting on Sunset Boulevard. With one-time Dillards drummer Dewey Martin, Buffalo Springfield – named after a steamroller company – were complete. Here were three elements of the Wild West, as it happened. They supported The Byrds at the Orange County Fairground in April 1966, blew them offstage, then settled into legendary status during a residency at the Whiskey Go Go.

David Downing described how the rivalry between Stills and Young manifested itself into what they wore onstage, which centred on yet more Americana: "Stills was the manic blond cowboy, sometimes in Confederate guise, while Young had become the brooding Indian." It's an image which fed directly into Young's song 'Broken Arrow', and more generally into images of darkness and paranoia and defeat. Throughout Young's career, the country – and country music – has always been a refuge, but also a place from which to then escape, while the city is a place of increasing violence but also excitement. Years later, 'Mirror Ball' took him back to the psychedelic ballrooms of Buffalo Springfield at its height. The downfall of the hippie dream is another obsession. When Furay sang Neil's lines "city lights at a county fair/never shine but always glare" on the first Springfield album, it brought a new note into rock music, beautifully precise but oddly unsettling.

Stills brought country sounds into the band, in particular on his song 'Go And Say Goodbye', and there's a twang to the singing, a yearning quality to that peerless first album. It all sounds too serious to be pop music. A sense of impending chaos is encapsulated in the opening track, 'For What It's Worth'. Here are sad songs, about failure and impotence, performed with a sweetness and a delicacy at odds with their more splenetic live gigs of the time. On *Buffalo Springfield Again*, banjo leads us back into Stills' last vocal on 'Bluebird' after a duel between lead guitars, while Furay edges closer still to country on 'A Child's Claim To Fame', with James Burton on dobro. The scraps and tatters of *Last Time Around* include Richie's 'Kind Woman', which is C&W in all but name – it could almost be Gram Parsons. Poco starts here. When Buffalo Springfield split asunder, the sparks flew everywhere.

At the Monterey Festival, David Crosby – then still with The Byrds – temporarily took Neil's place in the band, and Crosby, Stills And Nash were just a thought away. A mysterious solo debut saw Young looking back to his origins ("I used to be a folk singer keeping managers alive") and forward via the past on ambient orchestral pieces like 'String Quartet From Whiskey Boot Hill'. Like Robbie Robertson, his view of Americana is skewed from coming from North of the border, which makes it all the more penetrating. The songs are those of a recluse, lost in luxuriant backings, courtesy of Jack Nitzsche, and the Poco rhythm section. His own voice is buried deep in the mix, as if he's trying not to be there at all. Like the sleeve design, Young is in a country landscape, but he still reflects the city inside.

This strange, dream-like atmosphere also seeped into the quieter sections of *Everyone Knows This Is Nowhere*. '(When You're On) The Losing End' is a country hoedown from which all the joy and life have been leached away, leaving only pain – his voice is speeded up like a chipmunk on the line "all right, this is different", leading into the break. Bobby Notkoff's spooky fiddle on 'Running Dry' and Robin Lane's haunting vocal on 'Round And Round' both have a country melancholy, bordering on melancholia. His new backing band have been renamed after an Indian chief, and they seem to have opened up Neil, both emotionally and musically. On the sleeve, he's out in the wilderness with his favourite dog and a clad in a lumberjack shirt, and the two long guitar workouts are imbued with the spirit of the Wild West: a gunshot slaying in 'Down By The River' and also a cowgirl's lament. By the time CS&N got to Woodstock, Neil Young was on board as well. His brooding 'Country Girl', on *Déjà Vu* (with its cover pose from the Civil War), took orchestral country to a new peak.

What he had already established was the template for alt country. It says everything that the tribute CD *This Note's For You, Too!* is a double, and still feels like the merest surface sweep. The bands chosen here – Slobberbone, Big In Iowa, The Golden Watusis and so many others – are themselves impossible to categorise. Neil's greatest legacy is his refusal to stay put. Even so, where his followers have tended to choose one thematic strand or the other – whether luxuriantly-arranged self-absorption or strange mythological narratives set to wild guitars – Young had already encompassed both. He continues to swing between the two, pedal steels one year and the sonic assault of *Weld* the next, taking vocoders, grunge and the Gulf War in his stride.

By that same token, Crosby, Stills And Nash still plough the same furrow, individually and collectively. Unlike Young, the wild card in their pack, they use country music as a colouring rather than as a spur for creativity. This is largely true of many other bands now pigeonholed as country rock, and as pleasant as their work still sounds we can deal with them quickly.

Richie Furay is now the pastor of a non-denominational Christian church (after another country rocker, Al Perkins, led him to the Lord), but looks back on Poco as more influential even than Buffalo Springfield. Also on board were Jim Messina, from the last Springfield line-up; future Eagle Randy Meisner; and Rusty Young, who "began playing pedal steel in about 1959. At the time, because it was a brand new instrument, there were no instructors. The only way to learn was to experiment with it." He took lessons in music theory from a jazz pianist and transposed what he learned. The new band debuted during "Hoot Night" at the LA Troubadour, played five songs, "and just blew the place apart".

In a bizarre case of record company politics, Atlantic and Epic swapped Graham Nash and Poco in a double transfer deal. *Pickin' Up The Pieces* still has a wonderful freshness, with pretty pedal steel played through a Leslie speaker to give it sustain, along with harmonious singing, Furay's pure tenor voice and even the odd banjo solo. This is good-time music with an acoustic/electric mix, and I love it dearly, but even so, somehow it's all play acting. Appropriately, the inner sleeve is drawn from Hollywood Westerns – a cowboy sings to the moon inside a lariat – and opens with a poem set to music. Country music is about togetherness, "picnic lunches' and happy folk "pickin' and a-grinnin'". Tell that to Dock Boggs. To be fair, Ritchie reckoned that "Jimmy made the group more country than I had ever envisaged it. I wanted it more rock 'n' roll." Messina had learned his trade from studio musicians like Joe Osborne, and the country pop here fed back into the Nashville machine, with the youthful joy here siphoned off and thrown away.

It all could have been so different. Rusty told *Omaha Rainbow* that, when he first got to LA, "there were a lot of little bunches of people getting together", and one of these was the original conjunction between Gene Clark and Doug Dillard with a string bassist and Bernie Leadon: "They had their band together and they were going to be real bluegrassy. The record was so different. I was disappointed because it didn't have the magic that the little tapes they made in their house did. Boy, that was the closest thing to what I would consider country rock that I have heard, ever, and it's never made it to a record." Poco themselves played soft-rock with rustic accents, never better than on 1972's *A Good Feeling To Know*, on which the music forms a counterpart to the copperplate lettering on the sleeve, warm and ornate and slightly antique.

1974's *Live* separates the two elements, with country on one side, with a fine banjo and steel duet on 'Foggy Mountain Breakdown', and with rock on the other, driven by guitarist Paul Cotton. It all comes together on 'Rose Of Cimarron', which has dobro at the beginning and banjo at the end, with a Hollywood orchestra and guitar pyrotechnics between but with no rough edges anywhere. It's very palatable, but somehow castrated. The likes of Loggins and Messina smoothed this down further into mellow inanities. This way for John Denver.

A band much closer to the original mountain music was Kaleidoscope, who mixed and matched bluegrass, cajun and Cab Calloway. This was world music years before its time, in which violin and dobro mesh with oud and bouzouki, played with a spirit which belongs totally to the Sixties. Chris Darrow was the journeyman of the band: "My job was…to pull it all together." The folk boom had driven him to explore deeper, and hearing a record by Earl Taylor And His Stony Mountain Boys changed his life: "That band sent me into outer space, especially the mandolin sound, which just tinkled my brain." Darrow formed The Re-Organised Dry City Players, and these merged into David Lindley's Mad Mountain Ramblers into a kind of Claremount supergroup.

Frank Zappa and John Stewart were around town at the time, which makes you wonder quite what this revival fuelled in fields far removed from mountain music. Certainly The Mothers Of Invention have a wildness and weird humour about them which could well draw on old-time music. As for The Ramblers: "Our favourite group at that time was The Country Gentlemen. They were one of the few bluegrass groups with a style of their own. We were getting into some pretty avante-garde stuff ourselves...hot bluegrass with old-timey music thrown in."

Fenrus Epp – aka Max Buda, aka Chester Crill – was even odder than his name(s), and joined from The Indestructible Old-Timey String Band. Lindley, a lead guitarist and fiddle player, had just left The Rodents, Beatles' copyists of the direst stripe. As we have seen, he was also a champion banjo player, and joined Richard Greene in The Dry City Scat Band. Solomon Feldthouse, meanwhile, was a beatnik who lived in a garage: "It was like seeing a phoenix rise from the ashes to see him get out of his bed," Epp told an incredulous Mac Garry. "He had this cardboard-coloured skin and no eyes when he first woke up." He was either a gypsy or Jewish or a flamenco dancer, depending in which legend you believed. He would also bring his own troupe of belly dancers to liven up out-of-town gigs. I think we're starting to get a flavour of what these guys were like, and it certainly wasn't The Eagles.

Their music was made to match, comprising long, far-Eastern jams interspersed with fiery psychedelia and old-time Americana. Somehow, it all makes sense. *Side Trips* follows a weird drug song like 'Pulsating Dream', sounding like The Byrds flying supersonic, with the truly sombre 'Oh Death'. A fiddle scrapes, percussion sounds like clods of earth dropping on a coffin, and a man pleads for his very soul: "Oh death, can't you spare me over for another year?" 'Egyptian Gardens' suddenly veers from harem music to a banjo-led jig from the Appalachians. This is timeless stuff. 'Please' was covered twice by the English folk rock band Eclection, the second time with the honorary black Appalachian Dorris Henderson as lead singer. Throw in the old-style delights of 'Hesitation Blues' and 'Minnie The Moocher' and you have 26 minutes or so of aural dislocation, with the band looking like a cross between The Bonzos and a string band from the hills. They sound that way, too.

A Beacon From Mars was even stranger, with the Celtic folk of 'Greenwood Sidee', Lindley's arrangement of 'Baldheaded End Of A Broom' back from his Dry City Scat Band days, and the swinging cajun of Doug Kershaw's 'Louisiana Man'. The title track is a variant on 'Smokestack Lightning', which sounds like it's just about to blow up into a psychedelic freak-out when it quietens down and slows to a near halt, before growing extremely sinister. There are fiddles everywhere, even on the far-Eastern improvisation 'Taxim'.

Finest of all is their third album, *Incredible*. The band had immersed themselves in folk music for a year, building up to an appearance at Newport, and so 'Petite Fleur' is a cajun song – in French, of course – which breaks into a barn dance.

After snatch of lusty laughter worthy of Sid James we're into the echoing 'Banjo', a virtuoso instrumental. Flip sides, then, and 'Cuckoo' – a traditional song also found on the Harry Smith *Anthology* – has never been performed with such a heavy electric thump, sung with such venom, or ornamented with so liquid a West Coast solo. The third verse brings things around to Vietnam, and past and present coalesce. Then a bitter laughter and lights out.

Kaleidoscope reformed in 1976 with *When Scopes Collide*, mixing cowboy songs – like a tough, no-nonsense 'Ghost Riders In The Sky' – with songs like the traditional 'Man Of Constant Sorrow', as sad as a wasted life. Lindley was gone for good, but he continues to come at you out of left field. A recent CD taped in Japan, with just electric guitar and drums, ploughs through cajun, trad folk and ethnic material, seemingly sung by a werewolf. He moved to England for a couple of years, and then joined Jackson Browne, but he keeps his Appalachian experiments separate. To quote the *Rough Guide*, he still makes "weird music for the non-conformist mind" when playing solo.

Chris Darrow hides behind a mask of himself on *Under My Own Disguise*, recorded on both sides of the Atlantic, but there's no hiding the warmth of his particular take on country rock. He sings along with his fiddle on 'Old Scratch', "a song about the Devil", with synth weaving in at the end. In the previous year he had run the gamut, recording with the reggae band Greyhound, with Breton harpist Alan Stivell, and with Shirley Collins, complete with a medieval consort, as well as with members of The Elton John Band and Fairport Convention. Only Darrow could pull off that combination at the time, let alone make it all so amiably relaxed and yet likely to chill you to the bone just when you were least expecting it. Later albums were merely bland in comparison.

This is also a charge sometimes levelled at Michael Nesmith, who escaped from The Monkees to pioneer a sweet form of country rock, with only a small cult audience for his pains. Nesmith played a mix of folk and country under the name Michael Blessing, even before he put on his woolly hat and acted the John Lennon figure in teen TV. *Mojo* makes the frightening suggestion that he might have beaten Gram Parsons to inventing country rock, and so "the majority of Americana bands would be Nesmith-cheery, effortless and good-natured". The Eagles captured the big bucks from this same approach, at God-knows-what cost to their souls. It was a style which ended up exerting more of an influence on the likes of Travis Tritt rather than, say, Wilco.

Although I enjoy Nesmith's music (who couldn't?), particularly as a pleasant background burr, I find his views of greater interest still. The sage of The Monkees is still working things out. While still a small furry primate, Mike recorded 'Listen To The Band' in Nashville with a studio bunch who later became Area Code 615. As he told *Zigzag*: "I've had good success in putting together bands. Area Code 615 was the first I ever tried." But weren't they there already? He discovered early that Nashville session men play by the clock, "ten-to-one and two-to-five, they go in, they pick, leave for lunch, come back, pick, go home to dinner, come back, pick, and that's it. The wealth of Nashville musicians is like the economic base of a nation in Africa."

Perhaps as a result, his own albums were recorded in LA and built around local pedal steel hero "Red" Rhodes: "He has the velvet touch." California and Tennessee represent the two extremes of country music; they "are left and right politically and emotionally. LA has a carefree 'dance all night' attitude, whereas Nashville is very matriarchal, all about roots, family and 'Stand By Your Man'." His first album with The First National Band, *Magnetic South*, still sounds amazingly fresh, right down to its "short intermission…while you turn the record over", with Nesmith's light vocals over a sprightly backing sounding live in the studio, playful and even cuddly.

He brings a country twang, with Red Rhodes adding a country whine to what is otherwise jovial soft rock. It's the kind of record that brings a smile to your face, disarming any criticisms with its sheer *joie de vivre*. 'Joanne' is the obvious highlight, sung in a lovely falsetto, but even that new song remains the kind of plaintive fare which could have been recorded in the Fifties. Then, towards the end of 'Hollywood', the whole thing becomes very strange, almost psychedelic. 'One Rose' follows, which is back to traditional Nashville, but as gorgeous as it is we somehow don't trust him any more. This is a man playing games, and we're not quite sure of the rules any more.

A clock ticks away on 'Beyond The Blue Horizon', a man yawns, a door slams, chickens cluck, a tractor starts up, a fiddle and pedal steel spark into life, a man hums, and then Nesmith comes in with a vocal so redolent of happiness that you feel like melting in his arms. This is one of the most enjoyable, enigmatic and cleanly-played albums in the whole of the country canon. Nesmith pays tribute to a "musical triumvirate": Hank Williams, Jerry Lee Lewis and Jimmie Rodgers. "Somehow I always get back to them." All three learned a way to sing to their audience directly, "free from euphemisms and alive with their own emotions". He thanks Chet Atkins, too, "who gave us strength".

Loose Salute is more of the same, self-written apart from his jogtrot version of Patsy Cline's 'I Fall To Pieces', sung without a trace of irony. Being Nesmith, the album opens with a song which brings a reggae beat (and accent) into country pop, but somehow that crystalline clarity of the first album is missing. It seems to have become an indulgence, not a passion, and then suddenly he's singing 'Conversations' as if his life depended on it, and there…are…weird gaps…between the…verses. 'Listen To The Band' starts very quietly and then grows louder, like it's coming in from another room, but it's still background music when it comes to full strength. Red revs up his pedal steel at one point, like a motorbike.

The band has been augmented with musicians from Elvis' Las Vegas combo (whom Emmylou Harris would later waylay) on *Nevada Fighter*, which completes the trilogy. "That was the idea, red, white and blue, colours of the flag, see?" Yes, but why does the previous cover show a general sitting on a rat, with a tail in just those colours? Especially one with a tri-partite tail?

The back cover here is an endless highway to distant hills, totally empty of traffic and with an incomprehensible poem by "Papa Nes" superimposed on it. The album is dedicated to International Harvesters – Neil, are you listening? – and the Navajo Indians. It is a brave move to open an album with 'Grand Ennui', which turns out to be a Dylanesque tale of escape, but it helps when you can follow it with perhaps your greatest song, 'Propinquity'. The band are back in focus, and this is Nesmith's greatest influence, seen at its best on later British pub rock bands like Deke Leonard's Iceberg and Help Yourself: tight but loose, light but funky. There's also more of Mike's heaven-sent falsetto on 'Here I Am'.

It seemed that Nesmith's inner wellspring was drying up, though, and this is confirmed by *Tantamount To Treason* (which describes this musical abortion accurately), which was credited to The Second National Band, with Jose Feliciano, no less, on congas. The recipe for home brew on the back mixes in details of the musicians, and 'Highway 99 With Melange' is the musical equivalent, a sub-John Cage cut-up followed by a witless narration. It's worse than the Monkees at their most unfunny, which is going some. Did brave settlers die for this? 'Bonaparte's Retreat', which opens to military drumming and Dillards-style vocal harmonies, is a song about fiddles playing an old English folk tune (with not a fiddle in earshot) and has the line about meeting a girl he "did see" rhyming with "down in Dixie". It ends with the inside of a piano being scraped – along with the bottom of a barrel, perhaps. I hereby award this song the most witless ever to use the Appalachian tradition as a launching point. Red Rhodes mimics a phone ringing on the next track, and I turned the record off at that point, never allowing it to darken my turntable again.

Maybe the Nesmith who winks at you under the cover of a cowboy hat on *Pretty Much Your Standard Ranch House Stash* knows something we don't. Do we have another Gene Clark on our hands, exploring the mysteries of the cosmos through country music? Having read Michael's verbal burblings on the inside cover, it's more likely that such music is what one critic called "affable cowboy fare", and nothing more. Try this for size: "Logic, which is probably one of the subtlest traps going…that whole two plus two trip…the logical development that leads to fear of anything outside itself." Billy Graham appears on bass and fiddle, but one presumes that this isn't the evangelist. The songs are back to Nesmith's maddening best, and really there's no one to touch him on a jovial strum with an ache at its heart. 'The Back Porch And A Fruit Jar Full Of Iced Tea' is eight minutes of back-porch heaven, combining the traditional recitation 'The FFV' – "his eyes were covered up with blood" – with Bill Monroe's song 'Uncle Pen'. All over again, Nesmith sounds like he means it.

It may be that, given his family wealth (not to mention a second fortune made as a pioneer of pop video), Michael really doesn't have to try that hard, or maybe he even tries too hard. Anything to avoid the fate of such rich kids as Gram Parsons, of whom he once said: "There's nothing left for them to do but just gorge themselves on excessive living. The closer they are to death, the better they feel about it."

This is the polar opposite of the poor Appalachian farmer, for whom danger is a way of life and one not asked for. Maybe more of The Monkees' pop gloss rubbed off on Nesmith's later work than he realised. As his sleeve note to the ironically-titled album *And The Hits Keep On Coming* – a semi-acoustic delight – puts it: "I have tried to make music as honest and beautiful as I know how…but I am afraid to admit that I did it for me." He sits in a weed-choked sitting room, surrounded by beautiful women (is he a Mormon?) and clutching a copy of *Bury My Heart At Wounded Knee*. The chorus of the first song could stand for a whole generation: "The closeness is gone."

The same words could equally apply to the singing career of Linda Ronstadt, but with a happy twist at the end. As she told Pete Frame: "I guess it all stems from my grandfather, who was a rancher and a self-taught musician" from Tucson. She still has his guitar, a "real old, beautiful Martin, with a rosewood back and an ebony fretboard".

Linda was heavily influenced by Mexican music – "I speak a little Spanish" – and formed a group, The New Union Ramblers, with her sister and brother, with whom she played at local coffee houses. She helped to bring Nesmith's songs to a wider audience, although she first heard 'Different Drum' via The Greenbriar Boys. With her first real band, The Stone Poneys, she was a pioneer of this new musical hybrid. "Apart from Hearts And Flowers and a few lesser-known groups, nobody was doing country rock, and I was sure it could cross over and take off, but nobody believed it except me." Literally a few weeks later, Gram Parsons joined The Byrds and the floodgates opened. "I used to see The Flying Burrito Brothers when they first started off", and she had known Clarence White since she was 16. A year later, she became a regular at LA's Ash Grove folk club, along with Ry Cooder, Taj Mahal and The Byrds. As she said later, it was an innocent time, and "all about sitting around in little embroidered dresses and listening to Elizabethan folk ballads".

Linda chose most of the songs for The Stone Poneys, and included several songs by the young Tim Buckley. 'Morning Glory' – which she called 'Hobo' – "was about our house, this groovy little beach house which I really loved". She moved out and he moved in, and wrote that haunted, magical song. The Stone Poneys' three albums are now very hard to find, and sound over-orchestrated to 21st-century ears, but Ronstadt's voice is crystalline – folk, rather than country – and utterly devastating. Her first solo album proper, 1969's *Hand Sown…Home Grown*, has Linda on the seashore and in front of a run-down cabin, with her trademark bare feet and looks of an angel. There's still too much orchestra, and a strange mix of singer/songwriter fare by Dylan, Fred Neil and Randy Newman even, but country rock peeps through on the likes of the exuberant 'The Only Mama That'll Walk The Line', with a wonderful fuzz guitar solo. Linda is starting to rock out.

Unlike up-and-coming rivals like Joni Mitchell, Rondstadt relies on outside songwriters, but John D Loudermilk's 'Break My Mind' punches harder than The Burritos ever did. With great pedal steel and bar-room piano, she sails over the lot without seeming to break sweat. 'We Need A Whole Lot More Of Jesus (And A Lot Less Rock And Roll)' is peerless, and you almost believe her. Linda is less queenly than Emmylou, and gets right into the material. *Silk Purse* saw her recording in Nashville, with Mel Tillis on the playlist, although the front cover, depicting Ronstadt posing prettily in a pig sty (no sexist slur intended – Pete Asher remembers her as always "an extremely determined woman") is bizarre. The rocking element has been toned down (Wayne Moss is listed as one of the recording engineers), and for once the sleeve notes are nothing less than accurate: "She can pounce on her music...dig Hank Williams' brand of blues and cry with Johnny Cash."

She can change the pace radically mid-song, like a champion racing driver, and without missing a beat. There are lots of fiddles, a straight country weepie in 'I'm Leaving It All Up To You', and the traditional song 'Life Is Like A Mountain Railway'. Here The Beechwood Rangers add mountain harmonies, and Ronstadt's voice has never sounded lovelier. Most impressive of all is the way in which she gets right under the skin of the more emotionally troubled products of what was then called "new country": Paul Siebel's mournful 'Louise', and 'He Dark The Sun' (as it is titled here) by Gene Clark and Bernie Leadon. It was prescient. As she told Joe Smith, one night at the Troubadour "I was on my way to the bathroom, during a hootenanny, and this band Shilo starts doing my exact version of of 'Silver Threads And Golden Needles'. I was flabbergasted. Shilo ultimately became The Eagles".

First, though, they became her backing band, and Bernie Leadon, Randy Meisner, Glenn Frey and Don Henley all played on her third solo album, self titled and more laid back than before. Moving to Asylum and being put under the charge of Peter Asher further smoothed down her initial wildness, and it was a formula which eventually gained her a million seller on 1974's *Heart Like A Wheel*. Blandness was encroaching, though, its nadir being her attempts to go new wave by covering Elvis Costello's 'Alison', complete with synths. It was a confirmation of everything that country buff Costello most hated in American culture.

It was also a role in which she did not seem comfortable, having too much of the real country spirit, which is difficult to confine into exact measures: "The Eagles backed me up, but I was the one who was inconsistent onstage. I could do a real good show in one town, and the next night would be like the first time I'd ever gotten up onstage. I was never comfortable doing what I'd done the night before. My roots are folk roots." Even when singing *The Pirates Of Penzance* on Broadway, or revisiting her childhood influences in *Canciones De Mi Padre (Songs Of My Father)*, she reveals that attribute of a truly great singer: of being able to throw herself emotionally in at the deep end and come up swimming. It's instructive to listen to her version of Dolly Parton's 'I Will Always Love You'. Compared with the more famous cover version by Whitney Houston, a funeral parlour favourite, Ronstadt understates the song, bringing in some country sadness, aching rather than braying.

The three greatest female voices in country music – Parton, Rondstadt and Emmylou Harris – began to get back to their roots with an acoustic band for *Trio*, and then the same again, with diminishing rates of success. This cleared the air for Dolly's return to bluegrass, and for Linda and Emmylou to record *Western Wall/The Tucson Sessions*, both of which projects took more risks. Harris waxes sexy, singing about being "the crack of dawn" (a million men stiffen at the thought), and then attempts to 'Raise The Dead', or Hank Williams and Bill Monroe, while Ronstadt broods on 'Falling Down'. As Phil Sutcliffe puts it, they both convey "through steady grace what old bluesmen do through weather and whiskey". *Folk Roots* uses it as a stick with which to beat the CMA Awards, from which nightmare memory nobody seems able to escape. Here is an antidote to all "that Nashville decadence…sheer awfulness…tacky, overblown presentation of underwhelming, often off-key performances by plastic caricatures… Against it even the excesses of Eurovision seems like good taste." Once started, though, he can't stop, going on to lambast the "bizarre" sequence in which The Dixie Chicks presided over a scene in which "big-legged line dancers in mini-kilts did a sort of Kentucky Riverdance routine whilst Peter Pan rejects hurtled around on wobbly wires". At it's worst, the Harris-Ronstadt collaboration is merely "an Eaglesesque country rock jog", which is mildness incarnate.

Linda, who herself took drugs "from time to time", told the inimitable Barney Hoskyns – a man who has walked in the shadows himself – to "be regular and orderly in your life in order that you may be violent and original in your work". She had just moved back to Tucson, and *Feels Like Home*, a "country rocking affair" which was then her latest solo album, does just that. It began as a Trio project, along with the likes of David Lindley, David Grisman and Alison Krauss, but "we were really limited to traditional material and old-timey, pre-bluegrass stuff because of the combination of our voices".

Then Dolly dropped out, and so the remaining two "decided to take the record apart". Hence AP Carter's 'Lover's Return' and Neil Young's 'After The Goldrush' sharing the same silver disc. Somehow it all still works, even if the country roots are now buried deeper in the mix. Times change. Her father has recently retired as Tucson's chief of police, and Ronstadt is now a record producer in her own right, seizing the levers of production on Jimmy Webb's comeback album, *Suspending Disbelief*, one of her proudest achievements. As with all of the people whom this book has identified as heroic, "I'll do music always. If I don't make records, I'll be sitting here in my living room with my brother Pete and my brother Mike and my cousin John and we'll be playing music." That old back porch seems to beckon still.

One of the missing links between bluegrass and country rock was the LA band Hearts And Flowers, who played what they themselves described as "Georgia country folk meets Hawaiian ukelele folk rock". 1967's *Now Is The Time For* is wispy folk rock which could only have come from California and from that year, although two of the band pose in cowboy hats, bootlace ties and with unfathomable cool on the cover. They were an acoustic all-singing trio, with misty, psychedelic backings provided by Larry Murray, Dave Dawson on autoharp and Rick Cunha, formerly of The Scotsville Squirrel Barkers. Donovan and Tim Hardin meet Hoyt Axton on the soundtrack, but there's an odd edge throughout, such as that on 'The View From Ward Three', with a ticking clock and eerie downward runs on the autoharp.

Cunha was replaced on their second album, *Of Horses, Kids and Forgotten Women*, by Bernie Leadon, another former Barker. A tinkling, tingling affair, this album should not be blamed for bringing 'Two Little Boys' to the attention of Rolf Harris, although it's still a capital offence. A song from the American Civil War, learned from The Country Gentlemen and here rearranged by all three singers to harpsichord chords, it's dedicated "to both sides (of anything)". The Aussie's cover version is an abomination, an outrage, an instrument of torture, serving as a dreadful reminder that even historic Americana can poison the system if given a boy-scout chumminess and sung too briskly.

Another influential track here is Arlo Guthrie's 'Highway In The Wind', the subtle orchestration of which certainly points the way forward to Poco's 'Rose Of Cimmaron', although there's no banjo. Leadon describes the harmonica-led 'When I Was a Cowboy' as follows: "Wrote piecemeal by us. Is about some more horses and Jesse James and stuff. Dedicated to Gene Autrey, 'cause he bought Martin guitars during the depression." Next stop The Eagles, although they were already much too cynical to start an album – as both do here – with the same Christmas cracker message: "In this time of ours, we wonder if an end to hate we will ever see." Probably not, but it's a nice thought.

Don Henley was the singing drummer of Shiloh who had begun life as a Dixieland jazz band from Texas which later evolved into a rock act: "We were hair pioneers. I was the first guy in town to smoke grass and have my hair touch my ears." It was Kenny Rogers, no less, who suggested that they start to play original material and head for LA. Henley joined a much older tradition, moving to the promised land: "California was the dream of success…the music of The Beach Boys and The Byrds."

Hanging around the Troubadour – as he later told Joe Smith in *Off The Record* – "was kind of pathetic really. But one night Glenn Frey invited me over to his table and bought me a beer." It sounds like a seduction, which in some ways it was, although Frey's first reaction was to think Henley "just a fucked-up little punk".

Born in Detroit, Frey had been with John David Souther in the acoustic duo Longbranch Pennywhistle, singing "these bizarre minor-key songs" which brought him cult status, but "me and my partner are breaking up, and there's this guy named David Geffen, and there may be a deal in the works if a band can be put together". This is hardly hippie idealism, but it *was* 1971. The times were a-changing, and The Eagles would exemplify the new spirit of what one could call accurately the Geffen years. "In the meantime, do you want to go on the road with Linda Ronstadt and make 200 bucks a week?"

The two started "plotting and planning" and handpicked their colleagues, bringing in Randy Meisner (the son of sharecroppers) and Bernie Leadon from Poco and The Burritos respectively. Well, that's one story; another has an inebriated Bernie gatecrashing a Ronstadt show at Disneyland, of all places, and then climbing onto the stage and joining in uninvited. "Glenn said we needed to get those guys because they could play the kind of country rock we were all so interested in." It was a brilliantly simple idea. Rather than being used as a link with "authenticity", like The New Lost City Ramblers, banjo and pedal steel would now be used as musical colouring over a hard-driving West Coast rock group. (If you're expecting a puritanical rant here, you've come to the wrong book.) When Robert Christgau described their debut as "suave and synthetic, brilliant but false", he was right on the money without realising it: this was the exact game plan.

The early Eagles albums still possess huge excitement, representing country music with a red-hot poker shoved up its backside, just as punk, new psychedelia and techno would also do in their turn. This is The Alabama 3 at a different time, under the influence of different chemicals. Of more interest is the fact that the debut LP was recorded over in London with producer Glyn Johns, who had immediately realised their potential when he heard them playing acoustically one night. (Maybe things aren't that far from the folk tradition, after all.) He ensured that they played virtually live in the studio, which is part of the reason why the album still sparkles on any sound system worth its salt, with a good mix of careful vocal interplay and understated backings.

Everyone was determined that this should not be just another slice of "limp-wristed LA country rock". Step this way, Poco and The Flying Burrito Brothers, both by now parodies of how they had started out. It seems to be something endemic in country rock. What The Eagles lost as they turned into a stadium act *par excellence* was the witchy Carlos Castenada element, so carefully reflected in their very name and on the cover of their debut album, photographed at Joshua Tree. The band are grouped around a camp fire, like cowboys of old, except that they were more than high geographically: "The peyote was starting to come on and keep us awake...gave you that acid-like speed effect...those pictures were well stoned." As yet, the band lack a dominant lead guitarist, but what set them apart from the start was their emphasis on honing their craft. As Frey put it: "It wasn't a planned move that we recorded an album full of singles, but we did set out to record 10 good songs."

They include 'Take It Easy', by LA folkie Jackson Browne, with whom Glenn Frey once shared accommodation in Echo Park, and 'Train Leaves Here This Morning', by the immortal Gene Clark. The Eagles plunge headlong into the Wild West for *Desperado*, recorded in Notting Hill in the Wild West of London, a subtle concept

325

album in which themes and tunes repeat and mutate. There is a great deal more acoustic playing, with banjo and slide guitar and dobro, and the melancholy at the heart of the band gets its most sustained outing here. On the front cover, The Eagles pose as outlaws, as unsmiling and nasty a bunch as Hollywood ever faked up, while on the back cover they are seemingly brought to book, dead and in the dust. The rock star as gunman is a hopelessly romantic pose (except in rap, where it is all too true to life, and the corpses are real), but on this album the idea achieves a degree of grace it really doesn't deserve. As Frey observed: "The thread between outlaw and rock star that we were trying to get across was working."

Sam Peckinpah adopted the storyline, intending to film it at Hollywood, but never got around to making the movie, worse luck. The album sold poorly, and The Eagles started to move towards more guitars and less twang, with Joe Walsh coming in and Bernie Leadon going out. Walsh was on board for the modern folk tale that is 'Hotel California', meeting *la belle dame sans merci* "on a dark desert highway". It's pure Appalachian myth, an encounter with the spirit world from which "you can never leave". Or perhaps worse: there is a theory that this is all about the Church of Satan, with the mysterious figure in the balcony Anton LaVey, its leader and the master in whose "chambers they gathered for the feast".

More to the point is the line that "we haven't had that spirit here since 1969". Ex-hippies, too, are now desperados, trapped in a downward spiral from that time of hope, enslaved by drugs like cocaine and using sweet country rock music to help them come down from the Sixties. Remember that Alabama 3 lyric about using whatever drug you needed to stop you from screaming out in unspeakable agony? The Eagles, anyone? The last song on the same album, 'The Last Resort', is an embittered history of California and the lost dreams it has engendered. Henley sings it as a slow lament: "Someone laid the mountains low while the town got high." Don Felder plays pedal steel, and it sounds like someone weeping: "There is no more New Frontier."

One night on stage, Felder looked across at Glenn Frey and said "only three more songs till I kiss your ass, pal". Frey could hardly wait. "We're out there singing 'Best of My Love' but inside both of us are thinking, 'As soon as this is over, I'm gonna kill him'. That was when I knew I had to get out." The Eagles have reformed since, but never for very long.

It was an unplugged performance which got them back together, and the CD souvenir of the 'Hell Freezes Over' tour (as in "we will never stand on the same stage again together until…") tones down the electrics to the benefit of the songs. *Common Thread* was a tribute album by contemporary country musicians, and is an indication of The Eagles' continuing influence on the casual dress, soft rock and crafted lyrics which characterise new Nashville. Leadon aside, the Eagles were never really country musicians, so this is particularly ironic.

One of the most interesting of their contemporaries was The Pure Prairie League, named after a women's temperance society in an Errol Flynn movie. The band is much the same, pretending to be country music but in a fun way. Their songs never rush to a conclusion. Lighter on their musical feet than The Eagles, they have two great assets: pedal steel player John Call and lead singer Craig Fuller. Fuller is given to sweet stretches of melancholy (which, as he was briefly imprisoned as a conscientious objector, is hardly surprising). When he left after two albums – one of which, *Bustin' Out*, was graced by Mick Ronson's string arrangements – the band went into a rapid decline. Vince Gill, who hosted the 1999 CMA Awards, nursed their final years. Each album cover boasts a cartoon by Norman Rockwell of a run-down cowboy, old and in the way. On their debut, he clutched an old 78rpm disc titled 'Dreams Of Long Ago'. It was about as close as they ever got to genuine old-time music, but a record company flyer claims "their high, wild, confident country rock comes from a place where rock and country and bluegrass converge". You could add to that folk ballads, Southern blues, and a touch of Celtic cross-rhythm on 'You're Between Me'. Craig Fuller joined American Flyer, along with Doug Yule from The Velvet Underground, but failed to leave the ground.

Cowboy were pioneers rather than followers, welding the light touch of the new West Coast cowboys to a tougher sound. Their second album was partly recorded at the Capricorn studio in Alabama, which would see a stampede of Southern boogie merchants over the next decade, many of whom have since rebranded themselves under the country banner. Cowboy were more subtle, lauded by one critic as the first of a new breed of "thoughtful" country rockers, and the excellent compilation CD *A Different Time* neatly indicates the way in which the genre changed over the decade.

First, though, we have *Reach For The Sky*, a 1970 album drawn from their time in a hippie commune, which is largely acoustic, back-porch music with bluegrass trimmings. The following year's *Five'll Getcha Ten* sees more experimental material, with one song in 7/4 time and a dobro solo from Duane Allmann. By 1974, something had gone out of rock music – a freshness, a sense of adventure – and so those looking for such things had to search the margins, like country fusion. *Boyer And Talton* rocks more heavily and takes lot more risks, introducing a jazz coda to one song, along with an "electrical bluegrass fusion". This is music which is happy to be in the minority.

Their fourth album, *Cowboy*, came out in 1977, a year which tolled the death knell for anything laid-back or merely well-played. The once shaggy-haired hippies of the first album now look primped and permed and middle aged. All dress in white, like The Mahavishnu Orchestra or a dodgy religious cult. The music is sophisticated but no longer dangerous. A grace note to all of this is a track from Tommy Talton's *Happy To Be Alive*: 'It Might Be The Rain' starts quietly, weary and washed out and totally magnificent. This is the way to alt country. There you go, a history of a music sub-culture in four acts and an epilogue.

The first album by The Outlaws is marketed as "brutal rock 'n' roll", and there's not a pedal steel or fiddle in sight, but this Georgia band are imbued with a country spirit. 'Knoxville Girl' is pure electric bluegrass, although to see the song copyrighted to the band's lead singer is a matter of amusement. It's followed by nine minutes or so of 'Green Grass And High Tides', a title ripped off from a Rolling Stones compilation (there are all kinds of thefts from the tradition, hereabouts) for a track with stinging dual lead guitars. The Outlaws' music is shallow, meaningless and derivative, and I love it.

Redwing's first album has Ralph J Gleason comparing them to The Band, and, although they're nothing like that good, listening to them is like putting on a pair of comfortable old socks. On 'Hogtied', Tom Phillips gets a pedal steel effect on slide guitar. Like Gomez now, they're a little too affable for their own good. Goose Creek Symphony are much closer to Garth Hudson and crew and are an understated delight, with lots of organ, two country fiddles and unfunky brass. In *Words Of Earnest* they pose around a pulpit, with an ancient banjo taking its place alongside a jar of moonshine, sweetcorn and a picket fence on the front cover collage. "When I was a young boy, I lived in the mountains and had a lot of fun...with guitars pickin' and fiddles playin'." This is good, solid, three-dimensional music which didn't seem to appear again in the States until the alt country revolution, and now it's everywhere.

Beware, though, as you leaf through those old stacks of country rock vinyl. For each one-off like Goose Creek Symphony, there are a dozen Little River Bands, who are like The Eagles with soap and water.

Don't pass by Mason Proffit, though: their first album, *Wanted*, boasts steel guitar, banjo and fiddle, and there is a lynching depicted on the back cover, illustrating their macabre singalong 'Two Hangmen'. Subtle, it's not. Marshall Uncle Sam dispatches both 'I'm A Freak', whose crime is to set the inhabitants of Tombstone "thinkin'", and the hangman first sent to set him swinging, and who tells the tale. The band also perform the traditional folk song 'Stewball', slowly and with feeling, in a country twang.

June 1969 saw a gig by a pick-up band called Bobby Ace And The Cards at San Francisco's California Hall, with most of The Grateful Dead, along with John Dawson, David Nelson and Peter Grant on pedal steel, but without Pigpen. The acoustic set comprised versions of traditional mountain songs and Everly Brother covers, plus the debut of Garcia and Hunter's 'Dire Wolf', which is about as far in subject material and atmosphere from 'Dark Star' as you could get – from the edge of the cosmos to a desperate game of cards in a cabin in the back woods of Fennario, with a murderous animal spirit coming for its due. It was a new song that clutched at all kinds of old folk memories, in the "black and bloody mire"; sombre yet oddly joyful.

As Garcia put it: "We were out of our pretentious thing. We weren't feeling so much like an experimental music group but more like a good old band." Such material started to stray into live Dead sets. Hunter had been turned around by Robbie Robertson's songs for The Band, imbued with Americana: "I just said 'Oh yeah, this is the direction. This is the way for us, with all our folk roots, our country and bluegrass roots." For Jerry, it was just another facet of their vast repertoire of musical voices, "one of the possibilities".

The Dead took informal singing lessons from CSN&Y, kept their new songs short, and produced the two most perfect studio albums of their career. For once they all sing in tune, while being fully in tune with their material, whereas in-concert attempts to mimic black music in particular were often little better than a joke, like blackface routines all over again.

Garcia and Hunter were sharing a house, which helped the sense of together-ness, and carefully reworked these new songs like rustic pioneers. The material was then worked on further and acoustically by other members, so that the actual recording process was short and painless. "I was thinking, let's try a really close-to-the-bone approach, like the way they recorded C&W records. We're kind of on the far fringe of it, but we're part of that California Bakersfield school. Don Rich [Buck Owen's guitarist] was one of my favourites."

Gary's brother Mikal Gilmore – who knows plenty about death – described *Workingman's Dead* as a parable about America, and how it almost fell apart. Here, backings are unobtrusive, with acoustic guitars, pedal steel, lightly-played drums and electric bass. Garcia's electric guitar embroiders the music rather than dominating it, and everything is subservient to Hunter's gnomic lyrics. Each song is like a campfire tale. The closest parallel is Dylan's *John Wesley Harding*, with its simple rhyme schemes, strong rhythms and with every word written in blood. Here are songs about surviving Altamont – "this darkness gotta give" – and how the Sixties' sense of community was fraying, tested to destruction by greed and drugs. The vocals are anonymous enough to make The Dead a mouthpiece for its multitude of followers.

'Uncle John's Band' supposedly describes the proprietor of a flea circus and his charges, "little critters in uniforms you could only see under a magnifying glass", but The New Lost City Ramblers were also in Hunter's mind. John Cohen's nickname was 'Uncle', and Garcia came to many of their early gigs, soaking up the old music.

Here it all comes flooding back. 'Cumberland Blues' takes its cue from Appalachian tradition – there's always someone waiting to steal your shift. Hunter's proudest moment as a lyricist was when a retired Kentucky miner asked him what the "guy who wrote this songs would've thought if he'd ever known something like The Grateful Dead was gonna do it". The word "something" here is particularly priceless.

'Black Peter' started briskly in Hunter's mind, but when he came to put music to it Garcia gave it a mournful twist – it is, after all, about a man on his death bed. 'Casey Jones' is based on accurate research, but is one of many Hunter/Garcia songs which then lift off from a detail of US legend or history like a skyrocket. It's also as infectious as a rash. The real Jones foreswore alcohol, let alone cocaine and speed, but the song is about much more than it first seems, and the ghost of Neal Cassidy from the Acid Tests is invoked, not to mention the freaks of the turn of the 1970s: "Trouble ahead and trouble behind."

Robert Hunter, now in his anecdotage, recalls that, when the movie *American Beauty* came out, the plan was to put a photo on the back with the band holding pistols: "They were getting into guns at the time, target shooting. For example, we got a gold record and went and shot it up. I saw that photo, and that was one of the few times I really asserted myself with the band and said no. These were incendiary and revolutionary times, and I did not want this band to be making that statement." Along with Jefferson Airplane, The Dead "could have been the final match that lit the fuse, and we went real consciously the other way".

With their countryish lilt, and with outside musicians like John Dawson and David Nelson along for the ride, this was a record which exuded warmth and friend-liness. As Garcia commented: 'They're good tunes. Every one of 'em's a gem, I modestly admit." For Hunter, it was a conscious decision not to "get hung up with effects and weirdness", but to emulate instead "old Buck Owens records from Bakersfield, nice, raw, simple, straight-ahead music. Nothing flashy." It was an attempt to record "heartland music".

It was also a time of growing troubles, now that Mickey Hart's father had cleaned out the band's bank account and Jerry's mother had been fatally wounded in an auto-mobile accident. For Hunter, "there's a lot of heartbreak on that record", especially on Garcia's singing on 'Brokedown Palace', about the spirit leaving a dying body: "There is no emotion more appealing than the bittersweet when it's truly, truly spoken." This is just as true of 'Box Of Rain', written to order for Phil Lesh to sing to his dying father – as Appalachian a gesture as can possibly be imagined.

Here family duty meets musical ritual, and the box of rain remains a symbol which cannot quite be explained, hence its power. The lyrics for this rite of passage are as profound as any ever produced by a rock group, embodying sentiments which are literally as old as the hills. By some weird act of synchronicity, this was the last song ever to be played by The Dead onstage. It is now their obituary, and Garcia's too: "Such a long, long time to be gone, and a short time to be there."

Even so, this is a more joyful album than *Workingman's Dead*, and 'Friend Of The Devil' is a rogue's lament, with no apologies. 'Ripple' is pure bluegrass abstrac-tion – "there is a fountain that was not made by the hands of men" – but was written in London. Back at the birthplace of that mountain mythology, Hunter "felt I'd come home to some psychic place. Maybe the home of Robin Hood and Peter Pan." The band sing with a smile, and they all chant wordlessly at the end, women included.

American Beauty is about how they found the courage and talent to stick together, in Hunter's words "a shared sense of direction that was in tune with the times. The Band, The Byrds, Poco, CSNY and Dylan were all exploring traditional music augmented by the power of rock 'n' roll, and we were continuing to evolve what we believed to be the logical next step in American music." The cover paint-ing reads either 'beauty' or 'reality', depending on how you look at it. Psychedelia has not been abandoned, merely internalised.

A third album was planned to complete the trilogy, but never materialised, although much of the material turned up on stage and is captured on the live triple album *Europe '72*. 'He's Gone' is more of the same, "and nothing's gonna bring him back". 'Jack Straw' is more complex, an Appalachian murder tale, but the name in question also belongs to a key figure in the Great Revolt of 1381, and his memory in turn inspired a childrens' game and the description of any man of no consequence. Here, Hunter provides another twist to the legend. What he and The Dead began to do – in a seemingly endless series of live CDs and night-long concerts – was put together an epic America, where black and white (both in skin colour and morality) knew no distinction.

Here alone we have 'Brown-Eyed Women', the tale of hard times as experienced by a bootlegger back during the Depression, and 'Ramble On Rose', peppered with people both real and fictional, from Jack The Ripper to Wolfman Jack the DJ: "I know this song, it ain't ever going to end" – and of course live it didn't, with a new variant each night. It's much like the way in which Bob Dylan has played endless variations on the mood and, in some cases, the words of his songs, so that the live variants of 'Tangled Up In Blue' alone could fill a book. When the two got together in concert, the results were strangely disappointing, as each seemed too nervous about compromising the other to take their usual risks onstage.

Apart from Stephen Peters' lyric-by-lyric description, which traces each song carefully down the years, no critic seems yet to have grasped how monumental the ambition of those later Dead concerts was. Hardcore fans, on the other hand, need no prompting. 'Tennessee Jed' is about a convict in shackles, and shares the inbred surrealism of Dylan's *Basement Tapes*. It also shares much with The New Lost City Ramblers song 'Way Down The Old Plank Road'. Like Dylan, Hunter has been around for long enough to trap such ancient shards of folk wisdom in his brain and then recycle them as something rich and strange.

So has Jerry Garcia: "When I get ready to go on the road, I make up cassettes of all my favourite music. Country and western stuff. Ali Akbar Khan. Crosby, Stills And Nash. I love American music. I love Indian music, too. I even love English music. What I think of as being the English sound, the real sound, is like Pentangle, because it's very much that sort of madrigal, Elizabethan thing, very crisp. Economical. But it's not in any of the trends. It's more basic." The closest The Dead got to this sound was in the *Terrapin Station* suite, orchestrated by Paul Buckminster, which opens with a soldier and a sailor fighting for a lady "down in Carlisle". In this story, which draws on genuine folk ballads, only the latter is brave enough to dare all, and when he proves successful, "the lady fairly leapt at him", showing a lack of restraint at odds with the tradition, which emphasises modesty.

Hunter began working on this project "with an invocation to the Muse", and it later came to incorporate extra lyrics like 'Jack O'Roses', but it remained a source of contention that The Dead never saw the whole thing through. The English magazine *Dark Star* released his solo acoustic rendition of the whole cycle, as it then was. The whole thing is a cosmic fantasy, like Spirit's much more brutal *Potatoland*, but it all seems a little artificial. Weir described the band's studio version as "English court music", but it fails to connect to its time. Myths need to be relevant. It's a truth too painful to be told that Hunter just can't sing, although *Tales Of The Great Rum Runners* is saved by its backing musicians. His later work should be filed under research. Stick to reading his book of lyrics, which stand up just fine.

On 'Children's Lament', Hunter plays Scottish bagpipes like a blind man trying to paint. If you ever want to clear a party... Much more fruitful was Garcia's dabblings in country music. He had played pedal steel on 'Teach Your Children' by Crosby, Stills, Nash And Young, and for him "pedal steel was an instrument that was on my mind since back in the days when I was a banjo player". It did not prove as physically exhausting as playing electric guitar: "You just sit down, and it's all very close work. It's more like working out with a sewing machine. It's not such a totally physical trip. It's little motions. I can play it for hours in a row without hardly noticing it." He began to play with support band New Riders Of The Purple Sage just to warm up.

1981's live double album *Dead Reckoning* is an all-acoustic look backward at the band's folk dimensions, mixing in traditional material – like 'Dark Hollow' and 'Jack-A-Roe', and songs by Charlie Monroe and Elizabeth Cotton – with the Dead's own quieter side, all performed as if asleep. Some of these titles were duplicated by Dylan in his own roughly contemporaneous revisiting of his roots. Happy Traum once described such music as "semi-traditional", and Ken Hunt wisely points out that The Dead have always specialised in American music of all genres: "They will just as easily quote from Miles Davis' 'Sketches Of Spain' as perform the Child ballad 'Jack-A-Roe' or Marty Robbins' 'El Paso'." The trouble is that sometimes they level down rather than up.

The best of Garcia's collaborations with Hunter are beginning to enter the tradition in their own right. Norma Waterson recorded 'Black Muddy River' almost as if this plaintive classic was already hundreds of years old. It marks a poignant end to their songs about roses, as the last one of summer "pricks my finger". By another stroke of synchronicity, it was the last song which Garcia ever sang in public. Hunter wrote that "it's just a good look into the deep dark well", and it's very much a song of middle age. The tragedy was that Jerry had so few years left to "dream me a dream of my own".

The Dead played their last concert in the summer of 1995, and Eric Pooley describes how Garcia could derive grace and beauty from his declining powers. I suddenly think of Dock Boggs, raging at the dying of the light. Jerry's "courage was something to see. He no longer knew if his fingers would do his bidding, but he played on, like Clarence Ashley or ol' Lightnin' Hopkins or Duke Ellington at the end of their lives, because playing music for people is what these gentlemen did."

Part of the restitution of The Dead to the kind of cool audience – who had long abandoned it to those cult devotees who claimed ownership – was 1991's tribute album *Deadicated*. Here were the likes of Dwight Yoakam storming through 'Truckin', and David Lindley helping Warren Zevon on a version of 'Casey Jones' which is to be relished. Lyle Lovett sings 'Friend Of The Devil' without imposing too much personality on it, but The Cowboy Junkies' rendition of 'To Lay Me Down' digs into the song with a scalpel. Modern country starts here.

As to The New Riders, their work now sounds irremediably old fashioned, yet plaintive. It's the Wild West in soft focus and airbrushed. Back when they bisected The Dead's acoustic and electric incarnations every night they were powered by the parent band's rhythm section, but then Spencer Dryden came in from Jefferson Airplane on drums and Buddy Cage later replaced Garcia on pedal steel. Their self-titled debut album from 1971 is the best of the bunch, though a live bootleg from the same year, with Garcia along for the ride, is more lively.

The Adventures Of Panama Red was produced by Norbert Putnam, who kicks this most laid-back of bands up the creative backside and plays the dope card for all it's worth, uttering references to searching all the "joints" in town, and mounting his white horse "Mescalito". The arrival of Skip Battin on bass was the equivalent in country rock of vultures starting to hover overhead and the sun growing awfully warm. However lazy the music became, they certainly knew how to dress a sleeve, from the cartoon inside *Panama Red* to *Gypsy Cowboy* – depicting an exhausted cowboy resting by a dead tree in Monument Valley, with five monochrome desperadoes on the back cover – and the startling *Brujo*, on which the desert blooms.

Old And In The Way were recorded at the Boarding House in 1973 in front of a lively audience by Owsley Stanley, of all people, the pioneering LSD manufacturer. One doubts that there is any family connection with The Stanley Brothers, although Carter's intense 'White Dove' is one of the delights on offer. What Owsley synthesises here is something even more rare and strange than his liquid sunshine. Here is straight bluegrass, with a dream team of Garcia on banjo, Peter Rowan on guitar and vocals, David Grisman on mandolin and Vassar Clements on fiddle. John Kahn plays stand-up bass, and the front cover is a cartoon of this grade-A combo in patched jeans, playing in the corner of a grocery store. (Barefoot Jerry's, perhaps?) 'Panama Red' sparkles in this company, as do the gentle vocal harmonies on 'Wild Horses'. The instruments chuckle and glide, and no one tries to show off. One can only imagine how many Dead fans subsequently followed the music back to its source. A second album's worth of material emerged over 20 years later as *That High Lonesome Sound*, released after Garcia's death.

What comes over is the lead guitarist's sheer love for this music, stemming right from his adolesence: "I was a bluegrass *freak*, you know! Brought along our tape recorders and taped the shows." Hence The Dead's own tolerance of those who felt the same about their music. He was similarly careful to give proper copyright acknowledgment to traditional material, 'Cold Rain And Snow' excepted. "I'm an old folkie", right from the coffee house days. As Bob Weir told Ken Hunt for *Swing 51*: "A large body of our presentation has direct lineage clear back to the ballad singing of Northern Ireland and Scotland. There are songs that we do that are direct renderings of Child ballads. If you trace that lineage through what happened in Appalachia...we really exist in a large part in that vein, in that tradition." Garcia points out that Elvis', 'Blue Moon Of Kentucky', is "a hop, skip and a jump from that tradition", while Dolly Parton's style of singing "is very close to traditional singers, to someone like Jean Ritchie. Her scales and ornamentation are very, very similar to Northern English."

As he got older, Garcia came back to such music with his Acoustic Band, recording songs by the likes of Jimmie Rodgers. In the early Nineties, he rejoined Grisman for three albums of acoustic duets. The second, *Not For Kids Only*, was a charming collection of childrens' tunes, like 'The Teddy Bear's Picnic', but the posthumously-released *Shady Grove* is my own touchstone. It gives me the same chill as The Stanley Brothers, with perfect acoustic harmonies and the music of two men who are totally at ease with each other reviving songs that were old before they were born. Here are the likes of 'Jackaroo' and that epic of cross-dressing, 'The Handsome Cabin Boy', plus songs reinterpreted by AL Lloyd and Ewan MacColl and The Clancy Brothers' 'Whiskey In The Jar', which Garcia took back to The Dead.

To complete another circle, the notes in the CD booklet are written by John Cohen, and he takes things right back to the influence of the Harry Smith *Anthology*: "This was the musical ambience from which Jerry and David emerged." He repeats Kenneth Rexroth's review of Carl Sandburg, and that old free America. The performances here "reconnect us all – folk singers, deadheads, university students, hillbillies, country and bluegrass musicians" – with the America of which Rexroth wrote and Sandburg sang. It is a culture which even contemporary "cynicism" cannot destroy.

Grisman told *Acoustic Guitar* that Garcia is naturally unpredictable as a guitarist, in just the way of which that Harry Smith would approve: "He's very melodic, but he puts in a lot of accidentals. He's got his own personality: tone is a lot of it. He's got his own sound with the electric guitar and it's not the same sound on acoustic guitar...but it's the same vibe." As to his voice, he now has "enough age on him that it's soulful". Mike Garris, from The Del McCoury Band, has confirmed to Grisman that Old And In The Way – despite their self-mocking name – have since opened the door for progressive elements in bluegrass: "We weren't looking at it that way at all."

Paddy Moloney phoned Garcia to ask him if he would appear on what became *Santiago*, a CD on which Irish music met that from Galicia. Years before, Jerry had told Paddy that his father "was of Galician descent, and his mother Irish". Moloney had just started to compose a suitable tune when he received a phone call to tell him that Garcia had just passed away. He continued working on this new piece, which he has since titled 'Jerry's Tune' – a final Celtic connection.

The dawning of a new decade saw many musicians follow The Grateful Dead in a headlong dash towards country music as the music of consolation. (Or was it a retreat?) Before The Youngbloods, Jesse Colin Young had made a debut album of white boy blues, but 1972's *Together* is a lovely thing indeed, with his bruised tenor set against chugging guitar, dobro and warm brass. The cover drawing is that of a lucky six-leaf clover, showing three examples of Nature at its most bountiful and three of man and woman in harmony. On the back, a tiny child plays with daddy's guitar. This all became sickly a few albums down the line, but for now the title track is fragile enough to make each pause count. At his best, Jesse has the wondrous ability to convey sheer happiness, like a bird singing on a branch, while exuding the sad realisation that all of this could come crashing down in a second's time: "Here comes the sun again, making diamonds in the rain."

In 'Grey Day', Jesse even makes bad weather seem redeeming – I mentally sing it to myself every morning that the sun doesn't shine, which is a lot of singing. The 'American Dreams' suite is an overview of the Sixties' flash and its comedown, and although Young has lost a vital elasticity in both voice and imagination it's still surprisingly tough at heart, refusing to retreat. "Who's going to run the country if we run away?" Reagan and Bush, that's who.

At its worst, it all descends to gloop. A whole generation of singer/songwriters who were once tougher than the rest spent the 1970s wrestling with this dilemma. The most comforting of them all, like a great woolly blanket, was James Taylor, swaddling up his own mental illness and heroin dependency on *Sweet Baby James*. Here is another rich man's child seeking redemption in a pedal steel guitar.

Red Rhodes, Chris Darrow and Randy Meisner from The Eagles are among the backing musicians. I remember being introduced to this album when it was still a cult item by a schoolfriend who had taken way too much LSD and pressed it on me like an evangelist with a bible. As I knew Taylor from his challenging and at times atonal album released on Apple, the album seemed at first like being swathed in cotton wool, and suspiciously country on top, but I gradually succumbed to its lazy charms, seeing the underlying courage. It was a way of keeping going, through "fire and rain", and I played it over and over again.

Compare it to Eric Andersen's wracked confession – also of seeing "fire and rain" – or to any real country music you can think of, and it all seems a little artificial. The "banjo on my knee" in Stephen Foster's 'Oh Susannah' here is purely notional. Put the lazy cry to the Lord in 'Lo And Behold' up against any of the genuine gospel desperation of the recent *Prayers From Hell* compilation, or even Dylan's *Basement* song of the same title, and it sounds petulant. "There is a young cowboy who lives on the range" is pure Hollywood, or Marie Antoinette playing with her sheep. A cross between a lullabye and self-admiration – naming yourself as a baby is sectionable – it nevertheless grabs at the heart.

This is pure therapy, and if "Sunny Skies hasn't a friend" the real frisson is between the cheerful sound and Taylor's miserable words. Ralph McTell pulled off much the same trick with his earlier and vastly underrated songs about mental disease, such as 'Michael In The Garden', which he crooned so softly. There is a hypnotic charm in Taylor's warm voice and the careful backings which I imagine heroin gives you at the start. It has also proved just about as difficult to shake off. This was the kind of music which punk rock evolved on this Earth to counteract.

It became part of many an old hippie's spiritual progress to plunge into country music, almost as a form of confession. By plugging into such a communal art form they could gain the strength to face their own inner demons. David Crosby's *If I Could Only Remember My Name* drew in "plenty of old friends from the old folkie days" to create an unselfish and self-questioning suite of songs. The very title suggests a humility previously unknown from the author of 'Mind Gardens', and includes odes about having two girlfriends at once. Here is a lush and resonant soundscape – ambient almost, like trance dance – over which Crosby sings, often wordlessly and in tones of pure delight. It is like being half awake in paradise. Here is the sort of inner world one imagines belongs to the serial soft-drugs abuser. Then the lyrics gradually reveal themselves: lost, weary and sad.

The album is dedicated to an old girlfriend, Christine Hinton, who had died tragically the year before. In the final song – or plainsong, rather, as it sounds like choirboy music – she comes back to visit him, like the dead lover at the end of 'She Moves Through The Fair'. Crosby's befuddled brain somehow takes him to inhabit the same place from which all of those Celtic ballads come. It can't be that far from the barely-conscious to the collective unconscious! At the centre of everything is 'Cowboy Movie', a spaghetti western in song, full of betrayals and missing links, in which dying outlaw tells how his gang robbed a train and then fell out over an Indian girl, who "nearly bit my thumb clean through". Musically, it's as if every great West Coast guitarist was jamming on the same stage, which is just about true.

It's hard to hear exactly what David is singing about, but phrases like "as we were walking back through the darkness" and "kind of old and weird now" detach themselves from the narrative and float away. This is supposedly an allegory about CSN&Y, with Crosby himself as "Fat Albert", Stills as "Eli", Nash as "Duke", Neil as "Young Billy" and Rita Coolidge as "The Raven" – that's the Western bit. Country music plays around the edges, most notably Garcia's finest-ever pedal steel break on 'Laughing', and it's part of the aural scenery, what *Mojo* calls "a banquet of unfamiliar modal sounds". As honey for the ears, this album knows no rival.

Crosby's own cowboy fixation was becoming real. In a contemporary photograph, he points a hand gun with an American flag draped over it at his own head. At home in LA, an intruder menaced him with a .38 for real: "I grabbed my piece, rolled off the bed, and opened up: put the first one through the wood and glass right next to his head, sprayed splinters all over him. I shot first and I won." Some years down the line, he ended up in a cell as nasty and brutish as any in Wild West mythology, and his autobiography *Long Time Gone* tells of his slow and painful rehabilitation, like a man climbing back out of the grave.

Neil Young is a man who has flirted with country music throughout a long career, never quite committing himself but never quite walking away. As he told *Mojo*, his main childhood memories in North Ontario are of "guys like Frankie Laine. There was also Rawhide and all that cowboy stuff. I used to walk by a railroad track on my way to school. There was even a real hobo's shack there." His first instrument was a ukelele, and he later took up the banjo. Still unreleased is the 1969 track 'It Might Have Been', a traditional English folk song reworked as a honky-tonk country ballad. On moving to America, however, he immersed himself in its mythologies, just like fellow Canadian Robbie Robertson.

This was never more true than on *After The Goldrush*, originally based around a film screenplay by Dean Stockwell, "all about the day of the great earthquake in Topanga Canyon". Here is Don Gibson's 'O Lonesome Me', 'Southern Man' (sung in the voice of an Alabama bigot) and the album closer 'Cripple Creek Ferry'.

Crazy Horse started as a psychedelic blues band, but their 1971 debut was pure country rock, with Danny Whitten's fragile 'I Don't Want To Talk About It' as tender as music can get. Neil's own first full-scale country excursion, *Harvest*, was recorded partly in Nashville with a new backing band, The Stray Gators, comprising our old friend Ken Buttrey on drums and Ben Keith on pedal steel, along with James Taylor, Linda Ronstadt and David Crosby – the Marin County élite were just as incestuous as Tennessee pickers. The cover lettering is carefully antique, and the back cover shows Neil playing with his band. The pedal steel dominating the set, but check-shirted Young is the centre of everyone's attention as he fires off a guitar solo.

The music is certainly less frenetic than Crazy Horse, and Neil's adolescent voice has the right kind of whine for C&W but it's somehow too edgy, too individual. Pedal steel is probably its nearest instrumental equivalent. Someone – maybe even Neil himself – plunks banjo on 'Old Man', but Young's country borrowings tend to be straight Nashville rather than mountain music (even if his seemingly endless list of unreleased songs includes one called 'Hillbilly Band').

He returned with much the same crew and a mournful harmonica 20 years later for *Harvest Moon*. The warm tones and the setting sun on the original cover have now become a rising moon set among muted colours, with Neil in the tatters of a crow. Much more emotionally true to country music – which tends to be more middle-aged regret than youthful questioning – this is one of the most heartbreaking albums I've heard, with Neil using largely acoustic mainstream country music for what it does best: evoke tender recollections of good times gone and love's decay. 'From Hank To Hendrix' is the killer, heading for divorce "California style" and full of shards of bitter wisdom: "I never believed in much, but I believed in you."

1985's *Old Ways* was largely recorded in rural Tennessee, and with Bela Fleck on banjo it reprises the favourite song of his childhood, then brings in the likes of

Willie Nelson and Waylon Jennings to share lead vocals. It's endlessly pleasant, and Young being Young there's the occasional cutting edge, as on 'Are There Any More Real Cowboys?' However, it mostly smacks of Neil on a creative vacation. When it doesn't, it's too much about himself – "it's hard to teach a dinosaur a new trick" – and not desperate enough, which is an odd thing to say of Young. Here is a man who owns a ranch and a buffalo herd, and can get his boots dirty whenever he likes – someone else will clean them. He walks down a country road on the cover, but doesn't seem to be going anywhere. When David Geffen threatened to sue Young for making deliberately uncommercial music, he countered with the threat to record nothing but country albums from then on. This album is on the Geffen label.

Young had earlier taken his Rolling Zuma Review back to the bars, and this fed through into side one of *American Stars And Bars*, a selection of C&W tunes. 'The Old Country Waltz' has a shuffle beat, crying violin and weeping pedal steel, and Neil does sound totally genuine in his misery: "I ain't got no excuses." 'Saddle Up The Palomino' is the other side of the coin, drunken bravado with a thumping beat.

The cover of that album could not draw a more brutal contrast, with a drunken Neil and girlfriend on one side, ugly with greed, and snowy peaks, a teepee and a noble Indian on the other. Here is Pocahontas all over again – "they killed us in our teepee, and they cut our women down" – but with no Marlon Brando in sight.

It Comes A Time was another country excursion, using much the same band with which Neil finally hit the Opry, but it's muted rather than Nashville. As Peter Doggett wrote of yet another country rock hybrid, Hawks And Doves: "It's possible to see it as a portrayal of two facets of Young's nature, one mystical and scholarly, the other most at home in a bar listening to country and western."

There is a third facet. 'Captain Kennedy' opens with plucked guitar and Neil trying to sound like a traditional folk singer. At first it sounds like an ancient naval ballad, but then mentions the year 1971. 'The Old Homestead' also sounds at first like something straight from the Appalachians, but Neil applies his usual twist, a musical saw whines, and the words get either sinister or nonsensical, depending on your tastes. It's a long way from "the floor where the cowboys dance" to a prehistoric bird flying through the air and a naked rider galloping. As for me, I'll stick with the musical saw.

The most shocking manifestation of Young's country side was his 'Tonight's The Night' tour (the album had not yet been deemed fit to release), in which he acted out the junkie lifestyle onstage and looked like a wild mountain man, deliberately baiting his audience. As one of his band commented later: "We started realising what the album was all about. It was like an Irish wake, or something." A performance at the LA Roxy starts slow as death, and then degenerates into drunken chaos. On the album, Ben Keith makes his pedal steel howl right after Neil tells how the phone call telling of Bruce Berry's death sent "a chill up and down my spine". He plays more soothingly on 'Roll Another Number', as Neil talk-sings "I'm not going back to Woodstock for a while" in a mock country accent.

Silver And Gold was publicised as the third part of the *Harvest* trilogy. As *NME* noted, though, it is now "the alt country harvest who nod dreamily in his direction". For *The Observer*, it is a "sparse meditation on the fragility and endurance of love and family". One track even looks back with fondness to an earlier band, 'Buffalo Springfield Again', and there were rumours of a one-off reunion. *Mojo* found Young "becalmed", but pleasantly so, with all of the old ingredients: "Warm and delicately-picked country-folk guitar. Rootsy harmonica. Winsome pedal steel." Particularly fine is the "spare, drifting, sometimes Celtic-sounding 'Red Sun'", with Emmylou Harris on backing vocals.

Jackson Browne was working on a "concept album of sorts, a tribute to bandits and desperadoes" when the project was handed over to The Eagles instead. *The Pretender* is an album haunted by the suicide of Browne's wife and the matching death of the hippie dream. The title track is highly prophetic, voiced by a proto-yuppie learning to surrender to the everyday "struggle for the legal tender". David Lindley plays slide guitar and Browne's laconic singing, full of an inner sadness, has influenced subsequent country singers while not being country itself. 'Here Come Those Tears Again' here was originally written as a C&W lament by his mother-in-law, Nancy Fansworth, but takes on an added melancholy in this context. As with the David Crosby album, this could be a visit from the dead, and the word "grateful" is not part of his vocabulary.

Browne began his musical career at the Paradox, a folk club "out there in the wasteland. John McEuan was always bringing in bluegrass players he'd found at some festival." The Nitty Gritty Dirt Band, who came from Long Beach, invited Browne to join them in February 1966. As he told *Zigzag*: "I was in The Dirt Band for six months." They were "a real fun band to be in", playing jug band music. "I was much more into my own songs, and so I left in July 1966. John McEuan replaced me, and within weeks they had a recording contract and weren't a jug band any more." Liberty Records demanded that they sang material which was more contemporary, adopting the standard record company dodge of finding something new and then changing it: "It was years before they returned to the kind of folk-based music that they felt most comfortable playing."

Photographs of the time show The Nitty Gritty Dirt Band dressed much like The Charlatans, but with less self-conscious cool. The music on their early albums is a strange mix of folk rock and vaudeville, with authenticity in either field notable by its absence. They were a largely acoustic band, and a publicity shot has them clowning around Bonzo Dog style, with banjo, autoharp, accordion, fiddle, clarinet and the like. Even their bass drum has an old wind-up gramophone painted on it. This is old-time music with smile on its lips.

The band lived in some disarray in a huge old mansion in the Hollywood hills called the Dirt House with the comedian Steve Martin, Duane and Greg Allman and The Sunshine Company. "A year or so after we started, we got a couple of electric instruments…and a year after that, we learned how to use them." Jeff Hanna was employed at MacCabe's Guitar Shop, and the band started with an impromptu jam there. They later added John McEuen and Les Thompson from The Wigmore City Moonshiners, and the jaunty bluegrass tune 'Dismal Swamp' appears on their debut. Even here there's an element of self-parody, as the title suggests.

The band headlined gigs at the Fillmore over the likes of Buffalo Springfield, although they were barely amplified onstage. To toughen up the sound, Chris Darrow was brought into the band for *Rare Junk* and a live album, as well as a brief appearance in the comic western *Paint Your Wagon*. The band broke up in early 1969, with Hanna and Darrow going off to join Linda Ronstadt's tour band long before The Eagles, while Jeff also played with Mike Nesmith – lots of things are coming full circle here. John McEuen went as far as to join Andy Williams, playing banjo during the jauntier moments of his Las Vegas show.

Within six months they were back together, now with Jim Ibbotson on board. "When I first got into the band out in Hollywood, we were cramming country music down the throats of hippies." McEuen told Pete Frame: "we had been interested in Doc Watson, folk and bluegrass, but we grew up listening to rock 'n' roll." The two elements combine on 1970's *Uncle Charlie And His Dog Teddy*, which opens with mountain banjo and a Mike Nesmith song. *Mojo* talked to Jeff Hanna, who admitted to the influence of *Music From Big Pink And Sweetheart Of The Rodeo* but wanting to take this a step further on. The band felt that "a lot of great music gets played when the tape isn't rolling. That spontaneity was lacking in commercial music. We wanted to capture that, and bring a less mainstream country thing." It was a bold step indeed for a band commonly regarded as little more than a joke, but perhaps that very fact gave them the freedom not to worry about losing face. You can't imagine The Eagles, for example, doing what they were doing here, combining a rock rhythm section "with traditional acoustic instruments – fiddle, banjo and harmonica – kind of Appalachian Mountain surf music".

The resulting album sounds like it was taped live, almost without the musicians knowing. All human life is here: chicken impersonations, introspective songs, traditional tunes and a banjo transcription of a Baroque piece – Buddy Holly meets AA Milne. The band are dressed as if from the 19th century and swap instruments throughout. There's a lot of studio banter, and the same mix of back-porch atmospherics and space-age musicianship as on The Youngblooods' *Elephant Mountain*. The mystery ingredient added here is Uncle Charlie, who is a real man and a greatuncle of their manager, William McEuen's wife.

The lynchpin was The Dirt Band's recording of Jerry Jeff Walker's 'Mr Bojangles', which triggered something in William's mind. Charlie sits proudly on the cover with his dog and his guitar, and appears on the record playing and reminiscing literally on his front porch in Springville. Side two opens with his rendition of the cowboy myth 'Jesse James', and then he talks about his life, with Teddy singing along on 'The Old Rugged Cross'. He's more melodic than Neil Young on a bad day. Then it's straight into 'Mr Bojangles', which has never before been so heart-warming: "I ain't too good on B flat." He sounds fine on everything else.

After Earl Scruggs heard *Uncle Charlie*, he sought the band out backstage one night in Nashville, "and that sowed the seed of doing an album that would bring together the traditional and contemporary sides of country music". Meanwhile, the band moved *en masse* to Colorado and set out to conquer the Midwest. John McEuen: "Where I live, there is a mountain on each side, and though nothing ever seems to happen there, it has everything I need."

All The Good Times added Nashville sounds, Hank Williams and a 'Civil War Trilogy' to the mix, but the real breakthrough was the triple album *Will The Circle Be Unbroken?* McEuen takes up the story, describing that, when Earl Scruggs expressed an interest, "we just flipped out of course – then he got Doc Watson along, and it sort of snowballed from there; it wasn't pre-planned at all". Recording took about ten days. "The original idea was to select a double album's worth of the best stuff, but it was all best stuff, so we ended up using about all of it. It's sort of like a portfolio of traditional country music."

No wonder that no less than *The Tennessean* hailed it as "the most important event in the history of Nashville". The album cover proclaims "Music forms a new circle", and we start off with a history of Nashville in 'Grand Ole Opry Song', sung and played joyfully. That is the key, here: a harmony between rednecks and long-hairs, with lots of studio tracks and Mother Maybelle working out with the band on 'Keep On The Sunny Side': "On the old record, I started it like this..."

For anyone expecting only mountain music, the format is relaxed enough to take in a goodly range of traditional material, while also ranging from Hank Williams to Merle Travis. 'I Am A Pilgrim' is much more cheerful than The Byrds, with a real country swing. Vassar Clements adds fiddle throughout, and the whole thing is wonderfully spontaneous: as Roy Acuff says, "let's do it the first time", for something is lost on every studio retake. The lovely affability of Doc Watson acts as a bridge between youth and age, and he praises Merle Travis for what he himself describes as "that old coal mine thing. I made it up in two weeks." The performances are relaxed and respectful, but never consumed with their own importance, and everyone piles in at the end on another Carter Family song, 'Will The Circle Be Unbroken?'. Maybelle sings dreamily, with a majesty which is her due.

Most people would have ended things there, but as if deliberately turning the page to start a new chapter, this is followed with Randy Scruggs – son of Earl, who himself seems to have been reborn on these sessions – playing an instrumental version of Joni Mitchell's 'Both Sides Now'. A song written by a woman, and one from north of the border, at that. What could be worse? 25 years on, another Canadian singer would out-sell all of the competition and dominate Nashville, and Shania didn't even live nearby.

When William McEuen told the record company what he was up to, they told him to stop work immediately as they had not officially authorised the sessions. With the same spirit as the original settlers, he simply kept going.

How do you follow perfection? With a double album, *Stars And Stripes Forever*, which features live retreads of old material, doo-wop, comic routines and an interview with Vassar Clements. The band "got into bluegrass before we got into anything else". "What do you hope to do with it?" "Mess it up." They laugh, then say: "Give it some drive." It's more than just switching on an electric banjo and playing 'Foggy Mountain Breakdown'. Johnny is "a bluegrass player who can play rock 'n' roll", while others in the band are "rock 'n' roll players who can play bluegrass". Vassar narrates 'The Mountain Whippoorwill (Or How Hillbilly Jim Won The Great Fiddlers' Prize)', a piece of comic doggerel about a fiddle contest up in the mountains.

On *Dream*, the band grow even more ambitious, releasing a concept album about a journey through time, complete with the sounds of bagpipes, thunder and rippling water sampled into the mix. Maybe they were trying too hard. Nashville failed to take them to its cold, cold heart, even after they cut their hair, shortened their name to The Dirt Band and sought a slicker image, with fewer acoustic instruments in the mix. It didn't work, so back came Jim Ibbotson and their full name. The 1985 album *Partners, Brothers And Friends* celebrated the band's sheer determination: "Its great to be part of something so good that's it's lasted so long."

1989's *Will The Circle Be Unbroken? Volume Two* opens with the unmistakeable voice of Johnny Cash, but as so many of the original participants had already moved on to the great hootenanny in the sky – Mother Maybelle among them – the participants here represent what is literally the next generation of country musicians. Johnny is accompanied by his daughter Roseanne and bassist Roy Huskey Jr repeats his father's role on the original album, although Jimmy Martin is back as himself and Chet Atkins brings the Nashville stamp of authenticity. Here, too, are singer/songwriters John Prine and John Hiatt, along with former members of The Band and The Byrds, still going forwards. The latest generation of bluegrass pioneers is represented by Sam Bush and Bela Fleck, while other guests range from Ricky Skaggs to Emmylou Harris. Here is great musicianship, but it lacks the epic feel of the original collaboration which made the mountains tremble.

When Jeff Hanna was interviewed by *New Country*, he could see that things had changed for good: "Country is the new pop music, so there's a lot of money at stake. When that sets in, people get less creative. Right now, the lowest common denominator is the hunk train." It is not something which appeals to him, or any other of the country rock pioneers who came to the music at a more idealistic time, and for more cogent reasons: "Maybe there's a string of integrity through it all that you don't break."

What's important at the end is to keep hold of your dignity. "If you can achieve that in this business, then you've really done something." The circle of genuine country music is still unbroken, and it keeps on turning. Sometimes in the strangest places.

Chapter Seven

New Country

One of the strange places in which country music began to surface was among various West Coast mavericks. Ry Cooder hand-crafted the Western movie soundtrack for the likes of Wim Wenders (in *Paris, Texas*) and Walter Hill, who called him "a uniquely American artist, the work displaying recurring patterns, moods and attitudes that are distinctly his own". On Hill's *The Long Riders*, he sought for a back-porch feeling, so that the traditional song 'I'm A Good Old Rebel' is retooled for a string band. Cooder was working at Americana before anyone even gave it a name, rediscovering oddities like 'FDR in Trinidad' and the dustbowl ballads of Into The Purple Valley. The more pared back Cooder gets, the more powerful he plays: his slide guitar on the traditional 'Billy The Kid' cuts you in two. Similarly, the more dispassionate his singing, the better it becomes: "I have a purely abstract interest in the past."

Another destroyer of nostalgia is John Cale, whose *Walking On Locusts* uses pedal steel and "woozy" fiddle deliberately out of context. Cale always sings as if on the edge of self-control, as on 'Cable Hogue', his tribute to Sam Peckinpah, like a man shouting in the dark. This is from an album on which he appears in a strait-jacket. There are other forms of rebellion.

Jesse Winchester fled the draft to Canada, then spent his years of enforced exile crafting songs of sweet nostalgia, like 'Brand New Tennessee Waltz'. It's undercut by paranoia: "they'll catch you wherever you're hid". When allowed back home, he laid down *A Touch On The Rainy Side* in Nasvhille, and recorded with Emmylou Harris. His own tour band became country boogie merchants The Amazing Rhythm Aces.

They exemplify a whole strand of Seventies music, which saw white folks trying on soul music for size, never quite getting to its heart. It took particularly pernicious root in Britain, where it fuelled the pub rock boom. In a different universe were Little Feat, a band of mixed race who slithered on the edge of Lowell George's slide guitar, seemingly without effort and with a terrifying power. You always wondered what exactly inspired them. George was the enigma at the band's heart (when Craig Fuller later take his place, they became merely competent), and his skewed songs mythologise modern America, exploring the "grubby flipside" of trucking music. Heroism plays no part in his world: in 'Willin'', which the band describe as "a little C&W song that Lowell wrote", merely keeping going was something to achieve. If anyone questions why Lowell is mentioned here, just listen to his deeply soulful version of Hank Williams' 'Lonesome Whistle' on *Hoy, Hoy*, or indeed the mix of pain and pride in anything the man sang.

This chapter is starting like a series of footnotes – it will settle down when we reach Texas, but I might as well mention the truly bizarre *Hank Wilson's Back* in which Leon Russell attempts an act of ventriloquism. Personally, I reckon Uncle Charlie's dog gets closer. It's not the technique that counts, it's the feeling. On a similar note, I would suggest that any masochist out there track down Mason Williams' *Sharepickers*, on which the Irish mouth music of 'Little Beggar Man' and the "bluegrass" of 'Orange Blossom Special' get ground down to the same syrup. As Mason writes: "You've got to think of this record as being like a recording ranch with a crop of music. Having a record deal is like owning land. I found some sharepickers to help me get the most out of my record." It's enough to make you into a communist.

Stranger than strange is the totally wonderful Michael Hurley, the closest thing to a hillbilly musician currently treading the boards. He has drunk deeply from the well of old time music, but whereas his friends The Holy Modal Rounders play games with it, Hurley seems to inhabit his odd little songs. On *Armchair Boogie*, he really becomes that werewolf, "stepping along" with a howl in his throat and a tear in his eye, puzzled about "how much I love the maid as I tear off her clothes". Robin Remaily's fiddle adds just the right touch of pathos, and Hurley's unearthly, wordless chorus makes the blood run cold. Hurley grew up in rural New Jersey, bummed around in Greenwich Village, then got ill. Death haunts the edges of his songs, and for Robert Christgau he writes "about the afterlife better than anyone else". He is also a master of lulling you into a sense of false security and then throwing in a line like "when I learned to drink your blood, friend, it took years". (The use of the word "friend" is particularly unsettling.) More to the point, he's kept on going, recycling his greatest hits through a succession of off-centre record labels, from Folkways to Raccoon and Eugene Chadbourne's Fundamental, and God bless them all.

Hurley has the total self-absorption of the true eccentric, seen also in the hillbilly cartoons which form his second career: Boone and Jocko are holy fools, straight out of Appalachian folklore. For Christgau, "his old-timey feel is devoid of camp or nostalgia", and Michael has wandered America, fathering children and singing for dimes, playing scratchy banjo and fiddle in the crook of his arm. He can get that slightly out-of-tune sound which defines true country. The mutant heir of Hank Williams, he was once described as country's version of alternative rock, although he's naturally strange rather than wilfully eccentric. Julian Cope is particularly partial to 'Sweedeedee', while I don't think anyone has bettered the infectious simplicity of 'Slurf Song', his paean to food from *Have Moicy*, shared with other folk degenerates: "We fill up our guts/and we turn it into shit/then we get rid of it." I defy you not to sing along or tap your feet. Or eat real soon.

Hurley has turned himself into a cottage industry, putting out cassettes on his own Bellemeade label. A recent CD compilation of truck songs, old Bob Wills tunes and songs from his own ceaseless imagination, was subtitled "Return To The Land Of Lo-Fi". It ends with 'Sweet Thing', on which he seems to be playing a bagpipe tune on an ancient fiddle. 'Ruben's Train' is an "old Appalachian fiddle tune" played on a fretless banjo, and sung as if each word is piercing his heart, like a young Dock Boggs. The only more dreadful thought than that there could be a world in which no one made this kind of record is that there was one in which you had to hear it from morning to night.

Another man to derive amusement for the drugged mind was John Hartford, who played at local square dances, worked on a Mississippi riverboat, then hit Nashville as a session player, with songs like 'I've Heard That Tear-Stained Monologue You Do There By The Door Before You Go' and wordplay like that same song's "when the punchline reaches out and punches me". His much-covered 'Gentle On My Mind' flows dreamily, with uncharacteristic poetic imagery like something from Bob Lind. On his debut album, however, it follows directly on from a song called 'The Wart', a high-speed race between his voice and banjo, and presumably bankrolled a whole sequence of uncommercial albums which are now highly treasured by those in the know, none more so than *Aero-Plain*.

On the cover of this album, he wears a pilot's goggles and adopts a blank stare. Hartford entered the studio with a crack acoustic band, comprising our old friend the fiddler Vassar Clements, Norman Blake on guitar and mandolin, Tut Taylor on dobro and Ricky Skaggs as the joker in the pack on electric bass. He then instructed his band to play whatever came into their minds, and without the benefit of being able to listen to the playbacks. "A tune would start, and I would stand there and then I would look down and discover my hands busy at the music and that I was just two eyeballs floating in it." It was as close as modern Nashville studio musicians could get to the old back-porch free-fall. David Bromberg was brought in to act as God, keeping them going until enough decent stuff was in the can.

Sam Bush was just one young bluegrass musician turned on by this brief flash of light, like a kingfisher glimpsed and then gone. He saw the band play live: "Some may call it newgrass. I call it a mind-blowing musical experience." This free-flight jamming carried over to the album, and captures forever a moment in time when "there were no music videos, only two bluegrass magazines [*only two?*] and musicians were breaking boundaries...just for the love of the music". The results are warm and flowing, and yet sharp enough to dissolve any blandness in John's vocals, his one sin. Skaggs is left out when the others form a gospel quartet to sing an old Alfred Brumley song as if the whole thing is a radio broadcast. This is music in love with the past. The most prominent song is 'Tear Down The Grand Ole Opry', proving that you can always rely on the rebels to respect tradition most: "Right across from the wax museum, they used to line up around the block...Broad Street will never be the same." Nevertheless, down it came.

Paul Siebel had a genuine love for country from the start, though he spent some time in Greenwich Village as a folk singer. The magnificent *Woodsmoke And Oranges* is as evocative as its title, with stellar playing from Richard Greene, who duels with the singer for the high notes. Poignancy is his trademark, especially on 'Louise', a tender tribute to a small-town hooker. Siebel was country's answer to David Ackles: both men were too sensitive for their own good, burning out while lesser talents marched on. It just makes his Elektra debut all the more precious.

John Prine doesn't so much sing as growl. *The Guardian* reckoned that he had the voice of a "bulldog chewing a holly bush", but with it came a bulldog's determination. Prine emerged in the Chicago folk clubs, where the semi-fatal "new Dylan" tag was first attached to him, but country music was deep in his soul from the start. He learnt guitar from his brother Dave, who played in the style of The New City Ramblers: "When you play a Carter Family tune, you feel like a master. Right away, I started making up words and writing quasi-Carter Family songs." He also admitted that he shared three guitar styles with a younger member of that dynasty, Carlene Carter, namely: "fast, slow and calypso".

Prine recorded his debut album in Memphis, not Nashville – hip rather than hick – and it suits the toughness in his voice and his material, comprising everyday songs of working men. 'Illegal Smile' is a dope smoker's anthem, although John claimed unconvincingly that it was about his own tendency to daydream. 'Sam Stone' is a whole movie set to music, about a Vietnam vet who burns out young and turns to heavier stimulants: "There's a hole in daddy's arm/where all the money goes." There's lots of wordplay in his early songs, but it's reined back, bitten off short.

"John Prine is so good," Kris Kristofferson half-joked, "we may have to break his thumbs." The music is built to match, tough but witty. There's plenty of pedal steel in the sound, but Leo LeBlanc is not a Nashville picker: "his steel playing stays closer to the rhythm section than a Weldon Myrick". Prine might have grown up in Chicago, but his parents had emigrated from Western Kentucky, and John spent his summers back there, in a small town called Paradise. It was close to Beechcreek, where Johnny Cash came to record the coalmining section of his concept album *Ride This Train*.

'Paradise' is also the bitterly ironic title of Prine's song about a "backwards old town", close to Green River, where a mining company arrived with "the world's biggest shovel" and Eden disappeared: "Mr Peabody's coal train has hauled it away". Prine sings in a kind of lost innocence – with, yes, the subtlety of a young Dylan, also bemoaning what strip mining had done to Duluth – and to an Appalachian backing of acoustic guitars, fiddle and bass, with no drums. No wonder that The Everly

Brothers later covered this song, and Bill Monroe – who was born across the river – told him: "I thought it was a song I overlooked from the Twenties." In the excellent booklet to Prine's totally essential two-CD anthology *Great Days*, he fleshes things out further. While he was away serving in the army, this "Disney-looking town, [in which] there was one black man in town, Bubby Short, who looked like Uncle Remus", was wiped off the map by a coal company. John brought his father a tape of his new song. "He went into the next room, and sat in the dark while it was on. I asked him why, and he said he wanted to pretend it was on the jukebox." Prine is a romantic at his savage heart, and the song ends: "When I die, let my ashes float down the Green River." It's now a bluegrass classic.

The title of Prine's second LP was *Diamonds In The Rough*, a Carter Family song based on an old Appalachian hymn, and the music here is built to match, with dobro, banjo and fiddle. Prine shows himself as the new Hank Williams on 'Yes I Guess They Oughtta Name A Drink After You', funny but sad, too, and with not a word wasted. On the title track, he sings three-part harmony with brother Dave and long-time colleague Steve Goodman, who had been particularly upset at the break up of the English folk harmony trio The Young Tradition, whose Peter Bellamy once instructed me to buy the complete Carter Family output. It's all one circle, ever widening.

David Fricke writes about this album as part of Prine's life-long search for "the perfect recorded balance between his country and folk instincts", and after its relative commercial failure he rocked harder. On the cover of *Sweet Revenge*, he sprawls in an open-topped car, rumpled and bearded, with a scuffed pair of cowboy boots. "He used to sing me 'Blood On The Saddle'," goes one song, dedicated to his grandfather. It's like a template for Steve Earle's tougher efforts, and largely recorded in Nashville, with a driving cover version of Merle Travis' 'Nine-Pound Hammer'. Prine's determination to make every album sound different confused his audience, even if it served to assuage some inner restlessness. The next album was produced by Booker T, and the highlight of a messy and much-interrupted recording career was 1986's *German Afternoon*, another return to largely acoustic music and his Kentucky roots. He recut 'Paradise', and revisited The Carter Family. A recent battle with cancer of the neck perhaps made people realise how precious is Prine's talent, not to mention his bloody-minded determination. No wonder his band is called The Lost Dogs.

The Missing Years was described as "a collection of wry, dusty tales which helped define the genre of alternative country". *No Depression* was among the magazines to recently heap praise on *In Spite of Ourselves*, an album of duets with the likes of Dolores Keane, Lucinda Williams, and Emmylou Harris, on what he described as "these meetin', cheatin' and retreatin' songs". He also toured with Iris Dement in support, and joined her for her wicked parody of George Jones and Tammy Wynette's 1974 hit 'We're Not The Jet Set'. Lines like "Our Bach and

Tchaikovsky are Haggard and Husky" were sent from heaven. So, too, was Prine's title song, a saga of the modern everyday couple muddling through, with Dement getting all the best lines: "He ain't got laid in a month of Sundays/caught him once and he was sniffin' my undies."

To find a comparison with John Prine, you need to look far outside Nashville and at another master of the spoken word, the late Ian Dury. Both are craftsmen who can put exactly the right word in precisely the right place. As Prine described it, "it's more of an editing process with me. There's a lot of words there and I'm trying to figure out how to leave out the wrong ones. It's like I'm clipping around a hedge." Both Prine and Dury deal with the sometimes sordid matter of the human condition, neither can sing in any accepted sense, and yet both use their voices like great comic actors, and any audience can recognise what they both share: a huge and generous heart.

There was a matching joy in a musical movement concurrent with Prine's emergence from the folk clubs, and one too that looked back to an earlier form of country music as its life-force. Country swing re-emerged through the eccentric delights of former Charlatan Dan Hicks, with his Hot Licks, and Commander Cody And His Lost Planet Airmen.

Backwards into the future. In a time of psychic uncertainty, people could relate to a clowns onstage performing musical tricks. The Hot Licks began by reworking Charlatans classics such as 'How Can I Miss You When You Won't Go Away?'. Hicks was born in Little Rock, and felt a little "detached" in Haight Ashbury. As he told *Relix*: "I wanted to play guitar more, and play the kind of music where you could hear the words." The new band started by playing coffee houses, and called his new sound "folk swing", though others reckoned it "sarcastic, harmony-ridden 1930s soft-shoe rock", with smooth female voices in the chorus. Dan delivers the lyrics tongue in cheek, with a twang and a yodel, and as he said of one number onstage: "This is an instrumental, but it's got some words to it." Almost everything is in a 4/4 shuffle beat.

Despite her name, Sid Page was one of the first female instrumentalists in psychedelic pop, and is heard to best advantage on the live album *Where's The Money?*, itself well sampled on the compilation CD *Return To Hicksville*. Maryann Price sings Johnny Mercer's slick 'I'm An Old Cowhand (From The Rio Grande)' with lap steel, sweet country fiddle and a chuckle in her throat, while Dan's own 'My Old-Timey Baby' opens with some banter, and he then sings a piece of instant nostalgia. There's none of Bob Wills' feral wildness here.

Hicks keeps going, continuing to deal with serious subjects in an oblique, comical way, with lyrics like "My mother died from asbestos/My father's name was Estes/and I don't know if that messed us/up." Thomas Dolby covered 'I Scare Myself' as a precursor of techno, and as Dan told Barney Hoskyns, some people see the Hot Licks as a precursor for sophisticated nostalgia, "things like kd lang, but I feel we were just sort of there". You would, Dan, you just would.

Lost In The Ozone, the debut album by Commander Cody, opens with 'Back To Tennessee', and among the band is West Virginia Creeper, on pedal steel. Cody, under his real name of George Frayne, began pounding the ivories with The Fantastic Surfing Beavers. The Airmen formed in Michigan before moving to San Francisco, where their easy, flowing mixture of western swing, truckers songs and rockabilly now sounds like a try-out for Americana. It's low-voltage stuff best taken live, as on *Deep From The Heart Of Texas*, recorded at the Armadillo World Headquarters in Austin. During their first trip to Memphis, they raided the Sun warehouse for a pile of rare 78s – 'Flying Saucers Rock 'n' Roll later went down well on stage, "though we couldn't understand a word he said but the crazy beat" – which George later fell on and smashed. Their own classic doper's song 'Down To Seeds And Stems (Again)' was based on a Merle Haggard tune, which is a neat way of turning the tables. During a later recording session in Nashville, it was Wayne Moss who came up with the idea which they recorded 'Daddy's Drinking Up Our Christmas' as a novelty single, at the same time that "we were doing our full C&W sell-out at the CMA convention". Nobody was fooled: this is a bunch of stoned hippies, still not welcome in Muskogee. On one country station, the DJ announced: "Well, folks,you'll never guess what the cat just dragged in. Commander Cody. Scruffy old hippie."

The only friendly people were the likes of Waylon and Willie, who "saw all us hippies doing it", loosened up their image, and took "all the bucks home... Those weren't accepted as talents by the people in Nashville...they were too ugly. As soon as hicks started growing hair, people started paying more attention to them."

The band's greatest legacy is the new combination they forged between *Hot Licks, Cold Steel And Trucker's Favourites*, as the title of their second album describes it . As Cody told *Swing 51*: "In the history of country music the first recordings to feature a full drum kit and electric bass guitar were truck drivin' numbers. We liked the beat, we tried it, it worked." Compared with Cody, Asleep At The Wheel were a more controlled, more backward looking bunch, but were far more musically competent. The band was – and is – dominated by the smooth voice of Ray Benson, who has put together two tribute albums for his frontman, Bob Wills. Guests on the second range from The Squirrel Nut Zippers to The Dixie Chicks, and the whole thing is full of infectious charm.

As for Asleep At The Wheel, they moved from West Virginia to Austin in the early 1970s, and recreated western swing better than anyone, with pedal steel and fiddle, tinkling piano and string bass. Their debut album, Comin' Right At Ya, was released in 1973. "Even then, we didn't want to be compartmentalised." Another formative influence was Moon Mullican, a blues player, "and he was funky too. He'd get down with everybody." Benson remains a great enthusiast for the old music. As he told *New Country*: "what we're talking about here is folk music – music of the folks. This ain't Joan Baez folk music, not to put her down. But what I'm saying is that this is music that folks sing." He has always done the same: "You're not a star, you're just a dance band. You provide music for social gatherings: the tribe gets together and you play the music." Alvin Crow And The Pleasant Valley Boys were another young band acting old, while The Ozark Mountain Daredevils came from Missouri and were once described as The Eagles fronted by Jed Clampett – there was mountain music mixed up in their rock 'n' roll.

Meanwhile, the cutting edge of American rock music moved south to Capricorn records, and produced guitar-fuelled boogie. Duane and Gregg Allman were born in Nashville, where their father was an army lieutenant who came home from the Korean War for Christmas and picked up a hitchhiker, who promptly murdered him. That mixture of helpfulness and extreme violence could only be found in Tennessee. The family moved then to Florida, and the boys fell in love with R&B. The closest they came to country music was when The Nitty Gritty Dirt Band took them under their wing. Part of The Allman Brothers' sonic guitar attack, though, came from Richard Betts, whose father played fiddle for square dances and taught his son to play.

Richard fell under the spell of western swing, and later repaid the debt with the stone delight of his solo album *Highway Call*. *Dark Star* described it as "two sides of beautiful, swinging, country music", and it has all the flow of the Allmans at their best, with none of the overload. It is also a perfect balance between Macon, Georgia – where it was recorded – and Nashville, courtesy of Vassar Clements and steel player John Hughey from the Conway Twitty band. 'Hand Picked' stretches over most of a side of vinyl, and country instrumentals really don't come any finer. There's a lovely lightness of touch, with Vassar floating like a butterfly and then stinging like a bee.

Another fine fiddler, Buddy Spicher, turns up on the debut by another Capricorn band, Blue Jug, who exercised much more care in creating tableaux of Southern life than their rivals, at times appearing like a home-grown Band. Also worthy of note were The Atlanta Rhythm Section, an eclectic bunch who proudly sang "We like reggae, we dig country, classical music's a gas/we play the blues in three-quarter time." There's a sting in the tail, though: "But they don't want to hear that jazz/they want boogie...so we boogie." Like most of their compatriots, even this spikey crew succumbed to producing FM fodder, what Steve Burgess described as being "hermetically sealed, no throbbing allowed". Southern rock *did* keep hillbilly alive, though, even if sometimes in disguise. Even the Allmans at least stressed sibling togetherness.

The Marshall Tucker Band hailed from Spartanburg in the Blue Ridge Mountains, and could have more accurately been called The Caldwell Brothers Band rather than being named after a blind piano tuner. Their debut album contains the hoe-down 'Hillbilly Band'. As Tommy Caldwell said, "when we could do what we wanted, we came back to the country". Charlie Daniels came from North Carolina, and started as a country fiddler, playing on Dylan's *Nashville Skyline* and in Leonard Cohen's tour band. He then embraced Southern boogie and, as Bill Malone puts it, "this big, gruff, tobacco-chewing, outspoken musician embodied good-old-boy traits almost to the point of caricature. He was nationalistic, hedonistic, macho...and lovable."

Singing in a definitive Southern accent, he also played up his love of western swing on *Fire On The Mountain*, while 'The Devil Went Down To Georgia' was an update of an old folk theme, portraying Satan as a fiddle player – no wonder bible-bashers tried to ban the instrument. Daniels wrote about a changing land in 'Carolina, I Remember You', a nostalgic look back to his home state before it was opened up by the super-highways. Too rough around the edges for some country fans, he lights up the screen when *Urban Cowboy* features part of his stage show.

Another country boy to jump on the Southern rock bandwagon was Hank Williams Jr, who swaggered through hedonistic anthems like 'Whiskey Bent And Hell Bound'. Meanwhile, the greatest (hidden) country band of them all were Lynryd Skynyrd. On *Endangered Species*, they finally came clean, stripping classic songs like 'Sweet Home Alabama' – their answer in song to Neil Young's 'Southern Man' – down to acoustic guitars, dobro and mandolin. As Gary Rossington told *New Country*: "we were all raised on country music as well as the blues". In turn, modern stars like The Mavericks, Travis Tritt and Wynona Judd piled in to record a tribute album, *Skynyrd Frynds*, to a band once seen as interlopers. Growing up in Texas, Clint Black saw Skynyrd as something very close to country, though "they were writing very strong lyrics. They sounded like a band, but...something that was arranged by the songwriter type, where all the parts work together".

Ronnie Van Zant was the son of a truck driver, and devoured Merle Haggard songs as part of his intention to write his own lyrics about working-class life and Southern pride. Here was a boy whose favourite Hollywood cowboy was Ronald Reagan, but who wore his hair long and wanted his band to sound like a cross between Free and The Rolling Stones. He sang punchily to a loud but sweet thrust of three lead guitars, which producer Al Kooper honed to perfection. If you want hard rock, make this your first port of call – muscle and intelligence combined.

Although Skynyrd took to the stage in front of a huge Confederate flag, the cowboy-hatted Van Zant was certainly no racist, and his lyrics carefully picked at such matters. Here is a band which urged its followers to throw their handguns into the sea and attacked the redneck mentality from within, while at the same time exuding Southern pride. Like the Allmans, this was a band who grew an extra dimension in concert. On their double live CD *One More From The Road*, they introduce new member Steve Gaines as an "Okie", before going on to sing 'T For Texas', "an old song by Jimmie Rodgers". To complete the myth, Gaines and Van Zandt were both killed with extreme violence in a plane crash in 1977, a few days after the release of *Street Survivors*, on which the band are surrounded by flames. It does seem that embracing country values exposes you to all kinds of dangers and tragedy.

It's just as if it's all part of Pat Campbell's 'The Deal' (to quote the title of perhaps the most distressing of all country recitations), in which a man urges God to take his life and spare that of his wife and new-born son. A church-like organ plays as Pat half whispers about "complications" and what he offers up in the chapel. God assents: "my legs gave way and suddenly I began to fall" just as the doctor bends over him and says to the nurse "it's too bad he won't know of the miracle that's happened". Tom Petty put it better when he brought down the volume, cooled down The Heartbreakers and sadly emoted: "The young 'uns call it country/the yankees call it dumb/but everything is done with a Southern accent/where I come from."

The boogie tradition continues in the form of The Bottle Rockets, who fuse it with country folk and write humourous songs with a serious message at their heart. They started out just like Lynyrd Skynyrd and every new country-influenced band worth its salt. As they told *No Depression*: "So that was our big plan, to get down in the trenches and decide to be country. But we didn't want to learn country songs, we wanted to take what we knew and write our own country songs."

Back in Nashville, Billy Sherrill had created a music machine worthy of Tamla Motown, manufacturing a string of hit singles. The likes of Tammy Wynette, Charlie Rich and Tanya Tucker were the puppets, while Billy pulled the strings – and smothered his discs with them. He rejected any high-falutin' ideas of art, like those long-haired Beatles had spawned with *Sergeant Pepper*: "Hit singles are the best concept for albums in the world." The singer is less important than the song. "Finding the right song is the rough part of the record business. Recording is just the gravy." In a way he's right: almost all of the greatest country singers have also written their own material, or stolen it from the very best traditional sources. While Sherrill gives high praise to the likes of Hank Williams, "to say we can't broaden the appeal is ludicrous". The problem is that he essentially narrowed it to a middle-of-the-road, *Readers' Digest*-style clientele.

Billy co-wrote 'Stand By Your Man' with Tammy Wynette, and never can its opening line – "sometimes it's hard to be a woman" – have rung more true than in her own sad life. The record is muted, with weeping pedal steel in duet with a vocal which sobs in tune. Tammy sings with a catch in her throat, occasionally drops her voice down for a quiet aside, and then belts out the chorus with real spunk. She emotes with such evident sincerity that you fear for her sanity. This is confessional poetry, like a downmarket Sylvia Plath. Born in the Delta, Tammy picked cotton and learned to play the bass fiddle. She later trained as a beautician, married young, and gave birth to a child with spinal meningitis. This awful event opens her autobiography, which is more of a survival manual than light entertainment: "Sometimes I feel so angry and hostile that I want to shake my fist at a heaven that will justify this unbearable cruelty."

The book also reveals her credentials as part of the Celtic diaspora: "I come from solid English-Irish stock, generations of hard-working, practical people who put their faith in God and their sweat in the land." For a woman who once spelt D.I.V.O.R.C.E. out loud, she certainly could pick 'em. Tammy's second husband traded nude pictures of her to pornographic magazines, so she left him. Big mistake: husband number three was George Jones, who took pot shots at her with his rifle and once beat her so badly she had to pick up a CMA award wearing a wig to hide the bruises. And he sings gospel songs with such feeling! She had a series of horrible stomach operations (by the end "they were running out of places to put catheters"), was mysteriously kidnapped and beaten up, and then became addicted to painkillers.

Towards the end, one journalist caught a club gig and reported that "her face looked like she was dead already. I couldn't bear to watch. Her voice was thin and croaky, and she couldn't hit the high notes." Even when she reached the deep peace of the grave, they wouldn't let her be. Her family had her dug up again in pursuance of a law suit. All this happened to a woman who once sang 'Don't Liberate Me'. One of the bravest things she did was to collaborate with The KLF on 'Justified And Ancient', singing the utterly nonsensical words "all bound for Mu Mu Land" as if she meant every one. Is the joke on her, or them? A white voice raps away behind her, and you suddenly sense The Alabama 3 waiting in the wings. Out of the studio, Tammy cooked The KLF grits and asked of Bill Drummond, "You're from Scotland. Can you tell me why I have such a large lesbian following there?" Maybe they simply recognised a fellow Celt.

Dolly Parton's father was a tobacco farmer of Scotch-Irish extraction, while her mother was part Cherokee. She was born on Locust Ridge in Tennessee, started writing songs at the age of five, and listened to the Grand Ole Opry on a battery-operated radio – you couldn't invent this. Her grandfather was a fiddle-playing preacher, and she first sang in public in her local tabernacle: "Our services would be mostly music. The old hymns. They were just about the biggest things we did, recreation-wise."

Dolly has since made rich use of her rural upbringing, with her lyrics sounding like a dream: "sitting on the front porch on a summer afternoon, in a straight-back chair on two legs, leaned against the wall". Part of Parton's wide appeal is the way she can radiate pure joy or bleak despair at will. Her voice is still full of its original twang and snap, and it soars like a lark ascending. If you don't respond, you must be dead. Her songs often deal with life's abject cruelty, updating the mountain canon but staying true to it.

Even her starring role in Hollywood's *9 To 5* – which brought out the essential humour of the woman – was in a story about how office workers dealt with an oppressive boss, and the matching album contains her version of Merle Travis' 'Dark As A Dungeon', focusing on an earlier form of slave labour. Ironically, Dolly herself was almost swallowed up by Nashville slickness, but *Trio* proved the first step in her bid for freedom. Her voice once again glided and chuckled over banjos, fiddles, mountain dulcimers and songs by Jimmie Rodgers and Jean Ritchie's utterly devastating 'Dear Companion', plus 'Rosewood Casket' and 'Farther Along'. On the first, about love surviving death, the arrangement is credited to Parton's mother. For Emmylou and Linda, these were heartfelt performances; for Dolly, it was simply part of her heritage reborn.

Under the smooth surface of Nashville in the 1970s, all kinds of strange tensions were simmering. Old-time music might have been thought dead and buried, but it continued to poke above the ground. Weird as can be are 'Rocky Top', as performed by The Nashville Brass, who sounding like a colliery band on downers with steel guitar and banjo; The Oak Ridge Boys' 'An Old-Time Family Bluegrass Band', which is basically gospel gone choral; and the early works of C&W Lolita Tanya Tucker. From the age of 14, weird old men were putting words into her mouth, in what John Morthland called *"American Gothic*'s last stand". In 'Blood Red And Going Down' she watches her father kill his mother and her lover, cool as a cucumber and to a dying steel guitar: "At times like this a child of ten never knows exactly what to say." Tanya is sexually sophisticated beyond her years, as she describes 'The Man That Turned My Mama On' (in ladies' shoes, no less), and in 'Would You Lay With Me (In A Field of Stone)', she turns seductress herself – "if my lips were dry/would you wet them dear/in the midnight hour" – over Billy Sherrill's sweeping strings.

That song was written by David Alan Coe, and is indicative of a whole new breed of (male) country songwriter, who were as tough as a cowpoke's saddle but tender with it. Mickey Newbury wrote the ultimate example of Americana in 'An American Trilogy'. As sung live at Montezuma Hall, he opens with a simple Celtic filigree on his acoustic guitar, and then links together three fragments from the folk tradition of the Civil War: being born in Dixie, achieving glory and a peaceful death, and ending with a whistled coda. In three minutes, it somehow evokes the birth of modern America. He sings tenderly, but with a catch in his throat.

Some of Mickey's albums now sound a little too lush, as do his poetics, but at his best – like the atmospheric *Looks Like Rain,* a suite linked by "rain and train sound effects courtesy of Mystic Moods Orchestra" – he seems able to enter a dream world of his own making. Newbury continues to term himself a folk singer, and the live album is wonderfully bare, less dated than his studio work. *Rusty Tracks,* meanwhile, features further reworkings of American traditional songs.

Elsewhere, Jimmy Buffet was writing his "90 per cent autobiographical" story-songs with a touch of western swing. Here is an intelligent man acting dumb – you really can't beat a title like 'My Head Hurts, My Feet Stink And I Don't Love Jesus', or the jovial way he sings it. Harry Chapin told his "new greatest stories live" – he's dead now – with long raps between, including 'Old Folkie', which is blatantly about Pete Seeger. The song sounds folksy now, even if now unbearably sentimental, and Chapin makes the great man sound like a relic, a sad failure, "singing for some hopeless cause/shouting at the mountain top".

Tougher by far is Steve Young, who in his proud lament 'Montgomery In The Rain' wants only "to go by Hank's tombstone/and cry me up a thunderstorm chain". He is joined by bluegrass quintet The Last Mile Ramblers on 'The White Trash Song', a song which could define Appalachian life, with references to a rural dawn and "little squirrels a-barking like they thought they was a mountain lion". Broken-down cars litter his front yard, and his woman gone off with a gospel singer up in Nashville, Tennessee. (These last two words sung with vehemence.) He pauses only for some fierce banjo. "I was born a child of these muddy roads."

Much the same atmosphere seeps through the cover of *The Outlaws*, an old, tattered and frayed "wanted" poster, a relic of the Wild West, featuring the bearded and unsmiling trio of Willie Nelson, Waylon Jennings and Tompall Glaser – collars up or hiding under nasty hats – and the merely unsmiling Jessi Colter. The Outlaws were a brilliant marketing device, but were also much more. What started as a nickname (itself from a Lee Clayton song, 'Ladies Love Outlaws', as recorded by Waylon) became a sales pitch, but one that pitched real country into the rock marketplace, much as Island records did with Bob Marley and rebel reggae. In both cases, it also enabled the artists in question to grab control of their own work. Just as importantly, the image of long hair, soft drugs and fistfights proved to be a *lingua franca*, and these already grizzled veterans became touchstones for a younger generation.

And so they remain. To see Willie Nelson singing solo to an old guitar on *Later...* was almost literally to see God, just as to hear his bare session for the Andy Kershaw radio show was to hear a prophet in the wilderness. It's therefore all the more disconcerting to see photos of the young Nashville songwriter with short hair, a suit and a crocodile grin. Nelson has aged into magnificence.

He was true country, though, right from the start. Willie's family moved from Arkansas to Abbott, Texas, in the very year that the stock market collapsed. As he tells it in *I Didn't Come Here And I Ain't Leaving*, an autobiography which rings with his own voice – wacky, wise and mystical round the edges – his mother's family, part Indian, were "talented moonshiners as well as musicians. Her folks used to run hideouts in the mountains where outlaws could come and find safety." His father was from the Ozarks, which "in those times were full of English and Irish who were moving west in large numbers", after the US army had cleared the land of its natives. The Nelsons "brought their folk music with them from the old country. They had a tradition as storytellers and singers and dancers and fiddle players."

Following that same heritage, Willie's grandparents both taught at singing school, adopting the old shape-note method, and his grandad would soothe the young Willie to sleep with songs like 'She'll Be Coming Round The Mountain'. At the age of two, his parents bought him a tin mandolin, equipped with real strings, and by the time he was five he could be found singing 'When Irish Eyes Are Smiling' in public. He also learned early how to pick cotton, and not just "for exercise".

A more fitting career began in 1960 when he sold 'Family Bible', a song about his musical childhood – "I can hear my mother softly singing/Rock of Ages" – for $50, and it hit the charts. On his own 1971 version, there's banjo, steel guitar, honky-tonk piano and sad fiddle, although this version is too fast and cheerful for its own good. Not Willie, though: he sings as if only to himself. He later moved to Nashville, although he refused to wear rhinestones, raised hogs as a second income and recorded some demos of which Spencer Leigh reckoned: "The tracks are either bleak, very bleak, or unbearably bleak. Leonard Cohen and The Smiths have got nothing on this lot." At this time, he made his cash writing songs like 'Crazy' for Patsy Cline, and playing bass guitar with Ray Price.

His own recordings, produced by Chet Atkins, by now sound formulaic, although his voice could already break your heart. He knows exactly where to pause for dramatic effect, neatly picking out each syllable like a master carpenter knowing exactly where to bang in each nail. This is closer to jazz singing than hillbilly, except in the way in which he can plunge from the high notes to deep down low. Jim Reeves, anyone? It's like the feeling you get when the aeroplane you're on suddenly plunges a few thousand feet. The bog-standard backings – which Willie reckoned were decided by a computer in New York – sound as if they could be coming from another room.

It was only when Nelson left Nashville for Austin, and began to record with his own band, that his vocal style – "they'd say, 'He's not singing, he's talking'" – began to gain an audience. His last gasp for RCA, *Yesterday's Wine*, was a concept album about life and death, and this seemed to open the floodgates: "I'm finally standing upright on the ground/after taking several readings/I'm surprised to find my mind's still fairly sound." It opens with Willie talking with God; he did, after all, once teach religion before he began to exemplify it.

He then released the gospel album *The Troublemaker*, and the rockier *Shotgun Willie* soon followed, with songs by Bob Wills and a New York, soul-inspired production. Nelson was by now the thinking person's country star: side one of *Phases And Stages* is told from the woman's point of view, while side two is told from the man's. The original single, 'Phases, Stages, Circles, Cycles And Scenes', is sung to an acoustic guitar, and it draws you in as would a snake charmer. Willie has always had that hypnotic power, and by now his voice has shucked off any Nashville mannerisms, playing off the rhythm of his band, clipping the notes short. "A lot of people think I sing nasal. It's not true…actually it's the sound that comes from deep down in the diaphragm. That's where you get the most strength." Just listen to 'Stardust', his extraordinary colonisation of the classic song recorded with Booker T. Here country meets blues meets jazz, and all so mellow that it sounds as if "Willie's at home, sitting on his porch, while bald eagles fly above". He sings as if he's praying, or just about to be sick, it's that intense. He's doing what hillbillies always did, taking old songs and making them his own.

The most spectacular example is the *Red-Headed Stranger* album. As a man who had himself been nicknamed 'Booger Red' in childhood, he was particularly fascinated by the ballad of that name. His wife suggested that he write some new songs around it, and so tells the story of a preacher who shoots his unfaithful lover dead and then takes off on the road, recycling cowboy songs from the Thirties and Forties as he goes. There's even some saloon piano. The whole thing can be read as a horse opera, a kind of autobiography or religious parable. It works on every level. He told his band only to play what they thought was necessary, to get the barest feel he could. CBS at first tried to cover it up with strings, but good sense prevailed. It remains a stunning achievement, even if the CD leaves out the story told in the form of a cartoon on the back. Willie appears on the front as an old cowboy, or maybe as he is today. It says much for his image that it could be either.

As he has aged into grandeur, Willie has developed his Tex-flamenco guitar playing on stripped-back albums like *Spirit*, drawing the admiration of no less than Richard Thompson: "He plays these terrible solos and leaves them alone, which takes a lot of guts these days." *Teatro* benefits from Daniel Lanois at the controls of the ghost train, while *Tougher Than Leather* is another suite of songs about the Wild West and reincaration. *Across The Borderline* is almost a revived folk revival, and Willie quotes Roger Miller: "we had a lot of folks on there". He features such fellow musicians at his Fourth Of July Picnics, but a whole bunch of unexpected names turned up on the alt rock "non-tribute" album *Twisted Willie*, from Jello Biafra to Steel Pole Bath Tub – all rebels together.

Waylon and Willie came together to warn 'Don't Cuss The Fiddle' – a song with deep roots, about brotherly love and witchcraft – "unless you want that fiddle out of tune; that picker there in trouble, boy, ain't nothing but another side of you". The *Waylon & Willie* LP is textured like an old photo album, and Chet Flippo writes that both men "invoke the sheer beauty and power of real, honest country music". Jennings was born in Lamb County, Texas, and his voice comes across clear and muscular in his autobiography, *Waylon*, with chapter headings like "Busted" and "This Outlaw Shit". It reads like he sings, and west Texas comes over as a threatening place, whose storms have entered Jennings' deepest nightmares: "I've seen chickens got to roost at noon, it'd be so dark. The noise the wind made haunts me to this day. It sounded like the end of time." He also admits that if you are lucky enough to be born in the Lone Star state, "You think that you are a little bit taller, a little bit smarter, and a little bit tougher than anybody else. It's a country unto itself."

The Jennings were from immigrant stock, "Irish and Black Dutch, and as God-fearing as they come. My dad was as close to being a preacher as he could without being a preacher." They belonged to the Church of Christ, as self-righteous a bunch as could be found, puritanical to the point of obsessiveness. Women were not allowed to speak in church, and music was banned. Part of Jennings was attracted to such extremities (one thinks of Jerry Lee and the usual Southern dichotomy of fighting and fucking on Saturday night, then going to church the next morning), but even he found it unsettling that his Grandma Tempe would go to church, then come home "put on her old feed-sack dress, grab some poor chicken by the neck, and wring its head off".

Mr Jennings played guitar in the Texas dance halls. He'd roast peanuts with his son, and they'd listen to the Grand Ole Opry together. When Bill Monroe came on, "Daddy would look at me and grin. He liked that high voice." He also played guitar in the same "thumb-and-finger plucking style" as Mother Maybelle Carter. Waylon is a wonderful example of a singer on the cusp of old and new country, before and after rock 'n' roll. He still remembers hearing Elvis on the radio for the first time and understanding what exactly he was fusing together: "The sound went straight up your spine." Presley sang like a black man, but the music was pure country. "Maybe it was the flapping of that big doghouse bass, all wood thump, and the slapback echo of the guitars wailin' and frailin' away. It just climbed straight through you."

Like Willie, he started life picking cotton, and remembers hearing a lonely steam train across the fields: "It sounds like death. The last time I was pulling cotton I was about 16. I said 'I didn't plant this shit, and I ain't never gonna pull it up no more.'" He quit on the spot, and left his gathering sack on the ground. "It may be there to this day."

He set out to be a professional musician, and hit paydirt one day when he hitched to Lubbock, and ran into Charles "Buddy" Holly. Only a year older than Waylon, he was singing in a country duo, "in classic Delmore/Louvin Brothers fashion", but Elvis' Sun sound inspired Buddy to add a bassist and a fiddle player. Holly called it "western and bop", an update of western swing, "when rural string-band music started colliding with the big-band jazz of the early Thirties". Jennings later joined his band, on bass: "We'd sit on the bus and sing old bluegrass songs."

Jennings gave up his seat to the Big Bopper on Holly's final flight on that snowy night in Iowa. His last, jokey comment to Buddy was "I hope your ol' plane crashes." It took him some time to get over that, and there is a deep sense of tragedy which has haunted Jennings' music ever since. It may well have pushed him towards some of the folky material he includes on the brilliant run of albums he made for RCA, from 1966's *Folk-Country* to 1969's *Country-Folk*, recorded with the Kimberlys. All are an odd but satisfying mix of tinkly backings and a big, tough voice with attitude. A typical line is "you're always embarrassed by the callouses here on my hands", but next up will be the lighter songs like The Beatles' 'I'm A Man Of Constant Sorrow' and even Dylan's 'Don't Think Twice'. All this from a youth whose cover photos looked confrontational even then, and who starred in the cash-in movie *Nashville Rebel*, having acted out the part for real while he roomed with Johny Cash. Like the man in black, there's something too dark and brooding to be simple entertainment, and a "poem" on the back of *Only The Greatest* relates how "his voice swells in complete loneliness, an almost impossible despair". He can also be very funny, in a rough kind of way.

At the dawn of the 1970s, the Nashvhille backings darken to match, notably on *Singer Of Sad Songs*, produced by Lee Hazlewood and with a beat more akin to rock music. Jennings issued the ultimatum to the effect that, if he wasn't given more artistic freedom and the chance to use his own tour band in the studio, he would simply record the same song over and over again until Chet Atkins released him. The real breakthrough was *Honky-Tonk Heroes*, with a bearded Jennings and heavy bass guitar. The album features songs by Billy Joe Shaver, who approached him one day at a drug- and liquor-crazed gathering at the Hillbilly Central recording studio and demanded the chance to write him an album. The one song not by him, and with added strings, is 'We Had It All', which one reviewer described as having the "feeling of being rapt in the American landscape". Or wrapped. Or maybe even ratted.

It's a serious point, though. These later albums give a real sense of the wide open spaces of a land – and a music – still up for grabs, none more so than *Dreaming My Dream*. It's still not exactly heavy rock, but the bitterness in 'Are You Sure Hank Did It This Way?' is like a cry for freedom: "Lord, it's the same old tune, fiddle and guitar/where do we take it from here?" As Waylon himself writes, with its "relentless four-on-the-floor rhythm, phased guitars and eerie drones", its lack of a fiddle break, and the see-sawing between two chords, this is nothing like country music as it was previously known. It's ironic, really, given the subject. The guitars are mixed together "so they sounded like one huge instrument". The driving drums and overall ambience are closer to The Velvet Underground than they are to the Hillbilly king.

At this time, Waylon literally used to walk around in Hank Williams' shoes, and once laid out on the back seat of the Cadillac in which he had died. In 1978, he quite rightly asked the musical question "Don't you think this outlaw bit's done got out of hand?" Nashville, as usual, had subverted a genuine feeling into a musical style. So where should country music go now? The answer, perhaps, came with the final track on the same album. 'Bob Wills Is Still The King' is recorded live in Austin, and there's a wonderful driving quality to the band, to which the crowd respond in kind.

On *I've Always Been Crazy*, Jennings is photographed like Charles Manson on a bad day, but he is his usual tough but humane self inside the sleeve, finally laying the ghost of Buddy Holly to rest with a medley of his songs and with The Crickets in support. More recently, Don Was produced his RCA comeback, and played stand-up bass with his shoes up, earning the reproof "Don I'm country, but not that country!" For all that, he recorded 'Mountain Man', a song about a man from Jackson Hole who cleans himself up for the love of a woman, although too proud to actually tell her.

Waylon's 1971 album *The Taker/Tulsa* featured songs by Kris Kristofferson, a man whom he and Nelson later joined in The Highwaymen, and of whom it was said that he "brought the bedroom to the Opry stage". I also remember seeing him booed offstage at the Isle Of Wight Festival, where his lugubrious singing and apparent attack on The Rolling Stones stank of country music intransigence, out of kilter with hippie idealism or, indeed, good music. He still can't sing in tune, but *The Austin Sessions* turns this to his advantage by taking his greatest hits (which have also aged into grandeur), slowing them down even further, and then partnering his grizzled old-timer growl with the sweet voices of Jackson Browne, Alison Krauss, Vince Gill and – in this context alone – Mark Knopfler and Steve Earle. Maybe they should invent a form of karaoke in which you can sing along with Kris – even the most out of tune among us would shine.

Just like the young Bob Dylan pretending to be an Okie, there is a sense that the son of an air force major general, former Rhodes scholar at Oxford (where he briefly joined the Larry Parnes stable of pretty young boy singers as Kris Carson), and one-time English professor at West Point is overdoing things a little. His chiselled features certainly make him a fine Hollywood cowboy, and here he sounds like country music's answer to Leonard Cohen. In 'The Pilgrim: Chapter 33', which opens "see him wasted on the sidewalk", Kristofferson helpfully drops the names Dennis Hopper, Johnny Cash, Jerry Jeff Walker, Rambling Jack Elliot and Paul Siebel, plus some names we've never heard of, and himself. He's lucky he's a big man, I reckon. But if Kristofferson represents any kind of continuation with mountain music, it's in the realm of celebrating self-destructiveness.

If anyone in this movement was a real outlaw – the type to be found in long-term incarceration, like Merle Haggard or Charles Manson – it was David Allan Coe. His claim to have killed a fellow inmate has never been proved, but a man who once appeared in cape and mask as the Mysterious Rhinestone Cowboy certainly looks the sort who would give you a Chinese burn just for fun. He often dressed as a biker, perhaps the closest thing to a cowboy we now have, and even jokes at the kind of low-down dives he plays, describing them as places "where bikers laugh at cowboys who are staring at the hippies who are praying that they'll get out alive" – this from a song with a chorus about his long hair not covering up his red neck. Indeed, there is more intelligence on show than in the whole of Kris Kristofferson, who hides his Oxford MA under his cowboy hat.

Songs like 'Take This Job And Shove It' explore the harsh underbelly of the American dream, with a side order of rough humour. Coe does a brilliant cover version of his friend Steve Goodman's 'You Never Even Call Me By My Name', which parodies the singing styles of Waylon, Charlie Pride and Merle so accurately that you find yourself searching the record sleeve to see if they're really there. It ends with the whole of C&W compressed into four lines: "I was drunk the day my mum got outta prison," and he goes to pick her up at the station, in his pickup truck, in the rain, but before he can, "she got run over by a Danville train".

In 'If That Ain't Country', Coe writes about blue-collar workers with more insight, though less romanticism, than Bruce Springsteen. Here is the true voice of the urban hillbilly family – the Simpsons, perhaps – with a dad who "sold used parts to make ends meet" and a mum who's "been to hell since junior went to jail". He ends by singing four unrelated lines in a parody of that high, lonesome sound, so that the great speckled bird meets the wild of life, although 'Tennessee Whiskey' is the closest he gets to the mountains. Perhaps Coe's most important song is 'Willie, Waylon And Me', which sees the axis of country moving from California to Texas – and who mentioned Nashville? "I heard The Burritos out in California could fly higher than The Byrds...The Eagles flew in from the West Coast; like The Byrds they were trying to be free." This hard man from Dallas, Texas, is similarly intent on "making music that is free".

This isn't true of just men, either. Jennings made much play of his marriage to fellow singer Jessi Colter, but more to my own tastes are two women you would never want to cross. Rattlesnake Annie is part Cherokee, and refuses to allow the rattlesnakes on her farm to be killed, although she wears the skeleton of one from her ear. She mixes country and blues in the old way, just as they were when she was born in West Tennessee and then sang them in Beale Street. 'Country Music Hall Of Pain' opens with pedal steel, and then Annie's surprisingly light voice chimes in, bemoaning her fate. She gained a European following, and even pushed back the boundaries of the genre by recording with Czech C&W singer Michael Tcny as Rattlesnake Annie And The Last Cowboy. Elizabeth Barraclough, meanwhile, sounds tough as leather, a blues shouter whose album is partly recorded in Nashville, with Buttrey And McCoy providing a launching pad for her spiteful and extremely sensual songs.

Something strange was stirring in Austin, that most cosmopolitan of all Texan towns. Outcasts from Janis Joplin had once come to sing at places like Threadgill's Bar. Now it was Willie Nelson. Jan Reid put down (sometimes literally) the whole scene in a still-relevant book, *The Improbable Rise Of Redneck Rock*, providing vivid pen-portraits, so that the cosmic cowboy singer Michael Murphey, from the Mojave desert, "was born to play his guitar under clear skies in a meadow for retarded kids".

In fact, along with the likes of Steve Fromholz and BW Stevenson, Murphey was responsible for starting a new style of poetic idealism. He also released an album called *Americana*, plus a series of cowboy folk-tales in song. John Denver joins in on *Swans Against The Sun* and duets on 'Mansion On The Hill', no less, while John McEuen plays all kinds of mountain instruments. Murphey uses far too many words, but lines like "the high, uncertain singing of the unknown rider's song" have a trace of mountain mysticism, although no Appalachian would ever sing like such a wimp. Up there, they shoot you for much less serious crimes.

The Texan music which has lasted is far grittier, and step forward Jerry Jeff Walker as a guiding presence. Born in New York, he went on the road as a folkie, joined the psychedelic band Circus Maximus, and then re-invented himself again as a deep-voiced country grumbler with the laid-back Lost Gonzo Band. "Hi Buckeroos", says Viva Terlingua, opening an album recorded live with a down-home feel, and complete with a collage of matching photos showing a woman teaching a young boy to

play the violin mountain style, Jerry wearing a cowboy hat, and a gnarled hand pointing to the sign announcing the session. His fiddle-led version of Guy Clark's
'Desperados' (with shades of Van Morrison's *Astral Weeks*) is so magnificent – like
an old-timer reminiscing on his death bed – that it massages your heart.

Jerry Jeff once said that "My goal is not to be on VH1 as one of the great
tragedies of all time." Townes Van Zandt, however, is just that. When his future wife,
Jeanene, first heard his records, "I thought the guy had lived for a thousand years.
His songs are almost like old English ballads." *No Depression* made a more sinister
interpretation: "Like Dock Boggs, he was obsessed with death." Elsewhere, he was
described as "country's Nick Drake". 1969's *Our Mother The Mountain* looks and
sounds at first like standard hippie singer/songwriter fare, but then you notice the
hardness in his eye – in the shadow of a cowboy hat – and the intense way in which
he sings lines like "maybe I'll go insane, I've got to stop the pain". Just like Drake in
fact, he sings songs of self-immersion to careful string arrangements, but this time
from Nashville. Nick's haunted landscapes were all deep in his own mind, but here
there is real sense of place, and it's pure wilderness in every sense, another variation on that high, lonesome sound.

'Snake Mountain Blues', 'My Proud Mountains' ("my home is Colorado…where
rivers like gypsies, down her black canyons fall") and the title track all hymn the solitary life, and by the time *The Late Great Townes Van Zandt* appeared in 1973 Townes
had taken up residence in a tin-roofed shack in Tennessee, where he lived on raccoon meat. The title suggested Townes' coming demise, picked out in pitch-black
gothic script, and with an unsmiling Van Zandt hiding in an alcove. It almost became
a marketing device, with a later disc titled *In Pain*. When Townes actually passed
away, his record company brought out *A Far Cry From Dead*. He sings like a man
with no emotion. Do we have one of Mike Hurley's revenants here? He once said
"People will only know who I am after I am dead." Certainly, his cult is now growing.

On the album in question, Nashville's finest provide a backdrop of fiddles and
brisk guitars to more outgoing fare like 'Pancho And Lefty', a cowboy ballad set near
the border. Pancho, the outlaw who dies quickly and silently and enters myth, is
happier than Lefty, who hangs onto his existence like a rat: "He just did what he had
to do, and now he's growing old." Nothing can beat the nasty, matter-of-fact way in
which Townes suggest that the *federales* let Lefty go, "out of kindness, I suppose".
The kindness of the torture rack.

'The Silver Ships Of Andilar' is a tale of naval disaster ("one by one we died
alone, some by hunger, some by steel") which has the weight and authority of a
Celtic ballad. As Guy Clark admiringly put it: "[Van Zandt's] melodies are based on
real traditional country music and blues, coupled with his own take on stuff. He
wasn't derivative." What he did was to act as a transmitter for such mysteries for a
while, and then pass them on. There's always someone doing it, usually in the backwoods somewhere, whether Seattle or Brixton. It used to be called the oral folk

tradition. Townes later reckoned, rightly, that: "I'm the mould that grunge grew out of." Mudhoney covered his songs, and he was working on an album with Steve Shelley of Sonic Youth when he died. In just the same way, Dinosaur Jr, Bob Mould and other musical degenerates slurped down the doom and gloom of Richard Thompson. The mavericks of one generation become the proud fathers of the next.

And they usually choose to be obscure. Like Gram Parsons, Townes was born into a life of privilege. His father, the vice president of an oil company, came home crying one day because he had had to lay off 3,000 men (his present day equivalent would probably boast about it). This was one of founding families of Fort Worth, and Townes was about the closest it's possible to get to Texan royalty, but he chose to walk out of university and into the wilderness. There were inner demons to assuage, as great as those within any mountain man. "When he drank, he did crazy stuff", and he later spent six months in mental hospital, just like James Taylor.

He lived for a while with Roky Erickson, who was hardly a force for stability, and then, as Adam Sweeting wrote beautifully in *The Guardian*, "toured the southern states, half hobo, half musician, making just about enough to eat and get drunk, sleeping on peoples' couches, fascinated by the dream of freedom". Here is Lefty, then, no Mexican bandit but a wandering folk bard: "Living on the road my friend/was going to keep you free and clean/now you wear your skin like iron and your breath's as hard as kerosene." There is an extraordinary interview taken in his semi-rancid log cabin, which he rented for $30 a month – no plumbing, no phone – and which is only possible to reach after trudging through miles of forest and over a homemade cattle guard. Townes is making a trellis for his morning glory saplings. He has already talked in the past about spells of "total loss of meaning and motivation", and the feeling that "if I had a machine and could just chop my hands off then everything could be fine".

Here on his front porch, he reckons – a little too emphatically – that his songs come not from his roots (he was constantly uprooted as a child) or his memory, of which he lacks 20 years, but hotlined from his subconscious: "Bukka White used to call them sky songs. It seems they just come through me." He makes the sound of lightning. "It goes from the top of my head out my right arm." He wrote one in a kind of frenzy, "so fast my hands were aching". This is exactly what the tradition is, forcing you on, and it says much that Doc Watson was one of the first to record a song by him before Emmylou brought fame to 'Pancho'.

Van Zandt is in his rightful place when he sings alone and intimately to a small audience, following a tradition which goes back to Homer, and this is captured on a series of live discs, the first of which is *Live At The Old Quarter, Huston*. Here is "the first song I ever wrote", called to nobody's great surprise 'Waiting 'round To Die', in which the reference to an outlaw being dragged back to Muskogee gets a half-suppressed chuckle from the audience. Take that, Merle. The next song is 'Tecumseh Valley', which he wrote "on a banjo", and if you want an example of the

Celtic ballad in transition, here it is. Townes is just a mouthpiece for something old and strange, which is currently in temporary possession of his vocal cords. "Sunshine walked before her", he sings. No wonder that Steve Earle once said that Townes was the best songwriter in the world, "and I'll stand on Bob Dylan's coffee table in my cowboy boots and say that". We're not talking belly laughs, though.

All of Van Zandt's albums seemed to need a period of time before they saw the light of day, like moonshine whisky. *Rear View Mirror* was recorded at the Blue Onion in Oklahoma in 1979, with a fiddle and second guitar, but wasn't released for 15 years. You couldn't get closer to mountain music, whatever his parentage. It was later augmented with a bonus track, 'Riding The Range', with British country band The Good Sons. The 1994 album *Roadsongs* goes back even further, spanning Hank Williams' 'You Win Again' and a new version of TC Ashley's 'The Coo Coo', from the Harry Smith *Anthology*. Townes proves that he is no ornithologist, but that he understands that the song is more about nesting habits: "I thought this song came from Scotland, but there are no coo coo birds in Scotland. It comes from South Carolina where there are plenty. I know a couple."

The idea for the moody arrangements on *No Deeper Blue*, a kind of lush Celtic melancholy, came in a dream. His voice has grown richer with age, and here uilleann pipes and tin whistle join steel guitar and fiddle. He has reached the point at which, in 'Marie', he doesn't so much relate the story of a bum on the street, whose girlfriend dies as he watches, as inhabit it. That young malcontent on the first album is now gone grey and stubbly. He squints at the camera with an Appalachian's suspicion. His lips turn up slightly at the ends, but he sure ain't smiling. "Getting to know him was a real gradual thing." 'Billy, Boney And Ma' is a bone-dry tale of a boy going to a battlefield and digging up a skeleton, which sits up and grins back at him. They team up, just like Pancho and Lefty, and the song has a kind of horrid perkiness, especially the sting in its tale.

As he grew older, Van Zandt became increasingly confined to his cabin. *No Direction* carried a graphic account of his final days: "he was in incredible pain" and in a wheelchair for those final sessions, but he faced down his demons. 'Sanitarium Blues' is about his teenage breakdown, and rhymes away the pain: "They hose you down, make sure you're clean, shoot you full of thorazine." *The Observer* noted how his vocals "are vari-speeded down to an eerie slur". Backings were provided posthumously by Nashville session men. A mesmerising performance at London's Borderline, with snow in the streets, proved to be his last ever gig. Townes had long claimed that he would die on New Year's Day, just like Hank Williams, and at the age of 52, just like his father. He was proved right on both counts.

Guy Clark was as close a friend as Townes ever had, another singer who could growl like a dog or purr like a cat but as different a songwriter as could be imagined. As he told *Acoustic Guitar*, in all of his songs "there's a chuckle, a ray of hope. They may be sad, but it's not doomsday." With Townes, however, it's nothing but.

Clark was raised in the Texan town of Monahans, and "got into playing traditional folk in the Sixties", mostly in Houston, where he met Jerry Jeff Walker. Guy moved on to Nashville via Los Angeles, where he worked at the dobro factory. *Old No 1* saw his twangy, intimate voice softened by Johnny Gimble's fiddle, dobro (obviously!) and Emmylou Harris on backing vocals, and so much more.

As part of the mission which she chose to inherit from Gram, Emmylou took over from Judy Collins as the main conduit between new songwriters and a mass audience, while her band acted as a finishing school. Guy Clark was the latest writing sensation, and *Old No 1* still sounds good, although Clark is too restrained a singer ever to fully let go of himself. As he later told *Folk Roots*, "I've got no reason to write unless I want to go playin' for somebody, and no reason to go playing unless I've got songs I've written", and his work straddles the categories of folk and country. Every song tells a story or evokes a scene, which can be as apparently mundane as a fiddle-playing contest – "country music in the park/as far as they can see" – with bluegrass interpolations.

No Depression once called Clark "the Lone Star state's Ernest Hemingway", because of his ability to get to "the cruel radiance of what is" and a matching epic grandeur. In 'Desperadoes Waiting For The Train', which is actually about youth and age (and, one presumes, a boy and his grandfather), Clark uses imagery from the Wild West as a shared vocabulary. 'The Last Gunfighter Ballad' takes on that myth direct to the sound of a cello: "I was thinking about the gunfighter days, how they only lasted between about 1875 and 1890, until someone invented smokeless powder that was a lot more powerful and reliable than the old black powder. Then people really started getting hurt and it was the end of an era." "At the turn of a joke", too.

On 'Dublin Blues', the tune is based on the Irish melody 'Handsome Molly' (U2 are among Clark's fans), while the lyrics invest old-time music with the same seriousness as Renaissance art. He boasts that he has witnessed the work of three old masters: "I have seen the David, I've seen the Mona Lisa too, and I have heard Doc Watson play 'Columbus Stockade Blues'. The recent *Cold Dog Soup* is a delight of acoustic guitars, mandolin, fiddle and banjo, with Emmylou Harris gliding in on harmony as only she can on Steve Earle's 'Fort Worth Blues', a lament for Townes Van Zandt which was written while overlooking Galway Bay. The title track takes Clark back to Mission Beach in the 1960s, with Tom Waits collecting the money and Townes at the bar, "full of angst and hillbilly *haiku*". 'Sis Draper', meanwhile, is pure hoe-down. The CD shows the musicians live in the studio, facing each other in a circle. An unbroken one, that's for sure.

Lubbock might still be best known as the birthplace of Buddy Holly, but it has spawned a more recent breed of Texan singer/songwriter, who use country music as a paintbox with which to make new images. This is true literally, in the case of Terry Allen, who received a Guggenheim Fellowship and has used music as a sideline, just like Captain Beefheart began to do before abandoning it completely. He has some of Von Vliet's wildness, and shares his refusal to make his lyrics simple or autobiographical. Allen is no dilettante, though, and wrote songs for the likes of Bobby Bare and 'New Delhi Freight Train' for Little Feat.

Born in Wichita, he grew up in a family of "epic bullshitters". His mother was a jazz pianist, and his father a wrestling promoter who also ran a dance hall. Friday night was blues night, with the young Terry watching the likes of BB King and T-Bone Walker open-mouthed, while the "Saturday Night Jamboree" saw Hank Williams and Hank Snow passing through, along with their tour bands. He remembers record burnings, with kids bringing their rock 'n'roll discs to the fairground to be cast to the flames. As he told Andy Kershaw, Lubbock has "a very harsh climate, so people have a lot of hard back on them, very tough-natured and tough-hearted but also real good-hearted, a lot of contradictions in the place."

Terry's songs are much the same. "The idea of storytelling affects everything I do." He self-consciously continues the oral folk tradition of the South, where "the highlight of any relaxation in a week's work would be going to church, or eating supper with people, telling stories. It also comes out of a culture that isn't very literate, so verbalising things becomes even more colourful." In his own family, Allen encountered tales which went right back to the original settlers. You can hear different waves of immigration slam up against each other. The journey across the Atlantic must have been like "going to Mars".

It has to be said immediately that Terry is better on words than he is on tunes, while his vocals have gradually improved from a low base. It's Robert Hunter all over again. In 1975 he cut *Juarez*, "a simple story" about four people who migrate from California to Mexico, the soundtrack to an imaginary movie. It was recently recast as a stage musical, and it's Andy Kershaw's favourite album of all time. I am very proud to own it myself, but I play it only rarely.

Allen tells Kershaw that the border is central to him. "The fantasy that's there a line that you can cross, and everything's going to be great – it was like a magnet to me. It's like a mirror of American culture, but it's a funhouse mirror that's very distorted." On the album, he starts by giving thumbnail sketches of each character – "Spanish Alice is a Mexican prostitute working the bars in Tijuana looking for ways into the USA' – and needless to say it all comes down to the spilling of human blood. Meanwhile, Allen's pitch-imperfect voice and largely unrelieved clunky piano playing are a little hard to take.

That said, however, *Lubbock on Everything* is totally extraordinary, a double LP song cycle which fits just fine onto one CD and seems to encompass all American life. It is therefore full of eccentrics, from the Fifties' DJ The Wolfman Of Del Rio to a flat-land farmer who flatpicks an old guitar and can "outsing, outpick, outplay, outdrink, outpray and outlay any of them Nashville stars". Rednecks, sleazy businessmen, lovelorn waitresses and goodtime girls – they're all here. As Allen says, you have to bring things down to "an individual human level...otherwise it's just bullshit". Backings this time around are provided courtesy of The Panhandle Mystery Band, including fiddler Richard Bowden of The Austin Lounge Lizards and The Bad Livers' Mark Rubin on upright bass and tuba.

Allen toured his *Bloodlines* album with BJ Cole on pedal steel, and a session for Kershaw featured Terry's son Bud on accordion, and Richard Bowden "on the fiddle": "If you've got a convertible, an empty road and a good radio station, you don't need a psychiatrist." Radio "was the only open door to the outside – that, and your first set of car keys". 'Blue Suede Shoes' was the first song he heard "that didn't have to do with family and church. It was one of the first songs to address you as a human." He follows Norma Waterson's version of the gospel song 'There Is A Fountain In God's Blood' with an impromptu 'Bloodlines', and it fits like a glove.

Human Remains features deadpan harmonies from Lucinda Williams. One reviewer praised 'Gone to Texas' as "greasy with guitar and fiddle". It's a bitter description of modern Nashville, "some cowboy fake who thinks that all it takes is a hat on his head and a Grammy in his hand". *Salivation*, meanwhile, deals with the Second Coming, and has a strong country flavour, including a "pedal steal" number, about drug addiction. It ends with the funereal 'Give Me The Flowers', which was first performed by Flatt And Scruggs. As Allen told *No Depression*, the album deals with "the collision of the need to damn and the need not to be damned. Basically, it's gospel with a limp and a lurch." The cover was found in a junk store. "I think it's supposed to be Jesus. It looks like his mouth is full of snuff."

No survey of modern Americana could ignore Allen. As he told *Mojo*: "I haven't lived in Texas since 1962, but I go back constantly. There's affection there, but affection with a razor blade in it. One of the surest ways that you show affection is to start cutting and slashing them verbally – and expecting it in return. That's a kind of west Texas thing, and it's kind of an Irish thing too." Terry worked with David Byrne on the soundtrack of *True Stories*, which also features Randy Erwin, a modern Roy Rogers who yodels and does rope tricks. He was even commissioned to wrote a new national anthem, along with Joe Ely, Butch Hancock and Jimmie Dale Gilmore. They played a 15-song set at the Smithsonian, but the nearest they got to their target was 'Slow Boat To Tokyo', about how America was becoming a Japanese colony.

Allen went to the same high school as Gilmore and Hancock, who were two years his junior, and Ely, whom he did not meet until the late 1970s. "I was the first to get out of Lubbock. I got my drivers' licence before they did." The local talent night was called "Nothing Else To Do".

He had been teaching art in California for some years when, in 1971, the three younger men formed The Flatlanders. They were all sharing a house at the time, and the band was so named because Lubbock is at the centre of the Great Plains. David Halley remembers that they had previously called themselves The Supernatural Playboys: "They dressed up like hayseeds, playing this really strange and interesting stringband music." Ely adds that "we'd joke about being a band that never played a paying gig", although they played the Kerrville Folk Festival and "ended up cutting some songs in Nashville, acoustically". Only one single emerged at the time, though, Gilmore's 'Dallas', credited to Jimmie Dale And The Flatlanders. Much later, Charly released an album's worth of material.

Here is old-timey music, strictly acoustic, with dobro, string bass and fiddle. Steve Wesson's musical saw adds a bizarre sound, like the wind whistling through the trees, and there is a mystical edge to the lyrics, making it sound like The Carter Family meeting Eastern religion. Jimmie Dale Gilmore sings lead vocals, with the others providing harmonies. Ely "smelled while we were in Nashville that there was something funny going on, so I didn't sign any of the contracts, because I felt that there was a snake in the grass somewhere. Jimmie got a bad taste of it all." They also laid down some tracks at Buddy Holly's father's Lubbock studio. Ely later joked that Wesson didn't know whether to join the carpenters' or the musicians' union. He uses his saw "for building houses now".

Ely later told *Omaha Rainbow* that it was the birth of the outlaw movement which most inspired him: "I was excited about stuff that Billy Joe Shaver was writing. I was excited about the sound that Waylon was getting, inspired by stuff that was in that nebulous country realm." What Joe added to all this was the energy of punk rock. *Dark Star* interviewed him when he was playing support to The Clash: "I was born in Armarillo, and growing up here I was hearing more Bob Wills stuff on the radio than Buddy Holly. Even when I came to Lubbock, I was about ten or eleven years old. Holly wasn't really an accepted part of the music there." Ely left Texas at the age of 16 and went on the road for the next ten years. "We'd be stomping up and down those old Texas plains up there, playing those old joints. When he was offered a recording contract, "we just went into the studio and laid those songs down". This is what makes his debut so brilliant.

The cover shows Joe wearing a cowboy hat, with a quizzical look in his eye. He's generous to his two fellow songwriters from The Flatlanders, but the sound is much tougher, more electric, and led by pedal steel and honky-tonk piano. Ely sings like a young Presley, tougher than you'll ever be. This is country filtered through rock 'n' roll, and Hancock's 'Tennessee's Not The State I'm In' is slow but punchy, a denial of Nashville values. Joe was part of a new wave of country singers, taking sustenance from the old music rather than Chet Atkins. As he told *Rock 'n' Reel*: "MCA made it known to me that they didn't want me to do a country album, just to do what I normally do. Since Steve Earle and Lyle Lovett recorded with MCA Nashville, the label had begun to take a wider view of things. They're interested in rootsy American music, instead of just straight country music."

Ely was joined by Texan accordion star Ponty Bone, and he's there on the energetic *Live Shots*, which was recorded on tour with The Clash, with Carlene Carter on guest vocals and Mickey Gallagher on keyboards, on loan from The Blockheads.

Mojo described Ely's return to form on his later album, *Letter To Laredo*, as "country music's answer to novelist Cormac McCarthy". As a songwriter, he's of the Hank Williams' school, making every word count. Here is a series of short stories set where Tex meets Mex, with flamenco guitar plus a stripped-down acoustic country band. As Joe told *Acoustic Guitar*: "My dad had a used clothing store in downtown Lubbock, and he would put me to work running the cash register. The Mexican labourers would come and buy these ten-cent pairs of shoes and stuff. I fell in love with the romance of Spanish guitars and accordions and all that."

Jimmie Dale Gilmore was born on a farm near Lubbock. His high cheekbones attest Cherokee blood, but his voice is quite unique, a soaring, beautiful thing, ranging from the operatics of Roy Orbison to the brisk honky tonk of his early albums. Not for nothing did he head the house band at Threadgills for three years. As he told Nicholas Dawidoff: "[country music] set the course for my life. It was such a joyous sound." That also describes the sound towards which he has edged his way more recently. *Braver New World* saw T-Bone Burnett add Vox organ to pedal steel and horns, the strutting blues of 'Black Snake Moan' – on which his voice skitters, like a stone over water – and sound effects which suggest alt country. "To me, the whole beginning of country music and its whole power came from its completely wild abandonment". What Jimmie defines as "braveness" in Hank Williams informs his own *One Endless Night*. It's like another door opening.

Gilmore sounds at one moment like a Fifties throwback and at the next like an old mountain man, and his own spiritual search invests that chilling tenor with the sort of qualities which Gene Clark tried to put into words. It's a little like The Mavericks on acid, Kurt Weill meeting The Grateful Dead to a shuffle beat. 'Ripple', with sobbing fiddle, is restored to its country roots.

Butch Hancock is much more akin to a folk singer, as nasal as the young Dylan and with the just same perky interjections of harmonica, like a second voice. He released a series of seemingly endless delights on his own Rainlight label, of which the title to *West Texas Waltzes And Dust-Blown Tractor Tunes* says it all, really. He attacks the songs like a prizefighter. These solo acoustic stories of farming life are as starkly beautiful as the photos of dead coyotes and wrecked barns which studded the booklet when it re-emerged on CD. Earthy lines like "that farmer's dog can only bark but this cold north wind can bite" are as far as you can get from singer/songwriter "poetry", but they have the conciseness and true-to-life quality of the real thing.

Butch was born on a cotton farm and studied to be an architect, but he is said to still live in a trailer. As he told Dawidoff: "In Lubbock, we grew up with two main things: God loves you and he's gonna send you to hell, and sex is bad and dirty and nasty and awful and you should save it for the one you love. You wonder why we're all crazy." *Rolling Stone* once described Butch as "at heart a west Texas mystic with an equal affinity for romantic border balladry and Zen paradox". More recently, he toured his "Health And Happiness Show" – in tribute to Hank Williams – with lead guitarist Richard Lloyd, once a member of Television and more recently adding the spice to Matthew Sweet's sugar.

According to *New Country*, their album *Instant Living* drops "front porch instrumentation in favour of an intuitive, wilfully wobbly and endearingly scruffy roux of American roots", paying homage to Crazy Horse and The Band – it's Dylan all over again. You can only be a solo folk troubadour for so long, though; it gets lonely. The earlier *Firewater* features fiddle, electric guitar and Jimmie Dale Gilmore on harmonies, and was recorded live at the Alamo Lounge in Austin, which has since demolished. This has the force and thrust of the very best bluegrass. The reason for this musical venom appears to be that the engineer messed up the first run-through, and so, "with grim faces full of determination", they went for it again, and how.

The latest heir to this strain of Texas mysticism is Ray Wylie Hubbard. *Crusade Of The Restless Knights* is not some long-lost prog rock LP but a deep-voiced growler with a driving, largely acoustic band, singing songs about death and redemption, one alone of which, 'After The Harvest', is described as "a mythological bluegrass Buddhist Gnostic gospel hymn". More to the point, it's got a good martial tune. This is some spiritual distance from Ray's hippie anthem *'(Up Against The Wall) Redneck Mother'*, which Jerry Jeff Walker covered back in 1973. That same humour redeems this album, too, so that, when Ray tours hell with the Devil, he finds there "country program directors and Nashville record executives". There's a good joke about Charlie Daniels, and a wise last line: "some get spiritual 'cause they see the light and some 'cause they feel the heat". Another starts brilliantly "my mama ran off with a bible salesman". 'The River Bed', meanwhile, is like an Appalachian horror tale, in which Hubbard meets a dead woman down by the water and is baptised to death, with eerie Celtic fiddle from Eamon McLoughlin.

While Hubbard is not known widely enough, there was a small but fanatical cult in the Seventies which followed John Stewart. Most of his work is now unlistenable, with the glorious exception of *California Bloodlines*, which is sentimental as hell, atrociously sung by a man who sounds like Johnny Cash with a head cold, but is still somehow a masterpiece. This is pure Americana, complete with a maid calling the children home. At times he sounds just like John Wayne: "Boys? Hell, they were men." When he gets patriotic on the title song, you'll laugh at him through your tears. He frames emotion in the past, thus purifying it, as the class of 1902 sings, "Oh, Mother Country, I do love you."

Stewart spent time with The Kingston Trio and wrote songs with John Denver, as well as 'Daydream Believer' for The Monkees. In early 1969, producer Nik Venet took him down to Nashville for the first time: "Back then, the only non-country people to record there before I did were Bob Dylan and Joan Baez." When Stewart namechecks them all, plus nicknames, at the end of 'Never Going Back' – "Good Time" Charley McCoy, Kenneth "Downwind" Buttrey and "Gentleman" Roy Green – you can almost hear the surprise in the studio, and hear the music levitate.

Venet told *Zigzag* that "those Nashville studio men have a marvellous way of sweating, but not through their shirts. It looks so effortless, because they have learnt to control their dance. Their trade and their art is right there in their fingers." He decided to record them live, with John Stewart standing beside them, "and I felt that his magnificent, horrible voice and his style of picking would fire the musicians". Stewart reckons that Nashville musicians are no longer so open: "They're overworked, now, and their enthusiasm seems to have dropped. On those sessions, they played with their hearts."

Something was stirring in the mid Seventies, something which would sweep away the likes of John Stewart forever. The nest from which these new wave rats emerged was in New York's Bowery. Country Blue Grass Blues was soon shortened to CBGBs, and certainly never featured Bill Monroe, but there is a kind of weird logic to the name of this small and run-down venue, which at times was literally a toilet. It offered a chance to see oddball acts acting like dumb hicks (cf The Ramones) or improvising visionary poetry. As Patti Smith said: "We felt that we were carrying on a tradition that groups like The Fugs had begun." Post-punk bands like Bongwater similarly seemed in tune to the likes of The Holy Modal Rounders. Suicide updated the murder ballad in their synthesiser-assisted rant 'Frankie Teardrop', in which a man kills his wife, his children and then himself. Sid Vicious merely took this to its logical conclusion, in real life.

A new, irreverent mood stalked the land. R Stevie Moore was the a Nashville bassist, and issued literally hundreds of cassettes from his home studio in New Jersey, representing part of the cottage industry that pure punk crystallised. Anyone could do it in much the same spirit that Harry Smith captured, after the event. Moore played C&W songs like 'I Love You So Much It Hurts' with mock seriousness, and gave an up-beat treatment of Dylan's 'Who Killed Davey Moore?' It was the tip of the iceberg.

Loudon Wainwright III had started as a folk troubadour, albeit one not afraid to laugh at his own pretensions, and had his greatest hit with the bluegrass parody 'Dead Skunk', about either roadkill or President Nixon. He recorded *Attempted Moustache* in Nashville, and the insert for *Unrequited* sees him sitting alone on a hotel bed with only a guitar and a banjo for company.

Subversion is his trademark, and so 'The Hardy Boys At The Y' – "a requited love song" – refers not to the updated cowboys of the TV series but gay men at the YMCA. Loudon later revived the of-the-moment political song (as perfected by Phil Ochs) on public TV, the gems of which are collected on *Social Studies*. Banjo and fiddle embroider 'What Gives', in which Sixties idols grow older, so that The Animals are now "vermin" and Gerry needs a pacemaker. One of the themes is that of children duetting with dead parents, and Hank Williams Jr is the first he mentions, singing with his dad, whose "cheating heart was cold".

Loudon was married for a time to Kate McGarrigle, who with her sister, Anna, combined their Irish heritage – via their father – with the French-Canadian folk music with which they grew up at first as part of The Mountain City Four, and then as taken up by the country elite. Even Maria Muldaur brought in Nashville's finest for her cover version of their 'Cool River'. The sisters themselves became embroiled with synthesisers and the like, but came to their senses with *Matapedia*, the title song of which inhabits the stranger side of life, where only folk and old-time music dare step with impunity. As Kate told *Mojo*, she fell in love but ran away from marriage. "Years later, he ran into my daughter; she was 17, and he mistook her for me. He thought he's seen a ghost." Linda Ronstadt and Emmylou joined the McGarrigles for the homespun *The McGarrigle Hour*, back-porch music as it should be played. Iris Dement realised the short distance between folk and old time country when she recorded her own spell-binding version of 'Our Town', from their debut album.

Categories fray and dissolve. Thus we have Steve Forbert – "born to late", to quote one of his finest songs – emerging at first with acoustic guitar, harmonica and a denim jacket, playing a gig at CBGB's and surviving to tell the tale, flirting with R&B, and then using Uncle Tupelo as his backing band on *Rocking Horse Road* and The Rough Squirrels on *Here's Your Pizza*.

A few years earlier, Southern white soul man James Luther Dickinson recorded the wild and jaw-dropping *Dixie Fried*, with covers of Paul Siebel's 'Louise', on where everybody acts drunk, and the traditional carney song 'O How She Dances', with what sound like tom-toms – a dry run for Tom Waits, perhaps. Nick Tosches wrote beautifully of this album as "a dark, gale-force re-working of some ancient Southern lyrics...warm, visceral graftings of Dock Boggs and a thousand more drunken voices of an older, more tenebrous South". The trouble with masterpieces is that, as we have seen so often here, their determination to cross musical boundaries means that they are difficult to market, and gain an audience slowly. They lodge in our hearts and minds in a way that – if we dare mention him – the likes of Garth Brooks never will.

Reserve your pity for singers like Steve Goodman, who wrote the classic train song 'City Of New Orleans', and whose modern ballads could span comedy and tragedy. He was the kind of man who, when Kris Kristofferson first "discovered" him, said: "Oh, but you've got to hear my buddy John Prine". After his death from leukemia, before which he wore a large cowboy hat to disguise the effects of chemotherapy, those at a benefit concert held in Steve's honour spanned popular music (and this book), including John Prine and Randy Newman, Jackson Browne and Jimmy Buffet, Rosanne Cash and Willie Nelson. Like his friend Prine, he remained a free agent, and the posthumously released *Easter Tapes* all too appropriately includes Cole Porter's 'Don't Fence Me In'.

It cuts both ways. Dan Fogelberg's double LP *The Innocent Age* is a "song cycle" put together with the greatest care, but its date of release – 1981 – means that, although a commercial success at the time, it is now out of time. The country-rock elite are here, Chris Hillman and Glenn Frey and Emmylou, but there's something smarmy in Fogelberg's voice, and something over-ripe in his lyrics which disable any attempt at grandeur. The album seems to be about growing up, if I read lines like "circling the nexus in a fevered dance with fate" right. I presume it's Dan himself who is referred to as "born in the valley/and raised in the trees/of western Kentucky". Maybe it's a squirrel. He uses an equine metaphor in a later verse, which seems to veer towards Aryan ideology, so that "the fire of a mare/and the strength of a stud" are born "in the blood". Dodgy.

I'm being a little unfair here, though, as Dan's voice can swoop like an eagle, and he is a master at achieving sound textures from piano or guitar. The more prosaic 'Same Old Lang Syne' is a delight, a story of meeting an old girlfriend in the frozen food section. The Scottish theme continues into the wordless 'Aireshire Lament', with celtic harp and violin. The final song is 'Ghosts', taking us on an all-too-familiar trip "down the ancient corridors/and through the gates of time", and as unghostly as anything I've ever heard. The Moody Blues at their worst – and I speak as an early admirer – do not plumb the depths of banality that are explored here. Like that band in its pomp, it all sounds absolutely gorgeous. Fogelberg is magnificent once he shuts his mouth and gets out his guitar. This album is often cited as an influence on country singers like the aforementioned Garth Brooks and Clint Black, who have similarly turned vacuousness into an art form. I rest my case.

Fogelberg remembers once being "a folk singer in a coffee house with moccasins" (in California, of course) before relocating to Nashville. He often played support to The Eagles, and his flat-picking style was closely influenced by Doc Watson. One reviewer noted the almost total lack of twang in Dan's voice, even on his bluegrass venture, 1985's *High Country Snows*, which he modestly admitted was his attempt "to nurture acoustic music, being a huge fan of these great players". Certainly he helped to bring on the likes of Ricky Skaggs and Vince Gill, "young cats who weren't really legit yet in Nashville".

If Fogelberg was stranded by time, the ironic charms of John Hiatt have taken him from Nashville to new wave and back again, surfing the zeitgeist. When he talked to *Q* he admitted to sounding "like a miserable son of a bitch". Then he laughed and assumed the voice of a seen-it-all dirt farmer: "I'm having the time of life now, but by golly it was hard when I started out!"

Hiatt grabbed the job of staff writer at Tree Publishing in Nashville, at the tender age of 16, and had songs recorded by the likes of Tracey Nelson and Three Day Night. He was signed up for two unsuccessful albums by Epic, and was then dropped. It didn't help that both albums were uncategorisable, and it was once rightly pointed out that he owed more to Van Morrison than Conway Twitty. Even so, songs with titles like 'I Killed An Ant With My Guitar' are unlike to grab the public's attention, except by rendering it helpless with laughter. Both albums are frankly a mess, and not even interesting with it. He's trying too hard.

John went back to working the folk circuit as a solo act, and in 1979 had a second bite of the cherry, this time as rival for Elvis Costello. He cut his hair, shortened his songs, and on the cover is depicted headless, holding a photo of his own head. Country music is notable by its absence. He was also briefly famous: "After I was let go from Geffen, I went back to Nashville. At that point I thought maybe it's time to just make records for a small concern and stop trying to grab the golden ring." He went back to Tennessee in the mid Eighties, and *Bring The Family* was cut in an LA studio with Ry Cooder playing his lonesome slide guitar, Jim Keltner on drums and Nick Lowe on bass, keeping things simple.

It's a classic, of course, even if the opening track sneers a little too hard at modern country. Hiatt wants to trade his cowboy boots in for some flash Italian footwear, and tells his sweetheart to "forget the mousse and hairspray". He's certainly right on the button when he sings "I don't think Ronnie Milsap's gonna ever record this song" (although personally I think that Milsap should have called his bluff). The song turns back on itself, too, with Hiatt admitting, with some relief, that after this excursion they can put the cow horns back on the Cadillac. It's like the story of his career.

The same miraculous line-up got together as a touring band called Little Village, and the results were like sludge. You can't win... Hiatt kept going, though, as Nashville troopers do, and 1995's *Walk On* initially had to be self-financed. *Mojo* wrote – with perhaps more truth than they knew – that "this is Hiatt getting back to the backwoods". It's a great album, all the same, mainly recorded in Franklin, Tennessee, with rustic photos on the sleeve, lots of mandolin, strong drums, and with tracks like 'Dust Down A Country Road' demonstrating that John's voice had grown deeper and richer with age, and seemingly more content, so that his flashes of righteous anger are all the more potent.

There are two surprises at the end. The first is an unlisted bonus track, 'Mile High', which he wrote "Out in Idaho somewhere, at the crack of dawn. I got out the acoustic and started playing those chords, and it was almost like an aural opiate." To follow, there are three minutes of sound effects: crickets chirp over the rumble of a distant thunderstorm, and then there is a frighteningly loud hum, which turns out to be an approaching train. It sure beats *The Innocent Age* for atmospherics.

Since Hiatt first began recording in Nashville in the mid Seventies, mainstream country music has seen huge commercial success, even if in so doing it viciously shed any remaining whispers of old-time music. Symbolic here is the moving of the Grand Ole Opry from the Ryman Auditorium – historic and intimate, but now showing its age and in a run-down area of town – to a squeaky clean, purpose-built auditorium out on the edge. Minnie Pearl cried on stage, but no one should undervalue how far 'hillbilly' music has come, or by how rocky a journey.

Loretta Lynn appeared on the cover of *Newsweek*, ditto Merle Haggard on *Time*, the USA's equivalent of elevation to the House of Lords. Bill Malone itemises the way in which politicians have jumped on the bandwagon, such as LBJ's Texas barbecues being "spiced with country music". His political rival, Richard Nixon, invited the likes of Haggard and Johnny Cash to sing at the White House. Given their criminal past and early poverty, this is an amazing progression. Cash refused to sing 'Okie From Muskogee', but only because he couldn't remember the words. At the time of Watergate, Tricky Dicky flew to Nashville to open the new Opry. If only he had been shot, it would have been a perfect example of Altman's cynical film coming to life.

This practice also reinforced the links between country music and right-wing politics in a lot of people's minds. To redress the myth, democrat contender Jimmie Carter received support from the likes of Johnny Cash, Willie Nelson, Tom T Hall and Loretta Lynn, and once elected had them singing on his own new back porch in uptown Washington. Jimmie would even step up onstage to join in on a chorus or two. Bill Clinton continued that tradition, but unfortunately brought his saxophone as well.

Ronald Reagan was as folksy as any country star ever dared, and he held the CMA's 25th birthday party at the White House, with a jam session on 'Lonesome Road Blues' including Ricky Skaggs, Bill Monroe and Grandpa Jones. Merle Haggard was there seemingly every week – after all, as Malone slyly points out, Reagan had officially pardoned him while he was Governor of California.

There was an increasing crossover between country and pop, and old-time musicians found it harder and harder to obtain work. The CMA was seen by many to be complicit in this. The nadir came in 1974 when Olivia Newton-John, barely a pop singer, was honoured as Best Female Country Singer of the year. In the Australian outback, perhaps, but worldwide? George Jones set up the Association Of Country Entertainers in rivalry, but it didn't last long. A more productive way forward was to adopt the old music's reaction to any crisis and write a song about it. Justin Tubb's 'What's Wrong With The Way We're Doing It Now?' said it all but received little airplay.

Those expecting an in-depth study of Barbara Mandrell here, complete with discography, fashion notes and song charts, have come to the wrong book. I will merely relate the fact that she released a single called 'I Was Country When Country Wasn't Cool' and then add Malone's acid comment "in a style that possessed no country flavour at all". Comparing her to Emmylou Harris, for example, is to put over-processed food against a wholemeal loaf, even if Barbara did once play steel guitar.

There were a few welcome signs of life in more traditional areas of country music. Riders In The Sky made cowboy songs popular again, while honky tonk was safe in the hands of my own personal favourite, George Strait. Yet another Texan, George grew up on a farm, took a degree in ranch management, and later took 'Right Or Wrong' – first performed by Bob Wills – to the top of the country charts.

Professor Malone ends his survey of country music with foreboding: "For every Ricky Skaggs, there are a dozen pop-influenced performers who demonstrate great commercial appeal while also winning the industry's highest awards." He sees such pop elements as a threat to real country music. Malone quotes the veteran DJ Hugh Cherry to the effect that "when you kill the roots of a tree, it dies".

I'm no farmer, but Bill should have more faith in the music he so obviously loves to bits. As his own survey shows, time after time it is the people coming out of popular music who seem to pledge themselves most deeply, whether they start as blackface minstrel, a back-porch singer or a speed-freak punk rocker. The most extraordinary twist in the story, however, is yet to come.

There is only time and space here to pick out some of the strangest outgrowths of British C&W, the very best and the very worst. Links between Britain and country music had not ceased when the original settlers went west, and it was a two-way process, however colonial it might now sometimes seem. US stars at jamborees like the annual Easter shows at Wembley remind me of Nazi officers in occupied France, glossier and more self-confident than the peasantry they have been sent to dominate but essentially contemptuous under their polite surface. As we progress through this chapter, it will begin to become clear why.

Before The Beatles reversed the flow, a handful of British stars went over to Nashville in fealty, and to join the production line. Helen Shapiro's effort is creditable, but when The Springfields went over in 1963 to record *Folk Songs From The Hills* they needn't really have bothered. A scratchy orchestra imitates bluegrass, and Dusty comes on like a dime-store Dolly Parton. 'Maggie' is an object lesson on how to misread the emotional temperature of a song – there's not enough grandeur here against which she can set off her bruised voice, although she tries hard enough. Too hard, perhaps. "My home is down in Tennessee", a male Springfield sings, slightly flat and in a London accent. 'Alone With You' skips from mountain shack to country bounce, has some tootling sax and fuzz guitar, and suddenly releases the tiger in Dusty's tank. The future queen of white soul is simply not the right kind of singer to convey humility.

Ringo Starr looks and sounds more naturally plaintive – it's his trademark – and does a creditable job on 'Act Naturally', tucked away on side two of *Help* and the ideal song to accompany a film soundtrack. George Harrison plays some nice guitar interjections, Chet Atkins style. After The Beatles split, Starr went over to Tennessee to record the creditable *Beaucoups Of Blues* album, while Pete Drake came over to London to play on George's *All Things Must Pass*, also agreeing to produce it. He gathered a batch of new songs for Ringo to choose from, including all of the usual suspects.

Much more conceptually interesting is the 1971 album *Heritage*, on which George Hamilton IV and Liverpool band The Hillsiders swap places. The latter were pioneers of English country rock, and can be heard on various Merseybeat anthologies from the early Sixties singing titles by not by Motown girl groups but George Jones and Buck Owens, and – most importantly of all – in their own accents. Here they back Hamilton on his idea of what constitutes an English folk song – 'Streets Of London' and Ewan MacColl's 'Dirty Old Town' – and bring fresh harmonies and a pedal steel guitar to their own material. Folk songs they ain't, though, even if the sleeve notes namecheck Cecil Sharp and the Pilgrim Fathers.

R&B oddballs The Downliners Sect whine their adenoids through *The Country Sect*, which merely ups the skiffle quotient. An EMI spokesman is quoted to saying that "this record could set the recording industry back ten years". 'Wolverton Mountain' is so weedy you could smoke it.

It's all a world away from that great ventriloquist Mick Jagger, tutored here by Gram Parsons, as he slurs and whoops his way through 'Country Honk' with sweet fiddle and a ramshackle vibe close to the real thing. Years later, after he has sung 'Dead Flowers' live on *Stripped*, Mick mutters that he "felt like a hillbilly for a moment".

Even more strangely, Nigel Kennedy's recent violin mangling of the Jimi Hendrix songbook is based on his supposition that the guitarist was influenced by folk and Celtic music. However, he fails to prove his point.

More fruitful are British responses to *The Basement Tapes*, ranging from the crunchy rotundities of Fairport on *Unhalfbricking* – they grab hold of the drunken humour, too – to a whole album, *Lo And Behold*, by what became McGuinness Flint, although they somehow lose both the playfulness and the terror. Much better is *Backwoods Progression* by jazz-rock guitarist turned pop star (and later stand-in Sex Pistol) Chris Spedding. He can't sing, but that's just part of the charm, as he takes off from 'Please, Mrs Henry' onto matching songs of his own. It's one of those albums which somehow seeps into your consciousness, and you can never quite get rid of it. These are warm sounds, and defiantly English, too.

That first quality also applies to the early Elton John albums, especially *Tumbleweed Connection*, although Elton's American accent seems ridiculous even back then. The Band's influence looms large, and a pedal steel also intervenes on 'Country Comfort'. Bernie Taupin never wrote better, re-mythologising the Wild West in the wilds of East Anglia. As Philip Norman points out, almost every track has "a cowboy or Mexican-border feel", but lines like "the herdsman and his torch" refer to Bernie's own father, who was a farmer. It rhymes with porch, though, and the "six-o-nine goes roaring past the creek" is pure Americana. Elton plays some great honky-tonk piano on 'Burn Down The Mission', which he then re-imported to the States.

Dusty Springfield re-appears as a backing singer on 'My Father's Gun', which Elton sings with a stately tenderness and which presents America as a land of mystery and grace. The solemnity befits a song which sets a boy's coming of age during the Civil War, with Elton fighting for the doomed and romantic South. (For much the same reasons, he later bought Watford football club.) Caleb Quaye plays liquid guitar, and an orchestra comes in almost stealthily. On the title page of the LP booklet, Elton wears a bootlace tie and looks like riverboat gambler, not like humble Reg Dwight from Pinner.

It's from such sidelong references and echoes that the depth of the penetration of US culture into post-war England can be understood. No band could have been more English than The Kinks, but their most self-revelatory album is called *Muswell Hillbillies*. It's a play on words, true, but the cockney in the title song reckons "my heart lives in old West Virginia", despite never having been there. It's a myth to hold up against the tower blocks of home. 'Oklahoma, USA', meanwhile, changes the hero's sex (Ray Davies often puts his most intimate thoughts into female dress) but says just the same. In her dreams, she's Doris Day.

The Small Faces were another quintessentially English band, but when they split Steve Marriott plunged into Humble Pie, a country rock band for a while, before they declined into hoggish boogie. Ronnie Lane went further and founded Slim Chance, a band which took to the road with a big top and evolved their own brand of pastoralism. So, too, did Traffic, among the first of many new bands to get it together in a country cottage, with Steve Winwood – from the concrete encampments of Birmingham – affecting a rustic hat onstage. Even Led Zeppelin dressed like gentlemen farmers at the Bath Festival, and put together some of their best songs in a remote Welsh cottage with no running water (except the constant rain). That Appalachian dream – along with a ready supply of mood enhancers – proved endlessly potent.

Even tougher souls were smitten, although the photos of an already portly Van Morrison hiding away in Woodstock in a series of extraordinary capes and hippie hats lingers long in the inner eye. With his genius for atmospheres, *Tupelo Honey* evokes the sweet indolence of such an existence.

The mythology underpinning C&W proved useful for those coming down from the Sixties' party, in England just as much as in LA. Eric Burdon croaks his way through 'Ring Of Fire' and turns it into a cry of inner pain, deadened briefly by Andy Summer's liquid guitar break. It's a world away from his fellow Animal Alan Price's yee-haw version of Randy Newman's 'My Old Kentucky Farm', or indeed his rumbustious 'When I Was A Cowboy', complete with hummed chorus and jovial flute. Somewhere in between is The Walker Brothers' *No Regrets*, on which Scott uses his haunting baritone to turn "Chris" Kristofferson's 'Got To Have You' (one presumes that this is Kris, Anglicised) into a mood epic, with sweeping pedal steel from BJ Cole. Like so much of Scott's work, it is pompous and majestic, risible and profound, deep and shallow, all at once. It's certainly not country music, however far you stretch the definition, and I promise that this is as far as we will stray.

But then, neither is much of what passes as straightforward British C&W. However well intentioned, it's simply crap. I bought *The British Bluegrass Album Volume One* in the spirit of enquiry and, while they all do it better than I could, I won't be rushing to buy volume two. There's a true British reserve at play here, and none of the savagery of the real thing. For that we need to look elsewhere. I must record here that the Chairman of the British Bluegrass Music Association lives in Perth, however, which pushes the Celtic connection further than even I would want to go.

Out of sheer sadism, I refer you to two albums I found in a charity shop comprising live recordings from Britain's Country Music Festival, both taped at Cecil Sharp House in the late Sixties. Whatever I paid for this, it was too much. Here we have Ramblin' Sid Chalker from Bromley, who is actually UK country star Brian Chalker having us on – except that his parodies are so bad that the joke is really on him. A one-time policeman and Pinkerton's detective, he went on to edit the UK's *Country Music Review* and write for *Melody Maker*, but this is like the Two Ronnies without the jokes. To follow, there's some inept banjo from The Morriss Boys String Band, and then Dave Plane from Orpington – who "has been singing for about ten years" – tracks down 'Pretty Polly' as a song originally from Gosport which got to him via America. The best that can be said is that he remembers the words (although he muffs up the guitar), but he sings like a psychopath, so remote is he from the lyric's emotion. It's one thing to be stern, like Dock Boggs, and quite another to be blank. It makes you weep to think of bleak Appalachian renditions of the same song. Or it makes you laugh until you fall over. Callow, disconnected and inept – those are just his good points. As I don't have volume one, I am spared the sound of Dave being joined by his Rhythm Ranchers, and I guess I'll just have to live with that loss. Forever.

Needless to say, both albums are on the Allegro label, which specialised in duff provincial orchestras and for which the phrase "cheap and nasty" could have been invented. Things haven't changed much since, either. *Mojo* recently reviewed *The Best Of British New Country*, and opined, that because the form is tied so inextricably to the American South, "UK imitations are often either intentionally comic or unintentionally comical", sometimes even both at once. It's not quite all this bad, however. In the 1950s, Karl Denver was seen by some as a British Hank Williams, and Dave Travis is joined on his budget outings by Dave Cousins, "one of the finest exponents of the five-string banjo in the country".

Cousins founded The Strawberry Hill Boys, Britain's first and maybe only decent bluegrass act, with Arthur Phillips appearing on mandolin. They later mutated into folk explorers The Strawbs, and on their first album – with Sandy Denny as guest vocalist – some of that atmosphere remains. A few years later, Rick Wakeman was in the band and bluegrass flew out the window. (One's worst nightmare would be a Wakeman concept show of happy Appalachian farmers, on ice.)

Old time music was then, as now, hard to find, but even back in the Fifties it was there if you looked hard enough. The Grand Ole Opry came over the airwaves via

Germany, and even before Collets' bookshop opened its folk and blues LP section in the basement of the their shop on London's Charing Cross Road there was an importer of hardcore original US bluegrass and honky-tonk LPs in darkest Islington. He bought them back at half price if you didn't like them.

It must have seemed like a visitation from another world when Gram Parsons' descended on Middle Earth. The sparks flew high and wide. Fairport Convention's Ashley Hutchings is a snappy dresser, much given to bootlace ties and Western boots, and his own cowboy fixation later emerged with songs like 'Bury My Eyeballs On Top Of Boot Hill'. Meanwhile, Fairport's country side was hidden away on radio sessions and at gigs. Sandy Denny turns Johnny Cash's 'I Still Miss Someone' into a gentle lament, and Iain Matthews sings briskly but sweetly on Gene Clark's 'Tried So Hard', while Richard Thompson picks guitar as clean as running water, just like his idol, Nashville obscurity Thumbs Carlile.

The oddest thing of all is their version of 'Billy The Orphan's Lonely Christmas' for the John Peel show, a recitation by American friend Marc Ellington, oozing mock sincerity. Fairport swallowed Americana and then built something new from it, so that Simon Nicol's magnificent song 'Shattering Live Experience' takes country prettiness and adds a dreamy element on top. One wonders exactly what kind of silver spoon the singer lacks. When Linda Ronstadt jammed with a later Fairport line-up, she was amazed to find that they knew all of the chords already. For a brief year between Sandy joining and the awful road crash, the band held traditional British folk songs and American country music in perfect balance. When I recently asked Ashley if they knew much bluegrass and old-time American music, he snorted like a horse and then gently explained that the band immersed themselves in exactly that music before psychedelia, before moving not so much beyond it as further into its spirit. Nicol was the young acoustic guitar whiz, as he proves on the sadly prophetic 'M1 Breakdown'. It's both a bluegrass instrumental and literally a van shuddering to a halt.

When the original band members gradually peeled off for solo careers, they took this freshness of response with them, so we have Nicol pouncing early on Nanci Griffiths' 'From A Distance'. Iain Matthews plunged in further, and formed Matthews' Southern Comfort with the English pedal steel player Gordon Huntley. He might have looked like an eccentric uncle onstage, but he provided the final sweetening to propel their version of 'Woodstock' to Number One.

Ian – or Iain, as he now spells his name, in order "to reflect my Celtic roots" – had always had a sharp pair of ears for American country songwriters, and the band's debut scarfed up the likes of 'D'Arcy Farrow' and Ian And Sylvia's 'Southern Comfort', which ends with a snatch of the traditional British folksong 'Nottamun Town'.

Although having pedal steel and Ian's voice together can sometimes be like overdosing on over-rich chocolate, there are some very interesting fusions going on here, with 'Blood Red Roses' a sea shanty sung (mainly) *a capella* in American accents and Matthews' own 'Ballad Of Obray Ramsey' the story of a Tennessee banjo picker. Tom Paley, from The New Lost City Ramblers, guests on just that instrument. Matthews took his love for the likes of Jesse Winchester, Jules Shear and his personal touchstone, Richard Farina, into carving out a laid-back solo career, interspersed with the country harmonies of plainsong, where he now appears alongside Andy Roberts and Clive Gregson. After many years' residence in the States, an American accent now overlays his North-of-England burr, but if he lacks the brutality of the true Appalachian then he is as good a male singer of the gentler side of country as you will find, especially if you can catch him solo and acoustic. He can radiate happiness like no one else.

One night, Hutchings announced a song by "an up-and-coming country writer from North London, Richard Thompson". Thompson is another pioneer of English singing who also loves country, re-inventing the tradition on *Henry The Human Fly*, and seeks in his own songs to reach the wisdom and verbal restraint of Hank Williams. ('A Heart Needs A Home' is up there in the pantheon.) The Thompson world-view is a bleak place indeed, where butcher boys will rob you in the cradle and only love keeps you going, but humour breaks through every now and then to keep you from going mad. Onstage, he and his wife Linda would suddenly break into 'Wild Side Of Life' and other country obscurities just as you were about to slash your wrists.

The fatalism of old-time music fuses with Islamic zeal in Richard's late-Seventies work, as if he was looking at the human condition from outside: "If I beat you black and blue/I'll regret it all in the morning." He has lightened up a little since, and has grown less compulsive to watch. *Industry*, though, was a brave album, investigating industrial decline, and which could just as easily have been set in Kentucky as in the Yorkshire coalfields, or what is left of them. By the same token, 'Strange Affair' – a hushed song about ageing and death – is as stark as anything by Dock Boggs, even if sweetened by Linda's soothing voice.

When the two split up, the songs that resulted proved gold dust in Nashville, with Linda's accusatory 'Telling Me Lies' appearing on the first *Trio* album and Richard's funny but bitter and totally unyielding 'Tear-Stained Letter' becoming almost a country standard. The break-up of marriages makes perfect country material, and Thompson was no slouch at drinking songs either, before he took the pledge.

Fairport drummer Dave Mattacks was drafted in when US bluegrass band Hickory Wind recorded an entire album of British folk. Travelling in the opposite direction were English folk rockers The Arizona Smoke Review, featuring American Bill Zorn on lead vocals and banjo, whose jolly *A Thundering On The Horizon* was an attempt to graft the drugged vibe of The New Riders Of The Purple Sage and bluegrass harmonies onto what eventually became the acoustic folk duo Show Of Hands. They were best encountered live. As the Seventies dawned, it became a fashion statement for young English musicians to dress like Wurzel Gummage and hang loose in the countryside – not so much The Wild Bunch as Robin Hood and his band of merrie men.

Soul singer Jess Roden swapped the satin suits of The Alan Bown Set to sing lead vocal in Bronco in a denim shirt and with ratty hair. Naming a band after a horse is probably not the best of ideas, and the wooden structure on the cover of *Country Home* could be either a log cabin or a play house. Like I said, this is play-acting. I saw Byzantium – almost inevitably – on a rickety stage at a free festival, and their two lead guitarists bopped around the stage like elves on speed, grinning at each other through their waist-length hair. Or so it seemed – I might well have been a little chemically altered myself. We all grew up, though, and one of them became Chas Jankel, Ian Dury's right-hand man in The Blockheads. The band's extravagantly-packaged concept album *Seasons Changing* still looks wonderful, but truth to tell the music inside now sounds wimpish in the extreme. As for Bronco, their two albums are so lacking in energy it's a wonder that they can bring themselves to circulate on the turntable.

By and large, in this world you eventually get your due. When listening to a pile of early-Seventies country rock vinyl, you hear honest strivers, like Gypsy, the warm pleasantries of Andy Roberts, or the anonymity of Harlan County, with Peter Skellern unrecognisable as himself on keyboards. Home's *Pause For A Hoarse Horse* has a great cover cartoon of a dismounted cowboy in Monument Valley, but the music feels like the horse: moribund. Starry-Eyed And Laughing have more thrust, but its still The Byrds with water. It's infectious, though, and there's some nice harpsichord. Mountain Line play surprisingly good British bluegrass, but when you read on the sleeve notes the outrageous boast that "they are getting across to a lot more people in this country than its American cousin ever did", you cast the album aside in disbelief. But what can still make the pulse race 30 years on?

Step forward first Cochise, whose album cover is a fold-out landscape of female breasts. 'Moment And The End' suddenly explodes into a duet by its composer, BJ Cole, on pedal steel and Mick Grabham's lead guitar, which lifts the hair on the back of the neck after all this time. Cole looks like a shaggy wolf as he bends with huge seriousness over his fretboard like a man doing the ironing. The track slows right down at the end, and BJ seems to go into himself, like a pedal steel version of John Fahey, and then the band comes back in hárd. It's not over yet, as he goes into a plangent rendition of 'Silent Night'.

This was the kind of odd melange which went under the term "progressive" in the early Seventies, but Cole kept on going to the wilder shores of musical experiment. On 1989's *Transparent Music*, he's lost his beard and plays material ranging from Erik Satie to Debussy and Ravel along with his own tunes, all electronically altered. He paid for such experiments later by acting as a fixer for visiting Nashville stars, setting up their tour bands. His most unexpected move was to join The Verve onstage for their last few months, and then assist Richard Ashcroft on his first solo album. *Mojo* reports on a recent gig with dance technician Luke Vibert, which was billed as "a night of Hawaiian, hip-hop, free jazz and expansive exotica". The two men sit hunched over their different boxes of mysteries, with Cole – now short-haired and intense – switching between "soothing country music tones and steelier lead fills".

The music is "short and tart", and includes some western swing. Andy Gill gets really carried away when the two are joined by a "heavily-tattooed percussionist", and Cole's hands, knees and feet are in constant motion, a "sonic chameleon" torturing his machine to produce sounds "a sharp as needles, as wild as beasts, and as dangerous as traffic". It's a long way from the British Country Music Festival. This is also true of Heads, Hands And Feet, which feature a young Albert Lee on rip-snorting lead guitar, on his way to play with The Crickets, Emmylou Harris and Hogan's Heroes. Try *Old Soldiers Never Die* for size.

The best British bands to forever be pigeonholed in the genre known as country rock exemplify a togetherness – both musical and communal – which the Thatcher years ensured could never be quite recaptured. I'll come to the totally wonderful Brinsley Schwarz in a minute, but meanwhile my top three, in ascending order, are as follows. Hold on while I adjust my anorak and prepare my critical flick-knife…

Before they were first polluted and then dismembered by their conjunction with the terminally wimpish Sutherland Brothers – the kind of folk who give folk music a bad name – Quiver were a nifty little combo, with the classic twin lead guitar line-up. Cal Batchelor was American and Tim Renwick (later to be a foot soldier in the great Pink Floyd civil war) English, thereby neatly fitting into this book. 'Gone In The Morning' is the band at their best, with nice pastoral lyrics and lyrical bass from future Attraction Bruce Thomas. Then Batchelor and Renwick are off, running rings around each other like old friends sparring and then coming to an agreement. It's followed by a short banjo instrumental, for anyone questioning the definition of "country" here.

The same sense of a band totally in tune with itself is the greatest asset of the still shockingly underrated Mighty Baby. Even Gram Parsons never sounded quite as vulnerable and lost as Ian Whiteman when he sings "I'm from the country and I'm so tired" on their first album. Even Clarence White didn't play guitar with the elasticity of Martin Stone on their second, sounding like a man chuckling one moment, and as if deep in thought the next. If anyone asked me to find the British equivalent to bluegrass, with that mix of cold expertise and warm feeling, I'd point them towards *A Jug Of Love*, which is hideously rare and without a banjo or fiddle in sight.

Help Yourself reign supreme, however, if purely as a British country band. As I wrote in *Let Them All Talk*, the theme of their first album is "life in the countryside, but unsentimentalised". *Strange Affair* is sleeker, less a magical collision between folk and country, but at its centre is a long instrumental which never quite settles down into a tune. 'Excerpts From "The All-Electric Fur Trapper"' is pure

Quicksilver, and illustrates a short story of that name written by future Ducks Deluxe frontman Sean Tyler. It's a mountain fantasy, of Jesus Colt and his Cherokee sweetheart, "integrating nicely in the high snows of Montana". It's also contemporary: when he goes outside to the backwoods toilet, he wipes his backside on an old Fender guitar catalogue.

'Beware The Shadow' is more Americana than country, but with a richness that no other British songwriter can match – the British Neil Young. Best of all is 'American Mother', a picture of a native woman by turns erotic, abstract, spiteful and majestic: "The DA comes for breakfast…" Richard Treece's guitar shivers in the background, and a police siren wails. This is followed by Malcolm's high, fragile voice on a bed of acoustic guitars, and a distant harmony. It starts "When I was wounded at the door", and the shivers crawl up your spine: "I recall an Irish song/that my father used to sing/when he was young." It's a song about illness and death, but also "of beauty and of grace". He recalls his mother singing to him, too, promising sleep.

All of this is sung to what sounds like a traditional tune, and which is so inexpressibly lovely that even I am stumped for words to describe it. (At last!) If this is the music I hear when I lie dying I won't be surprised, and I'll go out happy. In a perfect world, Morley should be as prolific as Bruce Springsteen, say. In fact, you know from what he sings and the way in which he sings it that anything more is a bonus. So far there is only *The Return Of Ken Whaley*, the fourth Help Yourself masterpiece in a row, and a record on which Morley takes country rock just about as far as it will go.

This album is almost atonal at times, like he's struggling to say the unsayable, as bitter as hell, and starts with just about the grossest verse I've ever heard. Let's just say that fingers are involved. We're on safer ground with 'Pioneer Of The West In The Head', though, not that I have a clue what it's all about. It's got a real twang, though. 'Blown Away' is about the Okies on one level, about the loss of compassion on another, and as a by-product (although it's hardly as serious) of country rock. This is an album as fearful as you'll ever hear. Later, the otherwise unknown and very Welsh Vivian Morris sings his own 'Virginia', which is about going home, and is a thing of rare beauty. (Shouldn't it be called 'Swansea', though?)

This is the central question about country music, and I have yet to face it. If a native Virginian were to sing in the same way about Plumstead, we would laugh like drains, and yet the word 'Virginia' acts as a shorthand for a special place which we all understand without quite knowing why. In just the same way, we can empathise with Van Morrison's search for the *Veedon Fleece* in the wilds of Ireland, although in this case it isn't real. Some place have resonance; others don't. Mike Harding's 'Rochdale Cowboy' is starting to look like a zen statement.

It's quite OK to wear a cowboy hat, spurs and a lassoo if you're English as long as you do it in an ironic, iconoclastic way. Just ask The Mekons. Do it straight and they'll probably lock you up. It's a paradox central to English imitations of country music, or indeed Japanese bluegrass. It's what made those albums from the British Country Music Festival so risible. Any British citizen who sings as if from Nashville and styles himself as a Wayne or a Randy or a Clint is damned from the start, if you ask me.

Charlie Landsborough is an ex-teacher and an excellent singer. He looks like a younger version of Willie Nelson and he sells lots of albums, but the fact that he comes from Liverpool means that cannot quite take him seriously. Meanwhile Malcom Morley comes from London, I presume, and I take him very seriously indeed.

When chatting to Bob Harris, Sean Kenny neatly sidestepped the question. Compared to Nashville, England is a cottage industry, but "we don't do too badly, considering". As a singer, Sean wants to "have a UK identity, to be a UK derivative of the Nashville scene". It sounds suspiciously like being colonised to me. Can you imagine any self-respecting Scot happy to be merely a "derivative" of London? Kenny hits the nail on the head about the music's appeal when he notes how it soaks up all other kinds of music, from jazz to heavy rock. More to the point, "it's the last bastion of the real song".

Maybe having an Celtic name helps make you more authentic, although here Sean talks with a Brummie accent. Ditto Wes McGhee, a rougher singer, who has had Joe Ely and Ponty Bone play in his band. His most heartfelt line is "I'd rather be in Texas", and now he is, although *Airmail* was recorded in London. Songs by Wes here include 'It's No Use Being A Fast Draw (If You Can't Shoot Straight)'. Steve Burgess described this track as a "back-porch, sloe-eyed burn". A satisfying album by any criteria, and it is ironic that a performer so well respected in the States (he even recorded a double live album in Austin) should be so little known in his native land. Perhaps it's because he doesn't try too hard to sound American, which is a good idea when you actually come from Lutterworth.

Hank Wangford tries much too hard, which is the whole point. With sidekicks like Brad Breath and Milton Keynes, and early record releases on his own Cow Pie label which sound like an afterthought, he can hardly be serious. Except he is. He's a natural born showman who pokes fun at the music he loves, which is the only adult way to approach it. *Wake Up Dead* was mostly written in Connemara, and although it's lightweight on the surface, the lyrics cut deep. 'Did You See Me Wave?' is dedicated to the memory of his old friend Gram Parsons, and is surprisingly savage ("forgot my knife/could have stuck it in you/taken your life"), especially for someone who sings like a country uncle of the Pet Shop Boys.

The next track is an unholy din, supposedly an example of high, lonesome yodelling from Mongolia, equally supposedly the ancestor of the Appalachian sound. When he tells you that it was learnt from Dalai Lama Jr, the penny finally drops. Or is this a double bluff? With Hank, you never quite know.

The same mind thought up Sincere Products: "brought to you with no regard to quality". This is all too true of his early albums, despite the musical craftsmen he employs, and the best thing about them is their back covers, chock full of parodies which can only be fully understood by someone fully initiated into country music. Wangford is really an update of the comic character at the early Opry. "Life's greatest fool", to quote Gene Clark.

Hank had supposedly first struck gold as guitar player with Stanley And His Famous Negroes, "an all-white band none too popular in the South". *Rodeo Radio* is the best short guide to country in print, no question: "I suspect C&W is really all about selling, and its celebrities are just singing businessmen." He talks further about the "dead hand of Nashville" in an interview with Norman Warwick. In America, he is told not to use the "archaic" term country and western: "matter of fact, we don't even want to call it country, we just want to call it American music". Update that to Americana, and you're there. He also notes that, "in Ireland, country music is very big because they'll let it all out. In Scotland, they'll let it all out." In England, we keep ourselves tightly buttoned, no one more so than the Cambridge-educated Dr Sam Hutt, one feels, who uses his comic persona to unleash all kinds of personal traumas.

Being serious for a change, he reveals to *Folk Roots* his excitement in discovering, during his researches for the BBC, that "a piece of fiddle music from the Northern Urals was exactly like a hoedown", or hearing a sad Korean song "which sounded like it came from the Hebrides".

I had just the same kind of buzz in the early Seventies, when I could walk into a select handful of London boozers – all outside the West End – and hear bands who adopted country sounds as part of a user-friendly set, getting right back to basics, and at basic prices, too. It was as if the honky tonks had suddenly landed in Britain. Appropriately, it was an American band, Eggs Over Easy, who started the process in 1971, and it was an Irish pub, the Tally Ho in Kentish Town, which they chose to approach. Their one surviving album is country swing with a lope.

The debut album by Brinsley Schwarz was one of the more dreadful imitations of CSN&Y, misinterpreting that band's definition of "wooden" music. It's all unreal, with fake showbiz mud on their boots. Nick Lowe's song 'Shining Brightly' shows an early gift for pastiche, starting out "Hey, warm and tall, brown Appalachian woman with your hand stretched out to the east wind. Can I stand by your side through eternity?" After a disastrous attempt to launch themselves at the Fillmore East, they retreated to a house in Northwood and re-emerged with *Despite It All*, demonstrating country rock as it should be played, organ-rich but with added fiddle and pedal steel. Lowe was now writing more simply and more realistically, about how his "country girl knows how to groove me". The whole band were big Clover fans, and they went back to basics, with lumberjack shirts and low-volume amps. There was still a suspicious glint in Nick Lowe's eyes, however, while funk and rock 'n' roll were seeping into the sound.

When he first saw Eggs Over Easy, Lowe was amazed at how they could choose to play a hundred or so songs, half of them not even their own. This was the ultimate taboo at the time, to become a covers band. It also set the whole scene alight. Bands and the audiences alike rediscovered that music could be fun, and as Ian Hoare puts it "they got back in touch with the physical aspect of the music, got people dancing". It was a return to rock and country, not country rock. They closed their set each night with Commander Cody's 'Home In My Hand'.

Bees Make Honey were a straightforward country band who mutated into something else on *Music Every Night* – sax jostled with pedal steel and dobro, and the rhythm section put a rocket up their collective backsides. It was a deliberate step back in time to the 1950s, upping the tempo and cutting down on the introspection.

People started smiling on stage again. Chilli Willi announced on their debut album that "we don't have no psychedelic show", and posed Martin Stone in front of the kind of wooden shed even at which the poorest Appalachian would sneer, while Phil Lithman has a fiddle in his hand and a chicken at his feet. Martin holds a dobro, and left Mighty Baby to their Sufi studies to party and get back to country picking. Bongos Over Balham is a blast of country swing, with fiddles, pedal steel, banjos and up-beat songs. It still sounds sprightly.

Chilli Willi were the very best kind of cultural tourists. It says it all that one unsuccessful applicant was "a bluegrass player, whereas we were old rock 'n' roll freaks who liked bluegrass music". Ace archivists Proper Records recently issued *I'll Be Home*, a wonderful ragbag of radio sessions, part of their set at the *Zigzag* fifth birthday party, and tracks produced by the headliner there, Michael Nesmith. The songs range from Jesse Winchester's 'Midnight Bus' to truckers' favourites, 'Choo-Choo Ch'Boogie' and a wild, live, fiddle-crazy 'Fire On The Mountain', which was followed by their own 'Drunken, Sunken Redneck Blues'. Nothing wears out its welcome.

The Chillis were the kind of band with which you fell in love on the spot, the sort who would mention at the end of the set that they had nowhere to "crash", and asked if anyone had a spare floor. They were certainly my own intro to hearing such country delights live, and it wiped away bad memories of Jim Reeves on the parental record player forever. Fun, frolics, and pharmaceuticals.

Pub rock opened the cupboard door on dusty old record collections, and let the light shine in. The Kursaal Flyers hid all kinds of country expertise in their ranks, veterans of such bands as Natchez Trace, The Bread And Cheese Hillbillies, Cow Pie and Thomahawk, but shuffled it up and added a wide-boy frontman. They toured England in 1975 in support of what was left of The Flying Burrito Brothers, but recorded for Jonathan King's UK label and gave 10cc a run for their money as writers of sharp lyrics and snappy tunes. Richie Bull was some kind of maestro on banjo, although he mainly played bass, and Vic Collins played steel guitar. '(I've Never Been To) Tennessee' is pure country corn with a twist: "Chet Atkins ain't the only saint who ever played guitar/and I'm going to be a great big country star". "Just like Gene Clark," Paul Shuttleworth adds, almost under his breath. How could anyone dislike a band whose comeback album was called *A Former Tour De Force Is Forced To Tour*, which welcomes back original member Dave Hatfield. Hatfield started off on string bass with The Morriss Boys String Band, whom we encountered at Britain's Third Country Music Festival. It all comes around, if you wait long enough.

Dire Straits' debut is really about a boy in the provinces who – on side two of the original vinyl – escapes to the delights and dangers of London, a double edge caught in 'Wild West End'. It's a source of imagery which Knopfler uses to describe modern life: "even a hero gets a bullet in the chest". Forming The Notting Hillbillies was a way to sidestep fame while using it to his own advantage, and it resurrected the spirit of The Duolian String Pickers, a two-man band with Steve Phillips. Old-time country meets country blues. *Missing...Presumed Having A Good Time* sees the band posing in front of a Wild West main street, but it's a deliberate trick, a two-dimensional paint-ed stage set. A cynic would say that the music is, too.

It's certainly low key, but the presence of The Louvin Brothers' 'Weapon of Prayer', The Delmore Brothers' 'Blues, Stay Away From Me' and some close male harmonies suggest a debt to those angel bands. Live at Ronnie Scott's, with Bobby Valentino guesting on fiddle, the band keep going until two am, and *The Guardian* noted how Knopfler could "suddenly dress up a country weepie with a fluid, aching guitar line". Like Ry Cooder, he has largely disappeared into the world of movie soundtracks, but a recent CD of duets with Chet Atkins was delightful, up to a point.

Dire Straits owe most of their success to people of a certain age reacting against the perceived danger of punk and the new wave, but country music inserted itself here, too. It's really like a strong case of herpes: very difficult to dislodge once it's got a foothold. The brains behind Stiff records was Jake Riviera, once manager of Chilli Willi, and Nick Lowe helped to set up the label. The former country boy was now the "Jesus Of Cool", but it didn't last.

Lowe became what he always had been, a tricksy singer whose enthusiasm draws the listener towards him, and a Nashville-style songwriter whose clever wordplay skates over ungovernable emotions. Writing 'The Beast In Me' for his for-mer father-in-law, Johnny Cash, was the logical culmination. It took years to complete, and "I don't know if I was still writing it for Johnny Cash or, by then, for me. But, my God, I was so thrilled when he cut it." Nick's own version on *The Impossible Bird* is solo and acoustic, and half whispered, as if uttered in the con-fession box. Some saw the whole album as return to country, but Lowe confessed to *New Country* that "I don't think I ever went away from it". Well, he would, would-n't he? "I like what I've always liked, which is a mix of C&W and R&B. There's a funny little grey hole where those two styles meet, and that's where pop music really lives." What he did plan was "a set of songs that were grown-up and big-heart-ed, and I devised a way of recording them right." Country music, then.

Carlene Carter once claimed to have put the first syllable "back in country". The smartly-dressed deb of her debut album, recorded in England with backings by The

Rumour and with new country songs by the likes of Rodney Crowell, was radically repackaged by Jake Riviera for his new label, F-Beat. By this time, Mother Maybelle's grand-daughter combined fishnet tights and cowboy boots and posed provocatively. *Musical Shapes* saw Rockpile and Clover giving the music a new-wave twist. The arrangement of a brisk 'Ring of Fire' is Bizet's *Carmen* on heat, and her own song, 'Appalachian Eyes', is a back-porch two-step with a touch of the Gary Glitters, while 'Foggy Mountain Top' adds pedal steel to a rockabilly beat. Carlene is only doing here what her grandparents did back in the 1930s: bringing old-time music up to date for her age. We all go out of style, in the end.

What *New Country* described as her "rowdy charisma" has served Carlene well back in Nashville, although she cuts her vocals at home in California, thanks to her allergy to Tennessee pollen. This embargo does not extend to her family heritage, though, and on *Little Acts Of Treason* she revisits The Carter Family song 'The Winding Stream', with her mother, two aunts and her daughter all singing along. Carlene might be rebellious, but she's still a member of the dynasty. All the same, AP's claim of moral purity might be a little stretched by some of her lyrics. She is a strong, independent-minded woman, just like great-aunt Sara.

Clover were also the unnamed band backing Elvis Costello on his debut album, also produced by Nick Lowe. Given Elvis' own pub-rock background, singing updated country rock in Flip City, this was all too appropriate. The young Declan McManus combined an Irish heritage with a love of country: both are embedded deeply in his work. When he formed The Attractions, the rhythm section was Pete Thomas from Chilli Willi and the John Stewart band, along with Bruce Thomas from Quiver. He later worked with The Confederates, some of whom had played with Gram Parsons. Costello once revealed that 'Heathen Town' is his answer song to The Burritos' 'Sin City'.

None of this quite explains why, when he went to Nashville to record *Almost Blue* under the unwatchful eyes of Billy Sherrill, he weighed it so heavily towards the singers of his parents' generation, the likes of Charlie Rich and George Jones. The whole thing smells like a personal indulgence, one that adds nothing to what has gone before. Two tracks stand out, neither of them from the original album: his softly-sung psychopath's confession in Leon Payne's 'Psycho' and the live and bruised version of what is here retitled 'I'm Your Toy', with Steve Nieve's tinkling grand piano and the warm sweep of the Royal Philharmonic Orchestra. Even this track feels more like a performance than a confession.

Originally dismissed as an Elvis clone, Clive Gregson has put together what is for me a much more emotionally satisfying body of work, full of gritty humour and what *New Country* once called "vaguely Gaelic-sounding ballads". His strange career path has seen him move from pub rock to the folk clubs – during his acoustic duo with Christine Collister – and on to Homegrown Records of Nashville. It's a case of have talent, will travel – much like the old settlers, really. Thus did former Flowerpot Man Roger Cook trade harmony crap in England with harmony crap with a slight twang in Nashville. It's much like the progress (or lack thereof) which Jimmy Nail sketched out in *Crocodile Shoes*, and that album sounds increasingly to me like just about the best British mainstream country music ever made, even if Jimmy has to strain for some of the notes. More to the point, he keeps his Geordie accent. Clever lyrics by Nail himself and Paddy McAloon (that Celtic twist again) recycle cowboy myths knowingly – "Honey, you are looking at your Shane" – and the shit-hot band behind him include BJ Cole, as if that's a surprise.

The Sex Pistols chose to fall apart at the end of a short tour of the South. Johnny Rotten's own account is that "the cowboys took it for the joke it was meant to be. We weren't there to destroy their way of life, or anything. Quite the opposite." The prince of anarchy admits to liking the people he meets in Georgia and Texas: "they're very individualistic, not a uniformed lump", even going as far as to go off one night with a girl in a cowboy hat who's just come out of prison. He finds an affinity, too, in their basic philosophy, of learning from one another, and enjoying life for what it is: "That might be an Irish way of thinking on my part." However, he does admit – under-exaggerating wildly – that there were fights in some of the redneck truckstops they visited.

There was a different kind of violence when The Pistols' former manager and art-school terrorist, Malcom McLaren, plundered Appalachian music for his experiments in theft – sorry, I meant sampling. 'Buffalo Girls' yokes together violently the call from a square dance and a hip-hop backing track. What is so annoying is that works.

What The Sex Pistols unleashed was a whole rash of electric hillbillies. Barely-trained musicians gleefully took up instruments they could hardly play. It was only a matter of time before they got around to traditional Irish folk music, then onto country.

The Pogues started as a joyous thrash, with updates of Celtic emigrant songs a speciality. If you play them back to back with an early Appalachian string band, the two are blood brothers, with exuberance trampling over any wrong notes. The former Nipple Erector Shane MacGowan started to write lyrics about the Irish diaspora. Best of all is his skewed romanticism on 'Fairytale Of New York', where a drunk in a New York jail sings 'The Rare Old Mountain Dew', and an old couple declare undying love by throwing insults at one another. It's worthy of John Prine at his seamy best. Shane captures a people stranded between continents: "The boys of the NYPD/were singing 'Galway Bay'", and making much the same point the track features Ewan MacColl's daughter on backing vocals. London Irish meets London Scottish.

Those who reckoned that The Pogues were inauthentic were confounded when they were joined by Terry Woods, a founding member of Sweeney's Men and an ace clawhammer-style banjo player, a man whose musical life had been devoted "to playing ethnic American folk music within an Irish context." Another new Pogue,

Philip Chevron, wrote the best modern song about Irish emigration, 'Thousands Are Sailing'. It asks poignantly: "Did the old songs taunt or cheer you/and did they still make you cry?" Chevron, formerly with Irish punk band The Radiators, needed to escape a land of "guilt and weeping effigies".

As with The Alabama 3, one of the methods of escape was to play at being a cowboy. The band flew to Spain to act in Alex Cox's Western, *Straight To Hell*, and MacGowan – who had begun to play the town drunk, in real life – later recorded his own slurred version of Lee Marvin's 'Wand'rin Star'. The Pogues kick-started a new "rogue folk" movement, and the biggest rogue of them all was Scottish wildman Champion Doug Veitch, billed as "the undisputed king of Caledonian cajun swing". He managed to upset country purists from the start, combining the influence of Jimmie Rodgers and dub reggae played at the speed of punk. Veitch remains the only man yet to draft in the Mad Professor to remix pedal steel and fiddle at his Peckham home studio. If you play the 12" single 'One Black Night' at 33rpm, Veitch actually sounds like a West Indian.

Another media phrase used to describe this short-lived movement was "Cowpunk". The likes of Helen And The Horns, The Skiff Skats and The Blueberry Hellebellies played updated skiffle, do-it-yourself music, and none were better than Terry And Gerry, with their wonderfully-titled album *From Lubbock To Clintwood East*. 'The Good, The Bad And The Usherette' begins with a *yippie-i-aye*, and is about a girl "who watches the world from the Odeon, Leicester Square", and falls in love with a screen cowboy.

The Boothill Foot-Tappers produced music which ranged from ska to country, but the album that survives them does not do justice to the band onstage, with accordions, washboards and ankle socks, three girls in huge hairdos and check shirts, and souped-up old-time music. They were also defiantly cockney, which added to the joke. Guitarist Kevin Walsh and banjo player Chris Thompson had gone along to a gig at Acton's Town Hall, and blagged themselves onto the bill: "We were bad, to be honest, but people got into the yee-haw thing." The name came after Kevin had visited the States and visited the graveyard in question.

Lash Lariat And The Long Riders paid homage to American string bands from before the war, and called their music "hillbilly boogie", which featured fiddle, banjo and string bass, of course. As they told *Folk Roots*: "we're playing C&W, but it's not what most people would understand by that term. We're playing a style of music that has its roots in America in the Thirties and the Forties. It's basically acoustic music, and it's melodic, infectious and energetic." *Time Out* inferred by the band's name that they were sado-masochists.

Nobody could say that of The Famous Potatoes, an eight-piece acoustic band from Westcliff-On-Sea, who claimed to play "soil music", blending bluegrass, skiffle, swing and gospel. They started playing music for barn dances, and then were fired up when they discovered the Twenties hillbilly record *Echoes Of The Ozarks*. As they told

Sean McGhee: "It was similar to what we were doing but it had something extra, a lot of swing and sparkle which we felt was missing from what we'd heard of English folk music. Those recordings were on old 78s, and are a bit hard on the ear, like you're hearing 50 or 60 years in the grooves!"

They are "excavating" old songs, and returning them to their dance roots. Some of these now sound a trifle sexist, with titles like "It's A Shame To Whip Your Wife On A Sunday', although the reaction of *Time Out* is not recorded. They identify two separate audiences in England: those who listen to new country, and "those who go down to their country-music clubs, which is a very middle-aged thing. The new people just can't stand all this dressing up as cowboys. People in America can't believe it. They find it quite bewildering when they come over."

There was a third way, though: taking cowboy dress and subverting it along with the music it supposedly accompanies. No-one did this better than The Mekons, who dressed up in stetsons, cowboy boots and Mexican jackets, like extras on a spaghetti western. Leeds University art students of the fiercest ideological stripe, they started life as one of the most basic punk bands ever. Some years down the track, they chose to adopt C&W, as if reflected through a cracked mirror.

The journey started with their 1983 single 'The English Dancing Master'. Tom Greenhalgh had bought an album of primal English barndance music, and even this fearless punk "just couldn't understand what was happening. It sounded out of tune. It was awful. But then after a while I gradually understood it." Two years later, they moved towards country on *Fear And Whiskey*, released on their own Sin label, a perfect parody of Sun and based in Coldharbour Lane. There's a real rockabilly beat, with lots of scratchy violins, ragged punk guitar and an amateur vibe throughout, as befits The Mekons' "anyone can do it" philosophy. On the cover an empty highway leads to a modern city in ruins, and inside Hank Williams' 'Lost Highway' is as ramshackle as an old cowshed. "Jonny Boy" Langford sounds like a football terrace hooligan as he sings the grim words, with a chuckle in his throat. The fiddle is jaunty, if a little rough and ready, and then Dick Taylor – on loan from The Pretty Things – plays one of his not-a-note-wasted guitar solos, and the whole thing seems to levitate. It wasn't so much a tribute as a deconstruction, with Hank's song left in ruins.

Edge Of The World has a cowgirl on the back cover, lots of accordion, a disconnected-sounding Sally Timms on backing vocals, and a wonderfully downbeat 'Sweet Dreams', which suddenly breaks off. Having paid tribute to Don Gibson, Hank's 'Alone And Forsaken' becomes a Velvet Underground-style drone, with impassive vocals – in a North-of-England accent, of course. The whole stance of the band depends on this comic incongruity between cramped English back streets and the wide open spaces of the Wild West. On the front sleeve here, a Leeds terrace is plonked down in Monument Valley, and horsemen surround burning double-decker buses drawn up in a circle, just like a wagon train.

A dedication to Richard Manuel reads "see you down the road", and they cover

The Band's 'The Shape I'm In' – bitterly ironic in the fact of Richard's suicide – on the live CD *New York*. Greil Marcus wrote that, whereas a sense of togetherness came naturally to those living in Big Pink, The Mekons are exiles in their own land. They resemble The Band more closely "in their seamless melding of rock 'n'roll, old country music and ancient British folk music", so that a "Celtic fiddle piece" turns out to be a Hank Williams song.

Honky Tonkin' quotes another of his songs, but it's difficult to imagine Hank giving you a reading list which includes Wittgenstein and Engels, let alone a book on transsexualism. The mixture is gloriously the same as before: punk folk with rough edges. The Mekons might be intellectuals, but they can't hold a tune to save their lives, the dreamily exact Sally Timms excepted. Sophie Bourbon from Chicago proved to be The Mekons' saviour, and the band relocated to that city to form Bloodshot Records and The Waco Brothers, "half Clash, half Johnny Cash".

Back in the USA, punk hit late and then set off in some equally surprising directions. Jason And The Nashville Scorchers, as they were first named, played the kind of fast country rock which originally attracted the cowpunk label. The title of their debut EP, *Reckless Country Soul*, is more appropriate, with one song by Hank Williams, one by Jimmie Rodgers and two by the band. Their music is an affectionate punch at Nashville's guts, raunchy but respectful. *Fervor* has the band slouching in semi-cowboy dress in front of original posters for Roy Acuff, Hank Williams and Bill Monroe. These might be young tearaways, but they're family, too: Warner Hodges' parents toured with Johnny Cash, Perry Baggs' father sang gospel, and Jeff Johnson was raised in the Blue Ridge Mountains. Their music sounds a little bloodless now, but back then, as they told *No Depression*, "literally you could go into certain places and do what we were doing with country music – forging it, melding it, slamming it together with punk rock and rock 'n' roll – and get beat up". They blazed a trail for the likes of Uncle Tupelo to follow.

REM became unusual superstars, with an upside-down sound where the bass player played the melodies and the guitarist provided colouring. The lead singer mumbled so that you could hardly hear a word he said, and when you did he didn't seem to make any sense. They blazed their own trail deep into American folklore, one that would also feed back into new country, years down the line.

Fables Of The Reconstruction was recorded in a rain-drenched London, with producer Joe Boyd firmly leaving them to their own devices. Largely composed at the last minute, it is an odd, evanescent album that matures with age. Stipe surrounded himself with "fables and nursery rhymes and Uncle Remus and old tales", entranced by the idea of stories and songs being passed down by word of mouth and then becoming "as much a part of a way of living or a particular area as the religion or the trees or the weather. I like the connection between that and the South." Added to the list here is 'Old Man Kensey', a real-life dog kidnapper – whether official or not is not made clear – who ransoms the dogs back to their owners and then gets drunk. 'Green Grow The Rushes' takes its title and much of its inspiration from a Scottish song, with lyrics by Robert Burns, which Stipe erroneously reckons was sung by US soldiers in Mexico back in 1846. Meanwhile, banjo punctuates the tale of Wendell Gee.

Country is always there, on the edge of the picture. Buck's mandolin illuminates 'Losing My Religion' on *Out Of Time*, and 'Country Feedback' is just that, a demo with pedal steel. It's also one of the most mysterious songs, even by this most mysterious of bands, a waking dream of terrible loss: "It's crazy what you could have had." Stipe came into the studio with no words prepared: "He just had two little drawings on a piece of paper – an Indian head and an arrow – and he just kind of shouted." REM's debts to Athens, Georgia, are legion, watching the trains go by in 'Carnival Of Sorts (Boxcars)', the graveyard in '1,000,000', even the man 'Gardening At Night' in suit and tie. According to Peter Buck, "spooky gospel, that's what we wanted to be".

On top of this, Stipe began to build his own personal mythology. The year before *Fables*, he spent much time listening to "cassettes recorded in Tennessee, in the mountains, Appalachian folk songs, field recordings...an old man with a fiddle, with a woman in the background with her hand on the stove". Dock Boggs, perhaps. As Buck added: "Country and hillbilly music's something that's just absorbed in REM. It's in the air down here, you just can't get away from it."

The Blasters were an extremely basic LA punk band featuring two brothers, Dave and Phil Alvin. Lead guitarist Dave went on to join X, who also numbered among their friends the young Dwight Yoakam, and encouraged their occasional forays into country music as The Knitters. The new wave Gram Parsons, anyone?

Dave Alvin studied at Long Beach under Gerald Locklin, America's greatest living poet, and although he dropped out of the course – he was a punk, for God's sake – he was later associated with the Illiterati Press. Back with The Blasters, Dave wrote the title track for their debut album, *American Music*, and then really hit his stride with 'Long White Cadillac', which Yoakam made his own. He has since made a line of distinguished solo albums, rich and warm with a largely acoustic sound, and as relaxed as only an old punk can be.

Blackjack David is another of those essential albums I told you about at the start. It leads off with the traditional song, ominous and driving, while 'Abilene' is a more bitter song by far than George Hamilton IV's Sixties chart topper, to which it doubtless refers. 'Mary Brown' is a kind of update of 'Matty Groves', except that it is only Lord Darnell – in this case a banker – who dies here.

It's all steeped in the passage of time, from ancient ballads to the story of a Vietnam vet: "My mother's family have been here since 1870, and my grandparents ran a dance hall back in 1902, so I knew all about California history." Meanwhile, brother Phil released *County Fair 2000*, a matching trawl through American musical history. A little black boy embraces a white girl on the cover, and the album similarly recognises no restrictions of colour, starting with rockabilly and then taking in dirt blues, R&B, and featuring the old time of 'Starlight', with Phil on banjo, and swing jazz. Phil seems to have a different voice – and band – for each song. A final medley yokes 'The Old Ragged Cross' with a Sun Ra tune, and The Dirty Dozen Brass Band play us out with the traditional 'Didn't He Ramble', *al fresco*. It's like compressing a whole music library onto one silver disc.

All kinds of oddballs were attracted into the country tent in this mythical county fair. Country Dick Montana had once been drummer with beat revivalists The Crawdaddys, but his new band The Beat Farmers have a rocket-thrust propulsion which Jason And The Scorchers would kill for. *Tales Of The New West* puts it to the service of all kinds of modern classics, from Lou Reed to John Stewart's 'Never Going Back', which makes up for in excitement here what it loses in delicacy. There is positively no voice-over at the end, but a punk thrash instead.

'Hippie Boy' features Chip and Tony Kinman from Rank And File, themselves former members of new wave band The Dils, who then joined with a very young Alejandro Escovedo on *Sundown*, one of the freshest meetings of new wave and country. The Kinmans went on to record as Cowboy Nation, with quiet retellings of dusty tales like 'Remember The Alamo' and traditional songs from the saddle like 'Old Paint' and 'Cowboy's Lament' (aka 'The Streets Of Laredo', and originally an Irish tune). Tony plays bass dobro, and Chip lonesome harmonica. *Mojo* described it as closer to Springsteen than Roy Rogers, and there is an underlying hardness to the songs here, as one would expect. "There's a late-night campfire glow to these melancholic, deep-voiced tunes, as bleak and vast as the prairies all around." It's also music which can send you fast asleep. However, one notes that, under the punk trappings, these brother acts – the Alvins and the Kinmans, even Mark and David Knopfler – aren't a universe away from the previous generation of Stanleys and Louvins. You can take the boy out of the country...

Lighter fare came from Colorblind James And The Death Valley Boys, the acoustic side of The Colorblind James Experience. You hear more clearly the parent band's debts to string-band music and the polka, and their Yankee wit on such as 'Jesus At The Still', which starts: "I'm not a bible scholar, I'm just a hillbilly." Funny, I thought the two were much the same. All is forgiven when Jesus appears, "arms around the jug/giving it a tug", and recommending the sour mash.

The Meat Puppets started as a thrash band, although even on their first album 'Tumblin' Tumbleweeds' betrayed their hidden country roots, and elements of bluegrass began to seep through on the likes of 'Confusion Fog', and in their dextrous picking. On top of a ramshackle rhythm section, such guitar-play falls sweet as rainwater on an old tin roof. (Dare I mention that Curt and Chris Kirkwood are yet another pair of punky brothers?)

The Residents had already issued their *Stars And Hank Forever* album, one side of which is a ritual music disembowelment of the great country star. On the cover of *God In Three Persons*, a naked girl kneels suggestively at the feet of a masked cowboy. Those fearing for the worst when the giant eyeballs toured *Cure-E*, their history of American music, through Europe were not to be disappointed. The curtain opened on three dancers silhouetted against the moon, with "100-gallon hats on their heads and an electric campfire at their feet". The resulting double LP devotes one whole, seemingly interminable side to 'Buckaroo Blues', comprising sound collages of the likes of 'From The Plains To Mexico' and 'Cowboy Waltz', seemingly sung by Donald Duck. Being The Residents, there is also a track called 'Saddle Sores'. An electronic coyote howls in the distance. *Carousel* on LSD.

Also out on the lunatic fringe, Rubber Rodeo dressed in country finery and used a small-label 12" EP to mate synthesiser with pedal steel and fiddle. Here, country punk stretches to a cover version of Dolly Parton's 'Jolene', and they later covered 'The Good, The Bad And The Ugly', but all the freshness leached away as soon as they signed to a major label. The Violent Femmes, too, were best when still on punk imprint Slash, and *Hallowed Ground* brings traditional folk music to the party, if such a word can be used for a singer with Gordon Gano's intensity. Even Australian desert-rockers The Triffids joined in this back-to-basics approach when they recorded *In The Pines* in a wool-shearing shack way out in the outback. There is a band that pre-dated the langorous style of alt country by a decade, with pedal steel by "Evil" Graham Lee.

Back in America, a whole new slew of bands had emerged from the so called Paisley Underground. As had happened with psychedelia first time around, and would happen again with acid house, many of those coming down got right on down to country music – you can hide fried eyes beneath a stetson. Steve Wynn took a sideways step from The Dream Syndicate to record the one-off album *The Lost Weekend*, by "Danny And Dusty", with Dan Stuart of Green On Red. Sid Griffin, from The Long Ryders, also helped out on dobro, and Stephen McCarthy played lap steel. The extremely palatable results are like an update of Dave Crosby's *If Only I Could Remember My Name*, abstract songs played by the cream of the West Coast élite.

Wynn went on to sound like Neil Young, while Green On Red plunged into the aural bloodbath that was *Here Come The Snakes*, recorded at the Sun studios with Jim Dickinson among the backing crew: "After five years, four apartments, three abortions, two cities and a dog, she left me." Dan Stuart told *Bucketfull of Brains* that Green On Red evolved out of The Serfers, which also gave birth to Naked Prey: "We just stayed together and played. It's like a family of in-bred Appalachians." In terms of songwriting: "I think we're pretty much into the Woodie Guthrie/Hank Williams tradition. Each song we write you can play on acoustic guitar." It's the last thing you'd think off when you listen to the stormy gig captured at the Town And Country Club.

Green On Red – by now just Dan Stuart and Chuck Prophet with backing musicians – joined up with Al Kooper on keyboards down in Nashville for *Scapegoats*, another dark masterpiece. On the cover, a stetson rests in the graveyard, as if its owner is six foot under. There are songs to match, concerning blowflies, making love in the rooster shack and psychopaths, and there's even a little of the Johnny Cash patented rhythmic tick. As to touring musicians: "we've started to use Ireland as a resource. In Ireland, country music isn't a dirty word, whereas in England they think you're some kind of *Deliverance* redneck."

Prophet went on to make sweet harmonies with Stephanie Finch on *Brother Aldo*. As to Naked Prey, they reduced 'Wichita Lineman' to a funereal pace, and seem to be involved in some kind of outdoor black magic ceremony on *Under The Blue Marlin*, but their music is mainly the same old meat and potatoes. Far stranger is the work of Howe Gelb, a visionary out in the desert. With a postal address in Tucson, the first Giant Sand(worms) album *Valley Of Rain* allies punk thrash and haphazard playing to the essence of C&W, like sudden immersion in an ice-cold shower. This is music with spikes. *Ballad Of A Thin Line Man* is still as dark as hell, but new singer Paula Jean Brown sours rather than sweetens, and Gelb calls all kinds of unnerving noises out of his feedback guitar. At times he sounds like the scratchiest of string bands all by himself.

Gelb talked to *Strange Things Are Happening* about how he mixes cowboy tales with a cinematic focus: "I like the idea of tracks being like they're small clips of film." He has long admired the "sparseness" of country stars like Merle Haggard and Hank Williams, and set up a separate *nom de plume*, The Band Of Rocky Blanchette, to make the *Heartland* LP, charming on the surface but rancid on a closer listen. "Let them try to save everyone/from the death squads/from the eye-gougers." Apocalypse is waiting in the wings. Being Howe, take nothing at all on face value – the sleeve credits Rainier on dobro and "howling", along with a "peddle steel" player, and some of the faces of that Thirties cowboy band on the inner sleeve look a little modern. "The songs were written a long time before we recorded them. Back then, there wasn't a lot of new country music – we ended up making music that we couldn't buy."

A second album by the same band includes Waylon Jennings' 'Trouble Man', Lucienda (*sic*) Williams on guest vocals, and bows out with Jimmie Davis' 'You Are My Sunshine', sung cracked and desperate. It even has a country monologue: "y'know, Blacky isn't here tonight". Howe took time out to record with Dwight Yoakam, "who came on a little too fast", but rather than follow him back into country history he prefers to look to the future: "The desert is unthinkable…it helped me to open up." There's a hole in the sky, and even Clint Eastwood or Neil Young "won't ever make a statement on this one/cause big guitars and big guns/won't make a dent in this one". It's a hole just about as large as your imagination, and in Howe Gelb's case that seems pretty near to infinite. Now if only he could sing as well as another of his heroes, David Allen Coe…

On *Sage Advice*, Howe's young daughter wanders among desert trees wearing a huge cowboy hat, and she duets with her father on one track by bashing on an upright piano in a way that's guaranteed to give you a headache – as is so much of

Gelb's music. So why do we seek him out, when there are a million Jim Reeves clogging up the bargain bins?

Another crazy outlaw is Russ Tolman, once of True West. *Drifters* is like a country-rock version of Television, with two lead guitars duelling at high noon. Tolman's own solo outing, *Totem Poles And Glory*, is considerably more raw, with what one critic described as "enough echo to fill the Grand Canyon." Tolman might rant and rave, but he totally lacks Gelb's fingers-down-the-blackboard edginess Appalachian style.

And still the wild men emerge from the wood. Blood On The Saddle were the most extreme of them all, although a name like that was hardly likely to see them singing Joni Mitchell songs. Album titles like *Poisoned Love* and *Fresh Blood* give a extra few clues as to their general demeanour. Punk speed is allied to what *Trouser Press* describes as them trashing their C&W idols, and to further tease out that analogy their idea of country is "Hank Williams OD-ing in the back of a car". Their westerns are strictly of the spaghetti genre: men murdering each other for a handful of dollars. Ex-Bangle Annette Zakinska sings over stand-up bass and yodels, which gives historical authenticity and makes their debut album "a rodeo where even the horses are doing speed". Any John Denver fan who has strayed in here by mistake will have just been dispatched humanely. Annette keeps on gamely performing songs like '(I Wish I Was A) Single Girl (Again)' like a real country star, almost, or the captain of the *Titanic*, "while her band, out of control, beat her to the finish".

Thin White Rope were almost courtly by comparison, although it has been said that this is the kind of country rock band which David Lynch would relish. There is certainly a troubling surrealism to match the high, lonesome sound of Guy Kyser's voice, which sounds like that of a man crossed with a wolf. They are world class merely as a covers band. On the mini CD *Squatters' Rights*, the band ooze twin-guitar honey all over The Byrds' 'Everybody's Been Burned' – Guy babbles in the middle, and then it all gets very menacing – and my own favourite flipside, 'I Knew I'd Want You'. Then you find they've mixed in a dose of strychnine: Gene Clark's cheerful optimism on the original has evaporated, and Kyser almost spits out "and then we'll be happy." Why do I suddenly think of The Dead Kennedys, and 'California Über Alles'?

Exploring The Axis opens with military-style drumming, and the band strut about in an open field. The music is like psychedelic guitar set to a metronome, and the wonderful sense of space you find in, say, early Quicksilver Messenger Service, is here a claustrophobic hole. There are touches of country guitar even here, and they open out on the semi-acoustic soundscape that provides the quiet bits of 'In The Spanish Cave'. Skeletons investigate a wreck, and the band emerge from the dark like a street gang. 'Mr Limpet' is a tribute to Marty Robbins, with his Spanish touches impacted like solid rock. There's a hoe-down going on hereabouts, but it might end with you being asked to walk the plank.

Kyser's new songs catch at the same unease as the photo of the iconic Monument Valley on the back of *Moonhead*, picturing a guitar propped upright on an open grave. And yet the band have such a rich soup of a sound that it draws you on. The *Red Sun* EP was recorded after a tour of Russia, and the experience of seeing state terrorism for real leaked onto the vinyl. (Maybe it was this example of Western emotional decadence which finally cracked the Iron Curtain.) Here we have vintage Americana by Lee Hazlewood, of course, along with Gene Pitney's 'Town Without Pity' and Marty Robbins' 'They're Hanging Me Tonight', every one a joker.

Thin White Rope's final gig was captured on *The One That Got Away* (so it didn't), and includes their encore version of 'Wreck Of The Ol 97', with twangy guitars, a hillbilly vocal and a shivery lead break of at least two notes. Then they're singing 'Roadrunner', sound like Motörhead with a world-class guitarist, and the moment has passed. The only bands still around like that seem to be from Wales, for some obscure reason. Nobody else, from Alabama to Travis, seems to take risks anymore.

A later entry in the grisly chronicle of country punk was taken up by The Chickasaw Mud Puppies, whose *White Dirt* was a good Southern romp – three-legged alligators, and all that – with production courtesy of Michael Stipe and a duo from Athens, Georgia, who pretended to be hillbillies and were more likely college professors on vacation. Yokels don't write songs called 'Lon Chaney'; they watch him on late-night TV. As *Rolling Stone* put it: "imagine the sound of field-hollerin' rednecks after they'd come upon a cache of B-52s records". In fact, it's probably better to imagine them than to actually hear the likes of 'Sailor, Beat The Blood Out'. Take a tip from one who knows.

Also worth a footnote are Lone Justice, once described as Linda Ronstadt on speed or Dolly Parton backed by The Blasters, which is more to the point – after inhaling helium, though. The whole thing has that hysterical, boxed-in sound of Eighties pop. Even with a country twang, it's not different enough.

The Long Ryders were Byrds derivatives, right down to the way they spelt their name – taken from a Western movie – but scuzzier round the edges, less optimistic, and with a sore throat. Lead singer Sid Griffin remains an enigma, singing lyrics steeped in Americana while mostly living largely in London. The band formed in LA from the remnants of The Unclaimed, and then Steve Wynn went off and formed The Dream Syndicate instead. Griffin had escaped his native Kentucky to join The Frosties, playing Small Faces and Kinks' songs. He steered the rest of the band through one mini album and three full-length efforts, all totally essential. If the Sixties country rock bands represented a drug-fuelled search for transcendence, this was the product of more cunning and less idealistic minds, half pastiche and half heartfelt tribute.

On the short but determined *10-5-60*, the band's punkish roots are sweetened

by banjo, steel guitar and autoharp, and that Byrdsian propulsion is firmly on the launch pad. They are not played gently, though, and the vocals are the very antithesis of Nashville cool. If Gram Parsons approached country with respect, this is a full-tilt drunken assault.

The front cover of *Native Sons* was a deliberate parody of *The Notorious Byrd Brothers*. Luckily, songs like 'Ivory Tower' and 'Tell It To The Judge On Sunday' are strong enough to back up the comparison. The back cover places pedal steel guitars, a banjo and an autoharp alongside the Vox amp, snare drum and Rickenbacker. A tour jacket labelled "Sin City" invokes the ghost of Parsons, hinting at the hidden dangers in the lifestyle whose shiny detritus all of this represents. As if to cement the resemblance, 20 years on, Gene Clark adds his high, lonesome voice to the proceedings.

As Griffin told Peter Doggett, the band covered both generations: "There were older people on the Southern California scene who were really thrilled that somebody was doing this. Punk fans liked the fact that we played with a punky energy, while the older guys liked the twelve-strings and the Clarence White-styled lead guitar. When we went out to Middle America and then England, the crowd became more or less just young people, but in California we had hippies from communes standing next to people with purple hair and shaved heads. It was a beautiful thing to see."

Their final two albums – the first recorded in rural Oxfordshire with the Kursaals' pedal steel maestro Will Birch, and the second back in Hollywood – saw the band becoming more overtly political. They were by this time a prime influence, particularly in the way in which they could jump back in time but still keep things relevant, so that 'Harriet Tubman's Gonna Carry Me Home' was about an escaped slave, described by Sid as "the Nelson Mandela of her time". Then the band seemed to break up for no real reason, and the hole they left has never been adequately filled.

Griffin was always a fan of traditional folk music. "I think country really owes a debt of gratitude to people like Seeger and Leadbelly and Cisco Houston because they kept all these songs going." They kept such songs alive. Roger McGuinn puts the words and music to a traditional song on his website, because he feels it's going to die out with his generation. Pete Seeger "already can't sing very much any more". Sid himself went on to form The Coal Porters, a low-key affair who now mainly deal with reviving music of the past, while he himself has written a book on Gram Parsons. He has become a chronicler of the music that he loves.

As Sid told Peter Doggett, he could never stop going out on the road: "Some of the greatest political discussions I've had since university have been in the back of a van." He loves the very idea of "a bunch of guys belching and throwing gum wrappers at them". It's a bit like trucking, but with better songs. "I admire people like Ernest Tubb, who died waiting for the next tour to start." But as the Nineties beckoned, the freewheeling attitude which makes Griffin such a refreshing interview

was starting to look extremely out of time. With country music retreating into a commercial, politically inert blandness, the rough enthusiasm of The Long Ryders and their like had become a spectre at the feast.

It was a time for consolidation and retrenchment. The "unplugged" format enabled Neil Young to hold a back-porch orgy of pump organ, accordion and dobro, and the same constraints enabled Dylan to rediscover himself. When the amps are switched off, there's nowhere to hide.

Loretta Lynn turned her Kentucky background and Cherokee heritage into a song, a book, an "authorised video biography", a soundtrack album and a feature film. They all told the same story: way back when "we were poor but we had life". It was an appealing myth for the New Depression. Loretta was a Seventies honky tonk star, a tough-minded woman who breached Nashville etiquette with songs like 'The Pill' and 'Don't Come Home A-Drinking' (With Lovin' On Your Mind)', but ultimately stayed inside the big tent.

There's a sense of uplift to her singing voice, which belies the descriptions of *Butcher Holler*. The road was paved with coal slag ("red dog"), and in the summer she would hold fireflies on her fingers and pretend that they were diamonds. "Most of the people were Irish – not the Catholic kind, the other kind – from families that kept moving west until they finally settled in the hills. There wasn't nobody to take taxes from 'em…so they grew into their own independent ways. They raised chickens and hogs, corn and berries. They didn't have no papers or listen to the news." As to welfare, it makes her spit: "Being poor really helped me."

It was in much the same spirit that Nashville now made its big move. The urban country movement was swept away, to be replaced with the new traditionalists: out went dress trousers and open-necked silk shirts, and in came neatly-pressed jeans and cowboy hats.

George Strait was the role model, and Randy Travis the hottest young dude in town, even though his head remained stetson-free. In fact, *Storms Of Life* is still the only album you really need to sum up the whole style. The work features sparse backings, carefully arranged so that whichever instrument is chosen to complement his voice at any one time – dobro, clarinet or pedal steel – it is choreographed just right. There's not an ounce of spontaneity, but there are no Jordanaires or saccharine string sections either. Only Nashville could write, produce and then sell you a song about being brought back by train to your home town in your coffin, and then being buried under the old oak tree – and then make you feel good about it!

Randy's voice is as stylised as grand opera, deeply masculine (no Boy Georges hereabouts), tender but tough and with a realism that pop music would simply never dare try. The direct way he launches into 'Reasons I Cheat' is breathtaking, and by the end of the song you actually feel sorry for this two-timing bastard. Travis comes from North Carolina, where his builder father constructed a music room, complete with a stage, on which his children could perform. Randy was a troublesome teenager, spent his time drinking, fighting, shooting and threatening (allegedly), and then lost all of his money on a turkey farm. He did a spell on probation, but music and a change of surname did the trick – that and taking country back to basics: "Those songs were laying around publishing companies, just waiting for someone to come by and pick them up." Which he did.

It revitalised the industry. As Tony Brown, head of A&R at MCA, Nashville – and a king behind the throne – told *Q*, from the Sixties to the early 1980s, "country music was getting watered down. Now, this new breed, they made a statement by using acoustic instruments again, cutting real stripped-down records, and it sounded cool: traditional, but contemporary." Certainly the sound of *Storms Of Life* is superb: understated, crisp and timeless. The likes of Hank Williams were proud to dress as country singers, but from the Seventies on "everybody who was in country didn't want to be associated with country", so they started dressing like pop singers so that they weren't mistaken for hillbillies. The new breed are happy to go back to that.

If only that had been true. It's like a politician's promise – best check your wallet. Brown is sick of TV shows which present country singers as hicks: "they'll have bales of hay, a couple of mules, a girl with a gingham dress. I don't think you have to be associated with cows and pigs and shit." *Mojo* looks back ten years later, and the cows and pigs have gone but the shit is still all around. In around 1990, Nashville moguls decided to remove from country radio all music made prior to 1986. "The older artists, no matter how viable, were tossed aside with the old records, the baby and the bathwater." The philosophy was that, if a new act didn't hit home with their first or second single, they were finished, thrown in the dumper. Songs began to tend towards the superficial: "instead of being torn, bleeding, from the heart, they are written straight from the wallet". Tradition was merely the name on the packet.

Not quite for everyone. Travis Tritt, "made myself a promise when I was just a kid/I'd mix Southern rock and country, and that's just what I did". Reba McEntire's 'For My Broken Heart' is also full of excellent story-telling and genuine tragedy – her tour band had just died in a plane crash. Alan Jackson sings pure honky tonk, and has an archaeological nose for old songs. In marketing terms, though, they all take second place.

At the very latest count, Garth Brooks has now sold 99 million records, and has to sell only only 9 million more to overtake The Beatles – not bad for a boy whose mother was a backing singer on *The Red Foley Show*, and a man who exudes vulnerability on his CD sleeves. Garth invented "stadium country", and old traditionalists like Kinky Friedman reckon him to be a kind of Antichrist: "He's the anti-Hank. Anybody who likes Hank for any reason would not like Garth Brooks. Country music crossed over and never came back." What I hear is a smooth singer with an appealing catch in his voice, but nothing special, even a little bit camp – "she was born to a mother trucker" – laughing at himself as he mimics deep emotion. This is Dan Fogelberg with a pedal steel.

There must be more to it than that, however, and certainly more than his fabled college course in advertising, with classes in marketing on the side. This is music for people with not too many records in their house, and has been put together with the precision you'd expect from a well-made vacuum cleaner: a slow song, then a fast song. Let's take *Fresh Horses*. It's beautifully arranged, with lots of pedal steel and fiddle, well packaged, well programmed. But there's something else.

I think the best clue is in an article in *New Country*, which talks of the "penchant for melodrama" in his work: "Women run into the sea and drown after hearing of their spouse's death. Adam and Eve are archetypes for cowboys." We're back with the traditional Celtic ballad, however much it might here be debased. Just about every song on this album tells a story, often with a supernatural edge. It rises to a crescendo on 'Ireland': "her eyes are the stars in heaven". The ancient sound of the hurdy gurdy mixes with fiddle and a modern rock band – which is just about as far from traditional country as you can ge – and even if the words here are literally nonsense (an unexplained battle, the narrator as saviour), they still stir the blood.

Garth took a huge tumble from public favour with *The Life Of Chris Gaines*, a sort of Ziggy Stardust without the brains, or indeed the songs. Now that he's made it, Brooks seems determined to resurrect every dodgy Seventies rock act, not that Bowie is that. A retread of *The Man Who Sold The World* would have been a yet bolder move – Garth in a dress. Even so, it was a shock to see country's biggest star in ballet tights, a shoulder-length wig and a straitjacket (admittedly, not all in the same photo). You confuse the country audience at your peril. Customers shouted "obscene responses" at retailers, and Capitol were forced to sell the CD at a bargain price. It still didn't move. Being perverse, it's my favourite of his albums, and the only one I intend to keep, but I listen to it an example of superior pop, expertly produced by Don Was. If I was a Garth Brooks fan, I'd be reaching for my gun.

Brooks was helped in his massive rise to fame by the concurrent craze for line dancing, which his exact music fitted like a shoe. Again, we were back to those old cornhuskings, the simple pleasures of moving in time together – and with no sexual commitment – which goes back to the dawn of ritual. It's bloody good for stress, too. Music went back to its original purpose: that of providing a pulse.

Meanwhile, in our tireless search for the real thing, we'll have to abandon Nashville again. Bruce Springsteen is a writer who exposes Garth Brooks for the lightweight he is. Despite having auditioned as an acoustic troubadour, Springsteen didn't go properly unplugged until *Nebraska*, but on that album he proved himself to be the true heir to the troubadour tradition of Woody Guthrie and, indeed, Hank Williams.

Dylan is undoubtedly the greater poet, but what Bruce showed here was his uncanny ability to wear the skin of the poor and the dispossessed. Dawidoff grasps this, too, as does Emmylou – "I really think of him as a country singer" – and Don Everly: "Ain't no working class in country anymore. But Springsteen, I can relate to that real well." The singer himself refers to his "South Jersey cowboy songs". Listening to the likes of The Louvin Brothers, he realised that "country asked all the right questions. Everything after *Born To Run* was shot full with a lot of country music – those questions." Nebraska deals with mass killers, small-town gangsters, a patrolman who lets his own brother escape over the border, all of whom tell their dreadful stories politely, and almost in a whisper. The use of "sir" is one of the most disquieting things here, along with Bruce's lonesome harmonica, sounding like the unquiet dead.

For Mikal Gilmore, whose brother Gary took his own walk out "on the edge of town", "it was a record about what can occur when normal people are forced to endure what cannot be endured". Until we come to understand how the people in these songs "came to their place of ruin", we will not start making a better world. Springsteen sings about what you won't read about in the papers. We are living in a more violent and unfair world than we were in the Sixties: "Your wife can't walk down the street at night. People keep guns in their homes. They live with a greater sense of apprehension, anxiety and fear." It's certainly a more adult response than Dave Crosby, still singing about wooden ships as if he's being radical. *Tom Joad* was more of the same, recorded at home in Beverly Hills with a pedal steel and a fiddle. Here are more tales of hard times, illegal immigrants and pointless violence, which tear at your heart.

If Hank Williams came back, this is the kind of music he would feel at home with, not that mouthed by some smoothie in a stetson. It's a matter of what you feel in your pulse, so trust that rather than the marketing men. Some of the freshest country music – as defined by its roots – has come from those often put in the folk box.

Nanci Griffiths once described her music as "folkabilly", with each album planned as a series of short stories. *There Is A Light Beyond These Woods* is pure folk music, clearly sung, but sounds a bit too much like a teacher (as Nanci trained to be) sitting out in front of her class with a guitar – the original steel magnolia, and a natural successor to Judy Collins, kind of clean. The rest of Nanci's career shows Nashville doing what it does best: taking that pellucid voice, choosing appropriate songs for it, surrounding it with backing musicians of the level of Bela Fleck and Mark O'Connor, providing subtle, bluegrass-flecked arrangements to match, and then marketing it. Her image is so laundered that it comes as a shock to hear about flashes of temper, let alone that her parents were friends of Roky Erikson's parents, or that she married young to a Vietnam vet with a heroin addiction. No wonder that so many of her songs are about the joys of escape.

Mojo reckoned that Griffith had created "an authentic contemporary style in the American troubadour tradition", and it's no coincidence that she has recently drawn closer to Irish music, recording with The Chieftains, and singing harmonies with Maura O'Connell. Dolores Keane appears on the stunning *Other Voices, Too*, a trawl through the past, linking Guy Clark and Sandy Denny, Ian and Sylvia (separately), Tom Russell, Woody Guthrie and traditional songs like 'Wasn't That A Mighty Storm'. On the recent *Dust Bowl Symphony*, the past is literally orchestrated.

Folk Roots reckons that Iris Dement's voice "cuts like a knife, takes you apart, then kisses it better", and I can't improve on that. *My Life* is exactly what it says: an album looking back on a childhood which has been stolen from her, first by the strict Pentecostal faith of her parents, and second by what happened when the whole family (she was the youngest of 14 children) were forced to move from their Arkansas farm to California, where her father could find work in a factory. Iris was three at the time, and it says much for the current Nashville mindset that some fans have questioned her credibility. Pearls before swine – Dement rings as true as anyone in this book, her voice an emotional yelp which twangs like knicker elastic, and if her interpretation of The Carter Family's 'Troublesome Waters' doesn't hotwire her to the tradition then AP was faking it, too.

Her debut album offered up the joyful hymn '50 Miles of Elbow Room', which Hitler would have loved, but it was her songwriting which most amazed. The tragic 'Our Town', which Kate Rusby turned into an English folk song, is graced by the presence of a fiddle, almost like a second voice. 'Mama's Opry' is about her mother failing to make the Ryman, and so recreating it at home: "Her Daddy played the fiddle and used to do the callin'...they'd move all my grandma's furniture around." This is great writing, plucking out details from childhood and putting it all into context.

My Life contains a written reminiscence of Iris finding her own father's fiddle, where it was hidden once he became "saved", "high upon a shelf, next to a stack of quilts". She boldly takes it to him, he plays a brief tune, and then passes it over to her brother. "He was the kind of person who made life difficult for himself by usually opting for the path of greatest resistance." Very Appalachian.

Iris was obviously the child of her father, and *The Way I Should* caused further waves of controversy, as it saw her broadening her focus out into politics. 'Letter To Mom' is about being abused by her mother's boyfriend, and she takes this kind of personal hurt into the public arena, with songs about yuppies, Vietnam and the Gulf, "we kill for oil and throw a party when we win". As she told *New Depression*, it "could get me killed."

With a voice like a blowtorch, when she's singing in front of a full electric band the results are certainly scary. What would be expected in the mouths of Jackson Browne or Natalie Merchant is unexpected here, and Dement brings the righteousness of gospel music to her coruscating words. Dawidoff, as usual, gets it spot on: like Merle Haggard (who co-writes one song here), she writes "regular people's songs rather than hillbilly or country music". It used to be called folk music, before the wimps got at it. Her stories are not so much "ballads as what in the tradition of

Loretta Lynn's 'One's On The Way' might be called life fragments". Nanci Griffith also expresses a great debt to Lynn's realism, praising the way in which she has given modern female country singers a voice. Maybe Loretta's harsh words about it being beneficial to grow up in poverty (and she wasn't just talking about a lack of money) isn't as far off beam as it at first seemed.

So which male singers have this same kind of passion, the kind that would set Garth Brook's western on fire? Only one I can think of, and he's the man with the quiff straight out of *Eraserhead*. Lyle Lovett is an update of the cool dude, embodied by many from Bob Wills to Dan Hicks, a man who sings about valuing his stetson above any woman (with a second joke contained in it, about the hat acts who seem to do just that) and sometimes to a bossa nova beat, with a cello and congas. This is more western than country, perhaps, and the spirit of western swing courses through his work. Like Randy Newman – who plays on *The Road To Ensenada*, as do Chris Hillman and Jackson Browne – he often tells stories in the third person, but unlike Randy this Texan farm boy found out about the local music scene from reading *The Improbable Rise of Redneck Rock*, and began singing in Houston coffee houses.

Lyle laconically told *New Country* that "I think I have the part of the country audience that might be interested in other singer/songwriters, that don't only listen to country." Pure country fans ignore him, which is their loss as such a mixture of pain and wit can only be found in Hank Williams himself. Lovett was generous enough to release a double CD of other Texan songwriters, and toured with a big band (to diminishing effect), but he's best of all with just a cello and his own songs for company.

One of my own Desert Island Discs would be the four tracks he laid down *just so* for the Kershaw show, and if anyone still bleats that this isn't country music, then I'd point out: a) the way Lovett sings "let's have a hand for that young cowboy"; b) the perfect timing with which the cello comes surging underneath; c) how it all turns into a love song, like a coin flipping over; d) the ache in Lyle's voice; e) his combination of clever wordplay and obvious emotion; f) the high, lonesome sound, even if it is so far away that you can't hear the words; and g) then punch him in the kidneys. Andy Kershaw can hold my coat!

Lucinda Williams is also helping to redefine the genre, but in a more visceral way. She can focus the same kind of full-on intensity as Iris Dement but in a dreamy and detached way, almost as if Karen Dalton had come back to life. Lucinda came up through the blues, as can be clearly heard on her first album for Folkways, where the influences are still partially undigested. 'The Great Speckled Bird' is the only real hint at what we have in store, which was described by *Rolling Stone* as "vital and mesmerising as her crystalline keening voice evokes the unsettling mystery of larger forces shaping our lives". *Happy Woman* Blues is a strange combination of country blues and folk, with fiddle, pedal steel and bottleneck guitar, and with a central ambiguity she just won't divulge.

All that Lucinda vouchsafes to Charlotte Grieg is that she grew up in Louisiana and learned much from her father, the writer Miller Williams: "Nothing is sacred, you write about everything." Her earliest memories are "the Child ballads, all those terribly dark murder and incest ballads". On top came Delta blues, then ZZ Top and The Allman Brothers, like layers on a trifle. When she came to perform, "I drew on everything from Robert Johnson to Cream." Nashville don't know quite what to do with her, as she fits no category exactly, which is the precise reason for her brilliance.

As to *Car Wheels On A Gravel Road*, the album I play first to anyone I'm trying to win over to modern country, a rich soup of memory and death and desire (just listen to the way she sings "my trinkets, and everything"), her own dad recognised that Lucinda was starting to dip into her childhood. "This is just the tip of the iceberg. I get excited just thinking about what she's going to come up with next." Williams has started to allow the mysteries of those ancient ballads to speak through her, and the result is mesmeric.

The only rival for such splenetic sexuality in popular music at the moment is another singer who sits uncomfortably in the country pigeonhole, for want of someplace better to dwell. Shelby Lynne spent years in the Nashville sweatshops, churning out product (her first ever single was a duet with George Jones), but *I Am Shelby Lynne* is quite something else. The arrogance of the assertion is justified by the contents (although her face looks like a mask), and confronts the viewer head on. There's not the slightest hint of a smile or a come-on, which goes against everything in the Nashville code.

This is the missing link between Memphis and country soul, featuring black rhythms but with dobro, mandolin and pedal steel for colouring. After a chorus which tests your speakers, she settles down – although that's not exactly the right way to describe it – into a cross between Dusty Springfield at her moody height and the coldest, bleakest country singer in the world. This is a voice which cuts but refuses to soothe. It's also an album which I find myself playing over and over again, with nothing else inbetween. Once it's in your CD tray, it seems to stick like glue – or something more sinister.

You listen to a song like 'Life Is Bad', with its charnel imagery, wiping away the blood – "tar and acid drip from an ice cream cone" – and you wonder what the world has done to her imagination. Then you read that, when she was 17, her father shot her mother dead and then turned the gun on himself. This isn't merely a freak-show in the Terry Melcher mould; the information illuminates the typhoon force of both her singing and imagery, not the other way round. There, living within one of the more inhumane of the Child ballads, is Shelby.

Victoria Williams is another victim of life who has got right up and punched it full in the face. This zany, back-porch kind of singer is unmistakeable thanks to a childlike voice, which has been described variously as "space cowgirl", emanating from "some largely undiscovered area at the back of the throat", and as something that "could curdle cows, let alone milk".

Since being diagnosed with multiple sclerosis, Victoria has turned the Sweet Relief concert held in her honour into a cause for others, and has been the recipient of a covers' LP, almost like an early pension. Nothing prepares you for the home-made spirit of her originals, however, which sound as if an entire human life was directly inscribed onto those microgrooves, lacking a whole layer of skin. In the profoundest sense, illness has been the making of Williams – what could be more 'country' than that? It has expunged any remnants of little-girl ickiness, so that *No Depression* described *Loose* as containing songs "as direct and honest as anything The Carter Family mined from their hills". There's the same kind of innocence, but forget their stern Christianity: Williams' erotic pantheism is much more in tune with the age. She covers Spirit's 'Nature's Way', which I have always taken to be about death, and nature's way of "retrieving you". Victoria plays banjo on the sleeve of *Musings Of A Creek Dipper*, which is darker around the edges. Even she admits that "it looks at a lot of life-death issues".

Williams sounds like a cross between Kate Bush and Björk. Why has no one chosen to remix her voice to a dance track, as it wavers in the wind? The direction she took next was in the opposite direction. A trio with boyfriend Mark Olson (once of the Jayhawks) and Mike Russell, with Victoria herself appearing for some reason as the punningly-named Mabel Allbright, The Original Harmony Ridge Creek Dippers made their debut album available only through a PO box address in Joshua Tree. Here Victoria and Mark live in a refurbished cabin, somewhere between the desert and the sky. The Dippers' music is tangy as wild honey, and as down-home as the dogs photographed on the back porch. 'Kai's Bristlecone Waltz' has a Celtic lilt, and a mountain sweetness.

To briefly separate out two more of my favourite current female singers, Mary Chapin Carpenter is credited with the invention of "therapy country", and the facts that she was born in Princeton, was educated at an Ivy League college and started singing in Washington DC have all combined to alienate some country fans. It doesn't help that one album starts off with a song about being "kinda in the mood to speak some French tonight", but whether she's folk or country is "really a question of timing. When I got a record deal, Nashville was signing a lot of singer/songwriters that had very deep roots in folk and contemporary acoustic music." She has since used Irish singer Paul Brady on tin whistle, and for me there is a quaver in her voice, and a bluegrass tinge to her backings which are simply not present in the work of her friend, Shawn Colvin – who revitalised Richard Thompson during her brief spell in his band – or a straight-up-and-down rock singer like Sheryl Crow. I'm never going to turn any of them away from my turntable.

Anyone doubting Rosanne Cash's heritage as Johnny's daughter, or that she'd been tutored by Mother Maybelle Carter to play guitar and autoharp, would have to either be mad or a current Nashville radio programmer. She escaped to New York, and husband Rodney Crowell – a man whose profound influence on all that is

Nashville we have not really had time to explore – helped her put together a series of conceptual, emotionally brutal records, none more naked than *Interiors*, about the break-up of their marriage. It starts "We crawled night and day through the tears and debris", and then gets sadder. *The Wheel* is a later masterpiece, although no more cheerful, with a particularly good song about throwing a bunch of roses from a lover into the fire: "I know no man I can trust." At her best, Rosanne gets close to the spirit of the old ballads, although there isn't much wit to leaven the pain.

Perhaps its all so subtle that I'm missing it, like the fact that *10-Song Demo* actually contains eleven tracks, all of them stripped down to bare bones. I listen to Rosanne Cash in much the spirit I listen to Eric Andersen, for a luxuriant sadness which never quite becomes self-pity, but I can't quite believe that things are really that bad – nothing that a good bottle of champagne and a viewing of *Duck Soup* wouldn't temporarily cure. With Shelby Lynne, or on the bleaker moments of Victoria Williams' cheery discs when she suddenly plunges into melancholy, I fear for their very souls.

So let's immerse ourselves for one last time in the healing spirit of bluegrass. Alison Krauss is a fiddle prodigy – voted Most Promising Country Fiddle Player (Midwest) by the age of twelve – who developed into as fine a vocalist as can currently be found, at first with the strictly acoustic Union Statement, who were not above bringing the odd Black Sabbath tune into their set. (They'd do the reverse in their home studio, making heavy metal versions of 'Blue Ridge Mountain Home' for private consumption.) Charlotte Grieg enthused over the dazzle of her voice, like "a young Dolly Parton or a melancholic Emmylou, yet wholly her own". Still not yet 30, it's interesting how the rather gawky girl in a shapeless dress on the sparkling collection *Now That I've Found You* has been groomed and shorn of both her band and her fiddle (in the cover pictures only, thank God) for *Forget About It*. The result is rather like the Trojan horse, with Krauss smuggling in bluegrass backings, her wonderfully sinuous violin playing and that voice with a chill at its heart, all into the country mainstream. However, the banjo's gone.

Ricky Skaggs went the other way after he left The Hot Band. He made a wonderful duet album with Tony Rice, but diluted his talent in a Faustian pact with Nashville. When he joined CBS in 1980, "I was pretty prohibited from doing anything other than commercial country music." They turned down his idea for a Christmas album, a gospel album, a bluegrass album, and an album of instrumentals, so why did they sign him up in the first place? Surely you don't hire a Rolls Royce then just use it to collect the shopping. Jamming with the likes of Elvis Costello helped him escape back to what he does best. Still devoutly religious – "I've got better, not bitter" – he hosted a radio programme called *Simple Life*, in which he takes famous country stars back to their roots, and returned to bluegrass with *Kentucky Thunder*.

As he told *Acoustic Guitar*: "When the front door's locked, go in the back door." The craze for Americana suddenly gave him a commercial focus: "I feel like I've been let out of prison", he said of *Bluegrass Rules*, released on his own label. *Ancient Tones* is more of the same, frenetic and meditative by turns, largely looking back to the masters – with whom Ricky trained – but with a new song about the Carolina mines and Skaggs' own instrumental, 'Connemara', written for his son's graduation. You can just imagine 1970-era Fairport let loose on it, and it definitely has that Celtic sparkle. Talking recently to *Country Music International*, he claims that the bluegrass influence seeped into his Nashville albums, almost without anyone noticing. He has also launched Ceili records – its Gaelic name signifying musicians jamming in a living room – which aims to "exploit" interest in acoustic roots while expanding into Celtic music. Bill Monroe once told Peter Rowan to listen out for "the ancient tones", from Ireland, Scotland and England.

Bela Fleck is about as far removed from Skaggs as could be imagined, a banjo virtuoso from Manhattan who joined The New Grass Revival and then, rather than take bluegrass back to its roots, propelled it into outer space. He was as comfortable with be-bop as he was playing in the Earl Scruggs style, and though I find a lot of his music perplexing, and some actively unpleasant, at his best he makes his ensembles fly. It's like seeing some precocious show-off on *University Challenge*: you just want them to slow down a bit and stop showing off. Yet he's only doing a Chet Atkins, taking a hick instrument, and showing how it can be combined with anything and still hold its own. The ultimate irony is that he now plays everywhere from Mongolia to Singapore, but back home in Nashville "there's very little work for banjo players in this town" (although he's just played a Garth Brooks section, for a man who can afford the very best). Talking of which, Bela likes playing bluegrass straight, too, and "when I play with Doc Watson, I find myself straightening right out".

The double CD *Live Art* is startling both for its dramatic sound quality and for the fact that every note of this music is actually being played in front of you, even if not in real time. 'Lochs Of Dread' starts as a kind of dub reggae, then goes into a Scottish reel, and then shifts to a series of jazz solos. After hearing the piece, you don't need to be told that this is "the tale of a Rasta Dude who has a bad dream concerning Scotland", but no one explains why. Other delights from the same concert are 'The Ballad Of Jed Clampett' and 'UFO Tofu'. And you thought 'Flying Saucer Rock 'n' Roll' was the last word in weirdness!

Even in the early days, Fleck was as likely to launch into Chick Corea's 'Spain' as in the old-timey tune 'Ain't Gonna Work Tomorrow', both of which appear on the same album. When playing with the likes of John Hartford he tends to keep it traditional, and *Roads* takes him to the quiet melancholy of 'Ireland'. After this, he formed The Flecktones along with a keyboard player, an electric bassist, and with Roy Wooten playing on drumitar (a guitar wired to electronic drums). And to think that Alison Krauss received death threats when she added a drummer to Union Station, and he wasn't even wired up. Bela explored weird time signatures and jammed with the likes of Branford Marsalis, but as *New Country* points out, rather than jazzing up his licks he has slowed them right down, so that "the percussive banjo melodies come to resemble single-note piano lines". The effect is startling, and would have knocked a back-porch Appalachian right off his stool. How exactly did you do that? Now show me.

If Bela Fleck is right on the rim of bluegrass, The Bad Livers are right off the map. Here are noise terrorists with banjos, and the natural successors to The Holy Modal Rounders, who "play it old and raw". They started playing bluegrass versions of Iggy Pop and Motörhead tunes, were described as "lightning-fast Deep Southern banjo thrash", but also recorded *Dust On The Bible*, a collection of gospel songs "like a pickin' party on a neighbour's porch". It has more genuine religious feeling than a whole shop full of Garth Brooks Christmas cash-ins, and indeed huge swathes of the Bad Livers' output is wonderfully listenable, even when they are inventing classics wholesale. 'Shit Creek' and 'Uncle Lucius' are unrecorded in the folk canon, while not many bluegrass originators are – like Mark Rubin – Jewish. To justify their depradations of the tradition, they quote Bill Monroe: "If a man can take a little bit of my music and put a little bit of himself in, and come up with something of his own, well that's all right by me."

A huge row erupted when Grant Alden, on reviewing their new CD *Blood And Mood*, wrote in *No Depression* that through "the new sterility of their sound, The Bad Livers have chosen to alter the dialogue they have enjoyed with their audience for the last decade". Where, Grant asks, is the "reckless emotion" that punk rock once offered? How can they surrender to machines?

This might seem a small matter, but it goes to the heart of everything that I am writing about in *Country Roads*. Alden starts his review by paying tribute to The Bad Livers as were – here were a band with roots. It is no coincidence that it was the sound of The Bad Livers which inspired him to lean over to a friend and whisper: "Let's start the magazine we've been talking about." And now, metaphorically, they have pissed in his face. On *Blood And Mood*, they have done an Alabama 3 and incorporated samples and drum loops and electronic bleeps. Alden's review is barely coherent, so full is it of anger and betrayal.

As one of those people who think that John Fahey threw away his genius when he started making sound collages, and as no great fan of The Residents, I agree with Grant in my heart. My brain, though, tells me that to move on you have to take just such giant leaps. After all, which hillbilly from Ulster or Glasgow or Liverpool first borrowed a guitar or a banjo, then realised it suited the old songs of home? Psychograss also play adventurous bluegrass. They adapt 'A Whiter Shade Of Pale', having opened with a new verse written by themselves, describing the Sixties: "those times were crazy too". I hated it when I first heard it, then loved it ever since. It was as inappropriate a move as The Bad Livers' magnificent album *Horses In The Mines*, dressed in a parody of the Folkways style. New wine in old bottles.

411

In just the same way, Tim O'Brien mines new meanings from an old song – it's called progress. He finds things in 'A Whiter Shade Of Pale' which its composers never meant, but which affect us living in the here and now. Here are the ideals of the Sixties, dying in front of our eyes in a song about ghosts. Psychograss clothe this historical piece in a yet more ancient style: bluegrass. Bill Monroe might well have codified it at some time during the last war, but it's a music whose roots go back centuries, and to another continent, one whose inhabitants were forced – by economic and religious necessity – to be "leaving for the coast". And as the years pass from its being laid down live – as it sounds – in the studio, this interpretation itself becomes part of history, another link in the chain. The song continues to mutate. Trying to stop such a process makes Grant Alden look like King Canute, commanding the waves to retreat from his kingly presence in vain. The tide must come in, and go out, and eventually the seashore will wear clean away.

Chapter Eight

Full Circle

It's all a matter of how you look at things. The CD of *Horses In The Mines* can be programmed in two ways: one sequence of numbers brings you what *New Country* describes as "a finger-blistering bluegrass album", while by playing it complete you can hear the "fondness for found noises and distorted vocals which got them the punk tag in the first place". It's like one of those paintings that looks first one thing, and then another, through to infinity.

Looked at one way, the kind of sophistication which has previously been associated more readily with folk music and the more advanced area of rock has fed through to the work of the more imaginative country singers. In Marty Stuart's *The Pilgrim*, great voices from the music's past – Johnny Cash, George Jones and Ralph Stanley – help dramatise Marty's ambitious honky-tonk, which is epic based on a true story. Being country, it will no longer matter that this involves suicide, adultery, Harlan County and trains. A great excuse for sound effects.

What Stuart grasps intuitively is that the story works on both the level of the everyday and the mythic, like all true C&W. The details of an illicit love affair, which survives everything else, are set against the timelessness of Stuart's update of 'I Am A Pilgrim'. His song cycle ends with a brief extract from Tennyson's poem about King Arthur. Marty is no fool. He is simply tapping into a mythology which is there for the taking. It lights up the lowest Nashville trash, let alone something as wonderful as this. Two events inspired Stuart to write it: the death of Bill Monroe and his own reading of Dawidoff's *In The Country of Country*.

You'll find the same intensity in Hal Ketchum's recent and mournful CD *Awaiting Redemption*, which was shelved for two years in favour of more commercial material from the singer. You'll find much the same thing on *The Trinity Session* by The Cowboy Junkies, with Margo Timmins apparently sleepwalking her way through songs like the traditional 'Mining For Gold', and a dead-slow 'I'm So Lonesome I Could Cry', recorded all through one mic in an old church, with the band sat around in a circle playing fiddle, mandolin and pedal steel. I remember that when the album came out, in the mid Eighties – it seemed unnaturally quiet, like a healing breeze.

It was part of a wider process in which rock musicians came to seek out the consolations of country. Minneapolis band The Replacements gradually shuffled off their punky trappings for a rootsier style, and one of the albums they did it on was called *Hootenanny*, which the sleeve explains is "a gathering together of all sorts of people". They sneer, of course, but it also must sound attractive when you're recording "at a warehouse in some godawful suburb north of Minneapolis". You also feel that The Replacements would need more than coffee to fuel them at such an event. Mark Eitzel and The American Music Club are about as depressive as you can get outside Joy Division, so what drifts all over the wracked, feedback-strewn soundscape of California, like perfumed smoke, is pedal steel guitar. The Walkabouts started out on Sub Pop, but their intense, desperate music really only came into emotional focus on albums like *Setting The Woods On Fire*, where country came into the equation, and *Satisfied Mind* is a largely acoustic run-through of songs by The Carter Family, Gene Clark, Nick Cave and straight from the tradition.

Once of Shockabilly, the maverick Eugene Chadbourne has showered the world with a seemingly endless stream of releases which have been described as "the oddest versions of country and folk music ever", including the free-form noise with which he intersperses his own perversions of C&W hits on *Country Music Of Southeastern Australia*. This isn't the kind of record your granny would like, unless her name is Kray. *Country Protest* brings in Patti Smith guitarist Lenny Kaye on pedal steel and the Red Clay Ramblers on bad-taste titles like 'The Shah Sleeps In Lee Harvey's Grave'. There's something compulsive about the way that even noise terrorists just can't leave country music alone. J Mascis of grunge merchants Dinosaur Jr revealed, like a secret cache of pornography, his love for Charlie Rich and Tammy Wynette: "Our initial concept for the band" – this is Dinosaur Jr, for God's sake, as out of control a bunch as ever fell over on a public stage – "was to be country stars who played really loud. 'Ear-bleeding country', that was our aim." We'll leave rock music right there, for this book at least.

You'd think, though, that at least the avante-folker Michelle Shocked would be immune to all this, but if you do you'd better avoid *Arkansas Traveller*, which is a riot of banjo, fiddle and accordion, with the track 'Cotton-Eyed Joe' an essential, performed here with two members of The Band on board as well. It's wonderful, and fortunately Michelle decided against wearing blackface and so here wears a straw hat and print dress instead – which, for her, is just as bizarre.

It all comes down to what Sally Timms said recently on Radio 4's *Front Row* (and I'm quoting from memory), that the joy of country culture is that you can take from it exactly what you want and discard the rest. It's like a giant toybox, and we are all kids at play.

kd lang thus identified a secret subtext in the work of Patsy Cline on *Shadowlands*, touching base with Owen Bradley in order to do so. Nashville and lang finally parted company after the singer's 'Meat Stinks' campaign, though she still idolises the music. "Country is not pop. You have to be a member of a political mind-set to be accepted." But isn't that to confuse the Nashville establishment with the music on which it feeds? Is it only me, too, who feels a little uneasy reading Owen's heartfelt thanks to kd for "digging me out of the woodwork", when he doesn't seem fully aware of the agenda going on here? lang's music is an exotic outcrop of a more general rise of girl power, way before Ginger Spice and her squeaky friends first tottered into view. With her band The Recliners, she worked her way through Western swing, honky tonk, rockabilly, country ballads and "wild polkas...with a certain modern edge". *Modern Twang* traces her influence on later gay and lesbian acts like Y'All, Ranch Romance and The Topp Twins.

Sharyn McCrumb has based an entire detective novel – and so much more – around the Judds, and she explains as well as anyone else both the joke – that the mother is as attractive as the daughter – and the underlying sadness of Naomi's fight with hepatitis. More to the point, their music is, to quote Adrian Cooke, "a modern, mountain-hillbilly sound, straight out of the hill of Kentucky". Nothing more, nothing less – except when Mark Knopfler comes over to lend a plectrum.

Again, I must cherry pick. Kathy Mattea started off as a Grateful Dead fan who knew *Workingman's Dead* from cover to cover. She then moved to Nashville, at first to be a tour guide at the Country Music Hall Of Fame. She is relevant here because of her long-time musical association with the Scottish folk singer Dougie Maclean, and their duet is one of the highlights of the Transatlantic Sessions TV series. Among the newer artists I particularly like is Kate Campbell – Rosaryville is like a gothic soap opera with some of the links missing.

The real delight of country music, though, is the way it can suddenly throw a song at you which lodges in your head, a twist of its tune or a nice verbal trick. Ciely Wright's 'Single White Female' sums up a whole social trend, while Gretchen Peters' 'The Secret Of Life' sums up, well, life itself, and with the matching full-length CD shows that songwriting talent in Nashville has not dried up; it has just changed sex.

The Dixie Chicks don't write their own songs, but they do play fiddle, banjo and dobro, and live on stage as well – no muso tokenism here. They've also been playing together for ten years, first in the teenage bluegrass band Blue Night Express and then as a five-piece cowgirl band in costume. Add the fact that Natalie Maines' father used to play steel guitar with the Joe Ely band, and that there are elements of bluegrass in there, along with lots of straight country, rock and even Celtic. 'Ready To Run' certainly sounds better than it looked as staged at the CMA Awards, with pipes, tin whistle and bodhran.

NME asked if they were from the "dirty, smelly, six-fingered mutant-hillbilly-out-of-*Deliverance* side of the country? Or are they just dyed-bonde Céline Dion clones, posing in crude hand-tooled cowboy boots?"

Puppyish rather than sexy, the trio are almost frightening in the way they exemplify their culture, naturally gifted instrumentally, singing matter-of-factly about divorce, even – on 'Goodbye Earl' – seeming to endorse murder by poisoning as an antidote to wife-beating. It's all in the genes, but at least they've kept the twang. 'Wide Open Spaces' is the essence of the Wild West boiled down, even if ostensibly about finding your own way in life. That's the thing about country music: it's so damned literate. It's also the kind of record a middle-aged man could have playing in his flat without anyone worrying, whereas if he was listening to the Spice Girls – let alone Boyzone – all kinds of unfortunate conclusions might be drawn.

Shania Twain seems to be playing on every 30-something's hi-fi I know, and if anyone has been hanging on hoping I'm out for her blood as the vampire sucking out the life blood out of country music then they've come to the wrong place. I admire persistence and good songwriting, although I have to admit that I'm not going to be queueing up for a ticket to see her.

What is interesting is to compare the cool sheen of *Come On Over* with the 1989 demos she made while still in Canada with LA producer Paul Sabu, and which have recently leaked out as *Wild And Wicked*. There's not a trace of country in them, whether Appalachian, mainstream or honky tonk – not the slightest hint of a twang. It's more like Elkie Brooks, or something from *Fame*, with a soundtrack by one of those identical Eighties rock bands with permed hair and leather trousers. When she later came to Nashville, she was just passing through. You can dress her up in a stetson and chaps on the cover of *Country Music And More* magazine (although she seems to have forgotten to put anything around the middle), but I can't smell any horse shit.

As someone once memorably put it, she is "more Madonna than Minnie Pearl". Shania's in-concert video shows a woman totally in control, as beautiful as a Greek deity, sure, but brisk rather than sexy. Country is there in her voice, and the odd touch of fiddle, but not in the songs, the rock rhythm track or the whole look of the thing. Why complain about her rock producer husband Robert John "Mutt" Lange – whose previous clients include The Boomtown Rats, Def Leppard and AC/DC – bringing in disco mixes and a rock rhythm section, with particular emphasis on the kick drum, when it's only rock 'n' roll to begin with? I don't get the snap of reality that I do even with The Dixie Chicks. But then, humankind cannot bear too much reality...

There is even an *Unauthorised Biography* CD, festooned with pictures and divided into "tracks" with titles like "Emerging Talent" and "Heaven Sent" and introduced by a man with a street trader's accent to the accompaniment of Sooty-style organ. VH1 has hosted its own video biography, and Tim Jones of *Record Collector* did the same in print. Here, then, is the gospel according to Shania, and how she has punched her way through the wall between pop and country.

The blessed infant was born in Windsor, Ontario, in 1965 under the name Eileen Edwards, and –crucial to us all – of Irish ancestry, through her mother. Scrape off the modern trappings and it is the archetypal rags-to-riches story of just about every Appalachian singer. Only the costumes change. Her father deserted them, and her mother moved Eileen and her elder sister, Jill, to the mining town of Timmins. She remarried, to an Ojibway Indian called Jerry Twain, but they were dirt poor: "We went to bed wearing our coats, literally freezing." by the age of three, young Eileen was singing on the table of a diner, and within a few years was performing at local hotels, even though "I was scared shitless, very shy, and I had terrible stagefright". Video footage says otherwise, however, presenting an infant looking much like Shirley Temple confidently working her way through C&W classics such as 'I'm So Lonesome I Could Cry'. One can sense a proud mother in the background, pushing. She lived the life, too, being given her first rifle at the age of eight and joining in on community moose hunts.

Shania's favourite album at the time was Elton John's *Goodbye Yellow Brick Road*, and she spent her teens singing in a Top 40 covers band. Every summer, however, she helped in her parents' tree-planting enterprise. During her breaks, she would "sit alone in the forest with my dog and a guitar and just write songs". Living in a cheap apartment, she didn't even have a back porch on which to practice.

What we need to complete the picture is a family tragedy, and when it came it was of classical Greek proportions, with her parents killed outright when their car was hit by a logging truck. To her eternal credit, Eileen gave up her singing career to come back and help raise her step-brothers, and then moved the whole family to Huntsville, in the Canadian wilderness. There she joined a Vegas-style revue at the Deerhurst Resort Theatre – amateur footage shows her belting out show tunes like a young Shirley Bassey – and made the heavily AOR demos with Paul Sabu, which were so much musical junk. Looking for a fresh start, she changed her first name to Shania, the Ojibway word for "I'm on the Way". It was a demo tape of her own country songs, with the twang put back, which brought her to the attention of Nashville music lawyer Richard Frank, and a new career.

Nashville being Nashville, they then tried to iron out all of the kinks which made her interesting. Producer Norro Wilson introduced her to the delights of all-day songwriting sessions, although even then her own writing was marginalised. The Canadian connection became a selling point, with the cover of *Shania Twain* seeing her with big hair and standing in the Arctic landscape with only a wolf for company. what rescued her from the conveyer belt was the mastery she showed for making music videos. The one that she made for 'What Made You Say That?' first grabbed the attention of Mutt Lange, and she later turned the sexist tables on Robert Palmer. In 'Which Bed Have You Been Under?', a flirtatious Twain wanders around men in a diner.

The resulting album, *The Woman In Me*, was, at $500,000, the most expensive album in country music history, and largely subsidised by Lange. It features subdued fiddle and pedal steel, but it also topped the pop charts, selling 13 million copies. The words aren't exactly Hank Williams, but they have a kind of plain-speaking integrity: "Any man of mine better disagree/when I say another woman's better looking than me." Shania bared her navel in publicity shots, and even survived a less welcoming kind of exposure when her home--town newspaper accused her of pretending to be a blood member of the Ojibway in order to court publicity. Such a heritage is now a career enhancement. As the video biography so charmingly puts it, her stage show sees her "singing her butt off for 24 hours", putting to flight any rumours that it was all studio technology, or that she is Mutt Lange's puppet. As long as you don't believe in any of it, her work is as bright as candyfloss and as disposable as popcorn. It cheers you up, and there's not a pedal steel in sight any more.

Talking to *No Depression*, Steve Earle puts it all in context: "You listen to a Shania Twain track, one of the singles, and put it against a Def Leppard single off Hysteria, and you'll see a lot of the same elements there. The same tricks are all there, the same kind of things with percussion and vocals. He knows what he's doing. And I admire what he does, from the part of me that makes records and tries to go in and get a performance on a record, to push those buttons in people. But he does it real mechanically, and sometimes I think it's cheatin' a little bit."

What the publicity-shy Mutt Lange has done so brilliantly, as he lurks somewhere in the shadows, is to create a new hybrid of stadium country, with lights and noise and action. It's the very opposite of *Unplugged*, a Disneyworld approach, with just about as much in common with The Carter Family as, say, The Corrs have with Irish traditional music.

The Corrs are a useful reference point, purveying stadium-friendly pop music which relies on a low-voltage sexuality. Young women rule. Here, too, are joie de vivre, good tunes, and exactly the same act every night, right down to the "spontaneous" remarks and Jim's piano solo with all the same wrong notes. The crossover market hates any rough edges. Talking to *Folk Roots* before they outgrew such things, James reckons: "I really do hope we can create our own niche", modern music "with an Irish influence...It's a blend of modern rhythm and technology with acoustic instruments and harmonies. The marrying of all these elements makes our sound." Just like Shania.

Meanwhile, Nashville has another superstar ready on the assembly line, and Shania's crown is teetering on the edge. "Move Over, Shania" was the headline which screamed from *The Observer* as they profiled Faith Hill, this "drop-dead gorgeous" but carefully bland artist (no songs about killing men in her repertoire) reveals that she was once Reba McIntyre's fan club secretary. Faith is part of a celebrity couple, married to fellow star Tim McGraw, and as for her new single, 'Breathe', "it's not Patsy Cline, it's not Loretta Lynn, but hopefully it's something that the British will dig". Her interviewer points out that, "unlike Loretta, Tammy and even Shania, she hasn't struggled from that dirt-poor, traditionally tragic background we've come to expect from our country queens". Instead, we get a list of

her favourite designers: "Gucci, Prada, Richard Tyler, Versace, Ralph Lauren..."
Suddenly, Shania seems close to Minnie Pearl after all.

Shania was voted Entertainer Of The Year at the CMA Awards. George Jones boy-
cotted proceedings (not that many people noticed), growling on a local radio show
that there were: "too many pop stars. They don't belong. This is not country
music." A Nashville newssheet accused the powers-that-be of promoting "pop
crap". Even the host on the night, Vince Gill – usuall Mr Mild – made a heartfelt plea:
"Don't lose sight of our roots." Indeed, there didn't seem to be too many dungarees, old patched dresses or floppy hats in the audience.

In doing so, he was picking up on a mood of nostalgia. The Mavericks were outsiders from Miami, but their smooth and semi-ironic country crooning slips down
easily, and the voice of Cuban-American Raul Malo is a beautiful thing, Roy Orbison
reborn. Here is the antithesis of the high, lonesome sound, from what has been
described as "The Beatles in a secret marriage with Herb Alpert". "I'm not a country musician," claims guitarist Nick Kane, "I'm rock 'n' roll."

Much tricksier, but playing the same game, are Lambchop, who, with up to 14
members, aren't so much a band as a musical collective, and who made a self-conscious decision to give countrypolitan a strong dose of LSD and see what emerged.
Their music at first sneaks up on you, with Kurt Wagner apparently talking to himself softly as pedal guitars weep in the background, interspersed with cocktail-lounge
soul. It sounds like Owen Bradley meets Curtis Mayfield, pleasant enough at first,
and then you start to notice what he's talking about (basically, bodily functions:
"there's some spit on the ceiling, and it's going to drop") and realise that the music
is all becoming a little to queasy. This is music by – and for – disturbed minds.

They started by taking the sum of their influences and instruments and seeing
where this led. Thus pedal steel joins euphonium and bongos. One ten-inch EP is
called *Hank*, while one CD is named after Michael Jackson's greatest hit and lasts
precisely 33 minutes and 33 seconds. Sometimes I think that it is only the fact that
they are natives of Nashville which gets them labelled as country at all. My own
favourite record of theirs is their first, *I Hope You're Sitting Down* (later re-released
as *Jack's Tulips*), with spooky organ and the same love of texture which ennobles
The High Llamas. *How I Quit Smoking* has a real string section, but Wagner sounds
less convinced by his own stories.

No Depression commented on their "quiet presence" onstage, while *Uncut* carries perhaps the most bizarre interview I have ever read. Wagner admits to a death
fixation, that he wants to make "the darkest, blackest record", and grins inanely
under a Co-op hat. How did he come to write a lyric as mundanely bizarre as
'Scamper'? Well, "I am a bad storyteller, or at least one who can never remember the
punchline." He then immediately disproves this: "I lay wood floors, that's my job –
and the idea was I was going to go to this woman's house, this elderly, shut-in

woman who had lost control of her bladder functions...she was lying in the house making this moaning sound." The job means that he sits down onstage "because I'm tired". I think this is enough to tell us that we don't have another Garth Brooks here.

Nixon was described as everything from "Nashphilly" to an alt country *Pet Sounds*, and is clearly a masterpiece is you can stand to listen to it. Tom Cox, for one, cannot, and claims that Kurt has one of those bad voices "which cry out to have someone put them out of their misery". As for me, sometimes they sound like paint drying, while at others it cheers me up to think that people can be so miserable and yet still make records. *Nixon* culminates with the traditional song 'The Butcher Boy' (usually known as 'Died For Love', back where it came from) set to a Velvet Underground drone and Burt Bacharach strings. The sight of the poor girl hanging gets Wagner quite worked up, or as close to that state as he is ever likely to be.

A simpler pleasure is the music of The Derailers, who take their starting point as the Bakersfield sound, with lost of twang, slicked-back hair and sharp suits. Dave Alvin produced their first studio album, which came complete with a free comb and tips on style. *Reverb Deluxe* had stretched out far enough to include a cover of Prince's 'Raspberry Beret'. Meanwhile, stranger things were stirring

Nick Cave is a kind of Australian hillbilly, dressing like a preacher and obsessed equally with the Old Testament and the murder of young girls: "I've always enjoyed writing songs about dead women. It's something that crops up that still holds some mystery, even to me." By turns horrific and comic, *Murder Ballads* is the logical extension of one aspect of the Harry Smith *Anthology*, although in the traditional song 'Henry Lee' it is the woman who wields the knife. Cave sings with eager savagery, but to make Kylie Minogue sound ghostly – as she does on their duet of death 'Where The Wild Roses Grow' – is really something.

Cave put together an evening in celebration of "The Harry Smith Project", at which Jarvis deadpanned 'The Coo Coo Bird' and 'Mississippi Boweevil Blues' (at one point departing from the script to shout "I shat in your ciabatta"), Brian Ferry oozed his way through 'John Henry', and Bobby Neuwirth became a mole in the ground. Van Dyke Parks made his debut on a London stage, chuckling through 'East Virginia', and Cave himself sang something with the McGarrigles which the *NME* described as "apocalyptic gospel". It was that sort of night, with people getting into that weird, old atmosphere, and throwing away their cool. There were weird conjunctions, too, like Irish oddball Gavin Friday and Margaret O'Hara duetting on 'The Ship Went Down', dedicated to the workforce of the Belfast shipyards. Hopefully, highlights will appear on disc some day, as they already have for the more staid US counterpart, with all of the usual suspects.

The *Anthology* itself re-emerged, this time on CD with acres of new footnotes. Even more exciting is Rykodisc's announcement that they are to issue the long-missing fourth record, which Smith planned but never released, and which would complete the alchemical pattern.

The Internet is the closest thing we now have to oral transmission, and is a chaotic treasury of folk tales. Kristin Hersh, formerly of the punk folk band Throwing Muses, chose to market *Murder, Misery And Then Goodnight* – her album of Appalachian ballads – only through the Internet and mail order, which made obtaining it seem all the more precious. It's a deeply troubling catalogue of murder and dismemberment, made all the more unsettling by the way in which she sings it, as if with child-like innocence, close indeed to those recordings which survive of old mountain women cackling out these same songs. Bill Malone reckons that such cradle songs were a way for a mother to "privately voice her longings, her joy, or her loneliness and pain" to her children.

Hersh takes up the point in a very revealing interview with *No Depression*. Her own parents were from Chattanooga, but moved up to Rhode Island. These are the songs they sang to her, and "when I began to compile some old family songs in the hope of giving a taste of my warm, fuzzy childhood, I was intrigued to find that my soundtrack had been…let's say evil." Here are songs where "the chick always dies. She's stabbed and poisoned and drowned." Her versions have none of the relish which Nick Cave brings to such material. The results are more terrifying still, a kind of emotional blankness.

She is quite happy to sing them to her own children, though. "It feels good to shout gross things. To moan along with the dying and then get back to the oatmeal cookies." Children have "their own built in sensors. I've never seen them too badly fooled." OK, so why does the duet with her son on 'Mama's Gonna Buy' put a chill down my spine, like those Sixties movies where the heroine enters a sinister doll's shop, or the smile of Anthony Perkins just before he puts on his mother's hair?

Hersh now reckons that Throwing Muses were "pretty much a combination of Appalachian folk music, Patti Smith, The Talking Heads and The Doors" – storytellers all. In just the same way, "the chord progressions that I do are always Celtic and country".

Kelly Joe Phelps has come to much the same conclusion, and on *Shine Eyed Mr Zen* he has pulled traditional material from "the Appalachian side of early recorded music. You can take the music of Roscoe Holcomb and put this alongside Skip James, and there's a certain correlation." The results have much of the hypnotic power of the young John Fahey, who supped at these same waters, but with slurred vocals on top. 'Dock Boggs Country Blues' is a slow, bottleneck stomp, with a sense of infinite longing.

The picture CD of Geoff Muldaur's *The Secret Handshake* depitcs a slightly off-centre banjo, and Geoff looks off-centre too, with a strange glint in his eyes. The music itself is a startling return to form, again from the blues side of the *Anthology*: Dock Boggs appears as a composer this time, with 'Mistreated Mama' sung to banjo, fiddle and wind ensemble. Somehow it all works, and lifts you about a foot in the air. Muldaur first saw Boggs live at Newport in 1963, and in suitably dramatic circumstances: "There was a lot of fog…and it was rolling in across the stage…and the stagelights were blue." It was a setting worthy of Wagner, but what emerged through the mist was an "ordinary fellow with a banjo. He started some strange modal plunking and then began a liturgical croaking…'Oh death, oh death, won't you spare me over 'til another year'…it gave me chills. All of us Cambridge folkies had heard him on the Smith *Anthology*, but there he was…living history." And here Geoff brings him back to life.

If anyone sums up what is now called Americana it is surely Tom Waits. He forces out 'Dirt In The Ground', on *Bone Machine*, over a funereal brass trio and string bass, and as if each word was a stab in the throat. Dock Boggs himself could not get darker than this, with Waits singing his own drear epitaph. The piano roll at the very end is a device to wake us from death. However, he's not always as gloomy as this, thank God. From *Swordfishtrombone* onwards, Waits found a way to integrate carnival, minstrel show, old-time country, blues and jazz musics to give clatter and grace to his strange tales from the gutter. Such rich subject matter – the underbelly of a nation – requires its own soundtrack, and bleaty-voiced David Thomas has similarly ventured out into the musical wilderness, scuffling for gold. After the blood-curdling yelps he perfected with Pere Ubu, he appeared playing accordion in a butcher's apron and a series of songs improvised afresh each night with The Pale Boys. When I shouted out a request for 'Non-Alignment Pact' he obliged, but to a polka beat.

The recent Mirror Man stage show was another attempt to recapture that old lost America, with plenty of spoken passages and a whole array of great but unexpected voices: Linda Thompson, Jakie Leven, Peter Hamill. The whole thing felt like a deep root around in the rotting jaw of Western culture, with players and singers arranged in a broad semi-circle, like an updated minstrel show. The stage was littered with gutted fridges, a mangled shopping trolley, traffic cones and scrap metal. Act One "happens in the space where you are and where you want to be, where the county seat is Nowheresville". Sounds like Appalachia, too.

That such eccentricities now have a context can be largely put down to one magazine, the Seattle-based *No Depression*, which grew out of an on-line Gram Parsons' Uncle Tupelo discussion group and which has played nursemaid to a whole torrent of new music. Meanwhile, under the sardonic Allan Jones, who has been on board this ship since the days in which UK country rock started to turn new wave, *Uncut* magazine has gradually turned itself into the British equivalent, not least through a superb series of free CDs introducing new and obscure bands.

The godfathers of such music – whether categorised as alt country, Americana or Woodchuck Nation – are Gram Parsons and Neil Young, rather than Hank Williams or Dock Boggs. There are lots of electric guitars and not too many banjos. Any weirdness is generally kept for the left-field lyrics, which go with the territory. The *NME* reckons that alt country "is the final resting place for all those rabid kids who used to go to gigs but have now settled down". If one can delineate its audience, they are rock fans of a certain age, with little time for dance music, seeking a music which can both surprise them, and settle them down in middle-aged comfort.

In the introduction to *Modern Twang*, the essential guide to the new sounds, David Goodman remembers joining the Columbia Music Club and getting *Sweetheart Of The Rodeo* and *John Wesley Harding* as part of his introductory offer, although this built on a collection of 78s given to him by his grandmother (the next best thing to having them sung to him on the back porch). Alt country was coined to differentiate this new music from the hate figures of Garth Brooks or Shania Twain, "instead drawing on and enhancing traditional country through the addition of contemporary styles and ideas".

Goodman traces the term back to a 1985 British cowpunk anthology, *Leather Chaps And Lace Petticoats: Welcome To Alternative Country*, and finds, to his surprise, that Costello's *Almost Blue* was a key recording, which "exposed punkers to country and not a few country fans (like me) to punk". He traces this through to "a host of innovators in new old-time", like The Horseflies, The Chicken Chokers and The Red Clay Ramblers.

Next we have the LA "Town South Of Bakersfield" movement, headlines by Dwight Yoakam, whose *Just Lookin' For A Hit* has his sobbing voice over a honky tonk electric band, best captured on 'Long White Cadillac', and the likes of Rosie Flores and Dale Watson. Goodman darts between the New York "rig rock" sound, with the likes of The World Famous Bluejays, the Boston scene – typified by The Swinging Steaks – and Washington DC bands such as The Wanktones, who were alter egos of punks The Slickee Boys. *Live At The Fontana Bowlarama* is punctuated by "the sound of bowling pins and other bowling alley noises".

This is typical of Goodman's book (which, apart from so much else, would serve as a discography for my own more modest effort), a bewildering variety of needle-sharp dissertations. Here are bands like the barely-believable Scroat Belly, and their key themes of "ignorance, violence and especially drunkenness", and Buck Naked And The Bare Bottom Boys. Inventor of pornobilly, Buck would come on stage dressed only in a "cowboy hat, pink cowboy boots and a toilet-plunger codpiece". Goodman carefully delineates each act into categories, like Hillbilly Bop, Psychocountry ("frenzied playing, deranged singing [including yelling, whooping and various animal sounds]" and demented lyrics) and White Trash Parody.

Reading too much of this in one go gives you vertigo, but where else could you find such a succinct career summary of the likes of The Legendary Stardust Cowboy? Discovered by two vacuum cleaner repairmen, he cut 'Paralysed' (21/2 minutes of unbridled chaos) and later low-seeling classics like 'My Underwear Froze On The Clothesline' before taking part in fellow maverick Eugene Chadbourne's C&W opera *Jesse Helms Busted With Pornography*.

My own account of alt country will by necessity be a briefer affair. Although it has encouraged the work of many new bands, the most heartening aspect of *No*

Depression has been the new lease of life it has given old campaigners like Chip Taylor, who was too uncool for *Detailed Twang*. The brother of actor Jon Voight, Chip had a long creative drought after writing songs like 'Wild Thing' and 'Angel Of The Morning', and became a full-time gambler, but his recovery is complete with the "bluntly autobiographic" *Seven Days In May*, and the double CD *London Sessions Bootleg*, combining electric songs taped in London with an acoustic session from New York and some Nashville overdubs. Lucinda Williams joins in, and the controlled wildness of the sound captures a new spirit coursing through country music. You can call it whatever you like.

If you call it *No Depression* then you need to go back to the three friends from smalltown America – Belleville, Illinois, to be exact – who got together to record an album of that name in 1990. Jay Farrar plays guitar, banjo and "Nashville guitar", Jeff Tweedy plays bass, and Mike Heidorn plays drums, with friends providing piano, "rice can" and pedal steel. The three appear out of focus and in monochrome, and you can't see any of their faces (they're blurred, out of shot or in shadow). They thank "everyone who ever bought us beer, let us sleep on their floor or came to see us play", and produce a sound which is a bit like slowed-down heavy metal. The lyrics are hard to catch, but a typical line is "watch shit go by".

The whole thing, needless to say, is magnificent. Its mix of guitar attack, urgent, twangy singing (mainly from Farrar), and the sense of being lost is close to the feeling The Saints evoked on 'I'm Stranded', right at the start of punk, when they were half a world away in Australia. Then, suddenly, we have an acoustic cover of The Carter Family's 'No Depression', and it's reborn – not an antique or something played out of respect but a cry for help. It's back into guitar noise for the next track, and the trio show their own roots in The Primitives, a punk covers band who wouldn't even talk to anyone who didn't like Black Flag. This isn't music that hangs around. They don't so much play guitar breaks as pure noise, and their next album, *Still Feel Gone*, is even harder, with massive drums and the feel of a live gig. A touch of banjo is just about the only concession to country here. You can see the band, at least, and they're suitable anonymous. This has the feel of a rock group going nowhere: "I sold my guitar to the girl next door."

The crucial breakthrough comes with *March 16-20, 1992*, carefully produced by Peter Buck from REM. After a punky start, 'Grindstone' suddenly slows right down and John Keane comes in on pedal steel. We're in an acoustic universe, with traditional songs like 'Satan Our Kingdom Must Come Down' and 'Moonshiner', and some new songs about social desolation to match the rusty front cover. The clenched-teeth anger with which Farrar sings is daunting, and Tweedy plays McCartney to his Lennon, sweeter and more melancholic. The feeling here is closer to Woody Guthrie than to Black Flag; it has just that sense of emotional desolation which we have seen time and time again in the greatest country music.

Anodyne adds Max Johnston on fiddle, and is amped up again, but something has changed. That melancholy is deep now, especially in Jay Farrar's singing, which is majestic in its intensity. The songs are self-written (one jaunty example is even about 'Acuff-Rose'), except for one, by Doug Sahm, who also guests. To cap it all, the album is recorded in a small studio in Austin, and yet still sounds live.

Just when it sounded like Uncle Tupelo were about to be the next REM, and after a show back near home in St Louis on May Day 1994 with new drummer Ken Coomer (thankfully captured on bootleg), they had split up. On that last night they opened with 'No Depression' and closed with some covers including songs by Neil Young and Lynyrd Skynyrd. In the liner notes, Jay bemoans the decline of country music: "We'd hear it through our parents, at family gatherings and stuff. But the definition of country we're talking about is definitely not the contemporary Nashville sound." Jay and Jeff share a ramshackle apartment, and figure that they can play the circuit for "another ten years or so", when "I'll probably work on the railroad like my dad". And Jimmie Rodgers, too.

They were not comfortable people, and a press call reduced one journalist almost to tears. Old hand John Tobler at least finds out that Coomer's father was Scotty Moore's accountant, and reckons that they possess "the correct theory and spirit, if rarely the application which most country music fans might expect". Peter Blackstock, co-editor of the magazine which took its name from their debut album, is more generous when he looks back in the company of *Folk Roots*: "Uncle Tupelo was the foundation of a new generation of bands around 1990. They were the galvanising influence…one of the few taking a more countrified approach to rock music, and it was the quality of the songs they were writing." Those who clustered around them included The Bottle Rockets and Gary Louris from The Jayhawks.

Jay Farrar formed Son Volt, with Mike Hiedorn back on drums. They debuted with *Trace*, with Dave Boquist on lap steel and fiddle and his brother on bass, and with Eric Haywood on pedal steel. The sound is as moody as hell and alternates between electric and acoustic, just like Neil Young, to whom these sombre songs bear comparison. *Straightaways* winds down from a roar to a whisper, with just Farrar's acoustic guitar and harmonica backing his lonesome voice on 'Way Down Watson'. Their third album, *Wide Swing Tremelo*, opens sharp enough to cut your ears open, and then settles into superior country rock which practice sessions in an abandoned lingerie warehouse have honed to near perfection. I could listen to this band forever.

Jeff Tweedy kept on with Uncle Tupelo but changed its name to Wilco, and then steered the band more towards pure pop on their debut *AM*. It's a great album to the glory of the human voice, with some very tuneful singing, but melancholy – let alone rough country punk – are present only fitfully. He opened up to *No Depression*: "I was still wanting Uncle Tupelo fans to love me", but "I never dug that whole sombre approach to making music. I think it should be fun. Music is entertainment. It can be serious, it can be sad, but for the most part I want to feel better." The parent band had become "more and more repressed to fit into Jay's world, which is a hard world to fit in, for anybody". It's Paul and John, all over again. Others approach "the lack of showmanship" of that band, but not him. He also refutes any idea of Uncle Tupelo as a pathfinding band, let alone a "visionary" one: "I think you can really hear a young band trying to decide whether or not it wants to be Dinosaur Jr or Hüsker Dü." Or even The Carter Family, Jeff. That's what set them apart.

Being There was an ambitious double album, starting with a twisted tribute to Peter Laughner of Pere Ubu, a man determined to die young from sex and drugs and rock 'n' roll, and who achieved this end. The whole thing has the musical self-confidence of The Beach Boys, or even The Beatles, and pedal steel is only present as a musical colouring. Tweedy is amazed that some people still regard them as a country rock band: "The instrumentation is very different. We managed to get some of the songs into an orchestrated pop realm." As to *Summer Teeth*, this is as "a dark pop record (with nothing country or twangy about it)", and by now they were, and remain, the finest rock band on the planet, but any connection with the underlying theme of this book is pretty peripheral.

Son Volt, and a whole generation of imitators, carry on the rough and ready aesthetic, whereas this music is as smooth as silk. Aurally, at least, 'She's A Jar' sounds like McCartney fluff until Tweedy oozes out the last line with menace: "she begs me not to hit her". His lyrics remain a kind of sung equivalent to the way in which David Lynch makes films. One tradition the band does continue, though, is that of enigmatic sleeve designs, with a Fifties radio set, an anonymous hand grasping a guitar neck, and what looks like a woman with her head pressed against a balloon all given starring roles. On the third album, the band stand around looking as gormless as possible, anti-stars from their hoods to their sensible shoes.

And then, out of the blue, there they are as Billy Bragg's band on *Mermaid Avenue*, helping to put tunes to a collection of previously-unpublished Woody Guthrie lyrics and sounding as rough as hell. This is hangover music, and you can almost feel the musicians gripping onto their instruments to keep themselves upright. It's *The Basement Tapes* all over again, crossed with The Rolling Thunder Review, with Tweedy and co playing The Band to Bragg's laconic Dylan, with manly choruses and fire in their bellies. Eliza Carthy comes in on fiddle to cement the Atlantic alliance, while Natalie Merchant plays at being Emmylou Harris. There's even some pedal steel.

Tweedy reunited with Farrar, plug Roger McGuinn, on three songs at a Harry Smith tribute show. His most fruitful sideshow, however, was Golden Smog, which was named after a cartoon band in an episode of *The Flintstones*. He joined after these anonymous jesters from Minneapolis – Soul Asylum's Dan Murphy, Gary Louris and Marc Perlman from The Jayhawks – had already released the *On Golden*

Smog EP of cover versions of the likes of Thin Lizzy's 'Cowboy Song' and The Rolling Stones' 'Backstreet Girl'. It was guaranteed to get up any punk's nostrils, much like what XTC did with The Dukes Of Stratosphere, or Robert Smith with The Glove, although with neither the fanatical attention to detail of the first nor the chilling psychodrama of the second.

The band had got together every six months or so in the late 1980s, and as Murphy told *No Depression*: "Everybody was really big on punk rock and hardcore. We went to this place and brought driftwood lamps, and wore ponchos, and we did these Eagles covers real quietly and we sang harmonies. And people just flipped." The start of alt rock, perhaps? They were just fun versions of songs from their childhoods – it was no coincidence that band members hid their real names by adopting pseudonyms based on the street names where they were born. The truth didn't take long to leak out.

Jeff joined for the CD *Down By The Old Mainstream*, and they issued a promo box which claimed to sum up *35 Years Of Golden Smog*. This is far more fun than Garth Brooks alter ego, and the CD booklet reproduces three of these supposedly lost records, *America's Newest Shitmakers* (a parody of The Kinks), *Swingin' Smog People* and *Temple Of The Smog*. Jody Stephens of Big Star joined for *Weird Tales*, which was packaged like the old fantasy magazine, and 'Until you Came Along' is the best Gene Clark imitation ever. David Goodman finds "these jingly jangly morning songs are a very pleasant walk down memory lane" for old Byrds fans everywhere.

Some people reckon that The Jayhawks are the best of all alt country bands, if indeed they come into that category at all. They are sharper and less sugary than Seventies forbears like The Eagles, but with the same sense of melody and dynamics. There's certainly a country twang.

Mark Olson grabbed guitarist Gary Louris from another Minneapolis band, rockabillies Safety Last, and their debut album *The Jayhawks* drew favourable comparisons with The Flying Burrito Brothers. They also backed Joe Henry, a kind of cross between Dylan and Van Morrison, opening his shows as themselves then joining Joe as a backing band. "I would have these brooding, claustrophobic songs, but their delivery was more like three-chord rock, all loose and splashy and great." Their second album in their own right, *Blue Earth*, left scene makers like David Goodman in no doubt that "they, not The Eagles, were the true successors to *Sweetheart Of The Rodeo*", although successive albums on Def American moved closer towards pure pop, with a full and rich electric guitar sound. Best of the lot is *Tomorrow The Green Grass*, "a sublime country pastorale". These CDs are packaged to evoke safety and a past musical age, with the band posing carefully on a dead tree trunk or in front of the wooden Hollywood Town Hall in the snow.

When Mark Olson left to spend more time with Victoria Williams, the band reformed and Gary Louris took over the reins, stating that he would "rather risk being silly instead of this safe, pure, timeless Midwestern prairie band". Out went the steel guitar, but *Sound Of Lies* adds a fiddler (Jessy Greene of The Geraldine Fibbers), and is a stone triumph, country rock with a vengeance, even if Louris threatened to throw out the baby with the bathwater. This is warm music, but the lyrics lay bare the break-up of a love affair with forensic skill: "Hurry up, it's late, and I'm dying in the shadows." *Mojo* glories in the way in which the music explodes "in a sunburst of strings and guitars as the band exclaim 'Baby I'm scared of you'!". Not that far from Uncle Tupelo, after all.

Uncle Tupelo's influence was particularly marked in North Carolina, in which Whiskeytown's lead singer, Ryan Adams, was a veteran of Ralegh's punk scene. Whiskeytown started out playing country covers of despairing anthems by the likes of Black Flag and Richard Hell. Therefore, in Adams' own words, "I started this damn country band/because punk rock was too hard to sing". Then, between the scorching *Faithless Street* and *Strangers' Almanac*, he found his voice, "fragile and blasted", with Alejandro Escovedo lending support. They still sound pretty rough and ready on *Rural Free Delivery*, however, like a hoe-down band punked up.

David Goodman notes how indebted Adams is to Gram Parsons, and the contrast between his own strained larynx and Caitlan Cary's fiddle, but others saw the band using country as a "shock device". But it's that which makes them so good, with pedal steel really having to work for its living against a click-clack rhythm section and Adams' rasp. Is Ryan genuinely self-destructive or just a good actor? Remembering what happened to Ian Curtis, one hopes the latter.

As for Escovedo, he started of with SF punks The Nuns, then joined Rank And File, and later went onstage backed by his own orchestra, whose live mix of electrics and rich violins and cellos is captured well on the live compilation *More Miles Than Money*, like Lyle Lovett with a severe head cold, covering songs by Iggy Pop, The Rolling Stones and Lou Reed. It's emotionally devastating, and thing of rare beauty. On *With These Hands* Willie Nelson lends a hand and Alejandro explores a Latin percussive groove, but there is also the traditional Irish motif of 'Nickel And A Spoon'.

Back in Carolina, The Backsliders were originally a honky tonk band, highlighted – as *Modern Twang* puts it – by the "searing punk-fuelled leads of Brad Rice". It's just a shame that they changed the title of what was going to be called *Hicktopia* at the last moment. It's no longer the front porch you practice on in the standard country biography; but the local punk band. Jolene were 'city-reared veterans of punk bands" who added a pedal steel played, while 6 String Drag were founded by Kenneth Roby of The Lubricators, although he added trombone and sax to the sound in homage to The Band. Steve Earle produced the results.

This kind of musical promiscuity is what makes alt country both so fascinating and so difficult to get a fix on. It's an odd music, almost more popular in Europe than it is back home in the United States, although it remains almost exclusively an American form and some of its more obscure acts are hard to track down in Europe. There's nothing more frustrating than reading a rave review in *No Depression* – or even just seeing a title like The Beacon Hillbillies' *More Songs Of Love And Murder* (a Blood Oranges offshoot, and as wonderful as it sounds, by the way) – and then find that you just can't get it in London town, let alone the provinces. There even seems to be a conspiracy among some fans and promoters to keep the secret to themselves.

A band like Big In Iowa (who are actually based in Ohio) have as big a following in Europe as anywhere, however, and are signed to Germany's Blue Rose label. Their album *Twisted* starts strong and then runs out of steam, but *Bangin' 'n' Knockin'* lets Bob Burns' drawling voice off the hook and contains a great cover of The Pure Prairie League's song 'Two League Highway'. They also play Neil Young's 'Cinnamon Girl', the anthem of the whole alt country scene. Forget the vocoder, though, please.

It can all get rather samey, and at its worst it sounds like Dire Straits on a not so good night, or even Racing Cars, forever shooting horses. I suddenly realise what this reminds me of: pub rock, back in town but with a steel guitar this time around. Take Farmer Not So John and you have the sound to perfection, with questing lyrics by lead singer Mack Linebaugh and guest appearances by the likes of Pete Rowan and Clive Gregson. The trick is to separate the Uncle Tupelo clones from bands who have something new to say.

Hence The Bottle Rockets, whose founder Brian Henneman actually played with the parent band, and who now sings "solid grain-belt rock and hard-hitting songs about hard-hit people", according to Goodman. The Gourds meanwhile are from Austin, with lots of accordion and much influenced by Joe Strummer. Aside from the sheer wildness of songs like 'I Ate The Haggis', and covers of everyone from David Bowie to Snoop Dogg, *Dem's Good Beeble* is like a supercharged Holy Modal Rounders, "a thousand miles of dirt track from Nashville".

The Old 97s had to look up the word "insurgent" when they were described as such, but had been in such un-Nashville combos as Killbilly and Peyote Cowboys in their home town of Dallas. They released *Hitchhike To Rome* – which included Bob Wills and Merle Haggard songs – on their own label, and "it went plywood" when it sold out its initial run of 1,000 copies. Rhett Miller reckoned: "I stopped believing in true love when Reagan was king", and on *Wreck Your Life* they serve up perfect "strum and twang", although it's a little too raw for my own taste.

And still they come. According to *Modern Twang*, Slobberbone began life in the back room of a liquor store and touch on "disturbing themes like boozing, wrenching heartache and brutal death". *Barrel Chested* is "flat-out, nose-bleeding, ear-ringing 'twang thrash'", but I think I'll pass. Suddenly Jim Reeves seems like not so bad an option.

Then there's The Geraldine Fibbers playing covers of the likes of Bobby Gentry, George Jones and Dolly Parton, but as if "you were looking into the morphine/alcohol-addicted soul of Hank Williams at his most tortured". No wonder, when we learn that lead singer Carla Bozulich was a teenage junkie who resorted to prostitution, reformed at the age of 21 and then fronted techno/industrial band Ethyl Meatplow as a dominatrix.

Or why not try Robbie Fulks, whose debut CD *Country Love Songs* is fronted with the photograph of a man about to bash his wife in the head with an axe? I've only got *The Very Best Of*, and although it's on the usually intimidating Bloodshot label he sounds cheerful enough, and insists that "the theme is fun, yours and mine". That is, until you start listening to the words.

Fulks hopes that "your enjoyment of my music exceeds the material gain it has afforded me". At the age of seven, he was handed a banjo by his folk-singing father in North Carolina, and that was that. Inspired by Costello, he formed The Trailer Trash Revue, which Goodman describes as "a parodic country outfit complete with dancing girls in bikinis". Now he sings carefully-crafted songs like 'Roots Rock Weirdos' and 'She Took A Lot Of Pills And Died', and is backed by a bar band called The Skeletons, who also backed Jonathan Richman on his *Goes Country* CD. Fulks is suitably succinct about what he thinks of Nashville in 'Fuck This Town', believing that it will flourish "as long as there's a moron market/and a faggot in a hat to sign". Nobody is rushing to put him in a cowboy hat.

Perhaps the most uncompromising of all is Sixteen Horsepower, hailing from Denver and led by preacher's grandson David Eugene Edwards. David Goodman labels tham as "gothic", and then really goes to town: "Every aspect of this band oozes darkness, desolation, grotesqueness…disturbing grainy tin-type images of their CD cover art…scruffy sullen appearance…creepy lap steel, haunting fiddle…" I think we've got the picture. *Low Estate* is also incredibly exciting, as David's barely-controlled singing echoes over banjo and wild electric guitar. Here is the American Nick Cave, and there are lots of quotations from the Bible on their CD titles alone. Even the jigs and reels are fervid and fevered.

Goodman sees the band transporting the listener back to "19th-century mining camps, run-down farms and urban slums", and it certainly isn't easy listening. *No Depression* finds "Appalachian jigs and flatland reels laced with remnants of Old Country polkas and cabaret adagios". It's a wonderfully rich sound, rancid around the edges. Edwards doesn't lighten up in interviews, either: "I have a duty, an obligation to do what I do. The music I'm making is for the people who need that." PJ Harvey's close collaborator John Parrish recognised the same emotional fanaticism here, and came over to produce *Low Estate* in an antique studio in a barn on the edge of a Louisiana bayou. I wouldn't have liked to have been there when the lights went out.

I prefer the gentler pleasures of alt country, typified by Calexico (comprising two members of Giant Sand), who produced a CD with a booklet on handmade paper and aural soundscapes to match, or even the bittersweet lo-fi of Neil Casal's tuneful odds and ends collection Field Recordings, which is really back-porch music with amps.

Blue Mountain were once described by *Folk Roots* as "ethnopunk", so that you can virtually hear the weight of a couple of centuries on Cary Hudson's shoulders "as the rocking chair creaks on the front porch". Cary and her husband, Laurie Stirratt, have a good dose of humour, too: "Poppa ate squirrel…Poppa ate everything in the house." Meanwhile, there's a Celtic flavour to 'Heart Of The Hidden Beach'.

Looking through the Americana section in Tower Records is often like overturning a stone and seeing what crawls out from underneath. Tarnation's Paula Frazer played in SF punk bands like Frightwig, but she is almost somnambulant on the band's debut *I'll Give You Something To Cry About*, her vocals "somewhere between Joan Baez and Tammy Wynette". Without old-time music to anchor it, though, I find *Gentle Creatures* is the kind of album which never quite makes it out of the speakers.

Hazledene is more entrenched in the bones of things, a "sensual alternative to Shania Twain", with two female guitarists/singers. Shawn Barton admits to a death obsession, which isn't too surprising when her band's debut is called *Digging You Up* and blasts melancholia at you: "I'm more into confronting the issue, however sick or sad it might be, and experiencing it because then at least I know that I'm alive. I'm not afraid of death." From the same recording session comes a fan-club-only CD called *Orphans*, which sees Hazledene cover songs by Thin Lizzy and Radiohead.

On and on they come. The Old Joe Clarks are husband-and-wife team Jill and Mike Coykendall from Kansas. They started by playing contemporary classical music in The Wichita New Music Ensemble, and then switched to lo-fi with the help of dobro and lap steel player Kurt Stevenson. The hushed *Town Of Ten* has been described as a "cross between The Cowboy Junkies and The Scud Mountain Boys tanked up on espresso".

The Scud Mountain Boys are even weirder. They began by jamming informally around Bruce Tull's kitchen table while pursuing a "proper" musical career as rock band The Scuds. They acted as their own support act, playing acoustically as The Scud Mountain Boys, and found to their amazement that this often went down better than the main set. Things now get very weird, with the band resurrecting their down-home sets on stage, sat around that self same kitchen table, and then going back to the original kitchen to record their debut album on eight-track. It sure beats a porch – it's warmer, for a start. Their whispered, moody sound is heard best on Sub Pop's *Massachusetts*, a kind of minimalist country. After they split, Joe Pernice and his brother Bob recorded the CD *Overcome By Happiness* with a full orchestra, "leaving 'alternative country' and warmed-over 'Americana' in its wake", as the liner notes so arrogantly claim. It still sounds pretty quiet and restrained to me, though, with strings to match. Truly gorgeous – but nothing to do with country music.

I personally blame Souled American, the original pioneers of lo-fi cowpunk, or "country 'n' strychnine" as *Trouser Press* like to call it. Sonny takes songs by the likes of The Louvin Brothers and Merle Travis about as fast as a coffin entering a cemetery, and about as lively, too. Bloodshot Records describe their own act Trailer Bride as "somnambulistic country", even if Melissa Swingle had formerly played with all-girl band Pussy Teeth. You really couldn't make up this stuff.

After all of that quiet melancholy, it's a great tonic to turn to Mojo Nixon (in reality Kirby McMillan, Jr), who emerged in Denver performing Woody Guthrie and Leadbelly songs in soup kitchens and "organising winos". Having put together the punk band Zebra 123, he was heading back from San Diego one day when he had what he later described grandly as the "Mojo Nixon revelation", "a vision in which eh performed 'front-porch boogie woogie'...to make your grandma buck dance...and hit you in the head with her purse". Paul, on the road to Damascus, had nothing on this.

David Goodman takes up the story of how Kirby "began berating the local music scene with his unique blend of demented hillbilly music and socio-political rants...like and amphetamine-crazed televangelist". He played acoustic guitar, with Skid Roper on washtub bass and washboard, and MTV screened some of his off-centre videos until 'Debbie Gibson Is Pregnant With My Two-Headed Love Child' proved too strong for their censors. For the rest of the story, read *Detailed Twang*. I'm the proud possessor of Mojo's album Sock Ray Blue, with the Toadliquors, supposedly volume three of 'Texas Prison Field Recordings'.

Here are such delights as 'I Don't Want No Cybersex' and 'Redneck Rampage', all as inauthentic as hell, silly rather than shocking, and a honky tonk delight. Only 'Drunk-Divorced Floozie (The Ballad Of Diana Spencer)' would be enough to get him beaten senseless in certain traditional areas of London's East End. The chorus goes on and on and on, until *Mojo* verbally shrugs "I guess it's all over". This is a man who can rhyme "there was blood in my urine" with the "holy shroud of Turin", and make this the opening lines of a love song. The 33rpm sticker is unremovable.

Country influences have even spread to bands who border on the avantegarde. The Willard Grant Conspiracy are a loose collective who play a richly textured "country noir". A soft baritone voice weaves hypnotic patterns with cellos and sonorous organ chords. The band emerged from the same Massachusetts scene as Throwing Muses and The Pixies, although singer Robert Fisher prefers to stress the influence of his growing up on the edge of the Mojave desert. As he told *NME*: "a lot of people think of the desert as a barren wasteland, but it's really more explosive than that. It's very subtle, but there are all these amazing colours and textures there." Cue Giant Sand.

Fisher began his career playing in noisy guitar bands like The Flower Tamers, but got quieter. He enjoys what he terms "Western music", but "alternative country" is a misnomer: "It's a label being applied to a lot of things that aren't really alternative and aren't country either." Mojave is the sort of music which just hangs poignantly in the air. Sylvie Simmons got a bit carried away, describing Robert's "six-feet-deep voice" and 'Sticky' as "an industrial band with a hillbilly violinist doing 'I Am The Walrus'", although this is exactly how it sounds. The earlier *3am Sunday @ Fortune Otto's* is in a handsome sleeve, and contains songs like 'If Bojangles Couldn't Dance' and closes on the seemingly interminable 'Chinese New Year (New York)', which is just that: the sound of endless firecrackers.

Mercury Rev started out more conceptually extreme, but *Deserter's Songs* inhabits a similar dreamscape. It takes its title from a reference in Greil Marcus' *Invisible Republic* by a hostile journalist to The Band's early work, and Levon Helm and Garth Hudson turn up playing here. This is the kind of band whose lead guitarist is nicknamed Grasshopper and who checks into a monastery every now and then for mental solace. This is psychedelia 30 years on, with a smile on its face and whistling and a bowed saw for contrast. The Flatlanders were even further ahead of their time than they realised.

Talking to *Uncut*, singer Jonathan Donahue reveals that he and Grasshopper are close neighbours in the Catskills to the surviving members of The Band: "We were just pursuing the timeless song, like they were." The reason that so many musicians still find *The Basement Tapes* so alluring is that it is the sound of songs before they become entombed on records, "a lot of laughter and giggles and rude comments and bathroom humour – it's that spur-of-the-moment, immediate imagination". Growing up in the same mountains, as they have, the late-Sixties work of Dylan and The Band "are like Biblical references to us. All those places are near us. Maggie's farm is just down the road from us. It's where we buy gas now."

Although he doesn't specifically mention the Harry Smith *Anthology*, Donahue admits that "all the music I listen to is from the Twenties and Thirties. Our frame of reference is at the very least 45 years off." It's not that far a trip from 'I Wish I Was A Mole In The Ground' to the opening track here, "Holes, dug by little moles, angry jealous/spies, got telephones for eyes" – or to *The Basement Tapes*, for that matter. Both are examples of American surrealism. The band have an alternative existence as The Harmony Rockets, and *Paralysed Mind Of The Archangel Void*, a 40-minute track which purports to be an ancient artefact, was recorded live on a cassette recorder. The return of trance rock.

Mark Linkous grew up in Virginia, fell in love with punk, formed The Dancing Hoods, and then made the extraordinary *Vivadixiesubmarinetransmissionplot*, based on a dream about General Lee. This is music that melts. Linkous tends to wear a cowboy hat, and reveres the writer Cormac McCarthy, whose trilogy of novels about the contemporary Wild West explore a world without meaning. This is appropriate, really, as Mark collapsed in a London hotel from an overdose of anti-depressants, was left clinically dead for a short while, and still has to use leg braces to walk. After the accident, he recorded the gentle *Good Morning Spider* back in Virginia, an album with an other-worldly feel.

The English magazine *Bucketfull Of Brains* asked him what he listened to as he was growing up: "Johnny Cash, George Jones and bluegrass was all around that part of Virginia. The Stanley Brothers are actually distant relatives of mine." It figures, somehow. Now he lives back there, too, "in the middle of nowhere. Actually, they do sell crack not far from where we live." The new moonshine. "There are a lot of poor black people that live around here – leftovers from the plantation era".

Country harmonies blow like a summer breeze through the more melodic and left-field bands to flirt with Sixties sounds – The Olivia Tremor Control or, best of all, The Green Pyjamas. Phish are like a cross between Sun Ra and The Grateful Dead (with a side order of The Youngbloods) who perform one-off live recreations of classic rock albums, and are probably the best improvising rock band on the planet. They did a country two-step on *A Picture Of Nectar*, and their sampler, *Stash*, sees the presence of Alison Krauss on dreamy vocals and Bela Fleck playing banjo on the jubilant 'Scent Of A Mule'.

Best known for live electric workouts, Phish retreated to the rural seclusion of Woodstock to record my own favourite of their many records, legal and illegal. *Illy Breathes* is their *American Beauty*, and although it starts out with their trademark wailing psychedelic guitar, it ends with some sparkling semi-acoustic songs, and a general feel of contentment throughout. Country music is just one of the elements or have been chopped and diced in their musical blender. It is a much more subtle use of the form than the schoolboyish antics of the likes of Ween, who hired a group of veteran Nashville session men to back them on songs like 'Help Me Scrape The Mucous Off My Brain'.

These are the kind of shock tactics which Ben Thompson explores in his book *Seven Years Of Plenty*, in which he celebrates the musicians who are a part of "Woodchuck Nation", a phrase he credits to Lambchop (who else?) on the sleeve notes to *I Hope You're Sitting Down*. Thompson argues that "some of the most bewitching music of the decade has actually been made by quiet American singing the body acoustic". If they have a mission, I would argue that it is to stay upright in their chairs. Ben then gets more pretentious, seeing an heroic attempt to "marry the maverick moral energy of the pre-Nirvana hardcore diaspora with the most ancient American songwriting traditions". It's something that I've traced here in the way that US punk turned into alt country: maybe someone just turned off the electricity.

Exhibit number one is Vic Chesnutt, from Athens, Georgia, the wheelchair-bound friend of Michael Stipe. The parched Southern voice manages not to betray a smile as it sings: "A chip on the shoulder usually means there is wood up above. The world of Vic Chesnutt is a warped and winsome place where words dance like puppets". I think we get the picture. Vic sometimes strikes me as moving freak-show (I use that adjective in both senses), a man who broke his neck while still a teenager and who learned to play the guitar with a pick superglued to a plaster cast. He was so drunk at his London debut that he almost fell off the stage.

Most of his CDs look as messy and amateur (not amateurish) as they sound, harshly-sung vignettes of small-town life. They really grab at something inside, though, which all the money in Nashville cannot buy. The best one to start with is *Is The Actor Happy?*, with John Keane on "additional skiffle pedal steel" and an ornate sound over which Vic muses and moans. Lambchop turn up as his backing band on *The Salesman And Bernadette*, a caustic country rock "song novella", but the plot's gone missing somewhere.

Another term for this kind of music – with Will Oldham its crown prince – is Melan country. Its presiding genius is Smog's Bill Callaghan, an American who spent his childhood in Yorkshire and of whom *The Observer* wrote "with his mournful, deadpan voice, he is 33 going on 70", and compares him to "Hank Williams' mournful muse". That's fine, but Hank at least moved sometimes. Ben Thompson comes up with "a less trustworthy Kris Kristofferson, the neglected lovechild of Jeffrey Dahmer and Carole King, the post-punk Leonard Cohen, a one-man acoustic Joy Division", and still doesn't quite get there.

This is music which is so slow and introverted (self-obsessed, some would say) that it sounds like the universe running down. He's at his best when he adopts C&W to buttress his melancholy, like the pedal steel which adds texture to his best album, *Red Apple Falls*, or *Knock Knock*, written in a remote South Carolina farmhouse and full of images like "I lay back in the tall grass/and let the ants cover me".

The British take on country is always going to be that of outsiders, schoolboys with their noses pressed right up against the glass of a sweetshop. Or, in the case of The Waco Brothers, lobbing a brick through it and seeing what they can grab. Led by the saturnine Jon Langford, The Wacos were named after the location of David Koresh's millennial cult, whose fortified compound was stormed by the FBI. Modern outlaws. The band grew out of Hillbilly Lovechild, itself a continuation of The Mekons, country punks with a Marxist agenda. *Uncut* once memorably described them as "five blokes pretending to be Hank Williams fronting the Clash", and on the cover of *Cowboy In Flames* (another Waco reference?), they dress in matching shirts, and their name is carved on a fan's hand.

The music is honky tonk with attitude and the odd yelp, released by Bloodshot records in the band's adopted home of Chicago. "We have set out to be the most extreme hard country band", Langford explained to *No Depression*. The label's early compilation *For A Life Of Sin* boasts Jon's painting 'Deck Of Cards' on its cover. They're better live, leaping up in the air in unison on each chorus, as there is no concession here to armchair listening, and Jonboy shouts rather than finesses a lyric.

The most savage and jaw-dropping song here is 'The Death Of Country Music', sung by one Iggy Yoachum (or maybe Dwight Pop). Over a bouncy beat, they rescue the bones of true country from "beneath the towers of Nashville in a black pool of neglect", grind them up and snort them like cocaine. Next, some black magic:

they sprinkle some of their own blood back on the corpses of George Jones and Johnny Cash (we're talking music here) to resurrect them, "skulls in false eyelashes". Hence the skeletal imagery of the packaging, like a post-punk Grateful Dead.

The Alabama 3 must know this record, not just for the charnel imagery but for the way that country classics are subverted, so that 'Take Me To The Fires' turns Hank Williams' 'I've Seen The Light' into the flames of hell. 'Wreck On The Highway' and Johnny Cash's 'Big River' are among the other songs to be wilfully distorted.

Mandolin player Traci Dear recalls that Johnny Cash was a favourite of his father's, a member of The Dubliners, who were "the tough boys of Irish pub drinking music, and Cash was one of the tough boys of American music. It was about blue-collar honesty." Steel guitarist Mark Durante adds twang, and there's some great bass playing. It's still hard-going at times, though.

This is very knowing music. The later *Waco World* has great one-liners like "That's why they're called bars, 'cause they keep me inside" and a sound totally of its own, which *Folk Roots* nevertheless compares with The Stones from around 1969, "when they were enamoured with country music". The band look like The Wild Bunch, or maybe The Mild Bunch, and their sound is neither honky tonk nor Nashville but real country, "with the kind of fire missing in too much music these days". Langford also fronted a spin-off band, Skull Orchard, with much the same line-up but focusing its lyrical attentions on the industrial wastelands of South Wales in which he grew up: "Land of my fathers/my fathers can have it."

Sally Timms is from the same musical collective, but in *Cowboy Sally's Twilight Laments For Lost Buckaroos* her honeyed voice slopes over fiddle and pedal steel like a British Emmylou. This might be self-confessed "art country" performed with what one critic described as "an edge of uneasiness" but something in the cool intensity of her method makes it all deeply emotional.

The reviewers melted at her feet. *Folk Roots* found old-style country, with the roots and spookiness "that Nashville has long lost", on a mixture of classic songs and new insurgent anthems: "'In Bristol Town One Bright Day' sounds like a straight outta Harry Smith trad ballad when in fact it's written by Robbie Fulks." There's a banjo accompaniment, too. *No Depression* stressed the third word in "country and *western*", a vibe which you never got on country radio any more, outside the odd George Strait song.

Then Bobby Reed gets really steamed up, just after he has described the tongue-in-cheek cover, with a "sexy 40-year-old British singer in a gingham dress, seated atop a bale of hay". After playing the CD all night, soiling it with his "oily fingerprints" – and god knows what else – "at dawn, the two halves of your brain are gently split apart by the strong stalk of a sunflower that has taken root in your frightened, newly-enlightened heart. Your visage seeks the light." Well, there's something in Sally's carefully-enunciated consonants – Julie Andrews with attitude, maybe – and the way in which she asks to be rocked to sleep, which does bring out the beast in me, too, but even so. As *Uncut* puts it: "Timms may bring an ironic eye to her material, but she genuinely engages with it. As with Shelby Lynne, she's fascinated by the country genre, wanting to be of it, yet transcend it." It takes us back to Sally's theory on Radio Four that country music is alluring because we can inscribe our own personality and image onto it. It can be exactly what we choose it to be. The album ends with a lullaby, endlessly repeated, "Goodnight little buckaroo…"

There have been other pan-Atlantic hybrids, although only Dave Peabody has gone so far as to call his 1985 album *Americana*, even though when it was recorded in London. He justifies himself as being "an Englishman hooked" on American culture.

Peter Bruntnell's *Normal For Bridgwater* includes Son Volt's Dave Boquist playing fiddle, and Eric Haywood on steel guitar. Signed to Boston's Slow River Records as their first British act, it is said of Bruntnell in his own publicity material that he "would be heralded as the second coming of Gram Parsons if he was from America and not South London". The album title refers to a town in Somerset, another candidate for England's own Appalachia, where doctors write it down on their case notes to denote "someone who's slightly crazy or unstable, because it's such a common condition there".

Peter loves pedal steel and the voice of Gillian Welch: "Oh, and my porch. I built it myself and it's great. I've been hanging out there with Gram Parsons blaring out of the stereo."

Julian Dawson is another Englishman whose albums are issued by an American company, in his case Nashville's Compass Records. He also produced Charlie Louvin's "comeback" album *The Longest Train*. He makes new music from old ingredients, as people always have: "I've got this English folk side with the modal harmonies, and the bluegrass kind of feel, and the blues feel. You just chop them around and make new music."

This is what Gomez are meant to do, although I find them too stodgy, and agree with *No Depression* that "their version of Americana is an ideal, imagined through various media rather than experienced first hand", which makes them cinematic rather than gritty. Even so, you have the kind of musical togetherness which can only be achieved by a band which lives communally and plays with full-blooded ease. Gomez are after something "like The Grateful Dead, the way they sang together loosely, so you can hear who did each harmony". They are getting closer on *Liquid Skin*, which has lots of banjo and which even enters Alabama 3 territory on the country and techno campfire ballad 'Revolutionary Kind'.

It's a musical sub-culture yet to come fully into focus. The Mojave 3 were once shoegazers Slowdance but now sprinkle steel guitars alongside the Scottish laments and country ballads. Scott 4, meanwhile, are more technically adventurous, bridging Krautrock and C&W. Even market leader Moby uses honky tonk on his soundtrack album *I Like To Score*, and uses country as part of his sound palette. His album *Play* is constructed around material lifted straight from the Harry Smith *Anthology*. However, you still can't beat The Alabama 3, or A3 as they now style themselves. I've just replayed *Exile On Coldharbour Lane*, and even after the odyssey on which their stage show set me off nine months or so ago, they sound as fresh as sailor and as serious as your life. There is no less feeling or authenticity in their music than in that of the hoariest hillbilly.

Gorky's Zygotic Mynci are part of the revival of Welsh culture, and after a typical gig they play Gram Parson's on the van stereo all the way back to Cardiff. Their own multi-dimensional music can stretch to a song like 'Heart Of Kentucky', which begins as a Chet Atkins pastiche and ends with a gaggle of old women beating up Kraftwerk.

So where is alt country bound? In *Rock 'n' Reel*, Kevin Russell reckons that "If Bob Wills was around today, he'd be alternative country. Willie and Merle, they're both alternative country now, aren't they? I don't really count that too much because every ship that sails is eventually going to sink." Maybe the country/techno interface is the new frontier, and if so, Beck is the youngest and meanest gunfighter in town.

Beck Hansen had a fractured childhood, as a white kid living with his Mexican step-father. For comfort, he turned to The Carter Family, of all things. As he told his biographer, Rob Jovanovic: "There's this whole tradition of beautiful religious music that I love." The Carters had "these really strange, really beautiful harmonies". The young Beck became immersed in the Harry Smith *Anthology*, and the same key word crops up when he reveals that "that faraway strange quality is definitely something I gravitated towards…I realised that a lot of strangeness is still out there". In 1988 he found it, bussing and hitching through the South, receiving death threats on the way, and arriving in New York with no money and nowhere to stay.

Hansen fell in with the anti-folk scene, which updated the chaotic stagecraft of The Fugs spat in Joan Baez's eye. Alongside the likes of Michelle Shocked, he would dominate any stage he stepped on, banging down hard with his boot and playing banjo and harmonica. This musical anit-movement has gone largely unreported, but just as no-one much was looking the long-awaited 'new Dylan' was up at the microphone. Beck distributed a rough and ready tape called *Banjo Music*, putting new words to old songs. Sound familiar? He and his new friends behaved as if the Sixties simply hadn't happened: "We were taking back the folk music that had got such a bad name, living out our fantasies of putrid homelessness and distilled malt liquor."

Songs could be about a packet of potato chips, or "waking up after having been sawn in half by a maniac – stuff like that". Beck notes laconically that "a lot of us were playing folk music because we couldn't afford all the instruments". He sounds like a whiskery old hillbilly when he reveals his songwriting methods: "Set your guitars and banjos on fire…smoke a pack of whiskey and it'll take care of itself."

Hence unfathomable lyrics like "like a tiger with no skin". The final breakthrough was to put all this to a hip-hop beat. Back home in LA, Beck briefly formed Ten Ton Ltd, who specialised in Carter Family and Louvin Brother songs. One day, the boxer Mike Tyson climbed on stage and pissed on their drum kit in a display of spontaneous criticism. Meanwhile, Beck's first album, the cassette-only release *Golden Feelings*, described itself as "genuinely fucked up, straight from the heart of spooking folky noisy unaffected tales of poverty and lucklessness".

Such material runs like a second voice through Beck's subsequent career so that, if the wordplay and musical promiscuity of his more widely-distributed works ever starts to run shallow, you can turn to *One Foot In The Grave*, on which Beck sounds like a cross between the young Dylan and Syd Barrett living in a shack together, or alternatively listen to the ten-inch album *A Western Harvest Field By Moonlight*, the cover of which is just as beautiful as it sounds. Thus we have an unaccompanied and distorted voice – possibly Appalachian – talk-singing one of the old songs, then you listen more closely and it's vintage Beck, with phrases like "cholesterol on your mouth".

This side of Beck hit the mainstream with *Mutations*, an album about decay. It uses the same trick as Lambchop, putting dissonant words to lush backings, but there's far more thrust to the music here. It's low-key music, whereas the early tapes and vinyl-only releases are lo-fi. Beck has cut down on the samples and the odd noises but he keeps his road hand, while Greg Leisz adds pedal steel to 'Canceled Check' just as he did on 'Sissynecks' on *Odelay*, and there's a harpsichord, too. *NME* reckoned that, "as Beck's ancient voice becomes all the more intimate, the mischievous angel takes a turn for the worse…tapping into a timeless mythology of melancholy". For all of that, Johnny Cash – with whom there is no disagreeing – considers that "he's got that mountain music in his blood".

The same could be said of Snakefarm, whose Anna Domino is a veteran of the hip Belgian label Les Disques De Crepuscule and has been a huge influence on the likes of Portishead. Here she dispatches murder ballads with the coolness of Kristen Hersh, but over trip-hop backings and with the odd hint of banjo and dobro. The result is like Portishead's country cousin, and oddly effective. Ian Anderson reckoned *Songs From My Funeral* to be as important a breakthrough as *Liege And Lief* 30 years before: "This is the record which brings Anglo-American traditional songs dancing into the next century with renewed life." Unlike his rival editor over at *No Depression*, Ian has no problem with pre-programmed sounds. Dance beats have freed up things, and songs like 'Tom Dooley' – done to death by coffee-house troubadours – "now sound very modern". They "come alive again".

He's so right. Just listen to the slinkiness Anna here injects into 'Streets Of Laredo'. 'Black Girl' starts with her humming to a banjo, but after the first verse a shuffle beat comes in, like the cavalry charging across the scene, and Anna's voice is distorted almost beyond recognition. Then we're back to the banjo. 'Banks of the Ohio' starts with sonorous cello, and Anna struts the words, like a wolf loping slowly across the snow. Sensuous or what? This does things to me which Shania Twain couldn't even imagine. The way she sings about poor little lamby having his eyes pecked out could lull a man to his death. Meanwhile, Michel Delory makes his guitar shimmer.

Like Hersh, Anna first heard these songs from her parents, and found them "spooky...the underlying sense of longing and loss are so strong". She admires Nick Cave, but, as she told *Folk Roots*, his death songs are mainly his own while "my record is what happened to songs after they got to America, when they sat around the Appalachians and got bent out of shape for a few hundred years". An earlier project saw her interpret Merle Travis' 'Sixteen Tons', and she intends to take this "new" set of songs on the road with a DJ/soundman and a specially filmed video track. It's a long way from Dock Boggs and having just a banjo for company.

Also out there on the cutting edge is Greg Garing, a kind of Appalachian version of Massive Attack. He has come to this point by a strange and circular route since first discovering folk music in his native Pennsylvania, weaving a path through Irish bands like Planxty and De Danaan and The Chieftains. As he told *Folk Roots*: "I fell in love with that, and from there I got into bluegrass." He moved to Nashville to "look for Bill Monroe... His uncle was a first generation Scottish fiddle player and that was the first music that Bill ever heard. So bluegrass came out of Celtic music and my musical progression exactly mirrored that development."

The young fanatic took a job at Opry Land while camping next to Monroe's club, Bluegrass Country. "I met all the old-timers. To me they were big stars, but they hadn't really had a career in 20 years, so it was easy to get to know them." Jimmy Martin was still going, "the rocker of bluegrass singing. He jumped around and screamed like no one else." He began to experiment with tape loops: "To me, trip-hop has that same lonesome sound. Tricky meets Hank Williams."

Garing confirms the theory I have already laid out, that the blues are a Celtic music, in part at least, stemming from when "the blacks and the Irish met on the railroads in the 1840s. African music, too, but those bendy notes and that shortened scale are from Irish music." It all connects, if you dig deep enough.

MJ Harris and Martyn Bates collaborated on *Murder Ballads (Drift)*, in which the likes of 'Lucy Wan' are stretched out over nightmarish and seemingly endless drones. 4 tracks and 63 minutes, and I've never got to the end of the CD. At first you think it is merely repetitive, and then something gradually starts creeping up the back of your neck, and if someone were to suddenly turn off the lights...

There were more lively treats on offer, those with energy levels only given to kids, or those acting like them, even if the Freighthoppers claimed (correctly) that "there were old bands who were just as wild as us". For Ian Anderson, here is "a young string band playing old-timey music" with real joy, "because it is natural, not as some academic revivalist crusade". The Hix are a more arty combo, in the line of earlier folk mavericks like The Horseflies, sly rather than respectful. "We started out playing a square dance. What old time has taught us is the groove, the instruments come together and they're all one thing."

Cordelia's Dad have a full-on electric attack, but you start to realise that virtually everything on *How Can I Sleep?* is from traditional American sources. They quieten things right down for an *a capella* version of 'Old Bedford Town', "from the singing of Mr Lee Monroe, presnell of Beech Mountain, North Carolina". They then proceed to put a new tune to a song which dates back to the War Of Independence, and then forget an old fiddle tune and so improvise a banjo jig instead. It's the irreverence which gets you. Over in England, Chumbawamba did much the same with anti-poll tax songs from the 14th century on *English Rebel Songs*, but they did it straight, almost as if the gesture was enough. Cordelia's Dad apply wit and daring on top, and the result is even more shocking. A later, all-acoustic album, *Spine*, was produced by grunge merchant Steve Albini. *Unplugged* never expected this!

It's a matter of the spirit, not the notes. Much the same applies to The Hot Club Of Cowtown, forcing together Bob Wills and Stefan Grapelli (not that far a distance, anyway), and using slap bass to stitch together fiddle and guitar. They have to be heard to be believed. Wayne Hancock does much the same for honky tonk, so that what he plays is both familiar and new. It's the essence of moving forward.

If anyone is trying to do the same with old-time music, buring himself so deep that you think he will never climb out, it is the deliberately mysterious figure of Will Oldham. Here is a man who inspires devotion and hatred in roughly equal measure, who changes his name from Palace to Palace Brothers to Palace Music to Palace Songs and then to Bonnie 'Prince' Billie, as only an egomaniac could. It doesn't help that he is also a professional grouch, telling *Mojo* that "I like old music, but it doesn't seem different to me from new music. As for Greil Marcus' vision of America, well fuck him".

If Oldham has a vision, it's so dark that I would never like to encounter it. What comes over in his music is a scratchy, melancholic, death-obsessed reverie, sometimes barely in tune, deeply suspect, and – almost as an afterthought – the closest that anyone now alive has ever come to recreating the inner world of Dock Boggs. This is music for the early hours of the morning – but lock away the razor first.

Under whatever name they appear, all of his albums are much the same, like Michael Hurley without the humour and full of unforgettable phrases: "Behind you, I have warned you, there are awful things." Or how about "I send my nose to you"? The packaging of the albums is equally opaque; *Palace Brothers* is the most infuriating, with Oldham's head dominating the shot but out of focus and hidden in darkness. Typical, somehow. Meanwhile, *I See A Darkness* presents a grinning human skull – just what you want to see in your local high street store.

Oldham's first song was written in tribute to The Mekons, but he was also an actor, and had played a starring role in *Matewan*. Allison Stewart puts to him the charge that he is acting still, "appropriating old folk constructs – the high, mournful vocals, the awkward lyrical formations, the preoccupation with grimly biblical, fire-and-brimstone subject matter", and he replies that it is a good thing he does-n't play folk music, then: "I don't live on a farm, I don't ride the rails. My parents didn't play the fiddle, or make me sing in a country choir." He just sounds as if he does – apart from the last charge; I agree that no country choir in his native Kentucky would have had him, no matter how desperate.

So why do I rate him so highly? Because even if he's as good a musical put-on as Dylan – which would be saying something – he has the same ability to make you shiver, the same sense of mystery. I cherish one critical comment on *Arise Therefore*, that it could be a back-porch recording if it weren't so primitive you doubted that there even was a porch. He has inspired mavericks far beyond the alt country world, artists like Arab Strap and Gorky's Zygotic Mynci, who have trans-lated his world view into broad Scots and the Welsh language respectively.

Although he can write a song called '(If I Could Fuck A) Mountain', which we have yet to see on the Nashville playlists, Will can also record something as spiritual and ethereal as the EP *Blue Lotus Feet*, described there as "devotional songs". The haunted beauty of *I See A Darkness* inhabits a world all of its own, with a cheery cho-rus sung over and over again: "Death to everyone is gonna come/It makes hosing much more fun." Don't ask! The sound here is louder and more electric than most of what has gone before, and yet Oldham's voice is still – to quote Andrew Male – like "a consumptive Neil Young trapped in the body of a dying possum". When he played at the Embassy Rooms in London, one of the highlights was '(I Was) Drunk At The Pulpit', a "lengthy, absorbing narrative of God-fearing whisky guzzlers". I just know that I would have walked the hundred miles to London to hear it.

Gillian Welch looks, dresses and sounds as rural as hell, but was brought up in LA, in some comfort. She would sing Irving Berlin around the family piano rather than Carter Family spirituals. Hearing The Stanley Brothers lit a touch paper inside her, although, as *No Depression* points out, her songs draw "as much on the Celtic origins of Appalachian music as on its hillbilly roots". Songs like 'Acony Bell' could almost be traditional ballads. Perhaps it was taking thinks a little too far to record much of *Revival* in mono, though, and then claim it wasn't a "retro thing". Welch has an aloofness which such material requires. *Hell Among The Yearlings* opens with a murder tale, bottoms out on 'My Morphine', and Gillian sounds sleepy throughout. It's majestic album, even if it is based on an Appalachia of the mind. When Welch and her guitarist, David Rawlings, played in North Carolina, people would come up and say "I haven't heard harmonies like that since my father passed away."

Freakwater have been described as "spooky", a "post-punk Carter Family", and accused of reminding one listener of "churchyards, grandparents and the dust that comes out of 19th-century bibles". Their two lead singers – leather-voiced Catherine Irwin and Janet Beveridge Bean, who floats above her like a ghost – both come from Louisville, also the home of the Kentucky Derby and birthplace of Will Oldham, although these facts are not connected. The two singers were also part of

Eleventh Dream Day, a band which at its best touched heights of psychedelia not often seen since the Sixties. Freakwater sound rough and ready, but they shocked Andy Kershaw when they came in to play a live session which couldn't be told apart from the recorded versions of the same songs.

Their early work is rather hit and miss, largely acoustic affairs memorably described by *No Depression* as "lonely, lovely ballads about divorce, hardship and dead babies". Something happened on *End Time*, a shimmering, intense and richly melodic affair, thanks to a string section, pedal steel and organ. Some of the trance rock of Eleventh Dream Day has seeped in, and at times it's even reminiscent of early Mad River. The electrics chimes in nicely with the Appalachian abandon of the two voices.

And so, just as you think it couldn't get any weirder, we get to The Handsome Family. Husband Brett and Rennie Sparks have been dubbed "the king and queen of quirk", and with lines like "Liza Minelli spent a month in her bed/certain that Skylab would fall on her head", who could disagree? The same song digs its own grave, and when the same duo tackle 'The House Carpenter' it's in the same deadpan vocals and with the same jog-trot backing. Welcome back, The Holy Modal Rounders.

It's not just kooky; this is probably what the moors murderers sounded like in the bath. Country gothic doesn't get more unnerving than this. It comes as no surprise to find out that Brett had such a severe breakdown in 1995 that he had to be tied to his bed in a mental hospital, diagnosed as a manic depressive. He is also a former born-again Christian, which figures. "He ate the cat litter", says Rennie fondly, herself a former acid head who fled New York. According to *Uncut*, she "employs the folk process in miniature, distilling her fables and laments from myths, legends and everyday events". Except that the folk process is in existence to set up a communal body of wisdom, as encoded in parables, and this is just entertaining crap.

I love it, by the way. To my ears, the compilation *Down In The Valley* is all that you will ever need of their early work. They are now working their wacky way through a trilogy, of which *Through The Trees* and *In The Air* have already been let out in public. Fred Mills points out how brilliant Brett is in parodying earlier country styles, as his own music "unfolds at an impossibly unhurried Nashville pace", largely through his completely unshockable voice. Thus do we have a fiddler's waltz, a "twangy, Johnny Cash-like shuffle", Jordanaires' gospel, Eddie Arnold and The Eagles. Just when you think this is all good twisted fun, in the style of *Mad* magazine, you get the murder ballad 'Up Falling Rock Hill', which *The Guardian* pins down as "visceral, sinsiter but ravishing in its darkness".

The same newspaper caught them at Manchester University, and watched fascinated as Brett, in goatee and glasses, set up his Macintosh G3, which had been pre-programmed with rhythm effects. Rennie passed the time by asking the audience if they had "any questions about insects?"

The weird can get predictable, even boring, but we must make one more pit-stop in hillbilly purgatory. The Blood Oranges were something very special indeed, a band years ahead of its time. *No Depression* reckoned that there was a dark quality to Cheri Knight's singing that was "profoundly life-affirming". Too heavy ever to be a bluegrass band – although mandolin player Jimmy Ryan also turned up in The Beacon Hillbillies – and stuffed with unsettling lyrics ("she wore a housecoat made of feathers and tar"), they had that subtle grasp of dynamics which every great rock band breathes. I hear a lot of early Fairport in them, but then I've been looking for bands with that kind of shivery precision ever since.

My favourite Blood Oranges release is the five-track CD *Lone Green*, in some part because of a splendid version of 'Shady Grove', but mainly because of its jaw-dropping sleeve, a painting from 1934 by Thomas Hart Benson (who elsewhere created those images of an idealised South) in which an old hillbilly menaces a young girl with a knife. Everything has gone subtly wrong here: the perspective is like something out of Bosch, and an impromptu music jam features halfwits and a fiddle player from whom you wouldn't accept a lift on the darkest and wettest of nights. The painting is titled 'Ballad Of The Jealous Lover Of Lone Green Valley', and I presume that fiddler and killer are the same man, thinking of murder as he grasps his bow.

Let's take a mental rest here with Cathryn Craig's *Port Songs*, a winsome but pleasant affair, with crickets and a dog barking, recorded live on her back porch in Nashville. I still can't seem to get the image of that murderous fiddler out of my mind, though…

And so quickly on to Mike Seeger, David Grisman and John Hartford, old friends all, who appear as Retrograss, helpfully glossed as "music shifted back in time". Here we have 'Maybelline', 'Hound Dawg' and 'Maggie's Farm', all performed bluegrass style, as if this is how they started life. Here, the lightness of touch means everything. The trio pose amicably with an old microphone and a wind-up gramophone. The idea of this came to Grisman whe he heard The Anachronistic Jazz Band playing John Coltrane in a Dixieland style.

Mike Seeger takes centre stage on his *Third Annual Farewell Reunion*, a massive series of duets and or more. He adds a banjo line that's as hard as frozen rain to Dylan's meandering 'Hollis Brown', but the thing that really sends the shivers racing up my spine is Jean Ritchie's 'Deep Shady Grove'. I think that, if I have undervalued anyone in this huge enterprise, it is Ritchie, solely on the basis of a couple of albums from the Seventies which I have in my possession. For such an important figure, copies of her prime work are now very hard to get hold of, and those who own them presumably will only part with them when they go on to the final shady grove in the sky. Here, Jean's voice wavers like a candle flame in the breeze, but with a hard edge which makes it all the more wrenching.

Ritchie also wrote the mournful 'Black Waters', a song on Jody Stecher's debut album, released when he was still a Marvelous Boy. At the age of 13, in New York, Stecher was reputed to play and sing better than Bill Monroe himself, a difficult claim to live up to. He has since pottered through bluegrass and Indian classical music. When Martin Carthy states that Stecher is "one of the very great singers alive", it's difficult to argue. Stecher remains the natural continuation of the old Appalachian balladeers, with his high-pitched, matter-of-fact vocals and dexterity on banjo, mandolin and oud, for something a bit different.

There is a quiet intensity to his performance on *Oh The Wind And Rain*, a concept CD of classic ballads, no less. The thrill for British listeners is that many are sourced from American variants on "original" versions, which means that the album is at the same time familiar and unfamiliar. 'Young Rapoleon' is a variant of 'Bonny Bunch Of Roses', charmingly mispronounced by the Tennessee mountain man who first performed it.

One of the great surprises of the last few years was Stacey Earle's debut CD, so nostalgic that it was divided into "side A" and "side B" and full of the sweet singing and acoustic guitar shuffle which Nashville seemed to have forgotten how to do. At the time of its release, her much more (in)famous brother Steve Earle was taking a walk on the mild side himself.

So much is made of Steve's toughness and bouts of heroin addiction and imprisonment that it makes Lou Reed sound like the dilettante he is, and you expect to hear some razorblade-chewing monster playing Black Sabbath riffs. Well, he might look that way on stage, but his voice is actually quite light, almost folky when he isn't trying to growl too hard. It has a definite twang. This, however, is not a man much given to pedal steel. He has the kind of voice which befits a man who couldn't afford an electric guitar when he was young, or make his acoustic sound like Jimi Hendrix, "but I could make it sound like Tim Buckley and Tim Hardin and Jimmie Rodgers, so I just started gravitating towards acoustic music".

Even now, it's the words which Earle sings that are so heavy. During a stunning gig with The Dukes at the Irish Centre in Leeds, in 1997, what I heard was subtle country rock with a dimension of pain and fear on top. It's impossible to separate the singer from his biography: a junkie from the age of 13, married five times (twice to the same woman), and a one-time crack cocaine addict.

Not that such personal details harmed record sales. Earle has crossed the invisible line into cult status. This is the man who once told *No Depression* that "I think Hank Williams' records have a lot more to do with The Sex Pistols than with Brooks And Dunn...It's really just about any kind of music that's real." He actually saw a date one the final Sex Pistols tour, and "I didn't think they were very good, but I thought it was kinda cool. And it had a big effect on me...Hey, this is supposed to be fucking fun."

Earle's great-grandmother came over from Ireland, and he continued the connection by playing with The Pogues on *Copperhead Road*, the title track of which opens with a Celtic-influenced drone on the synthesiser, sounding like bagpipes. Born in Virginia, Steve was raised in Texas, the perfect combination for a country singer. Having befriended Townes Van Zandt – "a real bad role model" – he moved to Nashville, and scuffled. *Guitar Town* sounds to me like a natural outgrowth of the Texan school of songwriting, especially that of Guy Clark, with whom he would occasionally play. Earle has never struck me as belonging to Nashville, even though he might record there.

He performed long, beautifully-constructed shows much more in the Bruce Springsteen mould, and on *Train A-Coming* – released after he had just served a term in prison – he played acoustic but raw material. He apologises to Doc Watson before launching into 'Hometown Blues', with help from Peter Rowan on mandolin and Roy Huskey on double bass, and with no drums. As he points out in the lyric booklet, he hates MTV: "This ain't my unplugged record! I made most of these songs up before I was plugged in the first place. I hitchhiked to Nashville from Texas in '74 and began my higher education in the pickin' parties that went on all night, nearly every night back then."

It was a habit he picked up again with The Del McCoury Band on *The Mountain*, which was strictly bluegrass. All of the songs here are by Earle, but there is none of the self-revelation from *I Feel Alright*, a whole song cycle "which just sort of poured out of me in a six-month period". He takes the listener through betrayal, pain and redemption, with Lucinda Williams jostling in for a final, joyful 'You're Still Standing There'. Life doesn't imitate art; between that record and the equally indispensable *El Corazon*, "I've had another marriage fail". He hasn't lost his snap, though, "and if Garth Brooks is a country singer then I'm not". He has taped a photo of Reba McEntire to the toilet seat in the rest room of his office, and once called Shania Twain "the highest-paid lap dancer in Nashville".

The title track of *The Mountain* takes him back to his Appalachian childhood, "before they knocked down the timber and strip-mined the coal". When I saw Steve and the boys circling around themselves on *Later...*, I thought that some of the man mountains in The Del McCoury Band – in whose huge hands mandolins and the like looked like little toys – made the serious Earle look positively beneficient. Especially when they grinned.

The album was a delight then and it's a delight now. It starts with a jokey "you want to be in the band, you've got to put your hat on", and the chuckling strings seem to release something in Steve's voice so that it sounds richer, more Kentucky. He has never before sounded so purely happy. He is also bidding for immortality: "I wanted to just write one song that would be performed by at least one band at every bluegrass festival," he says after he's hung up his plectrum. We shall see.

He reminisces about Bill Monroe walking onstage at the Tennessee Performing Arts Centre one night, uninvited, and taking over his show: "When I look back now, I believe this record was really born that night." He first played with The McCoury Band on *El Corazon*. Del had been on the road with Monroe in the early Sixties, and then formed The Dixie Pals, which he renamed when two of his sons joined.

The collaboration certainly gets the blood moving, not least on two transatlantic numbers, the barn-dance-friendly 'Connemara Breakdown' and the stately stroll 'Paddy On The Beat'. Iris Dement joins in on 'I'm Still In Love With You', and there's a keening quality to her voice – she sounds like a wild woman throwing herself on a hearse. The album is one that I wouldn't be without, even though it doesn't quite reach that realm of pure music which the very greatest bluegrass inhabits. As Earle says, this is his own "interpretation" of the music that Monroe invented. There's a lot of himself in it, too.

Steve uses old-time music as part of his armour against personal demons. A bootleg CD from Warwick University opens with his solo set, just guitar and harmonica, extremely good humoured and surprisingly Dylanesque, just as the very first tape of Dylan singing is pure Nashville corn. When the band come in, they perform 'I'm Looking Through You' bluegrass style – talk about bringing it all back home. The concert ends with 'Hillbilly Heaven', which Earle introduces with a throwaway "There are two sorts of songs: those about girls and those about roads." Galway is the setting for an earlier song, 'Halo Round The Moon', "from my next album, which will be louder". A few days later Earle was reputedly thrown off the tour by Del McCoury because of his personal habits. That's my boy...

He went back in the studio to produce a new CD, *Transcendental Blues*, with the Irish accordionist Sharon Shannon: "It's a record about changing, and it's a rock album because I missed playing loud."

If *The Mountain* is a worthy attempt at greatness, Dolly Parton's *The Grass Is Blue* is a full-blown masterpiece, and one that blew the CMA Awards apart. It was in many ways a follow up to *Hungry Again*, in which she first returned to her mountain roots. The double meaning is fully intentional, although it is doubtful that Dolly will ever again go without a meal for the lack of hard cash. What she hungers for here is recognition, and in the amazing urgency of her vocals here you can sense all of the frustration that Dolly felt when her records were ignored on country radio and she was dropped by her mainstream record label. How Nashville can drop its greatest asset in the public imagination (a sexist author would here refer to its greatest two assets, but that would be cheap) is a matter of wonder outside that closed circuit.

A recent TV interview with Melvyn Bragg failed to mention the album, but she revealed herself to be a magnolia with a steel tip, a genuinely unaffected woman who also controlled a business empire. It also filmed a Nashville DJ of such gratuitous ill grace, who trashed Dolly's life-work, that I longed for him to trip over his ego. He summed up an industry interested only in sales trends and character assassination. Dolly simply went off to the specialist label Sugar Hill, and made probably the greatest record of her whole career.

The supercharged acoustic combo of bluegrass' finest, including Jerry Douglas on dobro and Sam Bush on mandolin, came "leaping to its feet" after each vocal. Even the backing singers here turn out to be Alison Krauss and Patty Loveless, but what really knocks you out is the choice of material – Lester Flatt, The Louvin Brothers, Johnny Cash and Parton herself – and the way in which Dolly throws herself in at the deep end vocally. She really does bring tears to your eyes.

Sid Griffin, no less, reckons – with only the slightest note of reservation as a result of being forced to sit through all of those dreadful TV specials – that "rarely has this entertainment icon sung so beautifully". It must be rather like the return of the prodigal son – or, in this case, daughter – with Parton dwelling for years in the fleshpots of Nashville and now asking for credibility as well. Tom Cox has no such doubts, making a comparison with Gram Parsons to the effect that, when Dolly covers 'Cash On The Barrelhead', "she does it with a soul-deep flair worthy of a grievous angel". However ridiculous the wigs or inane the chat, it all shrivels up when you hear the way she just pauses long enough on 'Silver Dagger', and it stops your heart beating for just that same split second. Anyway, what was that about welcoming back the miscreant with a fatted calf?

No Depression certainly did, bless 'em. Parton tells them that "what brought me out of the Smokey Mountains was the fact that I loved songs and wanted to sing, and it was because of this that all the other stuff has really happened...But I already know, now, that country music does not want me anymore, as an artist." She will follow her own instincts, as ever. At least these temporary eclipses forces stars like herself, Johnny Cash, Merle Haggard and George Jones – the true greats – to come back fighting, as if reborn. How could she ever fail? When once asked how long it took her hairdresser to fix her blonde bouffant hair, she replied, quick as a flash: "I have no idea. I'm never there."

Most journeys eventually take you back to where you started, but the place of departure often looks completely different. Home is never quite how you thought it would be, in your memory or in your imagination. Who are those strangers who claim to be friends and relations? And who is that now sitting in your favourite chair?

After too many junk books and cash-in CDs, the market in Celtic culture, as a marketing shorthand, is in freefall. The Oysterband's Ian Telfer, a proud Scot in a band which is largely English, administered the sharpest jab to its solar plexus: "Never trust anybody who wants to sell your history back to you in bite-sized pieces. It has no nourishment." Telfer traces the word back to the early-19th-century Scottish "poet" Ossian, a bard of the Highlands, who was actually invented by two men, both called McPherson but otherwise unrelated. (It's details like that which make history worthwhile.) Mr and Mr McPherson wove together their forgery from scraps and ballads, many originating from Ireland. From then on it was tartan all the way, with Sir Walter Scott writing windy epics and Queen Victoria "capering" at Balmoral.

In a sudden historical shift, Ian jumps forward to Irish folk music in the 1960s, and the way in which nationalist politics "rebranded" the Catholic struggle, using the language of civil rights. An oppressed people were supposedly being trampled underfoot by the English (and this myth is still being peddled by those seeking money for arms to blow up innocents), and looked back to pre-history for succour. Telfer gets a little carried away, and compares the sudden popular taste for the Celtic with Adolf Hitler's taste for Grail mythology. Just look where that led…

From my own doctoral studies in mythology, I would say that most of Telfer's conclusions are – speaking strictly as a scholar – a load of bollocks. The taste for Celtic culture is much more to do with a post-hippie mysticism which does not wish to attach itself to any rigid religious dogma, preferring to float free. It has a lot to do with films like *Ryan's Daughter*, and indeed the very strange landscape of the west of Ireland which inspired artists in the first place. Blame – or praise – the Celtic revival under Yeats and Lady Synge; blame Van Morrison, if you have to; but I feel that the IRA don't really have too much to do with it, other than as a linked romantic myth.

The funniest thing of all is that Van Morrison's own parentage and demeanour are far closer to the Scots-Irish Protestants who went off to settle in the Appalachians – and have engaged in internecine disputes ever afterwards – than to those Irishmen who stayed at home and dozed in the Celtic sunset. For all that, the popularity of CDs like *Celtic Tribal Trance* owes more to illicit chemicals than to history. Folk Roots invented its own fake CD, its own Ossian so to speak, and few readers twigged that *From An Ambient Celtic Rainforest* by The Dolphin Children was a hoax. Some people even tried to order it.

Ian Telfer objects to having music reduced to "a soundtrack for the heritage industry". He cites Enya as an example, a woman with a beautiful voice "stripped of meaning anything whatsoever". Well, maybe if you spoke Gaelic, Telfer… But with that corrective in mind, it remains true that Celtic music continues to develop and grow, largely through influences filtering back from across the Atlantic, and I will finish with a few recent examples. They give me faith that the process sketched out in *Country Roads* is alive and well and in good voice.

In the late Sixties, Robin Williamson lived in a hippie commune an hour's drive from his native Edinburgh with the rest of The Incredible String Band. "As a youngster in Scotland, I discovered people like Jeannie Robertson. To me, folk music and folk tales embody the notion of the 'inspired voice', older mysteries coming through the singer or narrator. I try to communicate with that purity." The ISB came together in the Crown Bar in Lothian Street, with Mike Heron and banjo player Clive Palmer, and then moved to Clive's Incredible Folk Club in Glasgow. They have been described as a Celtic Holy Modal Rounders, and took just the same irrelevant (but oddly reverent) view of old-time music, taking from it what they chose. And giving something back.

From his early 'The First Girl I Loved' (later covered by Judy Collins), Williamson let the words and tunes of his songs take a meandering path, half Indian and half Irish. He "had an interesting in finding the threads that would link the music of the world". The band played acoustic world music years before it became fashionable, and Appalachian is part of the mix, so that Robin's 'My Name Is Death' is Dock Boggs on acid, sung in wonder rather than dread. On *The Hangman's Beautiful Daughter*, 'The Water Song' is derived from an old hymnal, but Williamson redirects it to a pantheist god(dess). Robert Graves' strange grammar of poetic myth, *The White Goddess*, is an eccentric attempt to unite classical and Welsh mythologies and is the key book behind such songs, also infusing The ISB's most ambitious work: the double LP *Wee Tam And The Big Huge*.

Even here, Mike Heron's 'Log Cabin Home In The Sky', with twin fiddles and odd harmonies, is pure old time, drawing on a Nonesuch hymnal. An album of dead men walking and "elephant madness" culminates with 'The Circle Is Unbroken'. Robing plays whistle and Irish harp, changes all of the words and the tune of the traditional song, but still keeps its spirit: "Scattered we were when the long night was breaking/but in bright morning converse again."

This "Scottish-Irish mongrel" has pursued such a vision ever since the reconverging of the Celtic nations, no less, and now lives in Wales, having first gone there to compose the music for a production of the *Mabinogion*. As he told *Swing 51*: "In fact, the earliest Welsh poems were written in Edinburgh." Working back, you get to this "lost heritage, which one conceives to have been rather magical. You have a respect for the bard or for the musician which endured in the country areas of Scotland and Ireland for a very long time."

He follows this over to America, where "what became bluegrass was very much a living tradition in this century...it's still continued into C&W in a very different way". Robin takes such connections back to a seventh-century Oghma stone found in Canada, with the Gaelic word for harp next to its picture. A native tribe living near the Fraser River "speak a dialect which has got a large number of Gaelic words still in it", possibly connected with Pince Madog, "the Welsh chap who went across in about the tenth century".

Williamson moved to Los Angeles in the late Seventies and made a series of albums with his Merry Band, based on the research in Barry Fells' book *America BC*. The cover of *American Stonehenge* sees the band crouched beneath a dolmen in upstate New York, "coyly labelled on a sign nearby 'glacial remains'. I never heard of such an artistic glacier myself." His own search is for "a contemporary Celtic music using the old instruments in a new way...an echo of the ages that rekindles the spirit with a shot of the real McCoy, as it were". The resulting music sparkles, with harps and whistles and bagpipes and fiddles, and every now and then displays Williamson's greatest gift: it makes your jaw drop with recognition. "It's all about inspired utterances. Rap tries to do the same thing."

On *A Glint At The Kindling*, Williamson puts new words to the traditional Irish tune 'Nancy's Whiskey' on 'Lough Foyle', a song about how he went with the army to Northern Ireland ("not far from Derry town) as a young man, but went drinking south of the border instead. It's Robin's humour which makes palatable what in anyone else might become pretentious or simply nonsensical. That and the way he can still suddenly throw his voice up an octave until you feel the pit of your stomach disintegrating. He continues his precarious existence as a one-man bard to this day, with a steady stream of concerts (in which you participate or else) and CDs of traditional folk tales and harp solos and memories of the Sixties. He seems to have abandoned his attempt to remythologise America, though.

On *A Job Of Journey Work*, Williamson goes back to where he started, on the 1960s Scottish folk circuit. Here he wilfully rewords songs like 'Nottamun Town' (almost ragtime here, like something by The Band), and approaches self-parody as he growls, laughs and hums. It's a lifetime's heritage. "Some of the tunes I heard Jimmy Shand style at country dances in the Western Isles, or maybe the back room of a certain Dublin pub laughingly known as the 'intensive care'. Some of the American stuff I learned while fiddle-playing for Tom Paley of The New Lost City Ramblers on a tour he did of the North-east about 1963, and of course Clive and I used to play jug-band and old-timey numbers." Reunited with Palmer 30 years on, Williamson could still achieve the "Appalachian wobble" of old on 'Rise Where The Rooster Crows'.

Shaun Davey's *The Brendan Voyage* is an orchestral suite with uilleann pipes played by Liam O'Flynn, possibly the first ever Irish visitor to North America. At times, its polite sounds are perhaps a little too close to Ian Telfer's idea of Celtic for comfort. Give me Robin Williamson's wild conjectures any time.

More to our point is the music of Maura O'Connell. Once of De Danaan, with whom she made 'My Irish Molly-O' her own, she now lives and records in Nashville. Maura has fronted many a bluegrass band over there, with players of the high quality of Bela Fleck and Mark O'Connor fighting to have the privilege of playing with her. On *Stories* she has kept her Irish accent and folk phrasing intact, but the CD is produced by the American country maestro Jerry Douglas, who also plays lap steel and dobro. The song choice divides down the middle, too, with the likes of Hal Ketchum and Mary Chapin Carpenter on one side and with Paul Brady on the other. To further complicate matters, Tim O'Brien and James Taylor guest.

The results should be awful, but it all dissolves on the cusp of O'Connell's rich voice. She has pulled off this miracle not just once but on just about every CD since her 1983 solo debut on Ogham, recorded in both Nashville and Dublin. Even if O'Connell jokes that the main connection is a shared and blatant "sentimentality", don't believe her. Sentiment, rather. She looks out for songs "where you can feel the writer's pain", and this seems a far more cogent link between Irish folk music and real country. Maura is archetypal of the kind of person who is now genuinely transatlantic, and this stretches far beyond music. Even when she went back to Ireland to record *Wandering Home*, an album of traditional Irish songs performed "with the fresh vigour of a born-again evangelist", it was with Jerry Douglas as producer.

I mention in passing the musical atrocity known to its adherents as "country and Irish". Everything that Maura O'Connell gets right, this genre gets wrong. Brendan Shine and his horrible labelmates – that's what I'm talking about. Such music is no more and no less than what it sets out to be: music made for sedate waltzes in Irish dance halls, all much the same, whether found in London or Kerry.

Dick Gaughan has Irish grandparents and a Highland Scots mother. He is also a traditional singer of rare magnificence. Perhaps his greatest album, *Handful Of Earth*, begins with 'Erin-Go-Bragh', the story of Duncan Campbell, a Highlander from Argyll who is mistaken one night for an Irishman by a bigoted policeman. "Well, I know you're a Pat by the cut of your hair/but you all turn to Scotsmen as soon as you're here." Duncan knocks him down and escapes back to the far North.

Links between these two Celtic kingdoms, Scotland and Ireland, echo throughout the CD. Just a few words sung by Gaughan would convince you of his Scottishness (many English audiences at first demanded subtitles), so to hear him sing 'Song For Ireland' and suchlike raises all kinds of questions about what Celticism exactly is, and how its individual nations relate to one another.

Like so many traditional singers who emerged in the 1970s, Gaughan has gradually come clean about his previously hidden rock 'n' roll past. In fact, he went further still on the recent *Redwood Cathedral*, taping his own fierce versions of John Townes Van Zandt's 'Pancho And Lefty' and 'Turn, Turn, Turn' from Ecclesiastes, via Pete Seeger and The Byrds. Dick was also a member of The Boys Of The Lough for a short time, an acoustic quartet drawn from both sides of the Irish Sea set up to perform traditional material from Scotland, Ireland and Shetland. The band's fiddle player and *de facto* leader, Shetland's own Aly Bain, brought his affable presence – and breathtaking instrumental skill – to bear when hosting two series on Scottish TV called *The Transatlantic Sessions*, featuring (seemingly) impromtu collaborations between American country and Celtic folk musicians, unplugged but full of good spirit. Videotapes of the result have been passed around like *samizdat* literature, and two CDs of music from the second series have recently emerged commercially. If you have enjoyed this book, or even if it has enraged you, give them a listen.

Here are Ricky Skaggs and Jerry Douglas, Nanci Griffith and Roseanne Cash, Maura O'Connell and Paul Brady. Lovely as most of it is, it tends to be either one thing or the other. Series one – seemingly beyond retrieval – was much more co-operative, so that mixed bands of Yanks and Celts (to put it crudely) intermingled musically. As with similar sessions set up to illustrate song migrations on the equally indispensible *Bringing It All Back Home*, the conjunctions are electrifying. To see Emmylou Harris singing along with an Irish chorus, or Kathy Mattea looking as if she is just about to eat up little Dougie MacLean whole, is so life-enhancing that maybe I simply dreamed it. Every now and then, such musical comminglings can produce a surprising offspring. With transatlantic partners, it's even better.

Rather than end on such a low note, let's return to the stern figure of Dick Gaughan and another song on Redwood Cathedral. 'Reconciliation' is a plea for peace in Ulster, written by Ron Kavana. If Mike Seeger is a secret hero of this history, then surely Kavana is another, and it's neat that they are from opposite sides of the pond.

Although he was brought up in Ireland, Ron told *Folk Roots* that "my mother is American, and my grandmother, who raised me lived most of her life in America...a great old woman, she knew all The Carter Family and Jimmie Rodgers". No wonder that Ron should become intrigued by the "romance of the West", moving there after his band Juice On The Loose broke up, "but when I got there I didn't like it at all". *From Galway To Graceland* – which, as its title suggests, deals with the way in which these two cultures clash – is dedicated to Dolores Kavana, born "southside of Chicago, 1926".

We have already encountered Kavana thanks to his magnificent archive work on the four-CD anthology of Irish dance musicians in America and then the two-CD *Irish Songs Of Rebellion And Resistance* with his Alias Acoustic Band. He moved from Ireland to London when he was 17, and joined Juice On The Loose as the lead singer. Their 1981 LP of that name is much more blues than country, one of the last gasps of pub rock, with Bam King from Mighty Baby playing on rhythm guitar. It all connects!

Kavana has made a bewildering amount of music since, mostly on the cusp of Irish and American music. Most cherishable is *Appalachian Beach Party*, with Jim Couza and The D'Urberville Ramblers, a collection of dance tunes from up in the hills. It's all in good fun: Ron has painted his cheeks like apples, and is thanked for the "funky mandolin leads of Ron Kavana". (Couza claims that "old-time music was always good-time music", which is far from true.) Ron then went on to record *Home Fire*, a return to his Irish heritage and to form Alias Ron Kavana, a roots band which proved extremely popular live. He also became one of the bit players who circled as satellites around the magnetic figure of Richard Thompson.

Kavana was asked to join The Pogues, but the offer fell through. Instead, he added an Irish piper to his own tour band and started writing lyrics as sharp as anyone, even Shane. *From Galway To Graceland* is the pinnacle of his fusion experiments, bringing in all kinds of music into the mix: reggae, cajun, blues and country – all grafted onto native Irish airs. On the sleeve, he thanks a whole series of American musician friends, and it reads like the index to this book, from The Bad Livers to David Lindley. You can tell the measure of a man by his friends. The title medley starts with the tune to 'Love Me Tender', here noted as the traditional Irish song 'Nora Lee', then Thompson's great song about dead Elvis, set to shimmery guitar, and on to 'Are You Lonesome Tonight?' Kavana sings as if haunted by his own ghosts, less tender and colder than Thompson's own rendition.

What a song! "From the West Coast of Ireland to West Tennessee" could be the subtitle of this book, and in his usual economical way Thompson says everything you need to know about the glamour of America as seen through the eyes of the poor and loveless. Maybe this is 'Sail Away' for the Irish diaspora.

Kavana went on to take a sabbatical, taking a degree in Irish studies, working on the film script of *Galway Girls* and the stage show *Irish Ways*. As to his double album of Irish traditional songs: "I wanted to put a contemporary spin on the material with some songs that offered hope for the future, rather than simply dwelling on the past."

The most fascinating of all of Kavana's side projects is *Dancin' To The Ceili Band* by The Bucks, who are basically Ron and his old friend Terry Woods. It is a wicked album, in just about every sense. It makes you laugh, it makes you cry, and it makes you think – you can't really ask for more than that from a CD. There's a sideswipe at Daniel O'Connell, an updated murder ballad – 'The Ghost Of Winters Gone' – and, best of all, 'What A Time', on which a concertina opens proceedings and then Ron and Terry come in singing in unison as slow as you like, but then a rhythm section starts up and everything gets cheerful. It's like Kavana's four-CD set on Irish music in America boiled down to about three minutes. Once again, the Flannagans play the Tub Of Blood, while "in the Appalachian mountains the tunes took on new names". It's as if everyone is dancing.

The greatest miracle of all is kept until the end. It's what has probably kept Ron going over the years – me, too, and you as well, I'm sure, if you've come the whole distance. On the railroads, down in the mines, in vaudeville halls and in work camps, "Irish music met black rhythms with a sound that shook the walls". It shook the world, too. Some called it crazy at the time. Some called it a miracle. "It's called rock 'n' roll of late."

Further Reading

Alden, Grant and Blackstock, Peter: *No Depression: An Introduction To Alternative Country Music (Whatever That Is)* (Dowling Press, 1998).

Allen, Bob: *George Jones: The Saga Of An American Singer* (Dolphin, 1984).

Allingham, William: *The Ballad Book: A Selection Of The Choicest British Ballads* (Sever & Francis, 1865).

Arnold, Byron: *Folksongs Of Alabama* (University Of Alabama Press, 1950).

Artis, Bob: *Bluegrass* (Hawthorn, 1975).

Asch, Moses and Others (ed): *Anthology Of American Folk Music. Songs transcribed from recorded performances that appear on the renowned Folkways recording* Anthology Of American Folk Music, *with historical and folkloric commentary on each* song (Oak Publications, 1973).

Barker, Garry: *Notes From A Native Son: Essays On The Appalachian Experience* (University Of Tennessee Press, 1995).

Barrand, Anthony: "Songs From The Hills Of Vermont", in *Country Dance & Song 11/12* (1981).

Barry, Phillips and others: *British Ballads From Maine: The Development Of Popular Songs With Texts And Airs* (Yale University Press, 1929).

Behan, Dominic: *Ireland Sings* (Essex Music, 1965).

Behan, Dominic: *The Singing Irish* (Scott Solomon, 1967).

Belden, HM: *Ballads And Songs* (University Of Missouri, 1940).

Bennahum, David: *kd lang: An Illustrated Biography* (Omnibus, 1993).

Bird, Brian: *Skiffle: The Story Of Folk-Song With A Jazz Beat* (Hale, 1958).

Bogdanovich, Peter: *John Ford* (Studio Vista, 1968).

Boyes, Georgina: *The Imagined Village: Culture, Ideology And The English Folk Revival* (Manchester University Press, 1993).

Bronson, Bertrand: *The Traditional Tunes Of The Child Ballads* (Princeton University Press, 1959-72, in four volumes).

Bronson, Bertrand: *The Ballad As Song* (University Of California, 1969).

Brown, Frank C: *The Frank C Brown Collection Of North Carolina Folklore* (Duke University Press,1952-64, in seven volumes).

Bruford, Alan: "Bring Out Your Corpus: Definitive Collections Of Scottish And Irish Folk-Songs", in *Tocher #36-7* (1981).

Brunvand, Jan Harold (ed): *American Folklore: An Encyclopedia* (Garland, 1996).

Buchan, David: *The Ballad And The Folk* (Routledge, 1972).

Buchan, Norman and Hall, Peter: *The Scottish Folksinger* (Collins, 1973).

Bull, Andy: *Coast To Coast: A Rock Fan's US Tour* (Black Swan, 1993).

Bunting, Edward: *The Ancient Music Of Ireland* (Hodges And Smith, 1840. Reprinted with "A General Collection Of The Ancient Music Of Ireland" (Walton's Piano And Musical Instruments Gallery, 1969).

Bunting, Edward: *Bunting's Ancient Music Of Ireland. Edited from the original manuscripts by Donal O'Sullivan and*

Micheal O'Suilleabhan (Cork University Press, 1983).

Burt, Olive: *American Murder Ballads And Their Stories* (OUP, 1958).

Burton, Thomas G: *Some Ballad Folks* (East Tennessee State University, 1978).

Cantwell, Robert: *Bluegrass Breakdown: The Making Of The Old Southern Sound* (Illinois University Press, 1984).

Cantwell, Robert: "Smith's Memory Theatre: The Folkways Anthology Of American Folk Music", in *New England Review* (spring/summer 1991).

Cantwell, Robert: *Ethnomimesis: Folklife And The Representation Of Culture* (University Of North Carolina Press, 1993).

Cantwell, Robert: *When We Were Good: The Folk Revival* (Harvard University Press, 1996).

Carr, Patrick (ed): *The Illustrated History Of Country Music. By the editors of* Country Music *magazine* (Doubleday, 1980).

Carson, Ciaran: *Last Night's Fun!: A Book About Irish Traditional Music* (Cape, 1996).

Cash, Rosanne: *Bodies Of Water* (Hyperion, 1996).

Ceol, A Journal Of Irish Music (various issues).

Chase, Richard: *American Folk-Tales And Songs, And Other Examples Of English-American Tradition As Preserved In The Appalachian Mountains And Elsewhere In The United States* (Signet, 1956).

Child, Francis James: *The English And Scottish Popular Ballads* (Mifflin & Co, in five volumes; Dover, 1965).

Clancy Brothers: *The Clancy Brothers And Tommy Makem Songbook* (Oak Publications, 1964).

Cohen, John and Seeger, Mike: *The New Lost City Ramblers Song Book* (Oak Publications, 1964).

Clifford, Theresa: *An Irish Folksinger's Album* (Curwen, 1957).

Coffin, Tristram Potter: *The British Traditional Ballad In North America* (American Folklore Society, 1950; revised edition 1963; third edition with supplement by Roger deV Renwick, Texas University Press, 1977).

Combs, Josiah: *Folk Songs Of The Southern United States* (University Of Texas Press, 1967).

Comstock Lode (various issues).

Copper, Bob: *A Song For Every Season* (Heinemann, 1971).

Copper, Bob: *Songs And Southern Breezes: Country Folk And Country Ways* (Heinemann, 1973; foreword by John Arlott).

Corbin, Everett: *Storm Over Nashville: A Case Against "Modern" Country Music* (Ashlar Press, 1980).

Country Music (various issues).

Cox, John Harrington: *Traditional Ballads Mainly From West Virginia* (American Folk Song Publications, 1939).

Cox, John Harrington: *Folk Songs Of The South* (Dover, 1967).

Cox, Marian Roalfe: *An Introduction To Folk-Lore* (David Nutt, 1897 [enlarged edition]).

Crofts, Andrew: *Crocodile Shoes: From The North East To The Wild West* (Pocket Books, 1996).

Crosby, David and Gottlieb, Carl: *Long Time Gone: The Autobiography* (Doubleday, 1988).

Dallas, Karl: "The Roots Of Tradition", in *The Electric Muse: The Story Of Folk Into Rock* (Methuen, 1975).

Dark Star (various issues).

Darling, Charles (ed): *The New American Songster: Traditional Ballads And Songs Of North America* (University Of America Press, 1983).

Davis, Arthur Kyle, Jr: *Traditional Ballads Of Virginia, Collected Under The Auspices Of The Virginia Folk-Lore Society* (Harvard University Press, 1929).

Davis, Arthur Kyle Jr: *Folk-Songs Of Virginia: A Descriptive Index And Classification Of Materials Collected Under The Auspices Of The Virginia Folk-Lore Society* (Duke University Press, 1949).

Dawidoff, Nicholas: *In The Country Of Country* (Faber).

Dean, MC (ed): *The Flying Cloud And 150 Other Old-Time Songs And Ballads Of Outdoor Men, Sailors, Lumberjacks, Soldiers, Men Of The Great Lakes, Railroadmen, Miners Etc* (The Quickprint, 1922; Norwood, 1973).

Dean-Smith, Margaret: *A Guide To English Folk Song Collections 1822-1952* (Liverpool University Press & EFDSS, 1954).

Deller, Fred and Thompson, Roy: *The Illustrated Encyclopedia Of Country Music* (Salamander, 1977).

Denselow, Robin: "Folk-Rock In Britain", in *The Electric Muse: The Story Of Folk Into Rock* (Methuen, 1975).

Deturk, David and Poulin, A (eds): *The American Folk Scene, Dimensions Of The Folksong Revival* (Dell, 1967).

Dickey, James: *Deliverance* (Hamish Hamilton, 1970).

Dorgan, Howard: *The Old Regular Baptists Of Central Appalachia: Brothers And Sisters In Hope* (Tennessee University

Press, 1989).

Dorn, Edward: *Gunslinger 1 & 2* (Fulcrum, 1970).

Duff, John: *The Irish In America* (Wadsworth Books, 1971).

Dugaw, Dianne: *The Anglo-American Ballad: A Folklore Casebook* (Garland, 1995).

Eddy, Mary O: *Ballads And Songs From Ohio* (J Augustin, 1939; Folklore Associates, 1964).

Erlewine, Michael and others (ed): *All Music Guide To Country* (Miller Freeman Books, 1997).

Escott, Colin: *Hank Williams.*

Fischer, David: *Albion's Seed, Four British Folkways In America* (OUP, 1989).

Flanders, Helen Hartness (ed): *A Garland Of Green Mountain Song* (Schirmer: American Folk-Song series, 1937).

Flanders, Helen Hartness (ed): *Ancient Ballads Traditionally Sung In New England* (University Of Philadelphia Press, 1961-5, in four volumes).

Flanders, Helen Hartness: *Vermont Folk-Songs And Ballads* (Stephen Daye Press, 1931; 1968).

Flanders, Helen Hartness and Olney, Margaret: *Migrant Ballads In New England* (Strauss & Young, 1953; 1968).

Flippo, Chet: *Your Cheating Heart* (Simon & Schuster, 1981).

Folk Review (various issues).

Folk Roots/F Roots (various issues).

Fong-Torres, Ben: *Hickory Wind: The Life And Times Of Gram Parsons* (Omnibus, 1994).

Ford, Ira: *Traditional Music In America* (EP Dutton, 1940; 1965).

Fox, C Milligan: *Songs Of The Irish Harpers* (Schirmer, 1910).

Frayling, Christopher: *Sergio Leone: Something To Do With Death* (Faber, 2000).

French, Philip: *Westerns: Aspects Of A Movie Genre* (Secker & Warburg, 1973).

Fuson, Harvey: *Ballads Of The Kentucky Highlands* (Mitre Press, 1931).

Gainer, Patrick: *Folk Songs From The West Virginia Hills* (Seneca Books, 1975).

Galvin, Patrick (pseudonym of SF Hagan): *Irish Songs Of Resistance 1169-1923* (Folklore Press, 1956; 1962).

Gardner, Emelyn and Chickering, Geraldine: *Ballads And Songs Of Southern Michigan* (University Of Michigan Press, 1939; 1967).

Glatt, John: *"Another Country" – The Chieftains: The Authorised Biography* (Century, 1997, pp 246-59).

Goodman, David: *Modern Twang: An Alternative Country Music Guide And Directory* (Dowling Press, 2000 [3rd edition]).

Graeme, Joy (Ed): *The Irish Songbook: Collected, Adapted, Written And Sung By The Clancy Brothers And Tommy Makem* (Collier Books, 1971).

Graves, Robert: *The English Ballad* (Ernest Benn Ltd, 1927).

Green, Douglas: *Country Roots: The Origins Of Country Music* (Hawthorn, 1976).

Greenway, John: *American Folksongs Of Protest* (1953).

Grey, Zane: *The Last Trail: A Story Of Early Days In The Ohio Valley* (Al Burt, 1909).

Griffin, Sid: "Sin City", in *Love Is The Drug: Living As A Pop Fan* (Penguin, 1994, edited by John Aizlewood).

Grissum, John: *Country Music, White Man's Blues* (Paperback Library, 1970).

Guralnick, Peter: *Lost Highways: Journeys And Arrivals Of American Musicians* (Godine, 1979).

Guthrie, Woody: *California To The New York Island: Being a pocketful of brags, blues, bad ban ballads, love songs, Okie laments and childrens' catcalls by...woven into a script suitable for a concert, clambake, hootenanny or community sing by Millard Lampebell* (Oak Publications For The Guthrie Childrens' Trust Fund, 1958).

Hall, Doug: *Country On CD: The Essential Guide* (Kyle Cathie, 1993).

Hall, Tom T: *The Storyteller's Nashville* (Doubleday, 1979).

Harker, Dave: *Fakesong: The Manufacture Of British "Folksong" 1700 To The Present Day* (Open University Press).

Harris, Stacey: *The Carter Family* (Lerner Publishing, 1978).

Haslam, Gerald: *Workin' Man Blues, Country Music In California* (University Of California, 1999).

Helm, Levon and Davis, Stephen: *This Wheel's On Fire: Levon Helm And The Story Of The Band* (Plexus, 1993).

Hemphill, Paul: *The Nashville Sound: Bright Lights And Country Music* (Simon & Schuster, 1970).

Heylin, Clinton: *Behind Closed Doors – Bob Dylan: The Recording Sessions 1960-1994* (Viking, 1995).

Heylin, Clinton: *Dylan's Daemon Lover: The Tangled Tale Of A 450-Year-Old Ballad* (Helter Skelter, 1999).

Hogg, Brian: *The History Of Scottish Rock And Pop* (Guinness, 1993).

Hoskyns, Barney: "Nashville Blue", in *Say It One More Time For The Brokenhearted: Country Soul In The American South* (Bloomsbury, 1987).

Hoskyns, Barney: "Redneck Soul, George Jones And The White Man's Blues", in *From A Whisper To A Scream: The Great Voices Of Popular Music* (Fontana, 1991).

Hoskyns, Barney: *Across The Great Divide: The Band And America* (Viking, 1993).

Howes, Frank: *Folk Music Of Britain…And Beyond* (Methuen, 1969).

Hubbard, Lester A: *Ballads And Songs From Utah* (University Of Utah Press, 1961).

Hudson, Arthur Palmer: *Folksongs Of Mississippi And Their Background* (North Carolina University Press, 1936).

Hughes, Herbert: *Irish Country Songs* (Boosey & Hawkes, 1909-36, in four volumes).

Hume, Martha: *You're So Cold I'm Turning Blue: Guide To The Greatest In Country Music* (Penguin, 1982).

Humphries, Patrick: *Meet On The Ledge: Fairport Convention – The Classic Years* (Eel Pie 1982; Virgin 1997 [revised]).

Hunter, Robert: *A Box Of Rain: Lyrics 1965-1993* (Viking 1990; Penguin, 1993 [with extra lyrics]).

Huntington, Gale (ed): *Sam Henry's Songs Of The People* (University Of Georgia Press, 1990).

Hutchings, Ashley (ed): *A Little Music: A Collection Of Folk-Songs, Instrumental Tunes And Dances* (Island Music, 1976).

Igliori, Paola (ed): *American Magus, Harry Smith – A Modern Alchemist* (Inanout Press, 1996). Includes an interview with John Cohen.

Ives, Burl: *Irish Songs* (Duell, Sloan & Pierce, 1955).

Johnston, Ian: *Bad Seed: The Biography Of Nick Cave* (Abacus, 1996).

Jones, Loyal: *Minstrel Of The Appalachians: The Story Of Bascom Lamar Lunsford* (Appalachian Consortium Press, 1984).

Jones, Paul: *The Irish Brigade* (Luce, 1969).

Journal Of American Folklore (various issues).

Journal Of Country Music (various issues).

Journal Of The Folk Song Society/Journal Of The English Folk-Dance And Song Society (various issues).

Jovanic, Rob: *Beck! On A Backwards River* (Virgin, 2000).

Karpeles, Maud: *Cecil Sharp: His Life And Work* (Routledge, 1967).

Karpeles, Maud (ed): "A Return Visit To The Appalachian Mountains" (journal of the EFDSS #6 [3], 1951).

Kennedy, Douglas: *In God's Country: Travels In The Bible Belt USA* (Unwin, 1989).

Kennedy, Peter: *Folksongs Of Britain And America* (Schirmer, 1975).

Kent, Nick: *The Dark Stuff: Selected Writings On Rock Music 1972-1993* (Penguin, 1994). Includes "The Killer In Aspic: Going To Hell With Jerry Lee Lewis In Hollywood" and "Neil Young And The Haphazard Highway That Leads To Unconditional Love".

Kephart, Horace: *Our Southern Highlanders* (1913).

Kerridge, Roy: *In The Deep South* (Michael Joseph, 1989).

Kesey, Ken and Babbs, Ken: *Last Go Round* (Black Swan, 1995).

Kincaid, Bradley: *My Favourite Mountain Ballads And Old-Time Songs* (WLS Radio, 1928).

Kincaid, Bradley: Favourite Old-Time Songs And Mountain Ballads (WLS Radio, 1929-30, in two volumes).

Kingsbury, Paul (ed): *The Country Reader: 25 Years Of* The Journal Of Country Music.

Koster, Rick: *Texas Music*.

Laing, Dave: "Troubadours And Stars", in *The Electric Muse: The Story Of Folk Into Rock* (Methuen, 1975).

Landy, Ellliott: *Woodstock Vision: The Spirit Of A Generation* (Continuuum, 1994).

Larkin, Colin (ed): *The Guinness Who's Who Of Country Music* (Guinness Publishing, 1993).

Laws, G Malcolm, Jr: *American Ballads From British Broadsides: A Guide For Students And Collectors Of Traditional Song* (American Folklore Society, 1957).

Laws, G Malcolm, Jr: *Native American Balladry: A Decriptive Study And A Bibliographical Syllabus* (University Of Texas Press for the American Folklore Society, 1950; 1964 [revised edition]).

Leach, Macedward and Coffin, Tristram (eds): *The Critics And The Ballad: Readings* (Southern Illinois University Press, 1961).

Leamer, Lawrence: *Three Chords And The Truth: Hope Heartbeat And Changing Fortunes In Nashville* (HarperCollins).

Leisner, Tony: *The Official Guide To Country Steps* (Chartwell, 1980).

Lewis, Jerry Lee and White, Charles: *Killer* (Century, 1993).

Library Of Congress: *Folk Music: A Catalog Of Folk Songs, Ballads, Dances, Instrumental Pieces, And Folk Tales Of The United States And Latin America On Phonograph Records* (Library Of Congress [Music Division], 1958).

Linscott, Eloise: *Folk Songs Of Old New England* (Macmillan, 1939; 1962).

Lloyd, AL: *Folk Song In England* (Lawrence & Wishart, 1975).

Lomax, Alan: *The Folk Songs Of North America In The English Language* (Doubleday, 1960).

Lomax, Alan: *The Penguin Book Of American Folk Songs* (Penguin, 1964).

Lomax, John: *Cowboy Songs And Other Frontier Ballads* (Macmillan, 1918; 1938 [revised edition]).

Lomax, John and Alan: *American Ballads And Folk Songs* (Macmillan, 1934).

Lomax, John and Alan: *Our Singing Country: A Second Volume Of American Ballads And Folk Songs* (Macmillan, 1941).

Lynn, Loretta with Vecsey, George: *Coal Miner's Daughter* (Warner, 1976).

MacArthur, Margaret: "The Search For More Songs From The Hills Of Vermont: Songs And Ballads Of The Atwood Family", in *Country Dance & Song* #11/12 (1981).

McCaffrey, Lawrence J: *The Irish Diaspora In America* (Indiana University Press, 1976).

McCarthy, Cormac: The Border Trilogy (Pan/Picador, 1993-1998).
   All The Pretty Horses ; *The Crossing*; *Cities Of The Plain*

MacColl, Ewan: *Folk Songs And Ballads Of Scotland* (Oak Publications, 1965).

MacColl, Ewan and Seeger, Peggy (eds): *Travellers' Songs From England & Scotland* (Tennessee University Press, 1977).

McCrumb, Sharyn: Elizabeth Macpherson mysteries, set in Appalachia and Scotland:
   Sick Of Shadows; Lovely In Her Bones; Highland Laddy Gone; Paying The Piper; The Windsor Knot; Missing Susan; Macpherson's Lament; If I'd Had Killed Him When I Met Him (Ballantine, 1995).

McCrumb, Sharyn: Ballad Books, set in Appalachia
   If Ever I Return, Pretty Peggy-O (Scribners, 1990).
   The Hangman's Beautiful Daughter (Scribners, 1992).
   She Walks These Hills (Scribners, 1994).
   Foggy Mountain Breakdown (Ballantine, 1997 [short stories]).
   The Rosewood Casket.
   The Ballad Of Frankie Silver (Hodder, 1998).

McIntosh, David: *Folk Songs And Singing Games Of The Illinois Ozarks* (Southern Illinois University Press, 1974).

McLean, Duncan: *Lone Star Swing* (Vintage, 1998).

MacMullan, Robert (writing as "North Antrim"): *Rowlock Rhymes And Songs Of Exile* (Quota Press, 1933, ed Sam Henry).

McNeil, WK: *Appalachian Images In Folk And Popular Culture* 1995).

Malone, Bill: *Country Music, USA* (University Of Texas Press, 1985).

Malone, Bill: *Singing Cowboys And Musical Mountaineers: Southern Culture And The Roots Of Country Music* (University Of Georgia Press, 1993).

Malone, Bill: *Southern Music, American Music* (University Of Kentucky Press, 1979).

Malone, Michael and Etulain, Richard: *The American West: A 20th-Century History* (University Of Nebraska, 1989).

Marcus, Greil: *Mystery Train: Images Of America In Rock 'n' Roll Music* (EP Dutton, 1975).

Marcus, Greil: *In The Fascist Bathroom: Writings On Punk 1977-1992* (Viking, 1993).

Marcus, Greil: *Invisible Republic: Bob Dylan's Basement Tapes* (Picador, 1997).

Matteson, Maurice and Mellinger, Edward (eds): *Beech Mountain Folk-Songs And Ballads* (Schirmer, 1936).

Meek, Bill: *The Land Of Liberties: Songs Of The Irish In America* (Gilbert Dalton, 1978).

Melhuish, Martin: *Celtic Tides: Traditional Music In A New Age* (Quarry Music Books, 1998).

Miles, Emma: *The Spirit Of The Mountains* (University Of Tennessee Press, 1905; 1975).

Miller, Kerby: *Emigrants And Exiles: Ireland And The Irish Exodus In North America* (OUP, 1985).

Miller, Kerby and Wagner, Paul: *Out Of Ireland: The Story Of Irish Emigration To America* (Aurum Press, 1994).

Minton, John: "'Our Goodman' In Blackface And 'The Maid' At The Sookey Jump: Two Afro-American Variants Of Child Ballads In Commercial Disc" (John Edwards Memorial Foundation Quarterly #65-6, 1982). The two performances in question are Coley Jones' 'Drunkard's Special' and Huddie Ledbetter's 'Gallis Pole'.

Moffat, Alfred: *The Minstrels Of Ireland* (Augener and Co, 1897).

Mojo (various issues).

Moore, Ethel and Chauncey, O: *Ballads And Folk Songs Of The Southwest. More than 600 titles, melodies and texts collected in Oklahoma* (University Of Oklahoma Press, 1964).

Morris, Gregory L (ed): *Talking Up A Storm: Voices Of The New West* (University Of Nebraska Press, 1994).

Morton, Robin: *Come Day, Go Day, God Send Sunday. The songs and life story, told in his own words, of John Maguire, traditional singer and farmer from County Fermanagh* (Routledge, 1973).

Munnelly, Tom: "The Singing Traditions Of Irish Travellers", in *Folk Music Journal* #3 (1), 1975).

Munro, Ailie: *The Folk Revival In Scotland* (Kahn & Averill, 1984). Includes Morag Macleod's "The Folk Revival In Gaelic Song".

Nash, Alanna: *Dolly* (Granada, 1979).

Nelson, Willie and Shrake, Bud: *I Didn't Come Here And I Ain't Leaving* (Macmillan, 1988).

Nettel, Reginald: *Sing A Song Of England: A Social History Of Traditional Song* (Phoenix House, 1954; 1969).

New Country (various issues).

No Depression (various issues).

Nygard, Holger: *The Ballad Of Heer Halewijn, Its Forms And Variations In Western Europe, A Study Of The History And Nature Of A Ballad* (Folklore Fellows Communications, 1958).

Oak Ridge Boys: *The Oak Ridge Boys: Our Story* (Contemporary Books, 1987).

O'Canainn, Tomas: *Traditional Music In Ireland* (Routledge, 1978).

O'Connor, Joseph: *Sweet Liberty: Travels In Irish America* (Picador, 1996).

O'Connor, Nuala: *Bringing It All Back Home: The Influence Of Irish Music* (BBC Books, 1991).

Oermann, Robert: *America's Music: The Roots Of Country* (Turner Publishing, 1996).

Okun, Milton: *Something To Sing About! The Personal Choices Of America's Folk Singers* (Macmillan, 1968).

O'Lochlainn, Colm: *Irish Street Ballads* (Three Candles, 1939; Citadel Press, 1960).

O'Lochlainn, Colm: *More Irish Street Ballads* (Three Candles, 1965).

Omaha Rainbow (various issues).

Otto, JS and Burns, AM: "Black And White Cultural Interaction In The Early 20th-Century South: Race And Hillbilly Music", in *Phylon* #35 (1974).

Owens, William: *Texas Folk Songs* (Texas Folk Lore Society, 1950).

Palmer, Roy (ed): *Folk Songs Collected By Ralph Vaughan Williams* (Dent, 1983).

Palmer, Roy: *Room For Company* (Cambridge University Press, 1971).

Palmer, Roy: *A Touch On The Times: Songs Of Social Change 1770-1914* (Penguin, 1974).

Palmer, Roy (ed): *Love Is Pleasing: Songs Of Courtship And Marriage* (Cambridge University Press, 1974).

Palmer, Roy: The Sound Of History, Songs And Social Comment (OUP, 1988).

Pankake, Marcia and Jon: *A Prairie Home Companion Folk Song Book* (Viking, 1998; introduction by Garrison Keillor).

Patterson, Daniel and Zug, Charles (eds): *Arts In Earnest: North Carolina Folklore* (Duke University Press, 1990).

Pegg, Bob: *Rites And Riots: Folk Customs Of Britain And Europe* (Blandford, 1981).

Peters, Harry: *Folk Songs Out Of Wisconsin: An Illustrated Compendium* (State Historical Society Of Wisconsin, 1977).

Peters, Stephen: *What A Long Strange Trip: The Stories Behind Every Grateful Dead Song.*

Peterson, Richard: *Creating Country Music, Fabricating Authenticity.*

Peterson, Walter: *Mountain Ballads And Old-Time Songs* (MM Cole, 1931).

Planxty: *The Songs Of Planxty* (Mews Music, 1976).

Porterfield, Nolan: *Jimmie Rodgers: The Life And Times Of America's Blue Yodeler* (University Of Illinois Press, 1979).

Pound, Louise: *American Ballads And Songs* (Scribners, 1922; 1972).

Prendergast, Mark: *Irish Rock, Roots, Personalities, Directions* (O'Brien Press, 1987).

Price, Steven: *Old As The Hills: The Story Of Bluegrass Music* (Viking, 1975).

Purslow, Frank: *Marrow Bones: English Folk Songs From The Hammond And Gardiner Mss* (EFDS Publications, 1965).

Rainey, Leo: *Songs Of The Ozark Folk (The Ozarks Mountaineer*, 1976).

Randolph, Vance: *Ozark Folksongs* (State Historical Society Of Missouri, 1946-50, in four volumes; 1980 [revised edition]; 1982 [abridged and edited by N Cohen]).

Reeves, James: *The Idiom Of The People. English traditional verse edited with an introduction and notes from the manuscripts of Cecil J Sharp* (Macmillan, 1958).

Reeves, James: *The Everlasting Circle. English traditional verse edited with an introduction and notes from the manuscripts of S Baring-Gould, Jed Hammond and George B Gardiner* (Heinemann, 1960).

Reid, Jan: *The Improbable Rise Of Red Neck Rock* (Heidelberg).

Renwick, Roger deV: *English Folk Poetry: Structure And Meaning* (Batsford, 1980).

Richardson, Ethel and Spaeth, Sigmund: *American Mountain Songs* (Greenberg, 1927; 1955).

Riese, Randall: *Nashville Babylon* (Congdon & Weed, 1988).

Riley, Jeannie C: *From Harper Valley To The Mountaintop* (Chosen Books, 1978).

Ritchie, Jean: *Folk Songs Of The Southern Appalachians* (Oak Publications, 1965).

Roberts, Leonard: *Sang Branch Settlers: Folksongs And Tales Of A Kentucky Mountain Family* (University Of Texas Press, 1974).

Rogan, Johnny: *The Byrds, Timeless Flight Revisited – The Sequel* (Rogan House, 1997).

Rosenbaum, Art: *Folk Visions And Voices: Traditional Music And Song In N Georgia* (University Of Georgia Press, 1983).

Rosenberg, Neil: *Bluegrass: A History* (University Of Illinois Press, 1985).

Rosenberg, Neil (ed): *Transforming Tradition: Folk Music Revivals Examined* (University Of Illinois Press, 1993).

Sample, Tex: *White Soul, Country Music – The Church And Working Americans* (Abingdon Press, 1996).

Sandburg, Carl: *The American Songbag* (Harcourt Brace, 1927).

Sandburg, Carl: *Carl Sandburg's New American Songbag* (Broadcast Music, 1950).

Sarris, Andrew: *The John Ford Movie Mystery* (Secker & Warburg, 1976).

Savage, Candace: *Cowgirls* (Bloomsbury, 1996).

Scarborough, Dorothy: *A Song Catcher In The Southern Mountains: American Folk Songs Of British Ancestry* (Columbia University Press, 1937, Repr 1966).

Schlappi, Elizabeth: *Roy Acuff: The Smokey Mountain Boy* (Pelican, 1978).

Scobey, Lola: *Willie Nelson, Country Outlaw* (Zebra Books, 1982).

Scofield, Twilio: *An American Sampler: The Lore Of The Land, Or Our Traditions In Song, History, Foodways And Custom* (Cutthroat Press, 1981).

Scott, John: *The Ballad Of America* (Bantam, 1966).

Seeger, Peggy: *Folk Songs Of Peggy Seeger* (Oak, 1964).

Seeger, Peggy And MacColl, Ewan (eds): *The Singing Island: A Collection Of English And Scots Folksongs* (Mills Music, 1960).

Shannon, William V: *The American Irish: A Political And Social Portrait* (University Of Massachusetts Press, 1963).

Shapiro, Marc: *The Long Run: The Story Of The Eagles* (Omnibus, 1995).

Sharp, Cecil J: *English Folk-Song: Some Conclusions* (Novello, 1907; 1965 [fourth edition, revised, with an appreciation by Ralph Vaughan Williams]).

Sharp, Cecil J: *English County Folk Songs* (Novello, 1908-12, in five volumes; 1961 [omnibus edition]).

Sharp, Cecil J (compiler): *English Folk-Songs From The Southern Appalachians. Comprising 274 songs and ballads with 968 tunes, including 39 tunes contributed by Olive Campbell* (OUP, 1932 [second edition, in two volumes]). Edited by Maud Karpeles.

Sharp, Cecil J and Karpeles, Maud: *80 English Folk-Songs From The Southern Appalachians* (Faber & Faber, 1968).

Sharp, Cecil J: *Cecil Sharp's Collection Of English Folk Songs* (OUP, 1974, in two volumes). Edited by Maud Karpeles.

Sharp, Cecil J: *The Crystal Spring: English Folk Songs Collected By Cecil Sharp* (OUP, 1975, in two volumes). Edited by Maud Karpeles.

Shellans, Herbert: *Folksongs Of The Blue Ridge Mountains: Traditional Songs As Sung By The People Of The Blue Ridge Mountains Country* (Oak Publications, 1968).

Shelton, Robert: "Something Happened In America", in *The Electric Muse: The Story Of Folk Into Rock* (Methuen, 1975).

Shields, Hugh: "William Allingham And Folk Song', in *Hermathena* #117 (1974).

Shields, Hugh: *Shamrock, Rose And Thistles: Folk Singing In North Derry* (Blackstaff Press, 1981).

Shoemaker, Henry: *Mountain Minstrels Of Pennsylvania* (Newman F McGirr, 1931).

Silber, Irwin and Robinson, Earl: *Songs Of The Great American West* (Macmillan, 1967).

Sing Out (various issues).

Smith, Harry: *American Magus, Harry Smith – A Modern Alchemist* (Inandout Press, 1996). Edited by P Igliori.

Smith, Harry: *Think Of The Self Speaking, Harry Smith – Selected Interviews* (Elbow Press, 1999). Edited by R Singh.

Smith, Henry Nash: *Virgin Land: The American West As Symbol And Myth* (Harvard University Press, 1950).

Smith, Lee: *Oral History* (Picador, 1989).

Smith, Reed: *South Carolina Ballads* (Harvard University Press, 1928).

Spaeth, Sigmund: *A History Of Popular Music In America* (Random House, 1948).

Stewart, Bob: *Where Is Saint George? Pagan Imagery In English Folksong* (Moonraker, 1977).

Stout, Earl (ed): *Folklore From Iowa* (American Folklore Society, 1936).

Sturgis, Edith and Hughes, Robert: *Songs From The Hills Of Vermont* (Schirmer, 1919).

Thompson, Harold: *Body, Boots & Britches: Folktales, Ballads And Speech From County New York* (Lippincott, 1939; 1962).

Tichi, Cecelia: *High Lonesome: The American Culture Of Country Music* (North Carolina University Press, 1994).

Tosches, Nick: *Country: The Biggest Music In America* (Stein & Day, 1977). Reissued in Britain as *Country: Living Legends And Dying Metaphors In America's Biggest Music* (Secker & Warburg).

Townsend, CR: *San Antonio Rose: The Life And Music Of Bob Wills* (1976).

Tunney, Paddy: *The Stone Fiddle: My Way To Traditional Song* (Gilbert Dalton, 1979).

Turner, Steve: *Hungry For Heaven: Rock And Roll And The Search For Redemption* (Virgin, 1988; Hodder & Stoughton 1995 [revised edition]).

Unterberger, Richie: *Music USA, The Rough Guide* (Rough Guides, 1999).

Van der Merwe, Peter: *Origins Of The Popular Style: The Antecedents Of 20th-Century Popular Music* (OUP, 1989).

Vassal, Jacques: *Electric Children: Roots And Branches Of Modern Folkrock* (Muller, 1976).

Vaughan, Andrew: *The World Of Country Music* (Studio Editions, 1992).

Vaughan, Andrew: *Who's Who In New Country Music* (Omnibus, 1989).

Vaughan Williams, Ralph: *"National Music" And Other Essays* (OUP, 1963). Title essay first published in 1934.

Vaughan Williams, Ralph and Lloyd, AL: *The Penguin Book Of English Folk Songs* (Penguin, 1959).

Walsh, Stephen: *Heartache Spoken Here: An Off-Beat Journey Through Country And Western Music, Britain And Divorce* (Penguin, 1997).

Wangford, Hank: *Lost Cowboys, From Patagonia To The Alamo* (Gollancz, 1995).

Warner, Anne: *Traditional American Folk Songs, From The Anne And Frank Warner Collection* (Syracuse University Press, 1984).

Wells, Evelyn: *The Ballad Tree: A Study Of British And American Ballads, Their Folklore, Verse And Music* (Ronald Press Company, 1950).

Wetmore, Susannah and Bartholemew, Marshall: *Mountain Songs Of North Carolina* (Schirmer, 1926).

Wheeler, Mary and Bridge, Clara: *Kentucky Mountain Folk-Songs* (Boston Music Company, 1937).

Williams, Alfred: *Folk Songs Of The Upper Thames* (Duckworth, 1923).

Williams, Hank Jr: *Living Proof: An Autobiography* (GP Putnam, 1979).

Wittke, Carl: *The Irish In America* (Russell & Russell, 1970).

Wolfe, Charles: *A Good-Natured Riot: The Birth Of The Grand Ole Opry* (Vanderbilt Univerity Press, 1999).

Woods, Fred: *Folk Revival: The Rediscovery Of A National Music* (Blandford Press, 1979).

Wootton, Richard: *Honky Tonkin': A Travel Guide To American Music* (Travelaid, 1980 [third edition]).

Wright, Robert (ed): *Irish Emigrant Songs And Ballads* (Bowling Green University, 1975).

Wyman, Loraine and Brockway, Howard: *Lonesome Tunes: Folk Songs From The Kentucky Mountains* (HW Gray, 1916).

Wyman, Loraine and Brockway, Howard: *20 Kentucky Mountain Songs* (Oliver Ditson Company, 1920).

Wynette, Tammy and Dew, Joan: *Stand By Your Man: An Autobiography* (Hutchinson, 1979).

Zigzag (various issues).

Index

Ace, Bobby (And The Cards) 328
Ackers, Robert 88
Ackles, David 33, 231, 288, 346
Acuff, Roy 100, 104, 117, 130, 131, 151, 187, 222, 393
Adams, Ryan 428
Adcock, Eddie 249
Afro-Celtic Sound System 96
Ahern, Brian 278
Alabama 3, The 14-8, 20, 40, 85, 90, 109, 120, 129, 132, 139, 149, 195, 258, 267, 312, 325-6, 353, 391, 436, 438
Aladdin Laddies, The 122
Alan, Tom 110
Albin, Peter 302
Albin, Rodney 299
Albini, Steve 441
Alden, Grant 411, 412
Alias Acoustic Band 453
Alk, Howard 281
Allen Brothers, The 142
Allen, Barbara 41, 46
Allen, Red 245
Allen, Terry 223, 294, 367, 365-6
Allison, Mose 235
Allman Brothers, The 141, 133, 327, 339, 350-1
Almanac Singers, The 161, 246
Altman, Robert 38, 39, 240, 375
Alvin, Dave 232, 394-5
Alvin, Phil 21, 394-5
Amazing Rhythm Aces, The 343
American Flyer 327
Amis, Kingsley 168
Andersen, Eric 196, 199, 200, 251, 291, 335, 409, 194-5
Andersen, Lindsay 119
Anderson, "Whispering Bill" 239
Anderson, Ian 175, 440, 96
Anderson, Lynn 38
Angel Band, The 113, 276
Animals, The 371
Area Code 615 198, 213, 214, 309, 312, 318
Arizona Smoke Review, The 381
Armstrong, Louis 77, 91-2

Army, The 197
Arnold, Eddie 137, 143, 309
Aronowitz, Al 218
Asch, Moses 161
Ashcroft, Richard 382
Asher, Pete 322
Ashley, Clarence "Tom" 78, 164, 171, 202, 243, 332
Asleep At The Wheel 124, 349
Assembly Of God, The 100
Asylum 322
Atkins, Chet 41, 79, 90, 126, 136-7, 151, 193, 285, 297, 319, 342, 356, 359, 368, 376, 38-8, 410
Atkins, James 136
Atkinson, David 62
Atlanta Rhythm Section, The 350
Au Go Go Singers, The 313
Austin Lounge Lizards, The 367
Austin, James 268
Autrey, Gene 114-5, 117-8, 152, 228, 324
Axton, Hoyt 190, 237, 255-6, 324
Ayers, Kevin 216

Babitz, Eve 268
Bacall, Lauren 221
Bad Livers, The 467, 411
Baez, Joan 65, 80, 82, 110, 166, 179, 188-90, 214, 250, 274, 281, 349, 370
Baggs, Perry 393
Bailey, DeFord 40, 98
Bain, Aly 452
Bakersfield Brass, The 231
Bakunin, Mikhail 103
Ball, Earl 259, 261
Ball, EC 167
Banana And The Bunch 310
Band, The 39, 59, 169, 185, 195, 206-7, 217-21, 267, 287, 310, 328-30, 342, 370, 377, 393, 414
Barbarians, The 228
Barber, Chris 173
Bare, Bobby 23, 222-3, 366
Barefoot Jerry 217, 221, 289, 297, 214-6

Barnard, Junior 124
Barraclough, Elizabeth 361
Barraclough, Nick 13
Barrett, Syd 72, 307
Barth, Bill 177
Barton, Shawn 430
Batchelor, Cal 383
Battin, Skip 289-90, 333
Bauer, Joe 309
Baxter, Andrew 71
Baxter, Glen 239
Baxter, Jim 71
Baxter, Les (Balladeers) 256
Bay Singers, The 313-4
Beach Boys, The 235, 238, 324
Beacon Hillbillies, The 429, 444
Bean, Janet Beveridge 442-3
Beat Farmers, The 395
Beatles, The 15, 36, 79, 143, 148, 153, 157, 174, 204, 206, 209, 231, 233, 243, 249, 251, 256-7, 283, 297, 303, 352, 358, 376, 402
Beau Brummels, The 153, 309
Beck 13, 91, 97, 184, 229, 275, 276, 307, 438-9
Beckett, Barry 141
Bee Gees, The 131
Beecher, Bonnie 186
Beefeaters, The 254
Bees Make Honey 387
Beland, John 270
Bell, Max 214, 216-7
Bellamy, Peter 175, 203
Benet, Steven Vincent 120
Bennett, Tony 131
Benson, Ray 124, 349-50
Benson, Thomas Hart 160
Berline, Byron 251, 265, 270, 272-3, 282, 284
Berry, Bruce 338
Berry, Chuck 140, 152, 221, 244, 276
Betts, Dicky 141
Betts, Richard 350
Beverly Hillbillies, The 84, 116
Biafra, Jello 357
Bibb, Leon 163

Big Bopper, The 358
Big Brother And The Holding
   Company 302
Big In Iowa 315, 429
Bigsby, Paul 126
Bilk, Acker 162
Billy The Kid 33
Binkley Brother Dixie
   Clodhoppers, The 71
Birch, Will 400
Bird, Elmer 73
Bird, Louis 73
Black Mountain Boys, The 302
Black Shirts, The 100
Black, Bill 143, 218
Black, Clint 51, 232, 351, 373
Black, Mary 52-3
Blackstock, Peter 425
Blackwood Brothers, The 143, 146
Blade, Brian 279
Blake, Norman 345
Blake, William 185
Blaster, The 394
Blessing, Michael 318
Blood Oranges, The 166, 444
Bloodshot 124
Bloomfield, Michael 253
Blue Grass Boys, The 106-10, 241,
   247, 291
Blue Jug 350
Blue Mink 222
Blue Mountain 431
Blue Ridge Rangers, The 311
Blue Sky Boys, The 102, 151
Blue Southern Ramblers, The 308
Blue, David 195-6, 200, 281
Blues Project, The 196
Blur 17
Boeing Duveen And The Beautiful
   Soup 272
Boggs, Dock 78, 89, 94-8, 106,
   126, 130, 146, 160, 164, 170, 171,
   173, 182, 184, 202, 212, 243, 266,
   274, 287, 290, 310, 316, 332, 345,
   362, 372, 379, 381, 394, 421-2,
   440, 441
Boiled In Lead 166
Bolick, Bill and Earl 102
Bone, Ponty 368, 385
Bongos Over Balham 387
Bongwater 371
Bono 93
Bonzo Dog (Doo Dah) Band 124,
   157, 72, 317, 339
Booker T 221, 347, 356
Boone, Daniel 32
Boothill Foot-Tappers, The 391
Boquist, Dave 425, 437
Borges, Jorge Luis 31-2
Boswell, Eve 174
Bothy Band, The 291
Bottle Rockets, The 352, 425,
   429
Bourbon, Sophie 393
Bowden, Richard 367
Bowie, David 226
Bown, Alan (Set) 382
Boxcar Willie 222
Boyd, Joe 393

Boys Of The Lough 291
Boyzone 152
Bozulich, Carla 430
Bradley, Hank 298
Bradley, Lou 234
Bradley, Owen 128, 136, 414
Brady, Paul 52, 211, 408, 451
Bragg, Billy 173-4, 191, 426
Bragg, William 170
Brand, Oscar 164
Brando, Marlon 84, 200
Brasfield, Uncle Cyp 127-8
Bratland, Sondre 46
Brautigan, Richard 309
Bread And Cheese Hillbillies, The
   387
Bremnes, Kari 46
Brinsley Schwarz 383, 386
Broadway 41
Brogues, The 303
Bromberg, David 194, 211, 345
Bronson, Charles 37
Brooks, Garth 13, 19, 21, 43, 51,
   282, 372, 373, 402-3, 406, 410,
   420, 423
Brooks, Mel 300
Broonzy, Big Bill 164
Brown, Milton 122
Brown, Paula Jean 397
Brown, Rabbit 182
Brown, Tim 38
Brown, Tony 402
Browne, Jackson 290, 318, 325,
   339, 360, 372, 405
Bruce, Lenny 175
Brumley, Alfred 345
Bruntnell, Peter 437
Bryant, Boudleaux 128, 273-5
Bryant, Felice 128, 245, 273, 151
Bryant, Jimmy 125
Bubble Puppy 312
Buck Naked And The Bare
   Bottom Boys 423
Buck, Peter 394, 424
Buckeroos, The 230
Buckland, John 186
Buckley, Jeff 184
Buckley, Tim 264, 321, 445
Buckminster, Paul 331
Bucks, The 454
Buda, Max 319
Buffalo Springfield 202, 265, 313,
   314, 315, 340
Buffet, Jimmy 354, 372
Bull, Andy 43
Bull, Richie 387
Bull, Sandy 183, 178-9
Burdon, Eric 299, 378
Burgess, Steve 214, 215, 284, 286,
   350, 385
Burke, Kevin 46-3
Burnett, Dick 76-7
Burnett, T-Bone 369
Burns, Robert 64, 213, 394
Burr, Raymond 96
Burton, James 197, 201, 253, 268,
   277, 314
Busby's Bayou Boys 242
Busey, Gary 149

Bush, Roger 252, 253, 270, 284,
   304
Bush, Sam 165, 173, 278, 296, 342,
   447, 345-6
Butler, Wayne 205
Butterfield Blues Band, The 253
Butterfield, Paul 92, 253
Buttrey And McCoy 209, 361
Buttrey, Kenny 204-5, 213, 214,
   337, 370
Byrds, The 28, 37, 39, 100, 111,
   152-3, 176, 188, 191, 240, 251,
   252, 254-5, 258, 260-3, 265, 268-
   9, 271-2, 280, 282-4, 286, 288,
   290-1, 314, 317, 321, 324, 330,
   341-2, 361, 382, 398
Byrne, David 367

Caddle, Samuel 54
Cage, John 320
Cahill, Martin 53
Caldwell, Tommy 350
Cale, John 292, 343
Calexico 430
Call, John 327
Callaghan, Bill 435
Callahan Brothers, The 102
Calloway, Cab 316
Campbell, Glen 125, 153, 193, 222,
   234-5, 238, 260, 303-4
Campbell, Kate 415
Campbell, Olive 57, 58
Campbell, Pat 352
Canned Heat 178
Cantwell, Robert 81, 169, 170,
   188
Captain Beefheart 275, 366, 307-8
Carawan, Guy 162
Carlile, Kenneth 139, 380
Carlton, Gaither 85
Carpenter, Mary Chapin 93, 408,
   451
Carpenters, The 131
Carroll, Lewis 158, 272
Carson, "Fiddlin'" John 100-1
Carson, Ciaran 52, 56, 83, 112
Carson, Fiddlin' John 69-70
Carson, Kris 360
Carter Family, The 14, 24-5, 27, 65,
   79, 80-3, 90, 92, 98, 100, 102,
   104, 107-8, 110, 141, 145, 150,
   162-3, 168, 170, 178, 180, 184,
   186, 203, 206, 212, 216, 226, 243,
   245, 248, 279, 298, 299, 346, 347,
   368, 389, 405, 408, 414, 418, 424,
   438
Carter, Anita 82
Carter, AP 24, 66, 76, 79, 81, 82,
   92, 276, 278, 323
Carter, Carlene 80, 82, 136, 346,
   368, 388, 389
Carter, Helen 82
Carter, June 82, 225-7, 264
Carter, Maybelle 24, 79, 81-2, 103,
   108, 145, 163, 170, 222, 226, 341-
   2, 358, 389, 408
Carter, President James 375
Carter, Sara 24, 79, 81-2, 91, 389
Carthy, Eliza 165, 190, 245, 426

Carthy, Martin 53, 73, 82, 164, 174, 185, 190, 211, 245, 445
Cary, Caitlan 428
Casell, Chuck 271
Cash, Johnny 15, 19, 26, 33-6, 41, 80, 82, 84, 120, 129, 145-6, 151, 163, 164, 180, 187, 189, 198, 200, 205, 206, 209, 22-31, 238, 259, 286, 297-8, 305, 307, 322, 342, 346, 358, 360, 370, 375, 380, 388, 393, 413, 436, 439
Cash, Rosanne 372, 408-9
Cassidy, Neal 329
Castenada, Carlos 325
Cave, Nick 97, 165, 166, 177, 194, 414, 420, 421, 440
CBGBs 371-2
Cecil Sharp 243
Chad Mitchell Trio, The 28
Chadbourne, Eugene 344, 414
Chalker, Brian 379
Chapin, Harry 354
Chaplin, Charlie 182
Chaplin, Geraldine 38
Chapman, Roger 272
Chapman, Sam 100
Charlatans, The 169, 193, 284, 298, 303, 339, 348
Charles River Valley Boys 196
Charles, Ray 139-40, 256
Charter, Sam 86
Cheery, Hugh 65
Cherokee Cowboys, The 230
Chesnutt, Vic 434-5
Chevron, Phil 391
Cheyenne Mountain Dancers 30
Chickasaw Mud Puppies, The 399
Chieftains, The 213, 405, 440
Child 61-82, 84, 95, 181, 191, 194, 332, 334, 407
Childs, Rob 275
Chilli Willi 387, 388, 389
Chip, Yellowstone 113
Christgau, Robert 325, 344
Christian, Charlie 294
Chumbawamba 441
Ciambotti, Johnny 312
Cippolina, John 298, 303-4
Circus Maximus 361
Clampett, Jed 117
Clancy Brothers, The 158-60, 163, 334
Clancy, Liam 159
Clapton, Eric 91, 97, 141, 241, 266
Clark, Gene 251, 25-7, 286-8, 282-3, 285, 316, 320, 322, 325, 369, 380, 386-7, 400, 414
Clark, Guy 48, 362, 364-5, 405
Clark, Roy 236
Clarke, Michael 257, 268, 284, 287
Clash, The 154, 174, 221, 301, 368
Clayderman, Richard 126
Clayson, Alan 173
Clayton, Lee 355
Clayton, Paul 177, 185, 243
Clements, Vassar 110, 244, 333, 341-2, 345, 350

Clift, Montgomery 36
Clifton, Bill 243, 247, 250
Clinch Mountain Boys, The 112
Cline, Patsy 13, 127, 138, 271, 294, 319, 356, 414
Clinton, Bill 19, 248, 375
Clover 312, 386
Coal Porters, The 275, 400
Cochise 382
Cocker, Jarvis 165, 238
Coe, David Allan 13, 21, 23, 240, 354, 360-1
Cohen, Anne 75
Cohen, John 78, 84, 87, 101, 168, 169, 246, 329, 334
Cohen, Leonard 196-7, 228, 286, 351, 356, 360
Cohen, Mike 248
Cohen, Norm 75
Cohen, Nudie 173, 267, 275
Cohn, Nik 18, 128, 139
Cole, BJ 16, 367, 382-3, 390
Cole, Nat King 90
Coleman, Michael 156-7
Collie, DJ Bill 145
Collins, Judy 164, 192, 200, 255, 277, 365, 404, 190-1
Collins, Shirley 166-8, 202, 318
Collins, Vic 387
Collister, Christine 389
Colorblind James And The Death Valley Boys 395
Colorblind James Experience, The 395
Colter, Jessi 26, 355, 361
Coltrane, John 139, 293, 294, 301
Colum, Padraic 52
Colvin, Shawn 408
Colyer, Bill 173
Colyer, Ken 173
Commander Cody And His Lost Planet Airmen 348-9, 387
Confederate Mountaineers, The 242
Confederates, The 389
Connolly, Billy 28
Cooder, Ry 36, 39, 271, 321, 343, 374, 388
Cook, Roger 131, 222, 390
Cooke, Adrian 415
Cooley, "Spade" 124
Coolidge, Rita 336
Coombes, Ada 167
Coomer, Ken 425
Coon Creek Girls, The 102, 243, 246
Coon, Walter And His Joy Boys 71
Cooper, Fennimore 32
Copas, Cowboy 138, 230
Cope, Julian 344
Copperhead 304
Coppers, The 82
Corbitt, Jerry 308-9
Cordelia's Dad 441
Cornelius, Ron 197
Corrs, The 11, 418
Costello, Elvis 104, 138, 141, 166, 212, 234, 275, 276, 322, 374, 389

Cotten, Elizabeth 162, 170, 332
Cotton, Paul 316
Country Boys, The 254
Country Gazette, The 270, 284
Country Gentlemen, The 172, 242, 249, 317, 324
Country Joe And The Fish 214, 304-5
Cousins, Dave 379
Couza, Jim 453
Cow Pie 387
Cowboy 327
Cowboy Junkies, The 275, 333, 413
Cowboy Nation 395
Cox, Alex 391
Cox, Harry 243
Cox, Tom 420, 448
Crackers, The 39, 218
Craig, Cathryn 444
Cramer, Floyd 179, 195
Crazy Hickory Nuts, The 102
Crazy Horse 108, 337, 370
Crickets, The 148, 359, 383
Crockett, Davy 26, 114, 118
Crosby, Bing 104, 115, 123, 206, 233
Crosby, David 42, 180, 258, 265, 275, 287, 314, 336-7, 339, 404, 255-6
Crosby, Stills And Nash (And Young) 315, 329-30, 332, 336
Crow, Alvin (And The Pleasant Valley Boys) 350
Crow, Sheryl 275, 408
Crowe, JD 293
Crowell, Rodney 277, 279-80, 389, 408-9
Crowley, Aleister 165
Crudup, Arthur 259
Crumb, Robert 207
Crystal, Billy 31
Cumberland Mountain Entertainers, The 94
Cunha, Rick 324
Curtis, Ian 428
Cyrus, Billy Ray 282

D'Urberville Ramblers, The 453
Daley, Mick 54
Dalhert, Vernon 69, 76, 118
Dalton, Karen 193-4
Dalton, Lacy J 22-5, 141
Daly, Jackie 157
Dancing Hoods, The 433
Daniell, George 75
Daniels, Charlie 29, 30, 33, 133, 197, 350, 370
Danko, Rick 204, 218-20, 287
Danzig, Glen 229
Darin, Bobby 255
Darling, Eric 179, 191
Darlington, Andy 198
Darrow, Chris 259, 316, 318, 335, 340
Davey, Shaun 451
Davies, Ray 378
Davis, Jesse Ed 285
Davis, Jimmie 100

Davis, Miles 332
Davis, Sammy 219
Davis, Sammy Jr 230
Dawidoff, Nicholas 24, 79, 92, 102, 107, 136, 145, 150, 171, 172, 230, 232, 276, 280, 369, 404, 413, 225-6
Dawson, Dave 324
Dawson, John 328, 330
Dawson, Julian 151, 437
Day, Doris 42, 118, 290, 378
De Caro, Nick 288
De Danaan 47, 157, 158, 213, 440, 451
De Stael, Madame 50
Dean, James 272
Dear, Traci 436
Debussy, Claude 382
Delaney And Bonnie 266
Delaney, Clayton 236
Deliverance 12
Delmore Brothers, The 102, 142, 151, 244, 388
Delroy, Michael 440
Dement, Iris 46, 232, 347, 372, 405, 447, 348
Denny, Sandy 151, 189, 191, 192, 379, 380, 405
Denver, John 316, 370, 398
Denver, Karl 379
Depp, Johnny 228
Derailers, The 238, 420
Devlin, Barry 158
diCaprio, Leonardo 45
Dickens, Hazel 245-7, 279
Dickey, James 306
Dickinson, James Luther 254, 256, 372
Dickson, Roger 258
Diddley, Bo 303
Dietrich, Marlene 115
Dillard, Doug 249, 250, 251, 262, 283, 287, 316, 284
Dillard, Rodney 249
Dillards, The 249, 250-1, 263, 313-4, 321
Dillon, John 26
Dils, The 395
Dinosaur Jr 363
Dinosaurs, The 304
Dire Straits 388
Dire Straits 429
Dirt Band, The 342
Dirty Dozen Brass Band, The 395
Disney, Walt 52, 115, 227
Dixie Chicks, The 11-2, 124, 165, 323, 349, 415-6
Dixie Mountain Boys, The 243
Dixie Sacred Singers, The 99
Dixon, Willie 141
Docker Hill Boys, The 289
Doggett, Peter 23, 142-3, 234, 276, 307, 338, 400
Dolar, Packie 155
Dolby, Thomas 348
Dolphin Children, The 449
Dolphy, Eric 294
Domino, Anna 439-40

Donahue, Jonathan 433
Donegan, Lonnie 32, 173-4, 224
Donovan 185, 193, 324
Doors, The 191, 305, 421
Dorsey Orchestra, The 124
Douglas, Jerry 47, 447, 451
Douglass, Greg 296
Down Homers, The 142
Downing, David 314
Downliners Sect, The 377
Dozier, Holland 193
Drake, Guy 240
Drake, Nick 178, 362
Drake, Peter 205, 376
Dream Syndicate, The 396, 399
Drifting Cowboys, The 130, 134
Driftwood, Jimmy 174, 216, 224, 229
Drummond, Bill 353
Dry City Scat Band, The 317
Dryden, Spencer 333
Du Noyer, Paul 23-4, 131
Dubliners, The 436
Dudley, Dave 240, 121-2
Duffey 249
Duffy, John 242
Dukes, The 445
Dun, Aidan 65
Duncan, Gary 303
Duncan, Tommy 123-4
Dunford, Uncle Eck 71-2
Dunlop, Ian 271
Duolian String Pickers, The 388
Durante, Mark 436
Dury, Ian 348, 382
Dvorak, Antonin 56
Dylan, Bob 22, 25, 26, 36, 39, 59, 76, 78, 86, 87-8, 91, 93, 96, 102-3, 105-8, 110, 129, 141, 144, 146, 159, 161-6, 169, 17-5, 182-90, 192, 194, 196-8, 199, 203-5, 207-15, 220, 222, 225-6, 229, 232, 242, 243, 245, 248, 250, 253-5, 257, 259-60, 264, 274, 278-82, 285, 287, 290-1, 296-7, 306, 321, 329, 331-2, 335, 346, 350, 358, 360, 364, 369, 370-1, 401

Eagles, The 268, 273, 317, 322, 324-8, 335, 340, 350, 361, 427
Earle, Stacey 445
Earle, Steve 13, 17, 93, 104, 134, 225, 273, 278, 280, 347, 360, 364-5, 368, 418, 428, 445-7
Earp, Wyatt 32
Earth Opera 291, 294
Eastwood, Clint 36, 38, 130
Eclection 202
Eco, Umberto 71
Edcock, Eddie 242
Edwards, David Eugene 430
Edwards, Ethan 34, 154
Eggs Over Easy 386
Eitzel, Mark 414
Electric Flag, The 297
Eleventh Day Dream 443
Elgar, Edward 56, 172
Eliot, Marc 200

Ellington, Duke 259, 332
Ellington, Marc 380
Elliot, Ron 153, 309
Elliott, Rambling Jack 162, 164, 182-3, 201, 254, 281, 360
Ellis, Don (Orchestra) 111
Ely, Joe 148, 149, 232, 367-9, 385, 415
Emery, Ralph 264
England, John 57
English Folk Song Society, The 56-7, 60
Eno, Brian 36
Enya 449
Epp, Fenrus 317
Epstein, Brian 243
Erickson, Roky 312-3, 363
Erwin, Randy 367
Escott, Colin 27-8, 130-2
Escoveda, Alejandro 124, 207, 395, 428
Etheridge, Chris 197, 269-70, 284, 289
Evans, Dale 115
Evans, Rusty 181
Even Dozen, The 180
Everly Brothers, The 52, 54, 104, 151-3, 187, 198, 214, 235, 260, 271, 328, 346-7, 404
Everly, Ike 104, 126, 151

Fahey, John 164-6, 177-9, 382, 411, 421
Faier, Billy 248
Fairport 166, 191, 203, 207, 260, 283, 380, 444
Fairport Convention 189, 202, 220, 270, 318, 380
Faith And Disease 227
Fallen Angels, The 266, 270, 273
Family 272
Fansworth, Nancy 339
Fantastic Expedition, The 251, 283, 284
Fantastic Surfing Beavers, The 349
Farina, Mimi 237
Farina, Richard 196, 381
Farrar, Jay 307, 424-6
Faust, Luke 177, 182
Felder, Don 326
Feldthouse, Solomon 317
Feliciano, Jose 320
Feller, Sid 139
Fells, Barry 450
Fender, Freddie 240
Fender, Leo 127
Ferry, Bryan 165
Fesperman, Dan 19
Fields, WC 115
Filson, John 27
Fisher, Robert 432-3
Flamin' Groovies, The 312
Flanagan Brothers, The 155, 157, 160
Flatlanders, The 367-8, 433
Flatt And Scruggs 163, 206, 244, 247-9, 254, 367
Flatt, Lester 104, 106-11, 230, 244

Fleck, Bela 337, 342, 404, 410-1, 451
Fletcher, Curley 113
Flip City 389
Flippo, Chet 130, 357
Fludd, Robert 165
Flying Burrito Brothers, The 253, 259, 263, 265-71, 279, 284, 289, 321, 325, 361, 389
Flynn, Errol 326
Fogelberg, Dan 372-3
Fogerty, John 231, 270, 311
Foggy Mountain Boys, The 107
Foley, Red 127-8, 131, 143, 221, 402
Folsom, Lowell 128
Fonda, Henry 37
Fonda, Peter 37, 259
Fong-Torres, Ben 266, 268, 273
Fontana, DJ 144
Forbert, Steve 372
Ford, Henry 75, 98
Ford, Jim 238
Ford, John 33, 35, 119, 201, 256, 294
Formby, George 91
Foster, Stephen 85, 335
Fowley, Kim 289
Fox, James 268
Foxworthy, Jeff 18-9
Frame, Pete 270, 303, 321, 340
Frank, Jackson C 203
Franklin, Aretha 141
Franklin, Benjamin 26
Frayne, George 349
Frazer, Paula 430
Frazier, Charles 55
Freakwater 97, 442-3
Free 351
Freeny's Barn Dance Band 71
Freiburg, David 256, 299
Freidman, Kinky 240, 281, 402
French, Philip 32
Frey, Glenn 268, 322, 324-6, 373
Fricke, David 347
Frightwigs 430
Fritts, Donnie 141
Frizzel, Lefty 93
Fromholz, Steve 361
Frosties, The 399
Fruit Jar Drinkers, The 99
Fugs, The 174-5, 371, 438
Fulks, Robbie 124, 430, 436
Fuller, Blind Boy 41
Fuller, Craig 327, 343
Furay, Richie 265, 273, 314-6
Furry Freak Brothers, The 313
Fyrebyrds, The 287

Gable, Clark 36
Gaines, Steve 351
Gallagher, Mickey 368
Gallup, Cliff 148
Garbutt, Vin 250-1
Garcia, Jerry 212, 252-4, 293, 294, 299-302, 328-30, 332-4, 336
Garfunkel, Art 203
Garing, Greg 440
Garland, Hamlin 33

Garrett, Patrick 33
Garris, Mike 334
Garry, Mac 317
Gaughan, Dick 73, 452-3
Gavin, Frankie 47, 156-7
Gayden, Mac 214-5, 217
Gaye, Marvin 23
Geffen, David 196, 286, 325, 338
Gelb, Howe 199, 397-8
Geldof, Bob 51
Gentry, Bobby 235-6
George, Boy 21
George, Lowell 292, 343-4
Georgia Wildcats, The 77
Geraldine Fibbers, The 429-30
Gerrard, Alice 246, 279
Giant Sand 199, 217, 430
Gibson, Bob 200
Gibson, Clifford 92
Gibson, Don 136-9, 276, 337, 392
Gill, Andy 383
Gill, Vince 11, 12, 14, 232, 280, 327, 360, 373, 419
Gillespie, Bobby 238
Gilley, Mickey 88
Gilliland, Henry 69
Gilmore, Jimmie Dale 124, 172, 294, 367-70
Gilmore, Mikal 131, 301, 329, 404
Gimble, Johnny 123, 365
Ginsberg, Allen 281
Glackin, Paddy 53
Gladden, Texas 168
Glaser Brothers, The 119
Glaser, Tompall 260, 355
Gleason, Ralph J 299, 328
Globe Propaganda 303
Glover, Jim 200
Gentry, Bobbie 206
Golden Smog 426
Golden State Boys, The 254, 282
Golliwogs, The 311
Gomez 328, 437
Good Sons, The 364
Goodman, David 423, 427-30, 432
Goodman, Steve 347, 360, 372
Goose Creek Symphony 328
Gorky's Zygotic Mynci 438
Gosdin Brothers, The 264
Gosdin, Rex 254, 283
Gosdin, Vern 254, 283
Grabham, Mick 382
Graham, Bill 214, 320
Graham, Davey 202
Grainger, Percy 57
Grant, Marshall 225
Grant, Peter 328
Grateful Dead, The 77, 90, 153, 166, 207, 231, 247, 252, 293, 299-302, 328-35, 369
Graves, Buck 110-1
Graves, Robert 175
Graves, Uncle "Josh" 110
Gray, Otto 122
Gray, Tom 242
Grech, Rick 272-3
Green On Red 396
Green, Al 130

Green, Archie 75, 103
Green, Roy 370
Greenbaum, Norman 180
Greenbriar Boys, The 171, 173, 188-9, 321
Greene, Herb 298
Greene, Jessy 428
Greene, Richard 241, 286, 291, 346
Greenhalgh, Tom 392
Greer, Dolly 85
Greer, Sophronie 85
Gregson, Clive 381, 389
Greyhound 318
Grieg, Charlotte 406, 409
Grieg, Edvard 56
Grier, David 106
Griffin, Sid 255, 275, 399-401, 448
Griffith, Mark 152
Griffith, Nanci 21, 43, 163, 194, 380, 404, 406, 279-80
Grisman, David 157, 246, 291-4, 323, 333-4, 444
Grossman, Albert 255
Guilbeau, Gib 253, 270, 288
Gunning, Sarah 103
Guralnick, Peter 163
Guthrie, Arlo 47, 197, 324
Guthrie, Woody 20, 44, 48, 82, 103, 109, 131, 160-3, 169, 173, 175, 182-3, 186, 194, 200-1, 209, 232, 254, 264, 281, 304, 405, 426, 432, 298-9

Haggard, Merle 40, 93-4, 115, 124-5, 153, 201, 223, 231-4, 240, 244, 259-61, 271, 273, 280, 286, 301-2, 306, 308, 310-11, 349, 351, 360, 363, 374-5, 405, 429
Haley, Alex 45
Haley, Bill 142-3, 166
Hall, Rick 141
Hall, Stuart 153-5, 167, 170-1
Hall, Tom T 236-7, 245, 375
Halley, David 367
Hamill, Peter 421
Hamilton IV, George 88, 376-7
Hammon, Maggie 47
Hammond, Lawrence 186, 308-9
Hancock, Butch 367, 369
Hancock, Wayne 135, 441
Handcox, John 103
Handsome Family, The 20, 97, 271, 443
Haney, Carlton 247
Hanna, Jeff 339, 342
Hardin, Andrew 46
Hardin, Glen D 277
Hardin, John Wesley 32, 197-8
Hardin, Tim 180, 197-8, 251, 262, 310, 324, 445
Harding, Mike 113, 115, 384
Harper, Roy 209, 297
Harris, Bob 13, 135, 213, 221, 385
Harris, Doctor John 214
Harris, Emmylou 28, 33, 52-3, 65, 86, 130, 163, 188, 220, 232, 261, 270-1, 273-5, 276-80, 297, 319,

322-3, 339, 342-3, 347, 354, 363, 365, 372-3, 375, 383, 404
Harrison, George 376
Hart Valley Drifters, The 302
Hart, Mickey 330
Hartford, John 109, 345, 444
Harvey, PJ 430
Haskell, Jimmie 235
Hatfield, Dave 388
Hawkins, Hawkshaw 138
Hawkins, Ronnie 204, 218
Hawks And Doves 338
Hawks, The 39, 204
Hawkwind 14
Haworth, Speedy 127
Hay, George D 98, 127
Hayes, Dennis 53
Hayes, Martin 177
Hayes, Red 222
Hays, Lee 161
Haywood, Eric 437
Hazledene 430
Hazlewood, Lee 237-8, 260, 266, 399
Heads, Hands And Feet 383
Hearts And Flowers 323-4
Heckle, "Texas" Bob 118
Heidorn, Mike 424
Hell, Richard 221
Helm, Levon 33, 204, 206-7, 217-21, 433
Help Yourself 304, 320, 383-4
Helstrom, Echo 186
Henderson, Dave 250
Henderson, Dorris 201-2, 317
Hendrix, Jimi 106, 271, 299, 377, 445
Henley, Don 322, 324
Henneman, Brian 429
Henry, Bart 253
Henry, Joe 237
Henry, John 46, 225
Henske, Judy 192
Hentoff, Nat 188
Heron, Mike 449-50
Hersh, Kristin 421
Hester, Carolyn 192
Heylin, Clinton 52, 186-7, 206-9
Hiatt, John 342, 373-4
Hickock, "Wild" Bill 33
Hickory Wind 381
Hicks, Dan 348, 298
Hicks, Ray 82-3
Hiedorn, Mike 425
Highwaymen, The 359
Hill, Billy 116
Hill, Don 83
Hill, Faith 418-9
Hill, Joe 160-1
Hill, Joel Scott 289
Hill, Walter 343
Hillbilly Lovechild 435
Hillman, Chris 254, 257-8, 261, 264-5, 268-9, 271, 273, 276, 282-3, 373
Hillmen, The 254
Hillsiders, The 376-7
Hinton, Christine 336
Hinton, Eddie 101, 141

Hinton, Sam 166, 255
Hirschy, Gerri 140
Hitchcock, Alfred 203
Hitchcock, Robyn 307
Hitler, Adolf 449
Hix, The 440-1
Hodges, Warner 393
Hofner, Adolph 125, 313
Hogg, Brian 179
Holcomb, Roscoe 78, 87, 173, 186, 206, 421
Holland, Jools 11
Holly, Buddy 148-9, 201, 340, 358-9, 365, 368
Holmes, Oliver Wendell 32
Holy Modal Rounders, The 37, 174-6, 344, 371, 411
Holzman, Jac 191
Homeland Harmony Quartet, The 142
Homer 55
Hope, Bob 31
Hopkins, Al 74-585
Hopkins, Lightnin' 332
Hopper, Dennis 37, 360
Hornby, Nick 42
Horovitz, Mike 174
Horseflies, The 170, 440
Horslips, The 158
Horstman, Dorothy 20
Horton, Johnny 117, 224
Hoskyns, Barney 101, 140-1, 227, 229, 259, 267-8, 274, 323
Hot Band, The 277-8, 280, 409
Hot Burrito Review, The 270
Hot Club Of Cowtown, The 441
Hot Licks, The 348
Houston, Cisco 161
Houston, Whitney 322
Howard, Harlan 239
Howling Wolf 91
Hubbard, Ray Wylie 208, 218, 220-1, 223, 328, 370, 433
Hughes, Ted 271
Hughey, John 350
Humble Pie 378
Humblebums, The 28
Humperdinck, Engelbert 134
Humphries, Barry 144
Hunt, Ken 167, 332, 334
Hunter, George 298, 303
Hunter, Robert 300, 302, 328-32, 366
Huntley, Gordon 380
Hurley, Michael 93, 287, 344-5, 441
Hurt, "Mississippi" John 89, 100
Huskey, Kenni 231
Huskey, Roy 446
Huskey, Roy Jr 342
Hutchings, Ashley 202, 220, 262, 380
Hutt, Dr Sam 277, 386
Hyde, Karl 164
Hynde, Chrissie 275

Ian And Sylvia 120, 183, 206, 380
Ibbotson, Jim 340, 342
Ibsen, Henrik 264

Incredible String Band, The 174, 268, 449-50
Indestructible Old-Timey String Band, The 317
Insect Trust, The 182
International Submarine Band, The 259, 271, 297
Into The Purple Valley 343
Irish Ramblers, The 255
Irwin, Catherine 442-3
Ives, Burl 161-2

J Geils Band, The 271
J-Band, The 180
Jackson, Alan 12, 232, 402
Jackson, Andrew 103
Jackson, David 284
Jackson, Ronnie 230
Jacobsen, Erik 180
Jagger, Mick 162, 224, 268, 377
James, Frank 33
James, Jesse 33, 42, 312, 324
James, Skip 177
Jan And Dean 193
Jankel, Chas 382
Jansch, Bert 166, 189
Jason Rindenberg (And The Scorchers) 131, 393, 395
Jayhawks, The 425, 427
Jayne, Mitch 249-51
Jefferson Airplane 45, 199, 299, 303, 330
Jefferson, Thomas 67-8
Jenkins, Snuffy 108, 247
Jennings, Waylon 26, 148, 198, 338, 349, 355, 357-9, 360-1, 397
Jet Set, The 254
Jewel 234
Jimenez, Flaco 294
John, Elton 318, 377-8, 417
Johnson, Blind Willie 177
Johnson, Jeff 393
Johnson, Matt 132
Johnson, Robert 68, 94, 130, 166
Johnston, Bob 197, 205
Johnston, Max 425
Jolene 428
Jones, "Prince" Brian 299
Jones, Allan 421
Jones, Coley 41, 165
Jones, George 13, 19, 23, 26, 80, 129, 133-4, 141, 193, 230, 247, 266-7, 271-3, 275, 311, 347, 353, 375, 377, 389, 407, 413, 419
Jones, Glenn 177
Jones, Grandpa 175
Jones, Louis 78
Jones, Nic 211
Jones, Sam 100
Jones, Spike 124, 166
Jones, Tim 416
Joplin, Janis 22, 141, 195, 198, 361
Jordanaires, The 109
Jovanovic, Rob 438
Judd, Wynona 351
Judds, The 14
Juice On The Loose 453

Kahn, John 333
Kaleidoscope 259, 316, 318
Kane, Michael 310-1
Kane, Nick 419
Kantner, Paul 199, 256
Karnes, Alfred 72
Karpeles, Maud 57-60, 167
Kaufman, Phil 274-5
Kaukonen, Jorma 299
Kavana, Ron 154-5, 453-4
Kaye, Lenny 414
Kaye, Thomas Jefferson 285, 287
Kazee, Buell 78, 164-5
Kean, John 424
Keane, Dolores 46, 53, 347, 405
Keane, John 435, 93
Keillor, Garrison 87, 136
Keith, Ben 337-8
Keith, Bill 241, 291-2
Kelley, Kevin 262
Keltner, Jim 374
Kennedy, Bap 132
Kennedy, John F 158, 176, 193, 200
Kennedy, Nigel 377
Kennerley, Paul 26, 33, 78
Kenny, Sean 385
Kentucky Colonels, The 252-4, 270, 291, 301, 304, 312
Kentucky Mountain Boys, The 254
Kentucky Pardners, The 106
Kentucky Ramblers, The 73
Kerouac, Jack 281
Kerridge, Roy 43-50
Kershaw, Andy 13, 135, 211, 238-9, 355, 366-7, 406, 443
Kershaw, Doug 222, 235, 240, 317
Kesey, Ken 289
Ketchum, Hal 248, 413, 451
Kettle, Martin 82
Killbilly 429
Kimmell, John 157-8
Kincaid, Bradley 77-8, 117, 152
King Harvest 220
King, Clydie 285
King, Pee Wee 128
King, Reg (And The Action) 215
King, Stephen 206
Kingston Trio, The 163, 237, 370
Kinman, Chip and Tony 395
Kipling, Rudyard 203
Kirby, Robert 33
Kirkwood, Curt and Chris 395
Kiss Switch 227
Kitt, Eartha 41, 192
KLF, The 353
Knight, Cheri 444
Knopfler, David 395
Knopfler, Mark 360, 388, 395, 415
Koerner, "Spider" John 179
Konikoff, Sandy 204
Kooper, Al 204-5, 351, 396
Korner, Alexis 173, 243
Kraemer, Pete 299
Krauss, Alison 12, 172, 323, 360, 409, 410, 447
Kristofferson, Kris 20-1, 115, 210,

228, 230-1, 237, 240, 346, 359-60, 372, 378
Kursaal Flyers, The 387
Kweskin, Jim 183
Kyser, Guy 398-9

LaFarge, Peter 41, 226
Laine, Frankie 118
Lambchop 419-20, 434-5, 439
Lambert, Curley 109
Lambert, Kit 243
Landsborough, Charlie 385
Landy, Elliott 221
Lane, Robin 315
lang, kd 42, 348, 414
Lange, Robert John "Mutt" 416-8
Langford, "Johnny Boy" 392
Langford, Jon 124, 435
Langhorne, Bruce 159, 189, 192
Lanois, Daniel 278, 357
Lash Lariat And The Long Riders 391
Last Real Texas Blues Band, The 313
Laughner, Peter 426
Laurel And Hardy 31, 71, 115
LaVey, Anton 326
Lawrence, Stephen 17
Lawson, Doyle 249
Laydon, John 55
Leadbelly 161, 173, 254, 265, 400, 432
Leadon, Bernie 26, 259, 263, 265, 269, 283, 316, 322, 324-6
LeBlanc, Leo 346
Led Zeppelin 144, 174, 189, 202, 291, 378
Ledford, Lily May 102
Lee Valley String Band, The 54
Lee, Albert 33, 152, 289, 383
Lee, Arthur 305
Lee, Brenda 221
Legends, The 258
Leisner, Tony 30
Leisz, Greg 439
Lennon, John 39, 144, 251, 297
Leonard, Deke (Iceberg) 320
Leone, Sergio 36-7, 267
Lesh, Phil 301
Leven, Jakie 421
Levinger, Lowell (Banana) 309
Levy, Jacques 264, 280
Lewis and Clark 26
Lewis, "Pops" 245
Lewis, Furry 100
Lewis, Jerry Lee 21, 88, 133, 146-8, 152, 285, 319, 357
Lewis, Peter 305
Light Crust Doughboys, The 122
Lightfoot, Gordon 209
Lilly, Everett and Mitchell, "Bea" 241
Limelighters, The 255
Lincoln, Abraham 103
Linde, Dennis 214, 217
Lindley, David 316-8, 323-3, 339
Linkous, Mark 433-4
Lipscomb, Mance 88, 101
Lithman, Phil 387

Little Feat 216, 343, 366
Little Richard 147, 175, 186
Little Village 374
Lloyd, AL 162, 174, 334
Lloyd, Dorothy 30
Lloyd, Richard 370
Lloyd-Weber, Andrew 47, 264
Locklin, Gerald 21, 45
Logan, Tex 296
Lomax III, John 274
Lomax, Alan 72-3, 83, 90, 103, 108, 166-8, 181, 184, 203, 212-3, 228, 243
Lomax, John 103, 113, 228, 113
Lone Justice 399
Lonesome Pine Fiddlers, The 245
Long Ryders, The 287, 303, 399-400
Lost City Ramblers, The 212, 308
Lost Dogs, The 347
Lost Gonzo Band, The 361
Loudermilk, John D 141, 235, 239, 322
Louris, Gary 425, 427-8
Louvin Brothers, The 145, 149-52, 244, 273-4, 276, 282, 388, 432
Love 191
Love Affair 217
Love, Larry 15
Love, Reverend Wayne 16
Loveless, Patty 447
Lovett, Lyle 333, 368
Lovin' Spoonful, The 180
Lowe, Nick 135, 228-9, 272, 374, 386-9
Lunsford, Bascar 72, 248
Lydon, John 55
Lynn, Loretta 19, 21, 38, 220, 239, 374, 375, 401, 406
Lynne, Shelby 407, 409, 437
Lynyrd Skynyrd 351-2, 425

MacColl, Ewan 166, 191, 334, 377
MacColl, Kirsty 390
MacGowan, Shane 390-1
Mack, Leroy 252
MacKenzie, Scott 299
Maclean, Dougie 415
Macon, "Uncle" Dave 98-9, 40, 96, 168, 176, 249
Macon, Dorris 98
MacPherson, Bill 40
Mad River 308
Maddox Brothers And Rose, The 230, 304
Magaha, Mack 173
Magee, Harvey 215
Maguire, Barry 171
Maguire, John 61
Maguire, Leo 157
Mainer's Mountaineers 102-3, 109
Maines, Natalie 415
Makem, Sara 64-5
Maken, Tommy 156-60
Male, Andrew 442
Malone, Bill C 65-6, 68-9, 74-8, 102-3, 111, 114, 122, 125, 127-8, 135-6, 138, 141, 160, 223, 226, 230, 239-43, 248, 351, 374-6, 421

Malone, Red 127
Maloney, Mick 156
Maloney, Paddy 53
Man 304
Mandrell, Barbara 375
Mangurian, David 83
Manners, Zeke 116
Manness, Jay Dee 259
Mansfield, Brian 279
Mansfield, David 281
Manson, Charles 37, 286, 290, 297, 359, 360
Manson, The Reverend Charles 56
Manuel, Richard 220, 218-9, 287, 392-3
Marcus, Greil 94, 97, 145, 165, 166, 205, 205, 306, 393, 433, 441
Marks, Larry 200
Marley, Bob 355
Marriott, Steve 378
Marsalis, Branford 411
Marsh, Dave 206
Marshall Tucker Band, The 350
Martin, Dean 145, 229
Martin, Dewey 314
Martin, Grady 111, 148, 249, 293, 305, 310, 440
Martin, Steve 339
Martindale, Wink 63
Marvin, Lee 113, 307, 391
Marx Brothers, The 31
Marx, Groucho 115
Marx, Karl 103
Mason Proffit 328
Massive Attack 15
Mattacks, Dave 381
Mattea, Kathy 47, 134, 415
Matthews' Southern Comfort 152, 380
Matthews, Iain 272, 380-1
Mavericks, The 11, 275, 351, 369, 419
Mayall, Gaz 14
Mayall, John 14
McAuliff, Leon (And His Cimarron Boys) 138
McBryde, Martina 12
McCarthy, Cormac 433
McCartney, Paul 251, 297
McClinton, Delbert 276
McCormick, John 157
McCoury, Del 47, 134, 166, 172, 293, 334, 446-7
McCoy, Charlie 205, 370
McCrumb, Sharyn 40, 56, 182, 415
McDill, Bob 223
McDonagh, Johnny "Ringo" 157
McDonald, "Country" Joe 299, 304
McDowell, Mississippi Fred 17
McEuen, John 339-42, 361
McEuen, William 340-2
McFee, John 312
McGarrigle Sisters 85-6, 279, 371-2
McGhee, Brownie 101
McGhee, Sean 392
McGhee, Wes 385
McGuinn, Jim 191, 256-65, 280-1
McGuinn, Roger 291, 400, 426

McIntyre, Reba 11, 13, 418
McLaren, Malcolm 99, 390
McLaughlin, John 290
McLean, Don 196
McLean, Duncan 124
McLoughlin, Eamon 370
McReynolds Brothers 244, 249
McTell, Blind Willie 101
McTell, Ralph 336
Meagher, Thomas 51
Meat Puppets, The 313, 395
Meek, Joe 116, 162
Meeks, Gus 62
Meisner, Randy 322, 325, 335
Mekons, The 124, 179, 384, 392-3, 435
Melcher, Terry 271, 290-1
Melton, Barry 298
Meltzer, David 311
Mercer, Johnny 115, 348
Merchant, Natalie 405, 426
Mercury Rev 433
Mercy, Miss 268
Messina, Terri 287
Meyers, Augie 313
Michelle Shocked 172, 414, 438
Mighty Baby 215, 284, 383, 387, 453
Miller, Buddy 276
Miller, Glenn (Orchestra) 124
Miller, Jerry 305
Miller, Rhett 429
Miller, Roger 76, 139, 171, 230, 357
Mills, Mike 132
Mingus, Charlie 16
Minogue, Kylie 420
Mississippi Sheiks, The 100
Misunderstood, The 303-4
Mitchell, Chad 255
Mitchell, Joni 120, 194, 273, 281, 290, 321, 341, 398
Mitchum, Robert 16
Moby 437-8
Moby Grape 305-6
Mojave 3, The 437
Molly, Aunt 103
Moloney, Paddy 334
Monkees, The 257, 318, 320-1, 370
Monroe Band, The 293
Monroe Brothers, The 48, 102, 151, 95, 99, 104-6, 108-10, 112-3, 123, 131, 144-5, 153, 161, 165-6, 172, 176, 213, 236, 241, 245-6, 248, 278, 280, 283, 291-3, 297, 320, 323, 347, 358, 371, 375, 393, 410-2, 440, 446
Monroe, Charlie 332
Monroe, Marilyn 36
Montana, Patsy 42, 116
Montgomery, Bob 148
Moody, Dwight 67
Moore, R Stevie 371
Moore, Scotty 143-4, 218
Morricone, Ennio 36
Morris Brothers, The 247
Morris, Vivian 384
Morrison, Jim 300, 305
Morrison, Van 49, 83, 93, 106, 195, 198, 221, 362, 373, 378, 384, 449

Morriss Boys String Band, The 379, 388
Morrissey 288
Morse, Ella Mae 89, 90
Morthland, John 354
Morton, Tex 114
Moseley, Bob 306
Moss, Wayne 205, 213, 215-7, 309, 349
Mothers, Of Invention, The 317
Mould, Bob 363
Mounce, John 84
Mountain City Four, The 372
Mountain Line 382
MTV 43
Muldaur, Geoff 421
Muldaur, Maria 293, 372
Muleskinner 291, 293
Mullican, Moon 349
Munde, Alan 272
Mungo Jerry 16
Munich Mountaineers, The 222
Munny, William 36
Murphey, Michael 110, 119, 166, 361
Murphy, Dan 426-7
Murphy, Pat 157
Murray, Larry 324

N-Sync 13
Nail, Jimmy 43, 390
Naked Prey 397
Nash Ramblers, The 278
Nash, Graham 316, 336
Nashville Brass, The 354
Nashville Grass 110
Nashville Teens, The 141, 147
Nashville Washboard Band, The 90
Nashville West 253, 263
Natchez Trace 387
Neil, Fred 182, 191, 193-4, 199, 310, 321
Nelson, David 302, 328, 330
Nelson, Ricky 149, 259
Nelson, Tracey 373
Nelson, Willie 11, 23, 32, 36, 41, 138, 230, 232, 234, 239, 297, 312, 338, 349, 355-7, 361, 372, 375, 385, 428
Nelson, Willy 120
Nesmith, Michael 93, 110, 318-21, 340, 387
Neuwirth, Bob 198-9, 281
New Christie Minstrels, The 163, 256
New City Ramblers, The 346
New Grass Revival 410
New Kentucky Colonels, The 253
New Lost City Ramblers, The 165, 169, 173, 175, 254, 298, 325, 329, 331, 381, 451
New Riders Of The Purple Sage, The 289, 293, 302, 332-3, 381
New Union Ramblers, The 321
Newbury, Mickey 354, 193
Newman, Randy 39, 40, 153, 220, 321, 372, 378
Newton-John, Olivia 375

Nicol, Simon 380
Nitty Gritty Dirt Band, The 111, 339-40, 342, 350
Nitzsche, Jack 315
Nix, Hoyle And His Cowboy Band 125-6
Nixon, Mojo 432
Nolan, Bob 116
Norman, Philip 377
Notkoff, Bobby 194, 315
Notting Hillbillies, The 388
Nuns, The 428
Nyro, Laura 236

O'Brien, Tim 46-8, 52, 412, 451
O'Byrne, Ellen 155
O'Connell, Daniel 51, 454
O'Connell, Maura 157, 405, 451-2
O'Connor, Charles 158
O'Connor, Joseph 51-2, 54, 56, 66, 88, 157-8
O'Connor, Mark 53, 172, 293, 404, 451
O'Connor, Nuala 48
O'Flynn, Liam 54
O'Hagan, Sean 275
O'Hara, Mary Margaret 165
O'Hara, Maureen 35
O'Keefe, Danny 47
O'Neill, Captain Francis J 156
O'Suillebhain, Michael 49
Oak Ridge Boys, The 88, 354
Oasis 17
Ochs, Phil 76, 183, 191, 199-201, 232, 281, 371
Odetta 160, 194, 255
Oklahoma Cowboys, The 122
Old And In The Way 333-4
Old Joe Clarks, The 431
Oldham, Spooner 140
Oldham, Will 35-6, 435, 441-2
Oliver, Paul 101, 166
Olivia Tremor Control, The 434
Olsen, Mark 237, 276, 408, 427
Orbison, Roy 148, 369
Orton, Beth 165
Osborne Brothers, The 244-5, 249, 316
Osborne, Sonny 245
Otis, Johnny 291
Outlaws, The 355, 327-8
Owens, Buck 125, 222, 230-1, 259, 262, 268, 282, 329-30, 377
Oysterband, The 448

Padel, Ruth 80-2, 101, 134, 168, 194
Page, Jimmy 174, 189
Page, Patti 128
Page, Sid 348
Paisley Underground, The 396
Palance, Jack 31
Paley, Tom 168-9, 174, 177, 212, 250, 381, 451
Palmer, Bruce 314
Palmer, Clive 449, 451
Panhandle Mystery Band, The 367
Pankake, Jon 87, 94, 166

Pankake, Marcia 87
Pardon, Walter 243
Parker, Charlie 253
Parks, Van Dyke 165, 201, 238, 420
Parmley, Don 254
Parnes, Larry 360
Parrish, John 430
Parsons, Gene 39, 253, 263, 265, 266, 288, 289
Parsons, Gram 21, 77, 100, 150, 231, 240, 258-78, 280, 285-6, 297, 318, 320, 321, 363, 365, 377, 380, 383, 385, 389, 400, 422, 428, 448
Parton, Dolly 11-13, 19, 105, 129, 173, 192, 232, 247, 276, 279, 322-3, 353-4, 376, 396, 447-8
Patton, Charlie 178
Paul, Les 139
Paxton, Tom 182, 191
Paycheck, Johnny 21
Payne, Leon 138, 145, 214, 389
Payne, Rufus "Tee-Tot" 129-30
Peabody, Dave 437
Pearl, Minnie 220, 374
Peckinpah, Sam 14, 326
Pederson, Herb 251, 282
Peel, John 148, 297, 303, 380
Peer, Ralph 69, 70, 74-5, 79, 81, 91, 102, 102
Penn, Dan 140
Pentangle 202, 264, 331, 166
Pere Ubu 421, 426
Perkins, Al 270, 282, 315
Perkins, Carl 145-6, 148, 225
Perkins, Luther 225
Pet Shop Boys 385
Pete, Blind 90
Pete, Sneaky 269-70, 284
Peter And Gordon 256
Peter, Paul And Mary 28, 164
Peters, Gretchen 415
Peters, Stephen 331
Petty, Norman 148
Petty, Tom (And The Heartbreakers) 229, 281, 352
Peyote Cowboys 429
Phillips, Arthur 379
Phillips, John 255
Phillips, Michelle 255
Phillips, Sam 143, 218
Phillips, Steve 388
Phillips, Tom 328
Phipps, Ernest 72-3
Phish 434
Pickens, JP 311
Pickett, Bobby "Boris" 275
Pierce, Webb 275
Pigpen 300-1, 328
Pike County Boys, The 246
Pine Valley Boys, The 282
Pine Valley Cosmonauts, The 227
Pitney, Gene 273, 399
Place, Jeff 166
Plane, Dave 379
Plant, Robert 307
Planxty 47, 291, 440

Plastic Ono Band, The 290
Plath, Sylvia 271, 352
Platt, John 308
Poco 315, 324-5, 330
Pogues, The 390-1, 445, 453
Poole, Charlie 85, 77, 106, 168, 172, 175
Pooley, Eric 301, 332
Porter, Cole 85, 115, 372
Portishead 15
Poss, Barry 282
Power, Fiddlin Cowan And Family 72
Powers, Chet 302, 310
Presley, Elvis 43, 88, 90, 106, 112, 127, 129-30, 141, 143-6, 201, 210, 218, 224, 226, 233, 239, 259, 263, 266, 284, 297, 309, 319, 334, 358,
Pretty Things, The 392
Price, Maryann 348
Price, Ray 230, 356
Price, Stephen 241
Pride, Charley 38, 41, 90, 101, 237, 360
Primal Scream 238, 265
Primitives, The 424
Prine, Dave 346-7
Prine, John 16, 163, 342, 346-8, 372, 390
Prins, Kitty 222
Progressive Bluegrassers, The 248
Prophet, Chuck 396-7
Puckett, Riley 77, 169
Pure Prairie League, The 326-7, 429
Putnam, Norbert 141, 213, 333

Quarrymen, The 174
Quaye, Caleb 378
Quicksilver Messenger Service 193, 298-9, 302, 304
Quiver 383, 389

Radiators, The 391
Raitt, Bonnie 29
Ralph, Nick 253
Ramblers, The 169, 317
Ramsey, Evelyn 55
Ramsey, Obray 293
Randulph, Boots 148
Rank And File 395, 428
Rapp, Tom 287
Rare Bird 197
Rattlesnake Annie 361
Rawlings, David 442
Ray, Billy 253
Ray, Jean 200
Reagan, Ronald 31, 132, 201, 351, 375
Recliners, The 415
Red Clay Ramblers, The 414
Red Headed Fiddlers, The 71
Redding, Otis 130, 213, 294
Reed, Bobby 436
Reed, Bud and Ola Belle 241
Reed, Colonel George 266
Reed, Jimmy 196, 254
Reed, Lou 395, 445

Reese, Florence 103
Reeves, Goebel 113
Reeves, Jim 13, 96, 126, 137-9, 143, 146-7, 157, 387
Reich, Steve 164
Reid, Jan 361
REM 132, 281, 393, 424
Remaily, Robin 344
Remain, The 151
Renbourne, John 202
Reno, Don 247, 252, 253, 383
Replacements, The 414
Residents, The 395-6, 411
Retrograss 444
Rexroth, Kenneth 301, 334
Reynolds, Burt 38
Rhodes, Red 258, 319, 320, 335
Rice, Larry 254, 282
Rice, Tim 153
Rice, Tony 204, 254, 282, 293, 409
Rich, Charlie 141, 352, 389, 414
Rich, Don 231, 329
Richards, Keith 265, 268-9, 272, 274, 276
Richey, Kim 11, 134
Richman, Jonathan 430
Riddle, Leslie 81
Riddle, Nelson (Orchestra) 90
Riders In The Sky 375
Riders Of The Purple Sage, The 116
Riese, Randall 42
Riley, Billy Lee 146
Riley, Jeannie C 236, 239-40
Rinzler, Ralph 85, 171, 173, 187, 189, 241, 243
Rissik, Andrew 33
Ritchie, Jean 64-5, 107, 181-2, 202-3, 248, 277, 334, 353-4, 444
Ritter, Maurice "Tex" 116-7
Rivera, Scarlet 281
Rivers, Johnny 166
Riviera, Jake 388-9
Robardes, Jason 37
Robbins, Hargus "Pig" 205
Robbins, Marty 38, 119-20, 206, 332, 398-9
Robbins, Mitch 31
Robbins, Tom 277
Roberts, Andy 272, 381-2
Roberts, Rick 270, 273
Robertson, Eck 69
Robertson, Jamie 205
Robertson, John 258
Robertson, Robbie 26, 209, 218-21, 278, 314, 328, 337
Robins, Marty 118
Robison, Carson 76
Roby, Kenneth 428
Rock Bottom Remainders, The 206
Rock, Kid 18
Rockwell, Norman 327
Rocky Mountaineers, The 114
Roden, Jess 382
Rodents, The 317
Rodgers, Aaron 24
Rodgers, Jimmie 13, 24-5, 77, 79, 89, 90-5, 98, 100, 102-4, 106, 114-

5, 117, 137, 145, 153, 163, 172, 187, 199, 208, 212, 222, 228-9, 231, 233, 239, 266, 271, 311, 319, 334, 353, 391, 393, 445,
Rodgers, The 351
Rogan, Johnny 254, 263, 285-8
Rogers, Kenny 312, 324
Rogers, Lelan 312
Rogers, Roy 113-4, 116, 268, 303, 367, 395
Rogers, Will 93, 117
Rogie, SE 31, 239
Rolling Stones, The 148, 174, 204, 265, 269, 273, 275, 285, 298, 328, 351, 360
Rolling Thunder Review, The 162, 190, 199, 210
Ronson, Mick 327
Ronstadt, Linda 86, 214, 279, 321-3, 325, 337, 340, 354, 372, 380, 381
Rooney, Jim 43
Roosevelt, Franklin D 160
Roper, Skid 432
Rose, Fred 104, 129, 150
Rossington, Gary 351
Rotten, Johnny 217
Rough Squirrels, The 372
Rowan, Peter 106, 163, 241, 291-7, 410, 446
Roy, Little 245
Rubber Rodeo 396
Rubin, Mark 367, 411
Rumour, The 388-9
Rusby, Kate 405
Rush, Tom 179, 191, 196
Russell, CM 304
Russell, Jane 115
Russell, Kevin 438
Russell, Leon 257, 270, 311, 344
Russell, Mike 408
Russell, Tom 45-8, 87, 120, 232, 237, 405
Russell, Tony 101
Ruth, Babe 133, 287
Ruts, The 15
Ryan, Jimmy 444

Safety Last 427
Sahm, Doug 313, 425
Sainte-Marie, Buffy 41-2, 192-3, 196, 297-8
Sam, Marshall Uncle 328
Sample, Tex 18-21, 28
Sandburg, Carl 86, 87, 334
Sanders, Ed 174, 290
Sankey, Ira 67
Savage, Candace 42
Saverley, Arthur 104
Sayles, John 246
Schmidt, Rick von 169
Schultz, Arnold 104
Schwarz, Tracy 169
Scopes, John T 76
Scoppa, Bud 265, 270
Scotsville Squirrel Barkers, The 254, 282, 324
Scott 4 437
Scott, Ronnie 388

Scruggs, Earl 23, 47, 99, 104, 106, 108-11, 136, 217, 243-4, 247, 249, 255, 341, 410
Scruggs, Randy 341
Scud Mountain Boys, The 431
Scuds, The 431
Searchers, The 256
Sebastian, John 180, 183, 225
Secombe, Sir Harry 126
Second National Band, The 320
Seeger, Charles 161
Seeger, Mike 94-7, 109, 160, 168, 169, 171, 179, 212, 241, 245-6, 254, 279, 308, 444
Seeger, Pete 158, 161-3, 170, 175, 179, 182, 197, 254, 257, 354, 400
Seekers, The 164, 256
Seldom Scene, The 242, 279
Selvin, Joel 299
Serpent Power 311
Sex Pistols, The 55, 94, 147, 165, 390
Shakespeare, William 41, 128, 288
Shamblin, Eldon 123
Shamrock Band, The 158
Shanley, Eleanor 158
Shannon, Sharon 447
Shanty Boys, The 248
Sharon And The Students 203
Sharp, Cecil 56-63, 83, 167, 181, 310, 377
Shaver, Billy 368
Shaw, Lloyd 30
Shear, Jules 381
Shelton Brothers, The 147
Shelton, Allen 244
Shelton, BF 73
Shelton, Peter 243
Shepard, Sam 210, 281
Shepherd, Bill 95
Sherman, General 24
Sherrill, Billy 22, 141, 276, 352, 354, 389
Shilo 322, 324
Shilohs, The 259
Shiva's Headband 312
Short, Bubby 347
Show Of Hands 381
Shuttleworth, Paul 387
Siebel, Paul 322, 346, 360, 372
Silverados, The 286
Silverstein, Shel 192, 222, 223, 225
Simmons, Sylvie 432-3
Simon, Joe 140
Simon, John 218
Simon, Paul 174, 185, 203, 277
Sinatra, Frank 55, 129
Sinatra, Nancy 237
Sincere Products 385
Sir Douglas Quintet, The 313
Six-String Drag 428
Sixteen Horsepower 430
Skaggs, Ricky 13, 53, 65, 112, 136, 242, 248-9, 277, 280, 296, 345, 373, 375-6, 409-10
Skeletons, The 430
Skellern, Peter 382
Skillet Lickers, The 77, 160, 206, 243

Sky, Patrick 41, 196
Skyboat 217
Slack, Freddie (orchestra) 89
Slaughter, Marion Try 69
Sledge, Percy 140
Slim Chance 378
Slobberbone 315, 429
Slone, Bobby 252
Slowdance 437
Small Faces, The 378
Smith, Bessie 124
Smith, Harry 47, 59, 81, 89, 97,
    154, 156, 165-7, 169, 174-6, 178,
    182, 184, 186, 205, 210, 212, 246,
    296-7, 318, 334, 364, 371, 420-1,
    426-7 433, 438
Smith, Joe 322, 324
Smith, Lee 55
Smith, Mamie 69
Smith, Orriel 163
Smith, Patti 195, 281, 371, 414,
    421
Smith, Warren 63-4
Smiths, The 288, 300, 356
Snakefarm 439
Snow, Hank 25, 38, 93, 114, 143,
    197, 206, 240, 366
Snow, Kilby 185
Snow, Mat 211
Soles, Steve 199
Son Volt 425-6
Sonic Youth 238
Sons Of The Pioneers, The 114,
    244
Sopwith Camel, The 180, 299
Sorrells, Rosalie 63, 194
Souled American 431
South, Joe 205
Souther, JD 268
Sparks, Brett and Rennie 443
Sparks, Larry 248
Spence, Skip 72, 176, 297, 303,
    305-7
Spicher, Buddy 350
Spinners, The 174
Spiral Tribe 14
Spragg, Rob 17
Sprague, Carl 113
Springfield, Dusty 256, 377-8
Springfields, The 376
Springsteen, Bruce 53, 77, 280,
    360, 384, 395, 403-4
Sprung, Roger 248
Squires, The 314
Squirrel Nut Zippers, The 349
Stampfel, Peter 165, 175-6, 180,
    182-3
Stanely, Ralph 249
Stanley And His Famous Negroes
    386
Stanley Brothers, The 111-2, 115,
    178, 186, 243-4, 248, 254, 333-4,
    434
Stanley, Owsley 333
Stanshall, Viv 146
Star, Bella 42
Starling, John 279
Starr, Ringo 237, 376
Starry-Eyed And Laughing 382

Statesman Quartet, The 131
Statler Brothers, The 88
Steagall, Red 121
Stecher, Jody 73, 166, 293, 444-5
Steel Pole Bath Tub 357
Steele, Tommy 173
Steeleye Span 185, 220
Steinbeck, John 101, 231
Steiner, Rudolph 165
Stephens, Jody 427
Stepp, Bill 74
Stepp, WM 73
Steppenwolf 37, 237
Steve Miller Band, The 311-2
Stevenson, BW 361
Stevenson, Don 305
Stewart, Allison 441
Stewart, James 33, 96
Stewart, John 250, 317, 370-1, 389,
    395
Stills, Stephen 180, 191, 202, 282,
    313-4, 336
Stipe, Michael 394, 399, 434
Stivell, Alan 318
Stone Poneys, The 321
Stone, Martin 262, 272, 383, 387
Stoneman Family, The 242
Stoneman's Blue Ridge
    Cornshuckers 71-2
Stoneman, Ernest "Pop" 242
Stoney Mountain Boys, The 243
Stooges, The 191, 221
Strait, George 31-2, 375, 401
Strange Creek Singers, The 170
Strangers, The 232
Strauss, Levi 29
Strawbs, The 292, 379
Stray Gators, The 337
Stringbean 99, 104
Strong, Luther 73
Strummer, Joe 85, 174
Strzelecki, Henry 204
Stuart, Dan 396
Stuart, Marty 173, 413
Suicide 371
Sullivan, Dan 155
Summer, Andy 378
Summer, Marion 244
Sundowners, The 200
Sunshine Company, The 339
Sutcliffe, Phil 323
Sutherland Brothers, The 383
Swaggart, Jimmy 21
Swan, Billy 214
Swarbrick, Dave 185
Sweeney, Joel 68
Sweeney, Paddy 156
Sweeny's Men 203, 390
Sweeting, Adam 363

Talking Heads, The 421
Tamla Motown 23
Tams, John 162
Tannenbaum, Chaim 86
Tanner, Jim 77
Tarlton, Jimmie 164
Tashian, Barry 151
Taupin, Bernie 33, 377
Tawney, Cyril 53

Taylor, Earl (And His Stony
    Mountain Boys) 316
Taylor Kentucky Boys, The 101
Taylor, Chip 424
Taylor, Dick 392
Taylor, James 76, 335-7, 363, 451
Taylor, Tut 345
Tcny, Michael 361
Television 370, 398
Telfer, Ian 448-9
Ten Ton Ltd 439
Teneva Ramblers, The 91
Tennessee Three, The 225
Terlingua, Viva 361
Terry And The Pirates 304
Terry, Sonny 90, 161
Tex Hat, Connie 222
Texas Jewboys 240
Texas Playboys, The 122, 124
Textones, The 288
Thatcher, Margaret 132
The Old 97s 429
The The 132
Thin White Rope 398-9
13th Floor Elevators, The 312
Thomahawk 387
Thomas, Bruce 383, 389
Thomas, David 421
Thompson, "Hank" 125
Thompson, "Uncle" Jimmy 98
Thompson, Ben 434
Thompson, Bobby 213, 222, 244
Thompson, Chris 391
Thompson, Les 340
Thompson, Linda 421
Thompson, Richard 53, 131, 139,
    146, 151, 155, 262, 357, 363, 380-
    1, 408, 453-4
Thompson, Uncle Jimmy 67
Three Day Night 373
Three Johns, The 124
Throwing Muses 421
Thunder Mountain Tub Thumpers,
    The 302
Tillis, Mel 304, 311, 322
Timmins, Margo 413
Timms, Sally 124, 392-3, 414, 436-7
Tiny Tim 38, 208
Tobler, John 281, 309, 425
Tolman, Russ 398
Tosches, Nick 24, 40-1, 63, 100,
    147, 372, 54-5
Touhey, Patsy 156
Townsend, Pete 129
Traffic 378
Trailer Trash Revue, The 430
Traum, Happy 181, 183, 332
Travers, Mary 164
Travis, Merle 79, 110, 126-7, 163,
    166, 242, 299, 341, 347, 353, 432
Travis, Randy 136, 401-2
Travolta, John 29, 115
Treece, Richard 304, 384
Tremeloes, The 207
Tricky 15
Triffids, The 396
Trio 279, 323
Tritt, Travis 51, 318, 351, 402
True West 398

Tubb, Ernest 93, 114, 125, 127-8, 131, 240
Tubb, Justin 375
Tucker, Tanya 237, 352, 354
Tullis, Kyle 270
Tullock, "Cousin Jake" 110
Turner, Frederick Jackson 33
Twain, Shania 116, 192, 197, 225, 297, 416-9, 423
Tweedy, Jeff 424-7
Twiggy 38
Twitty, Conway 21, 43, 201, 218, 350, 373
Tyler, Sean 384
Tyson, Ian 120-1

U2 36, 51, 224, 278
Unclaimed, The 399
Uncle Tupelo 372, 393, 425, 425, 428

Valente, Dino 182, 194, 256, 302
Valentino, Bobby 388
Valley Boys, The 312
Van Gogh, Vincent 238
Van Ronk, Dave 46, 177, 179, 200
Van Zandt, Townes 193, 362-5, 446
Van Zant, Ronnie 351
Vassal, Jacques 64, 171, 197
Vaughan, James 67, 109
Vee, Bobby 186
Veitch, Doug 391
Velvet Underground, The 274, 327, 359, 392
Venet, Nik 370-1
Verve, The 382
Vibert, Luke 383
Vicious, Sid 55, 371
Vidal, Gore 201
Village People, The 34
Village Vanguards, The 259
Vincent, Gene 44, 148
Violent Femmes, The 396
Vipers Skiffle Group, The 174
Virginia Reelers, The 70
Virginia Trio, The 244
Voight, John 29, 38

Waco Brothers, The 393, 435-6
Wagner, Kurt 419
Wagoner, Porter 173, 221, 257
Wainwright III, Loudon 85, 228
Wainwright, Martha 86
Wainwright, Rufus 86
Waits, Tom 228, 372, 421
Wakeman, Rick 379
Walkabouts, The 414
Walker Brothers, The 152, 378
Walker's Corbin Ramblers 68
Walker, Jerry Jeff 163, 340, 360-2, 365, 370
Walker, Scott 378
Walker, T-Bone 366
Walker, Thomas 32
Wallace, George 38-9, 240
Wallace, Sir William 294
Waller, Charlie 242
Walsh, Joe 326
Walsh, Kevin 391

Walsh, Stephen 42
Walters, John L 164
Wangford, Hank 14, 150, 272, 385
Ward, Ed 166, 313
Ward, Wade 168
Warlocks, The 298-300
Warwick, Norman 386
Was, Don 359, 403
Wasserman, Rob 293
Waters, Muddy 17, 218
Waters, Sneezy 131
Waterson Family, The 245
Waterson, Norma 82, 332, 367
Watson, Annie 84
Watson, Doc 84-5, 95-6, 126, 160, 171-4, 180, 202-4, 212, 248, 252-3, 313, 340-1, 363, 365, 373, 410, 446
Watts, Isaac 66
Wayne Love, Reverend 267
Wayne, John 34-6, 76, 105, 115, 117, 133, 200, 227, 303, 370
Weavers, The 161, 179
Webb, Dean 249
Webb, Jimmy 234-5, 323
Weber, Steve 175
Weir, Bob 332, 334, 301-2
Weissberg, Eric 173, 177, 210
Welch, Gillian 79, 248, 275, 279, 437, 442
Wells, Kitty 42, 125, 127, 151, 246
Wenders, Wim 343
West Virginia Creeper 349
West, Mae 115
West, Speedy 125
Westbrook, John 92
Western Caravan, The 126
Whiplash Band, The 309
Whiskey, Nancy 170
Whiskeytown 275, 428
White Girls, The 277
White, Bukka 363
White, Clarence 39, 197, 201, 252-4, 257-8, 263-6, 269, 271, 274, 283-4, 288-9, 291, 293, 321, 383
White, John 160-1
White, Pat 154-5, 158
White, Roland 241, 252, 291
Whiteley, Keith 248-9
Whiteman, Ian 383
Whitman, Slim 93, 116, 222
Whitman, Walt 46
Whittaker, Roger 76
Whitten, Danny 337
Whittier, Henry 69-70
Who, The 129, 243, 299
Whyton, Wally 174
Wiggins, Ella May 103
Wigmore City Moonshiners, The 340
Wilburn Bros, The 127-8, 221, 240
Wilco 269, 275, 318, 425
Wild Stallions, The 296
Wildwood Boys, The 302
Wilheim, Mike 298
Wilkie, David 88
Willard Grant Conspiracy, The 432
Williams III, Hank 135
Williams, Andy 340

Williams, Hank 12-6, 20, 25, 44, 55-6, 77, 80-1, 89, 92, 100, 104, 116-7, 126, 128-9, 130-2, 134-7, 139-0, 145, 148, 182, 187, 197, 200-1, 206, 208-9, 222-3, 226, 229-30, 233, 235, 253, 258-9, 267-8, 271, 274, 283, 311, 313, 319, 322-3, 341, 344, 347, 352, 359, 364, 366, 369, 381, 392-3, 402, 404, 422
Williams, Hank Jnr 132-3, 351, 371
Williams, Larry 270
Williams, Lucinda 11, 131, 193, 242, 275, 279-80, 347, 367, 406-7
Williams, Mason 344
Williams, Miller 406-7
Williams, Stacey 187
Williams, Tex 126
Williams, Victoria 199, 237, 276, 407-8
Williamson, Nigel 276
Williamson, Robin 192, 294, 449-51
Williamson, Sonny Boy 218
Wills, Bob 13, 77, 81, 122-4, 138, 199, 233, 234, 294, 348, 356, 359, 368, 375, 429, 438, 441
Wilson, Brian 235, 285
Wilson, Norro 417
Winchester, Jesse 220, 343, 381, 387
Winger, Debra 30
Wingfield, Pete 152
Winwood, Steve 378
Wise, Chubby 104
Wiseman, Mac 172
Wissberg, Eric 164
Wolf, Howling 17
Wolfe, Charles 101
Wolfman Jack 331
Wonder, Stevie 285
Woods, Terry 203, 454
Wordsworth, William 27
Wren, Christopher 226
Wright, Ciely 13, 415
Wynette, Tammy 13, 38, 52, 268, 347, 352-3, 414
Wynn, Steve 399

Yakonovsky, Zal 180
Yates, Mike 55
Yearwood, Trisha 12
Yeats, WB 191
Yes 285
Yoachum, Iggy 435
Yoakam, Dwight 12, 61, 93, 231, 239, 248, 259, 276, 333, 423
York, John 288
Young Tradition, The 347
Young, Jesse Colin 196, 308-10, 335
Young, Neil 108, 136, 180, 196, 313-5, 323, 336-7, 338-9, 351, 401, 422, 425, 429, 442
Young, Preston 109
Young, Steve 110, 120, 288, 355
Youngbloods, The 176, 335, 340
Yule, Doug 327

Zakinska, Annette 398
Zappa, Frank 306, 317
Zevon, Warren 333
Zuckerman, Matthew 185, 209